POLICE IN AMERICAN SOCIETY

Bassim Hamadeh, CEO and Publisher
Mieka Portier, Acquisitions Editor
Sean Adams, Project Editor
Jackie Bignotti, Senior Graphic Designer
Alisa Muñoz, Licensing Associate
Natalie Piccotti, Director of Marketing
Kassie Graves, Vice President of Editorial
Jamie Giganti, Director of Academic Publishing

ISBN: 978-1-5165-2614-7 (pbk) / 978-1-5165-2615-4 (br)

POLICE IN AMERICAN SOCIETY

SELECTED READINGS FOR THE STUDENT PRACTITIONER

FIRST EDITION

HOWARD E. WILLIAMS

Texas State University—San Marcos

cognella® | ACADEMIC PUBLISHING

CONTENTS

INTRODUCTION

Managing the Police in Post-Ferguson America

BY HOWARD E. WILLIAMS

C hanges in societal expectations require attendant changes in the role of government. Archetypal changes are typical of social evolution. As economic conditions, social demands, and political mandates change, so do the roles of government. Police, as an institution, are not exempt from those stresses. Indeed, because they are the most visible symbol of government's domestic power and authority, the police often feel the most pressure to reform. Across the United States, the first two decades of the 21st century have witnessed increasing calls for fundamental change in the police role, but this is not a new phenomenon. History has demonstrated time and again that the role of police in American society is subject to change. There have been at least three distinct eras of American policing, each characterized by unique philosophies, policies, and management practices. Change is endemic to police service.

Pressures to redefine the police role come from many sources: the public, legislative bodies, the media, the courts, and police themselves. Whether such pressures in the 21st century mark the naissance of a new era in policing or simply define a new period within the current era remains to be seen. Historians will be the arbiters of that debate. However, one issue is clear—police administrators must be cognizant of changing demands regarding police services and heed calls to reexamine police functions. At stake is the legitimacy of the police role in post-Ferguson America.

HISTORICAL CHANGES IN POLICING PHILOSOPHY

Pleas for police reform are common in American history. Consequently, policing has evolved through clearly recognized eras. Although the earliest police departments reportedly formed according to Sir Robert Peele's altruistic principles, struggle for political survival marked the political era of policing. Administrators in the political era, circa 1840 to 1930, managed primarily through political patronage (Uchida, 2011). The commonly accepted list of Peele's principles that purportedly identified the ideals of policing were largely an invention of mid- to late-20th-century textbooks (Lentz & Chaires, 2007). During the political era, police activity was dependent on the demands of political bosses. Patrol officers were expected to maintain order in neighborhoods and to control the "dangerous class" of people (i.e., the people who threatened the political machine). Police managers dictated tactics and strategies that were intended to ensure the reelection of the political officials in a ward or precinct, thereby ensuring their own job security. Newly elected politicians usually meant wholesale changes in police management, so administrators ran their departments accordingly. Political machines recruited and maintained police officers. Reciprocally, management required officers to encourage citizens to vote for certain candidates, discourage them from voting for others, and, occasionally, assist in rigging elections (Kelling & Moore, 1988).

Standards within municipalities varied widely in recruit selection, training, rules and regulations, levels of enforcement, and police-citizen relations. Minority communities were often legally and politically powerless. Members of those minority communities therefore received few of the policing benefits that were directed to those with more political influence (Williams & Murphy, 1990). The difficulties of managing police departments in the political era were numerous: the chief of police lacked the power and authority to initiate effective change, officers had little or no education, training was limited, officers often resented proposals for change, political machines were difficult to break, and it was almost impossible for management to divorce policing from party politics (Uchida, 2011).

The corruption and inequities of the political era gave rise to reform efforts in the early 20th century. Reformers began to view politicization of the police as a problem to overcome, not as a legitimate basis of authority. Richard Sylvester, August Vollmer, and O. W. Wilson, among others, led calls for reform in 1920s and 1930s. During the reform era that followed, from 1930 through the late 1970s, the law, as opposed to political or citizen demands, established the base of police authority, and police began to reject the idea that political leaders should make tactical decisions (Kelling & Moore, 1988). Police departments became autonomous departments within government, and police themselves began to view political influence as a form of corruption. Police work focused on law enforcement and abandoned the broader social services common to the political era. The logical consequence for police administration was to narrow the police function to fighting crime, thus allowing police to concentrate on prevention of crime and apprehension of offenders.

One of the most important goals of police management during the reform era was to reduce the discretionary excesses of the political era by reorganizing according to the concepts of Frederick Taylor's scientific theory: division of labor and strict bureaucratic control. The Taylorism movement provided the impetus to standardize police training, limit discretion, and require professional detachment in police-citizen contacts. Advancements in technology and administration improved services and added to the carefully crafted image of the professional police officer. However, the reform era suffered from two important but unintended consequences. The first of these was the development of a police subculture that caused officers to feel alienated from administrators, the media, and the public. As a result, trust turned inward, contributing to the blue wall of silence. Second, the impersonal professional style of policing often exacerbated strained police-community relations (Uchida, 2011).

Once again, however, public dissatisfaction with police services resulted in calls for reform. In the 1970s, experiments on alternative police tactics, such as foot or bicycle patrols, coupled with social research into the relationship between fear of crime and public disorder, created new opportunities for the police to address concerns regarding the rising crime rates that had plagued the country through the 1960s. Police learned that information obtained from citizens was an important factor in improving police response to crime and in reducing public fear of crime. Citizens appreciated the opportunity to provide police with information regarding crime and disorder in their communities, and police came to realize that it was beneficial in terms of police-community relations to obtain authorization from communities to address disorder in neighborhoods. Herman Goldstein (1979) and James Q. Wilson and George Kelling (1982) led the call for police to engage in proactive policing and problem solving to supplement responding to calls for service that drove police operations during the reform era. The community policing era was born in the 1980s when police recognized that the benefits of public problem solving contradicted the crime-control tenets that dominated the reform era. Problem solving was antithetical to the routinized and standard bureaucratic rigidity previously thought necessary to control abuses of discretion.

The law continued to be the major legitimizing basis for police, but management placed a renewed emphasis on community and political authority. Administrators emphasized training in order maintenance, conflict resolution, and problem solving. They decentralized decision making, encouraged participative management, and increased involvement of police executives in planning and implementation. Fewer levels of supervisory authority were necessary, so agencies reorganized to reflect the new realities of managing in the community policing era. Unfortunately, the community policing era also revived one major criticism of the political era—the benefits of community policing were directed at those with greater political influence, and the needs of those with lesser influence were often ignored.

It is clear from the historical evidence that calls for police reforms are not new. The current calls for change are merely a continuation of a process that has lasted more than 150 years. The paradigm of policing in America has continuously changed as police endeavored to provide the public with the service it demanded. To students of police history, the resulting progress was obvious. In an early assessment of police, Bruce Smith (1940) noted that extant police forces in the United States had improved significantly from their historical predecessors in Europe. Specifically, Smith referred to France's *Sûreté Nationale*, founded by Eugène François Vidocq (aka François Eugène Vidocq) in 1812, and Jonathan Wild's thief-takers of early 19th-century London. Vidocq was renowned for his advances in police practices, such as undercover tactics, criminology, interrogation, and ballistics. However, Vidocq himself was a criminal who had spent several terms in prison for mostly petty offenses, and he hired mostly reformed criminals to work for him at the *Sûreté* (Ramsland, 2006). Wild had become known as the "Thief-Taker General." Thief-takers, forerunners to the London Metropolitan Police, were private individuals who were hired to capture criminals. Wild was an underworld figure who posed as a crime fighter but who was working both sides of the law by collecting rewards for the recovery of property that he or his confederates had stolen (Cyriax, Wilson, & Wilson, 2009). Smith argued that the continuous improvement of policing services over time justified expectations of further improvement.

Thirty years later, Egon Bittner (1970) argued that events of the previous three decades had proved Smith to be correct. Bittner claimed that brutality and corruption, once endemic features of American policing, had been reduced to sporadic levels and that police reforms had become internal goals that police executives actively sought. Since then, police have made continuous and significant improvements in professionalism. Nevertheless, even as police services continued to improve, public demands for accountability and transparency became even greater.

More recently, academics and practitioners have argued that policing has entered a fourth era, but the debate is not yet resolved on what that era will be. In the wake of the terrorist attacks on September 11, 2001, police agencies across the country found themselves adapting to a new homeland security role. This new role in American policing, tentatively dubbed the homeland security era, was a response to more than just the events of 9/11. It was also a response to changes brought about by various political, economic, and social factors (Oliver, 2006). Still later, research revealed that significant information-based policing strategies had emerged during the 1990s and had become predominant during the early 21st century. These strategies, ostensibly called the information era, included evidence-based policing, intelligence-led policing, and predictive policing (Hooper, 2014). Most recently, high-profile events, and the associated public and political turmoil that followed, have raised the question of whether American policing is entering a post-Ferguson era.

THE EVENTS IN FERGUSON, MISSOURI

At approximately noon on August 9, 2014, in Ferguson, Missouri, Officer Darren Wilson, a White police officer employed with the Ferguson Police Department, shot and killed Michael Brown, an 18-year-old Black man, who had reportedly just robbed a local store. A friend of Brown's named Dorian Johnson, who was with Brown when the shooting occurred, shortly thereafter offered his version of the event to the news media. Johnson claimed that Wilson had accosted him and Brown as they walked in the street. He claimed that Wilson grabbed and threatened to shoot Brown. When Brown broke free and started to run away, Wilson started shooting at Brown, hitting him in the back. Brown stopped, raised his hands in surrender, and told Wilson that he did not have a gun. Johnson claimed that Wilson then shot Brown several times, killing him. The national news media widely distributed Johnson's account of the event, portraying it as a White police officer unjustifiably shooting and killing an unarmed Black man. Public reaction was swift and predictable. In Ferguson, protests, some peaceful and some violent, lasted more than a week. Protestors chanted, "Hands up, don't shoot." Police critics across the country, including members of Congress, adopted the phrase when discussing the state of police-community relations in the United States.

However, investigations by the St. Louis County grand jury and by the U.S. Department of Justice later concluded that Johnson's account of the shooting was inaccurate. Those investigative bodies determined that Wilson's account of the event, which was supported by several eyewitnesses and the by the forensic evidence, was more credible (U.S. Department of Justice, 2015; St. Louis County District Attorney's Office, 2014). Wilson claimed that Brown had assaulted him and tried to take his service firearm while he (Wilson) was still seated in his car. When Brown started walking away, Wilson followed to arrest him for the assault. Brown turned around and charged at Wilson, and Wilson then shot him. The grand jury and the Justice Department found that Wilson's shooting of Brown was legally justifiable.

Early media reports on the shooting—the impetus for protests, riots, and nationwide criticism of Wilson and of the police, generally—were factually wrong, according to the investigations that followed. Nevertheless, a Pandora's box was opened, and the damage to police-community relations in America was done. Following the announcement on November 24, 2014, that the grand jury returned no indictment of Wilson, rioting again erupted in Ferguson, and protests and demonstrations occurred across the country. On March 4, 2015, the Justice Department reported that it had concluded its investigation, and it cleared Wilson of civil rights violations in the shooting. That announcement did little to restore faith in the police.

OTHER HIGH-PROFILE EVENTS

The quality of police-community relations has waxed and waned over time. Michael Brown's shooting was not the first police-citizen contact resulting in violent criticism of police behavior, and it would not be the last. The late 1960s and early 1970s were remembered for rising crime rates and civil rights riots. In 1967, President Lyndon Johnson established the President's Commission on Law Enforcement and Administration of Justice, a group of 19 people he charged with making recommendations to reform the American criminal justice system. In their final report, commission members called on officials of the criminal justice system to reexamine what they do, being honest with the public and with themselves about the system's shortcomings (President's Commission on Law Enforcement and Administration of Justice, 1967).

Additionally, Johnson formed the National Advisory Commission on Civil Disorders, better known as the Kerner Commission, to examine the causes and government response to the race riots of 1967. The Commission's report, the Report of the National Advisory Commission on Civil Disorders (National Advisory Commission on Civil Disorders, 1968), better known as the Kerner Report, concluded that the riots were not the result of a single incident but of a compilation of several prior incidents. In half of those riots, the prior incidents, which increased tensions and ultimately led to violence, were police actions. The commission recognized 12 deeply held causal grievances in cities that experienced major rioting. The number one grievance was police practices. The commission found several additional problems with police departments: police conduct included brutality, harassment, and abuse of power; training and supervision was inadequate; police-community relations were poor; and employment of minority officers lagged behind growth of the population.

On March 3, 1991, George Holliday videotaped four White Los Angeles police officers beating Rodney Glen King, a Black man, following a high-speed chase. Holliday shared his videotape with a local television station, and the scene was broadcast across the world. On March 14, 1991, the Los Angeles County District Attorney's Office obtained grand jury indictments on four officers for excessive force. On April 29, 1992, the trial jury acquitted three of the officers of all charges. The jury acquitted a fourth officer of one charge, but jury members could not agree on one other charge. In protest of the verdicts, for the next six days Los Angeles was plagued by violent rioting.

In the wake of the King beating, Los Angeles mayor Tom Bradley formed the Independent Commission on the Los Angeles Police Department, otherwise known as the Christopher Commission, to conduct an examination of the structure and operation of the Los Angeles Police Department. Among other concerns, the Commission found a significant number of officers who repeatedly used excessive force against the public and who persistently ignored the policy guidelines of the department regarding force. The Commission noted police management's failure to control those officers. This failure of management was at the heart of many of the Los Angeles Police Department's police-community relations problems (Independent Commission on the Los Angeles Police Department, 1991).

The Michael Brown shooting was the bellwether event of a new age of police-community relations, and it presaged the need for police executives to reconsider methods and philosophies. However, other recent incidents have raised questions about police practices. On July 17, 2014, Eric Garner died after New York police officers tried to arrest him for selling untaxed cigarettes on the sidewalk. The officers had reportedly used an unauthorized neck restraint hold to subdue the man when he resisted arrest. On July 10, 2015, a trooper with the Texas Department of Public Safety arrested Sandra Bland for what began as a simple traffic violation. She later committed suicide by hanging herself in her jail cell.

The Garner and Bland incidents are just two examples among many. Each new questionable and highly publicized police-citizen encounter challenges the legitimacy of the police role in society. It is the responsibility of police practitioners to protect and bolster the legitimate role of police in society.

REINFORCING POLICE LEGITIMACY

Police departments do not compete with other institutions in an economic sense. Instead, they exist to serve the will of their sovereign, that is, those people and organizations whose views are significant and who can substantially affect the well-being of the organization (Crank & Langworthy, 1992). In the interest of organizational survival, police must assent to the interests of the people and the institutions that control the assets needed for continued operation. Thus, police legitimacy depends on the views of legislative bodies, the courts, and, most importantly, the public. When conflicts arise and are not well managed, they can intensify into climates wherein the department loses legitimacy within the institutional environment. Such conditions usually result in the removal and replacement of the chief executive with a new chief who carries a mandate to recover the agency's legitimacy. In some cases, the agency becomes subject to restrictive mandates, such as consent decrees. In extreme cases, the department can cease to exist.

Legitimacy is important to the police for several reasons. First, if the police are to be effective in their mission, they need public support and cooperation. Without voluntary cooperation, the police find it far more difficult to maintain order or to investigate and suppress crime. Second, voluntary support and cooperation is directly correlated with the public's positive judgments about police legitimacy. People cooperate most with the police when they view them as legitimate legal authorities who are entitled to be obeyed. Third, the way police conduct their activities is a key antecedent of the public's judgments about their legitimacy and the exercise of their authority. Such procedural-justice judgments are central to public evaluations of the legitimacy of the police role. These judgments influence evaluations separately from assessments of the police mission per se (Tyler, 2004).

Post-Ferguson events have demonstrated mounting concerns about police legitimacy. The time has not yet come to demand dramatic changes in policing. To avoid creating disastrous unintentional consequences, such change should come only after considerable reflection and debate about the ramifications of proposed change efforts. It is time, however, to address criticisms of police and to explore better ways to deliver police services. Purposive change requires conscious, planned, and deliberate efforts, but the police do not control many of the social, economic, and political factors that foment discontent. Regardless, to avoid crescive change and to ensure legitimacy and organizational survival, executives must reexamine the four major functions under their control that influence and perpetuate police culture: police professionalism and accountability, recruiting and hiring, ethics, and use of force.

PROFESSIONALISM AND ACCOUNTABILITY

The model of professional policing promulgated in the reform era was technocratic, rigid, and often cynical. Policing was deliberately removed from communities when the police insisted that they knew better than residents how their communities should be policed (Stone & Travis, 2011). This professional model of policing failed to produce acceptable levels of public safety. The rise of the community policing era sought to replace the professional model of the reform era with a new model, one that was attuned to the needs of the community. That transformation has been incomplete. The post-Ferguson period is the time to reinvigorate the transition and to produce truly professional officers at all levels of the organization who are capable of complex and creative problem solving and who are accountable for their actions.

Across the country, police executives seek to increase their legitimacy by committing themselves to stricter accountability for their operational effectiveness and their conduct. A commitment to accountability requires an acceptance of an obligation to account for police actions at all levels of supervision and oversight, including the chain of command, citizen review boards, city councils and county commissions, state legislatures, inspectors general, government auditors, and courts (Stone & Travis, 2011). Accountability once referred only to the process of investigating civilian complaints and disciplining officers for misconduct. Today, however, chief executives view accountability as how they are held to task for managing the three Cs of policing—crime, cost, and conduct.

More police agencies have begun conducting public surveys to hold themselves accountable for reducing reported crime and for reducing fear of crime in neighborhoods and among vulnerable residents. Cost-conscious departments have begun finding new and more cost-effective ways to deliver police services, such as permitting online reporting of minor incidents and shifting some work to nonsworn employees. Finally, police executives have begun to publicly take responsibility for the conduct of their personnel. This requires chief executives to apologize promptly for clear cases of misconduct and take the initiative to explain controversial conduct that they consider legal and appropriate.

In practical terms, research shows benefits of requiring police to engage in dialogue that adopts the principles of procedural justice during citizen contacts—encouraging citizen participation, remaining neutral in decision making, conveying trustworthy motives, and demonstrating dignity and respect (Mazerolle, Bennett, Davis, Sergeant, & Manning, 2013). That process begins with recruiting and hiring people who are right for the job and who can subscribe to the tenets of procedural justice.

RECRUITING AND HIRING

Police agencies face three principle challenges in meeting recruiting and hiring goals: increasing attrition, decreasing sources of recruits, and expanding responsibilities (Wilson, 2012). Retiring baby boomers, continuing military activations, changing generational expectations of careers, and budget crises all contribute to increasing attrition in police organizations. Meanwhile, sources of recruits are decreasing because of decreases in the pool of qualified applicants, changing generational expectations of careers, increasing competition for qualified applicants, and expanding skill requirements. In addition, new roles in community policing, homeland security, and emerging crimes increase police responsibilities and create a demand for new and ever-increasing skill sets. As these challenges increase, police managers must find new and innovative ways to recruit qualified candidates to the service.

One continuing debate regarding police officers is the requirement for a college education as a prerequisite for employment. College education appears significantly to reduce the likelihood of use of force, but whether an education provides other job-related skills advantages remains unclear (Rydberg & Terrill, 2010). A policy requiring a college degree would streamline the hiring process by reducing the number of applicants, but whether a department could recruit and hire enough college graduates to maintain staffing requirements is unknown (Decker & Huckabee, 2002).

For more than 50 years, police departments have tried to recruit and hire more minorities and women to better reflect the demographics of the public they serve, but current recruiting and hiring processes have proven unsatisfactory in diversifying the workforce. Barriers to Black police applicants include the initial application, the written exam, and the background investigation (Kringen & Kringen, 2015). Black applicants are more likely to self-select out of the process in lieu of testing, and during background investigation, Blacks disqualify at greater rates for economic, educational, and criminal reasons. Despite women having made great strides in increasing representation in many institutions such as law, politics, and the economy, they have been less successful in policing. Police departments have had difficulty hiring and retaining female officers (Shelly, Marabito & Tobin-Gurley, 2011).

Once recruits have been hired, questions arise of the best way to train them for the job to come. Striking is the paradox of police training: police work in a free and democratic society, but they are trained in a paramilitary, punitive, and authoritarian environment (Birzer, 2003). Some evidence suggests abandoning the strict pedagogic format currently prevalent in police training environments in favor of a more andragogic and problem-solving orientation.

ETHICS

Unfortunately, police academies traditionally have not made ethics training an important part of their curriculum, usually devoting no more than just a few hours to this critical topic (Johnson & Cox, 2004). Even then, lectures are often merely demands to comport themselves according to the published rules and regulations or to adhere to a one-page code of ethics. Requiring adherence to rules and regulations is not ethics training, it is a call for personal discipline. Such an approach is far too simplistic. By the nature of their office, the police make decisions that few others outside of policing ever confront. Police ethics must be concerned with making critical decisions under stressful, dynamic, and evolving situations. There is seldom time for pensive reflection to decide on a course of action. Consequently, police encounter decision-making situations that are outside the parameters of normal life experiences and for which they have not been adequately prepared.

Police organizations must make ethics an integral part of the decision-making process. This approach requires changes in recruiting and selection, in the training curriculum, and in the organizational justice process. Police administrators and trainers must encourage vigorous discussions of ethical approaches to develop virtue-oriented ethical constructs.

USE OF FORCE

Perhaps the greatest threat to police legitimacy is the public's view of how police use force to accomplish their mission. What defines the police is not so much what they do, but how they do it (Klockars, 1985). Bittner (1970) postulated that the role of police in society is defined by their legitimate use of coercive force. In establishing limits to police use of coercive force, the Supreme Court has acknowledged that the Fourth Amendment to the Constitution recognizes that the right of the police to make an arrest "necessarily carries with it the right to use some degree of physical coercion or threat thereof to effect it" (*Graham v. Conner*, 1989, at 396). The Supreme Court has ruled that any use of force to seize a person must be analyzed under the reasonableness standard of the Fourth Amendment. The test of whether an officer's use of force was reasonable is whether the officer's actions are objectively reasonable considering the facts and circumstances confronting him or her. This analysis must be undertaken without regard to the officer's underlying intent or motivation. "An officer's evil intentions will not make a Fourth Amendment violation out of an objectively reasonable use of force; nor will an officer's good intentions make an objectively unreasonable use of force constitutional" (*Graham v. Conner*, 1989, at 397).

Regardless of an officer's evil or good intentions, it is axiomatic that the use of coercive force insinuates the possibility of inflicting on someone serious injury or death. To determine whether an officer used any greater force than was reasonable under given circumstances, the courts must examine the totality of circumstances at the time of the arrest or detention (*Graham v. Connor*, 1989; *Saucier v. Katz*, 2001; *Tennessee v. Garner*, 1985). Fourth Amendment jurisprudence addresses misuse of governmental authority, not accidental effects of otherwise lawful government conduct (*Brower v. County of Inyo*, 1989). Consequently, the law does not require law enforcement officers to calculate the least intrusive means of responding to an exigent situation; it requires only that they act within the range of conduct that the courts identify as reasonable (*Scott v. Henrich*, 1994).

The differences between what the law permits, what department policies prescribe, and what the public tolerates is significant to questions of police legitimacy. Law and policy form ahead of the use of force, and, consequently, departments can train officers on preapproved tactics. Police organizations cannot train to accommodate public opinion, which forms only after the fact. Thus, law and policy are based on precedent and regulations, but public opinion is based on the ambiguities of personal preference. Often, those two do not coincide. Citizens who do not approve of the behavior of an officer often do not understand that the officer violated no law or rule of the department and cannot be criminally charged or disciplined. It is this incongruence that leads citizens to lose faith in the police to behave in ways they perceive to be acceptable. The time is ripe for administrators to revisit policies and training to reduce the gap between legal requirements and public acceptance of police use of force.

THE READINGS

It is not the purpose of this essay to deliberate in depth the topics that affect the public's view of police legitimacy. That charge is left for the readings that follow in this anthology. However, it is the purpose of this endeavor to elucidate why it is important for police practitioners and students of policing to discuss the environment in which the police labor today. History clearly demonstrates that change is inevitable. It behooves the police to lead the change effort rather than to resist it. Only then can the police initiate purposive change that facilitates their goals and objectives. Otherwise, crescive change is thrust on them, and the police might not find that change to be helpful or beneficial.

REFERENCES

Birzer, M. L. (2003). The theory of andragogy applied to police training. *Policing: An International Journal of Police Strategies & Management, 26,* 29–42.

Bittner, E. (1970). *The functions of the police in modern society.* Chevy Chase, MD: US National Institute of Mental Health, Center for Studies of Crime and Delinquency.

Brower v. County of Inyo, 489 U.S. 593 (1989)

Crank, J. P., & Langworthy, R. (1992). An institutional perspective of policing. *Journal of Criminal Law & Criminology, 83*(2), 338–363.

Cyriax, O., Wilson, C., & Wilson, D. (2009). *The encyclopedia of crime.* New York: Overlook Press.

Decker, L. K., & Huckabee, R. G. (2002). Raising the age and education requirements for police officers: Will too many women and minority candidates be excluded? *Policing: An International Journal of Police Strategies & Management, 25,* 789–802.

Goldstein, H. (1979). Improving policing: A problem-oriented approach. *Crime and Delinquency, 25,* 236–258.

Graham v. Connor, 490 U.S. 386 (1989)

Hooper, M. K. (2014). Acknowledging existence of a fourth era of policing: The information era. *Journal of Forensic Research and Crime Studies, 1,* 1–4.

Independent Commission on the Los Angeles Police Department. (1991). *Report of the Independent Commission on the Los Angeles Police Department.* Los Angeles: Author.

Johnson, T. A., & Cox, R. W., III. (2004). Police ethics: Organizational implications. *Public Integrity, 7,* 67–79.

Kelling, G. K., & Moore, M. H. (1988). *The evolving strategy of policing.* Washington, DC: US Department of Justice, National Institute of Justice.

Klockars, C. (1985). *The idea of police.* New York: Sage.

Kringen, A. L., & Kringen, J. A. (2015). Identifying barriers to black applicants in police employment screening. *Policing: A Journal of Policy and Practice, 9,* 15–25.

Lentz, S. A., & Chaires, R. H. (2007). The invention of Peel's principles: A study of policing "textbook" history. *Journal of Criminal Justice, 35*(1), 69–79.

Mazerolle, L., Bennett, S., Davis, J., Sergeant, E., & Manning, M. (2013). Procedural justice and police legitimacy: A systematic review of the research evidence. *Journal of Experimental Criminology, 9,* 245–274.

National Advisory Commission on Civil Disorders. (1968). *The Kerner report.* New York: *New York Times.*

Oliver, W. M. (2006). The fourth era of policing: Homeland security. *International Review of Law Computers & Technology, 20*(1 & 2), 49–62.

President's Commission on Law Enforcement and Administration of Justice. (1967). *The challenge of crime in a free society.* Washington, DC: US Government Printing Office.

Ramsland, K. (2006). François Eugène Vidocq: World's first undercover detective. *Forensic Examiner, 15*(2), 49–51.

Rydberg, J., & Terrill, W. (2010). The effect of higher education on police behavior. *Police Quarterly, 13,* 92–120.

Saucier v. Katz, 533 U.S. 194 (2001)

Scott v. Henrich, 39 F.3d 912 (9th Cir. 1994)

Shelly, T. O., Marabito, M. S., & Tobin-Gurley, J. (2011). Gendered institutions and gender roles: Understanding the experiences of women in policing, *Criminal Justice Studies, 24,* 351–367.

Smith, B. (1940). *Police systems in the United States.* New York: Harper.

St. Louis County District Attorney's Office. (2014). *State of Missouri v. Darren Wilson*: Grand jury transcripts. Retrieved from *New York Times* website: https://www.nytimes.com/interactive/2014/11/25/us/evidence-released-in-michael-brown-case.html

Stone, C., & Travis, J. (2011). Toward a new professionalism in policing. *Journal of the Institute of Justice International Studies, 13,* 11–32.

Tennessee v. Garner, 471 U.S. 1 (1985)

Tyler, T. R. (2004). Enhancing police legitimacy. *Annals of the American Academy of Political and Social Science, 593,* 84–99.

Uchida, C. (2011). The development of the American police: An historical overview. In R. Dunham, & G. Alpert (Eds.), *Critical issues in policing: Contemporary readings* (6th ed., pp. 14–30). Prospect Heights, IL: Waveland Press.

US Department of Justice. (2015). *Department of Justice report regarding the criminal investigation into the shooting death of Michael Brown by Ferguson, Missouri police officer Darren Wilson.* Washington, DC: Author.

Williams, H., & Murphy, P. V. (1990). *The evolving strategy of police: A minority view.* Washington, DC: US Department of Justice, National Institute of Justice.

Wilson, J. M. (2012). Articulating the dynamic police staffing challenge: An examination of supply and demand. *Policing: An International Journal of Police Strategies & Management, 35,* 327–355.

Wilson, J. Q., & Kelling, G. (1982). Broken windows: The police and neighborhood safety. *Atlantic Monthly, 29,* 29–38.

HISTORICAL PERSPECTIVE

Introduction

EGON BITTNER

In his assessment of the police, Bruce Smith wrote in 1940 that, in spite of the still rather bleak picture, "the lessons of history lean to the favorable side."[1] He pointed to the fact that the then existing police forces had moved a long way from the past associated with the notorious names of Vidocq and Jonathan Wild,[2] and he suggested that the uninterrupted progress justifies the expectation of further change for the better. It is fair to say that this hope has been vindicated by the events of the past 30 years. American police departments of today differ by a wide margin of improvement from those Smith studied in the late 1930's. The once endemic features of wanton brutality, corruption, and sloth have been reduced to a level of sporadic incidence, and their surviving vestiges have been denounced by even generally uncritical police apologists. Indeed, police reform, once a cause espoused exclusively by spokesmen from outside the law enforcement camp, has become an internal goal, actively sought and implemented by leading police officials.

---

1   Bruce Smith, *Police Systems in the United States*, New York: Harper & Row, 1960, second rev. ed., p. 3.
2   For descriptions of early European police practices, see Patrick Pringle, *The Thief-Takers*, London: Museum Press, 1958 and P. J. Stead, *Vidocq*, London: Staples Press, 1958. Early American urban police is described in Roger Lane, *Policing the City: Boston 1822–1885*, Cambridge, Mass.: Harvard University Press, 1967; and in the literature cited therein.

Egon Bittner, "Introduction," *The Functions of the Police in Modern Society: A Review of Background Factors, Current Practices, and Possible Role Models*, pp. 1–5. 1970.

Despite these widely acknowledged advances, however, the police continue to project as bad an image today as they have in the past.[3] In fact, the voices of criticism seem to have increased. The traditional critics have been joined by academic scholars and by some highly placed judges. Certain segments of American society, notably the ethnic minorities and the young people, who have only recently acquired a voice in public debate, express generally hostile attitudes toward the police. At the same time, news about rising crime rates and widely disseminated accounts about public disorders—ranging from peaceful protest to violent rebellion—contribute to the feeling that the police are not adequately prepared to face the tasks that confront them. As a result of all of this, the police problem has moved into the forefront of public attention, creating conditions in which highly consequential and long range decisions are apt to be formulated. For this reason, it is of utmost importance to bring as much clarity as possible to the ongoing debate now.

The survival of the unmitigatedly critical attitude toward the police, in the face of patent improvements, implies a concern of far greater complexity than the ordinary exchanges of denunciation and defense are likely to reveal. Surely the police are not bad in some such simple sense that those who have the power to eliminate existing shortcomings could do so if they would just set their minds to it. Nor is it reasonable to assume that all the persistent critics are merely devious or fickle. Instead, it would appear more probable that in the heat of polemics some facts and some judgments shifted out of line, that many polemic opponents argue from positions that are submerged in tacit and conflicting presuppositions, and the task of analysis and pending reform could only be advanced beyond its present impasse by first setting forth as unambiguously as possible the terms on which the police must be judged in general and in all the particulars of their practices. Without such prior specifications of the proper terms of critique, it will continue to take the form of a desultory array of animadversions. Moreover, such a critique, employing arbitrary and *ad hoc* criteria of judgment, will unavoidably alienate the police, will strengthen their defensive and distrustful posture, and will cause, at best, a patchwork of reform, the main effect of which will be to shift malpractice from one form to another.

The formulation of criteria for judging any kind of institutional practice, including the police, rather obviously calls for the solution of a logically prior problem. Clearly it is necessary that it be known *what* needs to be done before anyone can venture to say *how* it is to be done well. In the case of the police, this sets up the requirement of specifying the police role in society. Simple as this demand may seem on first glance,

---

3   J. Q. Wilson cites evidence that improvements undertaken under the leadership of America's foremost police reformer, O. W. Wilson, did not result in better public attitudes; see his "Police Morale, Reform, and Citizen Respect: The Chicago Case," in D. J. Bordua (ed.), *The Police: Six Sociological Essays*, New York: John Wiley & Sons, 1967, pp. 137–162.

it presents difficulties that are more commonly avoided than addressed. Were such avoidance explicit it might do little harm; unfortunately it is often obscured by specious programmatic idealizations. Thus, we are often told that the role of the police is supposed to center around law enforcement, crime control, and peacekeeping. The principal import of such statements is not to inform, but to maintain the pretense of understanding and agreement. Because such statements of function are abstract and do not restrict the interpretations that can be given to them, they can be as easily invoked to serve the polemic purposes of those who find fault with existing practices as of those who sound the fanfare of praise of the police. Nor is it very helpful to elaborate the official formulas in finer detail as long as the elaborations remain on the level of abstract moral, legal, or political theory. As David Hume has demonstrated long ago, all efforts at a transition from the *ought* to the *is* can be achieved speculatively only by unwarranted and arbitrary inferences,[4] with the result that those who begin by talking amicably suddenly and unaccountably find themselves locked in bitter enmity without knowing when their seeming agreement collapsed.

The point of all this is not that programmatic idealizations are not important, but that they are important precisely to the extent that there is agreement on how they are to be interpreted in actual practice. This is not an easy matter because references to practice can easily be subverted to serve the purposes of abstract theorizing. That is, many a theoretician is fully prepared to concede that what is perceived as *in principle desirable* needs to be perceived in ways that are attuned to realities, only to go on from this concession to the formulation of subsidiary rules concerning what is *in principle practical*. For example, Joseph Goldstein argued in an immensely important and justly influential paper that the law enforcement function of the police cannot be properly understood when considered solely in terms of principles of pure legality. Far from merely applying legal maxims in a ministerial manner, police employ discretion in invoking the law. Thus, they in effect draw the outer perimeter of law enforcement, a power that is certainly not officially assigned to them. Because policemen often make decisions that are essentially "invisible" and subject to no review, especially when they decide not to make arrests, Goldstein concluded that they should be brought under the control of some subsidiary rules, compliance with which would be insured by the scrutiny of an official agency.[5] While the proposal that discretion should be reviewable is meritorious, the hope that its scope can be curtailed by the formulation

4 David Hume, *A Treatise of Human Nature* (L. A. Selby Bigge, ed.), Oxford: Clarendon Press, 1896, Book 3, Part I, Section I.

5 Joseph Goldstein, "Police Discretion Not To Invoke the Criminal Process: Low Visibility Decisions in the Administration of Justice," *Yale Law Journal*, 69 (1960) 543–594; see also H. L. Packer, "Two Models of the Criminal Process," *University of Pennsylvania Law Review*, 113 (1964) 1–68; S. H. Kadish, "Legal Norm and Discretion in the Police and Sentencing Process," *Harvard Law Review*, 75 (1962) 904–931; and, W. R. LaFave, "The Police and Non-enforcement of the Law," *Wisconsin Law Review*, (1962) 104–137, 179–239.

of additional norms is misguided. Contrary to the belief of many jurists, new rules do not restrict discretion but merely shift its locus.

The main reason why the abstract formulations of the police mandate cannot be brought closer to the conditions of actual practice by more detailed rulemaking, even when such more detailed rules are devised under the aegis of in-principle-practicality, is that all formal rules of conduct are basically defeasible.[6] To say that rules are defeasible does not merely admit the existence of exceptions; it means asserting the far stronger claim that the domain of presumed jurisdiction of a legal rule is essentially open ended. While there may be a core of clarity about its application, this core is always and necessarily surrounded by uncertainty. Consequently, in real life—as opposed to certain simple games—the element of mootness can never be eliminated. And since it is imponderable what either total certainty or total uncertainty might mean in rule compliance, talk about the reduction of rule ambiguity has all the earmarks of image mongering. The realization that all legal rules are defeasible need not lead to what in contemporary jurisprudence is known as rule scepticism.[7] For as Edward Levy argued, "Legal reasoning has a logic of its own. Its structure fits it to give meaning to ambiguity and to test constantly whether the society has come to see new differences or similarities."[8] But the realization of the defeasibility of rules does indicate that the discernment of the function of a public agency, in our case the police, cannot be achieved by working down from broadly conceived programmatic idealizations, or, at least, that proceeding in this manner produces a quest of highly uncertain promise. No matter how far we descend on the hierarchy of more and more detailed formal instruction, there will always remain a step further down to go, and no measure of effort will ever succeed in eliminating, or even in meaningfully curtailing, the area of discretionary freedom of the agent whose duty it is to fit rules to cases. In the final analysis, we can send even the most completely instructed patrolman out on his round only if we have grounds for believing that he will know what the instructions mean when he faces a situation that appears to call for action.[9] We cannot spare him the task of judging the correctness of the fit. And if this is so in the final analysis, we should be well advised to take account of it in the first instance as well. Accordingly, instead of attempting

---

6   L. G. Boonin, "Concerning the Defeasibility of Legal Rules," *Philosophy and Phenomenological Research*, 26 (1966) 371–378.

7   The term "rule-scepticism" is part of the polemics of modern American jurisprudence; see F. S. Cohen, "Transcendental Nonsense and the Functional Approach," *Columbia Law Review*, 35 (1935) 809–849; see also Jerome Frank, *Courts on Trial: Myth and Reality in American Justice*, Princeton, N.J.; Princeton University Press, 1949.

8   E. H. Levi, *An Introduction to Legal Reasoning*, Chicago: University of Chicago Press, 1948, p. 104.

9   F. J. Remington writes, "Even the most careful revision, such as those accomplished in Wisconsin, Illinois, and Minnesota, will not produce a criminal code which is capable of mechanical application to the wide variety of situations which arise. Legislatures expect that law enforcement agencies will exercise good judgment in developing an enforcement program." at p. 362 of his "The Role of Police in a Democratic Society," *Journal of Criminal Law, Criminology and Police Science*, 56 (1965) 361–365.

to divine the role of the police from programmatic idealizations, we should seek to discern this role by looking to those reality conditions and practical circumstances to which the formulas presumably apply. Naturally, we cannot afford to forget the terms of the abstractly formulated mandate. We would not know what to look for if we did. But we will keep them in mind as something to be worked back to, rather than as a point of departure. In sum, the task we have set for ourselves is to elucidate the role of the police in modern American society by reviewing the exigencies located in practical reality which give rise to police responses, *and* by attempting to relate the actual routines of response to the moral aspirations of a democratic polity.

Three Eras of Policing

JAMES J. CHRISS

Human societies have always attempted to control the behavior of their members. Even among the most primitive tribes, there exist customs and beliefs which everyone accepts and which typically are adhered to, primarily out of fear of punishment for violating them. These systems of control are more or less informal, embodied in the stocks of knowledge members have about their world and how to act within it. Many of the beliefs and practices of early human beings would appall modern sensibilities, but it must be understood that such primitive practices did not emerge out of thin air. Rather, whatever has been reported or discovered about early human behavior is typically reflective of the environments within which these human groups lived. Virtually all acts taking place within human groups are collective attempts to survive given the limitations of environmental resources and the threats to life and limb, whether real or perceived.

For example, as William Graham Sumner (1906) summarizes in his book *Folkways*, in particular times and places in the human past cannibalism was an acceptable practice. Wherever cannibalism was found to be practiced, it was almost always a result of a defect in the food supply. In short, where food supplies are meager—especially when there is a shortage of meat—cannibalism may be practiced. Yet, even if a particular primitive group practices cannibalism, there are rules regarding who can and cannot be eaten, and under what conditions. For example, members of the same tribe rarely eat their own. Instead, they may eat the flesh of enemies or strangers. Under the harshest conditions, however, the males of the tribe may eat other members who are deemed sickly or weak, but almost never will they eat a woman (Sumner 1906, p. 330).

In the condition of the primitive tribe (or the even more remote "primal horde"; see, e.g., Giddings 1896), members of the group police themselves to the extent that the folkways—the norms and customs of the group—are known to all and are expected to be enforced by all. Only when disputes arise over some important event will higher authorities be called to judge the believability of one side or the other in the dispute. Overwhelmingly in primitive human societies, these esteemed authorities are the elders, and they gain their authority and prestige on the basis of tradition and the fact that they have survived to a relatively old age even in a harsh physical environment where average life expectancies are short. In short, even in the most primitive of societies there are typically patterns of association among members dedicated in certain crucial instances or social situations to the regulation of norms and to the sanctioning of members who violate these folkways, customs, or norms.

Good examples of this are various types of association among Native American tribes which serve explicitly political functions. Among the Plains Indians (including the Hidatsa, Crow, Mandan, Blackfoot, Dakota, and Pawnee), the work of government was carried out by associations of male members of the tribe. For example, an important event among these Plains Indians was the communal buffalo hunt, and the association in charge of the hunt was vested with the power to confiscate the kill of any hunter who did not abide by the ground rules (for example, starting the hunt too soon or taking more than his fair share). In extreme cases of malfeasance the offending parties could even be put to death. Buffalo hunt police could not act outside of their narrow jurisdiction associated with the activities of the hunt, and each year typically new members were named to the association (Krader 1968, p. 34).

In the long march out of human savagery, human beings slowly changed the way they controlled and coordinated the activities of fellow human beings. Rather than relying on informal control, whereby clans, families, or associations regulate the behavior of their own members and defend themselves against persons outside of the group, more advanced societies started relying on specialized agents to carry out control functions for the wider society. When societies move to more advanced stages, their populations grow larger and the informal systems of control based upon blood ties and familiarity between all members are rendered less effective. Some of the earliest systems of control in Britain and Colonial America that moved beyond pure informal control, such as "hue and cry," frankpledge groups, and "watch and ward," utilized aspects of law enforcement or policing, although the persons taking on these roles were not professionals nor were they trained in the specific tasks necessary to do the job.

EARLY POLICING IN LONDON

In Britain, for example, even as late as the late 1600s residents of city wards were expected to act as night watchmen if selected, and they were instructed to cry out and send an alarm if they observed anything suspicious. They were expected to provide this service free of charge, and anyone who shirked his or her duty faced heavy fines or other penalties in the Lord Mayor's Court (Fletcher 1850, p. 222). Over time, however, persons started resisting volunteering for watch and ward duty, and this necessitated developing special categories of watch persons, some of which received pay. By the early 1700s Britain passed the Watch Acts, whereby pay was given to night watchmen as supervised and regulated within each ward. This system of night policing stayed relatively intact until the 1830s, at which time, due to various changes in London specifically and Western society more generally—urbanization and industrialization being the two most important factors—the night watch was replaced by a more systematic and professional system of policing.

The early impetus toward modern municipal policing was embodied in Robert Peel's Metropolitan Police Act, which was passed by British parliament in 1829. Concomitant to the establishment of the new police force of metropolitan London, there was also a description of the expansion of police powers. Some of the new regulations specified as enforceable by the new police were as follows:

- The regulation of routes and conduct of persons driving stage-carriages and cattle during the hours of divine services;
- Public houses to remain shut on Sundays, Christmas day, and Good Friday;
- Liquor shall not be supplied to persons under sixteen years of age;
- Power is given to the police to enter unlicensed theatres, and to regulate the activities taking place in coffee houses and cook shops;
- Pawnbrokers who receive pledges from persons under the age of sixteen are subjected to penalties;
- Drunkards guilty of indecent behavior may be imprisoned (Fletcher 1850, pp. 235–236).

Also included was the specification of a vast array of "street offences" for which police could take persons into custody for their violation, including illegal posting of bills or other papers on public buildings, walls, or fences; prostitution, night-walking, or loitering; distribution or exhibition of profane, indecent, or obscene books or papers; and regulation of threatening, abusive, or insulting words or behavior which threaten to or actually "provoke a breach of the peace" (Fletcher 1850, p. 237).

The establishment of a sworn, paid police force in London was symbolic of the new levels of political control and oversight which the city of London was eager to establish, even in the face of opposition among many of its residents who felt, from the very beginning, that the police were either corrupt, inefficient, or simply inattentive to some of their sworn duties, particularly in the areas of "protecting" and "serving." This theme, namely, the ambivalence of the citizenry toward sworn police officers, has resonated and continues to resonate across most societies. In his massive study of poverty in turn-of-the-century London, Charles Booth (1970 [1902–1904]) commented frequently on the role of police in the lives of Londoners and the generally negative views of them shared especially among the poor. Booth quoted one resident of Bethnal Green as saying "[The police] won't interfere to stop the most hideous disorder in the streets." Another Bethnal Green resident complained of the police that there are not "half enough of them, and [they] see as little as possible," and that they are "afraid to assert themselves in a district like this" (Booth 1970 [1902–1904], p. 132).

Even with these negative sentiments, in some rough areas the police are seen by the residents as effective in maintaining at least a modicum of order on the streets, primarily by making a point of knowing "by name and sight" who the "rough" characters are. The police will generally not intervene in activities taking place within homes or other private areas, but if it spills out into the streets, such as a drunken brawl, the police will make a show of corralling the primary aggressors and giving them a good "going over" (Booth 1970 [1902–1904], p. 137). This order-maintenance strategy is still practiced by modern police, as confirmed in Bittner's (1967) study of policing in skid row where police apply a standard of "rough informality" to keep the regulars in line, thereby often avoiding the need to invoke their formal powers of arrest.

THE AMERICAN SITUATION

By the late 1830s American cities began establishing police forces modeled on the London Metropolitan police. The negative effects of urbanization and industrialization that had earlier prodded the development of policing in London were now starting to affect larger American cities in the East. In America, in fact, urbanization and industrialization combined with other factors to produce a unique set of social circumstances that shaped early American policing and made it somewhat distinct from the British model even as it was based upon it. As David Johnson (1981, pp. 22–25) points out, these other factors in America were nativism, racism, social reform, and politics.

Nativism refers to negative treatment or attitudes toward persons on the basis of their being perceived as outsiders, especially those of foreign birth. The influx of

Catholics, especially after the 1840s with the arrival of large numbers of Irish Catholics, led to high levels of social and economic discrimination against them. Many riots that occurred—in Boston in 1834, Philadelphia in 1844, and Louisville in 1855—can be traced to these and other forms of nativism.

Racism, against Blacks but also against Hispanics and American Indians (or Native Americans), was a staple of American life not only in the South, where slavery was legal until 1865, but also in parts of the country where Blacks were presumably "free" but nevertheless often mistreated. As Johnson (1981, p. 23) notes, between 1829 and 1850 five major race riots erupted in Philadelphia alone, all of which required military intervention.

Social reform also sparked violence, instigated primarily among those who looked unfavorably on the proposed reforms. The two major reforms leading to social unrest were the abolition of slavery and the temperance movement. The temperance movement caused class antagonisms between social reformers as "do-gooders" who tended to come from the higher strata of society, and middle- to lower-class Americans who viewed the attempt to restrict their drinking as an unacceptable infringement on their freedom. Slavery and the question of its abolition was a source of antagonism in America since its founding, culminating of course in the Civil War and continuing into the era of Reconstruction as freed African-Americans sought better opportunities wherever they could find them, including on the Western frontier.

Finally, these and other issues led to protracted *political battles*, as urban political leaders staked out positions on divisive issues, while opponents became entrenched on the opposite side. This was the beginning of American partisan politics, and by the time of their establishment in each local community, police departments were inexorably shaped by these varied political entanglements.

POLITICAL SPOILS[1]

Following Kelling and Moore (1988) with modifications developed by Chriss (2007b), there have been three eras of American policing, described as political spoils; reform and early professionalization; and community policing (1970s to present).[2]

The first phase of modern policing, running from the 1830s to the 1920s, is referred to as the *political spoils era*. In this earliest stage of development police departments were controlled by city government as well as ward bosses who wielded considerable influence not only on how police were to be used, but also who would be chosen as police officers. There was no pretense of choosing officers on the basis of objective criteria of competence or ability. Rather, officers during the first era were chosen on the basis of political loyalty and ascribed characteristics such as family connections, race or ethnicity, or friendship. Such close relations between city government and police officers produced an entitlement mentality among ward leaders and the administrative staff of the police organization, and because police were poorly paid, all parties tended to look the other way when officers engaged in questionable activities. As a result, patronage abuses abounded and police engaged in many under-the-table or quid pro quo arrangements with various constituents in the community.

As Kelling and Moore (1988) note, policing of the political spoils era was scrabbled together haphazardly and willy-nilly, as there were no organizational mandates yet established for proper police procedures or defining the role of police officers in the community. As a result, the political class within each local community determined goals and activities for the police, thus contributing to the fragmentation of policing and the great variability in police organization from community to community. Police were simply an appendage of the political machine, beholden to those in power at the moment. When a new administration came in, it was not uncommon to see a complete housecleaning take place as the new mayor or city hall put into position "their" men (and women) in policing roles.

During the political spoils era police provided a wide array of services, including crime control, order maintenance, and various social services such as running soup lines, providing temporary lodging for new arrivals to the city, and working with ward leaders to help find work, especially for newly arriving immigrants. Additionally, early police were not as centralized as later more professional departments organized along quasi-military design. This is because cities were divided into wards, and police departments into precincts. Precinct-level police managers worked closely with city ward leaders in hiring, firing, and assigning personnel. This meant that there were lots of quid pro quo arrangements.

Police had tremendous discretion out in the field since all they had to tie them back to the precinct house was the call box.[3] Fire call boxes started appearing in American cities as early as the 1860s (a glass front that any citizen could break to alarm the fire department), but police call boxes appeared about two decades later. Police call boxes were sealed boxes which a patrol officer could access with a key. The patrol officer would enter the call box and flip a switch to notify a central command center that his patrol was proceeding as normal and that no assistance was necessary. Police officers pulled a different box switch on their patrol route every thirty minutes. It also featured a telephone that officers could use to communicate problems to the central command. These earliest patrol routes were called Carney Blocks, named after an officer that devised the system. The police call box was painted blue, and illumination of the light at night provided an officer the location of the box in case of emergency if or when they needed to call for backup. Each box had a number affixed, and policemen quickly identified problem areas in neighborhoods by the unique call box number. All early police boxes were on party lines, so the beat cop would have to pull the box lever to identify which box he was at on the circuit. There was also a pointer in the early boxes for ambulance, paddy wagon, riot, fire, and other safety or order-related issues. The front door had a citizen's key, and any passerby could insert the key and call a wagon for any manner of accident or emergency.

The decentralization of early policing fit in well with foot patrol (walking a beat), and as they were directly visible and available citizen demands focused on them, while ward politicians focused on the organization more generally. Demand for police services appeared at street level, with respect to average citizen calls and encounters, and also at the precinct level, with regard to the local requirements for use of police personnel by ward bosses, city hall, and as directed by police administration.

Aside from the early call box, the primary program or technology for police during this era was foot patrol. A system of "rough informality" (Bittner 1967) was the rule of the day, and much "off the books" activities occurred, including the third degree, widespread use of police informants, and police being at the beck and whim of ward bosses and the political machine for whatever purposes they deemed appropriate. It was not uncommon, for example, for politicians to use detectives to get dirt on people. In this sense, the earliest policing tended to be more person-centered than offense-centered.

Finally, the expected outcomes of police work were crime and crowd control, order maintenance, and urban relief (where police dealt with such issues as poverty, homelessness, and "poor relief" more generally). This sounds much like the basic goals or expected outcomes of more modern policing, and in many ways it is. However, the major difference between policing in this first era and policing in later eras is the level of professionalization: in the earliest political spoils era there were no pretenses that police officers should be trained or that a certain class of individual was necessary to fill these roles. Although relatively well paid because of the real or potential danger of the work, nineteenth-century police were poorly trained, and virtually anyone with the right political connections and an inclination to violence could be lured into police work. With no real training, police had to learn "on the fly" and fashioned their own personal strategies for dealing with whatever or whomever they encountered in their day-to-day rounds (Lane 1992, p. 13).

Even so, police attempted to maintain a precarious balancing act between assuring citizen satisfaction (at the street level) and political satisfaction (at the precinct level). Since there were few if any rules in place to regulate the behavior of police or to recruit new members into the department, police had almost no checks on their personal behavior. Of course, the department could censure or punish members, including suspending or firing officers, but since there was no meaningful reporting of the department's activities, public accountability of the police was nonexistent. Attempts to change this set of conditions would occur in the next policing era.

REFORM AND EARLY PROFESSIONALIZATION

The second policing era ran from approximately the 1920s through the 1960s. This second era of policing, referred to as *reform and early professionalization*, was dedicated to correcting some of the problems associated with first-era policing, especially the patronage abuses, graft and corruption, and brutality which characterized early policing. In order to keep officers in line, more attention was given over to organizing departments along military lines, and the new forms of bureaucracy emerging under Taylorism was also useful in setting up a system of overt checks and balances to ensure that the actions of police met the expectations of the department as well as the wider community. Police were also concerned with gaining more autonomy, and they did this by placing greater distance between themselves and local political influence. And to address the graft and corruption, police moved away from an emphasis on foot patrol to more impersonal relations with citizens.

The impulse toward (early) professionalization resulted in a strategy whereby police felt they should no longer engage in the various activities that marked their work in the earlier era. Instead of running soup kitchens or dealing with runaway children, the police opted to professionalization through specialization, and the special role they chose was that of the crime fighter. With the mass production of the automobile beginning in the 1930s, police departments were able to kill two birds with one stone, in terms of both reform and early professionalization, by shifting the mode of patrol from foot to automobile. This created an instantaneous expansion of coverage for calls arriving through dispatch, but also quicker response times, hence further meeting the goals of professionalism and efficiency.

The other advantage of automobile patrol was that the police placed greater physical distance between themselves and citizens, and in so doing mitigated to some extent the graft and corruption of the previous era. But this professionalism was early, incipient, and provisional because there was not yet consideration given to systematically increasing the amount or content of training for police officers, as up to this time there was still the widespread sentiment that policing was a blue-collar job—a craft, not a profession—which could be filled by virtually any able-bodied person with an inclination to that sort of work. The move toward full professionalization, complete with attention to the educational background of police candidates and implementation of ongoing training, would not be realized until the community-policing era (to be discussed below).

VOLLMER, WILSON, AND BEYOND

Attention to some of the background elements of this second era of police reform and professionalization should be noted. Berkeley, CA police chief August Vollmer was one of the first to push for police reforms during the 1920s and early 1930s. Vollmer saw the police as guardians of societal morality, and the goodness of officers would be judged on the quality and integrity of their work. As chief of the Los Angeles Police Department, Vollmer wrote an annual summary of conditions in the department for the year 1924. Many of the themes of modern policing, including emphases on education, training, specialization, and efficiency were evident in Vollmer's 1924 report. One key passage is worth noting:

> If [police] were thoroughly trained for the service before being appointed, they would soon be able to teach, preach and write concerning the obligation that rests upon every individual in the community to cooperate in creating reverence for law. Accordingly a tentative outline of courses for policemen has been prepared and is on file at police headquarters. It has been found that specialization is necessary in modern police organizations. The duties are too varied and control of the multiplicity of details must be done through a staff of competent experts. Police departments cannot continue to operate as in the past and efficiency will be impossible until highly specialized functions are placed in the hands of persons who have been trained for their profession (Vollmer 1974 [1924], p. 11).

O.W. Wilson, Vollmer's protégé, wrote explicit texts on municipal police administration, following what J. Edgar Hoover had done at the federal level with the FBI. Hoover professionalized the investigative function of the bureau and pushed for more stringent educational and training requirements for FBI recruits. Although Hoover's FBI was the model of professionalization for state, county, and local policing after the 1930s, Hoover himself engaged in a range of improper behaviors—such as domestic spying on particular Americans for overtly political purposes—which required further reforms of the FBI beginning in the 1960s (Johnson et al. 2008).

Wilson's *Police Planning* stood as the "bible" for police management and organizational training for many decades after it was first published in 1952. Wilson also crafted the Law Enforcement Code of Ethics, adopted in 1956 by the Peace Officers' Association of California. Even today, this code of ethics (see Figure 2.1) is recited by a majority of police recruits newly graduating from their respective programs, albeit with some modifications of language to comport with today's sensibilities (e.g., dropping "God" at the end of the oath).

The reform aspects of this second era of policing are tied to several high-profile failures of the political spoils system which eventuated in the passage of the federal Pendleton Act in 1883. In 1865 President Abraham Lincoln was assassinated, largely because his handpicked bodyguard, a federal police officer by the name of John Parker, decided to go off drinking in a saloon while leaving Lincoln unattended next door at Ford's Theater. This gave John Wilkes Booth unfettered access to the president, who took the opportunity to shoot Lincoln in cold blood (Oates 1984). Sixteen years later, in the summer of 1881, a disgruntled office seeker, Charles Guiteau, shot President James A. Garfield, who died in September, 1881 from his wounds (Theriault 2003).

As a Law Enforcement Officer, my fundamental duty is to serve mankind; to safeguard lives and property; to protect the innocent against deception, the weak against oppression or intimidation, and the peaceful against violence or disorder; and to respect the Constitutional rights of all men to liberty, equality and justice.

I will keep my private life unsullied as an example to all; maintain courageous calm in the face of danger, scorn, or ridicule; develop self-restraint; and be constantly mindful of the welfare of others. Honest in thought and deed in both my personal and official life, I will be exemplary in obeying the laws of the land and the regulations of my department. Whatever I see or hear of a confidential nature or that is confided to me in my official capacity will be kept ever secret unless revelation is necessary in the performance of my duty.

I will never act officiously or permit personal feelings, prejudices, animosities, or friendships to influence my decisions. With no compromise for crime and with relentless prosecution of criminals, I will enforce the law courteously and appropriately without fear of favor, malice or ill will, never employing unnecessary force or violence and never accepting gratuities.

I recognize the badge of my office as a symbol of public faith, and I accept it as a public trust to be held so long as I am true to the ethics of police service. I will constantly strive to achieve these objectives and ideals, dedicating myself before God to my chosen profession...law enforcement.

Figure 2.1. O.W. Wilson's Code of Ethics (circa 1956)

By this time, the political patronage system, whereby persons were given positions of authority and trust without explicit guidelines in place to determine their fitness for the position, was in deep disarray, and the call for meaningful civil service reform was being taken seriously. The resulting Pendleton Act passed by Congress required that those seeking positions in federal government be selected by competitive testing. It was referred to as the merit system, the forerunner to the now well-established civil service examination (Hogenboom 1959). Although originally designed to screen applicants for federal positions, somewhat later state and local governments began following suit, including of course the screening of applicants for municipal policing positions.

By the time of the Progressive Era beginning in the 1890s, then, reformers rejected politics as the basis of local governance in general and police legitimacy in particular. New civil service regulations for hiring, firing, and promotion of public personnel were favored by progressives, thereby presumably eliminating informal "good old boys" networks while championing achievement over ascription. This also served to move police further away from the citizens they served as well as the influence of local politics. This also coincided with a new claim of special police knowledge and expertise, based on knowledge of law and professional responsibilities. As a result of such specialization and professionalization, police were seen as more autonomous and not beholden to city hall, ward bosses, or others seeking to use the police for personal or political purposes.

Additionally, this focus on the law meant that the police started narrowing their agenda to crime control and criminal apprehension. They became law enforcement agencies, rather than safety organizations or peace forces. From the perspective of the organization, there was no need for police to entangle themselves in the political, social, cultural, or economic conditions presumably contributing to disorder and crime. In other words, police should not try to solve root causes of crime because they are neither social workers nor behavioral scientists. They should merely use their technical legal expertise to combat crime. Specialization of this sort also meant that medical and emergency services were shifted to private providers and/or firefighting organizations. In sum, in the second-era police were no longer an agency of urban government, but now part of the criminal justice system.

Further, the organizational design for policing beginning in the early 1900s was influenced by Frederick Taylor's ideas regarding control and efficiency within large, formal organizations (Bendix 1947). Within this formal organizational or bureau-cratic model, the assumption is that workers are not all that interested in work, so economic incentives are the key. Conceptualizing police organization in this way implies that worker productivity is linked to employees' rewards. To achieve control of this process a specialized, well-regulated division of labor is required. The military command-and-control model of hierarchical, top-down, supervision of lower-level personnel was useful for these purposes, where emphasis is placed on a chain of command and explicit rules are designed for each officeholder. There is also an attempt to reduce officer discretion by holding up the universality of the criminal code applied to all persons equally (rather than specificity). This further implies a legalistic rather than a service orientation. Further refinements in the police division of labor give rise to specialized units such as vice, juvenile bureaus, drugs, tactical/SWAT, gangs, and the like.

And just as J. Edgar Hoover used propaganda methods to sell the public on the growing problem of urban crime and the need to invest more resources and trust in law enforcement at all levels of government, so too did police reformers discover that public relations and increased use of media could be effective in publicizing police activities and related public concerns, whether good or bad. The second era of policing established public relations as an integral aspect of police practice, and it grew in importance into the third, community-policing era. The group image that was presented was that police are first and foremost crime fighters. Foot patrol was deemed outmoded and inefficient, which also served to keep officers at arm's length from citizens. This also led to the increased reliance on the use of the squad car for routine police patrols. Additionally, centralization is an organizing element in second-era policing, insofar as citizens are expected to contact police headquarters rather than individual cops on a beat.

As mentioned above, during the reform and early professionalization era police claimed to be specialists in crime control, and it was also upon this basis that police professionalization was assured (Kelling and Moore 1988). August Vollmer initiated the development of a uniform system of crime classification, which was later codified by the International Association of Chiefs of Police (IACP) in 1930. This early attempt by the IACP to codify crime statistics was seen as so promising that the FBI took over the collection and reporting of crime statistics a year later, eventually becoming the Uniform Crime Reports (Mosher et al. 2002). Since then all police departments have measured their effectiveness against this standard, especially in terms of such key measures as the crime rate, clearance rate, response time in patrol and other field operations, and so forth. This was an effective reform strategy during the relatively stable 1940s and 1950s, but was somewhat rigid and inflexible in the face of rapid social changes occurring during the 1960s, especially with regard to rising crime rates during the decade, fueled largely by the baby boom (1946–1963; see Cohen and Land 1987). As defenders of the status quo, police could not adjust rapidly enough to the sweeping cultural and social changes occurring during the 1960s.

COMMUNITY POLICING

As mentioned above, the third era of policing, running from the 1970s to the present, is known as community-oriented or problem-oriented policing. Community-oriented policing (COP) or simply *community policing*, along with the closely-related problem-oriented policing (POP), emerged out of the social transitions of the 1960s. With new challenges to the status quo in the form of social movements such as feminism, civil rights, gay rights, as well as war and campus protests, the police were forced into high-profile and sometimes violent clashes with these and other groups, and as defenders of a status quo under siege they were easy targets for protests and demands for reform beyond those of the second era. It seemed that the professionalism upon which the police staked their claim in the previous era was badly out of touch with the realities of a new and rapidly changing urban landscape. Out of this came the impetus towards real reform, such as developing explicit guidelines for improved training and education of police, as well as attempts to recruit police candidates who matched more closely the sociodemographic characteristics of the populations they served, especially in the areas of gender and race.

Coming out of a tumultuous period of sometimes violent clashes with social movement actors, the police were certainly eager to retool their image and show themselves to be committed to solving problems besetting communities with a spirit of collaboration and mutual respect. This also meant that police would relinquish the claim of specialists in crime control and start taking on a variety of roles in the community, being especially keen to bolster their positive presence in the community through order maintenance, service, and a more scientific approach to studying and solving community problems. To pull off this new ability to take on multiple roles, urban policing became committed to improving educational requirements of their officers, not only in the area of "hard" skills (the newest police technologies) but also with regard to "soft skills" (training in human relations where police act like counselors, psychologists, social workers, and sociologists if need be).

To reiterate, in the third era of community policing police departments made a concerted effort to be more "user friendly," including the downplaying of automobile patrol in favor of foot patrols, bike patrols, and other "slower" forms of police response and presence. Police endeavored to get more information to citizens about the nature of police operations and of crime and disorder in their community. Police started taking an overt interest in fear of crime, studying ways to reduce or eliminate it. This led to a thriving "fear of crime" industry, in effect launching a partnership with higher education to conduct studies/surveys about citizen fears and wants. In sum, there was a push to work more closely with citizens to address issues of the community (Renauer 2007). Indeed, this problem-solving or problem-oriented focus of community policing is embodied in the SARA acronym, which represents the elements or stages of police work aimed at identifying and resolving problems in the community. SARA stands for:

- **Scanning**—Initial identification of community problems to be addressed;
- **Analysis**—Collecting information and analyzing the data;
- **Response**—Developing a strategy to address the underlying condition;
- **Assessment**—Evaluating the effectiveness of the intervention or response (White 2007, pp. 96–98).

This problem-solving methodology assumes that citizens are prepared to work alongside police in a collaborative effort to solve community problems. A recent meta-analysis of a number of published evaluations of problem-oriented policing initiatives found that, for the most part, the SARA method is effective in helping police respond to and alleviate the various problems they and citizens of the jurisdiction identify (Weisburd et al. 2010). Nevertheless, it is important to examine more closely not only this but other assumptions which underlie community policing. Riechers and Roberg (1990) have summarized this bundle of assumptions, which include:

- **Fear of crime**—Beyond the obvious problem of crime, police should also be concerned with citizen fear of crime and set up monitoring systems (such as citizen surveys) to measure it;
- **Active shaping of community norms**—In collaboration with citizens, police can and should actively shape community norms and standards;
- **Demand for police services**—The public demands that police be more involved in the issues of interest to them, and that these citizen demands can be measured and defined;
- **Initiation not domination**—Although police spearhead and initiate community services and programs that citizens want, police neither dominate nor dictate community standards (although they *do* shape and guide them based upon feedback from the citizenry);
- **Value-neutrality**—Police can act in a value-neutral way, consistent with the professional orientation of the previous (reform and early professionalization) policing era;
- **Organizational change**—The old top-down, command-and-control, quasi-military organizational structure can be transformed into a flatter, more organic, more user-friendly form, including increased use of citizens within the organization (or so-called "civilianization");

- **Higher-quality personnel**—With increased educational requirements and more stringent screening systems, a better class of people can be recruited into policing who are more attentive to community needs and demands;
- **Police as community leaders**—Although a complex and difficult undertaking, the project of community restoration and safety is one that the police are in the best position to fulfill (see also Reed 1999).

For the most part these are assumptions generated from the perspective of law enforcement practitioners themselves, and as such at least some of them may play more of a rhetorical function than reflecting the perspectives of actual citizens. For example, one of the assumptions above is that citizens "demand" community-policing programs and services, but the reality is that many citizens are at best apathetic about these services and at worst don't trust the police or simply want to be left alone (see Buerger 1994; Herbert 2006a).

THEMES IN COMMUNITY POLICING

Whether merely rhetorical or grounded in the actual operational realities of policing citizens in a community, and acknowledging the great diversity of community-policing programs taking place in particular communities (Skogan 1994), it is nevertheless possible to produce an even more narrowly focused view of the essential elements of community policing. Mastrofski (1998, pp. 162–166) argues that community policing can be distilled down to four fundamental themes: debureaucratization, professionalization, democratization, and service integration. Early in its history municipal policing adopted a quasi-military, bureaucratic model of organization which emphasized political control (especially in the first, political-spoils era), rules, strict adherence to proper communications and a chain of command, centralization (such as command-and-control imperatives emanating from police headquarters), and specialization (especially beginning in the second era of policing). By the 1970s and the emergence of the community-oriented policing era, there was a feeling that the legal and technical requirements of the old bureaucratic model of policing should give way to a more humanistic and *debureaucratized* organizational model. Rather than being distant from citizens and coldly efficient "snappy bureaucrats" (Klockars 1980) specializing in crime control, police are now expected to work side by side with citizens and other stakeholders in the community to solve community problems collectively.

The second theme, *professionalization*, actually began in the second policing era of reform and early professionalization (as summarized above). Yet, professionalization of the third era does not come by way of organizational rules or centralization of command, but by increasing educational requirements for police recruits and training officers in the newest technologists as well as in the vagaries of human behavior. Under this model, police are given even more autonomy to act, since their training is grounded not only in the technical aspects of police work but also in the scientific knowledge base of sociology, psychology, and other pertinent disciplines teaching human or "soft" skills. Indeed, under problem-oriented policing the police are rewarded more for taking initiative to formulate and solve problems in the community rather than the traditionally valued outcomes, namely the "good pinch" (i.e., arrests).

The third theme according to Mastrofski is *democratization*. Community-oriented policing could be described as a sort of democratic policing to the extent that there is an explicit attempt to get citizens more involved in the day-to-day operations of the police department. This appears not only with regard to the emergence of a number of community-policing programs which invite higher levels of citizen participation, but also citizen review boards as a crucial source of external accountability for police departments. Additionally, community policing coincides with the trend of civilianization, namely, the continuing increase in the number of civilians employed in police departments (Crank 1989). These civilian employees are said to act as important bridges or intermediaries between citizens of the community on the one hand and sworn police officers on the other.

A fourth theme of community policing is *service integration*. If police are now taking the approach of solving problems via collaboration with stakeholders in the community, they must do so under the condition that all key community resources should be brought to bear on these problems and that they should be integrated into a seamless whole (this is a concept borrowed from therapeutic practices such as drug-addiction counseling, child services, or clinical social work, namely, helping the client in need with the provision of all-encompassing "wraparound services"; see, e.g., Toffalo 2000). Hence, more than ever before police have developed organizational linkages not only with other city safety forces, but also with schools, social service agencies, housing services (especially in the case of housing authority police), businesses, and colleges and universities in the local area. In addition, police service provision is being made in increasingly intimate settings, as police are now spending more time in people's homes, whether for domestic violence or calls for assistant for family issues such as runaways, delinquency, abandonment, child support and custody cases, or missing persons.[4]

All of these ideal aspects of community policing—debureaucratization, professionalization, democratization, and service integration—are evident in one of the biggest and most ambitious experiments in community-policing implementation, namely, Chicago Alternative Policing Strategy (CAPS). As described by Skogan (2006a, p. 3), who has studied the program extensively, CAPS "features extensive resident involvement, a problem-solving approach toward tackling chronic crime and disorder problems, and coordination between police and a wide range of partner agencies." There are always operational realities impinging on the implementation of community policing, in that under certain conditions some aspects of the program are muted or less apparent than under other conditions. For example, like other large urban areas, Chicago has distinct areas of town that are predominantly White, Black, or Hispanic. Skogan (2006a) found that community-policing implementation and effectiveness varied along sociodemographic characteristics of the community, and race was one of those significant sociodemographic variables. Indeed, Skogan's (2006a) study of community-policing implementation in Chicago is subtitled "A Tale of Three Cities."

The short story is that, although community policing-implementation and involvement of the citizenry went well in White and Black communities, there were significant barriers to CAPS implementation in Latino communities. Why was this? First, Latinos were the youngest of the three groups, and as a rule young people do not participate in community-policing programs. Second, home ownership and length of time at residence was one of the strongest predictors of involvement in community-policing programs. But out of the three groups, Latinos had the lowest level of home ownership, and were more likely to move and hence possessed lower stakes in the program. Third, Spanish-speaking Latinos especially, even more so than their English-speaking counterparts, tended to retreat from involvement with the police because of immigration concerns. What this illustrates is that more needs to be understood about the conditions and factors which reduce or enhance citizen involvement in and commitment to community-oriented policing programs. We will return to this topic shortly.

BEYOND COMMUNITY POLICING?

Notice that there has been a shortening of the length of policing eras over time. Political spoils ran a full century (1830s to 1920s). Reform and early professionalization ran about fifty years (1920s to 1960s). The third, community-oriented policing, has had about a forty year run, from the 1970s to the present. And there is talk of the emergence of yet another era of policing, so-called post 9/11 policing (to be discussed in Chapter 5). These collapsing eras may simply be a function of the pressures to remain new and fresh, both from the perspective of police practitioners out in the field as well as scientists observing the police. It may indeed reflect the sort of modernist myopia which Lester F. Ward (1903) referred to long ago as the "illusion of the near." We "modern folk" are fond of talking about how, due to advances in technology as well as other factors, the pace of life is quickening. In policing as well as in many other areas of life, there is the idea that a newfangled "next big thing" is just around the corner, nurtured along by continuous improvement, best practices, and the sheer growth of knowledge. This reflects the idea that innovations and improvements in both technology and everyday life are happening so rapidly that things that used to be considered the "cutting edge" rapidly become obsolete.

There does seem to be some truth to the notion that modern societies continue to place an overweening premium on quickness, speed, and efficiency. Just the other day I plunked down an extra five dollars a month for a quicker DSL connection for my home Internet. In fact, French cultural theorist Paul Virilio made a nice career for himself placing this emphasis on speed and efficiency front and center in his writings. Virilio (1986) refers to his own study of speed as dromology (the science of the journey; see Haggerty 2006). One point Virilio makes in his dromological studies worth briefly noting is that high social status also brings with it the ability to have things literally at your fingertips. Those with money, power, and the right connections can speed up access to goods and services that the average person either could never access or would have to wait in line for for a very long time. And just as is the case for many other things, the wealthy and powerful are looked up to by those further down the status ladder, and they covet those things that they do not have. In effect, the middle and lower classes have a tendency of adopting and striving for the objects, resources, signs, and symbols that characterize the well-to-do.

Savvy entrepreneurs pick up on this, and set up marketing campaigns promising to give speedy access to things persons covet even if they can't afford them. The credit system functions as much as anything to allow mere commoners to keep up with the Joneses, and to maintain the outward appearance of a middle-class lifestyle. Lester Ward (1893) made note of this phenomenon in a general sense, which he called "the principle of deception." Influenced by Ward, a few years later and more famously economist Thorstein Veblen called it "conspicuous consumption." This emphasis on speed and quickness, which operates on both the consumption and production sides with regard to goods and services, is now a generalized phenomenon across society. This means that the police, too, are judged on how well they are keeping up with current trends, and how quickly and efficiently they make available to the public their various goods and services.

Rather than a passing fad (although granted it has been around for some forty years now), Wesley Skogan (2006c) believes community policing is pretty much here to stay. In fact, in many ways the argument made by proponents of community policing is that local governments, city leaders, and police administrators should resist temptations to give in to new fads, because presumably the major elements of community policing (described above) represent the way policing in a modern, industrial, and culturally diverse society ought to be done. This temptation is made even more palpable when tight budgets challenge the delivery of services and programs community-policing departments think they should be providing (Skogan 2006c).

Stephen Mastrofksi (2006) wonders how community policing, as a process or programmatic orientation, should be measured. Perhaps much of what passes for community policing is more rhetoric than reality. If indeed local communities decide for themselves which kinds of services and programs community-oriented policing departments should provide, how do we make sense of this massive diversity? There are ways of indirectly measuring such things as the level of citizen participation in community-policing programs, the extent to which local police departments are moving toward decentralization, and whether or not problem solving by the police, in collaboration with the citizenry, is really going on. Presumably research teams could go to local communities and survey residents about their needs and their view of the effectiveness of police services, as well as conducting on-site observations of the police in action (Mastrofski 2006, p. 49). Of course, the limitation of such approaches is the limitation of the case method in general, in that it is difficult to produce generalized knowledge about community policing from individual cases. Local communities have their own unique histories, needs, and resources, so implementation of community policing in any of these locations will likewise be limited by such realities.

MEASURING THE IMPLEMENTATION OF COMMUNITY POLICING

Yet even in the face of these difficulties, research continues to move forward regarding how to understand and conceptualize what community policing is doing, and to what extent it is being implemented community by community (Roberg 1994). Jeremy Wilson (2006), for example, has undertaken an ambitious effort to develop an empirical model for actually measuring the level of community-policing implementation in American cities. Wilson's (2006) review of the existing literature (e.g., King 1998; Maguire 2003; Maguire and Mastrofski 2000) led him to posit three broad factors that could explain the level of community-policing implementation (as measured in 1999):

- Organizational context, including such factors as size of the police department, the department's task or goal orientation (e.g., legalistic, service, or watchmen-oriented), demographic characteristics of the community being served, levels of funding for COP programs, and region;

- Organizational structure, including two main subvariables: *structural complexity* (e.g., number of stations or precincts, level of specialization within the department) and *structural control* (e.g., degree of centralization, degree of formalization, and administrative weight, or the proportion of total employees within the police organization assigned to administrative and technical support tasks; Wilson 2006, p. 64);
- Level of community-oriented policing (COP) implementation as measured in 1997.

After running appropriate statistical tests, Wilson (2006) found that some of these factors were significant in predicting community-policing implementation, while others were not. For example, with regard to organizational context, neither size of the department nor task scope affected COP implementation. Additionally, police chief turnover negatively affected COP implementation (that is, as police chief turnover increased COP implementation decreased). This seems to indicate that continuity of leadership of the police organization is important in creating a commitment to community policing over the long term.

One community characteristic affected COP implementation, and that was population mobility. Specifically, as population mobility increased COP implementation increased. Presumably high levels of population turnover creates more uncertainty within the police organization, as its planners and leaders may be uncertain about which services or orientations are appropriate for the community. In such a condition of uncertainty, police organizations may be more open to COP implementation. The funding variable was also significant: police departments which receive greater funding for specifically community-oriented programs and orientations are more likely to implement community policing. Region was also significant: police departments located in the western United States were more likely than departments in other regions to move toward COP implementation. Perhaps given the uneven and peculiar history of policing in the West (to be covered next chapter), western police departments are more progressive, innovative, and aligned with the philosophical orientation underlying COP implementation.

What about the organizational structure variables? First of all, structural complexity was insignificant: the number of stations or the degree of task specialization was not related to the level of COP implementation. The findings regarding structural control were mixed. On the one hand, neither centralization nor administrative weight affected the level of COP implementation. However, formalization did influence COP implementation: formal directives regarding COP implementation had a positive effect on actual COP implementation.

Finally, and no big surprise at all, the level of COP implementation in 1997 significantly predicted the level of COP implementation in 1999 as measured in the Law Enforcement Management and Administrative Statistics (LEMAS) survey. However, although statistically significant, the strength of the relationship was weaker than expected. This may have to do with the fact that police departments are not consistent, or that procedures vary from department to department, with regard to identifying community-policing programs, services, and orientations and reporting these in the LEMAS survey.

INFORMALLY EMBEDDED FORMALITY

It would seem that the positive relation between formality and the level of community-policing implementation is a somewhat counterintuitive or unexpected finding. Standard professional policing is driven by a top-down bureaucratic model shot through with formalized rules and operating procedures concerning how police are to act and which goals are to be pursued. Indeed, the highly formalized nature of policing of the second era viewed the police as "snappy bureaucrats" who pursued the goal of crime control and who, as highly-trained professionals, did not need "mere" citizens to help carry out their duties. Indeed, under traditional professionalization everyday citizens were barely tolerated, as they were described as "know-nothings" according to Van Maanen's (1978) famous typology. The third era of community policing was supposed to cut into this heavy formality, by the creation of flatter organizational hierarchies and the sincere effort to incorporate citizens of the police district into police planning, organization, and provision of services. This seemed to indicate that informality would be favored over stiff or mechanical formality, and therefore the number of rules in place guiding police activities would be minimized in favor of the human element and a more organic organizational structure, which would thereby also be open to negotiation, dynamism, and flux as conditions on the ground dictated.

But finding both higher formality *and* higher levels of community-policing implementation—as Wilson's (2006) research indicates—can be explained if we take into consideration the work of Arthur Stinchcombe (2001), who wrote a book on when and how formality works. Stinchcombe is correct to note that, traditionally, formality has been viewed negatively because of the perception that it somehow distorts and unduly restricts the agency and creativity of real flesh-and-blood human beings. The idea is that if an extra set of guidelines has to be developed to steer certain types of activity—as in the case of the myriad laws, ordinances, policy initiatives, and governmental regulations characteristic of modern living—then this is an *ipso facto* admission that the mere informal norms and rules of everyday life have somehow broken down and are no longer effective in generating social order or the "good life" more generally. From this perspective, the formalizations of law or bureaucratic regulation are seen at best as "necessary evils" but, if left unchecked, can eventually lead to an "iron cage" of stultifying routine and harsh rules which are enforced as ends in themselves (Weber 1978).

Although an important starting point, the Weberian tradition of bureaucracy, rationalization, and formalization has typically not been concerned with a fine-grained analysis of what these terms actually mean beyond common-sense under-standings, or what the analytical connections are between formality and informality. Formalization is an abstraction which dictates a set of rules or procedures for carry-ing out some type of work in some human social setting. But all formalizations have some unstated or tacit elements which allow human beings who are carrying out the directives to use their professional judgment—otherwise known as discretion—to complete the task at hand. For example, Stinchcombe notes that the highly for-malized procedures embodied in the blueprints for constructing a building leave certain bits of information out. Blueprints tend to be very precise about planning and construction, and graphical representations are provided concerning configu-ration of space and materials to be used. The size and location of the foundation, the load points, the nature of the subsoil upon which the building is to be erected, and the amount and type of concrete needed by building contractors are some of the many points formally designated and enumerated within blueprints. But much of the smaller details are left to the craft workers—plumbers, carpenters, stone masons, etc.—and these are not part of the blueprint. Stinchcombe (2001, p. 59) describes the types of informality that creep into the discretionary work of construc-tion craftpersons as follows:

> The actual floor [as constructed] may be easily an eighth of an inch off; a plumbing connection between a toilet and a waste line that is an eighth of an inch off can put a lot of sewage on the floor. Neither the exact location of the plumbing in the walls nor the exact location of the fixtures is described in the blueprints, and both are designed with adjustable connectors … so that they can be adapted to the building as built.

Likewise, drawing on the work of Llewellyn (2008), Stinchcombe notes that although the great majority of appellate decisions are based upon the technical aspects of law embedded in the procedures taking place in the lower court as well as general principles of precedent—indicating of course that judges maintain a high level of fidelity with the formalizations of law—about 9% of cases are decided on the basis of *obiter dicta* or "other reasons." This means that in about 10% of the cases, rather than relying on the formalizations of legal procedures and precedents, judges go "off the books" and use their professional discretion to decide these cases based upon hunch, instinct, a sense of fairness or social justice, mitigating circumstances, their training, or a whole host of additional possibilities. This is a condition Stinchcombe (2001) refers to as "informally embedded formality."

Returning to the case of Wilson's finding of the correlation between formality and the implementation of community policing, if we take the concept of informally embedded formality seriously, then what we see is that the rather abstract and elusive configuration of activities described as "community policing" are made better sense of by real flesh-and-blood human beings when a set of guidelines—a "connect-the-dots" for community policing if you will—are put into place, and clear paths are illuminated with regard to "how to do" community policing and recognizing it as such. Where such guidelines are lacking, all that is left for police practitioners to do is to rely on their standard understandings of traditional policing—which is done according to the formal dictates developed for such policing—while any attempts at community policing likely "slip through the cracks" because they are not anchored effectively within the abstractions of the formalities necessary to pull off this type of work.

CONCLUSION

In considering the work of Wilson (2006), it is clear that the project of identifying community-policing components and measuring to what extent they are being implemented in communities is an exceedingly complex undertaking. As thorough as Wilson's model is, it explains only about 28% of the variance in the relationship between the various variables he considered (organizational context, organizational structure, and level of prior COP implementation) and the outcome to be explained, namely later implementation of community policing. This is not the fault of Wilson, for there are a host of other variables which were not measured or which could not be brought into the model, and these missing or unmeasurable variables surely play a large part in reducing the robustness of the model's explanation. As is the case for research in most other areas of sociology and criminology, the issue of community-oriented policing and the factors associated with its level of implementation will require further analytical refinement and research out in the field.

NOTES

1 This section and later sections discussing the three eras of policing draw in part from Chriss (2007b, pp. 96–98).

2 There are several anomalies not adequately addressed in the Kelling and Moore (1988) three-era model of the history of American policing. First, there were slave patrols in the American south, stretching as far back as the 1740s, which took place well before the alleged first era of municipal policing beginning in the 1840s. These police forces acted to maintain the racial and social status quo of the southern slave system (see Hadden 2001; Williams and Murphy 2006). The second anomaly is the uneven development of municipal policing that took place west of the Mississippi, in what is known as the western frontier, beginning in 1857 in San Francisco, presumably the first western police department, as defined by the date of adoption of police uniforms (Monkkonen 1981). Although the story of policing in the Wild West is just now beginning to be told, there are several scholarly studies (see, e.g., Dykstra 1968; Gard 1949; Prassel 1972) of the more individualistic lawman versus gunslinger model which has, of course, been so widely depicted in movies and other popular accounts. Chapter 3 is devoted to studying the transition from the solitary lawman to the establishment of police departments across the western frontier. Nevertheless, even given these caveats and blind spots, as far as the three eras of policing are concerned, the Kelling and Moore (1988) typology is a useful approximation of how policing emerged over these periods.

3 For the history of the call box in particular and early police patrols in general, I draw upon Thale (2004). Another source of information on this topic was gleaned from Kelsey and Associates, an organization dedicated to the architectural history of Washington, DC. Part of this project involves a careful documentation of the history of fire and police call boxes in DC. This information can be found at https://www.washingtonhistory.com/?q=content/call-box-project.

4 Interestingly enough, the recent case of Anthony Sowell in Cleveland has brought the issue of police response to missing persons into the critical spotlight. Upwards of eleven bodies were discovered in and around Sowell's house, all African-American women living in poverty and who were either drug addicts or prostitutes. Some had gone missing for months or years, and although missing persons cases had been filed on most of them, police investigations came to a dead end. The implication here is that Cleveland police did not take these missing cases seriously because of the race of the missing persons. Hence, we also have another example of the ease with which criminal justice officials in general, and the police in particular, can be accused of biased or even racist actions.

BIBLIOGRAPHY

Adams, Ramon F. 1963. "Cowboys and Horses of the American West." Pp. 323–376 in *The Book of the American West*, edited by J. Monaghan and C.P. Hornung. New York: Julian Messner Inc.

Alpert, Geoffrey P. and Jeffrey J. Noble, Esq. 2009. "Lies, True Lies, and Conscious Deception: Police Officers and the Truth." *Police Quarterly* 12 (2):237–254.

Anderson, Elijah. 1999. *Code of the Street: Decency, Violence, and the Moral Life of the Inner City.* New York: Norton.

Anderson, G.S., A. Courtney, D. Plecas, and C. Chamberlin. 2005. "Multitasking Behaviors of General Duty Police Officers." *Police Practice and Research* 6 (1):39–48.

Ankony, Robert C. and Thomas M. Kelley. 1999. "The Impact of Perceived Alienation on Police Officers' Sense of Mastery and Subsequent Motivation for Proactive Enforcement." *Policing* 22 (2):120–132.

Arcuri, Alan F. 1977. "Criminal Justice: A Police Perspective." *Criminal Justice Review* 2 (1):15–21.

Atwood, Kay. 2008. *Chaining Oregon: Surveying the Public Lands of the Pacific Northwest, 1851–1855.* Blacksburg, VA: McDonald and Woodward Publishing.

Bailey, John and Lucía Dammert. 2006. "Public Security and Police Reform in the Americas." Pp. 1–23 in *Public Security and Police Reform in the Americas*, edited by J. Bailey and L. Dammert. Pittsburgh, PA: University of Pittsburgh Press.

Bales, Robert F. 1950. *Interaction Process Analysis: A Method for the Study of Small Groups.* Reading, MA: Addison-Wesley.

———. 1953. "The Equilibrium Problem in Small Groups." Pp. 111–161 in *Working Papers in the Theory of Action*, edited by T. Parsons, R.F. Bales, and E.A. Shils. New York: Free Press.

Ball, Durwood. 2001. *Army Regulars on the Western Frontier, 1848–1861.* Norman: University of Oklahoma Press.

Balogun, Julia, Pauline Gleadle, Veronica Hope Hailey, and Hugh Willmott. 2005. "Managing Change across Boundaries: Boundary-Shaking Practices." *British Journal of Management* 16:261–278.

Bannister, Robert C. 1987. *Sociology and Scientism.* Chapel Hill: University of North Carolina Press.

Barth, Alan. 1961. *Law Enforcement versus the Law.* New York: Collier Books. Bartlett, Richard A. 1962. *Great Surveys of the American West.* Norman: University of Oklahoma Press.

Bayley, David H. and Clifford D. Shearing. 2001. "The New Structure of Policing: Description, Conceptualization, and Research Agenda." *NIJ Research Report.* Washington, DC: National Institute of Justice.

Bayley, David H. and David Weisburd. 2009. "Cops and Spooks: The Role of the Police in Counterterrorism." Pp. 81–99 in *To Protect and to Serve: Policing in an Age of Terrorism*, edited by D. Weisburd, T.E. Feucht, I. Hakimi, L.F. Mock, and S. Perry. Dordrecht: Springer.

Belvedere, Kimberly, John L. Worrall, and Stephen G. Tibbetts. 2005. "Explaining Suspect Resistance in Police-Citizen Encounters." *Criminal Justice Review* 30 (1):30–44.

Benedict, William Reed, Douglas J. Bower, Ben Brown, and Roger Cunningham. 1999. "Small Town Surveys: Bridging the Gap between Police and the Community." *Journal of Contemporary Criminal Justice Review* 15 (2):144–154.

Bendix, Reinhard. 1947. "Bureaucracy: The Problem and Its Setting." *American Sociological Review* 12 (5):493–507.

Bennett, Trevor. 1995. "Identifying, Explaining, and Targeting Burglary 'Hot Spots.'" *European Journal on Criminal Policy and Research* 3 (3):113–123.

Benson, Bruce L. 1998. *To Serve and Protect: Privatization and Community in Criminal Justice.* New York: New York University Press.

———. "Contractual Nullification of Economically-Detrimental State-Made Laws." *Review of Austrian Economics* 19:149–187.

Bernard, Thomas J., Eugene A. Paoline, III, and Paul-Philippe Pare. 2005. "General Systems Theory and Criminal Justice." *Journal of Criminal Justice* 33:203–211.

Bitsakis, Eftichios. 1991. "Mass, Matter, and Energy: A Relativistic Approach." *Foundations of Physics* 21 (1):63–81.

Bittner, Egon. 1967. "The Police on Skid-Row: A Study of Police Keeping." *American Sociological Review* 32 (5):699–715.

———. 1970. *The Functions of the Police in Modern Society*. Chevy Chase, MD: National Institute of Mental Health.

———. 1990. *Aspects of Police Work*. Boston: Northeastern University Press. Black, Donald J. 1970. "Production of Crime Rates." *American Sociological Review* 35 (4):733–748.

———. 1971. "The Social Organization of Arrest." *Stanford Law Review* 23: 1087–1111.

———. 1976. *The Behavior of Law*. San Diego: Academic Press.

———. 1980. *The Manners and Customs of the Police*. New York: Academic Press.

Black, Donald J. and Albert J. Reiss, Jr. 1970. "Police Control of Juveniles." *American Sociological Review* 35 (1):63–77.

Bohannan, Paul. 1973. "The Differing Realms of the Law." Pp. 306–317 in *The Social Organization of Law*, edited by D. Black and M. Mileski. New York: Seminar Press.

Booth, Charles. 1970 [1902–1904]. *Life and Labour of the People in London*, final volume. New York: AMS Press.

Bordua, David J. and Albert J. Reiss, Jr. 1966. "Command, Control, and Charisma: Reflections on Police Bureaucracy." *American Journal of Sociology* 72 (1):68–76.

Brodeur, Jean-Paul. 1983. "High Policing and Low Policing: Some Remarks about the Policing of Political Activities." *Social Problems* 30:507– 521.

———. 2007a. "High and Low Policing in Post 9/11 Times." *Policing* 1:25–37.

———. 2007b. "An Encounter with Egon Bittner." *Crime, Law and Social Change* 48:105–132.

Brodeur, Jean-Paul and Stéphane Leman-Langlois. 2006. "Surveillance Fiction or Higher Policing?" Pp. 171–198 in *The New Politics of Surveillance and Visibility*, edited by K.D. Haggerty and R.V. Ericson. Toronto: University of Toronto Press.

Brown, Ben. 2007. "Community Policing in Post-September 11 America: A Comment on the Concept of Community-Oriented Counterterrorism." *Police Practice and Research* 8 (3):239–251.

Brown, Mary M. and Jeffrey L. Brudney. 2003. "Learning Organizations in the Public Sector? A Study of Police Agencies Employing Information and Technology to Advance Knowledge." *Public Administration Review* 63 (1):30–43.

Brown, Richard M. 1976. "The History of Vigilantism in America." Pp. 79–109 in *Vigilante Politics*, edited by H.J. Rosenbaum and P.C. Sedeberg. Philadelphia: University of Pennsylvania Press.

Brunson, Rod K. 2007. "'Police Don't Like Black People': African-American Young Men's Accumulated Police Experiences." *Criminology and Public Policy* 6 (1):71–101.

Buerger, Michael E. 1994. "The Limits of Community." Pp. 270–273 in *The Challenge of Community Policing*, edited by D.P. Rosenbaum. Thousand Oaks, CA: Sage.

Burgess, Ernest W. and Harvey J. Locke. 1945. *The Family, from Institution to Companionship*. New York: American Book Co.

Burris, Scott. 2006. "From Security to Health." Pp. 196–216 in *Democracy, Society and the Governance of Security*, edited by J. Wood and B. Dupont. Cambridge: Cambridge University Press.

Butler, Anne M. 1997. *Gendered Justice in the American West*. Urbana: University of Illinois Press.

Canlis, Michael N. 1961. "The Evolution of Law Enforcement in California." *Far Westerner* 2:1–13.

Carlson, Joseph R. 1995. "The Future Terrorists in America." *American Journal of Police* 14 (3–4):71–91.

Carro, D., S. Valera, and T. Vidal. 2010. "Perceived Insecurity in the Public Space: Personal, Social, and Environmental Variables." *Quality and Quantity* 44:303–314.

Chan, Janet B.L. 2001. "The Technological Game: How Information Technology Is Transforming Police Practice." *Criminal Justice* 1 (2):139–159.

———. 2007. "Making Sense of Police Reforms." *Theoretical Criminology* 11 (3):323–345.

Chappell, Allison T., John M. MacDonald, and Patrick W. Manz. 2006. "The Organizational Determinants of Police Arrest Decisions." *Crime and Delinquency* 52 (2):287–306.

Chriss, James J. 1994. "Spain on Status and Space: A Comment." *Sociological Theory* 12 (1):106–109.

————. 1999a. *Alvin W. Gouldner: Sociologist and Outlaw Marxist*. Aldershot, UK: Ashgate.

————. 1999b. "Introduction." Pp. 1–29 in *Counseling and the Therapeutic State*, edited by J.J. Chriss. New York: Aldine de Gruyter.

————. 2001. "Alvin W. Gouldner and Industrial Sociology at Columbia University." *Journal of the History of the Behavioral Sciences* 37 (3):241–259.

————. 2004. "The Perils of Risk Assessment." *Society* 41 (4):52–56.

————. 2005. "Mead, George Herbert." Pp. 486–491 in *Encyclopedia of Social Theory*, edited by G. Ritzer. Thousand Oaks, CA: Sage.

————. 2006. "The Place of Lester Ward among the Sociological Classics." *Journal of Classical Sociology* 6 (1):5–21.

————. 2007a. "The Functions of the Social Bond." *Sociological Quarterly* 48:689–712.

————. 2007b. *Social Control: An Introduction*. Cambridge, UK: Polity Press.

————. 2007c. "Norm of Reciprocity." Pp. 3227–3229 in *Blackwell Encyclopedia of Sociology*, Vol. 7, edited by G. Ritzer. Malden, MA: Blackwell.

————. 2008. "Addams, Ward, et al.: American Sociology Past to Present." *Journal of Classical Sociology* 8 (4):491–502.

Clarke, Ronald V. and Graeme R. Newman. 2007. "Police and the Prevention of Terrorism." *Policing* 1 (1):9–20.

Clutterbuck, Lindsay. 2006. "Countering Irish Republican Terrorism in Britain: Its Origin as a Police Function." *Terrorism and Political Violence* 18 (1):95–118.

Coates, William R. 1924. *A History of Cuyahoga County and the City of Cleveland*. Chicago: American Historical Society.

Cohen, Lawrence E. and Kenneth C. Land. 1987. "Age Structure and Crime: Symmetry versus Asymmetry and the Projection of Crime Rates through the 1990s." *American Sociological Review* 52 (2):170–183.

Comstock, Donald E. 1971. "Boundary Spanning Processes in Complex Organizations." Master's thesis, University of Denver.

Cooley, Charles H. 1930. *Sociological Theory and Social Research*. New York: H. Holt and Co.

Corra, Mamadi and David Willer. 2002. "The Gatekeeper." *Sociological Theory* 20 (2):180–207.

Crank, John P. 1989. "Civilianization in Small and Medium Police Departments in Illinois, 1973–1986." *Journal of Criminal Justice* 17 (3):167–177.

Crank, John P. 2003. "Institutional Theory of Police: A Review of the State of the Art." *Policing* 26:186–207.

Crank, John P. and Robert H. Langworthy. 1996. "Fragmented Centralization and the Organization of the Police." *Policing and Society* 6 (2):213–229.

Crant, J. Michael. 2000. "Proactive Behavior in Organizations." *Journal of Management* 26 (3):435–462.

Crawford, Adam. 2006. "Policing and Security as 'Club Goods': The New Enclosures?" Pp. 111–138 in *Democracy, Society and the Governance of Security*, edited by J. Wood and B. Dupont. Cambridge, UK: Cambridge University Press.

Crowther, Chris. 2000. "Thinking about the 'Underclass': Towards a Political Economy of Policing." *Theoretical Criminology* 4 (2):149–167. Culberson, William C. 1990. *Vigilantism: Political History of Private Power in America*. New York: Praeger.

Dal Fiore, Filippo. 2007. "Communities versus Networks: The Implications on Innovation and Social Change." *American Behavioral Scientist* 50 (7):857–866.

Daleiden, J. Robert. 2006. "A Clumsy Dance: The Political Economy of American Police and Policing." *Policing* 29 (4):602–624.

Davis, James A. 1961. "Compositional Effects, Role Systems, and the Survival of Small Discussion Groups." *Public Opinion Quarterly* 25 (4):574–584.

Davis, Rebecca. 1997. "What Fourth Amendment? HR 666 and the Satanic Expansion of the Good Faith Exception." *Policing* 20 (1):101–112.

De Lint, Willem. 2003. "Keeping Open Windows: Police as Access Brokers." *British Journal of Criminology* 43:379–397.

Deflem, Mathieu. 2002. "The Logic of Nazification: The Case of the International Criminal Police Commission ('Interpol')." *International Journal of Comparative Sociology* 43 (1):21–44.

———. 2004. "Social Control and the Policing of Terrorism: Foundations for a Sociology of Counterterrorism." *American Sociologist* 35 (2):75–92.

———. 2005. "'Wild Beasts without Nationality': The Uncertain Origins of Interpol, 1898–1910." Pp. 275–285 in *Handbook of Transnational Crime and Justice*, edited by P. Reichel. Thousand Oaks, CA: Sage.

Denhardt, Robert M. 1947. *The Horse of the Americas*. Norman: University of Oklahoma Press.

Dewey, John. 1896. "The Reflex Arc Concept in Psychology." *Psychological Review* 3:357–370.

Di Paola, Pietro. 2007. "The Spies Who Came in from the Heat: The International Surveillance of the Anarchists in London." *European History Quarterly* 37 (2):189–215.

Dickens, Charles. 1855. *Household Words: A Weekly Journal*, Vol. 10. London: Lenox Library.

DiMaggio, Paul J. and Walter W. Powell. 1983. "The Iron Cage Revisited: Institutional Isomorphism and Collective Rationality in Organizational Fields." *American Sociological Review* 48:147–160.

———. 1991. "Introduction." Pp. 1–38 in *The New Institutionalism in Organizational Analysis*, edited by W.W. Powell and P.J. DiMaggio. Chicago: University of Chicago Press.

Drabek, Thomas E. 1965. "Laboratory Simulation of a Police Communication System under Stress." Ph.D. diss., Ohio State University.

Durkheim, Emile. 1984 [1893]. *Division of Labor in Society*, translated by W.D. Halls. New York: Free Press.

Durose, Matthew R., Erica L. Smith, and Patrick A. Langan. 2007. "Contact between Police and the Public, 2005." Bureau of Justice Statistics. Washington, DC: U.S. Department of Justice.

Dykstra, Robert R. 1968. *The Cattle Towns*. New York: Alfred A. Knopf.

Eck, John E. 2006. "Science, Values, and Problem-Oriented Policing: Why Problem-Oriented Policing?" Pp. 117–132 in *Police Innovation: Contrasting Perspectives*, edited by D. Weisburd and A.A. Braga. Cambridge, UK: Cambridge University Press.

Eckberg, Douglas Lee and Lester Hill, Jr. 1979. "The Paradigm Concept and Sociology: A Critical Review." *American Sociological Review* 44:925– 937.

Elazar, Daniel J. 1996. "The Frontier as a Chain Reaction." Pp. 173–190 in *Frontiers in Regional Development*, edited by Y. Gradus and H. Lithwick. Lanham, MD: Rowman and Littefield.

Elliott, Mabel A. 1944. "Crime on the Frontier Mores." *American Sociological Review* 9:185–192.

Elliott, Mabel A. and Francis E. Merrill. 1950. *Social Disorganization*. New York: Harper.

Ellwood, Charles A. 1910. *Sociology and Modern Social Problems*. American Book Company.

Ericson, Richard V. 2007. "Rules in Policing: Five Perspectives." *Theoretical Criminology* 11 (3):367–401.

Fagan, Jeffrey and Tom R. Tyler. 2005. "Legal Socialization of Children and Adolescents." *Social Justice Research* 18 (3):217–241.

Fararo, Thomas J. and Kent A. McClelland. 2006. "Introduction: Control Systems Thinking in Sociological Theory." Pp. 1–27 in *Purpose, Meaning, and Action: Control Systems Theories in Sociology*, edited by K.A. McClelland and T.J. Fararo. New York: Palgrave.

Faris, Robert E.L. 1955. *Social Disorganization*. New York: Ronald Press Company.

Farr, James. 2004. "Social Capital: A Conceptual History." *Political Theory* 32 (1):6–33.

Feldman, Leonard C. 2002. "Redistribution, Recognition, and the State: The Irreducibly Political Dimension of Injustice." *Political Theory* 30 (3):410–440.

Felson, Richard B., Steven F. Messner, Anthony W. Hoskin, and Glenn Deane. 2002. "Reasons for Reporting and Not Reporting Domestic Violence to the Police." *Criminology* 40 (3):617–648.

Feucht, Thomas E., David Weisburd, Simon Perry, Lois Felson Mock, and Idit Hakimi. 2009. "Policing, Terrorism, and Beyond." Pp. 203–224 in *To Protect and to Serve: Policing in an Age of Terrorism*, edited by D. Weisburd, T.E. Feucht, I. Hakimi, L.F. Mock, and S. Perry. Dordrecht: Springer.

Fletcher, Joseph. 1850. "Statistical Account of the Police of the Metropolis." *Journal of the Statistical Society of London* 13 (3):221–267.

Foucault, Michel. 1978. *History of Sexuality*, Vol. 1, translated by R. Hurley. New York: Vantage.

Frank, James, Steven G. Brandl, and R. Cory Watkins. 1997. "The Content of Community Policing: A Comparison of the Daily Activities of Community and 'Beat' Officers." *Policing* 20 (4):716–728.

Frantzen, Durant and Claudia San Miguel. 2009. "Mandatory Arrest? Police Response to Domestic Violence Victims." *Policing* 32 (2):319–337. Frazer, Robert W. 1965. *Forts of the West: Military Forts and Presidios and Posts Commonly Called Forts West of the Mississippi River to 1898.* Norman: University of Oklahoma Press.

Friedman, Lawrence M. 2007. *Guarding Life's Dark Secrets: Legal and Social Control over Reputation, Propriety, and Privacy.* Stanford, CA: Stanford University Press.

Gabbay, Edmond. 1973. *Discretion in Criminal Justice.* London: White Eagle Press.

Gard, Wayne. 1949. *Frontier Justice.* Norman: University of Oklahoma Press.

———. 1963. "The Law of the American West." Pp. 261–322 in *The Book of the American West*, edited by J. Monaghan and C.P. Hornung. New York: Julian Messner Inc.

Garland, David. 2005. "Penal Excess and Surplus Meaning: Public Torture Lynchings in Twentieth-Century America." *Law and Society Review* 39 (4):793–833.

Garner, Joel H., Thomas Schade, John Hepburn, and John Buchanan. 1995. "Measuring the Continuum of Force Used by and against the Police." *Criminal Justice Review* 20 (2):146–168.

Gelsthorpe, Loraine and Nicola Padfield. 2003. "Introduction." Pp. 1–28 in *Exercising Discretion: Decision-Making in the Criminal Justice System and Beyond.* Devon, UK: Willan Publishing.

Gerstein, Lawrence H. 2006. "Counseling Psychology's Commitment to Strengths: Rhetoric or Reality?" *Counseling Psychologist* 34 (2):276– 292.

Giddens, Anthony. 1984. *The Constitution of Society: Outline of the Theory of Structuration.* Cambridge, UK: Polity Press.

Giddings, Franklin H. 1896. *Principles of Sociology.* New York: Macmillan.

———. 1922. "The Measurement of Social Forces." *Journal of Social Forces* 1 (1):1–6.

Girodo, Michel. 1998. "Undercover Probes of Police Corruption: Risk Factors in Proactive Internal Affairs Investigations." *Behavioral Sciences and the Law* 16:479–496.

Goeres-Gardner, Diane L. 2005. *Necktie Parties: Legal Executions in Oregon, 1851–1905.* Caldwell, ID: Caxton Press.

Goffman, Erving. 1963. *Behavior in Public Places.* New York: Free Press.

Gouldner, Alvin W. 1954. *Patterns of Industrial Bureaucracy.* Glencoe, IL: Free Press.

Gouldner, Alvin W. 1960. "The Norm of Reciprocity: A Preliminary Statement." *American Sociological Review* 25 (2):161–178.

———. 1970. *The Coming Crisis of Western Sociology.* New York: Avon.

Gowri, Aditi. 2003. "Community Policing is an Epicycle." *Policing* 26 (4):591–611.

Graybill, Andrew R. 2007. *Policing the Great Plains: Rangers, Mounties, and the North American Frontier, 1875–1910.* Lincoln: University of Nebraska Press.

Groeneveld, Richard F. 2005. *Arrest Discretion of Police Officers: The Impact of Varying Organizational Structures.* El Paso, TX: LFB Scholarly Publishing.

Guetzloe, Eleanor. 1992. "Violent, Aggressive, and Antisocial Students: What Are We Going To Do With Them?" *Preventing School Failure* 36 (3):4–9.

Hadden, Sally E. 2001. *Slave Patrols.* Cambridge, MA: Harvard University Press.

Haggerty, Kevin D. 2006. "Visible War: Surveillance, Speed, and Information War." Pp. 250–268 in *The New Politics of Surveillance and Visibility*, edited by R.V. Ericson and K.D. Haggerty. Toronto: University of Toronto Press.

Haines, Valerie A. 1992. "Spencer's Philosophy of Science." *British Journal of Sociology* 43 (2):155–172.

———. 2005. "Spencer, Herbert." Pp. 781–787 in *Encyclopedia of Social Theory*, Vol. 2, edited by G. Ritzer. Thousand Oaks, CA: Sage.

Hallwas, John E. 2008. *Dime Novel Desperadoes: The Notorious Maxwell Brothers.* Urbana: University of Illinois Press.

Hamilton, Peter. 1996. "Systems Theory." Pp. 143–170 in *Blackwell Companion to Social Theory*, edited by B.S. Turner. Oxford, UK: Blackwell.

Haupt, Edward J. 2001. "Laboratories for Experimental Psychology: Göttingen's Ascendancy over Leipzig in the 1890s." Pp. 205–250 in *Wilhelm Wundt in History*, edited by R.W. Rieber and D.K. Robinson. New York: Plenum.

Hawkins, Keith. 2003. "Order, Rationality, and Silence: Some Reflections on Criminal Justice Decision-Making." Pp. 186–219 in *Exercising Discretion: Decision-Making in the Criminal Justice System and Beyond*. Devon, UK: Willan Publishing.

Haywood, C. Robert. 1991. *Victorian West: Class and Culture in Kansas Cattle Towns*. Lawrence: University Press of Kansas.

Hays, Sharon. 1994. "Structure and Agency and the Sticky Problem of Culture." *Sociological Theory* 12 (1):57–72.

Henry, Vincent E. and Douglas H. King. 2004. "Improving Emergency Preparedness and Public-Safety Responses to Terrorism and Weapons of Mass Destruction." *Brief Treatment and Crisis Intervention* 4 (1):11–35.

Herbert, Steve. 2006a. *Citizens, Cops, and Power: Recognizing the Limits of Community*. Chicago: University of Chicago Press.

———. 2006b. "Police Subculture Reconsidered." *Criminology* 36 (2):343–370.

Hillery, George A., Jr. 1968. *Communal Organizations: A Study of Local Societies*. Chicago: University of Chicago Press.

Hirsch, Paul M. 1972. "Processing Fads and Fashions: An Organization-Set Analysis of Cultural Industry Systems." *American Journal of Sociology* 77 (4):639–659.

Hirsch, Paul and Michael Lounsbury. 1997. "Ending the Family Quarrel: Towards a Reconciliation of 'Old' and 'New' Institutionalism." *American Behavioral Scientist* 40 (4):406–418.

Hoffmann, Gabi and Paul Mazerolle. 2005. "Police Pursuits in Queensland: Research, Review, and Reform." *Policing* 28 (3):530–545.

Hogenboom, Ari. 1959. "The Pendleton Act and the Civil Service." *American Historical Review* 64 (2):301–318.

Huberts, Leo W.J.C., Terry Lamboo, and Maurice Punch. 2003. "Police Integrity in the Netherlands and the United States: Awareness and Alertness." *Police Practice and Research* 4 (3):217–232.

Hutcheon, Pat Duffy. 1972. "Value Theory: Towards Conceptual Clarification." *British Journal of Sociology* 23 (2):172–187.

Innes, Martin. 2005. "Why 'Soft' Policing is Hard: On the Curious Development of Reassurance Policing, How it Became Neighbourhood Policing and what this Signifies about the Politics of Police Reform." *Journal of Community and Applied Social Psychology* 15 (3):156–169.

———. "Policing Uncertainty: Countering Terror through Community Intelligence and Democratic Policing." *Annals of the American Academy of Political and Social Science* 605:222–241.

International Association of Chiefs of Police. 2005. "Post 9-11 Policing: The Crime Control–Homeland Security Paradigm." Washington, DC: US Department of Justice, Bureau of Justice Assistance, Office of Justice Programs.

Jackson, Arrick L. and John E. Wade. 2005. "Police Perceptions of Social Capital and Sense of Responsibility: An Explanation of Proactive Policing." *Policing* 28 (1):49–68.

James, Nathan. 2008. "Community Oriented Policing Services (COPS): Background, Legislation, and Issues." Congressional Report RL33308. Washington, DC: Congressional Research Service.

Joh, Elizabeth. 2004. "The Paradox of Private Policing." *Journal of Criminal Law and Criminology* 95 (1):49–131.

Johnson, David R. 1981. *American Law Enforcement: A History*. St. Louis, MO: Forum Press.

Johnson, Herbert A., Nancy Travis Wolfe, and Mark Jones. 2008. *History of Criminal Justice*, 4th ed. Newark, NJ: LexisNexis.

Johnston, Les. 1992. *The Rebirth of Private Policing*. London: Routledge.

Jones, Robert Huhn. 1961. *The Civil War in the Northwest: Nebraska, Wisconsin, Iowa, Minnesota, and the Dakotas*. Norman: University of Oklahoma Press.

Kaptein, Muel and Piet van Reenen. 2001. "Integrity Management of Police Organizations." *Policing* 24 (3):281–300.

Kelling, George L. 1999. *"Broken Windows" and Police Discretion*. Washington, DC: National Institute of Justice.

Kelling, George L. and Mark H. Moore. 1988. "The Evolving Strategy of Policing." In *Perspectives on Policing*, No. 4. Washington, DC: National Institute of Justice.

Kennedy, David M. 2006. "Old Wine in New Bottles: Policing and the Lessons of Pulling Levers." Pp. 155–170 in *Police Innovation: Contrasting Perspectives*, edited by D. Weisburd and A.A. Braga. Cambridge, UK: Cambridge University Press.

King, W.R. 1998. *Innovations in American Municipal Police Organizations*. Ph.D. diss., University of Cincinnati.

Kinkaid, Harold. 2007. "Functional Explanation and Evolutionary Social Science." Pp. 213–247 in *Philosophy of Anthropology and Sociology*, edited by S.P. Turner and M.W. Risjord. Amsterdam: North-Holland.

Klinger, David A. 1997. "Negotiating Order in Patrol Work: An Ecological Theory of Police Response to Deviance." *Criminology* 35 (2):277–306.

———. 2004. "Environment and Organization: Reviving a Perspective on the Police." *Annals of the American Academy of Political and Social Science* 593:119–136.

———. 2005. "Social Theory and the Street Cop: The Case of Deadly Force." *Ideas in American Policing* 7:1–15.

Klockars, Carl B. 1980. "The Dirty Harry Problem." *Annals of the American Academy of Political and Social Science* 452:33–47.

———. 2006. "Street Justice: Some Micro-Moral Reservations." Pp. 150–153 in *Police and Society: Touchstone Readings*, edited by V.E. Kappeler. Long Grove, IL: Waveland Press.

Klockars, Carl B., Sanja K. Ivkovic, and M.R. Haberfeld. 2006. *Enhancing Police Integrity*. Dordrecht: Springer.

Knapp Commission. 1973. *The Knapp Commission Report on Police Corruption*. New York: George Braziller.

Kowalski, Brian R. and Richard J. Lundman. 2007. "Vehicle Stops by Police for Driving while Black: Common Problems and Some Tentative Solutions." *Journal of Criminal Justice* 35 (2):165–181.

KPMG. 1996. *Report to the New York City Commission to Combat Police Corruption*. New York: NYC Commission to Combat Police Corruption.

Krader, Lawrence. 1968. *Formation of the State*. Englewood Cliffs, NJ: Prentice-Hall.

Kuhn, Thomas S. 1962. The *Structure of Scientific Revolutions*. Chicago: University of Chicago Press.

Lab, Steven P. 2007. *Crime Prevention: Approaches, Practices and Evaluations*, 6th ed. Albany, NY: LexisNexis.

LaFree, Gary and Laura Dugan. 2009. "Tracking Global Terrorism Trends, 1970–2004." Pp. 43–80 in *To Protect and to Serve: Policing in an Age of Terrorism*, edited by D. Weisburd, T.E. Feucht, I. Hakimi, L.F. Mock, and S. Perry. Dordrecht: Springer.

Lane, Roger. 1992. "Urban Police and Crime in Nineteenth-Century America." Pp. 1–50 in *Modern Policing*, edited by M. Tonry and N. Morris. Vol. 15 of *Crime and Justice*, edited by M. Tonry. Chicago: University of Chicago Press.

Leichtman, Ellen C. 2008. "Complex Harmony: The Military and Professional Models of Policing." *Critical Criminology* 16 (1):53–73.

Levi, Ron and John Hagan. 2006. "International Police." Pp. 207–247 in *The New Police Science: The Police Power in Domestic and International Governance*, edited by M.D. Dubber and M. Valverde. Stanford: Stanford University Press.

Lewis, Oscar. 1980. *San Francisco: Mission to Metropolis*, 2nd ed. San Diego, CA: Howell-North Books.

Librett, Mitch. 2008. "Wild Pigs and Outlaws: The Kindred Worlds of Policing and Outlaw Bikers." *Crime, Media, Culture* 4 (2):257–269.

Lidz, Victor. 2001. "Language and the 'Family' of Generalized Symbolic Media." 141–176 in *Talcott Parsons Today*, edited by A.J. Trevino. Lanham, MD: Rowman and Littlefield.

Liebling, Alison. 2000. "Prison Officers, Policing, and the Use of Discretion." *Theoretical Criminology* 4 (3):333–357.

Liebling, Alison and David Price. 2003. "Prison Officers and the Use of Discretion." Pp. 74–96 in *Exercising Discretion: Decision-Making in the Criminal Justice System and Beyond*. Devon, UK: Willan Publishing.

Linn, Edith. 2009. *Arrest Decisions: What Works for the Officer?* New York: Peter Lang.

Llewellyn, Karl N. 2008. *Jurisprudence: Realism in Theory and Practice*. New Brunswick: Transaction Publishers.

Loader, Ian. 2006. "Policing, Recognition, and Belonging." *Annals of the American Academy of Political and Social Science* 605:202–221.

Loader, Ian and Neil Walker. 2006. "Necessary Virtues: The Legitimate Place of the State in the Production of Security." Pp. 165–195 in *Democracy, Society and the Governance of Security*, edited by J. Wood and B. Dupont. Cambridge, UK: Cambridge University Press.

Maguire, E.R. 2003. *Organizational Structure in American Police Agencies: Context, Complexity, and Control*. Albany, NY: SUNY Press.

Maguire, E.R. and S.D. Mastrofski. 2000. "Patterns of Community Policing in the United States." *Police Quarterly* 3:4–45.

Manning, Peter K. 1978. "The Police: Mandate, Strategies, and Appearances." Pp. 7–32 in *Policing: A View from the Street*, edited by P.K. Manning and J. Van Maanen. Santa Monica, CA: Goodyear.

———. 1997. Police Work: The Social Organization of Policing, 2nd ed. Prospect Heights, IL: Waveland Press.

———. 1999. "A Dramaturgical Perspective." Pp. 49–125 in *Privatization of Policing: Two Views*, B. Forst and P.K. Manning. Washington, DC: Georgetown University Press.

———. 2006. "Two Case Studies of American Anti-Terrorism." Pp. 52–85 in *Democracy, Society and the Governance of Security*, edited by J. Wood and B. Dupont. Cambridge: Cambridge University Press.

Marks, D.E. and I.Y. Sun. 2007. "The Impact of 9/11 on Organizational Development among State and Local Enforcement Agencies." *Journal of Contemporary Criminal Justice* 23:159–173.

Marsh, Margaret. 1989. "From Separation to Togetherness: The Social Construction of Domestic Space in American Suburbs, 1840–1915." *Journal of American History* 76 (2):506–527.

Marx, Gary T. 1986. "The Interweaving of Public and Private Police in Undercover Work." Pp. 172–193 in *Private Policing*, edited by C.D. Shearing and P.C. Stenning. Newbury Park, CA: Sage.

———. 1992. "When the Guards Guard Themselves: Undercover Tactics Turned Inward." *Policing and Society* 2 (3):151–172.

Maslow, Abraham H. 1934. "The Effect of Varying Time Intervals between Acts with a Note on Proactive Inhibition." *Experimental Psychology* 17 (1):141–144.

Mastrofski, Stephen. 1998. "Community Policing and Police Organization Structure." Pp. 161–189 in *How to Recognize Good Policing*, edited by J. Brodeur. Thousand Oaks, CA: Sage.

———. 2004. "Controlling Street-Level Police Discretion." *Annals of the American Academy of Political and Social Science* 593:100–118.

———. 2006. "Community Policing: A Skeptical View." Pp. 44–73 in *Police Innovation: Contrasting Perspectives*, edited by D. Weisburd and A.A. Braga. Cambridge, UK: Cambridge University Press.

Mazerolle, Lorraine and Janet Ransley. 2006. "The Case for Third-Party Policing." Pp. 191–206 in *Police Innovation: Contrasting Perspectives*, edited by D. Weisburd and A.A. Braga. Cambridge, UK: Cambridge University Press.

McCallum, Henry D. and Frances T. McCallum. 1965. *The Wire that Fenced the West*. Norman: University of Oklahoma Press.

McConville, Mike and Chester Mirsky. 1995. "Guilty Plea Courts: A Social Disciplinary Model of Criminal Justice." *Social Problems* 42 (2):216–234.

McGrath, Roger D. 1984. *Gunfighters, Highwaymen, and Vigilantes: Violence on the Frontier*. Berkeley: University of California Press.

McKelvey, Blake. 1969. *The City in American History*. London: Allen and Unwin.

McMahon, Pamela M. 2000. "The Public Health Approach to the Prevention of Sexual Violence." *Sexual Abuse* 12 (1):27–36.

Mead, George H. 1934. *Mind, Self, and Society from the Standpoint of a Social Behaviorist*, edited by C.W. Morris. Chicago: University of Chicago Press.

Melbin, Murray. 1987. *Night as Frontier: Colonizing the World after Dark*. New York: Free Press.

Meliala, Adrianus. 2001. "The Notion of Sensitivity in Policing." *International Journal of the Sociology of Law* 29:99–111.

Merton, Robert K. 1957. "The Role-Set: Problems in Sociological Theory." *British Journal of Sociology* 8 (2):106–120.

———. 1968. *Social Theory and Social Structure*. New York: Free Press.

Meyer, J. and B. Rowan. 1977. "Institutional Organizations: Formal Structures as Myth and Ceremony." *American Journal of Sociology* 83:340–363.

Miller, Nyle H. and Joseph W. Snell. 1963. *Great Gunfighters of the Kansas Cowtowns, 1867–1886*. Lincoln: University of Nebraska Press.

Miolanti, John M. 1996. "Police Suicide: An Overview." *Police Studies* 19 (2):77–89.

Monkkonen, Eric H. 1981. *Police in Urban America, 1860–1920*. Cambridge, UK: Cambridge University Press.

———. 1988. *America becomes Urban: The Development of U.S. Cities and Towns, 1780–1980*. Berkeley: University of California Press.

Morgan, Dale. 1963. "Opening of the West: Explorers and Mountain Men." Pp. 9–82 in *The Book of the American West*, edited by J. Monaghan and C.P. Hornung. New York: Julian Messner Inc.

Mosher, Clayton J., Terance D. Miethe, and Dretha M. Phillips. 2002. *The Mismeasure of Crime*. Thousand Oaks, CA: Sage.

Moskos, Peter. 2008. *Cop in the Hood: My Year Policing Baltimore's Eastern District*. Princeton, NJ: Princeton University Press.

Muir, William Ker, Jr. 1977. *Police: Streetcorner Politicians*. Chicago: University of Chicago Press.

Mumford, Lewis. 1961. *The City in History*. New York: Harcourt, Brace, and World.

Murray, Henry A. 1951. "Toward a Classification of Interactions." Pp. 434–464 in *Toward a General Theory of Action*, edited by T. Parsons and E.A. Shils. Cambridge, MA: Harvard University Press.

Nacy, Michele J. 2000. *Members of the Regiment: Army Officers' Wives on the Western Frontier, 1865–1890*. Westport, CT: Greenwood Press.

National Commission on Terrorist Attacks upon the United States. 2004. "Law Enforcement, Counterterrorism, and Intelligence Collection in the United States Prior to 9/11." Staff Statement No. 9. Washington, DC.

Newham, Gareth. 2003. "Preventing Police Corruption: Lessons from the New York City Police Department." Johannesburg, RSA: Centre for the Study of Violence and Reconciliation.

Nickels, Ernest L. 2007. "A Note on the Status of Discretion in Police Research." *Journal of Criminal Justice* 35:570–578.

———. 2008. "Good Guys Wear Black: Uniform Color and Citizen Impressions of Police." *Policing* 31 (1):77–92.

Nobles, Gregory H. 1993. "The Frontier." Pp. 1183–1196 in *Encyclopedia of American Social History*, Vol. 2, edited by M.K. Cayton, E.J. Gorn, and P.W. Williams. New York: Charles Scribner's Sons.

Nolan, James J., Norman Conti, and Jack McDevitt. 2005. "Situational Policing." *FBI Law Enforcement Bulletin* 74 (11):1–9.

Novak, Kenneth J., Brad W. Smith, and James Frank. 2003. "Strange Bedfellows: Civil Liability and Aggressive Policing." *Policing* 26 (2): 352–368.

Nunn, Samuel. 2001a. "Cities, Space, and the New World of Urban Law Enforcement Technologies." *Journal of Urban Affairs* 23 (3-4):259–278.

———. 2001b. "Police Information Technology: Assessing the Effects of Computerization on Urban Police Functions." *Public Administration Review* 61 (2):221–234.

———. 2001c. "Police Technology in Cities: Changes and Challenges." *Technology and Society* 23:11–27.

———. 2003. "Seeking Tools for the War on Terror: A Critical Assessment of Emerging Technologies in Law Enforcement." *Policing* 26 (3):454–472.

Nye, F. Ivan. 1955. "What Patterns of Family Life?" *Coordinator* 4 (2):12–17.

Oaks, Dallin H. 1970. "Studying the Exclusionary Rule in Search and Seizure." *University of Chicago Law Review* 37:665–757.

Oates, Stephen B. 1984. *Abraham Lincoln, the Man behind the Myths*. New York: Harper and Row.

Odum, Howard W. 1922. "Editorial Notes." *Journal of Social Forces* 1 (1):56–61.

Ogburn, William F. 1922. *Social Change: With Respect to Culture and Original Nature*. New York: B.W. Huebsch.

———. 1929. "The Changing Family." *Publications of the American Sociological Society* 23:124–133.

———. 1933a. "The Influence of Invention and Discovery." Pp. 122–166 in *Recent Social Trends in the United States: Report of the President's Research Committee on Social Trends*. New York: McGraw-Hill.

———. 1933b. "The Family and Its Functions." Pp. 661–708 in *Recent Social Trends in the United States: Report of the President's Research Committee on Social Trends*. New York: McGraw-Hill.

———. 1937. "Culture and Sociology." *Social Forces* 16 (2):161–169.

Oliver, Amalya L. and Kathleen Montgomery. 2005. "Toward the Construction of a Profession's Boundaries: Creating a Networking Agenda." *Human Relations* 58 (9):1167–1184.

Oliver, Willard M. 2000. "The Third Generation of Community Policing: Moving through Innovation, Diffusion, and Institutionalization." *Police Quarterly* 3 (4):367–388.

———. 2006. "The Fourth Era of Policing: Homeland Security." *International Review of Law, Computers, and Technology* 20 (1-2):49–62.

Olson, James C. 1966. *History of Nebraska*. Lincoln: University of Nebraska Press.

O'Reilly, Conor and Graham Ellison. 2006. "'Eye Spy Private High': Reconceptualizing High Policing Theory." *British Journal of Criminology* 46:641–660.

Otterstrom, Samuel M. and Carville Earle. 2002. "The Settlement of the United States from 1790 to 1990: Divergent Rates of Growth and the End of the Frontier." *Journal of Interdisciplinary History* 33 (1):59–85.

Packer, Herbert. 1968. *The Limits of the Criminal Sanction*. Stanford, CA: Stanford University Press.

Palmiotto, Michael J. 2000. *Community Policing: A Policing Strategy for the 21ˢᵗ Century*. Gaithersburg, MD: Aspen Publishers.

Parsons, Talcott. 1937. *The Structure of Social Action*. New York: Free Press.

———. 1946. "The Science Legislation and the Role of the Social Sciences." *American Sociological Review* 11 (6):653–666.

———. 1951. *The Social System*. New York: Free Press.

———. 1960a. *Structure and Process in Modern Societies*. Glencoe, IL: Free Press.

———. 1960b. "Pattern Variables Revisited: A Response to Robert Dubin." *American Sociological Review* 25 (4):467–483.

———. 1961. "An Outline of the Social System." Pp. 30–79 in *Theories of Society*, edited by T. Parsons, E. Shills, K. Naegele, and J. Pitts. New York: Free Press.

———. 1966. "The Political Aspect of Social Structure and Process." Pp. 71–112 in *Varieties of Political Theory*, edited by D. Easton. Englewood Cliffs, NJ: Prentice Hall.

———. 1967a. "On the Concept of Political Power." Pp. 297–354 in *Sociological Theory and Modern Society*. New York: Free Press.

———. 1967b. "Some Reflections on the Place of Force in Social Process." Pp. 264–296 in *Sociological Theory and Modern Society*. New York: Free Press.

———. 1968. "An Overview." Pp. 319–335 in *American Sociology: Perspectives, Problems, Methods*, edited by T. Parsons. New York: Basic Books.

———. 1975. "Social Structure and the Symbolic Media of Interchange." Pp. 94–120 in *Approaches to the Study of Social Structure*, edited by P.M. Blau. New York: Free Press.

———. 1977. *The Evolution of Societies*. Englewood Cliffs, NJ: Prentice Hall.

———. 1991. "The Integration of Economic and Sociological Theory: The Marshall Lectures." *Sociological Inquiry* 61 (1):10–59.

———. 2007. *American Society: A Theory of the Societal Community*, edited by G. Sciortino. Boulder, CO: Paradigm Publishers.

Parsons, Talcott and Gerald M. Platt. 1973. *The American University*. Cambridge, MA: Harvard University Press.

Pearse, John and Gisli Gudjonsson. 1999. "Measuring Influential Police Interviewing Tactics: A Factor Analytic Approach." *Legal and Criminological Psychology* 4 (2):221–238.

Pegnato, Joseph A. 1997. "Is a Citizen a Customer?" *Public Productivity and Management Review* 20 (4):397–404.

Pelfrey, William V., Jr. 2005. "Parallels between Community Oriented Policing and the War on Terrorism: Lessons Learned." *Criminal Justice Studies* 18 (4):335–346.

Prassel, Frank Richard. 1972. *The Western Peace Officer: A Legacy of Law and Order*. Norman: University of Oklahoma Press.

Prenzler, Tim. 2006. "Senior Police Managers' Views on Integrity Testing, and Drug and Alcohol Testing." *Policing* 29 (3):394–407.

———. 2009. *Police Corruption: Preventing Misconduct and Maintaining Integrity*. Boca Raton, FL: CRC Press.

Prenzler, Tim and Carol Ronken. 2001. "Police Integrity Testing in Australia." *Criminal Justice* 1 (3):319–342.

Prothrow-Stith, Deborah. 1993. *Deadly Consequences*. New York: Harper Perennial.

Psathas, George. 1960. "Phase Movement and Equilibrium Tendencies in Interaction Process in Psychotherapy Groups." *Sociometry* 23 (2):177–194.

Rausch, Sharla and Gary LaFree. 2007. "The Growing Importance of Criminology in the Study of Terrorism." *The Criminologist* 32 (6):1, 3–5.

Reckless, Walter C. 1941. "The Implications of Prediction in Sociology." *American Sociological Review* 6 (4):471–477.

Redmond, Michael and Alok Baveja. 2002. "A Date-driven Software Tool for Enabling Cooperative Information Sharing among Police Departments." *European Journal of Operational Research* 141:660–678.

Reed, Wilson E. 1999. *The Politics of Community Policing: The Case of Seattle*. New York: Garland Publishing.

Reiss, Albert J., Jr. 1986. "The Legitimacy of Intrusion into Private Space." Pp. 19–44 in *Private Policing*, edited by C.D. Shearing and P.C. Stenning. Newbury Park, CA: Sage.

Renauer, Brian C. 2007. "Reducing Fear of Crime: Citizen, Police, or Government Responsibility?" *Police Quarterly* 10 (1):41–62.

Reynolds, Gerald William and Anthony Judge. 1968. *The Night the Police Went on Strike*. London: Weidenfeld and Nicolson.

Richardson, Heather Cox. 2007. *West from Appomattox: The Reconstruction of America after the Civil War*. New Haven, CT: Yale University Press.

Riechers, L.M. and R.R. Roberg. 1990. "Community Policing: A Critical Review of Underlying Assumptions." *Journal of Police Science and Administration* 17:105–114.

Rigakos, George S. and Georgios Papanicolaou. 2003. "The Political Economy of Greek Policing: Between Neo-Liberalism and the Sovereign State." *Policing and Society* 13 (3):271–304.

Riley, K. Jack, Gregory F. Treverton, Jeremy M. Wilson, and Lois M. Davis. 2005. *State and Local Intelligence in the War on Terrorism*. Santa Monica, CA: Rand Corporation.

Ritzer, George. 1975. *Sociology: A Multiple Paradigm Science*. Boston: Allyn and Bacon.

Roberg, Roy R. 1994. "Can Today's Police Organizations Effectively Implement Community Policing?" Pp. 249–257 in *The Challenge of Community Policing*, edited by D.P. Rosenbaum. Thousand Oaks, CA: Sage.

Rosa, Joseph G. 1993. *The Taming of the West: Age of the Gunfighter: Men and Weapons on the Frontier, 1840–1900*. New York: Smithmark.

———. 1996. *Wild Bill Hickok: The Man and His Myth*. Lawrence: University Press of Kansas.

Rosenbaum, Dennis P. 2006. "The Limits of Hot Spots Policing." Pp. 245–263 in *Police Innovation: Contrasting Perspectives*, edited by D. Weisburd and A.A. Braga. Cambridge, UK: Cambridge University Press.

Rosenfeld, Richard. 2009. "Homicide and Serious Assaults." Pp. 25–50 in *Oxford Handbook of Crime and Public Policy*, edited by M. Tonry. Oxford, UK: Oxford University Press.

Rosenfeld, Richard and Scott H. Decker. 1993. "Where Public Health and Law Enforcement Meet: Monitoring and Preventing Youth Violence." *American Journal of Police* 12:11–57.

Roth, Wendy D. and Jal D. Mehta. 2002. "The *Rashomon* Effect: Combining Positivist and Interpretivist Approaches in the Analysis of Contested Events." *Sociological Methods and Research* 31 (2):131–173.

Russell, Don. 1963. "Indians and Soldiers of the American West." Pp. 193–260 in *The Book of the American West*, edited by J. Monaghan and C.P. Hornung. New York: Julian Messner Inc.

Russell, James W. 1994. *After the Fifth Sun: Class and Race in North America*. Englewood Cliffs, NJ: Prentice Hall.

Sanders, Irwin T. 1958. *The Community: An Introduction to a Social System*. New York: Ronald Press.

Sanders, William B. 1979. "Police Occasions: A Study of Interaction Contexts." *Criminal Justice Review* 4 (1):1–13.

Schafer, Joseph A. and Thomas J. Martinelli. 2008. "First-line Supervisor's Perceptions of Police Integrity: The Measurement of Police Integrity Revisited." *Policing* 31 (2):306–323.

Schwab, William A. 1992. *The Sociology of Cities*. Englewood Cliffs, NJ: Prentice Hall.

Selznick, Philip. 1949. *TVA and the Grass Roots*. Berkeley: University of California Press.

———. 1957. *Leadership in Administration*. New York: Harper & Row. Sennett, Richard. 1990. *The Conscience of the Eye: The Design and Social Life of Cities*. New York: Knopf.

Seron, Carroll, Joseph Pereira, and Jean Kovath. 2004. "Judging Police Misconduct: 'Street Level' versus Professional Policing." *Law and Society Review* 38 (4):665–710.

Sharp, Arthur. 2000. "Smile You're on CCTV." *Law and Order* 48 (3):53–58.

Shearing, Clifford D. 2006. "Reflections on the Refusal to Acknowledge Private Governments." Pp. 11–32 in *Democracy, Society and the Governance of Security*, edited by J. Wood and B. Dupont. Cambridge: Cambridge University Press.

Shearing, Clifford D. and Philip C. Stenning. 1981. "Modern Private Security: Its Growth and Implications." *Crime and Justice* 3:193–245.

———. 1983. "Private Security: Its Implications for Social Control." *Social Problems* 30:125–138.

———. 1986. "Reframing Policing." Pp. 9–18 in *Private Policing*, edited by C.D. Shearing and P.C. Stenning. Newbury Park, CA: Sage.

Sherman, Lawrence W. and David Weisburd. 1995. "General Deterrent Effects of Police Patrol in Crime 'Hot Spots': A Randomized Controlled Trial." *Justice Quarterly* 12:626–648.

Short, James F. 1984. "The Social Fabric At Risk: Toward the Social Transformation of Risk Analysis." *American Sociological Review* 49 (6):711– 725.

Sklansky, David A. 2006. "Not Your Father's Police Department: Making Sense of the New Demographics of Law Enforcement." *Journal of Criminal Law and Criminology* 96 (3):1209–1243.

Skogan, Wesley G. 1994. "The Impact of Community Policing on Neighborhood Residents: A Cross-Site Analysis." Pp. 167–181 in *The Challenge of Community Policing*, edited by D.P. Rosenbaum. Thousand Oaks, CA: Sage.

———. 2006a. *Police and Community in Chicago: A Tale of Three Cities*. Oxford, UK: Oxford University Press.

———. 2006b. "Asymmetry in the Impact of Encounters with the Police." *Policing and Society* 16 (2):99–126.

———. 2006c. "The Promise of Community Policing." Pp. 27–43 in *Police Innovation: Contrasting Perspectives*, edited by D. Weisburd and A.A. Braga. Cambridge: Cambridge University Press.

Skogan, Wesley G. and Tracey L. Meares. 2004. "Lawful Policing." *Annals of the American Academy of Political and Social Science* 593:66–83.

Skolnick, Jerome H. 1966. *Justice without Trial: Law Enforcement in Democratic Society*. New York: Wiley.

Skolnick, Jerome H. and James F. Fyfe. 1993. *Above the Law: Police and the Excessive Use of Force*. New York: Free Press.

Small, Albion W. 1895. "Static and Dynamic Sociology." *American Journal of Sociology* 1 (2):195–209.

Smith, Brad W., Kenneth J. Novak, James Frank, and Christopher Lowenkamp. 2005. Explaining Police Officer Discretionary Activity." *Criminal Justice Review* 30 (3):325–346.

Smith, Michael R., Matthew Petrocelli, and Charlie Scheer. 2007. "Excessive Force, Civil Liability, and the Taser in the Nation's Courts: Implications for Law Enforcement Policy and Practice." *Policing* 30 (3):398– 422.

Spacks, Patricia Meyer. 2003. *Privacy: Concealing the Eighteenth-Century Self*. Chicago: University of Chicago Press.

Spain, Daphne. 1992. *Gendered Spaces*. Chapel Hill: University of North Carolina Press.

———. 1993. "Gendered Spaces and Women's Status." *Sociological Theory* 11 (2):137–151.

Spencer, Herbert. 1864. *First Principles*. New York: Appleton.

———. 1872 [1850]. *Social Statics*. New York: Appleton and Co.

Sprey, Jetse. 1966. "Family Disorganization: Toward a Conceptual Clarification." *Journal of Marriage and the Family* 28 (4):398–406.

Stanton, Tami and Joe Thesing. 2006. "Ominous Trend: Growth of Municipal Accident Response Fees." *NAMIC Issue Brief*. Washington, DC: National Association of Mutual Insurance Companies.

Stinchcombe, Arthur L. 2001. *When Formality Works*. Chicago: University of Chicago Press.

Stroshine, Meghan, Geoffrey Alpert, and Roger Dunham. 2008. "The Influence of 'Working Rules' on Police Supervision and Discretionary Decision Making." *Police Quarterly* 11 (3):315–337.

Sumner, William G. 1906. *Folkways*. Boston: Ginn & Company.

———. 1909. "The Family and Social Change." *American Journal of Sociology* 14 (5):577–591.

Sun, Ivan Y. 2003. "Officer Proactivity: A Comparison between Police Field Training Officers and Non-field Training Officers." *Journal of Criminal Justice* 31:265–277.

Taylor, Charles. 1994. "The Politics of Recognition." Pp. 25–73 in *Multiculturalism*, edited by A. Gutmann. Princeton, NJ: Princeton University Press.

Teasley, C.E. 1978. "Police Role Perceptions: Their Operationalization and Some Preliminary Findings." *Criminal Justice Review* 3 (1):17–29.

Terrill, William and Eugene A. Paoline, III. 2007. "Nonarrest Decision Making in Police–Citizen Encounters." *Police Quarterly* 10 (3):308–331.

Thacher, David. 2005. The Local Role in Homeland Security." *Law and Society Review* 39 (3):635–676.

Thacher, David and Martin Rein. 2004. "Managing Value Conflict in Public Policy." *Governance* 17 (4):457–486.

Thale, Christopher. 2004. Assigned to Patrol: Neighborhoods, Police, and Changing Deployment Practices in New York City before 1930. *Journal of Social History* 37 (4):1037–1064.

Theriault, Sean M. 2003. "Patronage, the Pendleton Act, and the Power of the People." *Journal of Politics* 65 (1):50–68.

Thompson, James D. 1967. *Organizations in Action*. New York: McGraw-Hill. Tilley, Charles. 1976. "Major Forms of Collective Action in Western Europe 1500–1975." *Theory and Society* 3 (3):365–375.

Toffalo, Douglas A. Della. 2000. "An Investigation of Treatment and Outcomes in Wraparound Services." *Journal of Child and Family Studies* 9 (3):351–361.

Turner, Frederick Jackson. 1996 [1920]. *The Frontier in American History*. New York: Dover.

Unruh, John D., Jr. 1978. *The Plains across: The Overland Immigrants and the Trans-Mississippi West, 1840–1860*. Urbana: University of Illinois Press.

Van Maanen, John. 1974. "Working the Street: A Developmental View of Police Behavior." Pp. 83–130 in *The Potential for Reform of Criminal Justice*, edited by H. Jacob. Beverly Hills, CA: Sage.

———. 1978. "The Asshole." Pp. 221–238 in *Policing: A View from the Street*, edited by P.K. Manning and J. Van Maanen. Santa Monica, CA: Goodyear.

Van Maanen, J. and B.T. Pentland. 1994. "Cops and Auditors: The Rhetoric of Records." Pp. 53–90 in *The Legalistic Organization*, edited by S.B. Sitkin and R.J. Bies. Beverly Hills: Sage.

Van Tassel, David D. and John J. Grabowski. 1987. *Encyclopedia of Cleveland History*. Bloomington: Indiana University Press.

Veblen, Thorstein. 1899. *The Theory of the Leisure Class*. New York: Macmillan.

Venkatesh, Sudhir Alladi. 2006. *Off the Books: The Underground Economy of the Urban Poor*. Cambridge, MA: Harvard University Press.

Virilio, Paul. 1986. *Speed and Politics*, translated by M. Polizotti. New York: Semiotext(e).

Vollmer, August. 1974 [1924]. *Law Enforcement in Los Angeles*. New York: Arno Press.

Wagner, Helmut. 1963. "Types of Sociological Theory: Toward a System of Classification." *American Sociological Review* 28 (5):735–742.

Walby, Sylvia. 2001. "From Community to Coalition: The Politics of Recognition as the Handmaiden of the Politics of Equality in an Era of Globalization." *Theory, Culture and Society* 18 (2–3):113–135.

Walker, Lynn. 2002. "Home Making: An Architectural Perspective." *Signs* 27 (3):823–835.

Walker, Samuel. 1993. *Taming the System: The Control of Discretion in Criminal Justice, 1950–1990*. New York: Oxford University Press.

Walsh, William F. 2001. "Compstat: An Analysis of an Emerging Police Managerial Paradigm." *Policing* 24 (3):347–362.

Ward, Lester F. 1883. *Dynamic Sociology; or, Applied Social Science as Based upon Statical Sociology and the Less Complex Sciences*, 2 vols. New York: D. Appleton and Co.

———. 1893. *Psychic Factors of Civilization*. Boston: Ginn & Company.

———. 1895. "Static and Dynamic Sociology." *Political Science Quarterly* 10 (2):203–220.

———. 1903. *Pure Sociology: A Treatise on the Origin and Spontaneous Development of Society*. New York: Macmillan.

———. 1906. *Applied Sociology: A Treatise on the Conscious Improvement of Society by Society*. Boston: Ginn & Company.

Webb, Vincent J. and Charles M. Katz. 1997. "Citizen Ratings of Community Policing Activities." *Policing* 20 (1):7–23.

Weber, Max. 1978. *Economy and Society*, vol. 2, edited by G. Roth and C. Wittich. Berkeley: University of California Press.

Weisburd, David and Anthony A. Braga. 2006. "Hot Spots Policing as a Model for Police Innovation." Pp. 225–244 in *Police Innovation: Contrasting Perspectives*, edited by D. Weisburd and A.A. Braga. Cambridge, UK: Cambridge University Press.

Weisburd, David, Cody W. Telep, Joshua C. Hinkle, and John E. Eck. 2010. "Is Problem-Oriented Policing Effective in Reducing Crime and Disorder? Findings from a Campbell Systematic Review." *Criminology and Public Policy* 9 (1):139–172.

Weisheit, Ralph A. and John M. Klofas. 1998. "The Public Health Approach to Illicit Drugs." *Criminal Justice Review* 23 (2):197–207.

Weitzer, Ronald. 2000. "White, Black, or Blue Cops? Race and Citizen Assessments of Police Officers." *Journal of Criminal Justice* 28 (4):313–324.

Weitzer, Ronald and Rod K. Brunson. 2009. "Strategic Responses to the Police among Inner-City Youth." *Sociological Quarterly* 50 (2):235–256.

Wells, Helen. 2008. "The Techno-Fix versus the Fair Cop: Procedural (In)Justice and Automated Speed Limit Enforcement." *British Journal of Criminology* 48:798–817.

Wender, Jonathan M. 2008. *Policing and the Poetics of Everyday Life*. Urbana, IL: University of Illinois Press.

Westley, William A. 1970. *Violence and the Police: A Sociological Study of Law, Custom, and Morality*. Cambridge, MA: MIT Press.

Wharton, Amy S. 1991. "Structure and Agency in Socialist-Feminist Theory." *Gender and Society* 5 (3):373–389.

White, Michael D. 2007. *Current Issues and Controversies in Policing*. Boston: Allyn and Bacon.

White, Michael D. and Justin Ready. 2007. "The Taser as a Less Lethal Force Alternative: Findings on Use and Effectiveness in a Large Metropolitan Police Agency." *Police Quarterly* 10 (2):170–191.

———. 2010. "The Impact of the Taser on Suspect Resistance: Identifying Predictors of Effectiveness." *Crime and Delinquency* 56 (1):70–102.

White, Welsh S. 2001. *Miranda's Waning Protections: Police Interrogation Practices after Dickerson*. Ann Arbor: University of Michigan Press. Willer, David and Henry A. Walker. 2007. *Building Experiments: Testing Social Theory*. Stanford, CA: Stanford University Press.

Williams, Hubert and Patrick V. Murphy. 2006. "The Evolving Strategy of Police: A Minority View." Pp. 27–50 in *The Police and Society*, 3rd ed., edited by V.E. Kappeler. Long Grove, IL: Waveland.

Williamson, Roger E. 2001. *Wichita Police Department, 1871–2000*. Wichita, KS: Wichita Police Benefit Fund Association.

Willis, James J., Stephen D. Mastrofski, and David Weisburd. 2007. "Making Sense of COMPSTAT: A Theory-Based Analysis of Organizational Change in Three Police Departments." *Law and Society Review* 41 (1):147–188.

Wilson, James Q. 1968. *Varieties of Police Behavior*. New York: Atheneum.

———. and George L. Kelling. 1982. "Broken Windows: Police and Neighborhood Safety." *Atlantic Monthly* 249 (3):29–38.

Wilson, Jeremy W. 2006. *Community Policing in America*. London: Routledge.

Wilson, O.W. 1958. *Police Planning*, 2nd ed. Springfield, IL: Charles C. Thomas.

Wingerd, Mary Lethert. 2001. *Claiming the City: Politics, Faith, and the Power of Place in St. Paul*. Ithaca, NY: Cornell University Press.

Winther, Oscar O. 1963. "Transportation in the American West." Pp. 83–136 in *The Book of the American West*, edited by J. Monaghan and C.P. Hornung. New York: Julian Messner Inc.

Wolf, Ross, Charlie Mesloh, Mark Henych, and L. Frank Thompson. 2009. "Police Use of Force and the Cumulative Force Factor." *Policing* 32 (4):739–757.

Wortley, Richard K. 2003. "Measuring Police Attitudes toward Discretion." *Criminal Justice and Behavior* 30 (5):538–558.

Wright, Will. 2001. *The Wild West: The Mythical Cowboy and Social Theory*. Thousand Oaks, CA: Sage.

Yan, Aimin and Meryl Reis Louis. 1999. "The Migration of Organizational Functions to the Work Unit Level: Buffering, Spanning, and Bridging up Boundaries." *Human Relations* 52 (1):25–47.

Yates, Douglas. 1978. *The Ungovernable City: The Politics of Urban Problems and Policy Making*. Cambridge, MA: MIT Press.

Yip, Kam-shing. 2006. "A Strengths Perspective in Working with an Adolescent with Self-cutting Behaviors." *Child and Adolescent Social Work Journal* 23 (2):134–146.

Zhao, Jihong "Solomon" and Kimberly D. Hassell. 2005. "Policing Styles and Organizational Priorities: Retesting Wilson's Theory of Local Political Culture." *Police Quarterly* 8 (4):411–430.

NEW APPROACHES

A Quick History of Cops in America

RADLEY BALKO

Democratic law tends more and more to be grounded upon the maxim that every citizen is, by nature, a traitor, a libertine, and a scoundrel. In order to dissuade him from his evildoing the police power is extended until it surpasses anything ever heard of in the oriental monarchies of antiquity.

—H. L. MENCKEN, *NOTES ON DEMOCRACY*

Colonial American towns were usually filled with people who came from the same place, worshiped at the same altar, and shared the same sense of right and wrong. Historian and criminologist Sam Walker writes, "Crime and sin were synonymous; an offense against God was an offense against society, and vice versa."[1] Predatory crimes like murder, rape, and robbery were almost nonexistent. Far more common were punishments for crimes like blasphemy, adultery, or drunkenness. Not surprisingly, law and policing in prerevolutionary America were modeled fairly closely on the English example. Given the rugged conditions of frontier living and the lack of civic structures, trial and punishment were relatively rare. Mores and shared values were generally sufficient, and when they weren't, shunning and other forms of informal justice usually worked to keep civic order. Not all colonial communities were the same, and laws varied from place to place depending on the prevailing religion and tradition, but there was little need for state agents to enforce the law. Communities tended to handle transgressors on their own. There were Crown-appointed sheriffs and constables, but again, they largely focused on administrative matters.

As the country grew, three distinctive policing traditions began to emerge, coinciding with three regions—the Northeast, the South, and the western frontier.

In the Northeast, as the cities grew larger and more diverse in the early eighteenth century, their residents encountered more crime. Throughout the seventeenth and eighteenth centuries, early American cities first installed *night watch patrols*, first voluntary and then paid. The night watches were fairly successful at rounding up drunks and preventing petty infractions, but the low-paying positions would prove inadequate when cities began to experience riots, mobs, and more serious crimes.

The Southern colonies were more agrarian, less compact, and more homogeneous than the colonies of the Northeast. The primary threat to public safety in the South—at least in the minds of whites—was the possibility of slave revolts. As a result, the first real organized policing systems in America arguably began in the South with *slave patrols*. The patrols were armed and uniformed, and typically had broad powers to arrest, search, and detain slaves. The slave patrols' main responsibilities were to guard against rebellions and to look for escaped slaves. They had the power to enter slave quarters at will, whether or not they had permission from the slaves' owner. They could even enforce some laws against plantation owners, such as laws prohibiting the education of slaves. By the middle of the eighteenth century, every Southern colony had passed laws formalizing slave patrols. It became the primary policing system in the South. In many jurisdictions—most notably Charleston, South Carolina—slave patrols would eventually morph into the official police force.

On the western frontier, early policing was more piecemeal. Northern settlers tended to congregate together and set up systems in the Northern tradition, while pioneers from the South followed the Southern tradition. But the expanse of the frontier didn't always accommodate either system. Often there was just too much ground to cover, and the territory was too sparsely populated. That gap was often filled by *vigilantes* and private police for hire. The vigilante groups came together in response to some threat to public order, then dissolved once the threat had subsided. As the name implies, they tended to operate outside the formal legal system and were naturally more prone to pop up where the legal system either didn't exist or was too weak to maintain order. In some cases, vigilante groups were better than no justice at all. In other cases, they were quite a bit worse.

_____

The first modern police force as we know it today was created in 1829 in London by Sir Robert Peel. He and his father had been pushing the idea for decades, but

British concerns over the nation's civil liberties tradition had repeatedly killed the idea. Concerned about the worsening conditions in the city, Parliament finally gave its approval in 1829, but only after Peel put in place assurances and checks to retain some local control over the force and ensure that police officers' responsibilities were limited to fighting crime and protecting individual rights—his task was to convince the city that a police force would not be an army enforcing the will of a centralized power.

The British police force began with three thousand officers. They wore uniforms to make themselves recognizable, but Peel made the uniforms blue to distinguish them from the red worn by the British military. Peel was sensitive to concerns about standing armies, but he also believed that a successful police force would need at least some of the structure and discipline of a military influence. Peel appointed a retired colonel as one of his two first supervising justices. Thus, the inaugural police force took on a military-like top-down administrative structure, and even borrowed some military titles. It's a tradition that continues in most police departments in the United States today.

Peel and his justices set out a strict code of conduct. Officers were to avoid confrontation when at all possible. They were to be civil and polite when interacting with citizens. Most of all, Peel hammered home the principle that his police force worked for the people of London, not against them. Nevertheless, it took a while for the public to warm to the idea.

Across the Atlantic in rapidly urbanizing America, larger cities began to adopt the British model, albeit with some Americanized adjustments. The first modern-style police department in the United States was established in New York in 1845. Boston and Philadelphia soon followed. New York began its experiment with eight hundred policemen. Fearing that the London force was already too much like an army, the New York cops began their patrols unarmed, and without uniforms. Early American police departments were also much more democratic than the system in London. Peel and his top aides handpicked the officers to work in London. In the United States, early police officers were nominated by ward leaders and political bosses, then appointed by the mayor. Cops were required to live in the wards they patrolled. All of this tended to make early police departments more like service agencies than law enforcement bodies. Since ward leaders were elected, they found they could pressure local commanders to prioritize police duties in ways that would help get them reelected. In some neighborhoods, police officers ran soup kitchens and homeless people were given shelter in police stations to sleep. This democratic style of policing also gave police (or more accurately, their commanders) discretion to enforce laws in ways that reflected the priorities of the communities they patrolled. Alcohol laws, for example, might be strictly enforced in one part of a city, but rarely if ever enforced in another.

In some ways, this wasn't all that dissimilar to the way laws had been enforced before police departments existed, when transgressions within a community were handled by its members. But there were some clear drawbacks. The job of police officer had quickly become a patronage position. The only qualification for becoming a cop was a political connection. Mass firings were common when power changed hands. The ethnicity of a ward's police force tended to be exclusively that of the majority of the ward's population. This could be problematic for, say, an Italian caught in a majority Irish neighborhood. Training was nonexistent, beatings were common, and, perhaps most importantly, the system had little effect on crime—neither preventing it nor helping to bring criminals to justice.

Ironically, the more centralized, less democratic London model proved to be more protective of individual rights than early American police departments. Centralization allowed Peel to set high, consistent hiring standards based on merit. Because he was so aware of the English public's fears about violations of their civil liberties, Peel knew that the survival of his police department was probably contingent on his ability to alleviate those fears.

And so by the end of the nineteenth century, London's "bobbies" (the nickname derived from Peel's name) had managed to win over the public within a couple of decades, while the reputation of the American police officer had hit bottom. With no training or standards, and with jobs based on patronage more than merit, the police in America were best known for corruption, brutality, and incompetence. Wealthy citizens looked instead to private organizations like the Pinkertons when they needed reliable security or knew of a crime they wanted solved.

By the early twentieth century, police reform had become a cause of the progressive movement, whose adherents saw corrupt cops as just another consequence of cities being run by political machines. There were two competing voices for reform. Progressive academics and elites wanted not only to rid police departments of patronage and corruption but to mandate a more paternalistic role for police. They wanted cops to enforce good habits and morals among the urban poor, especially immigrants.

The other voice for reform came from administrators within the law enforcement community. They too wanted to free police departments from the political machines, but they focused less on ideology and more on fighting crime. They wanted to give more freedom and autonomy to police chiefs, who were often held responsible for the actions of their officers but had very little power to actually change their behavior.

In the end, the administrators won the long-term debate by embracing the concept of *professionalism*. Through the adoption of best practices, they successfully transformed the job of police officer from a perk of patronage to a formal profession with its own standards, specialized knowledge, and higher personnel standards and entry requirements. To be a police officer was no longer just a job, it was a career. The first thirty or so years of the twentieth century saw the formation of professional societies like the Police Chiefs' Union; the sharing of knowledge and "police sciences" like fingerprinting; and the creation of specialized "squads" to tackle specific problems like alcohol, prostitution, and gambling.

The champion of the professionalism movement was August Vollmer, who served as chief of police in Berkeley, California, from 1905 to 1932. Vollmer pioneered the use of police radios, squad cars, bicycles, lie detector tests, and crime labs. As Walker writes, "The professionalism movement created the modern police organization: a centralized, authoritarian, bureaucracy focusing on crime control."[2]

But the morals-oriented progressives also had some victories, at least in the short term. They succeeded in passing anti-obscenity laws, and in some cities (most notably New York) they were able to put shutting down brothels, adult-book stores, and other sex-related businesses high on the list of police priorities. Their biggest victory was of course the Eighteenth Amendment, which banned the production, sale, and importation of alcohol.

The amendment was enforced by the Volstead Act, passed in 1919. The prohibition of alcohol has some clear parallels with the modern drug war. Homicides spiked during Prohibition, as did public corruption. The federal government had created a lucrative new black market. In legal markets, businesses compete by providing a better product, a less expensive product, or better customer service. In black markets, they compete by warring over turf. Disputes are settled with guns, not in courtrooms. As the bootleggers obtained bigger guns to war with one another, law enforcement agencies felt that they needed bigger guns to go after the criminals. In larger cities, the ensuing arms race produced heavily armed police forces.

Like today's drug prohibition, the Volstead Act was a failure. It almost certainly reduced the amount of alcohol the country consumed, but it came nowhere near stamping out booze entirely. The true believers responded by calling for tougher crackdowns and less coddling of bootleggers and drinkers. In his book *The Spirits of America*, journalist Eric Burns writes that some politicians and civic leaders suggested sending drunks and booze distributors to Siberia or the South Pole. Burns notes that David Blair, the federal commissioner of internal revenue at the time, "recommended that all American bootleggers be lined up in front of a firing squad and shot to death."[3] Foreshadowing the cries the country would hear from drug warriors sixty years later, Henry Ford wanted the military to enforce the laws against illicit substances. Anti-alcohol activist Clarence True Wilson demanded that the Harding administration call up the Marines, "arm them to the teeth and send them to the speakeasies. Give the people inside a few minutes to depart, and if they chose not to, open fire anyhow."[4]

But as hard as the temperance activists tried, they couldn't demonize and dehumanize drinkers the way drug warriors have since succeeded in denigrating drug offenders.

One likely reason was that the Volstead Act didn't criminalize the possession or consumption of alcohol, only its production and sale. So the feds could raid speakeasies, but they couldn't raid a home based on a tip that someone had a cupboard full of gin—unless they suspected there was a distillery inside. Since simply ingesting alcohol was not a criminal act, it was more difficult for Prohibition's supporters to cast drinkers as villains. The country was also more federalist in the 1920s. Even after the Eighteenth Amendment passed, some states, cities, and counties simply refused to enforce it.

After the repeal of Prohibition in 1933, the professionalism model returned to police departments.

Although some of the aims of professionalism may have been noble, the story of early American policing is one of overcorrection. While the professionalism reformers were able to end the patronage system, in some cities they managed to insulate police departments from politics altogether, making it difficult for mayors and city councils to hold police officials accountable. At the level of individual cops, the use of squad cars and radios clearly brought a lot of benefits, but could also isolate police officers from the residents of the communities they patrolled. Cops out walking beats could chat with citizens, form relationships, and become a part of the community. Squad cars gave cops a faceless and intimidating presence. They tended not to get out of them except in the event of problems or confrontations. Police and citizens interacted only when police were ticketing or questioning someone, or when a citizen was reporting a crime. In poorer communities, that could bring about an increasingly antagonistic relationship between cops and the citizens on their beats.[5]

Perhaps no police chief better illustrated that double-edged sword of professionalism than William Parker in Los Angeles. Parker took over the LAPD in 1950 and imposed a rigid, hierarchical, militaristic bureaucracy. He took on corruption in the department—successfully—and stressed efficiency and crime fighting above all else. Parker had also worked in public relations for the military for a time, and he used that experience to sell his ideas about policing to the public. He helped create the show *Dragnet,* a virtual commercial for Parker-style police management—or at least an idealized form of it.[6]

But Parker also loathed community policing, the idea that cops should have a stake in the communities they served. He preferred to have a wall between cop and community. That sentiment probably stemmed from the goal of ridding the department of the sort of localized interests that existed in the patronage era. But completely walling off cops from their communities presented its own problems. Making cops indifferent to the areas they patrolled, instilling in them the notion that they were all that stood between order and anarchy—all of this could make police view the citizens in their districts as at best the *other,* and at worst, the enemy. Consequently, while Parker's management rid the LAPD of political patronage and corruption, and instilled some needed structure and standards, he seemed oblivious to growing animosity toward police in the city's black and Latino populations.

Parker's efforts at instilling professionalism provide a good segue into the age of militarization for a couple of reasons. For one, as we'll see, when the racial tension in LA finally blew up in the form of the Watts riots, it went a long way toward scaring middle America about crime, to the point where they were willing to embrace an all-out "war" on crime and drugs to clean up the cities.

But Parker also had a much more direct impact on militarization. Shortly after taking office, the chief made a young LAPD cop barely a year into the job his personal chauffeur, and eventually his protégé. That set the young cop's career on a fast track. By the time of the Watts riots in 1965, Parker's young protégé would take command of the city police department's response. The experience would scar him. The protégé would eventually become LA's police chief himself. And in large part because of his experience in Watts, he did more to bring about today's militarized American police force than any other single person. His name was Daryl Gates.

There are two forms of police militarization: direct and indirect. *Direct militarization* is the use of the standing military for domestic policing. *Indirect militarization* happens when police agencies and police officers take on more and more characteristics of an army. Most of this book will focus on the latter form of police militarization, which began in the United States in the late 1960s, then accelerated in the 1980s. But the two forms of militarization are related, and they have become increasingly intertwined over the last thirty years. So it's worth looking briefly at direct militarization in the twentieth century as well.

As discussed in the previous chapter, direct militarization has a longer history in the United States but has been more limited in scope. One reason may be that deploying military forces domestically usually requires a formal declaration by the president, which means such deployments have been limited to self-contained events. By the middle of the twentieth century, federal troops had been deployed in response to dozens of domestic disturbances, but the incidents were highly visible, and once the crisis abated the troops left the scene.

One of the more significant policies to move the country toward direct militarization was the Militia Act of 1903—sometimes called the National Guard Act. The antifederalists, remember, advocated that the country rely on state militias for national defense. That didn't work out, but the militias stayed around and were often called up by state governors to dispel less threatening uprisings.

But the militias were also sometimes called into war. In fact, the 1903 law was a response to widespread sentiment that the militias had performed poorly during the Spanish-American War. The new law took what remained of the state militias and converted them into what is today the National Guard. It also established an office in the Pentagon to oversee the Guard and appropriated funds to run the office and train Guard troops. Guard units would still report to their respective states and could still be called up by their governors when needed. But if called up by the president and federalized, they wouldn't be noticeably different from the military. One legacy of the National Guard Act was to make some state governors more likely to request military help from the president and thus more reliant on the use of the military to quell disruptions. Military leaders weren't keen on this trend. They knew from history that sending soldiers to dispel citizens was usually a bad idea, and sowed ill will toward the Army among the public.

The ensuing confrontations between the military and labor protesters and strikers, antiwar activists, and other demonstrators certainly had that effect. Worse, they also sowed a certain contempt for protesters among some in the military.[7] That sentiment, along with public anxiety about World War I and the Red Scare fears of communists and anarchists that followed, opened up a brief period in American history when military leaders seemed more willing to intervene in domestic life than ever before.

The most infamous incident came in 1932. In June of that year, forty thousand World War I veterans and their supporters descended on Washington, DC, to demand the bonus payment they had been promised for their service. They set up camps on the Anacostia Flats, a marshy area across the river from the US Capitol, and named their makeshift city "Hooverville" to mock President Herbert Hoover. As the Bonus March began on July 28, 1932, there was an altercation in which police shot and killed two marching veterans. President Hoover responded by sending in the US Army. Two regiments and six tanks moved into the nation's capital, under the leadership of Gen. Douglas MacArthur and Maj. George S. Patton. Maj. Dwight Eisenhower went along as an aide to MacArthur. The protesters initially cheered the military, thinking the troops were there to support them. Those cheers quickly turned to screams when the troops charged the protesters with guns and tear gas.

When the protesters retreated back to Hooverville, Hoover ordered MacArthur to stand down. MacArthur defied the order and went after the protesters, razing the Hooverville shacks and chasing veterans, their families, and their supporters out of the makeshift town at the points of bayonets.[8] The sight of veterans being lied to and then bloodied by the same US Army in which they had served didn't sit well with the public. Angry condemnations rang out from newspapers, civil rights organizations, and veterans across the country.[9] The crackdown doomed Hoover's already dim prospects for reelection and turned what had been an ambivalent public firmly in support of the veterans.[10]

Later that year, Patton wrote a remarkable paper recounting the lessons he had learned from the Bonus March. Titled "Federal Troops in Domestic Disturbances," it revealed a startling contempt for free expression—and for civilians in general. The paper first assesses periods of unrest throughout history. Patton ridicules nations and empires that hesitated to use violence against citizen uprisings and praises those that did. "When the foolish and genial Louis XVI lost his head and the Seine ran crimson to the sea, the fault lay not with the people, but with the soldiers," Patton writes. "Yet less than ten years later, Napoleon with a 'whiff of grape shot' destroyed the mob and saved, only to usurp, the directorate." Patton attributes the success of the Bolshevik Revolution to "the hesitating and weak character of the Russian officers," which prevented them from properly slaughtering the Communists while they were merely protesters.

Most alarming are Patton's own suggestions and recommendations on how the military should handle domestic riots and uprisings. He calls the writ of habeas corpus "an item that rises to plague us" and recommends shooting captured rioters instead of turning them over to police to bring before "some misguided judge," who might release the rebellious citizen on a legal technicality. On establishing geographic bearings while breaking up a protest, Patton advises: "It may be desirable to fly over the city to become oriented. If fired upon while in the air, reply at once with small bombs and machine gun fire." Using all-caps for emphasis, he later writes, "When guarding buildings, mark a 'DEAD' line and announce clearly that those who cross it will be killed. Be sure to kill the first one who tries to cross it and to LEAVE HIM THERE to encourage the others."[11] Elsewhere he writes, "If it is necessary to use machine guns, aim at their feet. If you must fire, DO A GOOD JOB. A few casualties become martyrs; a large number becomes an object lesson."[12]

Patton and MacArthur rose through the ranks during the first Red Scare of 1919 to 1921, when the entire country crouched in a panicked fear of radicalism. This was the era of Woodrow Wilson's Sedition Act, the 1919 anarchist bombings, and the responding raids, arrests, and deportations of thousands by Attorney General A. Mitchell Palmer. Every violent labor clash heightened fears that America was on the brink of Bolshevism. Like a number of US political and civic leaders, many military leaders had soured on the notion of affording civil liberties to groups they believed were determined to overthrow the government. At a news conference after the Bonus March fiasco, for example, MacArthur showed no regret. He called the protesters a "mob" that was "animated by the essence of revolution." He said their aim was to take over the government and that "a reign of terror was being started" that, without military intervention, would have caused "insurgency and insurrection."[13]

It was not an uncommon sentiment in the military at the time. When the US Army made its *Basic Field Manual* available to the public for the first time in 1935, it included a section on strategies for handling domestic disturbances.[14] The recommendations were unsettling. The guide suggested firing *into* crowds instead of firing warning shots over their heads, and it included instructions on the use of chemical warfare, artillery, machine guns, mortars, grenades, tanks, and planes against American citizens.[15] Another military manual defined *democracy* as "a government of the masses. . . . Results in mobocracy . . . demagogism, license, agitation, discontent, anarchy." Newspaper editorials and political advocacy groups lashed out, arguing that the US Army had essentially published a how-to guide for waging war on its own people. The military responded, with some justification, that the manuals made no mention of when or under what circumstances these tactics—which were tactics of last resort—should be used in domestic disturbances.[16]

The backlash showed that there was still an ample reserve of public support for the broader principles behind the Third Amendment. The outrage grew loud enough that in early 1936, Army chief of staff general Malin Craig retracted the manual and ordered it removed from circulation. By 1941 much of the offending language had been either removed or replaced with instructions emphasizing the use of nonlethal force.[17] The military had overstepped, and when it was held to account, it retreated: the instructions were revised to strike a more appropriate tone, one more in line with its proper relationship with the American citizenry.

World War II put an end to concerns about Communists and anarchists. Protests died down, and with them the need to send troops to dispel those that got out of hand. But the period wasn't entirely calm. Racial tension mounted in some cities as black servicemen returned from the war to the same segregation, poverty, and limited opportunity they had experienced before they left. In Los Angeles, clashes between stationed Navy and Marine servicemen and the city's Latinos boiled over into the Zoot Suit Riots of 1943. Riots also broke out in Detroit, Chicago, and Harlem, but only the Detroit riots required federal intervention.

The first decade after the war was even quieter, as the economy boomed and veterans settled down with good jobs to start families. But things were about to change. Civil rights victories would inspire revolt in the South, and the counterculture and antiwar protesters were coming.

The new era began in Little Rock in 1957. The Supreme Court's 1954 decision in *Brown v. Board of Education* animated civil rights groups and angered segregationists. When nine black students attempted to attend classes at Central High School on September 4, Gov. Orval Faubus sent Arkansas National Guard troops to prevent them from entering the building.

There had been a number of incidents leading up to Little Rock in which efforts to integrate public facilities had also been met with violence. Until Little Rock, President Dwight Eisenhower had opposed sending federal troops to force integration, and he initially resisted sending soldiers to Arkansas as well.[18] Instead, he first held a face-to-face meeting with Faubus, thinking he could convince the governor to stand down. Faubus responded by pulling the troops entirely, allowing an angry mob to force the black students to withdraw from class on September 23.[19] Two days later, Eisenhower ordered troops from the 101st Airborne Division to escort the students to school. The soldiers were soon replaced by troops from the Arkansas National Guard, which Eisenhower had federalized. Those units stayed until the end of the school year. Beginning the following year, federal courts supervised the Little Rock school system's compliance with *Brown v. Board of Education* until 2007.[20]

Eisenhower's initial reluctance to send troops to Little Rock is often seen as a stain on his record, perhaps justifiably so. But Eisenhower had ridden alongside MacArthur at the Bonus March. In fact, he had advised MacArthur that there was something unseemly about the military's highest-ranking officer leading a charge against a citizen protest. It's possible that Eisenhower was reluctant to send troops south in 1957 because of what he saw in 1932 and the resulting public backlash. Eisenhower eventually did send troops into Little Rock because, he said, federal law was being "flouted with impunity" and he feared that the South could slip into anarchy if something wasn't done. He waited until he felt that sending in troops was his only option. Though an argument could be made that he waited too long, his actions also kept with the protections built into the Insurrection Act.[21]

By the 1960s, the civil rights, counterculture, and antiwar movements would be in full swing, leading the government to call repeatedly on the National Guard and occasionally on US troops to keep order in urban areas. Still, the principle of keeping the US military out of law enforcement remained largely intact. Despite the best efforts of too many politicians, the public still tended to recoil at the idea of putting soldiers on city streets, even for a brief time, much less for day-to-day law enforcement.

That's the good news. The bad news fills most of the rest of this book. While as a nation we have mostly done a good job of keeping the military out of law enforcement, we've done a poor job, to borrow a bit of martial rhetoric, of guarding our flanks. The biggest threat to the Symbolic Third Amendment today comes from indirect militarization. Instead of allowing our soldiers to serve as cops, we're turning our cops into soldiers. It's a threat that the Founders didn't anticipate, that nearly all politicians support, and that much of the public either seems to support or just hasn't given much attention.

No one made a decision to militarize the police in America. The change has come slowly, the result of a generation of politicians and public officials fanning and exploiting public fears by declaring war on abstractions like crime, drug use, and terrorism. The resulting policies have made those war metaphors increasingly real.

NOTES

1 Samuel Walker, *Popular Justice,* 2nd ed. (New York: Oxford University Press, 1998), p. 16.

2 Ibid., p. 170.

3 Eric Burns, *Spirits of America: A Social History of Alcohol* (Philadelphia: Temple University Press, 2004) p. 229.

4 Burns, *Spirits of America,* p. 229.

5 The history of early policing in the United States is from Walker, *Popular Justice;* Roger Lane, "Urban Police and Crime in Nineteenth-Century America," and Eric H. Monkkonen, "History of Urban Police," both in *Modern Policing,* ed. Michael Tonry and Norval Morris (Chicago: University of Chicago Press, 1992); Robert H. Langworthy and Lawrence F. Travis III, *Policing in America* (Englewood Cliffs, NJ: Prentice-Hall, 2003); Burns, *Spirits of America;* and Samuel Walker and Charles M. Katz, *The Police in America,* 7th ed. (New York: McGraw-Hill, 2011).

6 See Walker, *Popular Justice,* pp. 173–175.

7 Clayton Laurie and Ronald Cole, *The Role of Federal Military Forces in Domestic Disputes, 1877–1945* (Washington, DC: US Army, Center for Military History, 1997), p. 324.

8 The Bonus March is summarized from Roger Daniels, *The Bonus March: An Episode of the Great Depression* (Westport, CT: Greenwood Publishing, 1971).

9 "The Bonus Army: How a Protest Led to the GI Bill," *Radio Diaries* (National Public Radio), November 11, 2001, available at: http://www.npr.org/2011/11/11/142224795/the-bonus-army-how-a-protest-led-to-the-gi-bill (accessed August 10, 2012).

10 "1932 Bonus March," GlobalSecurity.org, available at: http:// www.globalsecurity.org/military/ops/bonus-march.htm (accessed September 1, 2012).

11 George S. Patton, "Federal Troops in Domestic Disturbances" (1932), available at: http://www.pattonhq.com/textfiles/federal.html.

12 Ibid.

13 Douglas MacArthur, remarks at a news conference, Washington, DC, July 28, 1932, transcript available at: http://www.wwnorton.com/college/history/america7/content/multimedia/ch29/research_01c.htm (accessed September 15, 2012).

14 US War Department, *Basic Field Manual,* vol. 7, *Military Law,* August 1, 1935, pt. 3, "Domestic Disturbances," pp. 14, 31–67, cited and summarized in Laurie and Cole, *The Role of Federal Military Forces,* p. 364.

15 Laurie and Cole, *The Role of Federal Military Forces,* p. 364.

16 Ibid.

17 Ibid., p. 365.

18 See Robert W. Coakley, *The Role of Federal Military Forces in Domestic Disorders, 1789–1878* (DIANE Publishing, 1996), pp. 17–38.

19 Farnsworth Fowle, "Little Rock Police, Deployed at Sunrise, Press Mob Back at School Barricades," *New York Times,* September 24, 1957.

20 Steve Barnes, "Federal Supervision of Race in Little Rock Schools Ends," *New York Times,* February 24, 2007.

21 W. H. Lawrence, "Eisenhower Irate; Says Federal Orders 'Cannot Be Flouted with Impunity'; Protection of Laws Denied; President Warns He'll Use Troops; Queried on Force Drafted in Washington," *New York Times,* September 24, 1957. For a thorough analysis of Eisenhower's deliberation, decision, and motives about sending troops to Little Rock, see Walker, *Popular Justice,* pp. 174–176.

Defining Intelligence-Led Policing

JERRY H. RATCLIFFE

The Audit Commission never defined intelligence-led policing, nor did the National Criminal Intelligence Service when they issued the first public documents on the National Intelligence Model (NIM). Indeed, definitions of intelligence-led policing are hard to find, and most publications tend to discuss the challenges and merits of intelligence-led policing without actually defining it (for example, see IACP 2002). The situation appears to be analogous to the statement by US Supreme Court Associate Justice Potter Stewart, who, in a 1964 ruling regarding hardcore pornography, wrote, 'I shall not today attempt further to define the kinds of material I understand to be embraced within that shorthand description; and perhaps I could never succeed in intelligibly doing so. But I know it when I see it.' There appears to be an unwritten assumption that police officers and crime intelligence analysts may not be able to define intelligence-led policing, but they know it when they see it. Yet, without care and clarification, the term intelligence-led policing could become 'trite and jargonistic' (Keelty 2004: 6).

This chapter aims to demystify intelligence-led policing and approach a definition in order to provide the conceptual apparatus for the rest of the book. However, in the process, I will also argue that intelligence-led policing is an evolving concept and the tenets of intelligence-led policing have shifted over time. Comparisons will be drawn with other significant frameworks for policing to determine better the similarities and differences with other styles of law enforcement management. The chapter concludes with an attempt at a definition of intelligence-led policing, in addition to identifying where it varies conceptually from the main current policing paradigms.

To distinguish intelligence-led policing from other models, the chapter takes the rather challenging approach of attempting to identify the central precepts of community policing, Compstat and problem-oriented policing for the purposes of comparison with intelligence-led policing. Such a venture is fraught with contention given that these concepts are sometimes interpreted differently by an audience passionate about policing and the conceptual models they advocate. It is not my intention to make the definitive statement of these other conceptual models; I leave that to others more versed in, and more articulate about, these paradigms. As Tilley (2003a) points out, any attempt to highlight the distinctive components of each policing model inevitably creates contrasts that are more stark than they often are on the ground. The aim here is to present the distinguishing characteristics of intelligence-led policing. In the process, I ask that the reader recognise that this requires both a considerable degree of generalisation and some latitude to attempt to distil into a few paragraphs the varying policing models employed across hundreds of different police departments in many countries.

RELATED POLICING FRAMEWORKS

Intelligence-led policing did not originate out of thin air as a new conceptual way of conducting the business of policing. It built on experiences from the past, the organisational climate of the time, and the aspirations of its architects. As such, it is influenced by the existing policing models of the time. A paradigm shift involves a change in the basic assumptions about a process (Kuhn 1962) and it is difficult to identify those current policing movements that constitute a paradigm shift from the existing mode of policing at the time. It is much easier to define the original model from which the approaches in this chapter have their genesis.

As stated in Chapter 2, the standard model of policing traditionally comprises random patrol, rapid uniformed response, deployment of officers to crime investigation once an offence has been detected, and reliance on law enforcement and the legal system as the primary means of trying to reduce crime (Weisburd and Eck 2004). Defined by a faith in the traditional hierarchical system, an aim of solving reported crime, and the practice in which police management organise units within police administrative boundaries in an attempt to improve police efficiency, the model has been the subject of extended criticism. This model, summarised later in the chapter in the first column of Table 4.1, will be the benchmark against which more recent conceptual frameworks for policing are measured.

In this section, I will discuss community policing, problem-oriented policing, and Compstat. Whether these frameworks constitute paradigm shifts or more modest variations to an earlier style of policing is a point for discussion; however, it is clear that they are significant movements in the current policing environment. Furthermore, they are all part of a reform movement in policing, one that sees the need for change due to the failings of more traditional methods of policing (Tilley 2003a). Each recognises that policing needs to be less reactive, but they differ in their conceptual philosophy as well as the tactics that emanate from each model.

Of course, there are differences between policing tactics and conceptual frameworks (or models) of policing. For example, increasing foot patrols, where officers spend more time out of their cars and more time engaging with the community on walking beats, is a tactic. Moving to a community policing ethos that emphasises foot patrol as one of its approaches is the adoption of a conceptual framework. Conducting surveillance of a suspect is a tactic. Moving to an intelligence-led policing philosophy that (among other things) emphasises greater use of surveillance to target prolific offenders identified and prioritised through a strategic assessment is adoption of a conceptual framework. While I address some of the main conceptual models, there are other approaches to crime reduction that have not reached the widespread diffusion of community policing or Compstat but nevertheless are potentially significant players in the way that we will police in the future. Examples include evidence-based policing (Sherman 2002), hot spot policing (Weisburd and Braga 2006a), broken windows theory (Wilson and Kelling 1982; Taylor 2001; Sousa and Kelling 2006), and third-party policing (Buerger 1998; Buerger and Green-Mazerolle 1998). There is not the space in this book to examine these additional strategies, though a recent book provides a useful overview (*Police Innovation: Contrasting Perspectives*, edited by Weisburd and Braga 2006b). These models conceptually differ, but the tactics they advocate (such as saturation patrols or greater use of civil enforcement) can be incorporated within broader frameworks such as problem-oriented policing. As the next sections show, there are some challenges in trying to decipher this 'terminological mess' (Ponsaers 2001: 271)!

COMMUNITY POLICING

The origins of community policing have been described in Chapter 2. This section seeks to identify the key ingredients of a community policing style, a task that is not as easy as it sounds. Community policing defies definition. Some academics and practitioners see it as a policing philosophy, while others define community polic-ing by the programmes that are associated with it. For example, neighbourhood mini-stations, customer satisfaction surveys, foot patrols, school visits, the Drug Abuse Resistance Education (DARE) programme, local newsletters and Neighbourhood Watch are all programmes that are commonly associated with community policing. However, these programmes do not articulate its vision. While rarely articulated explicitly, the core purpose of community policing has been to increase police legit-imacy in neighbourhoods that have lost confidence in the police (see Chapter 2). A central aim of community policing is to increase the legitimacy of formal governance and improve community satisfaction in policing services. For example, Deukmedjian and de Lint (2007) recount the difficulties the RCMP had in getting information from the East Indian Punjabi community in British Columbia in the wake of the 1985 ter-rorist bombing of Air India flight 182 while it was over the Atlantic. Suspecting the bomb originated in Vancouver but lacking suitable linguists, the RCMP investigation was hampered by inability to access information from the Punjabi community. The subsequent prosecution, the most extensive in RCMP history, resulted in not-guilty verdicts against the chief suspects. For a brief time, the RCMP – as with many police departments – looked to community policing to help them regain legitimacy and restore this community connection.

Community policing can be defined extremely loosely as, for example, 'a collab-oration between the police and the community that identifies and solves community problems' (CPC 1994). Alternatively, community policing can be conceptualised as 'an organisational strategy that leaves setting priorities and the means of achieving them largely to residents and the police who serve in their neighbourhoods' (Skogan 2006b: 27–28). Some authors are more descriptive:

> The main elements of a community policing philosophy might be summarized in a single sentence as a belief or intention held by the police that they should consult with and take account of the wishes of the public in determining and evaluating operational policing and that they should collaborate with the public in identifying and solving local problems. (Bennett 1994: 229)

Although it is tempting to determine that community policing is happening because there are Neighbourhood Watch meetings and foot patrols, this relegates community policing to a suite of tactics designed to address particular problems. Wesley Skogan, who has dedicated many years of research to community policing programmes, ar-gues that community policing cannot be defined by the specific programmes that are often the most visible component of the model, because these programmes can change depending on the needs of the community (Skogan 2006b). Community policing is therefore a moving target that, if it is being followed in the manner suggested, continually changes with the whims of the public in line with their concerns regarding community safety, concerns that are not necessarily the same as those of the police department and are not necessarily even measured by traditional police data sources. It is the fluid and diverse nature of the definition of community policing that makes it so widely applicable. Indeed, a definition may not be possible. It may be the case that

> Different elements of community policing appeal to different audiences, and it has led to fruitless debates over what community policing 'really' means. In fact, it is this ambiguity and flexibility that gives community policing its all-things-to-all-people character and has contributed to its political viability over two decades, embraced by public leaders across the political spectrum. (Mastrofski 2006: 44)

And embraced it has been. This style of policing 'has become so much a catch-phrase in modern policing throughout the world, that hardly any policing organisation wants to be seen as not participating' (Edwards 1999: 76). Community policing has become a truly international phenomenon. The 2006 Community Policing conference in Washington, DC, attracted over 1,300 participants from as far afield as Australia, Indonesia and Pakistan. But while universally popular, community policing appears to be something that is easier to say you are doing than to define what it is you do.

There is significant disagreement about what constitutes community policing; however, Taylor's (2006) review of a range of studies found some commonalities in the majority of definitions, such as organisational decentralisation, more autonomy to local officers, greater responsiveness to citizen input, and commitment to problem-solving and the building of local capacity to resist crime. Generally, from this and many other studies, we can summarise that the community policing model:

- increases the interaction between the police and the community, either directly through collaboration or simply through consultation;
- attempts to provide named and accountable officers who know their area;
- gives communities a greater hand in driving police priorities;
- enhances decision-making at the lowest ranks of the police service;
- regains the legitimacy of police in the eyes of the public;
- allows a social service ethos to predominate, in which perceptions of community safety take priority;
- gives precedence to solving community problems over reactive law enforcement.

Evaluations of community policing are themselves difficult to evaluate, in view of the difficulty in reaching agreement among scholars and practitioners as to whether a programme is a true community policing one:

> The success of community policing will never be evaluated. The reason is simple. Community policing means too many things to different people. Its practices are so varied that any evaluation will be partial or challengeable as not being authentic 'community policing'. (Bayley 1994a: 278)

Though it should be possible to measure (through surveys, for example) changes in community satisfaction with the police if increased legitimacy is the aim, most attempts at community policing have been implemented without a clear set of aims and objectives. This often results in failure. It has been argued that the RCMP were unable to integrate the community into their community policing alignment strategy and create an empowerment ethos within the organisation, and 'the shift in executive discourse toward intelligence-led policing was an outcome of irreconcilable failures perceived during adoption of community policing' (Deukmedjian 2006: 536).

We can examine community policing on two scales. First – in regard to the breadth of crime and disorder problems that the approach is targeted to resolve – community policing is philosophically empowered to tackle a wide array of problems. Thus, on a problem focus scale that runs from *narrow* (perhaps just a focus on specific types of organised crime) to *broad* (that encompasses a whole gamut from violence to public nuisance abatement, for example), community policing has broad application. Indeed, this array of application areas is so broad that some problems fall beyond what most police officers would consider to be issues for the police at all. As Trojanowicz noted, 'community officers are so well received that they often find themselves inundated with requests that go beyond the scope of traditional law enforcement' (1994: 259). Secondly – on a continuum that explores the target of police operations that runs from crime events to offenders – it is more closely aligned to addressing crime and disorder events. Indeed, a focus on offenders might bring the police into conflict with some parts of the community and, as a result, risk losing the legitimacy that community policing seeks to regain. Figure 4.1 graphically shows the conceptual location of community policing on these continuums.

In summary, given the broad nature of community policing initiatives, community policing is difficult to define. However, this also means that it is easy to adopt, at least at a nominal level: true community policing may be a significant challenge. With a strong community focus, it is oriented towards neighbourhoods as the primary scale of activity, and has a bottom-up focus due to the discretion and autonomy given to

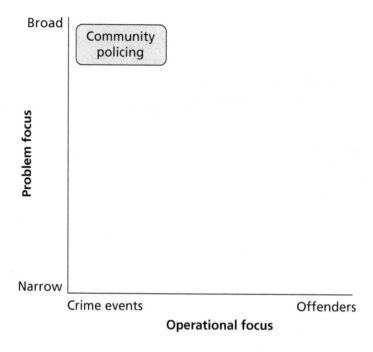

Figure 4.1 Two dimensions of community policing

patrol officers. It addresses a broad range of community issues (not just crime and disorder), and while the criteria for success are unclear and the subject of much discussion (see, for example, Mastrofski 2006; Skogan 2006b), a 'satisfied community' (Tilley 2003a: 326) and the expected outcome of an increase in perceived legitimacy of the police appear to be central aims. I have attempted to summarise these characteristics in Table 4.1.

PROBLEM-ORIENTED POLICING

Problem-oriented policing (POP) is considerably easier to define than community policing. The originator of problem-oriented policing, Professor Herman Goldstein, wrote that

> The emphasis in problem-oriented policing is on directing attention to the broad range of problems the community expects the police to handle – the problems that constitute the business of the police – and on how police can be more effective in dealing with them. ... It recognizes that the ultimate goal of the police is not simply to enforce the law, but to deal with problems effectively – ideally,

Table 4.1 Some generalised characteristics of five policing models

	Standard model of policing	Community policing	Problem-oriented policing	Compstat	Intelligence-led policing
Easily defined?	Yes	No	Fairly easy	Yes	Fairly easy, but still evolving
Easily adopted?	Yes	Superficially	Difficult	At the technical level, but managerially challenging	Managerially challenging
Orientation?	Police administrative units	Neighbourhoods	Problems	Police administrative units	Criminal groups, prolific and serious offenders
Hierarchical focus?	Top down	Bottom-up	As appropriate for the problem	Top down	Top down
Who determines priorities?	Police management	Community concerns/demands	Sometimes crime analysis, but varies from problem to problem	Police management from crime analysis	Police management from crime intelligence analysis
Target?	Offence detection	Unclear	Crime and disorder problems, and other areas of concern for police	Crime and disorder hot spots	Prolific offenders and crime problems, and other areas of concern for police
Criteria for success?	Increased detections and arrests	Satisfied community	Reduction of problem	Lower crime rates	Detection, reduction or disruption of criminal activity or problem
Expected benefit?	Increased efficiency	Increased police legitimacy	Reduced crime and other problems	Reduced crime (sometimes other problems)	Reduced crime and other problems

by preventing them from occurring in the first place. It therefore plunges the police into an in-depth study of the specific problems they confront. It invites consideration of a wide range of alternatives, in addition to criminal law, for responding to each specific problem. ... It looks to increased knowledge and thinking about the specific problems police confront as the driving force in fashioning police services. (Foreword, in Scott 2000: vi)

Some researchers suggest that problem-oriented policing is integral to definitions of community policing (Oliver and Bartgis 1998), and community and POP have often been bracketed together. In the US, the availability of funds from the federal government with which to conduct problem-oriented policing through community policing grants helped to establish problem-oriented policing, but it also caused some problems for POP's proponents. As Scott (2000: 1) writes, 'While the link between problem-solving and community policing in this large federal funding program has yielded many benefits, the linkage has also blurred the distinction between problem-oriented policing and community policing'. This section builds on the brief history of the development of problem-oriented policing from Chapter 2, and aims to clarify the similarities and distinct differences between problem-oriented policing and community policing in particular (also see Weisburd and Eck (2004) for an excellent review).

Problem-oriented policing is a conceptual approach that can address a vast array of policing issues. Problem-oriented policing requires police to delve deeper into the underlying problems that affect the safety and security of the community they serve. This requires police to be able to scan the broad array of information sources they have access to, including calls for service, recorded crime, informants and the community, and to reclassify these requests for assistance or action into aggregations not based on bureaucratic categories but as items associated with an underlying problem. The hope is that by attacking and resolving the underlying cause of an issue, the police can establish long-term solutions to problems, problems that plague communities and cause significant workload drains on the police department.

For better understanding of a problem when it is initially identified, police have to conduct a thorough analysis so that all potentially useful avenues of enquiry are covered. Often, but not always, this results in the identification of a solution that lies outside the direct policing domain. Law enforcement can be highly effective in reducing crime in the short term: for a simple example, consider static patrols by uniformed officers at crime hot spots. Static police patrols at a street corner drug market will reduce crime in the immediate vicinity of the location and can reduce both drug and violent crime (Lawton et al. 2005). However, it comes at a significant financial cost and is thus a short-term fix. When the cops leave, the underlying cause of why that street corner was a good location for drug dealing has not been addressed, and it is often easy for the site to return quickly to being a lucrative drug location (Rengert *et al.* 2005).

The central tenets of problem-oriented policing (see also www.popcenter.org) are as follows:

- Require officers and crime analysts to identify crime and disorder problems, and issues that cause harm to the community.
- Seek a thorough and detailed analysis of a problem before determining a possible solution.
- Allow that potential solutions to crime problems do not exclude the possibility of enforcement action by police, but often seek a long-term resolution that does not involve arrests.
- Resolution of the underlying issue is at least as important as alleviation of the harmful consequences of the problem.
- Greater decision-making and problem-solving freedom should be given to officers.
- Evaluation of the outcome of a solution is required in order to determine success.

Many problem-oriented policing practitioners used the SARA methodology to work through problem-solving. SARA involves:

- scanning: identifying recurring problems and how the ensuing consequences affect community safety;
- analysis: collecting and analysing all relevant data on the problem, with the objective of revealing ways to alter the causes of the problem;
- response: seeking out responses that might have worked elsewhere, identifying a range of local options, and then selecting and implementing specific activities that will resolve the problem;
- assessment: testing data collected before and after the response phase in order to determine whether the response reduced the problem and, if not, to identify new strategies that might work.

There are also variations based on SARA. For example, the RCMP used the acronym 'CAPRA' to signify *Clients Acquiring and analysing information, Partnership, Response, and Assessment* (Deukmedjian 2006).

As stated in Chapter 2, the adoption of problem-oriented policing has been at best a relatively slow emergence, and 'despite problem-oriented policing's wide appeal amongst senior officers, its implementation appears piecemeal in extent and halting in pace. The widespread transformation of problem-oriented policing rhetoric into practice cannot be expected anytime soon' (Townsley *et al.* 2003: 184). Braga and Weisburd (2006) go further by citing numerous studies that have identified a real disconnect with the aims of problem-oriented policing as articulated by Herman Goldstein (1979; 1990), yet contend that 'shallow' problem-solving responses can still be effective in crime control, and perhaps a less rigorous approach to the concept of problem-oriented policing is warranted.

One cause of the problem has been the inability to engage street-level officers in problem-solving. This does cause some difficulties for POP because it is sometimes (though not always) a bottom-up approach to crime control, resting greater responsibility in the lower ranks of the police service. Unfortunately, these same officers often defer to management for the identification and selection of problems; as happened when the RCMP attempted to implement a bottom-up style of community engagement (Deukmedjian and de Lint 2007). Furthermore, these officers usually have least control over resources. This lack of resources, or a mechanism to ask for them, resulting from the shift of emphasis from management to the front line, is seen as a 'structural difficulty' with problem-oriented policing (John and Maguire 2003: 65). It seems likely that it also influences priorities. Gundhus (2005) found that one Norwegian police station with a problem-solving preference was focused on low-level crime and public disorder concerns, whereas an organised crime unit with an intelligence-led policing inclination was more oriented towards national priorities and high-level crime and prosecution.

As with community policing, we can examine problem-oriented policing on the scale of the breadth of crime and disorder problems that the approach is targeted to resolve (the vertical axis in Figure 4.2). From a conceptual position, problem-oriented policing has a broad mandate though slightly less broad than community policing. In recent years, POP techniques have been applied to a growing variety of crime problems. For example, the Center for Problem Oriented Policing (www.popcenter.org) now has guides to address witness intimidation, bomb threats at schools, exploitation of trafficked women, meth labs, panhandling and prescription fraud. Furthermore, situational crime prevention techniques, closely aligned to problem-oriented policing, have featured in recent work on terrorism prevention (Clarke and Newman 2006; 2007). These topics reflect the broad applicability that Herman Goldstein intended. Problem-oriented policing places more emphasis on the crime events (collectively as a problem) than on arresting offenders (though a crackdown or arrest strategy is not out of the question, as Clarke and Eck 2005 point out). This realisation is reflected in the position of problem-oriented policing in Figure 4.2.

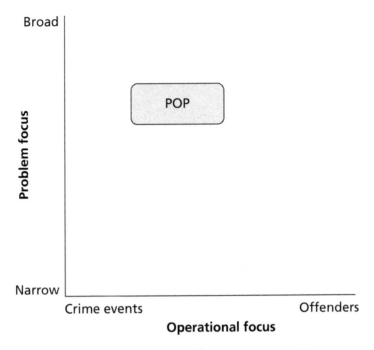

Figure 4.2 Two dimensions of problem-oriented policing (POP)

Problem-oriented policing therefore can be summarised as a conceptual framework that, while easy to define, is difficult to adopt. Adoption requires investment in analytical resources (both human and technical), a desire to move beyond responding to single incidents to addressing repeat calls for service as indicative of an underlying problem. It requires a police department to allow priorities to be grounded in analysis, and it demands a commitment to evidence as the basis for designing responses and evaluating outcomes. This all requires a considerable culture change within police departments, one where more autonomy is given to lower ranking officers, and where the reward structure rests less on arrests and more on alleviation of problems.

COMPSTAT

Compstat is a police managerial accountability mechanism. In a Compstat-oriented police department, mid-level commanders are made accountable to the executive level of the police department for the management of crime in their basic command units. By encouraging accountability, it is believed that precinct captains and managers will make use of regular, detailed crime intelligence and from this intelligence flow determine an appropriate crime reduction strategy.

Compstat is easy to define. The crime reduction mechanism of Compstat involves four principles:

- timely and accurate intelligence;
- effective tactics;
- rapid deployment;
- relentless follow-up and assessment.

When Compstat meetings started in early 1994, maps of crime in New York City were projected onto a wall. This allowed the meeting participants to concentrate on crime hot spots, and pressure was placed on precinct commanders to address emerging crime hot spots. Within Compstat, the application of the term *intelligence* is slightly at odds with how the word is more commonly used. Within the Compstat framework, *intelligence* more usually refers to mapped data and is more akin to *information* than the integrated crime intelligence that this book describes.

While crime data and geographical information systems (GIS) play a role in Compstat, it is more than data crunching: it is a marriage of crime mapping, operational strategy and accountability among mid-level commanders. In essence, it is a combined technical and managerial system (Moore 2003). As Silverman (2006) argues, the key to the success of Compstat was the organisational changes that allowed precinct commanders to have the freedom to try new tactics and approaches to crime reduction.

While mapping local crime hot spots forms the focus for timely and accurate intelligence (McGuire 2000), commanders must then devise effective tactics to combat new and ongoing crime concerns. Unlike with community policing, which devolves responsibilities to line officers, the pressure is squarely placed on these middle managers (Weisburd *et al.* 2006). In New York, Police Commissioner William Bratton replaced over a third of his precinct commanders within a year and a half: 'To Bratton, Compstat was police Darwinism – the fittest operational commanders survived and thrived, and the weakest lost their commands' (Walsh and Vito 2004: 60). Rapid deployment of resources is central to Compstat as, without a rapid response, the value of the 'timely' intelligence diminishes. The last part of Compstat often takes place at subsequent Compstat meetings where a review of the crime situation since the last meeting indicates the success (or not) of the previously-adopted tactics.

Compstat was associated with a significant reduction in crime in New York City (McDonald 2002), and as a result the strategy rapidly spread throughout the world, fuelled by media, public and law enforcement enthusiasm (Firman 2003). However, the accuracy of the claim that Compstat caused the significant reduction in crime that occurred in New York is difficult to determine (Moore 2003). For example, Levitt questions whether Compstat and other innovations encouraged by Bratton were responsible for the crime reduction in New York City in the early to mid-1990s, citing other possible explanations such as increased recruitment of police in the city, a levelling of the crack-cocaine market, and the delayed impact of the legalisation of abortion from the 1970s (Levitt 2004). Homicide rates in New York had already been dropping for four years before the introduction of Compstat, and crime rates were declining in Newark, New Jersey; Minneapolis, Minnesota; and Lowell, Massachusetts, prior to their police departments starting Compstat meetings (Weisburd et al. 2006).

In support of the crime reduction benefits of Compstat is a thorough empirical study from Australia, where the largest police department in the country, the New South Wales Police, introduced Compstat under the name 'Operation and Crime Review' (OCR). The OCR panels started in January 1998 and were based on the New York model. This involved a three-screen set-up, with maps and temporal trends graphically displayed in a large meeting room in Sydney, the state capital. Police local area commanders were not encouraged to adopt zero-tolerance tactics, but instead were to focus on hot times and places, search for illegal weapons and target repeat offenders, especially those with three or more convictions, those with outstanding arrest warrants, or those whom local intelligence officers suspected were active in the local crime scene (Chilvers and Weatherburn 2001b). In this last activity, it clearly shares similarities with the offender focus of intelligence-led policing. The researchers focused on burglary, a significant problem in Australia, and built a complex time series model that controlled for a number of other possible causes of any crime reduction. These included controls for the level of economic activity in the country, the local unemployment market, and the size of the local heroin-using population. The results suggest that OCRs were responsible for a significant reduction in burglaries across the state, and provide substantial evidence that much of the reduction in burglary was the result of targeting recidivist offenders (as much a supporting argument for intelligence-led policing). Recent work, also from Australia, has found that from inception in August 2001 until the end of June 2004, the Queensland Police Service's Operational Performance Review process cost AU$1,611,500 in salaries, equipment and travel; however, it was associated with reduced crime estimated at saving society AU$2,773,675, for an impressive overall cost benefit of over AU$1,000,000 (Mazerolle et al. 2007a).

There is growing evidence that any organisational changes – for example, organisational flexibility, data-driven decision making, and innovative problem solving – that represent any sort of substantive change from past management ideals remain a challenge for police departments (Fleming and Lafferty 2000; Weisburd et al. 2003; Willis et al. 2003). It has therefore been argued that, while the aims of Compstat remain laudable, in practice it is implemented in a manner that 'has been focused more on reinforcing and legitimating the traditional bureaucratic military model of police organisation than on innovation in the practices of policing' (Weisburd *et al.* 2006: 298). Furthermore, the use of mapping challenges police commanders to interpret intelligence products that are spatial in nature, and devise crime reduction strategies that are geographical in scope, something that few police commanders are trained to do (Ratcliffe 2004a).

Some researchers have noted that Compstat has a theatrical component whereby style and delivery in the large auditoriums where Compstat is played out can become a more effective means of surviving the meeting than providing substantive crime reduction. As a result, the crime reduction aspects can play a secondary role in the meeting. As Maple points out, during the Bratton days in New York City, it was more important to know what was going on and to be on top of the crime picture than to be effective at reducing crime (Maple and Mitchell 1999). Of course, these matters may be more issues of implementation than problems with the management strategy of Compstat itself; if Compstat does reduce crime, fixing the implementation issues may be time well spent.

In summary, we can say that Compstat is relatively easy to define, and fairly easy to adopt, because it does not require a significant cultural change within policing at the street level, though at the managerial level the change in culture and attitude can be significant. Some commentators claim Compstat requires organisational adaptations, while others argue that, in practice, Compstat reinforces the traditional hierarchy of law enforcement. It is oriented to the reduction in recorded crime across police administrative areas, and is driven by a top-down approach that reinforces the police command and control system. The aim is to reduce crime in police administrative areas such as districts, precincts or basic command units, and if crime figures are reduced (even if only in the short term), then this is an indication of success in crime reduction.

On the two continuums of operational and problem range, Compstat sits more towards the crime side (Magers 2004) and focuses on reducing violent, property and public disorder crime through strategies that tend to target crime reduction and suppression (Moore 2003) rather than specific offenders (though the targeting of individual criminals is not theoretically outside the remit of Compstat). In practice, the general aim of most Compstat sessions is to address street crime, such as robberies and assaults, and property crime, such as vehicle theft and burglary. Compstat has not been widely applied to more esoteric crime activity, such as organised crime or trans-national crime (though it has been proposed as a counter-terrorism tool; see Kelling and Bratton 2006), and it is not often applied to broader areas that community police units may address. This places Compstat on the problem/operational foci continuum as shown in Figure 4.3.

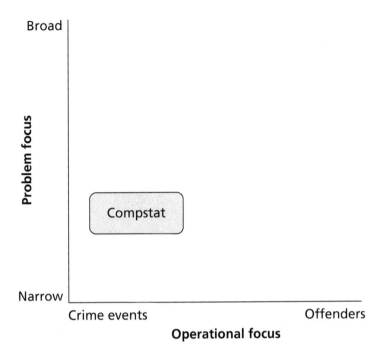

Figure 4.3 Two dimensions of Compstat

CONCEPTUAL CONFUSION

The previous sections have identified key movements in modern policing, approaches to the business of law enforcement that are often confused or merged with intelligence-led policing. However, as yet, we have not approached a definition of intelligence-led policing. To get there, we must wade through some of the conceptual fog that swirls around the business of policing. Generally, one has to infer the meaning of intelligence-led policing from researchers and practitioners who write about the subject. Some have sought to articulate their vision of intelligence-led policing as a new direction for policing, while others have tied intelligence-led policing to existing policing paradigms. More generally, there has been a lack of clarity in regard to policing paradigms and the frameworks by which academics and practitioners articulate their vision of how policing should function.

For example, it has been suggested that Compstat is a tool of community policing (Carter 2004), or that intelligence-led policing grew out of problem-oriented policing (Borglund and Nuldén 2006). Some writers have noted that proactive policing has built on the paradigm of community-based policing, using community policing as a foundation for intelligence-led policing (Clarke 2006), or that intelligence-led policing is synonymous with Compstat and Compstat is an evolution of community policing (Dannels and Smith 2001). There does, however, appear to be disagreement with a linking of community policing and Compstat. In particular, this perceived relationship runs counter to the 'undisguised contempt for some of the ideas behind the community policing paradigm' (Walsh and Vito 2004: 63) expressed by the originators of Compstat, William Bratton (1998) and his colleague Jack Maple (1999). Walsh and Vito conclude from their review of the writings of the key players from New York City that

> it is apparent Bratton, Maple and Mayor Giuliani were unsympathetic to the organizational message of community policing. They rejected this paradigm. From its very origin, Compstat was not designed as a vehicle to implement community policing. It was put into action to resolve the inability of community policing and of the nation's largest police department to address crime and to provide community security. (Walsh and Vito 2004: 65)

When broken down into constituent components, there are substantial differences between Compstat and community policing, and these are summarised in the earlier sections of this chapter, and in Table 4.1. In many of the same ways that there is confusion about the unique components of Compstat and community policing, so intelligence-led policing is significantly different from community policing. Here again, there is considerable confusion among commentators and practitioners.

For example, even though the development of intelligence-led policing was a repudiation of the crime focus of the community policing movement, there are still claims that there is a connection between intelligence-led policing and community policing (for a recent example, see McGarrell et al. 2007), that 'in many ways, intelligence-led policing is a new dimension of community policing, building on tactics and methodologies developed during years of community policing experimentation' (Carter 2004: 41), or that 'intelligence-led policing is a recent evolution from the strategies of community oriented policing and problem oriented policing' (Dannels and Smith 2001: 111). There is clearly a need for clarity in this conceptual area. Community policing emphasises increased contact with the public and the community and decentralisation of resources, yet Chris Hale and colleagues, with their considerable experience of intelligence-led policing with the Kent Policing Model (Anderson 1997), argue that an intelligence-led policing approach centralises resource control and would 'probably reduce numbers of officers in daily contact with local communities' (Hale et al. 2004: 303). Given that a central tenet of a proactive approach is less reliance on crime reporting and more crime recording taking place over the telephone, *reduced* contact with the public is a more likely outcome (Amey *et al.* 1996). Community policing and intelligence-led policing are different policing models that require an organisational realignment to move from one to the other (Deukmedjian 2006). Furthermore, community policing's central aim is an increase in police legitimacy, while intelligence-led policing strives first and foremost to reduce crime. These are substantial conceptual differences.

The Global Intelligence Working Group has one of the few definitions of intelligence-led policing, calling it 'the collection and analysis of information to produce an intelligence end product designed to inform law enforcement decision making at both the tactical and strategic levels' (GIWG 2003: 3-4). In this, they are linking intelligence-led policing to the intelligence cycle – a series of analytical steps by which information is converted into intelligence and disseminated to users (the intelligence cycle is described in Chapter 5). However, while the explicit linking of intelligence-led policing to the intelligence cycle is a fairly common phenomenon (Gill 1998; Dannels and Smith 2001), it may not be entirely accurate. The difficulty with directly associating intelligence-led policing with criminal intelligence or to the intelligence cycle is that these are processes for analysts, rather than a business model for the police service. This approach emphasises the *intelligence* in 'intelligence-led policing' rather than the *policing*.

This linking of intelligence products to the overarching conceptual framework is quite common. For instance, EUROPOL, in announcing the public version of the European Union's first Organised Crime Threat Assessment, claimed the threat assessment document 'is a core product of the intelligence-led policing concept and its drafting is one of EUROPOL's top priorities in 2006' (EUROPOL 2006: 3). While it may be a product, it is not the embodiment of the intelligence-led policing concept as it stands per se – welcome addition though it may be. There is no requirement of the police service (or anyone else) to action the intelligence, nor for the intelligence to be used to influence resource allocation. As a result, the development of an end product could be seen as the successful resolution of the process, yet singularly fail to influence policing or effect any crime reduction or disruption.

Overall, there is definitely a threat to intelligence-led policing, one that Osborne (2006) referred to in the intelligence world as 'diluting intelligence by calling everything intelligence'. Without clarity, there is certainly the chance that intelligence-led policing could suffer in the same definitional manner as community policing. As the following viewpoint from Deborah Osborne points out, a lack of clarity regarding the conceptual models that police departments employ has significant consequences for the quality of products that analysts produce.

VIEWPOINT
POLICING CONCEPTUAL FRAMEWORKS FROM THE ANALYST'S PERSPECTIVE
Deborah Osborne

Police managers have differing understandings of Compstat, community policing, problem-oriented policing (POP), and, now, intelligence-led policing. Whatever conceptual model employed, most law enforcement analysts, unlike their national security and military counterparts, receive little direction from law enforcement managers. They rely on outside training, their own particular expertise, and the influence of their peers in order to decide what types of analysis they will provide. Police managers and officers rarely go to analytical training and thus do not know what an analyst is supposed to do, could do, or what tools they need to do their job. The police management's adoption of one of the conceptual models may help analysts decide what to do in their agency, since analysts generally know what the concepts mean more than their commanders.

In agencies that focus on Compstat (or an adaptation of it) an analyst often becomes little more than a technician – someone who can produce statistics and pin maps on the computer. In this case, the analyst rarely analyzes – he or she is so busy creating descriptive data that there is no time for any in-depth analysis. Since Compstat focuses on timely, accurate intelligence, the analyst seldom, if ever, has time to do strategic assessments. Compstat management systems are more concerned with the here-and-now.

In community policing environments, the focus on the community's perception of problems makes it difficult for the analyst to objectively analyze all relevant data. Problems are determined by the community, not the data. Citizen surveys, citizens' complaints via 911 calls, and complaints to other political entities influence the direction of analysis. Community policing is supported by analysts through provision of community statistics and crime maps, which, as in Compstat models, is more description than analysis. Analysts may work with motivated community police officers to assess problems and recommend solutions, but more often on an individual case basis than system-wide.

Few analysts have the support, time and resources to conduct analysis for problem-oriented policing. In agencies that use POP as a model, generally officers choose projects and use analysts to help them obtain the data they need to work on their specific projects. While POP should integrate the analyst into every step of the process as an active member of the team, generally the analyst is not central to the process, but, rather, works on an as-needed basis.

True intelligence-led policing would expand and move the role of the analyst to centre stage. Adequate analytical staffing and tasking will be crucial to intelligence-led policing's success. Education and training focused on fully understanding analysis is mandatory for police officers and managers if we are to implement a concept that requires high-quality analysis. Officers need to know how to gather critical data and analysts need to know what officers need to affect change. Historically, analysts are blamed for producing irrelevant products, but this happens because – without the decision-makers' direction – the analyst is forced to be a mind-reader. Good results become based on lucky guesses. Analysts will be glad if intelligence-led policing can change that paradigm.

Deborah Osborne, a police analyst for ten years with the Buffalo Police Department (New York State), is 2007–08 President of the Society of Police Futurists International and author of the book Out of Bounds: Innovation and Change in Law Enforcement Intelligence Analysis.

INTELLIGENCE-LED POLICING DEFINED
ORIGINAL TENETS

Having just identified the need for a clear definition of intelligence-led policing, the next sections aim to approach an answer. The original articulation of intelligence-led policing by the Audit Commission (1993) and the Home Office (HMIC 1997), and as first operationalised by David Phillips, then Chief Constable of Kent Police, had the following central themes:

- *Target prolific and serious criminals.* 'The fundamental objective in recommending a clearer management framework … is to generate a capacity for proactive work which targets prolific and serious offenders' (Audit Commission 1993: 54).
- *Triage out most crime from further investigation.* 'The [Audit Commission] report … recommended the reduction of duplication in visits to crime scenes and the establishment of crime desks. These would handle all initial calls and screen out from further investigation, those where there would be no apparent benefit from doing so' (Heaton 2000: 345).
- *Make greater strategic use of surveillance and informants.* 'Even the smallest force needs access to a surveillance capacity … [and] one aspect of the enhanced supervisory role of [detective sergeants] should be to encourage detectives first to cultivate informants and then task them to produce information on high-priority crimes and criminals' (Audit Commission 1993: 57).
- *Position intelligence central to decision-making.* 'The intelligence function must be at the hub of operational policing activities' (HMIC 1997: 1).

This placed intelligence-led policing, at least initially, at the same level as Compstat on the problem focus continuum (Figure 4.4). While the Audit Commission used burglary as an example crime, and Phillips concentrated on property crime in Kent, intelligence-led policing also became associated with serious organised crime. As such, it did not initially address the wider array of policing problems to which it is now being applied. The initial model orientation therefore located intelligence-led policing to the middle right (ILP #1) of Figure 4.4.

REVISING THE ORIGINAL MODEL

These original components struck the initial tone; however, intelligence-led policing is definitionally an evolving concept. The last few years have seen a 'revisionist approach to intelligence-led policing' (Hale *et al.* 2004: 304), one that seeks to move intelligence-led policing more towards the crime-focus and problem-solving methodology of problem-oriented policing (Oakensen *et al.* 2002). This has been in line with government thinking in the last few years. The Home Office has articulated a more integrated model, with intelligence and problem-solving working hand-in-hand, such that 'whilst initial investigation into a crime is always undertaken, effective problem solving also requires the routine consideration of related intelligence' (HMIC 2000: 96). I reflected on this move towards integrating preventative problem-solving into intelligence-led policing when proposing a tentative early definition of intelligence-led policing as 'the application of criminal intelligence analysis as an objective decision-making tool in order to facilitate crime reduction and crime prevention through effective policing strategies and external partnership projects drawn from an evidential base' (Ratcliffe 2003: 3). The notion that intelligence-led policing was more an instrument than a philosophy found some support from Sheptycki, who, writing in 2005, defined intelligence-led policing as 'the technological effort to manage information about threats and risks in order to strategically manage the policing mission' (Sheptycki 2005).

But these definitions of intelligence-led policing as a tool or device do not do justice to the recent concerted efforts to position intelligence-led policing as a conceptual model that explains how the business of policing should be conducted, as exemplified by the National Intelligence Model. The recent revisions move intelligence-led policing away from being a tactic or tool to be employed as part of another conceptual model, and into the realm of a business model and conceptual philosophy for policing in its own right. These revisions also take a wider view of intelligence-led policing, such that it is increasingly being associated with the idea of identifying and analysing a problem (Hale et al. 2004). Given a greater acceptance of analysis at the core of decision-making, it was probably inevitable that the general processes would be applied to non-crime areas that are still within the domain of police, such as 'traffic, patrol and partnership activities' (Maguire and John 2006: 71). It was this thinking that inspired Merseyside Police to initiate a 'holistic strategy' that used an intelligence-led approach to all key areas of police business, not just crime (Barton and Evans 1999).

So, while still retaining the central notion that police should avoid getting bogged down in reactive, individual case investigations, intelligence-led policing is evolving into a managerial model of evidence-based, resource allocation decisions through prioritisation. It is also a philosophy that places greater emphasis on information sharing and collaborative, strategic solutions to crime problems, a concept that incorporates the 'reflexive notion of policing through partnerships' (Deukmedjian 2006: 531).

INTELLIGENCE-LED POLICING COMPONENTS

With the caveat that intelligence-led policing has been an evolving concept, we can infer the tenets of intelligence-led policing from published work, given that it is relatively detailed and well defined in this way (Hale et al. 2004). For example, intelligence-led policing is closely aligned with the UK National Intelligence Model, which is designed to prioritise targets for increased intelligence gathering, prevention strategies and enforcement tactics into a control strategy (NCIS 2000). This control strategy is the basis from which local police commanders set priorities for:

- the targeting of offenders;
- the management of crime and disorder hot spots;
- the investigation of linked series of crimes and incidents;
- the application of preventative measures. (NCIS 2000: 14).

The decision-making process is effectively a top-down one, with managers controlling uniform, traffic and detective resources and how they are deployed (Amey *et al.* 1996). Once those resources are deployed, Tilley (2003b) notes that increased arrests and reduced crime are expected benefits and indications of success. These realisations help to complete the intelligence-led policing column in Table 4.1.

The move towards a greater integration with problem-solving moves the target focus away from the far right of Figure 4.4, and to a more central position (while still retaining the offender slant). Greater use of intelligence targeting to a wider range of criminal activities, such as terrorism (IACP 2002; Loyka *et al.* 2005) and organised crime (Sheptycki 2004a; Harfield 2006; NJSP 2006a), broadens the range of applicable crime areas to which intelligence-led policing can be applied, and therefore the revised

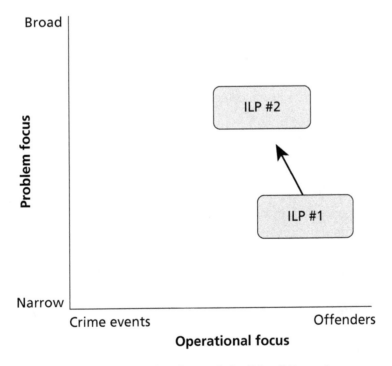

Figure 4.4 Two dimensions of intelligence-led policing (ILP) over time

location of intelligence-led policing on the two continuums of Figure 4.4 is reflected in the position of ILP #2.

A further piece of the puzzle is required before it is possible to attempt a definition of intelligence-led policing. The term *intelligence* has long been misunderstood within and outside law enforcement, and has often been associated with subterfuge and moral ambiguity. Moreover, it has also been misunderstood to mean the type of information gathered from informants or surveillance.

> A clear and general understanding of the meaning of the term 'intelligence', and an acceptance that it involves wider interpretations than perhaps traditional police-oriented explanations have allowed, is essential. This would include the interpretation of crime and incident data through analysis, and community information on a range of issues, as well as that more commonly used information gleaned from various sources on the activities of known or suspected active criminals. (Oakensen *et al.* 2002: 7)

Chapter 5 discusses the various definitions of intelligence, and how they can impact on the work of analysts; however, for now it is helpful to define *crime intelligence* as analysed information that blends data from crime analysis of crime patterns and criminal intelligence drawn from the behaviour of offenders. Here the term crime intelligence is used to reflect a realisation that good intelligence stems not only from knowledge about offenders (criminal intelligence) but also about crime events (crime analysis).

This all suggests that intelligence-led policing

- is a management philosophy/business model;
- aims to achieve crime reduction and prevention and to disrupt offender activity;
- employs a top-down management approach;
- combines crime analysis and criminal intelligence into crime intelligence;
- uses crime intelligence to objectively direct police resource decisions;
- focuses enforcement activities on prolific and serious offenders.

Furthermore, the model of intelligence-led policing practised in some places recognises the complementary nature of the long-term benefits of problem-oriented policing.

With these central tenets, intelligence-led policing is operationally the antithesis of community policing. Where community policing aims primarily for police legitimacy and is organisationally bottom-up and community centred, intelligence-led policing aims for crime reduction, is top-down and hierarchical, and uses crime intelligence to focus on offenders. Though there are stylistic similarities to Compstat (crime-fighting emphasis and organisationally hierarchical), the strategic approach to combating offender behaviour is substantively different. The offender focus differentiates intelligence-led policing from problem-oriented policing, even though this gap is shrinking as problem-solving becomes integrated into the crime disruption and prevention language of intelligence-led policing. Indeed, the 'revisionist' (Hale *et al.* 2004: 304) approach to intelligence-led policing has been increasingly to intertwine components of intelligence-led policing and problem-oriented policing. For example, Lancashire Constabulary explicitly sought to overlay intelligence-led policing (through the National Intelligence Model) over their existing problem-oriented policing approach (Maguire and John 2004).

Finally, it is sometimes said that police departments have been doing intelligence-led policing for a long time, but this is not the case. Intelligence has traditionally been used in police departments for case support, and not for strategic planning and resource allocation. The move from investigation-led intelligence to intelligence-led policing is the most significant and profound paradigm change in modern policing.

SUMMARY

Defining policing frameworks can be like trying to nail jelly to a tree. Various practitioners and commentators have tried to tie intelligence-led policing theoretically to existing conceptual frameworks of policing. However, if intelligence-led policing is truly a new paradigm in policing, then it should be recognised as significantly different from previous ways of policing (the policing models from this chapter are summarised in Figure 4.5). As said earlier, the degree of generalisation necessary even to try to conceptualise these comparative models into a simple framework highlights differences that are not always as severe in practice. Academics devote whole books to elucidating particular styles of policing, and many police departments operate models that are hybrids of these different approaches. The simplifications described herein should be interpreted as such.

From this chapter it should, however, be clear that there is a great deal of daylight separating intelligence-led policing and community policing (though see the GMAC PBM framework described in Chapter 7 for an example of an attempt to integrate more closely the business model aspects of intelligence-led policing with the collaborative ideals of community policing). If there is one fundamental difference between community policing and all of the conceptual frameworks for policing discussed in this chapter, it is that reduced crime is a by-product of successful community policing,

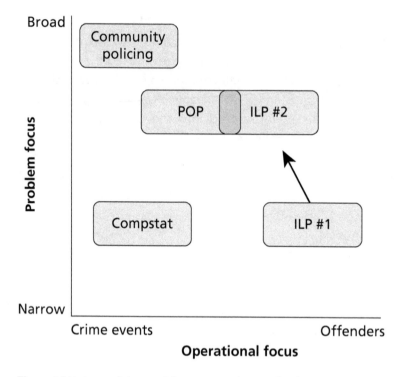

Figure 4.5 Various policing models represented on two focal continuums. POP: problem-oriented policing; ILP: intelligence-led policing

and not a primary aim. The primary aim of community policing is increased police legitimacy, whereas reduced crime is the primary aim of the other models.

While sharing some similarities, intelligence-led policing can have a broader problem range and more specific offender focus than Compstat. In many regards, intelligence-led policing tries to address many of the same problems as problem-oriented policing, though in a different organisational manner (more allied to traditional hierarchical command models) and with a greater emphasis on enforcement. In light of the philosophical revisions that have occurred in recent years and with a broader definition of intelligence, it is possible to propose a definition as follows:

> Intelligence-led policing is a business model and managerial philosophy where data analysis and crime intelligence are pivotal to an objective, decision-making framework that facilitates crime and problem reduction, disruption and prevention through both strategic management and effective enforcement strategies that target prolific and serious offenders.

Intelligence-led policing is thus a business model for policing that sees crime intelligence as a combination of what is more commonly known separately as crime analysis and criminal intelligence, and it works in an information management framework that allows analysts to influence decision-makers, and where a range of enforcement and longer-term, problem-solving prevention solutions are drawn from an evidence base that suggests their likely effectiveness. This definition also recognises the evolving nature of intelligence-led policing to be a more inclusive model able to incorporate areas of policing activity (such as accident reduction and missing person enquiries) that are not related to crime per se but are still significant problems for police agencies. With this evolution, intelligence-led policing is moving to become the 'all-crimes, all-hazards' business approach that is sought by many in policing.

There are a couple of points to note from this. Problem-oriented policing is usually defined according to its goal – reducing problems. Intelligence-led policing is too often defined according to the mechanism of how it is supposed to function. Therefore, the definition I propose here retains a similar goal-oriented approach; in other words, to use an objective, decision-making framework not as an end in itself, but as the means to achieve crime and problem reduction, disruption and prevention. Furthermore, Figure 4.5 shows a crossover of intelligence-led policing and problem-oriented policing. I share with a number of people the view that problem-oriented policing could benefit from greater use of crime intelligence and an offender focus, while intelligence-led policing could benefit from the strategic problem-solving capacities of problem-oriented policing.

The next chapters in this book will explore the role of analysts in making this vision a reality, and will introduce the 3-i model as a way to conceptualise how intelligence-led policing functions.

REFERENCES

9/11 Commission (2004) *The 9/11 Commission Report*. Washington, DC: National Commission on Terrorist Attacks Upon the United States.

ACC (2004) *Australian Crime Commission Corporate Plan 2004–2007*. Canberra: Australian Crime Commission.

ACC (2006) *Illicit Drug Data Report 2004–05*. Canberra: Australian Crime Commission.

ACPO (1975) *Report of the ACPO Subcommittee on Criminal Intelligence (Baumber report)*. London: Association of Chief Police Officers.

ACPO (1978) *Report of the ACPO Working Party on a Structure of Criminal Intelligence Officers (Pearce Report)*. London: Association of Chief Police Officers. ACPO (1986) *Report of the ACPO Working Party on Operational Intelligence (Ratcliffe Report)*. London: Association of Chief Police Officers.

Adlam, R. (2002) 'Governmental rationalities in police leadership: an essay exploring some of the "deep structure" in police leadership praxis', *Policing and Society*, 12 (1): 15–36.

AFP (2005) 'Targeting burglary', *Platypus Magazine*, June: 8–11.

Amey, P., Hale, C. and Uglow, S. (1996) 'Development and evaluation of a crime management model', Police Research Group: Police Research Series, Paper 18: 1–37.

Anderson, R. (1997) 'Intelligence-led policing: a British perspective', in A. Smith (ed). *Intelligence Led Policing: International Perspectives on Policing in the 21st Century*. Lawrenceville, NJ: International Association of Law Enforcement Intelligence Analysts, pp. 5–8.

Andrews, P. P. and Peterson, M. B. (1990) *Criminal Intelligence Analysis*. Loomis, CA: Palmer Enterprises.

Audit Commission (1993) *Helping With Enquiries: Tackling Crime Effectively*. London: HMSO.

Bakker, I. (2004) 'Police Knowledge Net: the development of a central knowledge database for the Dutch police', *4th Annual Conference of the European Society of Criminology*. Amsterdam, The Netherlands.

Barnett, A., Blumstein, A. and Farrington, D. P. (1987) 'Probabilistic models of youthful criminal careers', *Criminology*, 25 (1): 83–107.

Barton, A. and Evans, R. (1999) 'Proactive policing on Merseyside: briefing note', Police Research Group: Police Research Series, Paper 105: 1–2.

Bayley, D. H. (1994a) 'International differences in community policing', in D. P. Rosenbaum (ed), *The Challenge of Community Policing: Testing the Promises*. Thousand Oaks, CA: Sage, 278–281.

Bayley, D. H. (1994b) *Police for the Future*. New York: Oxford University Press.

Bayley, D. H. and Shearing, C. D. (1996) 'The future of policing', *Law and Society Review*, 30(3): 585–606.

Bennell, C. and Canter, D. (2002) 'Linking commercial burglaries by modus operandi: tests using regression and ROC analysis', *Science and Justice*, 42 (3): 153–164.

Bennett, T. (1994) 'Community policing on the ground: developments in Britain', in D. P. Rosenbaum (ed), *The Challenge of Community Policing: Testing the Promises*, Thousand Oaks, CA: Sage 224–246.

Bichard, M. (2004) *The Bichard Inquiry Report*. London: House of Commons. Biderman, A. D. and Reiss, A. J. (1967) 'On exploring the "dark figure" of crime', *Annals of the American Academy of Political and Social Science*, 374: 1–15.

Bigo, D. (2000) 'Liaison officers in Europe: new officers in the European security field', in J. W. E. Sheptycki (ed), *Issues in Transnational Policing*. London: Routledge, 67–99.

BJA (1998) *1998 Policy Clarification*. Washington, DC: Bureau of Justice Administration.

BJA (2005) *National Gang Threat Assessment 2005*. Washington, DC: Bureau of Justice Assistance.

Boba, R. (2005) *Crime Analysis and Crime Mapping*. Thousand Oaks, CA: Sage.

Bond, R. (2004) 'Methods and issues in risk and threat assessment', in J. H. Ratcliffe (ed), *Strategic Thinking in Criminal Intelligence*. Sydney: Federation Press, pp. 119–128.

Borglund, E. and Nuldén, U. (2006) 'Bits and pieces of information in police practice', *IRIS 29 – Paradigms, Politics, Paradoxes: 29th Information Systems Research Seminar in Scandinavia*.

BOTEC (2001) *Assessment of the HIDTA Program: High Intensity Drug Trafficking Areas*. Washington, DC: National Institute of Justice.

Bottomley, A. and Coleman, C. A. (1976) 'Criminal statistics: the police role in the discovery and detection of crime', *International Journal of Criminology and Penology*, 4: 33–58.

Bowers, K. J. and Johnson, S. D. (2003) 'Measuring the geographical displacement and diffusion of benefit effects of crime prevention activity', *Journal of Quantitative Criminology*, 19 (3): 275–301.

Bradley, D., Nixon, C. and Marks, M. (2006) 'What works, what doesn't work and what looks promising in police research networks', in J. Fleming and J. Wood (eds), *Fighting Crime Together: The Challenges of Policing and Security Networks*. Sydney: University of New South Wales Press, pp. 170–194.

Bradley, R. (1998) 'Public expectations and perceptions of policing', Police Research Group: Police Research Series, Paper 96: 1–24.

Braga, A. A. and Weisburd, D. (2006) 'Problem-oriented policing: the disconnect between principles and practice', in D. Weisburd and A. A. Braga (eds), *Police Innovation: Contrasting Perspectives*. New York: Cambridge University Press, pp. 133–152.

Brantingham, P. J. and Faust, F. L. (1976) 'A conceptual model of crime prevention', *Crime and Delinquency*, 22(3): 284–296.

Brantingham, P. L. and Brantingham, P. J. (1990) 'Situational crime prevention in practice', *Canadian Journal of Criminology*, 32 (1): 17–40.

Bratton, W. J. (1998) *Turnaround: How America's Top Cop Reversed the Crime Epidemic*. New York: Random House.

Bratton, W. J. (2006) 'Research: A practitioner's perspective, from the streets', *Western Criminology Review*, 7 (3): 1–6.

Bratton, W. J. (2007) 'Countering the radicalisation threat: an intelligence-led policing challenge'. *Testimony before the Subcommittee on Intelligence, Information Sharing and Terrorism Risk Assessment*. Washington DC: US House of Representatives Committee on Homeland Security.

Brodeur, J.-P. (1983) 'High policing and low policing: remarks about the policing of political activities', *Social Problems*, 30 (5): 507–520.

Brodeur, J.-P. and Dupont, B. (2006) 'Knowledge workers or "knowledge" workers?' *Policing and Society*, 16 (1): 7–26.

Brooks, J. (2001) 'Terrorism, organized crime, money laundering', *International Herald Tribune*, Tuesday, 30 October.

Brown, R., Clarke, R. V., Rix, B. and Sheptycki, J. (2004) *Tackling Organised Vehicle Crime: The Role of NCIS*. London: Home Office.

Brumwell, A. (2007) 'Mapping the cost of crime: area-based analysis of the economic and social cost of crime and implications for police and partnership working', *5th National Crime Mapping Conference*. London: Jill Dando Institute for Crime Science.

Buerger, M. E. (1998) 'The politics of third-party policing', in L. Green-Mazerolle and J. Roehl (eds), *Civil Remedies and Crime Prevention*. Monsey, NY: Criminal Justice Press, pp. 89–116.

Buerger, M. E. and Green-Mazerolle, L. (1998) 'Third party policing: a theoretical analysis of an emerging trend', *Justice Quarterly*, 15 (2): 301–327.

Burgess, E. W. (1916) 'Juvenile delinquency in a small city', *Journal of the American Institute of Criminal Law and Criminology*, 6: 724–728.

Burgess, E. W. (1925) 'The growth of the city: an introduction to a research project', in R. E. Park, E. W. Burgess and R. D. McKenzie (eds), *The City*. Chicago: University of Chicago Press, pp. 47–62.

Carter, D. L. (2004) *Law Enforcement Intelligence: A guide for State, Local, and Tribal Enforcement Agencies*. Washington, DC: Office of Community Oriented Policing Services.

Carter, D. L. (2005) 'The law enforcement intelligence function: State, local, and tribal agencies', *FBI Law Enforcement Bulletin*, 74 (6): 1–9.

Casey, J. (2004) 'Managing joint terrorism', *FBI Law Enforcement Bulletin*, 73 (11): 1–6.

Chainey, S. and Ratcliffe, J. H. (2005) *GIS and Crime Mapping*. London: John Wiley and Sons.

Chainey, S., Reid, S. and Stuart, N. (2003) 'When is a hotspot a hotspot? A procedure for creating statistically robust hotspot maps of crime', in D. B. Kidner, G. Higgs and S. D. White (eds), *Socio-Economic Applications of Geographic Information Science*, London: Taylor and Francis, pp. 21–36.

Chamlin, M. B. (1991) 'Research note: a longitudinal analysis of the arrest-crime relationship: a further examination of the tipping effect', *Justice Quarterly*, 8 (2): 187–200.

Chenery, S., Henshaw, C. and Pease, K. (1999) 'Illegal parking in disabled bays: a means of offender targeting', Briefing Note 1/99. London: Home Office Policing and Reducing Crime Unit.

Chilvers, M. and Weatherburn, D. (2001a) 'Do targeted arrests reduce crime?' *Contemporary Issues in Crime and Justice*. NSW Bureau of Crime Statistics and Research, Paper 63.

Chilvers, M. and Weatherburn, D. (2001b) 'Operation and Crime Review panels: their impact on break and enter', *Crime and Justice Statistics: Bureau Brief*. NSW Bureau of Crime Statistics and Research.

Christopher, S. (2004) 'A practitioner's perspective of UK strategic intelligence', in J. H. Ratcliffe (ed), *Strategic Thinking in Criminal Intelligence*. Sydney: Federation Press, pp. 176–192.

CISC (2006a) *2006 Annual Report on Organized Crime in Canada*. Ottawa: Criminal Intelligence Service Canada.

CISC (2006b) 'Criminal Intelligence Service Canada's 2006 annual report highlights organized crime threats in Canada', Press release, source http://cisc.gc.ca/media2006/news_release_2006_e.htm (accessed 10 October 2006).

CISC (2007) *Integrated Threat Assessment Methodology*. Ottawa: Criminal Intelligence Service Canada.

Clarke, C. (2006) 'Proactive policing: standing on the shoulders of community-based policing', *Police Practice and Research*, 7 (1): 3–17.

Clarke, R. V. (1992) (ed.), *Situational Crime Prevention: Successful Case Studies*. Albany, NY: Harrow and Heston.

Clarke, R. V. (2004) 'Technology, criminology and crime science', *European Journal on Criminal Policy and Research*, 10 (1): 55–63.

Clarke, R. V. and Eck, J. (2003) *Becoming a Problem Solving Crime Analyst*. London: Jill Dando Institute.

Clarke, R. V. and Eck, J. (2005) *Crime Analysis for Problem Solvers – in 60 Small Steps*. Washington, DC: Center for Problem Oriented Policing.

Clarke, R. V. and Harris, P. M. (1992) 'Auto theft and its prevention', *Crime and Justice*, 16: 1–54.

Clarke, R. V., Kemper, R. and Wyckoff, L. (2001) 'Controlling cell phone fraud in the US: lessons for the UK "Foresight" Prevention Initiative', *Security Journal*, 14 (1): 7–22.

Clarke, R. V. and Newman, G. R. (2006) *Outsmarting the Terrorists*. Westport, CT: Praeger Security International.

Clarke, R. V. and Newman, G. R. (2007) 'Policing and the prevention of terrorism', *Policing: A Journal of Policy and Practice*, 1 (1): 9–20.

Clarke, S. H. (1975) 'Some implications for North Carolina of recent research in juvenile delinquency', *Journal of Research in Crime and Delinquency*, 12 (1): 51–60.

Coleman, C. and Moynihan, J. (1996) *Understanding Crime Data*. Buckingham, UK: Open University Press.

Collier, P. M. (2006) 'Policing and the intelligent application of knowledge', *Public Money and Management*, 26 (2): 109–116.

Collier, P. M., Edwards, J. S. and Shaw, D. (2004) 'Communicating knowledge about police performance', *International Journal of Productivity and Performance Management*, 53 (5): 458–467.

Cooper, P. and Murphy, J. (1997) 'Ethical approaches for police officers when working with informants in the development of criminal intelligence in the United Kingdom', *Journal of Social Policy*, 26 (1): 1–20.

Cope, N. (2003) 'Crime analysis: principles and practice', in T. Newburn (ed.), *Handbook of Policing*. Cullompton: Willan Publishing, pp. 340–362.

Cope, N. (2004) 'Intelligence led policing or policing led intelligence?: integrating volume crime analysis into policing', *British Journal of Criminology*, 44 (2): 188–203.

Cordner, G. W. (1995) 'Community policing: elements and effects', *Police Forum*, 5 (3): 1–8.

Coumarelos, C. (1994) 'Juvenile offending: predicting persistence and determining the cost-effectiveness of interventions.' Sydney: NSW Bureau of Crime Statistics and Research.

CPC (1994) *Understanding Community Policing: A Framework for Action*. Washington DC: Community Policing Consortium.

Crawford, A. (1997) *The Local Governance of Crime: Appeals to Community and Partnerships*. Oxford: Clarendon Press.

Dannels, D. and Smith, H. (2001) 'Implementation challenges of intelligence-led policing in a quasi-rural county', *Journal of Crime and Justice*, 24 (2): 103–112.

Davenport, T. H. (1997) *Information Ecology: Mastering the Information and Knowledge Environment*. New York: Oxford University Press.

Davidoff, L. (1996) 'Police performance indicators', *Statistical Journal of the UN Economic Commission for Europe*, 13 (2): 161–169.

Dawson, D. (2007) 'New tool measures disruption to OC', *RCMP Gazette*, 69(1).

De Lint, W., O'Connor, D. and Cotter, R. (2007) 'Controlling the flow: security, exclusivity, and criminal intelligence in Ontario', *International Journal of the Sociology of Law*, 35 (1): 41–58.

Deukmedjian, J. E. (2006) 'Executive realignment of RCMP mission', *Canadian Journal of Criminology and Criminal Justice*, 48 (4): 523–542.

Deukmedjian, J. E. and de Lint, W. (2007) 'Community into Intelligence: Resolving information uptake in the RCMP', *Policing and Society*, 17 (3): 239–256.

Dixon, D. (1999) 'Reform, regression and the Royal Commission into the NSW Police Service', in D. Dixon (ed.), *A Culture of Corruption*. Sydney: Hawkins Press, pp. 138–179.

Docobo, J. (2005) 'Community policing as the primary prevention strategy for homeland security at the local law enforcement level', *Homeland Security Affairs*, 1(1): Article 4.

DOJ (1977) *Report of the Department of Justice Task Force to Review the FBI Martin Luther King, Jr. Security and Assassination Investigations*. Washington DC: Department of Justice.

DOJ (2005) *Fusion Center Guidelines*. Washington, DC: Department of Justice.

Dubourg, R. and Prichard, S. (2007) 'Organised crime: revenues, economic and social costs, and criminal assets available for seizure', Home Office Online Report 14/07. London: Home Office.

Dunnighan, C. and Norris, C. (1999) 'The detective, the snout, and the audit commission: the real costs in using informants', *Howard Journal of Criminal Justice*, 38(1): 67–86.

Dupont, B. (2003) 'Preserving Institutional Memory in Australian Police Services', *Trends and Issues in Crime and Criminal Justice*, No. 245: 1–6.

Dupont, B. (2004) 'Security in the age of networks', *Policing and Society*, 14 (1): 76–91.

Dupont, B. (2006) 'Mapping security networks: from metaphorical concept to empirical model', in J. Fleming and J. Wood (eds), *Fighting Crime Together: The Challenges of Policing and Security Networks*. Sydney: University of New South Wales Press), pp. 35–59.

Eck, J. E. (1997) 'What do those dots mean? Mapping theories with data', in D. Weisburd and T. McEwen (eds), *Crime Mapping and Crime Prevention*. Monsey, NY: Criminal Justice Press, pp. 379–406.

Eck, J. E. (2006) 'When is a bologna sandwich better than sex? A defense of small-n case study evaluations', *Journal of Experimental Criminology*, 2 (3): 345–362.

Eck, J. E., Chainey, S., Cameron, J. G., Leitner, M. and Wilson, R. E. (2005) *Mapping Crime: Understanding Hot Spots*. Washington, DC: National Institute of Justice.

Eck, J. E. and Maguire, E. R. (2000) 'Have changes in policing reduced violent crime? An assessment of the evidence', in A. Blumstein and J. Wallman (eds), *The Crime Drop in America*. Cambridge: Cambridge University Press, pp. 207–265.

Eck, J. E. and Spelman, W. (1987) 'Problem solving: problem-oriented policing in Newport News'. Washington, DC: Police Executive Research Forum.

Eck, J. E. and Weisburd, D. (1995) 'Crime places in crime theory', in D. Weisburd and J. E. Eck (eds), *Crime and Place*. Monsey, NY: Criminal Justice Press, pp. 1–33.

Edwards, C. (1999) *Changing Police Theories for 21st Century Societies*. Sydney: Federation Press.

Ericson, R. V. and Haggerty, K. D. (1997) *Policing the Risk Society*. Oxford: Clarendon Press.

EUROPOL (2006) *European Organised Crime Threat Assessment 2006*. The Hague: European Law Enforcement Organisation.

Everson, S. (2003) 'Repeat victimisation and prolific offending: chance or choice?'. *International Journal of Police Science and Management*, 5 (3): 180–194.

Ewart, B. W., Oatley, G. C. and Burn, K. (2005) 'Matching crimes using burglars' modus operandi: a test of three models', *International Journal of Police Science and Management*, 7 (3): 160–174.

Farrell, G., Chenery, S. and Pease, K. (1998) *Consolidating Police Crackdowns: Findings from an Anti-burglary Project*. London: Policing and Reducing Crime Unit, Research, Development and Statistics Directorate, Home Office.

Farrington, D. P. (1987) 'Predicting individual crime rates', *Crime and Justice*, 9: 55–101.

Farrington, D. P. (1990) 'Implications of criminal career research for the prevention of offending', *Journal of Adolescence*, 13: 93–113.

Farrington, D. P. (1992) 'Criminal career research in the United Kingdom', *British Journal of Criminology*, 32 (4): 521–536.

Farrington, D. P. (2003) 'Methodological quality standards for evaluation research', *Annals of the American Academy of Political and Social Science*, 587 (1): 49–68.

FBI (2004) *Strategic Plan 2004–2009*. Washington, DC: Federal Bureau of Investigation.

Felson, M. (1998) *Crime and Everyday Life: Impact and Implications for Society*. Thousand Oaks, CA: Pine Forge Press.

Fielding, N. G. (2005) 'Concepts and theory in community policing', *Howard Journal of Criminal Justice*, 44 (5): 460–472.

Firman, J. R. (2003) 'Deconstructing CompStat to clarify its intent', *Criminology and Public Policy*, 2 (3): 457–460.

Fleming, J. and Lafferty, G. (2000) 'New management techniques and restructuring for accountability in Australian police organisations', *Policing: An International Journal of Police Strategies and Management*, 23 (2): 154–168.

Flood, B. (2004) 'Strategic aspects of the UK National Intelligence Model', in J. H. Ratcliffe (ed) *Strategic Thinking in Criminal Intelligence*. Sydney: Federation Press, pp. 37–52.

Flood-Page, C., Campbell, S., Harrington, V. and Miller, J. (2000) *Youth Crime: Findings from the 1998/99 Youth Lifestyles Survey*. London: Home Office Research, Development and Statistics Directorate.

Ford Foundation (1996) *Innovations in American Government 1986–1996 Tenth Anniversary*. New York: Ford Foundation.

Forst, B. and Planty, M. (2000) 'What is the probability that the offender in a new case is in the MO file?', *International Journal of Police Science and Management*, 3 (2): 124–137.

Giannetti, W. J. (2007) 'What is Operation Safe Streets?', *IALEIA Journal*, 17 (1): 22–32.

Gill, P. (1998) 'Making sense of police intelligence? The use of a cybernetic model in analysing information and power in police intelligence processes', *Policing and Society*, 8 (3): 289–314.

Gill, P. (2000) *Rounding up the Usual Suspects? Developments in Contemporary Law Enforcement Intelligence*. Aldershot: Ashgate.

GIWG (2003) *The National Criminal Intelligence Sharing Plan*. Washington, DC: Department of Justice [Global Intelligence Working Group].

GIWG (2005) *The National Criminal Intelligence Sharing Plan* (revised June 2005). Washington, DC: Department of Justice [Global Intelligence Working Group].

Goldstein, H. (1979) 'Improving policing: a problem-oriented approach', *Crime and Delinquency*, 25 (2): 236–258.

Goldstein, H. (1990) *Problem-Oriented Policing*. New York: McGraw-Hill.

Goldstein, H. (2003) 'On further developing problem-oriented policing: The most critical need, the major impediments, and a proposal', in J. Knutsson (ed.) *Problem-Oriented Policing: From Innovation to Mainstream*. Monsey, NY: Criminal Justice Press, pp. 13–47.

Gottlieb, S., Arenberg, S. and Singh, R. (1998) *Crime Analysis: From First Report to Final Arrest*. Montclair, CA: Alpha Publishing.

Goudriaan, H., Wittebrood, K. and Nieuwbeerta, P. (2006) 'Neighbourhood characteristics and reporting crime: effects of social cohesion, confidence in police effectiveness and socio-economic disadvantage', *British Journal of Criminology*, 46 (4): 719–742.

Grabosky, P. (1992) 'Prosecutors, informants, and the integrity of the criminal justice system', *Current Issues in Criminal Justice*, 4 (1): 47–63.

Green, L. (1995) 'Cleaning up drug hot spots in Oakland, California: the displacement and diffusion effects', *Justice Quarterly*, 12 (4): 737–754.

Greene, J. R., Seamon, T. M. and Levy, P. R. (1995) 'Merging public and private security for collective benefit: Philadelphia's Center City District', *American Journal of Police*, 14 (2): 3–20.

Grieve, J. (2004) 'Developments in UK criminal intelligence', in J. H. Ratcliffe (ed.), *Strategic Thinking in Criminal Intelligence*. Sydney: Federation Press, pp. 25–36.

Guerry, A.-M. (1833) *Essai sur la statistique morale de la France: précédé d'un rapport à l'Académie des Sciences*. Paris: Chez Crochard.

Guidetti, R. A. (2006) 'Policing the Homeland: Choosing the Intelligent Option', Masters thesis. Monterey, CA: Naval Postgraduate School.

Gundhus, H. O. (2005) '"Catching" and "Targeting"': Risk-based policing, local culture and gendered practices', *Journal of Scandinavian Studies in Criminology and Crime Prevention*, 6 (2): 128–146.

Hale, C., Heaton, R. and Uglow, S. (2004) 'Uniform styles? Aspects of police centralisation in England and Wales', *Policing and Society*, 14 (4): 291–312.

Harfield, C. (2000) 'Pro-activity, partnership and prevention: the UK contribution to policing organised crime in Europe', *Police Journal*, 73: 107–117.

Harfield, C. (2006) 'SOCA: a paradigm shift in British policing', *British Journal of Criminology*, 46 (4): 743–761.

Heaton, R. (2000) 'The prospects for intelligence-led policing: some historical and quantitative considerations', *Policing and Society*, 9 (4): 337–356.

Heldon, C. E. (2004) 'Exploratory analysis tools', in J. H. Ratcliffe (ed.), *Strategic Thinking in Criminal Intelligence*. Sydney: Federation Press, 99–118.

Herrington, V. and Millie, A. (2006) 'Applying reassurance policing: is it "business as usual"?' *Policing and Society*, 16 (2): 146–163.

Higgins, O. (2004) 'Rising to the collection challenge', in J. H. Ratcliffe (ed.), *Strategic Thinking in Criminal Intelligence*. Sydney: Federation Press, pp. 70–85.

HMIC (1997) *Policing with Intelligence*. London: Her Majesty's Inspectorate of Constabulary.

HMIC (2000) *Calling Time on Crime*. London: Her Majesty's Inspectorate of Constabulary.

HMIC (2005) *Closing the Gap*. London: Her Majesty's Inspectorate of Constabulary.

Hobbs, D. (1997) 'Criminal collaboration: youth gangs, subcultures, professional criminals, and organized crime', in M. Maguire, R. Morgan and R. Reiner (eds), *The Oxford Handbook of Criminology*. Oxford: Clarendon Press, pp. 801–840.

Home Office (2004) *One Step Ahead: A 21st Century Strategy to Defeat Organised Crime*. London: Home Office.

Home Office (2006a) *Criminal Statistics 2005, England and Wales*. London: Office for Criminal Justice Reform.

Home Office (2006b) *Review of the Partnership Provisions of the Crime and Disorder Act 1998 – Report of Findings*. London: Home Office.

Horvath, F., Meesig, R. T. and Lee, Y. H. (2001) *National Survey of Police Policies and Practices Regarding the Criminal Investigations Process: Twenty-Five Years After Rand* (Final report [NCJRS 202902]). Washington DC: National Institute of Justice.

HOSB (1989) *Criminal and Custodial Careers of Those Born in 1953, 1958 and 1963*. London: Home Office.

Hough, M. and Lewis, H. (1989) 'Counting crime and analysing risks: the British Crime Survey', in D. J. Evans and D. T. Herbert (eds), *The Geography of Crime*. London: Routledge.

IACP (2002) 'Criminal intelligence sharing: a national plan for intelligence-led policing at the local, state and federal levels', *IACP Intelligence Summit*. Alexandria, VA: COPS and International Association of Chiefs of Police.

IALEIA (2004) *Law Enforcement Analytic Standards*. Richmond, VA: Global Justice Information Sharing Initiative.

Indermaur, D. (1996) 'Violent crime in Australia: interpreting the trends', *Trends and Issues in Crime and Criminal Justice*, 61: 1–6.

Innes, M. (2000) ' "Professionalizing" the role of the police informant: the British experience', *Policing and Society*, 9 (4): 357–384.

Innes, M. (2004) 'Reinventing tradition? Reassurance, neighbourhood security and policing', *Criminal Justice*, 4 (2): 151–171.

Innes, M., Fielding, N. and Cope, N. (2005) ' "The Appliance of Science?": The theory and practice of crime intelligence analysis', *British Journal of Criminology*, 45 (1): 39–57.

Ipsos MORI (2007) 'Research into Recent Crime Trends in Northern Ireland', May 2007. Belfast: Ipsos MORI on behalf of the Northern Ireland Policing Board and the Police Service of Northern Ireland.

Irwin, M. P. (2001) 'Policing organised crime', paper presented to the *4th National Outlook Symposium on Crime in Australia*. Canberra: Australian Institute of Criminology.

Jacobs, B. A. (1993) 'Undercover deception clues – A case of restrictive deterrence', *Criminology*, 31 (2): 281–299.

John, T. and Maguire, M. (2003) 'Rolling out the National Intelligence Model: key challenges', in K. Bullock and N. Tilley (eds), *Crime Reduction and Problem-oriented Policing*. Cullompton: Willan Publishing, pp. 38–68.

John, T. and Maguire, M. (2007) 'Criminal intelligence and the National Intelligence Model', in T. Newburn, T. Williamson and A. Wright (eds), *Handbook of Criminal Investigation*. Cullompton: Willan Publishing, pp. 176–202.

John, T., Morgan, C. and Rogers, C. (2006) 'The Greater Manchester Against Crime Partnership Business Model: an independent evaluation'. Glamorgan: Centre for Criminology, University of Glamorgan.

Johnson, B. D. and Natarajan, M. (1995) 'Strategies to avoid arrest: Crack sellers' response to intensified policing', *American Journal of Police*, 14 (3/4): 49–69.

Johnston, L. D., O'Malley, P. M., Bachman, J. G. and Schulenberg, J. E. (2005) *Monitoring the Future: National Results on Adolescent Drug Use: Overview of Key Findings, 2004*. Bethesda, MD: National Institute on Drug Abuse.

Johnston, R. (2005) *Analytic Culture in the US Intelligence Community: An Ethnographic Study*. Washington, DC: The Center for the Study of Intelligence, CIA.

Johnstone, P. (2004) 'Director General, National Criminal Intelligence Service (NCIS) of the United Kingdom (recently retired), John Abbott', *Police Practice and Research*, 5 (4/5): 407–414.

Jones, C. and Weatherburn, D. (2004) 'Evaluating police operations (1): A process and outcome evaluation of Operation Vendas'. Sydney: New South Wales Bureau of Crime Statistics and Research.

Keelty, M. (2004) 'Can intelligence always be right?' Presentation at the *13th Annual Conference of the Australian Institute of Professional Intelligence Officers*. Melbourne: AIPIO.

Keelty, M. (2006) 'International networking and regional engagement: An AFP perspective', in J. Fleming and J. Wood (eds), *Fighting Crime Together: The Challenges of Policing and Security Networks*. Sydney: University of New South Wales Press, pp. 116–132.

Kelling, G. L. and Bratton, W. J. (2006) 'Policing terrorism', *Civic Bulletin*, 43: 12.

Kelling, G. L., Pate, T., Dieckman, D. and Brown, C. E. (1974) *The Kansas City Preventative Patrol Experiment: A Summary Report*. Washington, DC: Police Foundation.

Kelling, G. L. and Wycoff, M. A. (2002) *Evolving Strategy of Policing: Case Studies of Strategic Change*. Washington, DC: National Institute of Justice.

Kerlikowske, R. G. (2007) 'Building a partnership strategy: improving information sharing with state and local law enforcement and the private sector'. Testimony before the Subcommittee on Intelligence, Information Sharing and Terrorism Risk Assessment. Washington, DC: US House of Representatives Committee on Homeland Security.

Koper, C. S. (1995) 'Just enough police presence: Reducing crime and disorderly behavior by optimizing patrol time in crime hot spots', *Justice Quarterly*, 12 (4): 649–672.

Krimmel, J. T. and Mele, M. (1998) 'Investigating stolen vehicle dump sites: An interrupted time series quasi experiment', *Policing: An International Journal of Police Strategies and Management*, 21 (3): 479–489.

Kuhn, T. S. (1962) *The Structure of Scientific Revolutions*. Chicago: University of Chicago Press.

Lab, S. P. (1988) *Crime Prevention: Approaches, Practices and Evaluations*. Cincinnati, OH: Anderson.

Lab, S. P. (2004) 'Crime prevention, politics, and the art of going nowhere fast', *Justice Quarterly*, 21 (4): 681–692.

Langworthy, R. H. (1989) 'Do stings control crime? An evaluation of a police fencing operation', *Justice Quarterly*, 6 (1): 27–45.

Lawton, B. A., Taylor, R. B. and Luongo, A. J. (2005) 'Police officers on drug corners in Philadelphia, drug crime, and violent crime: Intended, diffusion, and displacement impacts', *Justice Quarterly*, 22 (4): 427–451.

Laycock, G. (2001a) 'Research for police: who needs it?', *Trends and Issues in Crime and Criminal Justice*, 211: 1–6.

Laycock, G. (2001b) 'Scientists or politicians – who has the answer to crime?' Inaugural lecture of the Jill Dando Institute of Crime Science: University College London.

LEAA (1973) *Criminal Justice System – Report of the National Advisory Commission on Criminal Justice Standards and Goals.* Washington, DC: National Institute of Justice [Law Enforcement Assistance Administration].

Leigh, A., Read, T. and Tilley, N. (1996) 'Problem-oriented policing', Police Research Group: Crime Detection and Prevention Series, Paper 75: 1–62.

Leigh, A., Read, T. and Tilley, N. (1998) 'Brit Pop II: problem-orientated policing in practice', Police Research Group: Police Research Series, Paper 93: 1–60.

Levi, M. (2002) 'Money laundering and its regulation', *Annals of the American Academy of Political and Social Science*, 582: 181–194.

Levi, M. and Maguire, M. (2004) 'Reducing and preventing organised crime: An evidence-based critique', *Crime, Law and Social Change*, 41 (5): 397–469.

Levitt, S. D. (2004) 'Understanding why crime fell in the 1990s: Four factors that explain the decline in crime and six that do not', *Journal of Economic Perspectives*, 18 (1): 163–190.

Loyka, S. A., Faggiani, D. A. and Karchmer, C. (2005) *Protecting Your Community from Terrorism.* Vol. 4. *The Production and Sharing of Intelligence.* Washington, DC: COPS/PERF.

Mackay, D. and Ratcliffe, J. H. (2004) 'Intelligence products and their dissemination', in J. H. Ratcliffe (ed.), *Strategic Thinking in Criminal Intelligence.* Sydney: Federation Press, pp. 148–162.

Macpherson of Cluny (1999) *The Stephen Lawrence Enquiry, A Report by Sir William Macpherson of Cluny.* London: HMSO.

Magers, J. S. (2004) 'Compstat: A new paradigm for policing or a repudiation of community policing?' *Journal of Contemporary Criminal Justice*, 20 (1): 70–79.

Maguire, M. (2000) 'Policing by risks and targets: some dimensions and implications of intelligence-led crime control', *Policing and Society*, 9 (4): 315–336.

Maguire, M. and John, T. (1995) 'Intelligence, surveillance and informants: integrated approaches', Police Research Group: Crime Detection and Prevention Series, Paper 64: 1–58.

Maguire, M. and John, T. (1996) 'Covert and deceptive policing in England and Wales: issues in regulation and practice', *European Journal of Crime, Criminal Law and Criminal Justice*, 4: 316–334.

Maguire, M. and John, T. (2004) 'The National Intelligence Model: early implementation experience in three police force areas', Working Paper Series, Paper 50. Cardiff: Cardiff University.

Maguire, M. and John, T. (2006) 'Intelligence led policing, managerialism and community engagement: Competing priorities and the role of the National Intelligence Model in the UK', *Policing and Society*, 16 (1): 67–85.

Makkai, T., Ratcliffe, J. H., Veraar, K. and Collins, L. (2004) 'ACT recidivist offenders', *Research and Public Policy Series*, 54: 1–83.

Manning, P. (2000) 'Policing new social spaces', in J. W. E. Sheptycki (ed.), *Issues in Transnational Policing.* London: Routledge, pp. 177–200.

Maple, J. and Mitchell, C. (1999) *The Crime Fighter: Putting the Bad Guys out of Business.* New York: Doubleday.

Markle Foundation (2003) *Creating a Trusted Network for Homeland Security.* New York: Markle Foundation.

Marrin, S. (2007) 'At arm's length or at the elbow?: explaining the distance between analysts and decision makers', *International Journal of Intelligence and CounterIntelligence*, 20 (3): 401–414.

Marvell, T. B. and Moody, C. E. (1996) 'Specification problems, police levels, and crime rates', *Criminology*, 34 (4): 609–646.

Marx, G. T. (1988) *Undercover: Police Surveillance in America.* Berkeley: University of California Press.

Mastrofski, S. (2006) 'Community policing: A skeptical view', in D. Weisburd and A. A. Braga (eds), *Police Innovation: Contrasting Perspectives.* Chicago: Cambridge University Press, pp. 44–73.

Maxfield, M. (2001) 'Guide to frugal evaluation for criminal justice', Final grant report. Newark, NJ: Rutgers University.

Maxim (2006) 'Welcome to Murder City', *Maxim Magazine*, August 2006.

Mayhew, H. (1862) *London Labour and the London Poor.* London: Griffin Bohn.

Mayhew, P. and Adkins, G. (2003) 'Counting the costs of crime in Australia: an update', *Trends and Issues in Crime and Criminal Justice*, 247: 1–8.

Mayne, S. R. (1829) *Instructions to 'The New Police of the Metropolis'*. London: Metropolitan Police.

Mazerolle, L., Rombouts, S. and McBroom, J. (2007a) 'The impact of COMPSTAT on reported crime in Queensland', *Policing: An International Journal of Police Strategies and Management*, 30 (2): 237–256.

Mazerolle, L., Soole, D. and Rombouts, S. (2007b) 'Drug law enforcement: A review of the evaluation literature', *Police Quarterly*, 10 (2): 115–153.

Mazerolle, L., Soole, D. W. and Rombouts, S. (2007c) *Crime Prevention Research Review No. 1: Disrupting Street-Level Drug Markets*. Washington, DC: US Department of Justice (Office of Community Oriented Policing Services).

McCabe, S. and Sutcliffe, F. (1978) *Defining Crime: A Study of Police Decisions*. Oxford: Blackwell.

McDonald, P. P. (2002) *Managing Police Operations: Implementing the New York Crime Control Model – CompStat*. Belmont, CA: Wadsworth.

McDowell, D. (1998) *Strategic Intelligence: A Handbook for Practitioners, Managers and Users*. Cooma, NSW: Istana Enterprises.

McGarrell, E. F., Freilich, J. D. and Chermak, S. (2007) 'Intelligence-led policing as a framework for responding to terrorism', *Journal of Contemporary Criminal Justice*, 23 (2): 142–158.

McGuire, P. G. (2000) 'The New York Police Department COMPSTAT Process', in V. Goldsmith, P. G. McGuire, J. H. Mollenkopf and T. A. Ross (eds), *Analyzing Crime Patterns: Frontiers of Practice*. Thousand Oaks, CA: Sage, pp. 11–22.

McNamara, T. (2007) 'The over-classification and pseudo-classification of government information: the response of the program manager of the information sharing environment'. Testimony before the Subcommittee on Intelligence, Information Sharing and Terrorism Risk Assessment. Washington, DC: US House of Representatives Committee on Homeland Security.

McNamara, T. E. (2006) 'Information sharing environment implementation plan'. Washington, DC: Information Sharing Environment, Office of the Director of National Intelligence.

Mehrabian, A. and Ferris, S. R. (1967) 'Inference of attitudes from nonverbal communication in two channels', *Journal of Consulting Psychology*, 31 (3): 248–252.

Miller, J. (2007) 'In the front line in the war on terrorism', *City Journal*, 17 (3): 28–41.

Moore, M. H. (2003) 'Sizing up CompStat: an important administrative innovation in policing', *Criminology and Public Policy*, 2 (3): 469–494.

Morgan, R. and Newburn, T. (1997) *The Future of Policing*. Oxford: Oxford University Press.

Murphy, W. M. (2007) 'The over-classification and pseudo-classification of government information: the response of the program manager of the information sharing environment'. Testimony before the Subcommittee on Intelligence, Information Sharing and Terrorism Risk Assessment. Washington, DC: US House of Representatives Committee on Homeland Security.

NCIS (1999) *NCIS and the National Intelligence Model*. London: National Criminal Intelligence Service.

NCIS (2000) *The National Intelligence Model*. London: National Criminal Intelligence Service.

NCPE (2005a) *Guidance on the National Intelligence Model*. Wyboston, UK: National Centre for Policing Excellence on behalf of ACPO.

NCPE (2005b) *National Intelligence Model: Code of Practice*. London: National Centre for Policing Excellence.

NCPE (2005c) *National Intelligence Model: Minimum Standards*. London: National Centre for Policing Excellence.

NCPE (2006) *Guidance on the Management of Police Information*. Wyboston, UK: National Centre for Policing Excellence on behalf of ACPO.

Neville, E. (2000) 'The public's right to know – the individual's right to privacy', *Policing and Society*, 9 (4): 413–428.

Nicholas, S., Kershaw, C. and Walker, A. (2007) 'Crime in England and Wales 2006/07', HOSB 11/07. London: Home Office.

Nicholl, J. (2004) 'Task definition', in J. H. Ratcliffe (ed.), *Strategic Thinking in Criminal Intelligence*. Sydney: Federation Press, pp. 53–69.

NJSP (2005) 'New Jersey strategic assessment of organized crime threats'. Trenton, NJ: New Jersey State Police; Intelligence Section.

NJSP (2006a) 'Practical guide to intelligence-led policing'. Trenton, NJ: New Jersey State Police.

NJSP (2006b) 'State Police lead team of 500 officers to decapitate most violent set of Bloods street gang', Press release 25 July 2006. Trenton, NJ: New Jersey State Police.

NJSP (n.d.) 'Gangs in New Jersey: municipal law enforcement response to the 2004 and 2001 NJSP gang surveys'. Trenton, NJ: New Jersey State Police Intelligence Services Section.

Norris, C. and Dunnighan, C. (2000) 'Subterranean blues: conflict as an unintended consequence of the police use of informers', *Policing and Society*, 9 (4): 385–412.

Nunn, S., Quinet, K., Rowe, K. and Christ, D. (2006) 'Interdiction day: covert surveillance operations, drugs, and serious crime in an inner-city neighborhood', *Police Quarterly*, 9 (1): 73–99.

NZP (2002) 'Police strategic plan to 2006'. Wellington: New Zealand Police.

Oakensen, D., Mockford, R. and Pascoe, C. (2002) 'Does there have to be blood on the carpet? Integrating partnership, problem-solving and the National Intelligence Model in strategic and tactical police decision-making processes', *Police Research and Management*, 5 (4): 51–62.

Office of the Auditor-General, NZ (2006) 'New Zealand Police: dealing with dwelling burglary – follow-up audit'. Wellington, New Zealand: Audit New Zealand.

Oliver, W. M. and Bartgis, E. (1998) 'Community policing: a conceptual framework', *Policing: An International Journal of Police Strategies and Management*, 21 (3): 490–509.

Osborne, D. (2006) *Out of Bounds: Innovation and Change in Law Enforcement Intelligence Analysis*. Washington DC: Joint Military Intelligence College.

O'Shea, T. C. and Nicholls, K. (2002) 'Crime analysis in America', Final report. Washington, DC: Office of Community Oriented Policing Services.

O'Shea, T. C. and Nicholls, K. (2003) 'Crime analysis in America: findings and recommendations'. Washington, DC: Office of Community Oriented Policing Services.

Pawson, R. and Tilley, N. (1994) 'What works in evaluation research?', *British Journal of Criminology*, 34 (3): 291–306.

Pawson, R. and Tilley, N. (1997) *Realistic Evaluation*. London: Sage.

Petersilia, J. (1980) 'Criminal career research: a review of recent evidence', *Crime and Justice*, 2: 321–379.

Peterson, M. (2005) 'Intelligence-led policing: the new intelligence architecture'. Washington, DC: Bureau of Justice Assistance.

Petrosino, A., Turpin-Petrosino, C. and Buehler, J. (2003) ' "Scared Straight" and other juvenile awareness programs for preventing juvenile delinquency,' (Updated C2 Review). *Campbell Collaboration Reviews of Intervention and Policy Evaluations (C2-RIPE)*. Philadelphia, PA: Campbell Collaboration.

Ponsaers, P. (2001) 'Reading about "community (oriented) policing" and police models', *Policing: An International Journal of Police Strategies and Management*, 24 (4): 470–497.

Prunckun, J. H. W. (1996) 'The intelligence analyst as social scientist: A comparison of research methods', *Police Studies*, 19 (3): 67–80.

Quarmby, N. (2004) 'Futures work in strategic criminal intelligence', in J. H. Ratcliffe (ed.), *Strategic Thinking in Criminal Intelligence*. Sydney: Federation Press, pp. 129–147.

Quetelet, A. (1842) *A Treatise On Man*. Edinburgh: Chambers.

Ransom, H. H. (1980) 'Being intelligent about secret intelligence agencies', *American Political Science Review*, 74 (1): 141–148.

Ratcliffe, J. H. (2001) 'Policing Urban Burglary', *Trends and Issues in Crime and Criminal Justice*, 213: 1–6.

Ratcliffe, J. H. (2002a) 'Aoristic signatures and the temporal analysis of high volume crime patterns', *Journal of Quantitative Criminology*, 18 (1): 23–43.

Ratcliffe, J. H. (2002b) 'Burglary reduction and the myth of displacement', *Trends and Issues in Crime and Criminal Justice*, 232: 1–6.

Ratcliffe, J. H. (2002c) 'Damned if you don't, damned if you do: Crime mapping and its implications in the real world', *Policing and Society*, 12 (3): 211–225.

Ratcliffe, J. H. (2002d) 'Intelligence-led policing and the problems of turning rhetoric into practice', *Policing and Society*, 12 (1): 53–66.

Ratcliffe, J. H. (2003) 'Intelligence-led policing', *Trends and Issues in Crime and Criminal Justice*, 248: 1–6.

Ratcliffe, J. H. (2004a) 'Crime mapping and the training needs of law enforcement', *European Journal on Criminal Policy and Research*, 10 (1): 65–83.

Ratcliffe, J. H. (2004b) 'Intelligence research', in J. H. Ratcliffe (ed.), *Strategic Thinking in Criminal Intelligence*. Sydney: Federation Press, pp. 86–98.

Ratcliffe, J. H. (2004c) *Strategic Thinking in Criminal Intelligence*. Sydney: Federation Press.

Ratcliffe, J. H. (2004d) 'The structure of strategic thinking', in J. H. Ratcliffe (ed.), *Strategic Thinking in Criminal Intelligence*. Sydney: Federation Press, pp. 1–10.

Ratcliffe, J. H. (2005) 'The effectiveness of police intelligence management: a New Zealand case study', *Police Practice and Research*, 6 (5): 435–451.

Ratcliffe, J. H. (2006) 'Video surveillance of public places'. Washington, DC: Center for Problem Oriented Policing.

Ratcliffe, J. H. (2007) 'Integrated intelligence and crime analysis: enhanced information management for law enforcement leaders'. Washington, DC: Police Foundation.

Ratcliffe, J. H. (2008) 'Knowledge management challenges in the development of intelligence-led policing', in T. Williamson (ed.), *The Handbook of Knowledge-Based Policing: Current Conceptions and Future Directions*. Chichester: John Wiley and Sons, pp. 205–220.

Ratcliffe, J. H. (in press) 'Intelligence-led policing', in L. Mazerolle, R. Wortley and S. Rombouts (eds), *Foundations of Environmental Criminology and Crime Analysis*. Cullompton: Willan Publishing.

Ratcliffe, J. H. and Guidetti, R. A. (2008) 'State police investigative structure and the adoption of intelligence-led policing', *Policing: An International Journal of Police Strategies and Management*, 31(1).

Ratcliffe, J. H. and Makkai, T. (2004) 'Diffusion of benefits: evaluating a policing operation', *Trends and Issues in Crime and Criminal Justice*, 278: 1–6.

Ratcliffe, J. H. and McCullagh, M. J. (1998) 'Aoristic crime analysis', *International Journal of Geographical Information Science*, 12 (7): 751–764.

Ratcliffe, J. H. and McCullagh, M. J. (2001) 'Chasing ghosts? Police perception of high crime areas', *British Journal of Criminology*, 41 (2): 330–341.

Ratcliffe, J.H. and Taniguchi, T.A. (2008) 'Is crime higher around drug-gang street corners? Two spatial approaches to the relationship between gang set spaces and local crime levels', *Crime Patterns and Analysis*, 1(1).

Reiner, R. (1997) 'Policing and the police', in M. Maguire, R. Morgan and R. Reiner (eds), *The Oxford Handbook of Criminology*. Oxford: Clarendon Press, pp. 997–1049.

Rengert, G. F., Ratcliffe, J. H. and Chakravorty, S. (2005) *Policing Illegal Drug Markets: Geographic Approaches to Crime Reduction*. Monsey, NY: Criminal Justice Press.

Reuter, P. (1990) 'Can the borders be sealed?', in R. Weisheit (ed.), *Drugs, Crime and the Criminal Justice System*. Cincinnati, OH: Anderson Publishing, pp. 13–26.

Roach, J. (2007) 'Those who do big bad things also usually do little bad things: identifying active serious offenders using offender self-selection', *International Journal of Police Science and Management*, 9 (1): 66–79.

Rogers, K. (1998) 'Evaluating strategic intelligence assessments: some sextant readings for law enforcement', *Journal of the Australian Institute of Professional Intelligence Officers*, 7 (3): 23–36.

Rogerson, P. A. (2006) *Statistical Methods for Geography*. Thousand Oaks, CA: Sage.

Ross, N. (2005) 'Higher up the food chain: putting cops where they belong', paper presented to the *Problem Oriented Policing Conference 2005*. Charlotte, NC: www.popcenter.org.

Scarman, L. L. (1981) *Report of an Inquiry by the Right Honourable The Lord Scarman into the Brixton Disorders of 10–12 April 1981 (The Scarman Report)*. London: Her Majesty's Stationery Office.

Schneider, S. (2006) 'Privatizing economic crime enforcement: exploring the role of private sector investigative agencies in combating money laundering', *Policing and Society*, 16 (3): 285–312.

SCOCCI (1997) 'Guiding principles for law enforcement intelligence'. Sydney: Standing Advisory Committee on Organised Crime and Criminal Intelligence. Scott, J. (1998) ' "Performance culture": the return of reactive policing', *Policing and Society*, 8 (3): 269–288.

Scott, M.S. (2000) *Problem-Oriented Policing: Reflections on the First 20 Years*, October 2000. Washington, DC: COPS Office.

Sharp, D. (2005) 'Who needs theories in policing? An introduction to a special issue on policing', *Howard Journal of Criminal Justice*, 44 (5): 449–459.

Shaw, C. R. and McKay, H. D. (1942) *Juvenile Delinquency and Urban Areas*. Chicago: Chicago University Press.

Sheptycki, J. (2000) 'Introduction', in J. W. E. Sheptycki (ed.), *Issues in Transnational Policing*. London: Routledge, pp. 1–20.

Sheptycki, J. (2002) 'Accountability across the policing field: towards a general cartography of accountability for post-modern policing', *Policing and Society*, 12 (4): 323–338.

Sheptycki, J. (2003) 'The governance of organised crime in Canada', *Canadian Journal of Sociology-Cahiers Canadiens De Sociologie*, 28 (4): 489–516.

Sheptycki, J. (2004a) 'Organisational pathologies in police intelligence systems: some contributions to the lexicon of intelligence-led policing', *European Journal of Criminology*, 1 (3): 307–332.

Sheptycki, J. (2004b) 'Review of the influence of strategic intelligence on organised crime policy and practice'. London: Home Office Research and Statistics Directorate.

Sheptycki, J. (2005) 'Transnational policing', *Canadian Review of Policing Research*, 1: 1–7.

Sheptycki, J. (2007) 'High policing in the security control society', *Policing: A Journal of Policy and Practice*, 1 (1): 70–79.

Sheptycki, J. and Ratcliffe, J. H. (2004) 'Setting the strategic agenda', in J. H. Ratcliffe (ed.), *Strategic Thinking in Criminal Intelligence*. Sydney: Federation Press, pp. 194–216.

Sherman, L. W. (1986) 'Policing communities: what works?', in J. Albert, J. Reiss and M. Tonry (eds), *Communities and Crime*. Chicago: University of Chicago, pp. 343–386.

Sherman, L. W. (1990) 'Police crackdowns: Initial and residual deterrence', in M. Tonry and N. Morris (eds), *Crime and Justice: An Annual Review of Research*. Chicago: University of Chicago Press, pp. 1–48.

Sherman, L.W. (1998) 'Evidence-based policing'. Washington, DC: Police Foundation.

Sherman, L. W. (2002) 'Evidence-based policing: social organisation of information for social control', in E. Waring and D. Weisburd (eds), *Crime and Social Organization*. New Brunswick and London: Transaction Publishers, pp. 217–248.

Sherman, L. W. (2005) 'The use and usefulness of criminology, 1751–2005: enlightened justice and its failures', *Annals of the American Academy of Political and Social Science*, 600: 115–135.

Sherman, L. W., Gartin, P. and Buerger, M. E. (1989) 'Hot spots of predatory crime: Routine activities and the criminology of place', *Criminology*, 27 (1): 27–55.

Sherman, L. W., Gottfredson, D., MacKenzie, D., Eck, J., Reuter, P. and Bushway, S. (1998) 'Preventing crime: what works, what doesn't, what's promising'. Washington, DC: National Institute of Justice.

Sherman, L. W., Shaw, J. W. and Rogan, D. P. (1995) 'The Kansas City gun experiment'. Washington, DC: National Institute of Justice.

Sherman, L. W. and Weisburd, D. (1995) 'General deterrent effects of police patrol in crime "hot spots": A randomized, controlled trial', *Justice Quarterly*, 12 (4): 625–648.

Silverman, E. B. (2006) 'Compstat's innovation', in D. Weisburd and A. A. Braga (eds), *Police Innovation: Contrasting Perspectives*. New York: Cambridge University Press, pp. 267–283.

Silvestri, M. (2006) ' "Doing time": Becoming a police leader', *International Journal of Police Science and Management*, 8 (4): 266–281.

Skogan, W. G. (2006a) 'Asymmetry in the impact of encounters with police', *Policing and Society*, 16 (2): 99–126.

Skogan, W. G. (2006b) 'The promise of community policing', in D. Weisburd and A. A. Braga (eds), *Policing Innovation: Contrasting Perspectives*. New York: Cambridge University Press, pp. 27–43.

Skogan, W. G. and Hartnett, S. M. (1997) *Community Policing, Chicago Style*. New York: Oxford University Press.

Smith, P. (1995) 'On the unintended consequences of publishing performance data in the public sector', *International Journal of Public Administration*, 18 (2/3): 277–310.

SOCA (2006) *The UK Threat Assessment of Serious Organised Crime 2006/07*. London: Serious Organised Crime Agency.

Sousa, W. H. and Kelling, G. L. (2006) 'Of "broken windows," criminology, and criminal justice', in D. Weisburd and A. A. Braga (eds), *Police Innovation: Contrasting Perspectives*. New York: Cambridge University Press, pp. 77–97.

Spelman, W. and Brown, D. K. (1981) *Calling the Police – Citizen Reporting of Serious Crime*. Washington, DC: Police Executive Research Forum.

Spiller, S. (2006) 'The FBI's Field Intelligence Groups and Police', *FBI Law Enforcement Bulletin*, 75 (5): 1–6.

Stelfox, P. (1998) 'Policing lower levels of organised crime in England and Wales', *The Howard Journal*, 37 (4): 393–406.

Stevens, J. (2001) 'Intelligence-led policing'. Paper presented to the *2nd World Investigation of Crime Conference*. Durban, South Africa.

Taylor, B., Kowalyk, A. and Boba, R. (2007) 'The integration of crime analysis into law enforcement agencies', *Police Quarterly*, 10 (2): 154–169.

Taylor, R. B. (2001) *Breaking Away From Broken Windows*. Boulder, CO: Westview.

Taylor, R. B. (2006) 'Incivilities reduction policing, zero tolerance, and the retreat from coproduction: weak foundations and strong pressures', in D. Weisburd and A. A. Braga (eds), *Police Innovation: Contrasting Perspectives*. New York: Cambridge University Press, pp. 98–114.

Tilley, N. (1995) 'Thinking about crime prevention performance indicators'. Police Research Group: Crime Detection and Prevention Series, Paper 57: 1–35.

Tilley, N. (2003a) 'Community policing, problem-oriented policing and intelligence-led policing', in T. Newburn (ed.) *Handbook of Policing*. Cullompton: Willan Publishing, pp. 311–339.

Tilley, N. (2003b) *Problem-Oriented Policing, Intelligence-Led Policing and the National Intelligence Model*. London: Jill Dando Institute for Crime Science.

Tilley, N. (2004) 'Community policing and problem solving', in W. G. Skogan (ed.) *Community Policing (Can It Work?)*. Belmont, CA: Wadsworth, pp. 165–184.

Townsley, M., Johnson, S. and Pease, K. (2003) 'Problem orientation, problem solving and organisational change', in J. Knuttson, (ed.) *Problem-Oriented Policing: From Innovation to Mainstream*. Monsey, NY: Criminal Justice Press, pp. 183–212.

Townsley, M. and Pease, K. (2002) 'How efficiently can we target prolific offenders?', *International Journal of Police Science and Management*, 4(4): 323–331.

Trojanowicz, R. C. (1994) 'The future of community policing', in D. P. Rosenbaum (ed.) *The Challenge of Community Policing: Testing the Promises*. Thousand Oaks, CA: Sage, 258–262.

Vito, G. F., Walsh, W. F. and Kunselman, J. (2005) 'Compstat: the manager's perspective', *International Journal of Police Science and Management*, 7(3): 187–196.

Walsh, P. and Ratcliffe, J. H. (2005) 'Strategic criminal intelligence education: a collaborative approach', *IALEIA Journal*, 16(2): 152–166.

Walsh, W. F. (2001) 'Compstat: an analysis of an emerging police managerial paradigm', *Policing: An International Journal of Police Strategies and Management*, 24(3): 347–362.

Walsh, W. F. and Vito, G. F. (2004) 'The meaning of Compstat: analysis and response', *Journal of Contemporary Criminal Justice*, 20(1): 51–69.

Wardlaw, G. and Boughton, J. (2006) 'Intelligence-led policing: the AFP approach', in J. Fleming and J. Wood (eds), *Fighting Crime Together: The Challenges of Policing and Security Networks*. Sydney: University of New South Wales Press, 133–149.

Wartell, J. and McEwen, J. T. (2001) *Privacy in the Information Age: A Guide for Sharing Crime Maps and Spatial Data*. Washington, DC: Institute for Law and Justice.

Weatherburn, D. (2001) 'What causes crime?' Contemporary Issues in Crime and Justice (NSW Bureau of Crime Statistics and Research) No. 54, 1–12.

Weatherburn, D. (2004) *Law and Order in Australia: Rhetoric and Reality.* Sydney: Federation Press.

Weatherburn, D., Hua, J. and Moffatt, S. (2006) 'How much crime does prison stop? The incapacitation effect of prison on burglary', Contemporary Issues in Crime and Justice (NSW Bureau of Crime Statistics and Research), No. 93, 1–12.

Weatheritt, M. (1986) *Innovations in Policing.* Dover: Croom Helm.

Weisburd, D. and Braga, A. A. (2006a) 'Hot spots policing as a model for police innovation', in D. Weisburd and A. A. Braga (eds), *Police Innovation: Contrasting Perspectives.* New York: Cambridge University Press, pp. 225–244.

Weisburd, D. and Braga, A. A. (eds.) (2006b) *Police Innovation: Contrasting Perspectives.* New York: Cambridge University Press.

Weisburd, D., Bushway, S., Lum, C. and Yang, S.-M. (2004) 'Trajectories of crime at places: a longitudinal study of street segments in the city of Seattle', *Criminology,* 42 (2): 283–321.

Weisburd, D. and Eck, J. (2004) 'What can police do to reduce crime, disorder, and fear?', *Annals of the American Academy of Political and Social Science,* 593 (1): 43–65.

Weisburd, D. and Green, L. (1995) 'Policing drug hot spots: the Jersey City drug market analysis experiment', *Justice Quarterly,* 12 (4): 711–735.

Weisburd, D. and Lum, C. (2005) 'The diffusion of computerized crime mapping in policing: linking research and practice', *Police Practice and Research,* 6 (5): 419–434.

Weisburd, D., Mastrofski, S. D., McNally, A. M., Greenspan, R. and Willis, J. J. (2003) 'Reforming to preserve: CompStat and strategic problem solving in American policing', *Criminology and Public Policy,* 2 (3): 421–456.

Weisburd, D., Mastrofski, S.D., Willis, J. J. and Greenspan, R. (2006) 'Changing everything so that everything can remain the same: Compstat and American policing', in D. Weisburd and A. A. Braga (eds), *Police Innovation: Contrasting Perspectives.* New York: Cambridge University Press, 284–301.

Wellsmith, M. and Guille, H. (2005) 'Fixed penalty notices as a means of offender selection', *International Journal of Police Science and Management,* 7 (1): 36–43. White, J. R. (2004) *Defending the Homeland: Domestic Intelligence, Law Enforcement, and Security.* Belmont, CA: Wadsworth.

Williams, J. W. (2005) 'Governability matters: the private policing of economic crime and the challenge of democratic governance', *Policing and Society,* (15) 2: 187–211.

Willis, J. J., Mastrofski, S. D., Weisburd, D. and Greenspan, R. (2003) 'Compstat and organisational change in the Lowell Police Department: challenges and opportunities'. Washington DC: Police Foundation.

Wilson, D., Sharp, C. and Patterson, A. (2006) *Young People and Crime: Findings from the 2005 Offending, Crime and Justice Survey.* London: Home Office.

Wilson, J. Q. and Kelling, G. L. (1982) 'Broken windows: the police and neighborhood safety', *Atlantic Monthly,* March: 29–38.

Witzig, E. W. (2003) 'The new ViCAP: more user-friendly and used by more agencies', *FBI Law Enforcement Bulletin,* 72 (6): 1–7.

Wolfgang, M. E., Figlio, R. M. and Sellin, T. (1972) *Delinquency in a Birth Cohort.* Chicago: University of Chicago Press.

Wood, J. (1997) *Final Report of the Royal Commission into the NSW Police Service:* Vol. 1. *Corruption.* Sydney: RCNSWPS.

Wood, J. and Shearing, C. (2007) *Imagining Security.* Cullompton: Willan Publishing.

Wortley, R., Mazerolle, L. and Rombouts, S. (eds) (in press) *Environmental Criminology and Crime Analysis.* Cullompton: Willan Publishing.

Yokota, K. and Watanabe, S. (2002) 'Computer-based retrieval of suspects using similarity of *modus operandi*', *International Journal of Police Science and Management,* 4(1): 5–15.

LEGITIMACY

Elusive Legitimacy
Subservient, Separate, or Generative?

STEVE HERBERT

I t is the regular monthly meeting of a neighborhood council in Eastside. The neighborhood in question covers about a single square mile. Its residents are mostly middle-class homeowners, although there are also many multifamily dwellings. The racial composition of the neighborhood is majority white, but a sizeable minority population exists, comprising primarily Latinos and Asians.

In its meetings, the council addresses a fairly typical set of concerns: speeding cars on residential streets; possible negative externalities from a homeless shelter at a church; blighted homes; occasional graffiti. Because public safety concerns invariably form part of each meeting's agenda, a representative of the Seattle Police Department usually attends. The officer is usually included as a standing item on the agenda, typically to summarize recent crime events and to solicit questions and input from the residents.

On this night, the SPD representative is a lieutenant whose responsibilities include supervision of the precinct's Community Policing Team. After describing significant recent crimes in the area, the lieutenant asks for questions. One woman asks about a possible recent spate of car thefts from her block and wonders whether the lieutenant can confirm this statistically. The lieutenant claims ignorance, citing the fact that he only recently assumed his post. He does, however, reinforce the idea that the neighborhood is an attractive spot for car thieves. As an aside, he tries to explain this phenomenon in terms of the large number of "unsupervised youth" in the area.

This comment prompts a question. Asks one resident: "What happens to these kids when they are caught stealing a car?" The lieutenant leans into to his microphone, and in a stern voice says, "I'm going to tell you the truth, and it's going to irritate everyone in this room." He says that essentially nothing will happen to these kids, because the youth detention facility will not jail overnight a car thief or any other nonviolent offender. As a result, a car thief will "never see a minute" in jail until after the fifteenth arrest, when he might get ten days. The lieutenant describes this as "one of the weak links in the system." The only sound in response is a muttering in seeming support of the lieutenant's indignation.

COMMUNITY POLICING AND THE IDEAL OF POLICE RESPONSIVENESS

The legitimacy of community policing rests in significant part upon the long-treasured ideal of localized democracy. To self-actualize, citizens should come together and exert meaningful influence over the policy matters that affect them. Community policing can be legitimated as such an opportunity for urban residents to act in their collectively defined best interest. As we have seen, various impediments can render this vision illusory for urban neighborhoods. But even if neighborhoods could develop greater political capability, they would still need to exert sway over a state agency like the police. In other words, the police would need to integrate public input into their practices. They would need, to some extent, to render themselves subservient to the citizens they police.

The police, like all state agencies, stand in fundamental connection to the citizenry; they exist to provide service to the population. But, as with all state agencies, the precise nature of the relationship between police officers and the citizens they serve is not so straightforward. As with the political role of community, this is a matter of both normative theory and sociological reality. There is normative confusion about how state and society should relate, and there are significant on-the-ground dynamics that shape how these relations play out. In this chapter and the next, I seek to make this complex reality more clear.

Much of this complexity is attributable to different idealized models for state-society relations, each of which possesses tremendous legitimacy.[1] For instance, the general narrative of democracy suggests that state agencies like the police should be responsive to public input; they should do as they are directed by the citizenry. In such fashion, the state should understand itself as primarily *subservient* to its constituents.

However, the narrative of liberalism suggests that state agencies must possess a necessary autonomy from public input, the better to protect the rights of all citizens against the possibility of unjust majoritarianism. The state should strive toward some degree of neutrality, loyal primarily to the abstract rule of law. Otherwise, the rights and needs of the more marginalized will likely be threatened. For these reasons, the state must understand itself as importantly *separate* from society.

Yet respect for the rule of law is not the only means by which such state separation can occur. State actors often consider themselves possessors of unique bases of knowledge and authority. They thereby distinguish themselves from those they govern and assert that distinction in their daily practice. The police, for example, embrace the image of professional crime fighters, and they often expect deference to their unique authority. Separation here dons a professional guise and significantly structures state-society relations.

But subservience and separation do not exhaust the possibilities for the state-society relation. One could also argue that the state is *generative* of community. That is because the state, with its policies, helps determine the central characteristics of communities. Further, the state only understands "community" in particular ways, through the routines and epistemologies state actors use to filter public input. State actors also often characterize their work in terms of an overarching moralism that situates both state and society on a transcendental plane. This is particularly true of police officers, who thereby construct community as an entity in need of the protection that only their virtuous vanguard can provide.

The lieutenant's performance at the neighborhood council meeting displays all these modes of relation. To an extent, the lieutenant is being subservient. He takes time to come to the meeting, he provides information he thinks the residents will find useful, he opens himself to questions and discussion. He reinforces the implicit assumption that, as a public servant, he must make himself available to the citizenry and engage them on matters of public safety.

This nod to subservience is, however, not all that characterizes the lieutenant's behavior. He also positions himself as separate. He sits at the front of the room, in full uniform, and speaks in an authoritative voice. Behind him stands the majesty of the law, the rights it protects, the duties it imposes. He acts as if his authority is unquestionable. This sense of autonomous authority is exacerbated by the emotional and rhetorical force of his utterance. Already an intimidating force—bedecked as he is with uniform, badge, and a belt full of coercive tools—the lieutenant imposes himself further with his presentational style. He physically and symbolically sets himself apart from the public.

Yet the performance is also generative. The lieutenant invokes implicit notions of both the community and the larger moral terrain upon which he situates his work.

Community, in other words, is not separate from the state; rather, it is something that state actors, like the lieutenant, produce in their work. They render society sensible through certain organizational routines and moral architectures. In the lieutenant's case, it is his moral architecture that is most evident. Note the manner by which it leads him to assume a commonality in the group about his viewpoint. He says it will "irritate everyone in the room" because he believes everyone agrees that car thieves should be tracked down and removed to jail. He implicitly suggests that anyone who disagrees is suspect. The lieutenant's moral understanding renders the community a set of passive, like-minded good people who deserve better protection from the criminal justice system.

Thus, even though there were at this meeting elements of police responsiveness to the public and a sense in which the police were open to accountability, the lieutenant was not especially subservient. He used his institutional stature and his emotional rhetoric to short-circuit rather than promote debate about crime control policy. This was therefore not an instance of a vibrant project of deliberative democracy. Even though the lieutenant likely considers himself responsive to the citizenry, he does not approach the gathering as an open, respectful dialogue between similarly situated people. Rather, he constructs himself as society's protector and asserts his unique authority to quell a moral plague that troubles the otherwise peaceful community.

The lieutenant's performance is something of an overdrawn example, but it represents a pattern that was invariably repeated at police-community forums. Almost never did a police official seriously interrogate any suggestions from the public that the organization reorient its priorities or practices. Recall another lieutenant's performance at the Weed and Seed meeting described in the introduction. In that case, the lieutenant less loudly but no less effectively controlled the conversation by deflecting recommendations from the public. His use of these strategies may not have been entirely conscious, but it was effective nonetheless. In an interview, however, a precinct captain did acknowledge his desire to retain tight control over an upcoming community forum. If he surrendered any control, he suggested, he would get his "ass lit up." Similarly, after one such public meeting, another precinct captain expressed pleasure with how the meeting went: there was little discussion after his presentation and thus little need to respond to public concern. Such lack of enthusiasm for meaningful engagement with citizens obviously stands in opposition to the normative, democratic thrust of community policing.

In this chapter I illustrate how the police invoke different understandings of their relationship to the community and how these do not necessarily cohere. Most of all, I show how the police understand themselves as importantly separate from society. Of the three paths to state legitimacy outlined above, the police favor a self-understanding that emphasizes their autonomy. However, this is justified and perpetuated in terms other than those envisioned by liberal theorists. Although they do see themselves as neutral enforcers of an abstract, objective law that is ideally applied equally to all citizens, officers more robustly build a self-construction as members of a politically embattled institution whose unique base of expertise needs protection from the uninformed meddling of biased community activists. From this perspective, the police must stand separate from society because otherwise they will be enmeshed in political machinations that will negatively affect them. Officers repeatedly state a fear of being sacrificed on the altar of "politics," and thus seek to stiff-arm public participation to avoid that fate.

A complete explanation for why this is the case must wait until chapter 4. For now, the task is to understand how the police pursue and balance the drives to be subservient, separate, and generative.

THE POLICE-COMMUNITY CONNECTION: A NORMATIVE APPROACH

Even if concerns about the political capacity of community could be allayed, it remains uncertain how any communal group can and should interact with a state agency such as the police. What should be the balance of power between a community group and the police? Should the community direct what the police do? Or should the community play second fiddle, acting only via police directive? Or is a genuine partnership even possible, one in which the balance of power is equilibrated? How to strike a balance between subservience, separation, and generativity?

There is both normative and sociological heft to each of these approaches to the state-society connection. Each possesses legitimacy, and each influences interactions between communal groups and the police. It is therefore difficult to assess just how communities *should* interact with state agencies like the police. In this section, I review each of these three approaches in a bit more depth, and outline how each shapes how one might construct an ideal balance of power between community groups and the police.

SUBSERVIENT?

Iris Marion Young states succinctly the case for citizen influence over the policy-making process: "The normative legitimacy of a democratic decision depends on the degree to which those affected by it have been included in the decision-making processes and have had the opportunity to influence the outcomes."[2] Implicit in this normative formulation is an active citizen who deserves a place at the table at which policy is generated. Without so respecting the agency of its citizens, a state is not legitimate, according to democratic theorists like Young. A state must ensure that its dictates possess the imprimatur of the people it serves; it must respect the capacity for self-determination that inheres in each citizen.

This is particularly critical when one considers the coercive power state agencies possess, none more obviously than the police. As noted by such important theorists as Weber, Durkheim, and Habermas, coercion is an insufficient basis for rule.[3] Exercises of coercive power must invoke some greater good, some communally supported ideal. Otherwise, power is nakedly exposed and loses legitimacy. Citizen control of state agencies that exercise coercive power is thus critical to democratic states' quests for legitimacy.[4]

Such an assumption helps legitimate community policing. Recall that community policing efforts developed in response to tensions between the professionalized police and urban communities. Professional police were seen as too aloof and too often aggressive, orbiting somehow above the everyday concerns of citizens. Such citizens were not recognized as possessing a legitimate need to direct police operations. Rather, they were adjuncts to police operations, and their input was narrowly channeled by the dictates of professional practice. By contrast, legitimations of community policing are full of language of "co-production" and of "partnerships," language that heralds a citizenry active in the construction of police policy. An engaged and active citizenry can exercise self-determination through shaping the police's use of the state's coercive power.

The language of democracy thus reinforces the legitimacy of community policing; the police need to be responsive to the will of the community. Such an active citizenry is also endorsed by theorists of crime and social control who recognize the fundamentally communal nature of deviant activity.[5] If crime and disorder develop from communally based social patterns, then these patterns must be addressed. Such a logic, for example, drives various restorative justice programs.[6] The goal here is to respond to deviance by re-establishing communal connections. Deviant behavior is, by definition, a violation of communal norms. The goal in response could be to re-establish those norms and to reincorporate the offender into the fold. Implicit here is a notion of community members as effective agents who assume responsibility to reinforce bonds frayed by deviance.

In sum, a strong version of community power suggests that communal agents are primarily responsible for ensuring social control. They do this by reestablishing connections to those who deviate and by assuming a muscular role in overseeing the formal social control efforts of the police and other relevant state agencies. From this view, the police must understand themselves as importantly subservient to the community. They must avail themselves of public input, enable citizens to help construct police policy, allow citizen groups to evaluate their performance. Without such responsiveness, the police's quest for legitimacy might well suffer. There is thus a push from many quarters to open up the police to oversight from the citizenry, through such vehicles as police review boards.[7] At the neighborhood level, this could mean partnerships that are more genuinely shared projects of governance, not police-run exercises that marginalize community input. In these and other ways, the police are seen as within the parameters of citizen oversight.

SEPARATE?

This push toward subservience, however, faces resistance from those who fear the potential misdirections of an overly responsive state agency. Might a communal group be swayed by an unrepresentative and particularly passionate minority? Might it be motivated by its opposition to some other communal group that is perhaps not as well organized? If so, does a subservient state become inadvertently an unjust one by favoring one group's interests at the expense of another's? Might a minority group be unfairly disadvantaged in the process?

These concerns about the passions and partialities of communal political activity reinforce the liberal emphasis on a politically neutral state whose sway over civil society must face limits. These limits are made real through the creation and protection of various civil and political rights. These rights should prevent the state's intrusion into such matters as expression, assembly, and worship. A state thereby guarantees individuals and groups the chance to coalesce as they please, to pursue a range of political projects, to construct freely the "good life" they cherish. For liberals, individuals need autonomy to pursue their vision of the good. The state should thus be minimalist and neutral: minimalist, because it should rarely restrict one's freedom; neutral, because it should not promote its own version of the good to the possible exclusion of others. In important ways, then, the state needs to be separate from communal groups, constantly wary of how the pursuit of a parochial community agenda might lead to the usurpation of the legitimate rights of others.

This liberal protection of rights is not, of course, necessarily in conflict with the quest for democracy. Quite the opposite: civil liberties are often legitimated precisely because they provide the political space in which groups in civil society can construct and debate alternatives for state policy. Without such protections, the political agency of the citizenry cannot be realized. However, there are critical moments where these two approaches to legitimating the state may well come into conflict.[8] What to do when communities protest the construction of halfway houses for convicted sex offenders who are due to be released from prison? Should the state respond to the wishes of such communities, or protect the legally defined rights of ex-offenders? How to deal with the issue of jury nullification? Should juries strictly follow the letter of the law, or should they be empowered to actually nullify the law in question?

Political liberalism often emphasizes the procedures through which political discussion should ensue. The goal is to ensure that public discussion is fair, orderly, and protective of a plurality of groups. Thus, John Rawls exalts "public reason" as the mechanism for adjudicating political conflict.[9] The goal is to try to remove from public discussion as many metaphysical and moral questions as possible, to narrow the debate to those issues around which agreement is possible. As Jeffrey Isaac, Matthew Filner, and Jason Bivins summarize it, "Public reason is typically abstract and juridical; it is dispassionate and 'rational,' that is, oriented toward the uncoerced agreement of deliberative interlocutors; it is expressed in a way that is accessible to others in spite of their particular identities."[10] This should minimize the divisiveness of a plural society. But whatever calm is produced in the process comes at the price of a more open discussion. In this way, the state is to be shielded from the responsibility of adjudicating claims that originate in such moral discourses as religion. It is to be responsive to only those policy advocates that can articulate a case with an abstract logic embraceable by all. Constructed like this, liberalism restricts the extent of democratic debate and renders some citizen demands as beyond the political pale.

The extent of state responsiveness is relevant to considerations of the police-community connection. Many community-based groups that focus on issues of crime and disorder often do so in response to a particular threat, often embodied in a particular group.[11] What to do when teenagers are gathering in public space and engaging in voluble behavior that causes fear among some residents? What if there are suspicions amongst residents that some in that group are engaged in the sale of drugs or the trafficking of guns? How far should the police go in responding to these concerns? How do the police balance the various rights of the teenagers—the right to assembly, the right against intrusive searches and seizures—against their need to show that they take citizens' complaints seriously? Does a police force that takes civil liberties seriously threaten its own legitimacy?[12]

The drive to understand the police as importantly separate from society derives legitimacy not only from the need to protect civil liberties, but also from the police themselves, in their quest for professionalism. This is the second, and distinct, means by which separation can be legitimated. Indeed, the professional movement was initiated to increase the distance between the police and the communities they patrolled. In the machine-era of urban politics, officers were seen as too enmeshed in their neighborhoods, and thereby too easily corrupted. Professionalism was meant to make police more aloof, more controlled by legal and bureaucratic rules. Officers would thus be less corruptible. They would also be more efficient and effective in reducing crime.[13] This legacy of professionalism, and the separation from the community that it implies, lives on in police culture. Like other professions, the police seek to preserve a unique base of competence. From this base, they can resist community oversight.

The potential tension between subservience and separation derives, then, from both normative conflict and sociological practice; they can conflict as political ideals, they can conflict because of police adherence to ideals of professionalism. This is an intractable issue, because each ideal—of democratic decision making, of a neutral state that protects individual rights, of state actors who uphold professional norms— possesses considerable legitimacy. On those occasions when they do conflict, there is no ready calculus toward an ideal resolution. What complicates matters further is that there is yet a third way in which the state-society relation can be understood and legitimated.

GENERATIVE?

Rather than viewing the state as either subservient to or separate from society, one can also justifiably see it as fundamentally generative of society. In both democratic and liberal theory, there is an important sense in which state and society are distinct and need to remain so. But perhaps this helps us miss how the state is a basic creator of community. There are three ways in which this could be said to be true.

First, one could emphasize the extent to which state policy undergirds the conditions in which communities develop. Zoning policy, for example, critically shapes the class composition of a neighborhood, and thus helps construct a landscape of differentiated political capability. The provision of other social services, such as education, health care, and child care, also shape the well-being and political capacity of a community.[14] The formal social control apparatus is another contributing factor in a neighborhood's dynamic. One of the more potent critiques of the massive growth in incarceration in the United States is its impact on the male population of distressed neighborhoods. The absence of income earners and heads of families arguably increases those levels of distress.[15] In short, state policy structures urban dynamics significantly; the state helps generate the community that develops within a city's neighborhoods.

A second sense in which the state could be understood as generative of community emerges from discussions of governmentality. Working from an initial formulation by Foucault,[16] analysts of governmentality emphasize the means by which governance projects are constructed, rationalized, and implemented, particularly in liberal societies, where the political subject is presumed to be free. Projects of governmentality are thus, as Mitchell Dean puts it, "distinguished by trying to work through the freedom or capacities of the governed."[17] Analysts of governmentality place principal emphasis upon the rationalities of government: the expert knowledges upon which governmental programs draw and the implicit definitions of truth contained therein; the assumptions these knowledges make about the present and desired future state of the governed; the latent capacities within the governed that can be tapped in productive ways.[18]

Here our attention is drawn to how state agencies apprehend community. State actors employ certain grids of legibility upon the input they receive from the citizenry; they recognize some and not other forms of input as legitimate, they sort that input into categories, they react to it via certain prescribed routines.[19] James Scott provocatively refers to this broad phenomenon as "seeing like a state."[20] Community is thus not some independently existing entity, but is rendered sensible through a particular state epistemology.[21] The police are no different in this regard. As we will see, they construct community in particular ways that fundamentally impact the manner in which they respond to citizen concerns and demands.

There is yet a third way in which the state generates community. State efforts to improve legitimacy often involve trumpeting abstract ideals which state policy reinforces. These ideals are typically transcendent and moralized. Freedom, equality, justice, and opportunity are all obvious examples. Counterexamples are often mobilized as the target of state energies; terrorism is an evil because it restricts freedom, racial bias odious because it frustrates equal opportunity. In moralistically constructing state policy and its motivations, state actors create a more universal terrain that seeks to unite citizens into an overarching community. Various efforts to promote patriotism exemplify this. They work to create, in Anderson's words, an "imagined community" in whose name such dramatic action as war-making can be legitimated.[22]

Crime is one phenomenon often constructed in highly moralistic terms, in part to legitimate a robust formal social control apparatus.[23] As a moral plague, as an impediment to people's freedoms to possess property and to move safely through space, crime demands a strong state response. Certainly, the police understand their work in moralistic terms, as integral to a pitched struggle between the opposing forces of communal good and criminal evil.[24] By constructing this moral terrain, state actors like the police help to generate community. They seek to unite people around a common and transcendent vision of crime's genesis and suppression. Once placed upon this moral terrain, the citizenry are not primarily political subjects with rights and democratic potential, but instead potential victims who must be protected. These moralistic discourses work to limit the range of citizen discourses police officers consider legitimate; they are a set of ideological blinders with considerable consequences.

In each of these three ways—as creators of highly consequential state policy, as architects of an epistemology that defines legitimate forms of communal input, as protectors of transcendent goods—state actors generate community. These realities further complicate how best to understand, both normatively and sociologically, the relationship between state agencies like the police and the communities with whom they are meant to partner. The tension between subservience, separation, and generativity necessarily infuses the politics of community policing in ways that are not easily resolved.

THE POLICE-COMMUNITY RELATION: AN EMPIRICAL APPROACH

Just as we saw from debates about the political status of community, we see again normative disagreement, this time concerning the state-society relation. The state stands in no simple relation to its communities of constituents, and thus no single strategy for legitimation reveals itself unambiguously. The persistence of this ambiguity is even more obvious when one looks closely at actual police practice, including their encounters with the public. Such an examination reveals the presence of each of these modes of state-society connection. This renders even more illusory the simplistic narrative of a state eagerly responsive to citizen input.

There is ample reason to doubt that the police understand themselves, first and foremost, as subservient to the citizenry. Certainly, police-community forums in West Seattle are not instances of vibrant democracy. Instead, a predictable sequence of events occurs that limits open-ended discussion. Police officials arrive decked out in full uniform and place themselves at the front of the room. They are allocated a slot on the meeting's agenda, usually near the beginning. They outline the recent major crimes and explain their current or anticipated response. They tend to accentuate police successes; they trumpet the capture of any notorious alleged criminals. They often describe strategies for areas where longstanding problems are present, such as a home where suspected drug sales are occurring or a park that hosts anonymous sexual encounters.

After this monologue, the police solicit input. Sometimes audience members follow up on a situation the officer has already described, to ask a clarifying question or provide additional information. At other times, they ask questions about other phenomena of concern. Are there more abandoned cars on this block? Isn't graffiti becoming more of a problem on that street corner? In response, the police will explain their understandings of the pattern and indicate an interest in investigating further. Often, the officer will explain what limits their ability to investigate further. Perhaps there is disagreement with the Parks Department concerning how best to respond to anonymous sex in a park, perhaps the juvenile system does not stringently punish young thieves.

Discussion never emerged about the basic parameters of police action and authority. Rarely did citizens even attempt to so enlarge the discussion. The few attempts that did occur were ignored or deflected. The police's central mission and tactics were thus never open to debate; rather, they were a set of presumptions that necessarily limited the conversation. These forums were not instances where a true "partnership" was on display, where "co-production" was an ongoing reality.

Take, for example, a community council meeting at Blufftop, the public housing facility. Each of these monthly meetings included a presentation by the facility's police officer. Funded by the local housing authority, the officer focuses exclusively upon Blufftop. At this particular meeting, he wasted little time in proposing and propounding a new "no trespass" zone within the interior spaces of the sprawling complex. He argued that his encounters with people late at night led him to conclude that few were residents. Instead, he said, they were outsiders "without a legitimate purpose." His implication was obvious: they were there to traffic in drugs. The green spaces of the facility, in his words, were a "haven for unlawful activity." He wanted a means to police them effectively. The "no trespass" zone would allow him to cite any nonresidents found on the grounds during nighttime hours.

It was never clear just why the officer felt a need to get the council's approval for this measure; the nature of legal authority over these interior spaces seemed uncertain. It was also unclear whether residents could be cited for violating the proposed ordinance. The officer indicated that the law was "squishy" on this issue. Nonetheless, the residents quietly acquiesced to the plan. They asked only a few questions, none of which interrogated the plan's logic or consequences. When it finally came time for a vote, the president of the council tried to articulate the plan. After struggling to do so, she turned to the officer and said, "Whatever you want." The measure passed without dissent.

It may well be that the residents fully endorsed the officer's plan and agreed with his argument that loiterers were "broken windows" who needed to be removed. Indeed, interviews with some of these residents indicated that they were troubled by people they suspected of selling drugs. However, their lack of critical engagement with the officer's plan, their willingness to acquiesce to "whatever you want," was striking. To his credit, the officer sought community support for his plan, but what transpired was a cursory rubber stamp to a proposition that was wholly his own.

This consistent pattern of minimal discussion about police practices at community forums does not suggest that the police ignore public input. To a significant degree, police are responsive in this fashion; they recognize a degree of subservience to the citizenry they police. It is simply that this is not the only pathway to legitimacy that they develop. To understand how this is the case, I turn now to a review of the ways in which the various key projects of legitimacy—subservience, separation, and generativity—structure how the police understand and undertake their work.

THE PROJECT OF SUBSERVIENCE

In any society where the democratic impulse possesses legitimacy,[25] state agencies must engage in practices that demonstrate some subservience to the public. This is especially critical in the case of the police, given their tools of coercion. The specter of a "police state" is ever present with armed agents of government authority. An appearance of subservience offers reassurance that coercive authority will not be exercised arbitrarily. This is a particularly resonant theme in American political culture, where wariness of an overly intrusive state has a long and potent heritage.

There are several means by which the police demonstrate their willingness to be responsive to the citizenry. Perhaps the most obvious example is the process by which officers are dispatched. Citizens can access the police department quickly, by dialing 911, and request assistance. That assistance arrives with uncertain speed, but genuine emergencies generate as rapid a response as possible. When requests are numerous, police work can be largely determined by them—an officer simply spends a shift responding to call after call. Here, the citizen assumes the role of customer, and the officer the service provider. The officer's work pattern is compelled by citizen demands.

Indeed, many critics of the police, and many senior police officers, bemoan the power of calls for service to dictate police practice. If an officer simply bounces from call to call, she is unable to spend extended time understanding and addressing an ongoing issue in a given neighborhood. Thus, the arguable need emerges to go "beyond 911"[26] to enable officers time to engage in often extensive "problem solving" operations.[27] Senior officers argue that younger officers lack precisely these skills. As one veteran said, "These officers go to a call, write up a report, and then forget about it. They think that's police work." He argued that the ascent of the dispatch system limited the development of a broader set of useful skills and orientations. He, and others, also argued that "aggressive dispatch"—the drive to get an officer to a call as quickly as possible—necessarily meant that officers were often sent to areas outside their beats. Officers thus spend less time inside their beats, and are less able to establish close relations with residents. The goal of "beat integrity," of keeping officers within the areas for which they are responsible, is thwarted. In these ways, "aggressive dispatch" may work against community policing, which emphasizes close ties with the citizenry and prolonged efforts at collective problem solving.

Regardless of the merit of these arguments, it is clear that the dispatch system represents the most obvious and significant way by which police departments are responsive to the citizenry. That departments endeavor to respond to calls quickly indicates a recognition that such responsiveness is critical to police legitimacy. Similarly, the fact that police officials attend regular community meetings indicates a desire to also demonstrate subservience to public input. As noted above, these encounters always include a time for public comment. That the ensuing conversation is often constrained does not eliminate the fact that the exchange occurs, and that the police feel compelled to outline a response to the information they receive. Officers seek to demonstrate that the information will be acted upon somehow, that a citizen comment deserves as specific a rejoinder as possible.

This willingness to solicit and potentially act upon citizen concerns is exemplified in the various reports the public can file with the police. These range from concerns about alleged criminal activity, such as suspected drug sales, to concerns about police practice itself, such as when officers use what citizens perceive as excessive force. The degree of police responsiveness to these various reports is subject to debate; as we will see, many residents wonder if such reports receive any attention at all. But they do represent a desire by the police to solicit public input and to demonstrate, whether sincerely or not, a willingness to respond.

Similarly, the police often work with multi-agency task forces that are created to confront particularly intractable problems. In Seattle, these task forces are referred to as "Neighborhood Action Teams," or NATS, and involve representatives from various municipal agencies. This wide participation should enable the government to respond in a coordinated fashion to issues related to public safety, such as land use, sanitation, lighting and other infrastructure, and ongoing criminality. The police participate deeply in these projects, and sometimes even spearhead them. In such a fashion, the police demonstrate an apparent willingness to respond meaningfully to public complaints about areas of longstanding concern.

The desire to respond to continued complaints about such longstanding problems motivates much of the work labeled "community policing." Community police team members in Seattle are not expected to respond to calls for service. Instead, community police officers are assigned to monitor those situations that generate continuous complaints from residents. Absent such long-term attention, in theory, these problems will resist amelioration. In short, the community police officer's role is understood as essential to the department's ability to be responsive to public concerns.

These are the most prominent ways by which the police pursue legitimacy through subservience. They solicit and respond to public input, they seek to alleviate concerns about crime and disorder. Through their everyday practices and their public interaction, officers implicitly recognize the citizenry's substantive role. Without such attempts at demonstrating subservience, the police's quest for legitimacy would surely suffer.

However, the police place limits upon this seeming subservience. They also understand themselves as significantly separate from the public. The drive for separation springs from two distinct sources. One comes from liberalism's insistence on state respect for individual rights, and from the constitutional and legal order that protects those rights. The other comes from the quest by state agencies like the police to develop and maintain professional codes of conduct.

THE PROJECT OF SEPARATION I: LIBERALISM AND THE LEGAL ORDER

As I emphasized above, the doctrine of liberalism emphasizes a politically neutral state. The state must not tie itself to any particular vision of the good life, but should build and defend a set of rights that enable citizens to pursue a wide range of individual expression. The expression of these rights is necessarily limited, to ensure that one person's development of her free will does not limit another's. But the state should not interfere beyond this point; it should not foist any proscriptions upon its citizenry beyond those necessary for society to function with minimal disruption to the right of expression and the general maintenance of order. Hence the importance of constitutions to liberal states, for these provide the basic architecture of what the state can and cannot do. State actions are thereby not dictated entirely by democratic sentiment, but also by constitutional and legal rules. These rules help divorce the state from the project of strict subservience. Otherwise, the liberal logic goes, the state might capitulate to a majoritarian program that could diminish the liberties and rights of marginalized minorities.[28]

Consider the example of community policing. On the one hand, police departments engaged in community policing are meant to solicit input from localized groups and to respond strongly to that input. In the name of localized democracy, state agents and active citizens are to come together and "co-produce" solutions to problems of crime and disorder. But what happens if a particular neighborhood group's concern involves the actions of another social group? What if, for instance, a group of largely Anglo homeowners is upset at their Latino neighbors, who perhaps pack several residents into a small apartment, or who play music at somewhat high volume? Here the police's responsiveness should be tempered by the legal code. If the Latinos are in legal violation of resident codes or of a noise ordinance, then action can be taken. Otherwise, the police should not pursue subservience by running roughshod over the law.

Indeed, the police do regularly cite the legal code as the basis upon which they act or do not act. Take the example of anonymous sex in a local park. The park in question contains a few acres of woods, with a trail system running throughout. It reputedly hosts encounters between gay males. These encounters generate continual complaints by residents of the adjoining neighborhood. These complaints, in turn, motivate the community police officer for the area to limit the sexual activity. However, he considers himself significantly constrained by the legal code, which sets fairly strict guidelines for when he can arrest someone. He needs to witness a sexual act in progress. Here he faces long odds: it is hard to move through the woods noiselessly, and he does not have the time or resources to engage in surreptitious surveillance. His tactics rely instead upon the occasional walk through the woods. He hopes that his presence will scare off those who seek liaisons.

I observed him using this strategy one afternoon. During a walk through the woods, he literally crossed paths with a middle-aged male. The man turned tail when he saw the police uniform. The officer caught up to the man, and asked questions about his presence in the park. The man appeared nervous. The officer expressed little interest in what the man did in private, but explained how he wished to keep the park free of illegal activities. Lacking evidence for an arrest, the officer dismissed the man after a brief sermon. However, the officer later suggested that the man's nervousness was a positive sign. If others would become similarly fearful, the officer hoped, then the illicit encounters might well decline. But this was a strategy that was clearly circumscribed by legal restrictions.

The legal code also emerged around an issue that energized many activists in a high-crime neighborhood in Centralia. These activists focused their attention less on those who engaged in such activities as drug delivery, and more on the landlords of the apartments where these people lived. The activists believed, as did the police, that the landlords did an inadequate job of screening their tenants and of regulating their behavior. However, the activists and the police found themselves limited in what they could do, because of legal regulations surrounding enforcement of landlord obligations. Many of these landlords were able to lease to tenants who possessed Section 8 vouchers (i.e., federally subsidized grants for housing). This meant that federal regulations helped determine actionable violations on the part of a landlord. In addition, the City of Seattle had its own regulations surrounding issues of building safety and other concerns, such as noise or accumulating trash.

The confusion surrounding these legal matters was evident in a small meeting in this neighborhood, attended by a handful of active residents and representatives from the mayor's office, the local housing authority, and the city's Department of Construction and Land Use. The meeting was called to inform residents of some possible new regulations the housing authority hoped to enact to enable them to punish landlords more aggressively. But the meeting served to generate as much confusion as hope. During a wide-ranging, nonlinear conversation, several matters remained unclear: how much legal power the housing authority or the DCLU possessed; what happened when federal codes conflicted with local laws; what legal authority activists had to demand an official investigation of a given property or landlord; and how one could mobilize the police as part of such an effort. In short, the welter of legal authorities and regulations limited what state actors could do in addressing the loudly voiced concern of activists focused on reducing crime in their neighborhood.

In this and manifold other ways, the law helps separate state actors and the community: the former can never entirely respond to the latter's concerns. In the case of the allegedly irresponsible landlords, the legal rules were designed to limit the intrusion of government officials into private property and to ensure a sufficient supply of affordable housing. This is but one example of the role of law in structuring the police's response to community requests. Even when a well-organized group of activists makes a persuasive case that landlords are culpable for their tenants' misdeeds, the police still cannot act forcefully. They are prevented, by law, from acting on simple subservience.

THE PROJECT OF SEPARATION II: PROFESSIONALISM AND THE EXPECTATION OF DEFERENCE

The drive by state agencies, and especially the police, to separate themselves from the public stems from more than their legal authority. If liberal thought requires a state agency like the police to abide by legal regulations, and thus to be somewhat aloof from the vicissitudes of community pressure, it says very little about how such aloofness might be understood and legitimated by state actors themselves. Even minimal contact with police officers reveals the great extent to which they distinguish themselves from the wider public. They clearly see themselves as members of a unique group. Three principal factors fuel their construction of themselves as importantly separate from the citizenry: a desire for protection from community meddling; a felt need for undiminished authority in the situations they confront, in part to ensure their own safety; and a hope to attain status via comporting with standards of professional practice.

SEPARATION AS A MEANS OF PROTECTION   One afternoon, I was invited to share lunch with a group of officers in the precinct station's lounge. The lunch was prepared by a retired officer who enjoys coming to the precinct to cook a meal for the officers. The prospect of a warm, tasty, and free meal brings them together. I sat down to my plate of beef brisket and was introduced to the other officers at the table. One officer eyed me warily and promptly asked, "Are you a liberal or a conservative?" I had barely begun to answer when the officer launched into a monologue on the evils of the news media and its love affair with a small number of anti-police political activists. At issue, in particular, was media coverage of some then recent police shootings of African Americans. These shootings had generated much public criticism. The officer suggested that the media consistently discounted the sensibility of the shootings, most gallingly by not fully reporting the nature of the threat facing the officers involved. Other officers at the table murmured their assent, concurring with the broad argument that the media listens too closely to police critics and thus unfairly impugns the work of the police.

On another evening, I was asked to wait for a ride-along just inside the precinct station door, in an area where many officers mill about. One officer passed by a few times before stopping and only half-jokingly asking me, "Do you work for the mayor's office?" He said that he thought he saw me reading his name tag. He did not stick around to belabor the issue, but his point was clear: he was wary of the possibility that I could spy on him and use any information I might glean to punish him.

On yet another evening, I talked at length with an officer about efforts by some members of the Seattle City Council to conduct research to determine whether SPD officers engaged in "racial profiling." The council wanted to determine the racial composition of the citizens SPD officers stop for traffic violations, to determine whether a disproportionate number of those stopped are minorities. The officer was adamantly opposed to such a study, primarily because he distrusted the political motives of the council members. In his view, any such study would be rigged. As he put it, "If the City Council wants to find racial profiling, they will find it."

Each of these incidents illustrates a theme that was regularly sounded by the officers I encountered: that they are members of a politically vulnerable institution that can easily suffer the slings and arrows of ill-motivated activists and public officials. Officers express considerable fear that public meddling in police affairs will impact them most significantly in terms of punishments. This refrain was consistent—a plaintive wail that the police attract attention from uninformed whiners. These ostensive political operatives allegedly make baseless complaints about the police, thereby making the officers vulnerable to superiors who may sacrifice them to public pressure. Indeed, many officers assess their superiors largely on whether they protect the rank and file from such public pressure. Suspect superiors are castigated as too "political," too easily led to punish officers when the public complains. They want leaders to shield them from such pressure. From their perspective, the public is simply too ignorant to possess any power to determine their fate. The citizenry, many officers allege, can never understand the realities the police face and the necessary tactics they must employ. A police leader's job is thus to keep the public at bay, to insulate the officers from sanctions that might befall them should the public possess meaningful power.

In short, the police hope to be not only separate from the public, but actively protected from community intrusion into their affairs. Such intrusion, officers widely believe, can only bring negative consequences, including sanctions against officers whose split-second decisions will be scrutinized by ignorant and biased political activists. Thus, any talk by City Council members about racial profiling was seen as pandering to African-American activists who seek political benefits through ill-informed police bashing. If their superior officers did not protect them, they would be the fall guys for these machinations. As one officer ruefully observed, "Shit rolls downhill."

These dynamics fueled a set of political maneuvers by the police officers' union in Seattle. The officers were distressed that a new apparatus was established inside the organization to allow non-sworn civilians to investigate citizen complaints. The Office of Professional Accountability is the result of political efforts to provide some external oversight of police actions. The first high-profile case the OPA investigated involved an officer who detained a group of Asian Americans for jaywalking on a downtown street. Those detained alleged that the officer treated them rudely and that he singled them out because of their ethnicity. The OPA rejected the allegation of racial profiling in the incident, but did recommend that the officer be sanctioned for rudeness. The chief of police, less than a year into the job, accepted the OPA's recommendation. That led the rank and file to mobilize a vote expressing "no confidence" in the chief.[29] The message was clear: the officers expected the chief to protect them from such meddling by citizens, and publicly withdrew support from him when he appeared to sway too easily in the political winds.

This dramatic and well-publicized effort to highlight their alleged vulnerability to politics illustrates vividly a more pervasive sense in which the police understand themselves as embattled. Anything that smacks of "politics" is suspect, any effort in the name of civilian oversight represents an opening through which police opponents can seek the trophy of a punished officer.[30] Because even well-meaning citizens cannot understand the vagaries and challenges of the job, it hardly makes sense to the typical officer that anyone with an overt political agenda be given influence over police policy and conduct. Instead, the rank-and-file officer, charged with the task of responding quickly to situations where lives may hang in the balance, needs to be shielded from excessive community meddling. Separation from the public is thus understood as an important mechanism of protection.

SEPARATION AND AUTHORITY   Another means by which officers seek separation from the public is by expecting deference to their authority. When they arrive on a scene, the police expect those present to acquiesce to the officers' felt need to dictate the flow of action. They want citizens to obey orders and to comply with requests for information. The police believe they play a unique role in society, and they see their authority as critical to their success in that role. Citizens, in other words, need to recognize the police as a separate and powerful institution, and to defer accordingly.

In important respects, this desire for unquestioned authority is tied to officers' understandable preoccupation with safety. Given the unpredictable and potentially dangerous nature of some scenes to which they are summoned, officers sensibly hope to gain quick control amid chaos. Such successful dominion can thus reduce the possibility of danger. This functional connection between authority and safety is one I explore more in chapter 4. The important point to stress here is that a principal source of the separation the police construct between themselves and the citizenry is their desire for deference to their authority.

For example, in the story cited earlier of the man on the paths of the park known for illicit sexual encounters, the officer was quite distressed that the man initially sought to elude him. He berated the man for walking away, reminding him that it was "a good idea" to comply with a police request for a conversation. Another officer told me he derived great satisfaction from his job because, as he put it, "I like to win. I don't win them all, but I do win most of them." This officer is confident that, eventually, his authority will emerge triumphant, and he exults in that reality.

Indeed, the police regularly invoke their superior tactics and their capacity to exercise coercive force in describing their work. One officer described an encounter that occurred at a roll call attended by the mayor shortly before the World Trade Organization Ministerial Conference in 1999. According to the officer, the mayor attended roll call to urge restraint in the face of expected protestors. The officers responded derisively, and suggested to the mayor that he was underestimating the threat the protestors would pose to public order. The mayor reportedly bristled at these remarks, a reality that the officer dismissed. He said, "We have guns. We aren't bashful. Don't come into our station and expect us to shut up."

Another sergeant evinced much the same logic in concluding a dissection of an encounter I had just witnessed, wherein he negotiated a standoff between a shop owner and a towing company. The shop owner had parked his car in front of a fire hydrant near his shop, a violation that can be punished with an immediate towing. A traffic officer had ticketed the car, and summoned the tow company with which the city contracts. When the tow truck arrived, the shop owner hurried out to his car and occupied it. The truck operators stopped the tow and called the police because they would not tow the car with the owner inside. When they arrived, the police were told by the shop owner that he suffered from a heart condition, and thus any effort to remove him forcefully might cause a heart attack. For their part, the tow operators were unwilling to unhook the car without receiving payment from the car owner. The sergeant artfully negotiated a compromise, whereby the shop owner agreed to pay a reduced fee in exchange for the cessation of the tow. The sergeant explained his reasoning for seeking an amicable solution: "We try to avoid a fight. But if they really want to fight, we'll fight."[31]

At the limit, then, the police recognize their need to prevail, and will physically enforce that authority if necessary. Their understandable preference is for their authority to be immediately recognized and deferred to. Absent such deference, officers will assert their authority as they see fit. They recognize themselves as distinct and separate from the citizenry, possessors of a unique source of power that will be hegemonic.

SEPARATION AND PROFESSIONALISM Beyond their adherence to the law, then, the police reinforce a sense of distinction between themselves and the public by seeking protection from excessive political intrusion into their affairs and by embracing a self-construction as authoritative actors. An additional source of separation comes through the prestige associated with the status of a professional. Recall that the ideal for police organizations that preceded community policing, the professional model, stressed the unique bases of expertise the police could mobilize to reduce crime. The police sought to make themselves analogous to other high-status occupations. Just like doctors and lawyers are specially educated, so were police officers trained according to high standards that ensured an efficient workplace. This was tied to the effort to wage an effective war against crime. Because of their superior tactics, the police would consistently outwit criminals, and therefore deter future criminality.

Even if one could argue that community policing has supplanted the professional model,[32] the notion of the police as possessors of unique expertise clearly persists, and for officers this expertise reinforces a distinction between themselves and the public. For example, during a ride-along, a dispatcher asked an officer to respond to a citizen complaint about a group of men who were selling drugs on a street corner. The officer dismissed the call because the citizen "had not been trained" to detect drug sales. It would therefore likely be a waste of his time to respond. Another officer I accompanied observed a group of young men dispersing from a street corner as his cruiser drove past. This was a significant phenomenon, he asserted, one that only a "trained police officer" would notice. Their dispersal, he argues, is a clear signal that they are "up to no good." Why else, he wonders, would they be dispersing?

This notion of professional separation was reinforced subtly but powerfully at police-community forums. Each conversation between officers and members of the public focused on some matter related to crime and disorder. In each case, the officers controlled the conversation, reserved for themselves the last word, and discussed—often at length—the various measures they would take to address the issue at hand. If there were any obstacles to the police's effectiveness, these were invariably matters beyond police control: a too-lax system of punishment, an unresponsive bureaucracy, the delicate politics of arrests of homosexuals. In short, the police reinforced a notion of themselves as the expert professionals, able to deploy their unique set of knowledge, skills, and tactics to solve a problem beyond the scope of an ordinary citizen to confront.

In sum, then, the police construct themselves as a separate and powerful social group, and legitimate this distinction in potent and reinforcing ways: they are legal actors with allegiance to the legal code; they are members of a politically vulnerable group that deserves protection from ill-informed public meddling; they possess an authority to control situations to which the public should defer; they command a unique base of knowledge, and thus deserve an elevated professional status. From this position of separation from the public, it is obviously difficult for police to approach the citizenry as fully vested "partners" with whom they can "co-produce" strategies for crime reduction. In this way, subservience is limited by separation.

THE PROJECT OF GENERATIVITY

Subservience and separation do not exhaust the means by which the connection between the citizenry and the police is constructed. In each of these approaches, state and society are considered distinct, and the state is either responsive to or shielded from society. However, the two approaches neglect the significant ways in which society is very much a product of the state, how the two are not neatly distinguishable. As I elaborated above, there are three principal means by which the state generates community: by constructing policies that significantly determine the material realities within given neighborhoods; by establishing a set of routines and practices by which community input is understood and processed; and by constructing a moral universe that state and community together inhabit and seek to protect. Through these policies, practices, and discursive constructions, the line between state and society is blurred in ways that are critical to state efforts at legitimacy.

It is a point of some controversy whether the police do much to shape the material realities that exist in given neighborhoods. There is evidence that the police can help reduce the fear of crime, but the evidence that they can actually reduce crime is largely missing.[33] In terms of the structural dynamics that shape neighborhoods—the type and caliber of the housing stock, the localized labor market, the provision of social services—the police possess no impact whatsoever. So, the police's capacity to generate community primarily involves the epistemology they mobilize and the moralistic understandings they develop.

THE EPISTEMOLOGY OF COMMUNITY   The rhetoric of community policing suggests that the police can and should work closely with the "community." But just what does this term mean to the police? What do officers recognize as a community? Who do they consider capable of speaking for a community? In general terms, how do the police channel and make sense of the input they receive from the public?[34]

What was striking from my conversations with police officers was the fact that the term "community" possessed very little resonance. I regularly asked officers about the communities in the areas for which they were responsible. Were there identifiable such communities? Where were they? Of whom did they consist? Were they aware of any formally or informally organized community groups focused upon issues of crime and disorder? If so, how did they understand the connection between any such groups and the police?

These conversations revealed that the officers' geographies were structured primarily by those "problem locations" to which they were summoned most regularly. The key locales on their mental maps were the hot spots that elicited regular calls for service: a public housing facility; a block where outdoor drug sales were apparently common; a row of adjacent houses reputed to be home to gang members. In some cases, officers knew well many of the residents in these areas of particular concern. One officer, for example, took me down an especially notorious block and briefly described the residents of nearly every single building.

But that same officer knew almost nothing about areas to which he was not regularly summoned. As we drove along a major thoroughfare, he waved his hand at a neighborhood to our right and said, "That's all residential." That area, he implied, was full of stable homeowners, and thus of no interest. Indeed, nearly every officer with whom I rode spent their discretionary time either cruising along major streets or visiting hot spots. Neighborhoods that did not host ongoing problems were largely invisible.

The term "community" was not one that officers used regularly in describing their areas. It was not a term that emerged organically from our conversations about the geography of their beats. It was the extremely rare officer who possessed information about the informal dynamics in a given place, who could provide keen observations about the realities in any particular neighborhood.[35] Any such detailed knowledge was almost exclusively confined to community police team officers, although even many of those struggled to provide comprehensive explanations of ongoing problems. For their part, officers in regular patrol might know quite a lot about a particular problem location or two. Yet their knowledge was limited to the alleged perpetrators of those problems, and did not include the wider dynamics in the neighborhood. As I explore in detail in chapter 4, problems were largely considered the handiwork of a few "bad apples" who plagued an otherwise peaceable area. The term "community" was rarely discussed as either a constituent component of these problems or as a significant player in their resolution. As one patrol officer admitted, "I don't think too many of us spend much time thinking about community."

Even if "community" was not central to officers' understandings of place, still the police were regularly summoned by citizens who sought assistance with matters of concern. Invariably, these requests for assistance are filtered through a set of bureaucratic and cultural scripts; public comment is translated into a language that the police recognize. So community input does not exist independently of the police, but is sifted through officers' screening mechanisms.[36] The police actively construct community through these translation practices.

For example, an officer was summoned to a residence because of a "911 hangup" call. Someone in the house in question had called the emergency number, and then quickly hung up. Such a call becomes an emergency, for fear that the caller's request for help has been interrupted by a dangerous assailant. The officer hurried to the residence in question, and arrived simultaneously with his superior, a sergeant. A man who lives in the house with his wife was outside, repairing his car. He explained to the officers that their car was vandalized, and that his wife called the police department. The sergeant was visibly angry, and explained why a 911 hangup is an emergency call. Further, he explained how he and his officer were pulled away from other pressing matters to respond to this call. Dissatisfied with the man's explanation, the sergeant called the dispatcher to gather more specifics. The dispatcher could not provide any more information, but then the man's wife emerged from the house. She indicated that she did indeed dial 911, but hung up when she realized that there was a non-emergency number to call instead. Both she and her husband were profusely apologetic, although the officers remained visibly bothered throughout the conversation.

In this instance, we see quite clearly how the police's apprehension of public input is structured by various bureaucratic routines. What to the couple in question seems like an ordinary act—to hang up the phone when one realizes one has dialed a wrong number—becomes a matter of concern and frustration for the police. The sergeant, in particular, struggles to accept the fact that the couple failed to appreciate the implications of the woman's actions for the police. He works hard to understand precisely what happened, and explains, with detail and exasperation, how their actions were interpreted by the police. He obviously resents this needless interruption to his day, and he does little to disguise his feelings.[37]

In another case, I accompanied an officer who was part of a group responding to a call involving a domestic disturbance. A long sequence of events culminated in a recommendation that the man involved move his belongings out of his girlfriend's apartment. As the group waited for this task to be completed, a call came over the radio concerning a report that some shots were fired in a nearby neighborhood. The officer turned to me and explained that this was a "nothing" call. She indicated that unless there are several such reports, there is no sense in responding. Only then, she said, would the police know that this was a call of substance and thus worthy of response. I could not help but wonder about the resident who had phoned the police: did he or she believe this was a "nothing" call?

On yet another evening, an officer was summoned to an apartment to file a report of a stolen car. This would involve much paperwork, but he did not wish to do all of this at the residence in question. Instead, he pulled his car into a parking lot in a neighborhood that generates many calls for service, some of them involving violent crime. The officer was anxious to respond to any such calls. He reasoned that he did not want to be in an apartment doing paperwork when a priority call arose. He would rather minimize his time in the apartment to maximize his capacity to respond to an emergency. After several minutes spent doing paperwork in his car, he ultimately arrived at the apartment. There, we discovered that the owner of the stolen car was waiting for the police so that she could get to work. Further, she needed to arrange care for her small child. The officer's tardy arrival thus reduced her work time and complicated her life.

Each of these instances illustrates a broader point: that "community" and "community input" do not exist independently of the police's construction of them. In each case, the police translated a request for service into a particular form, one different from the form generated by the citizen. An innocent hang-up becomes an emergency, a frightening report about a weapon becomes a nothing call, a request for assistance on a stolen car becomes a restriction on an officer's ability to respond to something more interesting.

These sorts of disjunctures produce much tension between citizens and the police. What I wish to stress now is that the community and the police are not strictly separable entities. Instead, the police construct community through their various routines and epistemologies. In such fashion, the state generates community; it defines what, in practice, community actually means. Something similar occurs when the state constructs a moral understanding of its actions.

MORALITY AND THE POLICE-COMMUNITY RELATION   One of the most potent and consequential ways by which state actors construct community is by developing a set of moral justifications for their actions. Recall the lieutenant's performance discussed at the outset of this chapter. What made his rhetorical performance so powerful was the sense of moral indignation that undergirded it, the palpable outrage at a punishment apparatus unable to address the threat posed by unfettered car thieves. Cast onto this terrain, car thefts are far more than an inconvenience—they are a plague inflicted upon vulnerable citizens. Further, these citizens deserve more protection than they get. It is the state's moral obligation to do more. By casting criminality in such moralistic terms, the lieutenant fuses state and society in a particularly powerful way. No longer separate entities, each with some influence upon the other, state and society are situated together in a moral combat zone, a transcendental realm where good and evil battle. "Community" thus emerges not as a constellation of citizens with sufficient political agency to help oversee police policy, but rather as a site upon which the virtuous can defeat the unsavory. The police and the citizenry are implicitly joined in an unquestionable pursuit of a moral victory. Note how the lieutenant says, "I'm going to tell you the truth, and it's going to irritate everyone in this room." The possibility of dissent over the moral terms of the battle is inconceivable; state and society are joined in an overarching struggle to ensure that the good emerges victorious.

This sense of moralism is entrenched within the police's subculture. The coercive authority the police possess is often justified in terms of the abiding good that police work enables and protects. This narrative cloaks police authority in a penumbra of exalted justification; it legitimates coercion by emphasizing the greater good that coercion protects. One officer, for example, engaged in a rough search of an African-American man he thought might be connected to a robbery in a home occupied by a ten-year-old boy. After the man complained about the search, the officer legitimated his actions by emphasizing his need to respond to the mistreatment of a vulnerable child. He sought to absolve himself of guilt for his forceful behavior by connecting to the higher purpose of protecting the innocent.

This self-image, as protectors of the weak and vulnerable, is one that officers project frequently. One officer allowed a conversation about citizen oversight of the police to become a vehicle for his exasperation. He recalled an incident he had handled a few days earlier, where a child was under threat from his mother's boyfriend. When the officer arrived at the mother's home, he was astonished to find that she had barricaded herself into a room alone, leaving her child vulnerable. The officer noted that it was left to him to fulfill this basic responsibility of protecting her child. He drew a clear conclusion: if members of the public were unwilling to place themselves on the line for their own children, and wanted the police to do so instead, then they were in no position to criticize the police's work.

This exalted status for police and their crime-fighting work also makes it hard for officers to understand how they might appear to citizens as anything other than beneficent. One officer was astonished that a citizen complained to his captain because the officer stopped by for a "knock and talk." This is a practice whereby officers knock on the door of someone they think might be connected with a crime or might possess information about criminal activity. The officers use it to ferret out information, presumably with the compliance of the person involved. In his own view, the exasperated officer merely wanted to "have a conversation." Why, he wondered, would any complain about that? He could not understand why an officer in uniform symbolically represents something more than a casual conversant, why a citizen would possess anything other than complete faith in the police's mission.

A central part of this mission, for the police, is the exposure to danger that officers necessarily embrace. They are acutely aware of the risk they assume by inserting themselves into scenes of potential danger and violence. Even if many of them eagerly embrace this challenge—many are quick to respond to high-priority calls, with lights and sirens blazing, even from several miles away—they also exalt the potential sacrifice involved. It is of telling significance that officers who died in the line of duty are featured on wall displays in police precincts, a perpetual reminder of the life-threatening nature of police work. It is perhaps not surprising to hear a police officer refer to his colleagues as "men of honor." He knows that they are pledged to sacrifice themselves to defend the citizenry they are sworn to protect. Such sacrifices are made worthwhile by the moralistic language officers use to cloak their work; lives lost are legitimated because they preserve the greater good.

To situate their work firmly within the transcendental realm of the good is thus an understandable cultural response by officers to the dangers inherent in it. But such moralizing has implications for police-community relations. To so exalt their work is to thereby diminish the legitimacy of public oversight. If their work supports the greater good, then it lies beyond question. Recall again the lieutenant at the neighborhood council meeting. His outrage over the lax treatment of car thieves was implicitly a moral message about the danger of crime and the need to respond to it forcefully. The potency of this morality helped make it impossible for him to imagine a serious alternative to his framing of the situation. An alternate perspective on police work, perhaps one mobilized by critics, thus possesses little or no legitimacy and can be ignored or actively disparaged. Broad, open-ended discussions with the public about the direction of police policy and practice are hard to countenance.

In short, the separation between state and society is regularly blurred, in ways that restrict the reach of citizen oversight. State agencies like the police actively construct and situate the citizenry. Public input is filtered through various ordering schemes, community members are placed on a moralistic battleground where good faces evil. Community is thus not something separable from the state, but is generated by state actors like police officers. Through their definitional and moralistic work, the police construct community in particular ways, with telling impact on the nature of state-society relations.

CONCLUSION

A simple, uncomplicated, perhaps nostalgic vision of state-society relations infuses much of the rhetoric of community policing. According to this ideal, residents of urban neighborhoods can come together and develop a unified vision and resolution of their problems. Further, the police are to approach these neighborhoods in a spirit of responsiveness and cooperation. Officers should embrace neighborhood understandings of their concerns and should work as co-equal partners in crafting and executing strategies to address those concerns. The state should be subservient to a citizenry that exercises its political agency with alacrity and cohesion.

In some ways, the police respond to this imperative to subservience: they provide a range of services to meet the demands placed upon them. They respond to calls for service, they attend public meetings, they solicit citizen complaints and concerns via various mechanisms. But subservience by itself hardly characterizes the police-community relation; separation and generativity also figure large in the state-society connection. As much as the police demonstrate responsiveness, they also persistently reinforce a self-image as importantly separate from the citizenry. Such separation is often legitimated in terms of the police's need to enforce an abstract legal code that helps protect individual rights, and rightly so—the police do need, at times, to resist unjust demands from parochial social groups. But the drive for separation is fueled by other factors as well. Officers seek protection from their critics, they defend their authority to control the scenes to which they are summoned, they exalt their professional status vis-à-vis uninformed citizens.

Similarly, they exalt their work in terms of an overarching moralism that joins state and society together in an imagined community of virtue, wherein the evil stains of criminal pollution deserve an unquestioned vanquishing. In this way, and in a set of translation practices through which community input is rendered sensible, the police construct community in their everyday practices. Community is thus not something distinct from the police, but the result of a set of cultural understandings and bureaucratic routines.

In other words, the state is not simply a black box, a coherent object of abstract political theory. It is very much a social creation, developed through a complicated set of practices and cultural scripts. This reality complicates the police's pursuit of legitimacy. Whatever the resonance of the narrative of state subservience to legitimations of community policing, it is not the sole means of understanding the state-society relation. As the police demonstrate daily, any tendency toward subservience is balanced, and at times subverted, by the projects of separation and generativity. As a consequence, "community" stands in no simple relation to the police. A community may, at times, possess some capacity to mobilize a police response. But its members are frequently dismissed as either misinformed or the passive recipients of the police's expert and virtuous efforts.

The processes of separation and generativity thus limit the extent to which the "community" possesses meaningful oversight of the police. This becomes obvious when we open up the black box of the state and witness the competing imperatives toward police legitimacy. Another advantage of opening this black box is that it provides analytic purchase on the cultural dynamics of the police. Because these dynamics are a critical component of the police's stance toward the citizenry, particularly as part of community policing, they are the focus of chapter 4.

NOTES

1   I obviously oversimplify by referring to "the" state and to "society," as if these were self-contained, unitary entities. In much of this book, I am at pains to demonstrate quite the opposite: that both are complex and diversified. For instance, society is composed of a range of communities, which differ along numerous dimensions, such as location, wealth, education, race, and political capability. Similarly, the state is composed of varied institutions and actors whose relations are rarely unproblematic. However, for the purposes of normative assessment, the broad terms "state" and "society" are useful. They enable me to categorize the types of relations that might pertain between aspects of the state apparatus and members of the citizenry.

2   Iris Marion Young, *Inclusion and Democracy* (Oxford: Oxford University Press, 2000), 5.

3   Max Weber, *Economy and Society: An Outline of Interpretive Sociology*, ed. Guenther Roth and Claus Wittich (New York: Bedminster Press, 1968); Emile Durkheim, *The Division of Labor in Society* (New York: Free Press, 1984); Jürgen Habermas, *Legitimation Crisis* (Boston: Beacon Press, 1975). Peter Manning makes this point eloquently with respect to the police: "The continued deference of citizens to police authority in the absence of specific demands, commands, or laws designed to produce compliance or punish its absence is the source of police power." Manning, "Community Policing as a Drama of Control," in *Community Policing: Rhetoric or Reality?*, ed. Jack Greene and Stephen Mastrofski (New York: Praeger, 1988), 27–45.

4   Not surprisingly, Iris Marion Young highlights her democratic action by recounting her involvement in efforts to establish a civilian review board of police action. Young, *Inclusion and Democracy*.

5   Robert Bursik and Harold Grasmick, *Neighborhoods and Crime: The Dimensions of Effective Community Control* (New York: Lexington Books, 1993); Todd Clear and David Karp, *The Community Justice Ideal: Preventing Crime and Achieving Justice* (Boulder, Colo.: Westview Press, 1999); Lawrence Sherman, "Communities and Crime," in *Preventing Crime: What Works,*

What Doesn't, What's Promising, ed. Lawrence Sherman (Washington, D.C.: U.S. Department of Justice, 1997).

6 John Braithwaite, *Crime, Shame and Reintegration* (Cambridge: Cambridge University Press, 1989); John Perry, ed., *Repairing Communities through Restorative Justice* (Lanham, Md.: American Correctional Association, 2002).

7 A comprehensive overview of such efforts, and the issues they raise, can be found in Samuel Walker, *Police Accountability: The Role of Citizen Oversight* (Belmont, Calif.: Wadsworth, 2001).

8 Allen Buchanan, "Assessing the Communitarian Critique of Liberalism," *Ethics* 99 (1989): 852–82; Stephen Gardbaum, "Law, Politics and the Claims of Community," *Michigan Law Review* 90 (1991): 685–760; Will Kymlicka, *Contemporary Political Philosophy* (Oxford: Clarendon Press, 1990); J. Donald Moon, *Constructing Community: Moral Pluralism and Tragic Conflicts* (Princeton, N.J.: Princeton University Press, 1993).

9 John Rawls, *Political Liberalism* (New York: Columbia University Press, 1993).

10 Jeffrey Isaac, Matthew Filner, and Jason Bivins, "American Democracy and the New Christian Right: A Critique of Apolitical Liberalism," in *Democracy's Edges,* ed. Ian Shapiro and Casiano-Hacker Gorden (Cambridge: Cambridge University Press, 1999).

11 Stephen Mastrofski, "Community Policing as Reform: A Cautionary Tale," in *Community Policing: Rhetoric or Reality?,* ed. Jack Greene and Stephen Mastrofski (New York: Praeger, 1988), 47–67.

12 This tension highlights the distinction drawn by Herbert Packer between the due process and crime control models that can ostensibly govern criminal justice practices. In the former, criminal justice officials are strictly regulated by due process considerations and endeavor to follow all procedural rules. In the latter, those officials are encouraged to use their discretion more freely, and to move swiftly and surely against suspected offenders. Police departments that adhere to the due process model risk losing legitimacy by appearing insufficiently muscular; those more focused on crime control risk arousing concerns about an intrusive state. See Herbert Packer, *The Limits of the Criminal Sanction* (Stanford, Calif.: Stanford University Press, 1968). A more recent version of this debate emerged around the rise of "order maintenance" policing in such American cities as New York and Chicago. For a useful introduction to this debate, see Tracey Meares and Dan Kahan, *Urgent Times: Policing and Rights in Inner-City Communities* (Boston: Beacon Press, 1999).

13 Robert Fogelson, *Big-City Police* (Cambridge: Harvard University Press, 1977); Samuel Walker, *A Critical History of Police Reform* (Lexington, Ky.: Lexington Books, 1977).

14 Peter Dreier, John Mollenkopf, and Todd Swanstrom, *Place Matters: Metropolitics for the Twenty-first Century* (Lawrence: University of Kansas Press, 2001); Rutherford Platt, *Land Use and Society: Geography, Law and Public Policy* (Washington, D.C.: Island Press, 1996); Constance Perrin,

Everything in Its Place: Social Order and Land Use in America (Princeton, N.J.: Princeton University Press, 1977).

15 Jeffrey Fagan, "Crime, Law and the Community: Dynamics of Incarceration in New York City," in *The Future of Imprisonment,* ed. Michael Tonry (Oxford: Oxford University Press, 2004), 27–59; Becky Petit and Bruce Western, "Mass Imprisonment and the Life Course: Race and Class Inequality in U.S. Incarceration," *American Sociological Review* 69 (2004): 151–69.

16 Michel Foucault, "Governmentality," in *The Foucault Effect: Studies in Governmentality,* ed. Graham Burchell, Colin Gordon, and Peter Miller (Chicago: University of Chicago Press, 1991), 87–104.

17 Mitchell Dean, *Governmentality: Power and Rule in Modern Society* (London: Sage, 1999), 15.

18 Barbara Cruikshank, *The Will to Empower* (Ithaca, N.Y.: Cornell University Press, 1999); Dean, *Governmentality*; Wendy Larner, "Neo-Liberalism: Policy, Ideology, Governmentality," *Studies in Political Economy* 63 (2000): 5–25; Dan MacKinnon, "Managerialism, Governmentality and the State: A Neo-Foucauldian Approach to Local Economic Governance," *Political Geography* 19 (2000): 293–314; Mike Raco and Rob Imrie, "Governmentality and Rights and Responsibilities in Urban Policy," *Environment and Planning A* 32 (2000): 2187–2204; Nikolas Rose, *Powers of Freedom: Reforming Political Thought* (Cambridge: Cambridge University Press, 1999).

19 See also Peter Manning, *Symbolic Communication: Signifying Calls and the Police Response* (Cambridge, Mass.: MIT Press, 1988).

20 James Scott, *Seeing Like a State: How Certain Schemes to Improve the Human Condition Have Failed* (New Haven, Conn.: Yale University Press, 1998).

21 Richard Ericson and Kevin Haggerty document extensively how the various forms police are asked to complete in handling calls structure how officers understand and encode the realities they confront. See their *Policing the Risk Society* (Oxford: Oxford University Press, 1997). Their insightful analysis overstates the importance of the insurance industry and other external actors in shaping this police epistemology, at least in the context of policing in Seattle and other U.S. cities.

22 Benedict Anderson, *Imagined Communities: Reflections on the Spread of Nationalism* (London: Verso, 1991).

23 Katherine Beckett, *Making Crime Pay: Law and Order in Contemporary American Politics* (Oxford: Oxford University Press, 1997); Stuart Hall, Charles Critcher, Tony Jefferson, John Clarke, and Brian Roberts, *Policing the Crisis: Mugging, the State and Law and Order* (London: Macmillan, 1978).

24 See Steve Herbert, "Morality in Law Enforcement: Chasing 'Bad Guys' with the Los Angeles Police Department," *Law and Society Review* 30 (1996): 799–828.

25 Such a society today is largely unimaginable. As Ian Shapiro states, the "democratic idea is close to nonnegotiable in today's world." Shapiro, *The State of Democratic Theory* (Princeton, N.J.: Princeton University Press, 2003), 1.

26 Malcolm Sparrow, Mark Moore, and David Kennedy, *Beyond 911: A New Era for Policing* (New York: Basic Books, 1990).

27 Herman Goldstein, *Problem-Oriented Policing* (New York: McGraw-Hill, 1991).

28 Will Kymlicka, "Liberal Individualism and Liberal Neutrality," in *Communitarianism and Individualism*, ed. Shlomo Avineri and Avner de-Shalit (New York: Oxford University Press, 1992).

29 The chief's acceptance of the OPA's recommendation was not the only factor in the no-confidence vote. Critical also were his decisions during civil unrest during a Mardi Gras celebration in a downtown region. The chief did not send officers into a melee in the streets, for fear of sparking further turmoil. The decision backfired when one partygoer was bludgeoned to death. The rank and file interpreted the chief's reluctance to send in officers as further evidence that he was too cautious, too fearful of the negative consequences of strong assertions of police authority.

30 Police officers might do well to define politics more expansively, and less defensively. Take, for instance, the definition of politics offered by Stone and his co-authors: "The activity by which a diverse citizenry reconcile, put aside, or in some manner accommodate their differences in order to pursue their common well-being." Clarence Stone, Jeffrey Henig, Bryan Jones, and Carol Pierannunzi, *Building Civic Capacity: The Politics of Reforming Urban Schools* (Lawrence: University of Kansas Press, 2001), 6.

31 Egon Bittner uses more social scientific language to capture the same sentiment: "Police procedure is defined by the feature that it may not be opposed in its course, and that force can be used if it is opposed. This is what the existence of the police makes available to society." Bittner, *The Functions of the Police in Modern Society* (New York: Jason Aronson, 1975), 41.

32 The popularity of so-called "broken-windows" policing, also referred to as "order-maintenance" policing, suggests that perhaps community policing is not as hegemonic as it seems. Although broken-windows policing is often treated as analogous to community policing, the two are different, largely in terms of the role each envisions for citizen oversight of the police. The popularity of broken-windows policing makes clear that the professional moment is far from over. See Steve Herbert, "Policing the Contemporary City: Fixing Broken Windows or Shoring Up Neo-Liberalism?" *Theoretical Criminology* 5 (2001): 445–66.

33 In an exhaustive review of the literature, Eck and Maguire found little evidence that anything the police do reduces crime. John Eck and Edward Maguire, "Have Changes in Policing Reduced Violent Crime? An Assessment of the Evidence," in *The Crime Drop in America*, ed. Alfred Blumstein and Joel Wallman (Cambridge: Cambridge University Press, 2000), 207–65. The most commonly cited instances of some impact of police actions include so-called "hot spot" policing—where

officers concentrate heavy attention on known areas of criminality—and some problem-solving efforts where the police establish an understanding of particular underlying dynamics that can be ameliorated, often through redesign of the physical environment. See Lawrence Sherman, David Farrington, Bandon Welsh, and Denise Gottfredson. eds., *Evidence-Based Crime Prevention* (New York: Routledge, 2002). Whatever successes these strategies might yield, they are notable for the intensiveness of the time and resources they require and for their comparative rarity in the life of a typical urban police department.

34 Peter Manning notes the importance of the police's epistemological construction of the world they inhabit: "The environment in which the officers act is one they largely project, act in accord with, and thus reify." Manning, *Narc's Game: Organizational and Informational Limits on Drug Law Enforcement* (Cambridge, Mass.: MIT Press, 1980), 55.

35 Jewkes and Murcott found, in their analyses of bureaucrats involved in community programs, that these officials typically used metaphors of distance when discussing community. They saw themselves as sharply distinct from the communities with which they worked, and they interpreted their work as acting upon various groups. They also argued that these bureaucrats possessed little sense of what it was like to be inside these communities. Rachel Jewkes and Anne Murcott, "Meanings of Community," *Social Science and Medicine* 43 (1996): 555–63.

36 Manning, *Symbolic Communication.*

37 This scenario can arguably be read as, more than anything, a poorly executed bureaucratic exercise. The dispatcher, for instance, could call the number back to learn more about the situation, and thereby provide more information to the sergeant. Even so, the sergeant's behavior makes plain that he sees this incident in a very particular way, one conditioned by his experience as a police officer. Indeed, the strength of his orientation evidently makes it difficult for him to accept a decision by the wife that she may view as a simple and understandable mistake.

Organizational Legitimacy and the Policing Mandate

JOHNATHAN A. COOPER

All organizations require legitimacy in order to exist and operate (Suchman, 1995). As such, the acquisition and maintenance of legitimacy is an important research area. One way that organizations can acquire and hold on to legitimacy is by the efficient production of needed goods or services (Weber, 1947). This method is complicated for public sector organizations, however, such as the police. The police are faced with two dilemmas that limit the extent to which their legitimacy, as an organization, can be gained through the efficient production of a needed service. The first dilemma has to do with their public mandate. One public mandate the police must satisfy has been described as an "impossible mandate" (Manning, 1978). To wit, to fight crime. This mandate is, on the one hand, difficult to quantify, and, on the other hand, constantly being reinvented. As a nebulous goal and what amounts to a moving target, the police mandate does little in the way of allowing police agencies to evaluate the degree to which they are successfully providing a needed service. Even if the mandate were more concrete and static, police would still be hampered in their legitimacy-seeking efforts by the second dilemma: the tool provided them to accomplish their mandate. However innovative police programs may appear, at their heart remains that aspect most associated with police presence: the power to arrest, and its accompanying potential for the use of coercive force (Bittner, 1970) . This tool puts police in a double bind. First, by using arrest and/or coercive force too little or too often, they risk losing legitimacy (Kane, 2003). Second, it is an inefficient, and in many ways an ineffective, method for "fighting crime" (Manning, 1978). The nebulous and transient nature of the police mandate, combined with the limiting tool at their disposal for accomplishing this mandate, place police at a serious disadvantage in terms of acquiring and maintaining organizational legitimacy[1].

Law enforcement agencies may therefore turn to a different source of legitimacy, namely the institutional environment. An organization's institutional environment is composed of powerful sovereigns who dictate how an organization is to behave in both form and function (Suchman, 1995). For a police agency, sovereigns may include political actors, professional organizations, or even other influential police agencies or individual officers within an agency. By conforming to the expectations of these sovereigns, an agency is able to hold on to legitimacy. This process is known as isomorphism. Police scholars have already explored these ideas (for an overview, see Crank & Langworthy, 1992), and many have found both anecdotal and empirical support for this institutional framework (Crank, 2003). I contend that such research, while important and informative, is missing a vital element for understanding how isomorphic processes occur. More specifically, in understanding how police agencies seek to acquire and maintain legitimacy by conforming to institutional pressures, the territorial nature of police behavior must be taken into account. Police agencies are organized around areal units, and these units have an impact on their behavior (Klinger, 1997; Rubinstein, 1973). Whereas the police mandate outlines the goals and directs the behavior of the police, it is within specific territories that this behavior takes place. By accounting for the territoriality of the police, researchers can better understand how isomorphism defuses behavior across police agencies.

This framework may also be applied from an intraorganizational perspective. Despite scholars suggesting that isomorphism is both an intra- as well as an interorganizational phenomenon (Meyer & Rowan, 1977; Crank, 2003), most research on the police and isomorphism has taken place at the interorganizational level. Yet, large police agencies are essentially composed of several smaller organizations, which are delineated along territorial lines. Just as some influential police agencies may stand out as sovereigns within their institutional environment, so too may some influential police precincts (or individual officers) act as sovereigns within their agency, with behavioral norms emanating out from them spatially across precincts in an isomorphic process.

This chapter will develop and build on these theoretical themes. As this and the following chapter will demonstrate, the isomorphic literature, in tandem with a territorial understanding of police behavior, provide meaningful hypotheses towards the end

---

1   This book is focused, essentially, on one part of the police mandate. This is not to suggest that it is the only mandate, only a driving mandate that is particularly focused in the minds of the public, from whom the police garner so much of their legitimacy.

of understanding how arresting behavior can defuse across police precincts within an organization.

THE NATURE OF LEGITIMACY AND THE POLICE MANDATE

Suchman (1995) defined legitimacy as "a generalized perception or assumption that the actions of an entity are desirable, proper, or appropriate within some socially constructed system of norms, values, beliefs, and definitions" (p. 574). In this light, legitimacy is understood to be a normative concept that is contingent on cultural exigencies[2]. In discussing legitimacy, Weber (1964, p. 328) delineated the now well-known rational, traditional, and charismatic authorities. In addition, Weber also asserted that "[l]egitimacy may be ascribed to an order by those acting subject to it …" (p. 130). In synthesizing the literature since Weber, Suchman (1995) suggested three essential forms that legitimacy can take: pragmatic, moral, and cognitive. Pragmatic legitimacy "rests on the self-interested calculations of an organization's most immediate audiences" (p. 578), and subsumes Weber's rational authority. Moral legitimacy rests on the assumption that what an organization does is just, good, and right, and reflects Weber's emotional or affectual attitudes and traditional authority. Finally, Suchman's (1995) cognitive legitimacy explains that an organization is recognized as being necessary to the functioning of society, and corresponds with Weber's legal authority. That is, both cognitive and legal legitimacy assert that an organization's legitimacy stems from its value in maintaining some sort of *status quo* or, at minimum, from being an inevitable reality. Suchman (1995) suggests legitimacy becomes more difficult to obtain moving from pragmatic, to moral, to cognitive, but also becomes more powerful. Legitimacy is most powerful and unquestionable at the cognitive level, where it is simply taken-for-granted: when an organization has reached this level of legitimacy, the idea that society could exist without that organization is simply inconceivable.

Suchman's (1995) definition came after several generations of academic dialog. Initially, organizational theorists, drawing on the works of Weber's ideal bureaucratic

---

2   Tyler (2006) also discusses legitimacy in terms of the police. The way legitimacy is used here is distinct from how Tyler employs the term. For Tyler, legitimacy is the result of police following due process and acting justly and fairly towards citizens. The result of perceived police legitimacy is citizen obeisance to the law. For the institutional literature, police legitimacy is the result of a direct and demonstrable connection between their behavior and the fulfillment of their mandate - crime control, in short. It is important to note that this mandate comes, in part, from the public and their perceptions of police behavior. The result of police legitimacy is not obeisance to the law, but rather the police organization's access to resources necessary for their survival.

model, focused on the concept that formal organizations were created out of a necessity to navigate complex social and commercial relationships. These theorists drew on Weber's (1964) arguments for a rational bureaucratic system, where the most successful organizations are those which are rationally organized around quantifiable results: their structure and behavior are geared towards the efficient achievement of output. To the extent that an organization was able to efficiently achieve such outputs it could acquire and maintain legitimacy. Stated otherwise, a rational organization's legitimacy rests on its ability to effectively accomplish its mandate (Suchman, 1995). Meyer and Rowan (1977) criticized this vein of thought by pointing out that institutional theorists had ignored another source of the legitimacy of complex organizations as posited by Weber. Weber (1964) wrote, "Action, especially social action which involves social relationships, may be oriented by the actors to a belief (*Vorstellung*) in the existence of a 'legitimate order'" (p. 124). This posits that individuals and organizations behave according to shared beliefs as to what constitutes legitimacy that may or may not have anything to do with the efficient production of outputs. This shift changed the foundational understanding of organizational legitimacy from being the result of pure output oriented behavior to introducing social and cultural elements. It was now understood that there were multiple pathways to legitimacy, including the classic Weberian concept of a rational bureaucracy, but also including conforming behavior that matched with institutional expectations.

Legitimacy is important to understand because of what its acquisition means to an organization. As Blau and Meyer (1987) argue, legitimacy is tied to power, and power is tied to the acquisition of resources. Subsequently, legitimacy promotes organizational success and survival (Meyer & Rowan, 1977). All organizations that perform the same or similar functions compete for a number of resources, including revenue and customers. What is more, they compete for legitimacy (DiMaggio & Powell, 1983). To the degree that one organization acquires and maintains legitimacy while other organizations fail to do so, that organization will better succeed in the acquisition of all other resources. Suchman (1995), in summarizing the legitimacy literature, has pointed out that legitimacy brings stability, credibility, and support to an organization. In terms of support, an organization may acquire either active support or passive support (or both). Whereas active support refers to the actual and regular assistance from institutional constituents in goal achievement, passive support only requires that an organization is simply let alone to do what it is that they do, *sans* interference. The assumption is that the organization is acting in good faith (Meyer & Rowan, 1977). This assumption is one of the fruits of organizational legitimacy. Overall, legitimacy is necessary for an organization to survive.

POLICE LEGITIMACY

The legitimacy of the police traditionally has been garnered through their impact on crime. Indeed, the focus of Peel's Metropolitan Police was crime prevention (Manning, 1978; Uchida, 2005). Although this focus crossed over the Atlantic to several early 19th century United States cities, starting in the early 20th century police impact on crime became operationalized in quantifiable terms such as arrest numbers, calls for service, or response times (Reiss & Bordua, 1967; Skolnick & Fyfe, 1993). This reflected a shift to Weber's rational order of legitimacy: by demonstrating that their behavior was arithmetically associated with quantifiable changes in crime, police could be seen as vital and necessary. This behavior also manifested itself in legitimacy seeking behavior in line with Weber's traditional authority. Herbert (1997), for example, suggested that the law, bureaucratic regulations, a guiding value of machismo, maintaining safety on the job, demonstrating competence worthy of respect, and upholding a morality of good versus evil, each guide how police officers behave – that is, that police behavior was influenced by the notion of "what a cop" looked like and did: fight crime and bravely protect the innocent. This behavior, however, must play out under the "number's game" (Skolnick & Fyfe, 1993): Writing about the Philadelphia police, Rubinstein (1973) commented that "[t]he worth of a man to his platoon does not depend on his success in preventing crimes, arresting suspected felons, or even giving service without complaint or injury ... 'Activity' is the internal product of police work. It is the statistical measure which the sergeant uses to judge the productivity of his men ..." (pp. 43–44). Rubinstein continued: "Arrest activity is computed from what the patrolman 'puts on the books' and not by the disposition of his cases in court. Since activity is a measure of his work, his sergeant has no interest in what eventually happens to the cases" (pp. 44–45).

This system of assessment has at least two flaws. First, using arrest statistics as the primary example, they are artifacts of police behavior rather than of police impact (Manning, 1978). In most introductory criminal justice and methodology text books it is pointed out that *Crime in America* is often used as a measure of what police do as opposed to a measure of criminal activity (Lynch & Addington, 2007). This will most likely vary by type of crime. This means that as police increase their arresting behavior, the crime rate appears to increase, as well. This leads to calls for more arresting behavior. This pattern is subsumed by the second flaw, articulated by Manning (1978) as policing's impossible mandate: to engage in the "efficient, apolitical, and professional enforcement of the law" (p. 8).

THE POLICE MANDATE

Manning (1978) defines a *mandate* as an organization's right to define the parameters and technology of its occupation. He has argued that the police mandate is not, however, wholly in their hands. Rather, it is something thrust upon them by public expectations and political deliberation. Because the police are part of the executive branch of government, both of these processes are ultimately beyond their purview. However, Manning (1978) reminds us that American police themselves have accepted and expanded (or, perhaps narrowed) this mandate to a professional status, despite that doing so can severely threaten the legitimacy of the police (see note 2 above). This mandate, again according to Manning (1978), is an impossible one. The mandate communicates to officers the expectation that they can and should have a meaningful impact on the amount of crime that occurs in cities. This mandate is impossible not because police have no impact on crime whatsoever, but, as Herbert (2001) pointed out "… on their own, police can do little to reduce crime" (p. 449) when relying on traditional law enforcement techniques (Klofas, Hipple, & McGarrell, 2010). What is more, although efforts are made to quantify the police mandate, it ultimately remains nebulous (Klockars, 1986), precluding any systematic analysis of the state of crime *then* versus the state of crime *now* (DiIulio, 1995). The thrust of Manning's (1978) argument was that the police had placed themselves in a very difficult spot: they had promised a product that they were unable to deliver.

SOURCES AND CONSEQUENCES OF THE POLICE MANDATE

The model for American policing has its origins in Peel's London Metropolitan Police. Peel's vision for a unitary police force was transported across the Atlantic in piece-meal fashion in both form and function. For example, for Peel, the police prime directive was to prevent crime, and to do so avoiding legal sanctions and resorting to violence only in the most extreme of circumstances. During the formative years of policing in the United States, the American model did resemble the British model in terms of crime prevention and social assistance, though the American police remained exceptionally decentralized and politicized. In many instances, this led to laziness and corruption (Strecher, 1991; Walker, 1998). Through two waves of reform (first towards the end of the 1800s by the Progressives and then at the start of the 1900s by reformist police chiefs), police agencies attempted to ameliorate these faults through a professional-ization movement (Walker, 1998; White, 2007). Subsequently, American police rarely sought to prevent crime and, as the form of policing became more bureaucratized, came to rely extensively on legal sanctions and coercive force (Manning, 1977). This created a situation that stood in stark contrast to the British model.

Three changes to American policing accompanied this move to professionalize the police that would impact the mandate of police agencies (unless otherwise noted, this paragraph relies on Manning, 1977, pp. 97–98). The first change was the institutionalization of a national database of crime statistics. This effort was first spearheaded by the International Association of Chiefs of Police (IACP) and August Vollmer, and then taken up by the fledgling Federal Bureau of Investigation (Skolnick & Fyfe, 1993). Hoover employed the new crime statistics program (the Uniformed Crime Report or UCR, published as *Crime in America*) to highlight the FBI as *the* professional standard of crime fighting experts. Law enforcement agencies around the country took note of the FBI's new status, and soon began to emulate the FBI's training, techniques, and, most importantly, professional mandate. The second change came in how police agencies used the data from the UCR: the crime rate became the measuring rod by which police success would be judged. This had the effect of quantifying the mandate. Finally, police began to focus on the technological tools they could use to be professional crime fighters, including patrol cars, two way radios, and latent fingerprint recognition. These tools symbolized the police agencies' role as professional crime fighters who were specially trained and equipped to protect society from crime (Manning, 1977).

These changes had the cumulative effect of focusing the police officer role on crime fighting through crime rate statistics. Since the inception of the UCR, police have been judged according to numerical standards. This has included, among other things, arrest rates and crime rates, but has also extended to calls for service and response time (Rubenstein, 1978; what Skolnick and Fyfe [1993] refer to as "the numbers game"). This has also resulted in police officers focusing less on whether they have achieved their goals and more on what they are doing towards those ends. In this situation, the police mandate has pushed agencies into a means/end syndrome where the means actually become the ends (Goldstein, 1979). Police were *crime fighting experts*, a mandate which said little about *crime preventing or reducing*. Whether intended or not, this has had the ultimate consequence that police behavior became focused on serving themselves rather than on serving the public (Reiss & Bordua, 1967; Manning, 1978).

This focus on crime statistics and the concomitant expectation that police can and should be able to do something about it immediately (Bittner, 1970) is reinforced from a myriad of sources that have taken on a life of their own. This is to say that a citizen need not be aware of crime statistics as such to expect police to engage in crime fighting through crime rate statistics. The media play an important role in reifying myths about the police's role as the thin blue line between safety and anarchy (Manning, 1978; Potter & Kappeler, 2006) . There is also evidence that this mandate is communicated vigorously from the political environment (Wilson, 1968) and the organizational environment (Slovak, 1987; Kappeler, Sluder, & Alpert, 1998; Manning & Van Maanen, 1978). As Kappeler and colleagues (1998) state, "[i]n essence, police are selected, socialized, and placed into a working environment that instills within them an ideology and shared culture that breeds unprecedented conformity to the traditional police norms and values" (p. 84). For the police, then, the impossible mandate is more than an occupational dictum: it is a moral calling filled with value-laden responsibility. This is a calling that many, if not most, police officers bring with them to the job (Raganella & White, 2004), and that police take very seriously (White, et al. 2010). This mandate guides the behavior of police officers and forms the goals to which their behavior is aimed. However, that behavior takes place within unique territories that also have an impact. The next section takes up this topic.

TERRITORIALITY AND POLICING

Since at least the beginning of the 20th Century, most (if not virtually all) American police departments have deployed patrol officers in local beat areas (Walker & Katz, 2007). Indeed, although this deployment paradigm originated as a way of holding police officers accountable to their desk sergeants in the absence of portable radios (de Lint, 2000), assigning officers to local beats – often for months at a time – has had the perhaps unintended consequence of encouraging police work-groups to develop norms and occupational world views on the basis of territoriality (Klinger, 1997). Thus, while the external environment of the police organization requires them to adopt a crime-fighting mandate, it is through territoriality that police work-groups apply their knowledge of their local working environments in ways that allow them to try to achieve the crime control goals.

Territoriality refers to "how people manage the location they own, occupy, or use for varying periods of time" (Taylor, 1988, p. 1). Territoriality can therefore be understood as a strategy of control. Sack (1986) elaborates on this idea in this way: "Territoriality [is] defined as the attempt by an individual or group to affect, influence, or control people, phenomena, and relationships, by delimiting and asserting control over a geographic area" (p. 19). Weber (1964) posited that states are essentially social aggregates commissioned to maintain political borders. That is, they are commissioned to maintain a politically defined territory. Within these borders, the state must also safeguard the well-being of the body politic. Weber (2004) distinguished the state from other social aggregates by pointing out that the state possessed a monopoly on the use of force. As Bittner (1970) argued forty years ago, the use of force in coercing compliance is the central role of police officers. Police can therefore be understood as the literal manifestation of the state's monopoly on the use of force. Indeed, individual police officers are "the most visible aspect" of the government and "that aspect most likely to intervene directly" in the lives of citizens (Van Maanen, 1974, p. 84). In carrying out this role, the police organize and behave within territorial units (Herbert, 1997).

Large municipal police agencies typically divide their organizational hierarchy according to spatial units across the city. Precincts are supervised by mid-level managers; in turn, precincts comprise a collective of beats supervised by sergeants and patrolled by line officers. Throughout the United States there are variations on this organizational set up according to departmental size, geography, and the political environment, among other factors (Klinger, 1997), but the practice of organizing territorially is a constant across departments. The territories employed by police agencies are typically political rather than reflecting any organic sense of community as understood by citizens (Herbert, 2006; Klinger, 1997). The political boundaries layered over the municipal map become so important that officers may cease to understand the city in terms of neighborhoods or landmarks; instead, it becomes "a mosaic of linked districts" (Rubenstein, 1973, p. 26) to which the "patrolmen are tied inextricably" (Van Maanen, 1974, p. 113).

SOCIAL ECOLOGY AND POLICING

In general, the goals of police behavior are provided by the police mandate. The behavior designed to achieve these goals takes place within a territory. The contents of that territory will bear directly on the behavior of police officers. Early on, Whyte (1943) found that there were different rules for how police were to behave according to the kind of neighborhood in which they were patrolling. Smith (1986) was one of the first scholars to empirically document this phenomenon. Among his findings, police were most likely to initiate contact with suspects and suspicious persons in racially heterogeneous neighborhoods, but were less likely to do so in high crime areas. Similarly, he found that in lower-status neighborhoods, suspects were three times more likely to be arrested than in higher-status neighborhoods.

Klinger (1997), drawing on the negotiated order perspective, suggested that the degree to which officers invoke their law enforcement powers ultimately rests on a collection of formal and informal work rules that are common to all officers. These rules provide direction to officers in negotiating contacts with citizens, and arise because, first, line-level officers have a high level of autonomy, and second, labor is divided along territorial (that is, precinct and beat) lines. What is more, these two facets are influenced by the social environment of the precinct, the police organizational mandate, and a workload that cannot be ignored. Essentially, every precinct has a certain level of "normal deviance", and any crime that departs from this mean is considered deviant and treated more vigorously - that is, with more official action on the part of the officer. Klinger (1997) argued that as crime rates increase in a precinct, "work group rules will hold that deviant acts of a given level of seriousness should receive less vigorous police attention" (p. 296). Thus far, at least four studies that have explicitly tested Klinger's ecological framework have found significant support (Phillips & Sobol, 2010; Johnson & Olschansky, 2010; Sobol, 2010; Jackson & Boyd, 2005).

Kane's body of work has expanded this research agenda into other policing domains beyond the decision to arrest. For example, Kane (2002) found that police misconduct could be predicted by structural disadvantage, population mobility, and changes in the Latino population. In what can also be construed as a test of police territorial management, Kane (2005) found that, controlling for structural disadvantage, police were able to reduce rates in burglary and robbery, but, again, only up to a certain threshold. He also found that changes in Latino population were related to the allocation of police officers over time in New York City, but only up to a certain threshold (Kane, 2003). This finding is part of a larger literature that has consistently found similar racial and ethnic effects on police behavior. Drawing from a Weberian paradigm, Jacobs and O'Brien (1998) found that the police killings of Black citizens could be predicted, among other variables, by the economic inequality between Whites and Blacks. Jacobs and O'Brien (1998), as well as Kane (2002), suggest that one of the reasons that minority communities may be more vulnerable to police attention is because they lack the social capital necessary to muster resources against police violence. As Jacobs and O'Brien (1998) point out, without constraints, police violence is more probable than when under community constraints. It is important to note that these three studies (Kane, 2002, 2003; Jacobs and O'Brien, 1998) did control for a reactive hypothesis wherein police were simply responding to criminal activity within these communities.

Overall, literature in this domain has found that, without appropriate agency controls, minority communities are more prone to police violence compared to majority communities (Fyfe, 1982; Meehan & Ponder, 2002). Tying all these studies together (Kane, 2002, 2003, 2006; Jacobs & O'Brien, 1998) is the idea that the police and the social environment in which they work are bound together in an ecology: just as the environment impacts police behavior, such as misconduct, so too can police behavior impact overall patterns of citizen behavior, such as burglary and robbery. Importantly, the social environment under scrutiny in these studies (and others, e.g., Sherman, 1986; Smith, 1986) was the politically created and enforced boundaries of the police precinct.

What goes on in an officer's territory therefore guides his behavior: sometimes liberating it (e.g., *in this neighborhood, it's ok to …*), sometimes constraining it (e.g., *in this neighborhood, it's best not to …*). For example: a precinct with a particularly high crime rate will result in high levels of arrest. In such a neighborhood, the means of fulfilling the police mandate - arrest - is the accepted law enforcement response to high crime. In a precinct with lower rates of crime, however, arresting behavior may vary, because the mandate is more nebulous: *The crime rate here is relatively low, so should I, as an officer, arrest this individual for something that in a high crime area I normally would, because that's what's expected of me there? Or can I let this slide?* The answer is: it depends on a number of situational factors (Terrill & Reisig, 2003), precinct-level elements (Klinger, 1997), and ecological covariates (Kane, 2002, 2003, 2005). The difference between the two scenarios is largely a matter of what extra-legal reasons can enter the decision making picture. I submit that one such predictor is to be found in the overall institutional environment.

ISOMORPHISM AND THE INSTITUTIONAL ENVIRONMENT

According to Weber, one source of organizational legitimacy, which he coined *rational authority*, is drawn from an organization's ability to match its behavior to desired outcomes. Early theorists, therefore, argued that legitimacy was gained through the output-oriented success of organizations. The expansion of the bureaucratic model and the rational acquisition of legitimacy were first understood in terms of economic and international competition and the concomitant search for the efficient means of production. Organizational theorists argued that to the degree that what an organization did was rationally tied to its outcome, and that that outcome was achieved with maximal efficiency, it earned and maintained legitimacy. Many contemporary theorists suggest that the tie between what an organization does and its outcomes may have little or nothing to do with an organization's legitimacy. Rather, many modern organizational theorists argue that legitimacy is now less tied to efficiency and is more part of subordinating structure and operation to the institutional plane's *status quo* (DiMaggio & Powell, 1983). Just as Weber (1964) argued that bureaucracy was the inevitable iron cage of society, many modern organizational theorists suggest that the structure of organizations is inevitable because of the pressures exerted from the institutional environment (Meyer & Rowan, 1977; DiMaggio & Powell, 1983). Clarifying his definition of legitimacy, Suchman (1995) wrote: "… when one says that a certain pattern of behavior possesses legitimacy, one asserts that some group of observers, as a whole, accepts or supports what those observers perceive to be the behavioral pattern, as a whole" (p. 574).

This shift in understanding came about largely because researchers began to realize that a) not all organizations behaved according to their bureaucratic structure, and b) not all organizations had operational (that is, quantifiable and measurable) goals (Parsons, 1963; Meyer & Rowan, 1977; DiMaggio & Powell, 1983; Blau & Meyer, 1971). Yet, such organizations not only survived but in many cases thrived. Parsons (1963) offered one explanation for this paradox: He pointed out that society held intangible values that were reinforced by the political climate of that society. These values trickled down to organizations which ostensibly were set up to carry those values out. One problem with this process was, being intangible, the operationalization of these goals was *categorical* rather than *quantitative* (Meyer & Rowan, 1977). Unable to measure their goals, organizations were also unable to meet the bench-marks held up by a Weberian bureaucracy. This threatened their legitimacy, and hence their survival. Organizations, therefore, had to seek legitimacy elsewhere.

DiMaggio and Powell (1983) suggested that one way in which organizations acquire legitimacy is through isomorphism: "… [the] bureaucratization and other forms of organizational change [that] occur as the result of processes that make organizations more similar without necessarily making them more efficient" (p. 147). The point DiMaggio and Powell are making is that organizations copy one another not because another organization's operations or structures are seen as efficient means to a promising outcome, but simply because another organization may be perceived as legitimate. By copying it, an organization hopes to acquire legitimacy itself. In a very real sense, institutional isomorphism is the organizational equivalent of peer pressure: organizations make structural and behavioral changes according to the demands of their institutional environment to conform.

DiMaggio and Powell (1983) outlined three mechanisms of isomorphic change. Coercive isomorphism occurs whenever powerful stakeholders put pressure on an organization to adopt or drop specific policies, practices, or organizational elements. For example: the adoption of mandatory arrest policies in cases of domestic violence during the 1970s and 1980s were largely in response to law suits and the activist behavior of women's advocacy groups (Sherman, Schmidt, & Rogan, 1992). Mimetic isomorphism occurs whenever, in a bid to acquire legitimacy, organizations adopt the practices of similarly purposed organizations which are already seen as legitimate. This form of isomorphism is most common when "organizational technologies are poorly understood … when goals are ambiguous, or when the environment creates symbolic uncertainty" (p. 151). For example, the presence of paramilitary units in small town police departments which have no need of them may reflect efforts to imitate the police agencies from larger cities (Kraska & Cubellis, 1997). Finally, normative isomorphism occurs as a result of an organization seeking to couch its purpose and methods within the broader institutional environment, generally via professionalization. For example: as COMPSTAT has come to be understood as an effective *crime fighting tool*, its adoption has spread throughout the United States (Willis, Mastrofski, & Weisburd, 2007).

For all forms of isomorphism, entities already possessing legitimacy or holding the power to define an organization's legitimacy are called sovereigns (Meyer & Rowan, 1977). Sovereigns include *inter alia* other organizations with the same or similar goals. Sovereigns may also include individuals (Katz, 2001). This may be the case when there is a particularly charismatic chief or sheriff, such as Bratton, Arpaio, or Bouza. Additionally, this may occur whenever an officer is seen as a stand-up cop who is able to effect change. This, for example, occurred in Katz's (2001) study where the commanding officer of a new gang unit was able to endow that unit with legitimacy. Any entity perceived as legitimate may be considered a sovereign insofar as its or his influence is unduly strong on the behavior of others or other institutional entities.

According to the institutional perspective, organizations vie for legitimacy in light of the demands of sovereigns in order to survive (DiMaggio & Powell, 1983). Failure to conform to institutional standards may result in the inability to acquire legitimacy, the loss of organizational relevance, and disbanding – without any regard for efficient productivity or the ties between practices and outcomes. Sovereigns exist because they are perceived to either have legitimacy, or because they have some resource-advantage over other units in the environment. Their legitimacy can come from tradition, a charismatic leader, or from the socio-legal environment of the society of which they are a part (Weber, 1964).

Suchman (1995) extends this line of thinking by pointing out that there are at least three ways that an organization can respond to isomorphic pressure. An organization may simply conform to the expectations of their institutional environment. Or, they may select into another institutional environment more in line with the direction they want to take. Finally, an organization may attempt to manipulate their environment to ensure their own legitimacy and survival. In all three scenarios, *legitimacy* and its acquisition remain part of a socially constructed reality (Meyer & Rowan, 1977). This reality may have little or nothing to do with the efficient production of output-oriented goals. What matters is that organizations carry the appearance of conforming to the expectations of their institutional environment. Insofar as an organization successfully maintains the appearance of doing what is expected of it from the institutional environment, it can maintain legitimacy. This also has the effect of making organizations within the same institutional environment more similar to one another than different (DiMaggio and Powell, 1983).

REFERENCES

Alpert G. P., & Moore, M. H (1993). Measuring police performance in the new paradigm of policing. In J. J. Dilulio (Ed.), *Performance Measures for the Criminal Justice System* (pp. 215–232). Washington, D.C.: U.S. Government Printing Office.

Angell, J. E (1971). Toward an alternative to the classic police organizational arrangements: A democratic model. *Criminology, 9,* 185–206.

Anselin, L (1988). *Spatial econometrics: Methods and models.* Dordrecht, The Netherlands: Kluwer.

Anselin, L (1995). Local indicators of spatial association - LISA. *Geographical Analysis, 27,* 93–115.

Anselin, L (2003a). *An introduction to spatial autocorrelation analysis with GeoDa.* Retrieved from http://geodacenter.asu.edu/pdf/geodaGA.pdf

Anselin, L (2003b). *An introduction to spatial regression analysis in R.* Retrieved from http://www.dpi.inpe.br/sil/11_06_CST_310/Referencias/AnaliseEspacial_metodos/anselin_R.pdf

Anselin, L (2007). *Spatial regression analysis in R: A workbook.* Retrieved from http://geodacenter.asu.edu/system/files/rex1.pdf

Beck, N, Gleditsch, K. S, & Beardsley, K (2006). Space is more than geography: Using spatial econometrics in the study of political economy. *International Studies Quarterly, 50,* 27–44.

Bittner, E (1970). *The functions of the police in modern society: A review of background factors, current practices, and possible role models.* Chevy Chase, MD: National Institute of Mental Health, Center for Studies of Crime and Delinquency.

Black, D (1976). *The behavior of law.* New York: Academic Press.

Blalock, H (1967). *Towards a theory of minority group relations.* New York: Capricorn Books.

Blau, P. M, & Meyer, M. W (1987). *Bureaucracy in modern society* (3rd ed.). New York: Random House.

Bratton, W. J, & Malinowski, S (2008). Police performance management in practice: Taking COMPSTAT to the next level. *Policing: A Journal of Policy and Practice, 2,* 259–265.

Brooks, L. W (2005). Police discretionary behavior: A study of style. In R. G. Duham & G. P. Alpert (Eds). *Critical issues in policing: Contemporary readings* (pp. 89–105). Long Grove, IL: Waveland Press.

Bureau of Justice Statistics (2008). Law Enforcement Agency Profile for Washington Metropolitan Police Dept, DC. Retrieved online from http://www.bjs.gov/dataonline/Search/Law/Local/RunLawLocalAgencyProfile.cfm

Bursik, R. J., Jr., & Grasmick, H. G (1993). Economic deprivation and neighborhood crime rates, 1960–1980. *Law & Society Review, 27,* 263–283.

Chambliss, W, & Seidman, R (1982). *Law, order, and power* (2nd ed.). Reading, MA: Addison-Wesley.

Chappell, A. T, MacDonald, J. M, & Manx, P. W (2006). The organizational determinants of police arrest decisions. *Crime and Delinquency, 52,* 287–306.

Cook, T. D, & Campbell, D. T (1979). *Quasi-experimentation: Design & analysis issues for field settings.* Boston, MA: Houghton Mifflin.

Cordner, G (1999). Elements of community policing. In L. Gaines & G. Cordner (Eds.) *Policing perspectives: An anthology* (pp. 137–149). Los Angeles: Roxbury Publishing Company.

Crank, J. P (2003). Institutional theory of police: A review of the state of the art. *Policing: An International Journal of Police Strategies & Managmenet, 26,* 186–207.

Crank, J. P, & Caldero, M. A (2002). *Police and ethics: The corruption of noble cause.* Cincinnati, OH: Anderson Publishing.

Crank, J. P, & Langworthy, R (1992). An institutional perspective of policing. *Journal of Criminal Law & Criminology, 83,* 338–363.

Data Catalog (2011). *Data Catalog.* Retrieved from http://data.dc.gov/

De Lint, W. (2000). Autonomy, regulation and the police beat. *Social and legal studies: An international journal, 9,* 55–83.

Dilulio, J. J (1993). Measuring performance when there is no bottom line. In J. J. Dilulio (Ed.), *Performance Measures for the Criminal Justice System* (pp. 147–160). Washington, D.C.: U.S. Government Printing Office.

DiMaggio, P. J, & Powell, W. W (1983). The iron cage revisited: Institutional isomorphism and collective rationality in organizational fields. *American Sociological Review, 48*(2), 147–160.

Eck, J (1994). *Drug markets and drug places: A case-control study of the spatial structure of illicit drug dealing.* Unpublished doctoral dissertation, University of Maryland, College Park.

Eck, J, & Maguire, E (2000). Have changes in policing reduced violent crime. In A. Blumstein & J. Wallman (Eds.) *The crime drop in America* (pp. 207–265). New York: Cambridge University Press.

Elkins, Z, Buzman, A. T & Simmons, B (2008). Competing for capital: The diffusion of bilateral investment treaties, 1960–2000. *University of Illinois Law review, 265,* 265–304.

Federal Bureau of Investigation. (2010). *Crime in America.* Retrieved from http://www.fbi.gov/about-us/cjis/ucr/ucr

Fox, J (2008). *Applied regression analysis and generalized linear models* (2nd Ed.). Thousand Oaks, CA: Sage.

Fyfe, J. J (1982). Blind justice: Police shootings in Memphis. *The Journal of Criminal Law and Criminology, 73,* 707–722.

Giblin, M. J (2006). Structural elaboration and institutional isomorphism: The case of crime analysis units. *Policing: An International Journal of Police Strategies & Managment, 29,* 643–664.

Giblin, M. J, & Burruss, G. W (2009). Developing a measurement model of institutional processes in policing. *Policing: An International Journal of Police Strategies & Management, 32,* 351–376.

Gleditsch, K. S, & Ward, M. D (2000). War and peace in space and time: The role of democratization. *International Studies Quarterly, 44,* 1–29.

Goldstein, H. H (1979). Improving policing: A problem-oriented approach. *Crime and Delinquency, 25,* 236–258.

Gorman, A (2010, July). Arizona's immigration law isn't the only one. *Los Angeles Times.* Retrieved from http://articles.latimes.com/2010/jul/16/nation/la-na-immigration-states-20100717

Greene, J. (2003). Community policing and organizational change. In W. G. Skogan (Ed.) *Community policing: Can it work?* (pp. 30–54). Belmont, CA: Wadsworth.

Greene, J.R., & Taylor, R.B. (1988). Community-based policing and foot patrol: issues of theory and evaluation. In J.R. Greene & S.D. Mastrofski (Eds.) *Community Policing: Rhetoric or Reality* (pp. 195–224). New York: Praeger.

Haining, R (2003). *Spatial data analysis: Theory and practice.* Cambridge, UK: Cambridge University Press.

Herbert, S. K (1997). *Policing space: Territoriality and the Los Angeles Police Department.* Minneapolis: University of Minnesota Press.

Herbert, S. K (2001). Policing the contemporary city: Fixing broken windows or shoring up neo-liberalism? *Theoretical Criminology, 5,* 445–466.

Herbert, S. K (2006). *Citizens, cops, and power: Recognizing the limits of community.* Chicago: University of Chicago Press.

Hobbes, T (2009). *Leviathon.* New York: Oxford University Press.

Hunt, J (1985). Police accounts of normal force. *Urban Life and Culture, 13,* 315–341.

Jackson, A. L, & Boyd, L. M (2005). Minority-threat hypothesis and the workload hypothesis: A community-level examination of lenient policing in high crime communities. *Criminal Justice Studies, 18,* 29–50.

Jackson, P (1989). *Minority group threat, crime, and policing.* New York: Praeger.

Jacob, H (1984). *Using published data: Errors and remedies.* Thousand Oaks, CA: Sage.

Jacobs, D, & O'Brien, R. M. (1998). The determinants of deadly force: A structural analysis of police violence. *The American Journal of Sociology, 103,* 837–862.

Jenness, V, & Grattet, R (2005). The law-in-between: The effects of organizational perviousness on the policing of hate crime. *Social Problems, 52,* 337–359.

Johnson, R. R, & Olschansky, E. L (2010). The ecological theory of police response: A state police agency test. *Criminal Justice Studies, 23,* 119–131.

Kalven, H, & Zeisel, H (1966). *The American jury.* Boston: Little, Brown.

Kane, R (2011). The ecology of unhealthy places: Violence, birthweight, and the importance of territoriality in structurally disadvantaged communities. *Social Science & Medicine.* DOI: 10.1016/j. socscimed.2011.08.035

Kane, R J. (2002). The social ecology of police misconduct. *Criminology, 40,* 867–896.

Kane, R J. (2003). Social control in the metropolis: A community-level examination of the minority group-threat hypothesis. *Justice Quarterly, 20,* 265 – 295.

Kane, R J. (2006). On the limits of social control: Structural deterrence and the policing of "suppressible" crimes. *Justice Quarterly, 23,* 186–213.

Kane, R J., & Cronin, S (2011). Maintaining order under the rule of law: Occupational templates and police use of force. *Journal of Criminal Justice, 34,* 163–177.

Kane, R, Gustafson, J. L, & Bruell, C (2011). Racial encroachment and the formal control of space: Minority group-threat and misdemeanor arrests in urban communities. *Justice Quarterly,* 10.1080/07418825.2011.636376.

Kappeler, V. E, Sluder, R. D, & Alpert, G. P (1998). *Forces of deviance: Understanding the dark side of policing* (2nd ed.). Prospect Heights, IL: Waveland Press.

Katz, C M. (2001). The establishment of a police gang unit: An examination of organizational and environmental factors. *Criminology, 39,* 37–73.

Katz, C M., Maguire, E R., & Roncek, D. W (2002). The creation of specialized police gang units: A macro-level analysis of contingency, social threat and resource dependency explanations. *Policing: An International Journal of Police Strategies and Management, 25,* 472–506.

Kennedy, P (2008). *A guide to econometrics* (6th ed.). Malden, ME: Blackwell Publishing.

King, W. R (2009). Organizational failure and the disbanding of local police agencies. *Crime & Delinquency,* retrieved online at http://cad.sagepub.com/content/early/2009/09/08/0011128709344675.full .pdf+html

King G., Koehane, R,m & Verba, S. (1996). *Designing Social Inquiry: Scientific Inference in Qualitative Research.* Princeton University Press.

Klinger, D. A (1997). Negotiating order in patrol work: an ecological theory of police response to deviance. *Criminology, 35,* 277–306.

Klockars, C. C. B. (1986). Street justice: Some micro-moral reservations: Comment on Sykes. *Justice Quarterly, 3,* 513–516.

Klofas, J. M, Hipple, N. K, & McGarrell, E. F (2010). *The new criminal justice: American communities and the changing world of crime control.* New York: Routledge.

Kraska, P. B, & Cubellis, L. J (1997). Militarizing Mayberry and beyond: Making sense of American paramilitary policing. *Justice Quarterly, 14,* 607–629.

Kraska, P. B, & Kappeler, V. E (1997). Militarizing American police: The rise and normalization of paramilitary units. *Social Problems, 44,* 1–18.

Kubrin, C. E (2003). Structural covariates of homicide rates: Does type of homicide matter? *Journal of Research in Crime and Delinquency, 40,* 139–170.

Kuhn, T. (1962). *The Structure of Scientific Revolutions.* University of Chicago Press.

Land, K. C, & Deane G. (1992). On the large–sample estimation of regression models with spatial effects terms: A two–stage least squares approach. *Sociological Methodology, 22,* 221–248.

Land, K. C, McCal, P. L, & Cohen, L. E (1990). Structural covariates of homicide rates: Are there any invariances across time and social space. *American Journal of Sociology, 95,* 922–63.

Langworthy, R H. (1986). *The structure of police organizations.* New York: Praeger.

Leicht, K. T, & Jenkins, J. C (1998). Political resources and direct state intervention: The adoption of public venture capital programs in the American States, 1974–1990. *Social Forces, 76,* 1323–1345.

Levitt, S (2004). Understanding why crime fell in the 1990s: Four factors that explain the decline and six that do not. *Journal of Economic Perspectives, 18,* 163–190.

Lipsky, M (1980). *Street-level bureaucracy: Dilemmas of the individual in public services.* New York: Russell Sage Foundation.

Locke, J (1993). *Two treatises of government.* North Clarendon, VT: Tuttle Publishing

Long, J. S (1997). *Regression models for categorical and limited dependent variables.* Thousand Oaks, CA: Sage.

Lynch, J. P, & Addington, L. A (2007). *Understanding crime statistics: Revisiting the divergence of the NCVS and UCR.* New York: Cambridge University Press.

Lynch, J. P, Sabol, W. J, Planty, M, & Shelly, M (2002). *Crime, coercion and community: The effects of arrest and incarceration policies on informal social control in neighborhoods.* Washington, D.C.: National Criminal Justice Reference Service.

Maguire, ER. (1997). Structural change in large municipal police organizations during the community policing era. *Justice Quarterly, 14,* 547–576

Manning, P. K (1977). *Police work: The social organization of policing.* Cambridge, Mass: MIT Press.

Manning, P. K (1978). The police: Mandate, strategies, and appearances. In P. K. Manning, & J. Van Maanen (Eds.), *Policing: A view from the streets* (pp. 7–31). Santa Monica, CA: Goodyear Publishing Company.

Manning, P. K, & Van Maanen, J (1978). *Policing: A view from the street.* Santa Monica, CA: Goodyear Pub. Co.

Meehan, A. J & Ponder, M. C (2002). Race and place: The ecology of racial profiling African American motorists. *Justice Quarterly, 19,* 399–430.

Merton, R. K (1957). *Social theory and social structure.* Glencoe, Ill: Free Press.

Messner, S. F, and Anselin, L (2004). Spatial analyses of homicide with areal data. In Goodchild, M. and Janelle, D., editors, *Spatially Integrated Social Science* (pp. 127–144). Oxford University Press, New York, NY.

Metropolitan Police Department (2009). *Annual Report 2008.* Washington, D.C.: Metropolitan Police Department.

Metropolitan Police of the District of Columbia (n.d.). *Brief History of the MPDC.* Retrieved from http://mpdc.dc.gov/mpdc/cwp/view,a,1230,q,540333,mpdcNav_GID,1529,mpdcNav,%7C31458%7C.asp

Meyer, J. W, & Rowan, B (1977). Institutional organizations: Formal structure as myth and ceremony. *American Journal of Sociology, 83,* 340–363.

Meyer, J. W, & Scott, W. R (1992). *Organizational environments: Ritual and rationality.* Newbury Park, CA: Sage Publications.

Morenoff, J. D, & Sampson. R. J. (1997). Violent crime and the spatial dynamics of neighborhood transition: Chicago, 1970–1990. *Social Forces, 76,* 31–64.

Nielsen, A. L, Hill, T. D, French, M. T, Monique, N. H (2009). Racial/ethnic composition, social disorganization, and offsite alcohol availability in San Diego County, California. *Social Science Research, 39,* 165–175.

Ord, J. K, & Getis, A (1995). Local spatial autocorrelation statistics: Distributional issues and an application. *Geographical Analysis, 27,* 286–306.

Park, R. E, & Burgess, E. W (1967). *The city: Suggestions for investigation of human behavior in the urban environment.* Chicago: University of Chicago Press.

Parsons, T (1963). *Structure and process in modern societies.* New York: Free Press of Glencoe.

Pelfrey, W. V, Jr. (2005). Geographic information systems: Applications for police. In R. G. Dunham & G. P. Alpert (Eds.) *Critical issues in policing: Contemporary readings* (5th ed.) (pp. 217–228). Long Grove, IL: Waveland.

Phillips, S. W, & Sobol, J. J (2010). Police attitudes about the use of unnecessary force: An ecological examination. *Journal of Police and Criminal Psychology,* accessed online http://www.springerlink.com/content/t51m770h1w1u1472/fulltext.pdf

Piliavin, I, & Briar, S (1964). Police encounters with juveniles. *American Journal of Sociology, 70,* 206–214.

Potter, G. W, Kappeler, V. E (2006). *Constructing crime: Perspectives on making news and social problems* (2nd ed.). Long Grove, IL: Waveland Press.

Raganella, A. J, & White, M.D. (2004). Race, gender, and motivation for becoming a police officer: Implications for building a representative police department. *Journal of Criminal Justice, 32,* 501–513.

Reisig, M. D (2010). Community and problem-oriented policing. *Crime and Justice, 39,* 1–53.

Reiss, A. J, & Bordua, D. J (1967). Environment and organization: A perspective on the police. In D. J. Bordua (Ed.), *The police: Six sociological essays* (pp. 25–55). New York: John Wiley and Sons.

Reiss, A. J, Jr. (1971). *The police and the public.* New York: Yale University Press.

Reuss-Ianni, E (1982). *Two cultures of policing: Street cops and management cops.* New Brunswick, NJ: Transaction Publishers.

Rey, S. J (2004). *Geography 585: Quantitative Methods in Geographic Research.* San Diego, CA: Department of Geography.

Roberg, R. R, Novak, K. J, & Cordner, G W. (2005). *Police & society* (3rd ed.). Los Angeles: Roxbury.

Rosenfeld, R, Fornango, R, & Baumer, E (2005). Did ceasefire, COMPSTAT, and exile reduce homicide? *Criminology & Public Policy, 4,* 419–449.

Rosenfeld, R, Fornango, R, & Rengifo, A. F (2007). The impact of order-maintenance policing on New York City homicide and robbery rates. *Criminology, 45,* 355–384.

Rousseau, J (1992). *The social contract and the discourses.* New York: Random House

Rubinstein, J (1973). *City police.* New York: Farrar, Straus and Giroux.

Sack, R. D (1986). *Human territoriality: Its theory and history.* New York: Cambridge University Press.

Sampson, R. J (1997). Collective regulation of adolescent misbehavior: Validation results from eighty Chicago neighborhoods. *Journal of Adolescent Research 12,* 227–244.

Sampson R. J., & Groves W Byron. (1989). Community structure and crime: Testing social-disorganization theory. *American Journal of Sociology, 94,* 774–802.

Sampson, R. J, Raudenbush, S. W, & Earls, F (1997). Neighborhoods and violent crime: A multilevel study of collective efficacy. *Science, 277,* 918–924.

Sherman, L. W (1986). Policing communities: What works? In A. J. Reiss Jr., & M. Tonry (Eds.), *Communities and crime* (pp. 343–386). Chicago: University of Chicago Press.

Sherman, L. W, & Weisburd, D (1995). General deterrent effects of police patrol in crime "hot spots": A randomized, controlled trial. *Justice Quarterly, 12,* 625–648.

Sherman, L. W, Schmidt, J. D, & Rogan, D. P (1992). *Policing domestic violence: Experiments and dilemmas.* Detroit: The Free Press.

Skolnick, J. H (1966). *Justice without trial: Law enforcement in democratic society.* New York: John Wiley & Sons, Inc.

Skolnick, J. H, & Fyfe, J. J (1993). *Above the law: Police and the excessive use of force.* New York: Free Press.

Slovak, J. S (1987). Police organization and policing environment: Case study of a disjuncture. *Sociological Focus, 20,* 77–94.

Smith, D. A (1981). Street-level justice: Situational determinants of police arrest decisions. *Social Problems,* 167–177.

Smith, D. A (1986). The neighborhood context of police behavior. *Crime and Justice, 8,* 313–341.

Sobol, J. J (2010). The social ecology of police attitudes. *Policing, 33,* 253–269.

Spohn, C, & Cederblom, J (1991). Race and disparities in sentencing: A test of the liberation hypothesis. *Justice Quarterly, 8,* 305–327.

Strecher, V. G (1991). Histories and futures of policing: Readings and misreadings of a pivotal present. *Police Forum, 1,* 1–9.

Stroshine, M. S (2005). Information technology innovations in policing. In R. G. Dunham & G. P. Alpert (Eds.) *Critical issues in policing: Contemporary readings* (5th ed.) (pp. 172–183). Long Grove, IL: Waveland.

Suchman, M. C (1995). Managing legitimacy: Strategic and institutional approaches. *Academy of Management Review, 20,* 571–610.

Sykes, G. W (1986). Street justice: A moral defense of order maintenance policing. *Justice Quarterly, 3,* 497–512.

Taylor, R. B (1988). *Human territorial functioning: An empirical, evolutionary perspective on individual and small group territorial cognitions, behaviors, and consequences.* New York: Cambridge University Press.

Terrill, W, & Reisig, M. D (2003). Neighborhood context and police use of force. *Journal of Research in Crime and Delinquency, 40*, 291–321.

Thurman, Q, Zhao, J, & Giacomazzi, A. L (2001). *Community policing in a community era.* Los Angeles: Roxbury.

Tobler, W.R. (1970). A computer movie simulating urban growth in the Detroit region. *Economic Geography 46*, 234–240

Trojanowicz, R. C, & Bucqueroux, B (1990). *Community Policing: A Contemporary Perspective.* Cincinnati, OH: Anderson.

Tyler, T (2006). *Why people obey the law.* Princeton, NJ: Princeton University Press.

U. S. Census Bureau (2010). *District of Columbia.* Accessed online http://quickfacts.census.gov/qfd/states/11000.html.

Uchida, C. G (2005). The development of the American police: An historical overview. In R. G. Dunham, & G. P. Alpert (Eds.), *Critical issues in policing: Contemporary readings* (5th ed., pp. 20–40). Long Grove, IL: Waveland Press.

Van Maanen, J (1974). Working the street: A developmental view of police behavior. In H. Jacob (Ed.), *The potential for reform of criminal justice* (pp. 83–130). Beverly Hills, CA: Sage.

Walker, S, & Katz, C (2007). *The police in America: An introduction* (6th ed.). New York: McGraw Hill.

Walker, S (1993). *Taming the system: The control of discretion in criminal justice, 1950–1990.* New York: Oxford University Press.

Walker, S (1998). *Popular justice: A history of American criminal justice* (2nd ed.). New York: Oxford University Press.

Walker, S (2005). *The new world of police accountability.* Thousand Oaks, CA: Sage.

Walker, S (2012). *Sense and non-sense about crime, drugs, and communities.* Belmont, CA: Wadsworth/Cengage.

Walsh, W. F (2001). Compstat: An analysis of an emerging police managerial paradigm. *Policing, 24*, 347–362.

Wang, F (2006). *Quantitative methods and applications of GIS.* Boca Raton, FL: Taylor & Francis Goup.

Ward, M. D, & Gleditsch, K. S (2008). *Spatial regression models.* Thousand Oaks, CA: Sage.

Weber, M (1964). *The theory of social and economic organization.* New York: Free Press.

Weber, M. (2004). *The vocation lectures.* Indianapolis: Hackett Pub.

Weisburd, D, Mastrofski, S, McNally, AM, Greenspan, R, & Willis, J (2003). Reforming to preserve: COMPSTAT and strategic problem solving in American policing. *Criminology & Public Policy, 2*, 421–456.

White, M. D (2007). *Current issues and controversies in policing.* Boston: Pearson Allyn and Bacon.

White, M. D, Cooper, J. A, Saunders, J, & Raganella, A. J (2010). Motivations for becoming a police officer: Re-assessing officer attitudes and job satisfaction after six years on the street. *Journal of Criminal Justice, 38*, 520–530.

Whyte, W. F (1943). *Street corner society; the social structure of an Italian slum.* Chicago: Ill., University of Chicago Press.

Willis, J J., Mastrofski, S D., & Weisburd, D (2007). Making sense of COMPSTAT: A theory-based analysis of organizational change in three police departments. *Law & Society Review, 41*, 147–188.

Wilson, J. Q (1968). *Varieties of police behavior: The management of law and order in eight communities.* Cambridge, MA: Harvard University Press.

Wilson, J. Q, & Kelling, G. L (1982). Broken windows. *Atlantic Monthly, 249*(3), 29.

Wilson, W. J. (1987). *The truly disadvantaged: The inner city, the underclass, and public policy.* Chicago: University of Chicago Press.

Worrall, J. L, & Kovandzic, T. V (2007). COPS grants and crime revisited. *Criminology, 45*, 157–190.

Zhao, J, & Hassell, K. D (2005). Policing styles and organizational priorities: Retesting Wilson's theory of local political culture. *Police Quarterly, 8*, 411–430.

Zhao, J, & Thurman, QC (1997). Community policing in the US: where are we now? *Crime and Delinquency, 43*, 345–57.

Zhao, J, He, N, & Lovrich, N (2003). Community policing: Is it changing the basic functions of policing in the 1990s? A national follow-up study. *Justice Quarterly, 20,* 697–724.

Zhao, J, Lovrich, N P., & Robinson, T. H (2001). Community policing: Is it changing the basic functions of policing? Findings from a longitudinal study of 200+ municipal police agencies. *Journal of Criminal Justice, 29,* 365–377.

Zhao, J, Scheider, M. C, & Thurman, Q (2002). Funding community policing to reduce crime: Have COPS grants made a difference? *Criminology & Public Policy, 2,* 7–32.   *1-22*

Zhao, J, Thurman, Q, & Lovrich, N (1997). Community policing in the U.S.: Where are we now? *Crime and delinquency, 43,* 345–357.

Zimring, F. E (2007). *The great American crime decline.* New York: Oxford University Press.

Zimring, F. E, & Hawkins, G (1997). *Crime is not the problem: Lethal violence in America.* New York: Oxford University Press.

PROFESSIONALISM AND ACCOUNTABILITY

Toward a New Professionalism in Policing

*CHRISTOPHER STONE, & JEREMY TRAVIS, ***

INTRODUCTION

Across the United States, police organizations are striving for a new professionalism. Their leaders are committing themselves to stricter *accountability* for both their effectiveness and their conduct while they seek to increase their *legitimacy* in the eyes of those they police and to encourage continuous *innovation* in police practices. The traffic in these ideas, policies and practices is now so vigorous across the nation that it suggests a fourth element of this new professionalism: its *national coherence*. These four principles—accountability, legitimacy, innovation and coherence—are not new in themselves, but together they provide an account of developments in policing during the last 20 years that distinguishes the policing of the present era from that of 30, 50 or 100 years ago.

Many U.S. police organizations have realized important aspects of the new professionalism and many more have adopted its underlying values. The ambitions for accountability, legitimacy and innovation unite police

* This article was previously published as part of a series of papers titled New Perspectives in Policing by the National Institute of Justice (NIJ) and Harvard Kennedy School: Program in Criminal Justice Policy and Management, March 2011. © 2014 by authors, reprinted here by permission. Correspondence concerning this article should be addressed to ebalazon@jjay.cuny.edu.

organizations in disparate contexts: urban, suburban and rural, municipal, county, state and federal. With approximately 20,000 public police organizations in the United States, national coherence in American policing would be a signal achievement.[1] We do not see this new professionalism fully realized in any single department. We know how difficult it can be to narrow the gap between these ambitions and many deeply ingrained routines and practices. Much policing in the United States remains, in these terms, unprofessional, but professional ambition is itself a powerful force and it is at work almost everywhere.

We hear similar ambitions for accountability, legitimacy, innovation and coherence in other countries, from the state police organizations in Brazil and India to the South African Police Service, the French Gendarmerie and the Chilean Carabineros. A global police culture with these same four elements increasingly defines the ambitions of police leaders in most countries. In this paper, however, we focus on the trend in the United States.

To describe and illustrate the elements of this new professionalism, we draw on our own experiences working in and studying police organizations and on the deliberations of two Executive Sessions on Policing, both convened by the National Institute of Justice and Harvard University's Kennedy School of Government: the first from 1985 to 1992 and the second commencing in 2008 and continuing today.

WHY A NEW PROFESSIONALISM?

We offer the "New Professionalism" as a conceptual framework that can help chiefs, frontline police officers and members of the public alike understand and shape the work of police departments today and in the years ahead. Even as it remains a work in progress, the New Professionalism can help police chiefs and commissioners keep their organizations focused on why they are doing what they do, what doing it better might look like, and how they can prioritize the many competing demands for their time and resources. On the front lines, the New Professionalism can help police officers work together effectively, connect their daily work to the larger project of building a better society, and share their successes and frustrations with the communities they serve. In communities everywhere, the New Professionalism can help citizens understand individual police actions as part of larger strategies, and assess the demands

---

1   According to the Bureau of Justice Statistics, as of September 2004, 17,876 state and local law enforcement agencies with the equivalent of at least one full-time officer were operating in the United States. Reaves, B. (2007). *Census of Law Enforcement Agencies, 2004.* Washington, D.C.: U.S. Department of Justice, Office of Justice Programs, Bureau of Justice Statistics, 1.

and requests that police make for more public money, more legal authority and more public engagement in keeping communities safe. From all of these vantage points, the New Professionalism helps all of us see what is happening in policing, how we got here and where we are going.

Each of the four elements of the New Professionalism—accountability, legitimacy, innovation and national coherence—has something to offer police and the communities in which they work.

By a commitment to accountability we mean an acceptance of an obligation to account for police actions not only up the chain of command within police departments but also to civilian review boards, city councils and county commissioners, state legislatures, inspectors general, government auditors and courts. The obligation extends beyond these government entities to citizens directly: to journalists and editorial boards, resident associations, chambers of commerce—the whole range of community-based organizations.

By a commitment to legitimacy we mean a determination to police with the consent, cooperation and support of the people and communities being policed. Police receive their authority from the state and the law, but they also earn it from the public in each and every interaction. Although it is important to derive legitimacy from every part of the public, those citizens and groups most disaffected by past harms or present conditions have the greatest claims to attention on this score because their trust and confidence in the police is often weakest. Fortunately, research we discuss later in this paper suggests that police departments can strengthen their legitimacy among people of color in the United States and among young people of all races and ethnicities without compromising their effectiveness.[2] Indeed, effectiveness and legitimacy can be advanced together.

By a commitment to innovation we mean active investment of personnel and resources both in adapting policies and practices proven effective in other departments and in experimenting with new ideas in cooperation with a department's local partners. Empirical evidence is important here. Departments with a commitment to innovation look for evidence showing that practices developed elsewhere work, just as they embrace evaluation of the yet unproven practices they are testing.

By national coherence we mean that the departments exemplifying the New Professionalism are participating in national conversations about professional policing. They are training their officers, supervisors and leaders in practices and theories applicable in jurisdictions across the country. Not long ago, it was common to hear police officers insist that they could police effectively in their city, county or state only if they had come up through the ranks there: good policing was inherently parochial. Such

---

2   See the discussion at note 33, *infra*, and the sources referenced therein.

a belief belies a true professionalism. Inherent in the idea of the New Professionalism in policing is that police officers, supervisors and executives share a set of skills and follow a common set of protocols that have been accepted by the profession because they have been proven to be effective or legally required. That is not to say that local knowledge and understanding are unimportant—they are vital. But they are not everything. There is vital knowledge, understanding and practice common to good policing everywhere, and this common skill set defines police professionalism.

There are many definitions of professionalism and some debate about what it means for policing to be a profession. We take these up at the end of this paper, after putting the New Professionalism in historical context. For now, suffice it to say that for any profession to be worthy of that name, its members must not only develop transportable skills but also commit themselves both to a set of ethical precepts and to a discipline of continuous learning. A look back in history reveals how this meaning of "professional" contrasts with another use of the word employed in the early debates over community policing. The New Professionalism embraces and extends the best of community policing, whereas the "old professionalism" said to characterize policing in the 1960s and 1970s was seen as antithetical to community policing.

COMMUNITY POLICING AND THE NEW PROFESSIONALISM

Twenty-five years ago, when the elements of the New Professionalism began to emerge in urban American police departments, "community policing" was the organizing framework advanced to describe the new approach and new priorities. To most Americans who heard of the idea, community policing summoned up images of police walking the beat, riding on bicycles, or talking to groups of senior citizens and to young children in classrooms. These images adorn countless posters and brochures produced by individual police departments to explain community policing to local residents. They picture community policing as a specialized program: a few carefully selected officers taking pains to interact with "good" citizens while the rest of the police department does something else.

Inside police departments, however, and at the first Executive Session on Policing, community policing was being described as far more than the next new program. It was promoted as the organizing framework around which police departments were going to change everything they did. Community policing might look like a specialized program when a police department first adopts it, but that is "Phase One," as

Lee Brown, who led police departments in Atlanta, Houston and New York City before becoming mayor of Houston, wrote in a 1989 paper for the first Executive Session. Brown explained that "Phase Two":

> ... involves more sweeping and more comprehensive changes. ... It is the department's *style* that is being revamped. ... Although it is an operating style, community policing also is a *philosophy* of policing ... (emphasis in original).[3]

Brown went on to explain how, in Phase Two, community policing requires changes to every part of policing, including its supervision and management, training, investigations, performance evaluation, accountability and even its values. True community policing, Brown wrote, requires a focus on results rather than process; it forces decentralization, power sharing with community residents, the redesign of police beats, and giving a lower priority to calls for service. Malcolm Sparrow, a former Detective Chief Inspector in the English police service on the faculty of the Harvard Kennedy School, made the same point in even more dramatic language:

> Implementing community policing is not a simple policy change that can be effected by issuing a directive through the normal channels. It is not a mere restructuring of the force to provide the same service more efficiently. Nor is it a cosmetic decoration designed to impress the public and promote greater cooperation.
>
> For the police it is an entirely different way of life. It is a new way for police officers to see themselves and to understand their role in society. The task facing the police chief is nothing less than to change the fundamental culture of the organization.[4]

In this grand vision, the advent of community policing marked an epochal shift, replacing an earlier organizing framework: professional crime-fighting. And this, finally,

---

3   Brown, L. (1989, September). Community Policing: A Practical Guide for Police Officials. *Perspectives on Policing, no. 12.* Washington, D.C.; Cambridge, Mass.: U.S. Department of Justice, Office of Justice Programs, National Institute of Justice; & Harvard University, John F. Kennedy School of Government, Program in Criminal Justice Policy and Management. Hereinafter, publications in this series are identified by their number in the series, Perspectives on Policing. The entire set is available at: www.hks.harvard.edu/criminaljustice/executive_sessions/policing.htm.

4   Sparrow, M. (1988, November). Implementing Community Policing. *Perspectives on Policing, no. 9.* Washington, D.C.; Cambridge, Mass.: U.S. Department of Justice, Office of Justice Programs, National Institute of Justice; & Harvard University, John F. Kennedy School of Government, Program in Criminal Justice Policy and Management, 2.

is why the field today needs a "new" professionalism, for the original professionalism was—as an organizing framework at least—discarded in favor of community policing.

In their promotion of community policing and a focus on problem solving, the proponents of reform roundly criticized what they saw as the professional crime-fighting model, or simply the "professional model" of policing.[5] They saw the professional model as hidebound: too hierarchical in its management, too narrow in its response to crime and too much at odds with what police did. Led during the first Executive Session on Policing by the scholarship of three academics—Professors Mark Moore of the Harvard Kennedy School, George Kelling of Northeastern University and Robert Trojanowicz of Michigan State University—the champions of community policing contrasted their principles and methods to this "traditional," "classical," "reform" or, most commonly, "professional" style of policing.[6]

The criticisms made by Moore, Kelling and Trojanowicz of the then-dominant form of policing in U.S. cities were right on the mark, but by labeling this dominant form "professional" crime-fighting, they needlessly tarnished the concept of professionalism itself.[7] Looking back on these debates, it is easy to see that this so-called professional model of policing was at best a quasi-professionalism and at worst an entirely false professionalism. At the time, however, the critique from Moore, Kelling, Trojanowicz and others succeeded in giving professional policing a bad name, so much so that reformers in countries where policing was still entirely a matter of political

---

5   See, for example, Kelling, G.; &Moore, M. (1988, November). The Evolving Strategy of Policing. *Perspectives on Policing, no. 4.* Washington, D.C.; Cambridge, Mass.: U.S. Department of Justice, Office of Justice Programs, National Institute of Justice; & Harvard University, John F. Kennedy School of Government, Program in Criminal Justice Policy and Management, 6 (where the authors write specifically of "the professional model").

6   The first Executive Session on Policing convened 31 officials and scholars, but its 16 published papers were authored by only 13 participants. Mark Moore and George Kelling were authors or co-authors on six papers each; Robert Trojanowicz was co-author on three; Malcolm Sparrow, Robert Wasserman and Hubert Williams were authors or co-authors on two each. No one else appeared on more than one. Of the first six papers issued, all were authored or coauthored by Moore, Kelling and Trojanowicz, with no other co-authors; and through the end of 1992, the Executive Session published only three papers that were not authored or co-authored by Moore, Kelling or Trojanowicz. Other scholars played at least as great a role in the formulation of community policing during these years, including Herman Goldstein (who was a member of the first Executive Session) and David Bayley (who is a member of the second Executive Session), but neither wrote for the first Executive Session on Policing.

7   More recently, the Committee to Review Research on Police Policy and Practices convened by the National Research Council of the National Academies recounted the story in the same way, although choosing in its own analysis to refer to the professional model of policing as the "standard" model. See National Research Council, *Fairness and Effectiveness in Policing: The Evidence,* Committee to Review Research on Police Policy and Practices, Wesley Skogan and Kathleen Frydl, editors, Committee on Law and Justice, Division of Behavioral and Social Sciences and Education (Washington, D.C.: The National Academies Press, 2004), p. 85. (Community policing "is characterized as something that transforms the 'professional' model of policing, dominant since the end of World War II. ...")

patronage and a blunt instrument of political power began to ask if they could skip the professional stage of police evolution and proceed directly to community policing.[8]

Community policing was an important improvement on the style of policing it challenged in American cities, but it is time to correct two distortions inherited from that earlier debate. First, what community policing challenged in the 1980s was not a truly professional model of policing, but rather a technocratic, rigid, often cynical model of policing. Moreover, it reinforced pernicious biases deeply entrenched in the wider society. Both good and bad police work was performed in that mode, but it was hardly professional. Second, community policing was only part of the new model of policing emerging in the 1980s, with contemporaneous innovations occurring in technology, investigation and the disruption of organized crime. By reinterpreting the rise of community policing as part of a larger shift to a New Professionalism, we hope simultaneously to rescue the idea of professional policing from its frequently distorted form in the mid-20th century and to show how the elements of this New Professionalism might anchor a safer and more just society in the decades ahead.

THE SO-CALLED PROFESSIONALISM OF MID-20TH-CENTURY POLICING

Proponents of community policing in the 1980s labeled its mid-century predecessor as "professional crime-fighting," but what sort of policing were they describing? What were the characteristics of the mid-century policing they hoped to replace?

First, in its relationship to citizens, the previous mode of policing was deliberately removed from communities, insisting that police understood better than local residents how their communities should be policed. As George Kelling described it in the first paper in the Perspectives on Policing series, the police had long been seen as "a community's *professional* defense against crime and disorder: Citizens should leave control of crime and maintenance of order to police (emphasis added)."[9] Or, as a separate paper explained, "The proper role of citizens in crime control was to be relatively passive recipients of professional crime control services."[10] In contrast,

---

8   Police officials in Kenya, eager to implement a version of community policing, put this question to one of the authors of this paper in 2000, as did a leader in the military police of Rio de Janeiro in 2001.

9   Kelling, G. (1988, June). Police and Communities: The Quiet Revolution. *Perspectives on Policing, no. 1.* Washington, D.C.; Cambridge, Mass.: U.S. Department of Justice, Office of Justice Programs, National Institute of Justice; & Harvard University, John F. Kennedy School of Government, Program in Criminal Justice Policy and Management, 2–3.

10   Kelling, G., & Moore, M. The Evolving Strategy of Policing (note 5).

explained Kelling, under community policing, "the police are to stimulate and buttress a community's ability to produce attractive neighborhoods and protect them against predators."[11]

Second, in terms of tactics, the previous mode of policing relied on a limited set of routine activities. As another 1988 paper in the series explained, "Professional crime-fighting now relies predominantly on three tactics: (1) motorized patrol; (2) rapid response to calls for service; and (3) retrospective investigation of crimes."[12]

Third, the management structure of professional crime-fighting was centralized and top-down. Its management technique was command and control, aiming principally to keep police officers in line and out of trouble. As one paper described it, "the more traditional perspective of professional crime-fighting policing … emphasizes the maintenance of internal organizational controls."[13] And as another paper explained in more detail:

> In many respects, police organizations have typified the classical command-and-control organization that emphasized top-level decisionmaking: flow of orders from top-level executives down to line personnel, flow of information up from line personnel to executives, layers of dense supervision, unity of command, elaborate rules and regulations, elimination of discretion, and simplification of work tasks.[14]

This mid-century model of policing can be criticized as technocratic and rigid, but it was not all bad. The elevation of technical policing skills, the introduction of hiring standards, and the stricter supervision and discipline of police officers improved some police services and helped some police chiefs put distance between themselves and political ward bosses, corrupt mayors and local elites demanding special attention. Prioritizing 911 calls at least allocated police services to anyone with access to a telephone rather than only to those with political connections or in favor with the local

---

11 Kelling, G. Police and Communities: The Quiet Revolution (note 9), 2–3.

12 Moore, M., Trojanowicz, R., & Kelling, G. (1988, June). Crime and Policing, *Perspectives on Policing, no. 2.* Washington, D.C.; Cambridge, Mass.: U.S. Department of Justice, Office of Justice Programs, National Institute of Justice; & Harvard University, John F. Kennedy School of Government, Program in Criminal Justice Policy and Management.

13 Wasserman, R. & Moore, M. (1988, November). Values in Policing, *Perspectives on Policing, no. 8.* Washington, D.C.; Cambridge, Mass.: U.S. Department of Justice, Office of Justice Programs, National Institute of Justice; & Harvard University, John F. Kennedy School of Government, Program in Criminal Justice Policy and Management, 5.

14 Kelling, G.; Wasserman, R.; & Williams, H. (1988, November). Police Accountability and Community Policing, *Perspectives on Policing, no. 7.* Washington, D.C.; Cambridge, Mass.: U.S. Department of Justice, Office of Justice Programs, National Institute of Justice; & Harvard University, John F. Kennedy School of Government, Program in Criminal Justice Policy and Management, 2.

police. But these were incremental gains, and policing remained (and remains) closely tied to politics.[15]

Moreover, each of the three elements of so-called professional policing described here—its claim to technical expertise, its tactics and its management strategy—failed to produce adequate public safety. Rising crime and disorder in the 1960s and 1970s belied the technical expertise of the police, as did the repressive response to the civil rights and peace movements and the persistence of brutality on the street and during interrogations. A growing body of research evidence demonstrated the ineffectiveness of random patrol, the irrelevance of shortened response times to the vast majority of calls for service, and the inability of retrospective investigation to solve most crimes. As for command-and-control management, the work of frontline police officers, operating outside of line-of-sight supervision, proved ill-suited to this form of supervision.

Ironically, the command-and-control management techniques identified with "professional crime-fighting" were the antithesis of the practices generally used to manage professionals. Instead of depending on continuous training, ethical standards and professional pride to guide behavior, command-and-control structures treated frontline police officers like soldiers or factory workers, yet most of the time the job of policing looked nothing like soldiering or assembly-line production.

Even then, the advocates for community policing recognized that mid-century policing was hardly professional in its treatment of the officers on the street. They minced no words here, explaining that by the 1960s and 1970s, line officers were still

> managed in ways that were antithetical to professionalization ... patrol officers continued to have low status; their work was treated as if it were routinized and standardized; and petty rules governed issues such as hair length and off-duty behavior. ... the classical theory [of command-and-control management] ... denies too much of the real nature of police work, promulgates unsustainable myths about the nature and quality of police supervision, and creates

---

15 Daryl Gates, then-Police Chief in Los Angeles, explained more fully: "Chiefs today are unfortunately deeply tied to politics and politicians. It's a very sad commentary on local policing. How do chiefs refer to their mayor? 'My mayor.' 'Is your mayor going to win this election?' ... And if they do not, that is the last time we see that commissioner or chief. Gone, because of political whim, not his or her performance as a chief. So, if you do not think politics are tied into policing today, you are being very, very foolish." See Hartmann, F.; ed. (1988, November). Debating the Evolution of American Policing, *Perspectives on Policing, no. 5.* Washington, D.C.; Cambridge, Mass.: U.S. Department of Justice, Office of Justice Programs, National Institute of Justice; & Harvard University, John F. Kennedy School of Government, Program in Criminal Justice Policy and Management, 6.

too much cynicism in officers attempting to do creative problem solving. Its assumptions about workers are simply wrong.[16]

Of all the problems created by terming mid-century policing "professional," none was more glaring than its dissonance with the experience of African-Americans and other racial and ethnic minorities. Former New York City Police Commissioner Patrick Murphy and former Newark (NJ) Police Director Hubert Williams coauthored a 1990 essay in which they argued that for black Americans, the so-called professional model was infused with the racism that had biased policing since the organization of the police during slavery:

> The fact that the legal order not only countenanced but sustained slavery, segregation, and discrimination for most of our Nation's history—and the fact that the police were bound to uphold that order—set a pattern for police behavior and attitudes toward minority communities that has persisted until the present day. That pattern includes the idea that minorities have fewer civil rights, that the task of the police is to keep them under control, and that the police have little responsibility for protecting them from crime within their communities.[17]

Indeed, as Williams and Murphy pointed out, blacks were largely excluded from urban police departments in the same years that "professional" policing was taking hold, and those African-Americans who were hired as police officers were often given lesser powers than white officers. In New Orleans, the police department included 177 black officers in 1870, but this number fell to 27 by 1880, further fell to five by 1900, and to zero by 1910. New Orleans did not hire another black officer until 1950. Even by 1961, a third of U.S. police departments surveyed still limited the authority of black police officers to make felony arrests. By the end of that decade, anger at racial injustice had fueled riots in more than a dozen cities, and a Presidential commission had concluded that many of these riots, as Williams and Murphy underscored, "had

16 Kelling, G. & Moore, M. The Evolving Strategy of Policing (note 5), 9, 14.
17 Williams, H. & Murphy, P. (1990, January). The Evolving Strategy of Policing: A Minority View, *Perspectives on Policing, no. 13*. Washington, D.C., and Cambridge, Mass.: U.S. Department of Justice, Office of Justice Programs, National Institute of Justice, and Harvard University, John F. Kennedy School of Government, Program in Criminal Justice Policy and Management, 2. The significance of this particular publication is especially great as Murphy had served as president of the Police Foundation from 1973 to 1985, succeeded by Hubert Williams, who continues in that position today.

been precipitated by police actions, often cases of insensitivity, sometimes incidents of outright brutality."[18]

Today it is clear that the rise of community policing did not mark the end of professional policing, but rather its beginning. Little about policing in the mid-20th century was "professional." Its expertise was flawed, its techniques crude, its management techniques more military than professional, and it reinforced rather than challenged the racism of the wider society. Community policing, with its emphases on quality of service, decentralization of authority and community partnership, was more professional than the style of policing it attempted to displace.

The phrase "community policing" does not, however, adequately describe what replaced mid-century law enforcement and what continues to propel the most promising developments in policing today. What began to emerge in the 1980s was a new, truer, more robust professionalism of which community policing was and remains a part. The proponents of the term "community policing" were, in the 1980s, already aware of this problem with their language. They knew their "community policing" framework was merely a partial replacement for mid-century policing. Yet they resisted the broader labels suggested by their colleagues, clinging to their banner of community policing. Why?

THE ATTORNEY GENERAL AND THE PROFESSORS

Among the participants in the first Executive Session on Policing was Edwin Meese, then- Attorney General of the United States. Two years into the session, during the discussion of a paper by Professors Moore and Kelling tracing the evolution of policing strategies over the previous 100 years, an exchange between the Attorney General and Professor Moore captured not only the state of the debate in the policing field, but the reason that Moore and his academic colleagues adopted the phrase "community policing" to describe the broad changes they were both charting and championing.

Emphasizing the historical significance of these changes, Kelling and Moore had argued in their paper that American policing since the 1840s had begun in a "political" era in which policing and local politics had been intimately connected and in which police carried out a wide range of social and political functions, only some of which related to law enforcement. Policing had then passed through a "reform" era, reaching its zenith in the 1950s, in which professional crime-fighting became the dominant

18   *Ibid.,* pp. 9, 11.

organizational strategy. Then, just as the many failures of professional crime-fighting became apparent in the 1960s and 1970s, police departments, according to Kelling and Moore, were achieving new successes with the reintroduction of foot patrol and with experiments in "problem solving." Foot patrol proved both effective at reducing fear of crime and politically popular with residents, merchants and politicians, so much so that voters were willing to increase taxes to pay for it. At the same time, problem solving appeared to capture the imagination and enthusiasm of patrol officers, who liked working more holistically in partnership with residents to resolve neighborhood concerns. This led Kelling and Moore to the principal claim in their historical account: foot patrol, fear reduction, problem solving and partnerships with local residents were "not merely new police tactics." Instead, they constituted "a new organizational approach, properly called a community strategy."[19] Although some departments were introducing foot patrol or problem solving as mere add-ons to professional crime-fighting, their implications were far broader:

> We are arguing that policing is in a period of transition from a reform strategy to what we call a community strategy. The change involves more than making tactical or organizational adjustments and accommodations. Just as policing went through a basic change when it moved from the political to the reform strategy, it is going through a similar change now.[20]

Attorney General Meese was sympathetic but skeptical. "I think the paper is good, but perhaps a shade grandiose," he told its authors. "Suggesting that we have 'a whole new era' to be compared with the reform era is too grand an approach." Community policing, the Attorney General insisted, is "only one component of the whole picture."[21] The then-director of the National Institute of Justice, James K. "Chips" Stewart, suggested a different term, "problem-oriented" policing, because police were taking many initiatives, not merely creating community partnerships, to affirmatively identify and solve problems rather than waiting to respond to reports of crime.[22] Attorney General

---

19 Kelling, G. & Moore, M. The Evolving Strategy of Policing (note 5), 13.

20 *Ibid.*, p. 14.

21 Quoted in Hartmann, F. Debating the Evolution of American Policing (note 15), 3.

22 Problem solving was discussed frequently at the Executive Session, often as a component of community policing, but its importance as an independent thrust in police reform has been more widely recognized since then. Herman Goldstein, who coined the term "problemoriented policing," was careful to write at the time of the Executive Session that it "connects with the current move to redefine relationships between the police and community." Goldstein, H. (1990). *Problem-Oriented Policing.* New York: McGraw Hill, 3. Looking back on these discussions in 2003, Goldstein explained that in the years of the Executive Session, "the community policing movement grew rapidly in policing. One element of that movement supported the police becoming less legalistically-oriented: that police should redefine their role in ways that sought to achieve broader outcomes for those, especially victims, who turned to the police

Meese suggested "strategic policing" because the term embraced not only the work in communities but also the support that community work was going to require (especially the intelligence, surveillance and analysis functions) and the "specialist services that are going to focus on homicide, citywide burglary rings, car theft rings, and organized crime and terrorism." The Attorney General said that his concerns would disappear if the professors talked about community policing as a *part* of a new era of policing, rather than defining the era itself. If they did that, he concluded:

> Everybody would realize that this [community policing] is a very important contribution which, along with other things happening in the police field, marks a new era of strategic policing in which people are thinking about what they are doing.[23]

Not only did the professors continue to insist on using "community policing" to define the new era and its strategy, but they soon persuaded the field to do the same. Community policing became the slogan around which reformers rallied, eventually including President Bill Clinton, who put "community policing" at the heart of his national strategy to deal with crime and to provide unprecedented federal assistance to local police.

In response to Attorney General Meese's suggestion that the professors substitute the term "strategic policing," Professor Moore responded with a four-part argument. First, he agreed that the many elements of strategic policing and problem solving were an important part of the new era. Second, he predicted that most of these new strategies would take hold even without encouragement from leaders in the field or academics. Third, he predicted that police would find most uncomfortable the building of true partnerships with communities. He concluded, therefore, that labeling the entire package of innovations as community policing would give special prominence to the very aspect that would be most difficult for the police to adopt. In short, the name was a dare. As Moore said to the Attorney General:

> Let me say why we keep talking about this phrase "community policing." Let us imagine ... that there are two different fronts on which new investments in policing are likely to be made. One lies in

---

for help. Beat-level 'problem solving' was seen as supporting these efforts and therefore often incorporated into the community policing movement. As community policing and problem-oriented policing evolved alongside each other, the two concepts were intermingled. I contributed to some of the resulting confusion." Goldstein, H. (2003). "On Further Developing Problem-Oriented Policing: The Most Critical Need, The Major Impediments, and a Proposal," *Crime Prevention Studies* 15: 13–47, 45, note 2 (citation omitted), available at http://www.popcenter.org/library/crime-prevention/volume_15/01Goldstein.pdf.

23   Quoted in Hartmann, F. Debating the Evolution of American Policing (note 15), 3.

the direction of more thoughtful, more information-guided, more active attacks on particular crime problems. Some are local crime problems like robbery and burglary, and some turn out to be much bigger … [including] organized crime, terrorism, and sophisticated frauds. That is one frontier. In many respects it is a continuation of an increasingly thoughtful, professionalized, forensic, tactical-minded police department. The other front is … how to strike up a relationship with the community so that we can enlist their aid, focus on the problems that turn out to be important, and figure out a way to be accountable. … The first strand is captured by notions of strategic and problem-solving policing. The second strand is captured by the concept of community policing. … My judgment is that the problem solving, strategic thing will take care of itself because it is much more of a natural development in policing. If you are going to make a difference, you ought to describe a strategy that challenges the police in the areas in which they are least likely to make investments in repositioning themselves. That is this far more problematic area of fashioning a relationship with the community.[24]

The dare worked. Not everywhere, and not completely, but many American police departments took up the banner of community policing and found it possible to varying degrees to create partnerships with the communities they policed.[25] The successful marketing of community policing was solidified in the first presidential campaign and then the presidency of Bill Clinton, whose signature policing initiative—federal funding to add 100,000 cops to U.S. police departments—was managed by the newly created Office of Community Oriented Policing Services (COPS Office). With those funds, local police departments pursued hundreds of varieties of community partnerships, and the public came to understand that modern policing was community policing.

But Attorney General Meese was right. Community policing was only one part of the new era in American policing, and police departments did not, indeed could not, transform their entire organizations in service of local community priorities. There were too many things to do that did not fit neatly within that frame. Instead, departments began to change on many fronts at once: incorporating new forensic science

---

24   *Ibid.*, p. 5. In a later paper, Moore suggested, likely in jest, that one could term the new strategy "professional, strategic, community, problem-solving policing." Moore, M. & and Trojanowicz, R. (1988, November). Corporate Strategies for Policing. *Perspectives on Policing, no. 6.* Washington, D.C.; Cambridge, Mass.: U.S. Department of Justice, Office of Justice Programs, National Institute of Justice; & Harvard University, John F. Kennedy School of Government, Program in Criminal Justice Policy and Management, 14.

25   See, for example, Skogan, W. (2006). *Police and Community in Chicago: A Tale of Three Cities.* New York: Oxford University Press.

technology and new surveillance capabilities, building new information systems that allowed chiefs to hold local commanders accountable almost in real time for levels of crime in their districts, expanding the use of stop-and-search tactics, responding to criticisms of racial profiling, and managing heightened concern about terrorism. And every one of these innovations raised problems, at least in some departments, beyond the guidance that community policing principles provided.

As federal funding for community policing diminished after 2001, police leaders found themselves without a single organizing framework that could allow them to make sense of all of these developments. Soon the labels were proliferating: intelligence-led policing, evidence-based policing, pulling levers, hot-spot policing and predictive policing.[26] Some still argued that community policing, rightly understood, was a vessel capacious enough to contain all of these developments, but others believed that many of these tactics and strategies had become divorced from community engagement and participation. Community policing, in short, lost its power as a comprehensive, organizing concept and again became a single element in the complex and contentious field of policing.

Moreover, even in the Clinton years, community policing succeeded as a political slogan and provided a framework for important changes in police practice, but did not serve as the transformative paradigm that Moore and others thought was needed. Police leaders remain uncertain even to this day what they should ask of their communities. Despite books, trainings, conferences and countless new community policing initiatives, police departments became only marginally better at building broad, trusting, active partnerships with community residents, especially in high-crime neighborhoods. By the time of Barack Obama's election in 2008, community policing had not only lost most of the federal funding and priority it had enjoyed in the 1990s, but the power of the slogan to focus police attention, catalyze public support for police reform, and serve as an overarching philosophy was exhausted as well.

The New Professionalism can restore to the field an overarching, organizing framework. It brings together the strategic, problem-oriented, community partnership strands from the 1980s and 1990s, and incorporates many additional developments in policing in the new century. Still, the exchange between Attorney General Meese and Professor Moore is worth recalling, for it reminds us that some elements of reform are easier than others for police to integrate into their tradition-bound organizations. As the New Professionalism advances, reformers inside and outside police departments should focus on those aspects that will be most difficult for those departments to embrace.

---

26   See, for example, Weisburd, D.; Braga, A.; & eds. (2006). *Police Innovation: Contrasting Perspectives.* New York: Cambridge University Press.

THE NEW PROFESSIONALISM IN THE 21ST CENTURY

All four elements of the New Professionalism are already apparent in the values espoused by many police leaders in the United States and in the operations of several of their departments: accountability, legitimacy, innovation and national coherence. Indeed, the fourth is why the first three define a true professionalism: a collection of expertise, principles and practices that members of the profession recognize and honor.

INCREASED ACCOUNTABILITY

Police departments used to resist accountability; today, the best of them embrace it. Twenty years ago, the term "police accountability" generally referred to accountability for misconduct. To speak of police accountability was to ask who investigated civilian complaints, how chiefs disciplined officers for using excessive force, and so on—sensitive topics in policing. Police chiefs did not generally feel accountable for levels of crime.[27] The change today is dramatic, with increasing numbers of police chiefs feeling strong political pressure to reduce crime even as they contain costs. The best chiefs speak confidently about "the three C's": crime, cost and conduct. Police departments today are accountable for all three.

Consider accountability for crime. Originating in the New York Police Department (NYPD), the CompStat accountability process, in which chiefs in headquarters hold precinct and other area commanders accountable for continuing reductions in crime and achievement of other goals, is now a staple of police management in most large departments. The CompStat process focuses most intensely on "index crimes": homicide, rape, robbery, aggravated assault, burglary, larceny and motor vehicle theft. At the same time, neighborhood residents in local community meetings question police commanders most commonly about other problems, such as open-air drug markets, disorderly youth, vehicle traffic and noise. In still other forums with more specialized advocates, police executives are expected to account for their responses to domestic violence complaints and hate crimes. In these and other ways, police agencies are now routinely accountable for their ability—or inability—to reduce the volume of crime.

---

27   See Kelling, G.; Wasserman, R.; & Williams, H. Police Accountability and Community Policing (note 14), 1. ("Rising crime or fear of crime may be problematic for police administrators, but rarely does either threaten their survival.")

Accountability for cost is hardly new, but the costs of policing are receiving intense scrutiny across the United States as state and local governments cut their budgets. Although some police departments are resorting to familiar cost-cutting strategies—reducing civilian staff, slowing officer recruitment, limiting opportunities for officers to earn overtime and eliminating special programs—others are urging a more fundamental re-examination of how police departments are staffed and what work they do.[28] In Los Angeles, Chief of Police Charles Beck eliminated an entire citywide unit of 130 officers known as Crime Reduction and Enforcement of Warrants (CREW), used for tactical crime suppression. This allowed the department to maintain patrol officer levels in local police districts during a time of budget cuts, even though it deprived his executive team of a flexible resource for responding quickly to new crime hot spots. More than cost cutting, this is a serious bet on the value of district-level leadership, entailing a public accounting of how the department is managing costs in a tight fiscal environment.[29]

Finally, police leaders are taking responsibility for the conduct of their personnel: not only apologizing promptly for clear cases of misconduct, but also taking the initiative to explain controversial conduct that they consider legal and appropriate. For example, when the Los Angeles Police Department employed excessive force on a large scale at an immigrants-rights rally in MacArthur Park in May 2007, then-Police Chief William Bratton publicly confessed error within days, and followed up with strict discipline and reassignment of the top commander at the scene, who later resigned.[30] Perhaps a less obvious example is the NYPD's annual report on all firearms discharges, in which the department reports the facts and patterns in every discharge of a firearm by any of its officers. In the 2008 report, for example, the NYPD reported on 105 firearm discharges, the fewest in at least a decade. These included 49 discharges in "adversarial conflict" in which 12 subjects were killed and 18 injured. The report takes pains to put these police shootings in context, providing accounts of the incidents, information

---

28 See Gascón, G. & Foglesong, T. (2010, December). Making Policing More Affordable: Managing Costs and Measuring Value in Policing. Washington, D.C.; Cambridge, Mass.: U.S. Department of Justice, Office of Justice Programs, National Institute of Justice; & Harvard University, John F. Kennedy School of Government, Program in Criminal Justice Policy and Management, NCJ 231096.

29 Beck disbanded the Crime Reduction and Enforcement of Warrants task force (CREW), weathering criticism that this vital unit "comprised quick-strike troops that former Chief William Bratton used to focus on problem gangs and neighborhoods." Beck also reduced the size of other specialized, central units focused on gangs and drugs by 170 officers to maintain patrol levels in the districts. See Romero, D. (2010, February). "LAPD's Beck Shuffles Cops To Deal With Budget Crisis: No New Cars, No Unused Vacation Pay Possible." LA Weekly, available at: http://www.laweekly.com/news/lapds-beck-shuffles-cops-to-deal-with-budget-crisis-no-new-cars-no-unused-vacation-pay-possible-2397035.

30 See Board of Police Commissioners. (2007, October). Los Angeles Police Department, "An Examination of May Day 2007."

on the backgrounds of the officers and the subjects shot, and comparisons with earlier years.[31]

The embrace and expansion of accountability is likely to continue as part of the New Professionalism in policing, as it is in most professions. On crime, for example, we expect to see more police agencies conducting their own routine public surveys, as many do now, holding themselves accountable not only for reducing reported crime, but also for reducing fear and the perception that crime is a problem in particular neighborhoods or for especially vulnerable residents. The police department in Nashville has engaged a research firm to conduct surveys of residents and businesses every six months since 2005, tracking victimization as well as the percentage of respondents who consider crime their most serious problem, and sharing the results publicly.[32]

To decrease costs, police departments will likely accelerate the shifting of work to nonsworn, and therefore less expensive, specialist personnel, especially in crime investigation units that are currently staffed mostly with detectives. A range of new specialists, including civilian crime scene technicians, data analysts and victim liaisons, might well replace one-half or more of today's detectives. A wide range of new civilian roles could emerge, boosting the prominence of civilian police careers in much the same way that nurses and technicians have taken on many of the roles traditionally played by doctors within the medical profession. This move is already under way, but it proceeds haltingly and with frequent reversals because of the politics of police budgets in periods of fiscal constraint, when retaining sworn officers becomes an especially high priority for elected officials.

On issues of conduct, the New Professionalism may bring substantial reductions in the use of force—already apparent in several jurisdictions—as police departments become more proficient in analyzing the tactical precursors to use-of-force incidents. Already, some departments are reviewing uses of force not only to determine if the officers were justified in the moment that they pulled their triggers or struck a blow, but also to discern earlier tactical missteps that may have unnecessarily escalated a situation to the point where force was legitimately used. By moving beyond a focus on culpability and discipline to smarter policing that relies less on physical force, more departments can demonstrate their professionalism and better account for the force that they deploy.

Finally, we see a growing appreciation among police executives for their own accountability to frontline officers and other members of the organization. This is the least developed form of accountability, with too many police managers still speaking about

---

31 Three police officers were injured by subject gunfire, and none were killed in those incidents. See New York Police Department, "2008 Annual Firearms Discharge Report," 2009.

32 Personal communication from then-Police Chief Ronald Serpas, November 2009. A copy of the June 2009 survey report is on file with the Program in Criminal Justice Policy and Management at the Harvard Kennedy School.

doing battle with their unions and too many unions bragging about their control over chiefs. This familiar, bruising fight between labor and management obscures the beginnings of a more professional, constructive engagement between police unions and police executives, where leaders at every level are committed to disciplinary systems that are fair and perceived as fair, the development of rules with robust participation of frontline officers and staff, and codes of ethics and statements of values that speak to the aspirations of men and women throughout policing and are grounded in a participatory process.

LEGITIMACY

Every public-sector department makes some claim to legitimacy, and policing is no exception. In their account of professional crime-fighting of the mid-20th century, Professors Kelling and Moore identified the sources of legitimacy for policing as "the law" and the "professionalism" of the police. They contrasted these sources of legitimacy with early sources of legitimacy in urban politics. To free themselves from the corruptions of political manipulation, the police of mid-century America, the professors explained, claimed their legitimacy from enforcing the law in ways that were properly entrusted to their professional expertise. By contrast, community policing emphasized the legitimacy that could be derived from community approval and engagement.

The legitimacy of policing under the New Professionalism embraces all of these, recognizing that legitimacy is both conferred by law and democratic politics and earned by adhering to professional standards and winning the trust and confidence of the people policed. The New Professionalism, however, puts a special emphasis on the sources of earned legitimacy: professional integrity and public trust. The last of these—public legitimacy—extends a long-established principle of democratic policing and a tenet of community policing: policing by consent of the governed.

In recent decades, police have had only the weakest means to measure erosion of public legitimacy, mostly derived from the numbers of civilian complaints against the police. As every police officer and police scholar can agree, counting formal civilian complaints produces highly problematic statistics. Relatively few people who feel aggrieved in their encounters with the police make a formal complaint, so the complaints received are unlikely to be representative of wider patterns. Moreover, the police discount complaints from at least two categories of civilians: persistent offenders who use the complaint process to deter police from stopping them, and persistent complainers who file literally dozens of complaints annually. These complainants may be relatively few, but the stories about them circulate so widely among police officers that they undermine the ability of police commanders or outside oversight bodies to use numbers of civilian complaints as a credible measure of public dissatisfaction. Finally, adjudicating civilian complaints is so difficult that most complaints remain formally unsubstantiated, further undermining the process.

The problem is with the use of civilian complaints as the leading measure of public legitimacy, not with the goal of public legitimacy itself. Research conducted by New York University Professor Tom Tyler and others over the last two decades demonstrates that rigorous surveys can reliably measure legitimacy, and that doing so allows police departments to identify practices that can increase their legitimacy among those most disaffected: young people and members of ethnic and racial minority groups. Tyler and others demonstrate that police can employ even forceful tactics such as stop-and-frisk in ways that leave those subject to these tactics feeling that the police acted fairly and appropriately.[33] It is through the pursuit of public legitimacy, guided by repeated surveys that disaggregate results for specific racial, ethnic and age groups, that the New Professionalism can directly address the persistent distrust between ethnic and racial minorities and the police in the United States.

As the New Professionalism develops further, police departments will be able to use better surveys than are common today to measure public legitimacy, allowing them to make more appropriate and modest use of civilian complaints statistics. In 2007, then-Senator Barack Obama underscored the importance of this pillar of the New Professionalism when he promised that, as President, he would work for a criminal justice system that enjoyed the trust and confidence of citizens of every race, ethnicity and age.[34] Public surveys that capture the satisfaction of people in these discrete groups in their encounters with police and in their broader confidence in the police can help measure progress toward that goal.[35]

---

33 See, for example, Tyler, T. (2004). "Enhancing Police Legitimacy," *Annals of the American Academy of Political and Social Science* 593 (10) (2004): 84–99. See also Tyler, T.; ed. (2007). *Legitimacy and Criminal Justice: International Perspectives.* New York: Russell Sage Foundation.

34 See Obama, B. (2007, September). *Remarks at Howard University Convocation.* Available at http://www.barackobama .com/2007/09/28/remarks_of_senator_barack_obam_26.php, accessed October 14, 2010.

35 At a national level, the *Sourcebook of Criminal Justice Statistics* annually reports levels of "confidence" in the police as an institution by age, income, racial and ethnic group, and political affiliation. The results in 2009 showed that 63 percent of white adults had "a great deal" or "quite a lot" of confidence in the police, in contrast to 38 percent of black adults. If individual departments track the exact language of these national surveys, they can compare themselves with these national benchmarks. See Pastore, A. & Maguire, K.; eds. (2009). *Sourcebook of Criminal Justice Statistics,* Table 2.12.2009, available at http://www.albany.edu/sourcebook/pdf/t2122009.pdf, accessed August 2, 2010.

CONTINUOUS INNOVATION

One complaint about the old professionalism of mid-century policing is that it stifled innovation at the front lines of policing. Police managers were so concerned about the dangers of corruption and a loss of discipline that they suppressed the creative impulses of frontline officers who wanted to try new ways of solving crime problems and eliminating other conditions that caused people grief. Conversely, a complaint about community policing in the 1990s was that it left problem solving to the variable skills of frontline officers, with only rare examples of senior management investing in departmentwide problem solving or developing responses beyond the "generic" solutions of "patrolling, investigating, arresting, and prosecuting ... without benefit of rigorously derived knowledge about the effectiveness of what they do."[36]

Today, innovation at every level is essential for police agencies charged with preventing crimes and solving problems from terrorism to youth violence, vandalism, mortgage fraud, Internet gambling, drug dealing, extortion, drunk driving, intimate partner violence and so on. The last decade has seen innovation in the strategies, tactics and technologies that police employ against all of these, and in ways that police develop relationships within departments and with the public. Films and television series popularize innovations in forensic sciences, but equally dramatic are innovations in less-lethal weaponry, the use of "verbal judo" to control unruly people without physical force, direct engagement with neighborhood gangs and drug dealers to reduce crime, and recruiting techniques that can rapidly diversify the pool of applicants for police jobs. Other innovations boost attention to customer service at police stations, help supervisors identify officers at greater risk of engaging in misconduct, improve the outcomes of confrontations with mentally disturbed individuals, and provide more effective service to victims of persistent domestic violence and spousal abuse. It is a dizzying array.

The challenge of the New Professionalism is to encourage innovation within the bounds not only of the law but also of ethical values. The use of value statements to guide police behavior in place of the strict enforcement of detailed regulations continues to gain acceptance in the field, driven first by community policing and problem solving and more recently by reforms to disciplinary processes and closer collaborations between union leadership and police executives. As police departments reward innovators with recognition, resources and promotion, that trend will continue.

As part of the New Professionalism, departments can expand the range of incentives for innovation and build structures that encourage innovation as part of the routine work of police officers and senior management teams. These might include

---

36   Goldstein, H. "On Further Developing Problem-Oriented Policing" (note 22), 21.

community partnerships that go beyond the neighborhood activities of community policing, and joint ventures with other government departments, national and international nonprofit organizations, and private-sector companies. Such partnerships encourage police to see crime and crime problems in new forms and new places, well beyond the narrow confines of those reported to the police and recorded in the Uniform Crime Reports.

But innovation alone will not prove valuable without a way to learn from the process. All professions are distinguished from mere trades by their commitment to continuous learning through innovation, whether it is experimentation in medicine, the development of the common law, or the application of engineering breakthroughs in architecture. As Herman Goldstein wrote a few years ago in urging the importance of developing knowledge as part of police reform, "The building of a body of knowledge, on which good practice is based and with which practitioners are expected to be familiar, may be the most important element for acquiring truly professional status."[37]

Knowledge—its creation, dissemination and practical application—is essential to genuine professionalism. Police organizations need not only to encourage innovation but also to measure their outcomes, and reward and sustain innovations that succeed. They should encourage independent evaluations of their policies and tactics. Working with researchers, they should design experiments that rigorously test new ideas. Police organizations must then communicate the reasons for their successes widely and quickly throughout the profession. Formal partnerships with universities and nonprofit think tanks can help, and many departments have already built such partnerships.

All this suggests a new way of learning within policing. The pace of innovation and knowledge development today is simply too fast for police organizations to rely on recruit training and occasional specialized courses. Rather, police departments need to become learning organizations of professionals. For example, analysts in police agencies should not only be studying crime patterns but also analyzing what the police are doing about them and to what effect, informing the development of tailor-made strategies to deal with the underlying problems, and then sharing their analyses widely within the department in forms that busy frontline officers and supervisors can easily digest, retain and apply. Another example: frontline officers and rising managers should be rewarded for the professional habits of reading, learning and actively contributing to the expansion of knowledge in the field.[38]

---

37   Ibid., p. 46, note 3. Goldstein here describes it as "especially troubling" that the 20th century "professionalization" of policing had not included this element.

38   The idea of a "learning organization" goes well beyond what we expect of all professional organizations. For more about learning organizations, see Garvin, D. (2000). *Learning in Action: Putting the Learning Organization to Work.* Cambridge, Mass.: Harvard Business School Press.

NATIONAL COHERENCE

Achieving accountability for crime, cost and conduct; public legitimacy across social divisions; and continuous innovation and learning at every rank would mark a watershed in policing. These first three elements build on efforts begun with community policing, elevating them to a New Professionalism that infuses all of what police organizations do. To make that New Professionalism worthy of the name, however, requires one more step: achieving national coherence in this radically decentralized business. This element has not yet developed as far as the first three, but it has begun to grow.

Policing in the United States is notoriously parochial, entrusted to something close to 20,000 police departments—the precise number changes so quickly that there is no reliable count. Yet in the last three decades, policing has begun to develop features of a coherent field of professional work. The Police Foundation and Police Executive Research Forum have helped by nurturing national conversations among practitioners and researchers. These conversations took on greater intensity in the first Executive Session on Policing, and they became far more public when Bill Clinton, campaigning for the presidency in 1992, argued for using federal resources to spread community policing to every state. Since then, national discussions and debates about police practices and strategies have become commonplace, thanks in large part to the efforts of the COPS Office, the Office on Violence Against Women and the Office of Justice Programs—all within the Department of Justice—and the conversations hosted by the Major Cities Chiefs Association and other professional associations.[39] Many of the best-known brands in policing practices—"CompStat Meetings," "Fusion Centers" and even older brands like "Weed and Seed" programs—are national in name only, with each manifestation so different from the others that they contribute little to national coherence. Still, even these widely differing practices can create an appetite for more truly coherent practices in an extremely decentralized field.

Most other countries achieve at least some national coherence through a national police agency or a limited number of state police services. England, with only 43 local police services, has recently created the National Police Improvement Agency to assume a variety of shared functions and bring a greater degree of national coherence to policing. Canada uses a mixed model, in which municipalities and provinces contract with the Royal Canadian Mounted Police (RCMP) to provide local or provincial police

---

39   The Major Cities Chiefs Association comprises the chiefs of the 63 largest police departments in the United States and Canada (56 of the departments are in the United States; seven more are in Canada). Members include the chief executive officers of law enforcement agencies in U.S. cities with populations greater than 500,000, the chief executive officer of the largest law enforcement agency in each U.S. Standard Metropolitan Statistical Area with a population greater than 1.5 million, and the chiefs of police in the seven largest Canadian cities. For more information about the association, see the association's website, http://www.majorcitieschiefs.org.

services according to local specifications aiming to achieve locally negotiated goals. Large jurisdictions, such as the provinces of Ontario and Quebec and the cities of Toronto, Montreal and Vancouver, still choose to field their own police services, but the other provinces and many smaller cities contract with the RCMP.

Local control over local policing is deeply ingrained in American political culture, and we do not expect that to change. Some consolidation among the 80 percent of police agencies with fewer than 25 police officers could help residents of those communities receive more professional police services, but such consolidation will not do much for national coherence. Indeed, further progress toward national coherence through the New Professionalism may be necessary for this consolidation to be attractive.

Greater mobility among police departments for officers and professional staff could do more than consolidation to advance national coherence. True professionals are mobile across jurisdictions, even across national boundaries. Engineers, doctors and even lawyers can practice their professions and apply their skills and training almost anywhere. Many professions have local testing and licensing requirements, but reciprocity arrangements recognize that the training and skills of these licensed professionals are portable, and both individuals and organizations take advantage of this portability. Local experience has value in every profession, but local expertise can be balanced with wider knowledge and experience.

Only in the last few decades has it become common for big-city police chiefs to be recruited from outside of their departments and states, though even today most chiefs have spent their entire careers in the departments they lead. That trend needs to deepen, and the profession needs to find ways to encourage greater movement from place to place and across state lines at every stage of police careers. The obstacles are substantial. Police pension rules can create powerful disincentives for officers to move. In some states, such as California, the pension system does not block movement within the state, but creates disincentives for wider moves. In Massachusetts, state laws and contracts make it difficult for veteran officers and supervisors to move even within the state without loss in rank.

If the values of policing are really professional, not local, then departments need not worry that a workforce enjoying geographic mobility will become unskilled or undisciplined. Officers who have worked in the same community for a decade or more and who know the local people and their customs will be invaluable members of any police service, but that is true in many professions. What is needed is a genuine national coherence in the skills, training and accreditation of police professionals.[40]

---

[40] The issues of national coherence and professionalism can raise questions about minimum standards for police, especially educational standards. Should police officers be required to have a college degree? Should there be educational qualifications for promotion? In light of racial and ethnic differences in formal educational attainment,

At stake here is much more than the ability for some police officers to move from one department to another. Citizens should be entitled to professional performance from U.S. police officers wherever they find them. Not only should the definition of professional performance be constantly evolving, but the public—itself mobile across the country—should expect police officers everywhere to keep up with these developments.

This kind of coherence implies the development of national norms of how the police respond to situations, particularly to criminal activity, public disorder, political dissent or even a traffic infraction. Consider, for example, a routine traffic stop. This can be a tense moment for a police officer who does not know if the car's occupants were merely speeding or escaping the scene of a crime, just as it is an anxious moment for most drivers. A common protocol for how the police approach the vehicle, what they require of the driver, and how they respond as the encounter proceeds could not only save the lives of officers, but could help motorists as they drive from state to state avoid inadvertently alarming any officers who stop them. Such protocols have already begun to spread, but they could usefully be developed for a much wider range of situations.

The concept of a "protocol," familiar in the medical field, could prove useful in professional policing. Some may become standard because of research findings, others because of judicial decisions, still others because of advances in forensic science. As in medicine, the danger is that protocols will, in the hands of busy police professionals, replace nuanced diagnosis and a plan to address the problems at hand. Careful analysis of local problems and the custom crafting of solutions continue to be necessary. Still, once a tool becomes part of that solution, its use according to standard protocols can save lives, improve effectiveness, reduce costs and let everyone benefit from the accumulation of professional knowledge. Just as systematic evaluation and rigorous research can discipline innovation, they can strengthen national protocols.[41]

Increased mobility and stronger protocols are only two ways in which national coherence can advance. The attraction of the new professionalism is likely to feed

---

standards might be more appropriately focused on knowledge rather than years of schooling or formal degrees. Many professions allow apprenticeships to substitute for formal classroom education. The issues also raise questions of pension portability for line officers, which some states are beginning to address with the support of police unions. In general, we have been impressed that many police unions share the ambitions of the New Professionalism.

41   The recently created National Network for Safe Communities, which links more than 50 jurisdictions that are implementing a gang violence reduction strategy piloted in Boston and a drug market reduction strategy piloted in High Point, N.C., represents one such effort to move police practice from experimentation to application and adaptation of common, national protocols. See http://www.nnscommunities.org. A similar national effort, the Policing Research Platform Project, is collecting comprehensive data from new recruits, supervisors and entire police agencies to expand understanding of the career paths of police professionals and of quality policing. See https://www.nij.gov/topics/law-enforcement/administration/policing-platform/Pages/welcome.aspx.

a flowering of specialist professional associations, bachelor's and master's degree programs, professional journals and other features of professional infrastructure.

IS THE NEW PROFESSIONALISM REALLY NEW?

We return, finally, to the definitional question: What is professionalism? When an earlier generation of reformers described the police strategy of the mid20th century as professional crime-fighting, they may have been using the term "professional" merely as the opposite of "amateur." Perhaps they thought of professional police much as people think of professional athletes or professional actors. Through more rigorous selection, better training and tighter command, they had left the ranks of mere amateurs.

It is also likely that this earlier generation wanted to put distance between the police and partisan elected officials. Police departments live with a constant tension between serving the government leaders of the day, whether mayor, county executive or governor, and remaining independent of partisan politics. In the mid-20th century, reformers deployed the language of professionalism to help manage that tension, hoping to hold the local political machine at arm's length. That aim was laudable, but the claim was false. These departments were not professional.

We describe today's genuine police professionalism as "new" to distinguish it from the earlier rhetoric that mistakenly equated professionalism with an overreliance on technology, centralization of authority and insulation from the public. These features, found in much policing in the second half of the 20th century, do not define true professionalism.

Consider the parallel with the practice of medicine as a profession. In the 1960s and 1970s, U.S. doctors were often criticized as overly reliant on technology and distant from the patients whom they treated. A wave of reformers in medicine developed new specialties in family practice and championed medical education that trained doctors to communicate with patients respectfully, engaging patients more meaningfully in their own treatment. New roles for nurse practitioners and other health workers made the practice of medicine more humane. Family practice and other reforms aimed to build good relationships between medical practitioners and patients, just as community policing aimed to build good relationships between police and the people they served. But no one seriously suggests that doctors and nurses should abandon their identity as professionals. Instead, professionalism in medicine has come to embrace the respect for patients, accountability and innovations that are improving practice. Medicine has discovered its own new professionalism. So, too, has legal practice, in part through law school clinics that teach the importance of respectful client relationships alongside legal doctrine.

Similarly, in law enforcement, the New Professionalism embraces the respectful engagement of citizens and communities that lies at the core of community policing. Those who continue to champion the aspirations of community policing should understand the New Professionalism as aligned with their ambitions.[42] Moreover, the New Professionalism is clear about its expectations, whereas community policing has become so vague a term that it has lost its operational meaning. As Moore advised two decades ago, the New Professionalism focuses police attention on the very things that are most difficult to achieve: accountability, legitimacy, innovation and national coherence. Community engagement is essential at least to the first two of those and perhaps all four.

Much can be gained from a truer police professionalism. For the public, policing promises to become more effective, more responsive to the opinions of residents and less forceful, less brusque. For members of the police profession themselves, the work promises to become more stimulating with a greater emphasis on learning, innovation, ethics and professional mobility. But the greatest gains are for democratic societies generally and the American experiment in democracy more specifically.

A certain amount of force will always be a part of police work; a degree of coercion is necessary to keep order and enforce the law. What matters is whether policing—when it forcefully asserts its authority—makes democratic progress possible or impedes it. Professional policing enhances democratic progress when it accounts for what it does, achieves public support, learns through innovation and transcends parochialism. That is the promise of the New Professionalism.

---

42   See, for example, Sklansky, David, *The Persistent Pull of Police Professionalism*, to be published in this series. [National Institute of Justice (NIJ). BiblioGov (August 13, 2012)] Sklansky continues to identify "professionalism" in policing with the desire to centralize police authority, make use of the latest technology, and keep the public at a distance. He decries such professionalism and longs to engage police in questions of genuine partnership with communities. We agree with his ambition but disagree that he needs to strip police of their professional identity to achieve it. We believe the New Professionalism is a more accurate and more attractive banner for this effort than his "advanced community policing."

Operating Criminal Justice Agencies Under a Consent Decree

DARRELL L. ROSS

Beyond civil litigation filed by citizens or prisoners in state or federal courts, there are additional methods by which criminal justice personnel are scrutinized about performing their sworn duties. Congress has passed significant legislation authorizing the Department of Justice to initiate investigations and pursue litigation against correctional and police entities. In 1980, Congress passed the Civil Rights of Institutionalized Persons Act (CRIPA), 42 U.S.C. § 1997, which addresses investigations relating to conditions of confinement. In 1994, Congress promulgated Title 42 U.S.C. § 14141 as part of the Violent Crime Control and Law Enforcement Act, which prohibits government authorities or those acting on their behalf (including law enforcement officials) from engaging in a pattern or practice of conduct that deprives people of their constitutional rights.

The purpose of this chapter is to describe how these two pieces of legislation operate and affect criminal justice agencies. The issue of police misconduct and prisoner abuse is clearly a matter of social policy and legislation requiring assessment. These laws have had a significant impact on the criminal justice system and represent a major federal government intervention into the operations of criminal justice agencies. Legislation affects policy, and administrators and officers should be aware of the mechanics of these two statutes and address changes in their agency's operations as appropriate.

SECTION 14141

High-profile incidents, such as the Rodney King arrest (1991), the Amadou Diallo (1994) and Abner Louima (1997) incidents in New York, and the riots in Cincinnati after a police officer shot and killed an African-American youth (2001) have raised concerns about how the police treat citizens. In addition, the 2000 Rampart precinct scandal in Los Angeles, where a veteran officer, Rafael Perez, stole one million dollars' worth of cocaine only serves to convince the public that police corruption is rampant as well. These, among other incidents, have become popular examples that police pundits point toward in order to prove their contention that the police are corrupt and require federal regulation (U.S. Commission on Civil Rights, 2000).

These and other examples are frequently cited by police critics who make sweeping indictments alleging that the police profession is corrupt, that it hides behind the "blue curtain" of cover-up, and that it chronically uses excessive force. There is no question that acts of police misconduct have occasionally occurred and that excessive force has been used in some circumstances. There is no empirical evidence, however, to support claims that excessive force or officer misconduct occurs with statistically significant frequency (Ross, 2005). In his analysis, Ross found in 65 published articles on the police use of force from 1968 to 2004, including two Department of Justice national studies (1996 and 2001) and an International of Association Chiefs of Police independent national study (2001), that the use of any type of force is rare in police contacts with citizens. Moreover, he found that excessive force accusations, in contrast to public perception, were even rarer.

The United States Supreme Court has addressed proper police conduct in a series of landmark cases since the 1960s. The Court's interpretation of the "due process" rights of citizens has played a significant role in shaping social policy. For example, the Court's decisions in *Mapp v. Ohio* (1961) (which established the exclusionary rule) and *Terry v. Ohio* (1968) (which established standards for investigatory detentions and weapons pat-downs) placed restrictions on police in conducting searches and seizing evidence, and required police officers to follow legal procedures. These procedures are intended to properly guide officers and curb police misconduct. As shown in previous chapters, since the 1960s, citizens have used Title 42 U.S.C. § 1983 as the primary civil remedy for asserting legal claims against the police for alleged constitutional violations (Kappeler et al., 1993; Vaughn & Coome, 1995; Worrall, 2001; Ross, 2003; Silver, 2005). While § 1983 remains a viable mechanism to redress alleged governmental intrusions on citizens' rights, some scholars argue that it has only been partially successful in deterring or curbing police abuse of authority (Silveria, 2004; Walker, 2003; Kim, 2002; Levenson, 2001; Livingston, 1999). This argument, however, has been considerably weakened after the Court's decision in *Groh v. Ramirez* (2004), when it denied qualified immunity to an officer who relied on an invalid warrant that he had prepared, even though it was approved by a magistrate. The decision further warns against police abuse of power and sends a message to the police community regarding judicial intolerance of such misconduct.

Despite police reforms and commission reports about police practices over the past 50 years, advances in police practices, and court decisions, police misconduct still occasionally occurs. Seeking to remedy the issue, Congress enacted § 14141 of Title 42 as part of the Violent Crime Control and Law Enforcement Act in 1994. Section 14141 grants authority to the Department of Justice (DOJ) to pursue equitable and declaratory relief against police engaged in a "pattern and practice" that deprives individuals of their constitutional rights. Section 14141 does not authorize compensatory damage awards to citizen complaints, but rather gives the DOJ the power to initiate police reform by essentially dictating future management practices in that police entity (Silveria, 2004). In an initial assessment of the application of § 14141, Livingston (1999) argued and agreed with some police scholars that police reform will be most effective when reform involves not only simple adherence to the rules, but also a wholehearted embrace of change in organizational values and systems.

Section 14141 specifically authorizes the DOJ to bring a lawsuit against a police organization rather than individual officers. Beginning in 1996, the DOJ, initiated investigations of 22 police departments, which have resulted in seven consent decrees and six memorandums of agreement. One investigation was dropped. The DOJ is currently investigating eight police departments (DOJ, 2006).

BACKGROUND OF § 14141

PROVISIONS OF THE ACT

As a result of the Rodney King incident, Congress passed the Violent Crime Control Act in 1994. As part of this legislation, Congress gave authority to the United States Attorney General to investigate allegations of "patterns and practices" of police misconduct. Section 14141 substantially enhances the Department of Justice's statutory basis for intervening into the affairs of police departments. This provision allows the Special Litigation Section of the Civil Rights Division to investigate and bring a civil lawsuit against a police department when the Attorney General believes that constitutional violations based on patterns and practices have occurred. The fundamental purpose of § 14141 is to remedy systemic police abuse.

In establishing a claim, § 14141 requires the DOJ to demonstrate that a municipality or police department engaged in a "pattern or practice" of conduct by law enforcement officers that has deprived individuals of their constitutionally protected rights. Congress provided no explicit guidance nor has there been any judicial interpretation of § 14141, and defining a "pattern or practice" of misconduct can be problematic. There are, however, two components that shed light on the interpretation. First, the United States Supreme Court suggested in developing Title VII language that the term "pattern and practice" can mean "denoting something more than the mere occurrence of isolated or accidental or sporadic unlawful acts" (*Int'l Brotherhood of Teamsters v. United States,* 1977). In the police context, this can mean that a "pattern or practice" of conduct by police officers that violates constitutional rights would likely show that such conduct is a practice or custom that occurs frequently or regularly (Livingston, 1999). With such regularity of occurrence, a court could conclude that such abusive conduct is the *regular* practice rather than the *unusual* practice. The Supreme Court has also ruled in *Hazelwood School District v. United States* (1977) (a case predating § 1414) that a plaintiff can make a prima facie case of "pattern or practice" of discrimination simply through the introduction of statistical evidence. Because statistical evidence was sufficient proof of a "pattern or practice" of discrimination (in an educational setting), a plaintiff need not prove any overt institutional practice to satisfy the definition.

Second, in the predecessor to § 14141, the Judicial Committee Report in 1991 suggested that establishing a "pattern or practice" need not be based on extensive evidence of systematic repeated violations (H.R. Rep. 102). The report cited acts or omissions that constituted patterns and practices in illustrating the potential applicability of § 14141 to situations in which relief was formerly unavailable. For example, the Committee cited the Ninth Circuit Appellate Court's holding in *Mason County v. Davis* (1991). Affirming the lower court's decision, the appellate court determined that a § 1983 claim was valid when four separate plaintiffs showed a pattern of excessive force stemming from unconstitutional traffic stops performed by deputies over a period of nine months. Such a pattern of abuse demonstrated the inadequacies of training provided by the department for its officers.

CONSENT DECREE

Once allegations of constitutional violations emerge, the DOJ conducts a preliminary inquiry to determine the nature of the allegations. The DOJ may notify the agency or the municipality that it will be conducting a formal investigation. If the investigation reveals evidence of a pattern or practice of abuse, the DOJ may release a letter of general findings to announce its discovery, or it may simply walk away, stating that there is no evidence to support a claim.

There are several options available to the DOJ when a "pattern or practice" is established, in its opinion, under § 14141. First, the DOJ may file a lawsuit against the police agency, which may involve a lengthy litigation process. Second, a lawsuit may be filed with the expectation that the city will settle the case through a consent decree or settle it through a memorandum of agreement (MOA). While both are settlements, there are distinctions between them. Consent decrees serve as a court-ordered and court-enforceable settlements. A federal judge provides oversight of the consent decree, which normally lasts five years (Livingston, 1999). When a MOA is used to settle the DOJ claim, there is no judicial oversight. A municipality agrees in writing to comply with recommendations made by the DOJ, which threatens a future consent decree or litigation if the agency fails to comply with the agreement. Ostensibly, a consent decree is an MOA with teeth (Silveria, 2004). A Special Monitor is appointed by the court to serve as an independent auditor in consent decrees and MOAs. The Special Monitor reports on each defendant's compliance on a quarterly basis.

INVESTIGATION TRENDS OF § 14141

TRENDS

The trends of consent decrees and MOAs filed by the DOJ from 1996 to 2005 are shown in Table 8.1. The DOJ has conducted 22 investigations involving one state police agency, 18 municipalities, and two county sheriff's departments (DOJ Special Litigation Section, 2006). These investigations have resulted in seven consent decrees and six MOAs.

Considering the lack of congressional guidance on the definition of a "pattern or practice," policy patterns of § 14141 have differed significantly from the Clinton administration to the Bush administration. Under the Clinton administration, the first investigations occurred in 1996. Pittsburgh, Pennsylvania, and Steubenville, Ohio, were the first cities the DOJ investigated for practices and patterns of police misconduct. Both investigations resulted in five-year consent decrees commencing in 1997 and both cities successfully completed the period of judicial monitoring (Livingston, 1999). The third and final police agency placed under a consent decree during the Clinton administration was the New Jersey State Police in 1999. The consent decree specifically addressed racial profiling and methods to remedy such allegations (DOJ, 1999). Prior to 2001 and the George W. Bush administration, the

Table 8.1 Trends of Consent Decrees, MOAs and Investigations: 1997–2005

City/Year	CD	MOA	Investigation	Case Dropped
Albany, NY (2003)			X	
Bakerfield, CA			X	
Beacon, NY (2002)			X	
Buffalo, NY (2002)			X	
Cincinnati, OH (2002)		X		
Cleveland, OH	X			
Columbus, OH (2002)				X
Detroit, MI (2003)	X			
Highland Park, IL (2000)		X		
Los Angeles, CA (2001)	X			
Miami, FL (2001)			X	
Mount Prospect, IL (2003)			X	
Nassau County, (2001)		X		
NJ State Police (1999)	X			
Pittsburgh, PA (1997)	X			
Portland, ME (2003)			X	
Prince George's County, Mary Land (2004)			X	
Schenectady, NY (2003)			X	
Steubenville, OH (1997)	X			
Villa Rico, GA (2003)		X		
Virgin Island (2003)			X	
Washington, D.C.		X		

DOJ had initiated an investigation of the Los Angeles Police Department (LAPD), but they were placed on a consent decree during the first year of the Bush administration.

During the first three years of the Bush administration, more § 14141 investigations were completed than in the six years after its passage under the Clinton administration. Section 14141 investigations by the DOJ have increased under the Bush presidency. From 2001 to 2005, the DOJ conducted 18 § 14141 investigations. As a result, four agencies agreed to consent decrees, six agreed to MOAs, eight are still under investigation or monitoring, and the DOJ dropped the lawsuit in the Columbus, Ohio, investigation (DOJ, 2006). Investigations are still being conducted in accordance with § 14141, but the trends show that under the Bush administration the investigations are slightly more likely to result in a MOA.

Thus far, Columbus, Ohio, is the first city to challenge a § 14141 action in court. The city filed a motion to dismiss the action, claiming that § 14141 constituted an abuse of the government's power to enforce the Fourteenth Amendment (*United States v. City of Columbus*, 2001). Denying the motion, the federal district court held that § 14141 creates Congressional oversight to prevent violations of the Fourteenth Amendment. The case continued to drag on for several more years and the DOJ decided to drop the case under the Bush administration. This decision is important because it demonstrates an aggressive, adversarial approach to § 14141 enforcement (Silveria, 2004). A review of the contents of the MOA suggests a more "cooperative" strategy and policy approach to the enforcement of § 14141.

TYPES OF ALLEGATIONS MADE UNDER § 14141

Section 14141 allows the DOJ to file a lawsuit against a police entity for allegations of "pattern or practice" of police misconduct. The allegations must show that an individual's constitutional rights were violated. While such allegations may include a variety of claims, analysis of the consent decrees and MOAs reveal several levels of claims.

The first level of claims regarding police officer misconduct is a natural outgrowth of COP as it is the officer or officers who initiates the contact with the citizen. Common complaints typically include: using excessive force; false arrest and false imprisonment; and improper traffic stops, searches, and seizures of people. The second level of claims concerns practices condoned by departmental administrators. Common allegations may include: supervisors who condoned officer abuses; failed to implement or enforce policies; failed to train, supervise, and discipline officers; failed to investigate officer misconduct or citizen complaints; and failed to implement a risk management system that could assess officer practices of abuse.

The number of complaints and investigations conducted by the Special Litigation Section of the Department of Justice has decreased from former years. From 2006 to 2008, four such investigations were performed; two in 2008, one in 2007, and one in 2006 (DOJ, 2009). Common complaints investigated include the following topics: use of force involving Tasers, less-lethal equipment, and canines; use of force policies; multiple applications of the Taser; discipline practices; medical care; training of officers and supervisors; response to the mentally ill; conducting internal investigations of critical incidents; and incorporating early warning/risk management systems. No new consent decrees were activated with any police department by the DOJ during this period.

PRINCIPAL COMPONENTS OF § 14141 CONSENT DECREES

Each consent decree addresses unique and specific abuses identified by the DOJ investigation of a particular police entity, and forms the basis for the claim of a "pattern or practice" of police misconduct. While not every consent decree requires the police agency to address the same issue or the same number of issues, analysis of the six consent decrees reveals a total of 94 factors that have been addressed during the monitoring period. Many of these factors required by the DOJ during the duration of the consent decree were derived from the DOJ's report on *Good Policing* (DOJ, 2003).

Consent decrees mainly call for the revision or development of policies and procedures. Common policy areas generally include: use of force, citizen complaints, in-car video camera usage, conducting investigations, performing arrests, searching and obtaining warrants, conducting traffic stops, foot pursuits, and racial profiling.

The second general factor of each consent decree is the establishment of a data-driven information management system. These systems are designed to provide useful information about the activities of all officers and supervisors in the department in order to establish accountability measures. The data-management system is comprised of six separate elements, including: a risk management database and analysis; officer and supervisor database; citizen complaints; and an early identification system for problem officers. A separate tracking system must be designed and maintained that documents: police and citizen contacts, police use of force, traffic stops, citizen arrests, police misconduct, and police response to the mentally impaired. Each database requires an involved officer to complete and submit designated forms and reports documenting their actions in a given incident.

The use of a reporting system is a core component in the consent decree actions (Walker, 2003). It is integrated into the data-tracking/reporting system, the revised policy, the early identification system, investigation protocols, and the risk management assessment system. In many agencies this has meant a total revamping of their entire system.

The early identification system is designed to identify potential problem officers so supervisors can provide those officers with early intervention, normally through counseling or additional training by a supervisor. The system is integrated into the other database systems described above. The system provides supervisors with greater flexibility in addressing performance problems (Walker et al., 2000). The concept is supported by research that suggests that in any law enforcement agency a small number of officers are involved in a disproportionate percentage of problem incidents, such as citizen complaints, use-of-force incidents, civil lawsuits against the department, and other indicators of performance problems (Walker, 2001).

Another factor addresses establishing varying agency programs. Such programs can include: field officer training, in-service training, police response to the mentally impaired, community outreach, and employee assistance programs. Training is a core component in consent decrees and MOAs. Generally, the decrees do not stipulate the content of such training. Common training subject areas include: use of force; search and seizure laws; response to domestic violence, hostage and barricade situations; emotionally impaired persons; vehicle pursuits; communication skills; and training on racial, gender, and religious differences of community citizens. Supervisors must also attend the training.

Performing investigations represents the fourth major factor of the consent decree, and topic areas can include: criminal, civil, citizen complaints, disciplinary complaints, and internal affairs investigations. A majority of many of the decrees contain the requirement of performing use-of-force investigations. Citizen complaint investigations also must be addressed. After investigations are concluded, a report must be submitted that shows how the investigation was conducted and the evidentiary basis of the findings of the investigation. These provisions are designed to correct specific problems that are unique to a department's failure to conduct investigations or past failure to perform a thorough and complete investigation.

The fifth factor addresses administrative oversight of the entire consent decree. For each agency, an independent monitor is assigned by the court to provide quarterly monitoring progress of how the agency was complying with the components of the consent decree.

All reports must be entered into a database that tracks the unique components of each consent decree. Supervisors must dedicate time to analyze trends and patterns of officer activities that were identified in the previous sections. Supervisors must periodically monitor the documents that are to be part of the ongoing assessment of officers, including annual performance evaluations (Livingston, 1999). Quarterly reports must be prepared by supervisors documenting these assessments. Certain steps must be taken when an officer accumulates a number of use-of-force incidents, citizen complaints, or other incidents that may reveal conduct outside authorized policy requirements. For example, if an officer accumulates more than three citizen complaints within two years, he or she must be counseled and attend refresher training in the subject matter consistent with the complaint. More severe sanctions may be assessed depending upon the severity of the complaint. Documentation of the remediation must be entered into the early intervention system and the database. Supervisors must perform annual evaluations of every officer under their command.

MEMORANDUM OF AGREEMENT

Since 2001, DOJ investigations have increasingly resulted in memorandums of agreement (MOAs). MOAs are more conciliatory than consent decrees. They do not involve judicial monitoring as do consent decrees. While stipulations from consent decrees and MOAs may be similar, MOAs are more likely to address three primary topic areas beyond officer training and developing an early intervention warning system with all officers: (1) Policy and Procedure; (2) Citizen Complaints; and (3) Data Collection.

The first area addressed in an MOA is policy and procedure for performing investigations within the police department. All of the departments are required to revise their policies pursuant to the findings of the DOJ investigation.

Perhaps the most fundamental difference in the MOA is a change in the use-of-force policy. While police agencies today provide their officers with a use-of-force policy, revisions may have to be made, such as restricting the use of certain force techniques or equipment, reporting procedures, or tracking and analyzing force incidents. The Washington, D.C., MOA required the department to completely overhaul their use-of-force policy and bring it into compliance with applicable law and professional standards (DOJ, 2003). The city of Cincinnati was required to develop policy language that limited the use of pepper spray, the use of canines, and the use of the choke hold (DOJ, 2001). The Cleveland Police Department was required to address their procedures for using detainee holding cells and was also required to revise its lethal force policy (DOJ, 2002).

Previous complaints have been made that police frequently do not enforce their departmental policies. The problem may be that the officer in question is being investigated by his or her immediate supervisor, resulting in a less than thorough investigation. Thus, investigations into officer actions contrary to the policy are required in all MOAs to ensure the integrity of, and public confidence in, the investigation. The subject matter of investigations generally includes: use of force, citizen complaints, traffic stops, and searches and seizures. In Cincinnati, the MOA requires an investigation when an officer uses force. The officer must first notify his immediate supervisor, the supervisor must respond to the scene, and an investigator from internal affairs must respond to the scene of "serious" force incidents. The investigator may neither ask leading questions nor show preference to statements made by the officer, nor may they disregard a witness's or the arrestee's statement of the incident.

Another major component addressed in most of the MOAs is the handling of citizen complaints. Modifications to complaint procedures are required. The goal is to enhance citizen satisfaction in the outcome of the complaint process by providing more transparency in the process. In many of the MOAs, officers are required to carry complaint forms in their patrol vehicles and are required to inform citizens that they have a right to file a complaint about the officer's response. Investigations of citizen complaints must be performed and documented, and a report of the nature of the disposition and description of the evidentiary grounds used to determine the outcome of the investigation must be completed.

Data collection is also addressed by most MOAs. Data is required to be collected, analyzed, and assessed in a variety of topic areas, but is focused on traffic stops. This requirement has emerged from allegations that police have engaged in racial profiling practices during traffic stops. When an officer makes a traffic stop, he or she is required to submit a lengthy form documenting the nature of the stop. That information is submitted to a supervisor for review. The information is then entered into the database system for further analysis and it is also entered into the early intervention database.

CIVIL RIGHTS OF INSTITUTIONALIZED PERSONS ACT

The Civil Rights of Institutionalized Persons Act, 42 U.S.C. § 1997 et seq. (CRIPA) was passed by Congress in 1980 and is similar to § 14141. CRIPA authorizes the United States Attorney General to conduct investigations and litigation relating to conditions of confinement in state or locally operated institutions (excluding private facilities). Under the statute, the Special Section of the Civil Rights Section investigates covered facilities to determine whether there is a "pattern or practice" of violations of residents' federal rights (the Section is not authorized to represent individuals or to address specific individual cases). The intent of Congress in passing CRIPA, as identified in § 1997g, is to correct deplorable conditions and abuses of the use of force in institutions that amount to deprivations of rights protected by the United States Constitution.

Section 1997a grants discretionary authority to the Attorney General. Under this provision, whenever the Attorney General has reasonable cause to believe that any State or political subdivision of a State, official, employee, or agent thereof, or other person acting on behalf of a state or political subdivision of a State is subjecting persons residing in or confined to an institution to egregious or flagrant conditions that deprive such persons of rights protected by the Constitution, or that causes that person harm, may institute an investigation or civil action in a federal district court for equitable or declaratory relief. The legislation does not provide for monetary awards. Section 1997b stipulates that prior to performing an investigation at a facility, the Attorney General must provide notification in writing to the governor or chief executive officer that an investigation will be taking place. The announcement must also identify the allegations and supporting facts warranting the investigation.

Section 1997a of the Act defines *institution* as: "any facility or institution which is owned, operated, or managed by, or provides services on behalf of any State or political subdivision of a State." There are five types of "institutions" addressed under CRIPA: (1) jails and prisons, (2) juvenile correctional facilities, (3) mental health facilities, (4) developmental disability facilities, and (5) nursing homes. In accordance with CRIPA, the DOJ reviews complaints, conducts investigations, litigates civil actions that demonstrate a "pattern and practice" of abuse, enforces and monitors court orders, and monitors the progress toward compliance in consent decrees and settlements. The discussion in this chapter only addresses issues pertinent to jails, prisons, and juvenile facilities.

Since CRIPA's enactment in 1980, the DOJ has initiated 409 investigations, resulting in 120 consent decrees and settlements, involving about 240 facilities (Department of State, 2005). These investigations represent about 55 percent jails, prisons, and juvenile correctional facilities. CRIPA enforcement has been a priority with the DOJ since 1999 and there are 56 ongoing investigations. In 2004, 10 jails and six prisons were under consent decree and seven investigations of jails, prisons, and juvenile institutions were under way (DOJ, 2004).

Similar to § 14141, an investigation under CRIPA can result in a consent decree. Investigations into alleged "patterns or practices" that result in a consent decree generally address the following topics regarding prisoner rights: medical and mental health care (including suicide prevention); prisoner supervision and failure to protect (including population management); classification and prisoner discipline; policies and procedures; abuses of the use of force by officers/staff; food services; officer and supervisor training and performance evaluations; the process of conducting investigations of prisoner complaints; and quality of administrative management of the facility.

If an institution decides to enter into a consent decree after the DOJ investigation, a federal court will oversee the stipulations of the agreement and monitor the progress of the compliance with the orders, like § 14141 actions. Many of the consent decrees include an array of the above-described factors that the correctional entity must change, which would be specific to that institution, based on the DOJ's investigation. Failure to comply with the consent decree can result in extending federal oversight for a period of time determined by the court. The DOJ may also bring a civil action against the entity in federal court. Special monitors are appointed, as in § 14141 actions, to monitor the progress toward completion of the stipulations. The institution must provide periodic progress reports.

From 2006 to 2008, the Department of Justice performed 11 investigations regarding prisoner complaints in jails and prisons. Of these investigations, eight resulted in a memorandum of agreement with the agency; two resulted in settled agreements; and one resulted in a Court Order (DOJ, 2009). All but two of these actions involved county jails. Also during this period, the Department of Justice terminated consent decrees with eight jails. Further, the Department of Justice reported conducting 11 investigations regarding complaints occurring in juvenile facilities. The Department of Justice reported that one resulted in a court order; four resulted in settlement agreements; four resulted in memorandums of agreement; and the other two are pending.

The court's decision in *United States v. Terrell County, Georgia* (2006) provides an example of the federal government enforcing CRIPA. The federal government brought a legal action in accordance with CRIPA against a county, county sheriff, and other county officials, seeking a determination that county jail conditions were grossly deficient in violation of the Fourteenth Amendment. The district court granted the government's motion for summary judgment. The court held that the sheriff and other officials were deliberately indifferent to the jail's gross deficiencies in the areas of medical and mental health care for prisoners, protection of prisoners from harm, environmental health and safety of prisoners, and fire safety, in violation of the due process clause. The court remarked that the lack of funds is not a defense to, nor legal justification for, unconstitutional conditions of a jail, for the purpose of analyzing a deliberate indifference claim under the due process clause. Even if a defendant argued that it is planning or working toward construction of a new jail to remedy the unconstitutional conditions at the current facility, the failure to implement interim measures to alleviate those conditions demonstrates deliberate indifference.

DISCUSSION

These two statutes address the ongoing challenges of reforming criminal justice entities. Reforms have been attempted numerous times over the years. Formally, there have been two primary methods that have addressed abuses and misconduct. First, there have been several commission reports since the 1960s. Typically, incidents of alleged misconduct or riots generate an investigation, followed by "blue ribbon panel" reports calling for sweeping changes in the criminal justice agency involved. These reports have been successful in highlighting abuses, but they have not been successful in providing lasting solutions.

The second reform attempt has come through the judicial system. Title 42 U.S.C. § 1983 created a remedy for citizens and prisoners to challenge alleged constitutional rights violations by an officer and his or her supervisor. The United States Supreme Court, beginning with their decisions in *Monroe v. Pape* (1961) and *Monell v. Department of Social Services* (1978) has upheld this remedy. Numerous lawsuits have been filed during the last 40 years and the results of these lawsuits show that plaintiffs have been modestly successful in prevailing in civil rights actions (Kappeler et al., 1996; Ross, 1997). Critics complain, however, that the judicial system has been inconsistent in awarding claims on behalf of plaintiffs and that state laws generally indemnify the officers in the majority of punitive damage awards (Levenson, 2001; Silveria, 2000). Such claims, however, are not fully supported. At least two studies have found that plaintiffs have prevailed in civil lawsuits against the police in 48 percent of cases (Kappeler et al., 1996; Ross, 1998) in 45 percent of cases in correctional litigation.

The courts have fashioned other remedies to curb or punish officer misconduct. The exclusionary rule, developed by the United States Supreme Court in *Mapp v. Ohio* (1961), requires that police officers comply with the requirements of the Fourth Amendment (search and seizure) as well as the Fifth and Sixth Amendments (self-incrimination). It provides that evidence obtained unlawfully by police officers may not be used in a criminal proceeding. The Court ruled that it is the law that sets a criminal free—nothing can destroy a government more quickly than its own failure to follow the law.

It has been argued that exceptions to the exclusionary rule have weakened its ability to deter police abuse (Livingston, 1999; Walker, 2003). This argument, however, has been shown to be misleading. Davies (1985) and Orfield (1987) conducted independent studies that concluded that the exclusion of evidence in cases involving murder, rape, and other violent crimes is exceedingly rare. Orfield also noted that the more serious the crime, the greater the officer's desire to follow the legal procedures, thereby showing the deterrence effect of the exclusionary rule. The American Bar Association (1998) found in a study of police officers and prosecutors that since the *Mapp* decision, police officers generally follow the procedures of the rule and that it has enhanced professionalism. Levenson (1999) observed that there is no evidence and no reason to believe that a police officer will be any less motivated to lie in an administrative hearing, where his reputation and job position are at risk, than in a criminal proceeding where the court threatens to exclude evidence.

There are a variety of laws on the books (i.e., obstruction, perjury, planting evidence, etc.) that allow criminal prosecution of officers who engage in misconduct that rises to the level of criminal behavior. For example, the United States Department of State (2005) chronicles a selection of 18 criminal prosecutions as examples of police and correctional officers sentenced for crimes of abuse from 1999 to 2005. While any law or court standard directing officer conduct can be violated, the ultimate responsibility lies with the individual officer, supervisors, prosecutors, and the courts to ensure that the rule is followed. Prosecutors have the absolute discretion to refuse to prosecute cases if they suspect police misconduct. *Brady v. Maryland* (1963) requires the prosecutor to disclose evidence that may exonerate a defendant and that could be used to impeach a government witness, so a prosecutor has greater motivation to "look behind the curtain." For more than 40 years, however, the exclusionary rule has generally served as a successful spur toward professionalizing the police and curbing abuse (Kamisar, 2003). For example, two officers were convicted and sentenced to prison on federal charges for the Rodney King beating (Levenson, 2001), even after acquittal on state charges. Officer Rafael Perez of the Rampart Precinct of the Los Angeles Police Department was also sentenced to state prison for his participation in the scandal (Boyer, 2001).

UNDERMINING DEMOCRATIC ACCOUNTABILITY

Consent decrees in general, and operating a criminal justice agency by consent decree have a profound effect on public policy. "Policy, wrote Kaufan (1960) is enunciated in rhetoric, and is realized in action." With its passage of CRIPA and § 14141, Congress has ushered in a new model of attempting to curb abuses or misconduct without fully considering the consequences of their handiwork. Management by consent decree represents the new paradigm of attempting to address misconduct and accountability at a federal level, rather than at the local or state levels. There is no question that police and correctional officers are human and abuses have occurred. Officer misconduct cannot be condoned and guilty officers should be held accountable. But the question emerges as to whether § 14141 and CRIPA represent the appropriate social mechanism by which to address allegations of abuse. After years of DOJ investigations and consent decrees, it remains questionable as to whether such federal intervention is effective in bringing lasting reforms to criminal justice agencies. There are several reasons for caution and skepticism about forcing consent decrees on police and correctional agencies and whether it represents legitimate social policy.

One question that begs to be answered is whether every solution should be a federal solution in a country that is founded on the principle of federalism. Federalism is defined as a political system in which power is divided and shared between the national/central government and the states (regional units) in order to limit the power of government. Policing by decree undermines that accountability of government to its constituents and therefore it becomes less responsive (Sandler & Schoenbrod, 2003).

Consent decrees by their intrinsic nature are settlements negotiated behind closed doors, although they become public record upon filing in the court proceedings. It has been suggested that because a potential consent decree requires the cooperation of the police entity in crafting equitable relief, such an agreement does not implicate a "strong" degree of federalism (Kim, 2002). When such important policy decisions are made behind closed doors under threat of a major lawsuit by the federal government, officials become indebted to them and to a minority of community constituents. This represents a policy consequence that results in the government failing to represent the public as a whole. A major power shift occurs when policy-making responsibility is stripped from the local or state government and transferred to the federal government and to the federal courts. Such an action violates the principle of limited government and turns the judiciary into a super-legislature. Subsequently, this frequently leaves governments less capable of responding to the legitimate desires of the public and makes elected officials less accountable to the public. Rabkin (1997) suggests that "the more government is accountable to private litigants, the less it can be accountable to anyone else. Limiting the choices of government officials limits their responsibility, for they cannot be responsible for choices they are not allowed to make."

Entering into a consent decree shifts power from the affected government to the DOJ and the courts. Neither the United States Constitution nor state constitutions allow one legislative body to bind the next, by either contract or budgetary appropriation (McConnell, 1987). Governments may not contract away the power to change policy. Citizens who may have legitimate concerns with governmental policies are unable to approach employees of the DOJ and the federal judge, neither of which are elected officials. Moreover, a consent decree is shifted away from concerns of local voters to the specific concerns of technocrats (Sandler & Schoenbrod, 2003). Consent decree investigations can take years to conduct and conclude. Police agencies essentially lose their rights to a speedy judicial process. Once the contents of the decree are issued police executives are bound by the stipulations.

UNDERMINING POLICE EXECUTIVE LEADERSHIP

Consent decrees have been used as a remedy in the United States during the past 40 years in a majority of prison and jail condition cases in an attempt to reform the prison and jail system. Jails and prisons have been subject to consent decree accountability for longer than their police counterparts. It is debatable whether these decrees have brought lasting reforms to correctional institutions, because the decrees have not accomplished all of their objectives (Sandler & Schoenbrod, 2003). Dilulio (1990) observed in his review of prison consent decrees that successful accomplishments were accounted for by small incremental advances and compromises rather than full-scale assaults. What this means is that when judges act like legislatures, they are more likely to succeed. This, however, exceeds the boundaries of judicial responsibility and allows the judge to assume to the role of a super legislature. Ironically, Congress restricted the use of consent decrees in corrections and limited judicial intervention when it passed the Prison Litigation Reform Act (1996), which ostensibly reduces the filing of "frivolous" prisoner lawsuits and terminates existing consent decrees of correctional facilities. Yet despite the passage of the PLRA, the DOJ continues to pursue investigations into correctional institutions.

A major consequence of consent decrees is that they cannot ensure effective leadership within the agency that is necessary for ongoing reforms to be accomplished, and may even undercut opportunities for such leadership to emerge (Livingston, 1999; Walker, 2003). Glazer (1979) remarked that court orders that are aimed at restructuring public institutions normally result in a decline in staff morale, an increase in staff turnover, and an increase in the unruliness of clientele groups, which undermines police authority by the entire consent process. Wilson (1989) noted that consent decrees aggravate the unfortunate tendency of bureaucracies to focus on counting things rather than helping people. Such appears to be the case with the new paradigm of performing criminal justice responsibilities by decree.

In the only study conducted to date on the impact of police consent decrees, the Vera Institute of Justice (Davis et al., 2002) surveyed a sample of police officers, supervisors, and community leaders in the city of Pittsburgh regarding their perceptions about the outcome of the decree. Generally, community leaders (40%) perceived that the police treated citizens better than before the consent decree, that the decree was a useful tool in improving police practices and accountability, and that they had greater confidence in the police. Citizen complaints declined by 50 percent overall. Supervisors reported that community-oriented policing efforts were detrimentally affected. Their concern emerged from the fact that they were strapped with a great deal of paperwork that kept them from spending quality time with their officers and providing leadership. Although a majority of supervisors reported that the early warning intervention system assisted in identifying problem officers sooner, discipline of officers declined by 45 percent.

The most significant negative impact of the decree was felt by line officers. They commented that their morale had been detrimentally affected, that they were more reluctant to use force and reluctant to make traffic stops. While the use of sick time declined slightly, there was an increase in officers leaving the department. Generally, officers reported that they were less likely to engage in proactive policing strategies. During the five years, arrests declined by 40 percent, clearance rates of arrests declined by 35 percent, traffic summonses declined by 35 percent, and arrests of African-American suspects dropped by 15 percent. There was no noticeable change in the occurrence of Part I or Part II crimes.

COSTS

Start-up and maintenance costs linked with successful compliance with consent decrees are enormous. It is estimated that the LAPD consent decree may cost between $30 and $50 million annually, meaning that over five years, they could pay out more than

$250 million (Levenson, 2001). The Cincinnati consent decree cost approximately $13 million in start-up costs and more than $20 million annually to ensure compliance with the stipulations (Walker, 2003). Without financial assistance from either the state or the federal government, municipalities will be unable to implement or maintain the requirements of the consent decree. Correctional departments have experienced the same problem in funding the associated costs with making the necessary changes consistent with the consent decrees. State and county budgets have had to be realigned and other funding priorities have been neglected in order to comply with a consent decree.

The financial problem is a congressional one. Congress has repeatedly been criticized by state governors for creating unfunded mandates for the states. The United States Supreme Court determined in *Printz v. United States* (1997), in overturning a portion of the Brady Handgun Violence Prevention Act, that by requiring state governments to absorb the financial burden of implementing a federal regulatory program, Congress can take credit for solving problems without having to ask their constituents to pay for the solutions and without raising taxes. Even when the municipalities are not forced to absorb the implementation costs, they are still put in a position of taking the blame for its burdensome effects. Having shifted the blame to local and state officials, Congress is not compelled to consider the negative consequences of their mandate.

Conversely, it is costly for the DOJ to conduct investigations. Since the 1990s, conducting investigations into allegations of misconduct in criminal justice agencies has been a major priority of the DOJ (Department of State, 2005). While costs for conducting such investigations have not been published, the following questions arise: "Does it make sound public policy to spend millions in conducting these investigations?" and "Does it make good public policy for DOJ attorneys to spend their time and budget conducting these investigations?" Clearly these are important questions that require detailed assessment if future investigations are performed.

RESPONSE

It remains debatable whether operating correctional institutions or policing under a consent decree will prove to be effective in bringing about lasting reforms to the criminal justice system. As a matter of practice, patterns of police abuse of citizens or prisoners should not be condoned and an organizational culture that allows such misconduct should be held accountable. Police and correctional officers must be accountable for following the law and proper procedures in performing their duties. Governments cannot be above the law, but federal intervention fails to provide the appropriate social policy to bring about long-term and lasting reforms. The incremental gains are not justified by the immense costs and the long-term threat to our system of democracy.

There are lessons to be learned from the consent decrees, and criminal justice managers should take these lessons into consideration. Administrators are encouraged to voluntarily undertake the following proactive strategies in order to increase their accountability. These strategies align with risk-management principles discussed in Chapter 5 through Chapter 7.

Because consent decrees require a monitor to review the compliance and progress toward the stipulations, administrators should first create a compliance officer position to oversee departmental activities. The compliance officer should report to the chief executive of the department (Schmidt, 2005; Ross, 2003). This position could be a supervisor who would be responsible for ensuring that policies and practices are implemented properly and tracks and assesses pertinent departmental information. Second, administrators should consider instituting a data tracking system designed to record information about the performance of officers and supervisors. Systematically collecting and assessing data about calls for service, arrests, use of force, traffic stops, and pursuits can be instrumental in providing police supervisors with valuable information to use in leading the organization and provide early warning of marginal officer performance. The same type of system could be used to track pertinent information in correctional institutions as well.

Third, administrators should voluntarily review and revise policies and procedures on a regular basis. As the law changes, policies should also be changed in order for officers and supervisors to perform their duties within legal parameters. Fourth, intersecting the data tracking system with the early intervention system has the potential to transform the organizational culture and department. It can raise the standard of officer conduct and supervisory accountability in maintaining proper officer performance and identifying problem employees early. The system provides supervisors with more flexibility in addressing appropriate intervention strategies to keep officer conduct from progressing further thus requiring more severe sanctions. It serves to maintain accountability of officers and supervisors and assists in reducing allegations of failure to supervise or discipline officers.

Fifth, in compliance with the United States Supreme Court decision in *City of Canton v. Harris* (1989), administrators should endeavor to provide their officers with ongoing training commensurate with their duties and in accordance with state requirements. Training should be documented in the data tracking system and designed to address frequently occurring situations, agency policies, and high-profile topics, such as: use of force, pursuits, arrests with or without warrants, domestic violence calls, traffic stops, ethical behavior, and conducting felony arrests. Correctional agencies should also address high-profile subjects as: use of force, responding to special needs prisoners, searches, disturbance control, special threat group management, escapes, medical and psychological care issues of prisoners, transportation of prisoners, and security functions, to mention a few. Sixth, agencies should ensure that investigations into citizen and prisoner complaints and incidents of officer use of force are performed properly, pursuant to policy and the appropriate legal standard. Administrators should consider using an external agency to perform investigations when high-profile cases occur.

The compliance officer should perform regular inspections and audits to ensure that departmental regulations are being followed to prevent any patterns of abuse from occurring. Implementing and maintaining such a system provides a proactive framework with several benefits. Administrators as agency leaders must set the tone for proper conduct and create a department culture that protects constitutional rights of citizens. Public education about such efforts could help to improve public confidence in police and protect it from frivolous complaints. This assures the public that officers are adhering to departmental policies and that supervisors are enforcing them properly, underscoring accountability. It demonstrates to the community that the department has voluntarily undertaken a system of self-governance without being threatened by a lawsuit or judicial intervention.

A fundamental component of the criminal justice profession is that administrators have the responsibility and the right to manage their own departments as other professions do. Criminal justice agencies in the United States have made significant changes since the 1960s, but the new era of consent decrees overshadows and discounts these accomplishments. Rather than the decree stipulations becoming the "standard," leaders of criminal justice agencies will be well served to study the stipulations and work toward making appropriate changes in their department as warranted. Voluntarily incorporating these features and changing agency practices as needed exhibits a policy that underscores professionalism, proactive leadership, and ensures that the agency can be accountable without forced federal intervention. Information provided by the Department of Justice shows a trend of such investigations and resulting consent decrees to be decreasing slightly. Proactive efforts by administrators based on lessons learned from past investigations appear to be affecting these declining trends. Administrators are encouraged to review these investigations and to continue to manage their departments in ways that place them in the best position to defend against complaints of misconduct.

REFERENCES

Bayley, D.H. (1988). "Community Policing: A Report from the Devil's Advocate." In J.R. Green & S.D. Mastrofski (eds.), *Community Policing: Rhetoric or Reality* ? New York, NY: Praeger.

Bayley, D.H. & C.D. Shearing (1996). "The Future of Policing." Law and Society Review 30:585–605.

Bentham. J. (1789; 1948). *The Principles of Morals and Legislation.* New York, NY: Hafner Publishing Company.

Boyer, P.J. (2001). "Testimony on Police Misconduct Ignited the Biggest Scandal in the History of L.A.P.D.: Is it the Real Story?" *The New Yorker* May 21:60.

Bracey, D. (1992). "Police Corruption and Community Relations: Community Policing." *Police Studies* 15:179–183.

Catialno, S.M. (2005). *Criminal Victimization: National Crime Victimization Survey*. Washington, DC: Bureau of Justice Statistics.

Civil Rights of Institutionalized Persons Act (1980), Title 42 U.S.C. § 1997.

Davies, T.Y. (1985). "A Hard Look at What We Know (and Still Need to Learn) About the Costs of the Exclusionary Rule: The NIJ Study and Other Studies of Lost Arrests." American Board Foundation Research 610–645.

Department of Justice (2009). *Settlements and Consent Decrees (2006–2008)*. Washington, DC: Special Litigation Division of the Civil Rights Division. www.doj.org.

Dilulio, J.J. Jr. (1990). *Courts, Corrections and the Constitution*. New York, NY: Oxford University Press.

Glazer, N. (1979). "The Judiciary and Social Policy." In L.J. Theberge (ed.), *The Judiciary in a Democratic Society*. Lexington, MA: Lexington Books.

Greenfeld, P.A. Langan & S.K. Smith (1997). *Police Use of Force: Collection of National Data*. Washington, DC: U.S. Department of Justice.

H.R. Rep. No. 102–104, 102d Congress, 1st Session at 406, 1911 WL 206794, at 138–39 (1991).

International Association of Chiefs of Police (2001). *Police Use of Force in America*. Alexandria, VA: Author.

Kamisar, Y. (2003). "In Defense of the Search and Seizure Exclusionary Rule." *Harvard Journal of Law and Public Policy* 1:119–138.

Kappeler, V.E., S.F. Kappeler & R.V. del Carmen (1996). "A Content Analysis of Police Civil Liability Cases: Decisions of the Federal District Courts, 1978–1990." *Journal of Criminal Justice* 21:325–337.

Kaufman, H. (1960). *The Forest Ranger: A Study in Administrative Behavior*. Baltimore, MD: Johns Hopkins University Press.

Kim, E. (2002). "Vindicating Civil Rights Under 42 U.S.C. 14141: Guidance From Procedures in Complex Litigation." *29 Hastings Constitutional Law Quarterly* 767:1–34.

Klockars, C.B. (1988). "The Rhetoric of Community Policing." In J.R. Green & S.D. Mastrofski (eds.), *Community-Oriented Policing: An Alternative Strategy*. Washington, DC: International City Managers Association.

Langham, P.A., L.A. Greenfeld, S.K. Smith, M.R. Duros & J.L. Levin (2001). *Contacts Between Police and the Public: Findings from the 1999 National Survey*. Washington, DC: U.S. Department of Justice.

Levenson, L.L. (2001). "Police Corruption and New Models for Reform." 35 *Suffolk University Law Review* 1:1–41.

Levenson, L.L. (1999). "Administrative Replacements: How Much Can They Do?" 26 *Pepperdine Law Review* 879–881.

Livingston, D. (1999). "Police Reform and the Department of Justice: An Essay on Accountability." *Buffalo Criminal Law Review* 2:817–859.

Longmeadow Press. (1981, originally published 1851). *The Works of Charles Dickens*. London, UK: Octopus Books Limited.

McConnell, M.W. (1987). "Why Hold Elections? Using Consent Decrees to Insulate Policies from Political Change." *University of Chicago Legal Forum* 295.

Nagel, R.F. (2001). *The Implosion of American Federalism*. Oxford, UK: Oxford University Press.

Orfield, Jr., M.W. (1987). "Comment: The Exclusionary Rule and Deterrence: An Empirical Study of Chicago Narcotics Officers." *54 University of Chicago Law Review* 1015–1055.

Prison Litigation Reform Act (1996). Public L. No. 104–134, Statute 1321, Codified at 18 U.S.C. § 3626.

Rabkin, J.A. (1989). *Judicial Compulsions: How Public Law Distorts Public Policy*. New York, NY: Basic Books.

Rosen, J. (1998). "Search and Seizure." *New Republic* March 27:10.

Ross, D.L. (2005). "A Content Analysis of the Emerging Trends in the Use of Non-Lethal Force Research in Policing." *Law Enforcement Executive Forum* 5:121–149.

Ross, D.L. (2003). *Civil Liability in Criminal Justice*, Third Edition. Cincinnati, OH: Anderson Publishing Co.

Ross, D.L. (2003). "Emerging Trends in Police Failure to Train Liability." *Policing: An International Journal of Police Strategies and Management* 2:169–193.

Ross, D.L. (1997). "Emerging Trends in Correctional Civil Liability Cases: A Content Analysis of Federal Court Decisions of Title 42 United States Code Section 1983: 1970–1994." *Journal of Criminal Justice* 25:501–515.

Sandler, D. & D. Schodendbrod (2003). *Democracy by Decree*. New Haven, CT: Yale University Press.

Schmidt, W. (2004). "Criminal Justice Compliance Officer." *Journal of Law Enforcement Executive Forum* 5:1–14.

Silver, I. (2005). *Police Civil Liability*. New York, NY: Matthew Bender & Co.

Silveria, M.J. (2004). "An Unexpected Application of 42 U.S.C. 14141: Using Investigative Findings for 1983." 52 *UCLA Law Review* 601:1–30.

U.S. Commission on Civil Rights (2000). *Revisiting Who Is Guarding the Guardians?: A Report on Police Practices & Civil Rights in America*. Washington, DC: Author.

United States Department of Justice Web site (2006). www.DOJ.gov. Civil Rights Special Litigation Division. html. Accessed February 2006.

United States Department of Justice (2003). *Principles of Good Policing: Avoiding Violence Between Police and Citizens*. Washington DC: United States Department of Justice.

United States Department of State (2005). *Second Periodic Report of the United States of America to the Committee Against Torture*. Washington, DC: U.S. Department of State.

Vaughn, M.S. and L.F. Coomes (1995). "Police Civil Liability Under Section 1983: When Do Police Officers Act Under Color of Law?" *Journal of Criminal Justice* 23:395–415.

Walker, S. (2003). "New Approaches to Ensuring the Legitimacy of Police Conduct: The New Paradigm of Police Accountability: The U.S. Justice Department 'Pattern or Practice' Suits in Context." 22 *Saint Louis University Public Law Review* 3:1–43.

Walker, S. (2001). "Early Warning Systems for Police: Responding to the Problem Police Officer." *Research in Brief*. Washington, DC: U.S. Department of Justice.

Walker, S., G.P. Alpert & D.J. Kenney (2000). "Early Warning Systems for Police: Concept, History, and Issues." *Police Quarterly* 2:132–152.

Wilson, J.Q. (1989). *Bureaucracy: What Government Agencies Do and Why They Do It*. New York, NY: Basic Books.

Wilson, J.Q. (1985). *Thinking About Crime*. New York, NY: Vintage Books.

Worrall, J.L. and O. Marenin (1998). "Emerging Liability Issues in the Implementation and Adoption of Community-Oriented Policing." *Policing: An International Journal of Police Strategies and Management* 1:1221–136.

Worrall, J.L. (2001). "Culpability Standards in Section 1983 Litigation against Criminal Justice Officials When and Why Mental State Matters." *Crime & Delinquency* 47:28–59.

CASES CITED

Brady v. Maryland, 373 U.S. 83 (1963)
City of Canton v. Harris, 489 U.S. 378 (1989)
Groh v. Ramirez, 540 U.S. 551 (2004)
Hazelwood School District v. United States, 433 U.S. 299 (1977)
International Brotherhood of Teamsters v. United States, 431 U.S. 324 (1977)
Mason County v. Davis, 927 F. 2d 1473 (9th Cir. 1991)
Mapp v. Ohio, 367 U.S. 643 (1961)
Monroe v. Pape, 365 U.S. 167 (1961)
Monell v. Department of Social Services of New York, 436 U.S. 658 (1978)
Printz v. United States, 512 U.S. 898 (1997)
Terry v. Ohio, 392 U.S. 1 (1968)
United States v. City of Columbus, No. CIV A. 2: 99CV1097 (S.D. Ohio 2000)
United States v. Terrell County, Ga., 457 F. Supp. 2d 1359 (M.D. Ga. 2006)

RECRUITING

Factors Affecting the Supply of Police Recruits

JEREMY M. WILSON, BERNARD D. ROSTKER, AND CHA-CHI FAN

E ach year, police departments throughout the United States recruit new personnel. While it is common for departments to share information with others about their programs in an effort to discern "best practices," there is little systematic analysis of characteristics of successful recruiting programs. Departments seldom collect data or implement programs in a way that rigorously controls for changes over time. Similarly, cross-department comparisons are usually descriptive and seldom use statistical techniques to control for differences in departments; that is, departments rarely conduct rigorous cross-sectional analysis.

Police recruitment practices have evolved over time. The first moves toward professionalization occurred with the 1931 recommendations of the Wickersham Commission, which advocated elimination of the spoils system (Alpert, 1991; Walker, 1997). As police agencies moved toward merit-based hiring, they faced dual problems of liability for law enforcement behavior and concerns over discrimination in police work, leading to adoption of more scientific methods in recruitment, culminating in the 1967 forma-tion of the Law Enforcement Assistance Administration (Fyfe et al., 1997; Hogue, Black, and Sigler, 1994; Scrivner, 2006). This system was challenged in the mid-1970s when research indicated that the skills officers required for their work differed from those for which recruits were screened, trained, and tested (Goldstein, 1977). This led the Commission on Accreditation

Jeremy M. Wilson, Bernard D. Rostker, and Cha-Chi Fan, "Factors Affecting the Supply of Police Recruits," *Recruiting and Retaining America's Finest: Evidence-Based Lessons from Police Workforce Planning*, pp. 41–57, 105–113. Copyright © 2010 by RAND Corporation. Reprinted with permission.

for Law Enforcement Agencies to put forth recommendations for diversifying forces. Evaluation processes today may either "select out" candidates (that is, identify flaws disqualifying candidates) or "select in" candidates (that is, identify positive qualities that make applicants attractive candidates). Controversies over these approaches and their merit have persisted throughout the community policing era (Scrivner, 2006). As a result, police recruitment is often not uniform but reflects fragmentary approaches (Orrick, 2008b; Scrivner, 2006; White and Escobar, 2008).

To identify what approaches may be most effective for police recruitment today, in this chapter, using the data from our survey, we attempt a cross-sectional analysis that controls for differing features of agencies and their communities. In particular, we explore the determinants of the supply of police recruits—why recruits join police departments—and the impact that various programs have on that supply.

WHY RECRUITS JOIN POLICE DEPARTMENTS: THE BASIC MODEL

Our models rely on economic theories of occupational choice, which recognize the importance of both cash attractions, such as compensation, and noncash attractions, such as taste for particular work. Such economic models have proven to be useful for practical management. Indeed, such models have guided the military in managing its manpower needs since the advent of the all-volunteer force (see, for example, Fechter, 1970).

AN ECONOMIC MODEL OF WHY RECRUITS JOIN POLICE DEPARTMENTS

An economic model holds that each potential police recruit may choose to apply or not to apply to a police department. In principle, each action carries with it a set of cash and noncash costs and benefits. The model assumes that the potential recruit chooses the specific course of action that provides the highest net cash and noncash benefits. It also assumes that potential recruits can evaluate noncash costs and benefits in cash terms. In other words, it assumes the potential recruit is able to stipulate the number of dollars of additional pay, or cash benefits, required to offset the noncash cost associated with joining the police department. Given these assumptions, we can postulate that the potential police recruit can determine a "reservation wage" making

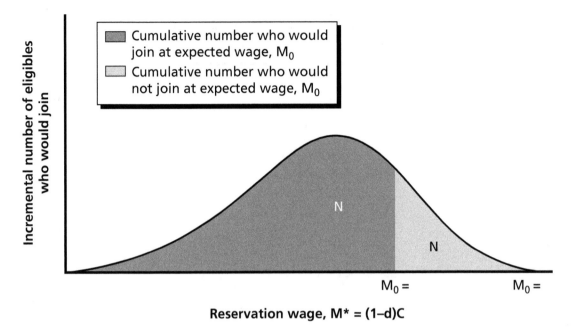

Figure 9.1 Frequency Distribution of Potential Recruits Classified by Their Reservation Wage

the sum of the cash and noncash benefits from joining the police department equal to the sum of that for not joining.[1] The reservation wage is the wage at which a potential recruit would be indifferent to joining or not joining the department. If the actual wage offered is above the reservation wage, the potential recruit will join the department. If it is not, the potential recruit will not join.

The wage at which a potential recruit would be willing to join a department will vary by individual differences in "taste" for or interest in police work. Individuals who are more interested in police work will be willing to accept a lower wage for it. In principle, all potential recruits may be arrayed by their reservation wages, creating a frequency distribution like that in Figure 9.1. The shaded area under the frequency distribution can be transformed into points on the police supply curve, as shown in Figure 9.2. The entire police supply curve in Figure 9.2 displays the number of recruits who would be willing to join the department at each alternative police wage, other things held constant.[2]

---

1   For other examples of models using the concept of reservation wages, see Gordon and Blinder, 1980, and Eckstein and Wolpin, 1989.

2   If a normal curve best approximates the basic distribution of tastes, the cumulative distribution function of that curve (Figure 9.1) is the familiar upward-sloping S-shaped supply curve (Figure 9.2).

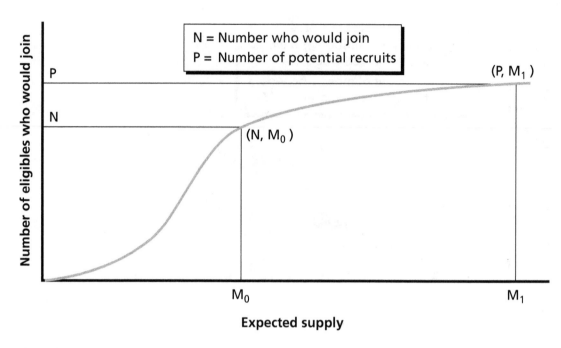

Figure 9.2 Aggregate Police Supply Curve

A SIMPLE MATHEMATICAL MODEL OF WHY RECRUITS JOIN POLICE DEPARTMENTS

In mathematical terms, we can specify the supply function as follows:

$$A = f(M, C, T, P),$$

where

A = number of applicants

M = expected cash or monetary return for joining the police department

C = the expected cash or monetary return for not joining the police department—i.e., the opportunity cost of joining

T = net taste for police work

P = the size of the city, i.e., a scale factor.

We hypothesize that the number of recruits is a positive function of the wages offered by the police department and a negative function of the wage of nonpolice alternatives. In other words, all else equal, the higher police wages are, the more likely a potential recruit will join a police agency, but the higher nonpolice wages are, the more likely a potential police recruit will take work elsewhere. The number of police recruits will also be positively related to the net taste for police work and the scale factor, for which we use city population as a proxy. Larger cities are not only more likely to offer more varied police careers but also have more persons in the workforce.

THE BASIC ECONOMETRIC MODEL

We fitted an ordinary least squares regression model using our 2007 survey and community-level data. To the above function, we added a measure of unemployment to reflect the condition of the local labor market. To measure the specific police labor market, we also added the number of vacancies. Using logarithms for each variable so as to interpret the magnitude of effects in percentage terms,[3] the wage elasticity of supply can be estimated as the coefficient α_1 in the equation

$$\text{Log applicants} = \alpha_0 + \alpha_1 \log M + \alpha_2 \log P + \alpha_3 \log C + \alpha_4 \log\_UER + \alpha_5 \log\_V + \varepsilon,$$

where

applicants = number of recruits who applied

M	=	starting yearly compensation at the local police department
P	=	size of the city
C	=	average yearly compensation in all jobs in the area
UER	=	average yearly unemployment rate in the area
V	=	police department vacancies
ε	=	error term
α_1	=	$\log(\delta A/\delta M)$ = *Elasticity of supply*, which measures the percent change in the number of applicants in response to a percent change in wages offered—e.g., if $\alpha_1 = 10$, a 10 percent change in starting compensation would result in a 10 percent change in the number of applicants.

RESULTS FOR THE BASIC ECONOMETRIC MODEL

Table 9.1 shows results for estimating the basic model for all applicants.[4] This model "explains" about 55 percent of the differences among police departments in our sample.

---

3   While the "double-log" model is helpful in that effects can be interpreted in percentage terms, it also assumes the elasticity coefficients remain constant at each level of the independent variables (Gujarati, 2003). Our limited sample size did not permit thorough testing of how well this functional form fit the data, but it is commonly used in models of demand and production (Greene, 2000).

4   Similar to the nonresponse analyses for individual variables, we tested for systematic differences between the agencies represented in the basic model and the target population on the various agency and community characteristics. The sample was equivalent to the population on all measures except region. The proportion of agencies in the sample located in the northeastern United States was less than in the population (p = 0.10), suggesting that they were underrepresented in the sample.

Table 9.1 Econometric Results for Basic Model of Police Applicants

	Coefficient	Standard Error
Observations	64	—
R-squared	0.546	—
Log of the starting yearly compensation at the local police department	1.053***	0.382
Log of the size of the city	0.797***	0.168
Log of the average yearly compensation in all jobs in the area	0.152	0.174
Log of the average yearly unemploy-ment rate in the area	0.330	0.254
Log of the police department vacancies	0.138	0.131
Constant	−17.226***	4.487

* indicates a statistically significant difference at $p < 0.1$; **, a significant difference at $p < 0.05$; and ***, a significant difference at $p < 0.01$.

NOTE: Coefficients are unstandardized. Neither multicollinearity nor heteroscedasticity were detected in the model.

Sixty-four departments provided data that could be used to estimate a single supply curve for all applicants. Our analysis is generally consistent with economists' view of the importance of cash benefits in choosing a job. Even after accounting for the size of the cities represented in our sample and, we assume, the total number of persons looking and able to apply for police work, the compensation offered by police departments is a statistically significant explanation of the numbers of applicants. Area mean wages, a proxy for wages paid by other employers in the area, and area unemployment rates, a proxy for the general state of employment in the area, are not statistically significant.

Some measurement problems may be hiding the true relationship. We know the value of the starting yearly compensation at each department in the survey, but not the actual alternatives that prospective recruits have. General area wages and unemployment are only proxies.

It is hardly surprising to learn that police departments paying higher starting wages get more recruits. There are many examples of the importance of compensation. For example,

- In 2005 a New York City arbiter cut starting pay for New York City police officers from nearly $36,000 to $25,100 (Wilson and Grammich, 2009). By 2007, the NYPD was 2,000 recruits short of its goal of 2,800, with many new officers planning to take better-paying suburban jobs as soon as they could ("Getting Out of Dodge,"

2008). A restoration of the $35,881 salary for new officers helped the department meet a reduced hiring goal of 1,250 in 2008 (Proffer, 2008).

- Arlington County, Virginia, reported meeting a four-year hiring goal and reaching full strength after increasing starting pay several times. As the department chief told a local reporter, "If we were ever going to fill these positions, we would have to improve salary competitiveness" (Armstrong, 2006). After the pay increases were approved, "We saw an immediate improvement in the quality of applicants and in the flow of applications."

Yet, when asked the effect of higher compensation on recruiting, most departments in our survey indicated that there was no effect on their ability to meet recruiting goals, even though other data provided by the departments suggested that a 10 percent increase in compensation yielded about an 11 percent increase in the number of applicants. This may indicate how difficult it is to determine or discern the impact of policy changes without an appropriate analysis of empirical data.

The positive effect of city population on police recruiting when controlling for other variables may reflect not only a greater absolute number of available potential applicants but also, as noted, a greater variety of available policing careers appealing to those with tastes for such work. We consider this further below.

IMPACT OF THE CRIME RATE ON POLICE RECRUITING

Our basic model above includes only labor-market variables, such as those on compensation and unemployment. Yet the underlying theory holds that "taste" for the job also influences a recruit's decision to join a department. Taste could include the desire for adventurous or nonroutine work or the desire and opportunity to make a community safer (Raganella and White, 2004; Stone and Tuffin, 2000; Slater and Reiser, 1988; Martin, 1980; Van Maanen, 1973). We cannot directly measure individual taste for or interest in police work, but we can measure some characteristics that distinguish police work, individual departments, and opportunity to help make a community safer. We might, in particular, expect local crime rates to affect recruiting police jobs. To assess the effects of crime on local police recruiting, we used three measures: rate of violent crimes per 100,000 residents, rate of property crimes, and rate of all crimes. Because, as Table 9.2 shows, these three measures of crime are highly correlated, and we wished to determine whether particular types of crime might affect recruiting, we

Table 9.2 Crime Rate Correlation Matrix

	Violent Crime Rate	Property Crime Rate	Total Crime Rate
Violent Crime Rate	1	N/A	N/A
Property Crime Rate	0.7045	1	N/A
Total Crime Rate	0.8102	0.9868	1

constructed three separate models to assess their effects: one for violent crime, one for property crime, and one for total crime.

Controlling for both labor-market variables and crime rates shows that crime rates—violent, property, and total—boost recruiting.[5] Each column in Table 9.3 represents a different model: The base model does not include a crime rate, while the remaining three columns model the effect of the violent crime rate, the property crime rate, and the total crime rate on police recruiting.

More demanding, and less safe, work does not make potential recruits less inclined to be police officers but rather more inclined. As with that in larger cities, perhaps police work in areas of greater crime, regardless of size, appeals more to persons with a taste for police work or a desire and opportunity to make a community safer.

POLICE DEPARTMENT EFFORTS TO IMPROVE RECRUITING

Police departments, of course, can make their own efforts to recruit officers regardless of local conditions. We consider below tools that departments may wish to use in their recruiting, including recruiters and budgets for them, advertising, and incentives.

---

5 Similar to the core regression model, the samples of agencies represented in the crime models were equivalent to the target population on all agency and community measures except region. Agencies in the northeastern United States were underrepresented (p = 0.06 for each model). We attempted to explore the instability of the yearly compensation variable, which was statistically significant in the models containing property and total crime rates but not the basic or violent crime–rate model. Our tests did not find multicollinearity or heteroscedasticity in any of the models. Nevertheless, when we employed bootstrapping to estimate these regression models, the yearly compensation variable was not statistically significant in any. This suggests that the instability of this variable might be due to an insufficient sample size.

Table 9.3 Econometric Results for Basic Model of Police Recruits with Crime Rates Included

	Basic Model	With Violent Crime Rate	With Property Crime Rate	With Total Crime Rate
Observations	64	61	60	60
R-squared	0.546	0.592	0.595	0.599
Log of the starting yearly compensation at the local police department (standard error)	1.053*** (0.382)	1.288*** (0.384)	1.257*** (0.375)	1.281*** (0.376)
Log of the size of the city (standard error)	0.797*** (0.168)	0.821*** (0.181)	0.834*** (0.164)	0.835*** (0.165)
Log of the average yearly compensation in all jobs in the area (standard error)	0.152 (0.174)	0.155 (0.151)	0.258* (0.141)	0.245* (0.141)
Log of the average yearly unemployment rate in the area (standard error)	0.330 (0.254)	0.073 (0.267)	0.228 (0.257)	0.186 (0.258)
Log of the police department vacancies (standard error)	0.138 (0.131)	0.080 (0.120)	0.116 (0.117)	0.108 (0.116)
Log of the crime rate (standard error)	—	0.392*** (0.126)	0.455*** (0.159)	0.488*** (0.157)
Constant (standard error)	−17.226*** (4.487)	−22.067*** (4.543)	−24.608*** (5.360)	−25.000*** (5.400)

*, **, and *** indicate a statistically significant difference at the 0.1, 0.05, and 0.01 levels, respectively, indicating that the observed difference is likely not due to chance.

NOTE: Coefficients are unstandardized. Neither multicollinearity nor heteroscedasticity were detected in the models.

RECRUITERS AND RECRUITING BUDGET

Of the 70 departments in our survey sample, 55 have full-time recruiters. Fifteen departments had no full-time recruiters, but the average number per agency was four (Figure 9.3). On average, departments in our survey employed one recruiter per 100,000 residents, with one agency employing 14 per 100,000 residents. Statistical analysis not shown found no significant relationship between the numbers of recruiters, whether civilian or sworn officers, and of applications. We also found no evidence of a relationship between recruiting budgets and applications.

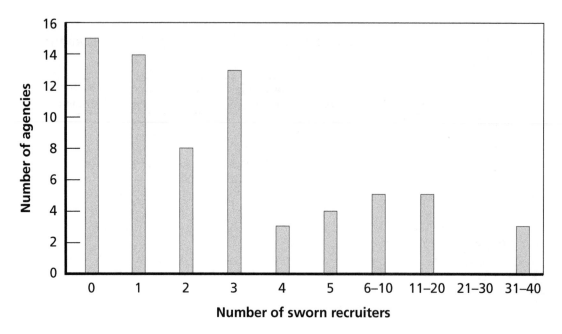

Figure 9.3 Number of Full-Time Sworn Recruiters

ADVERTISING

Departments reported using a wide variety of advertising in their recruiting efforts. Among the most common means are career fairs, Internet postings, posters, and mass media, such as newspapers, radio, and television (Figure 9.4).

To test the effects of differing forms of advertising on recruiting, we constructed a multivariate model that included labor-force variables and variables for forms of advertising that were used by 20 to 50 agencies in our sample.[6] The only advertising variable to have any statistically significant effect on recruiting was television advertising, and the effect was positive (Table 9.4).

The effect of television advertising was unexplainably large. The 0.471 coefficient translates into a 60 percent increase in applicants as a result of television advertising.[7] We can conclude that other means of advertising included in our model do not appear to have been effective, but we note again that there were several methods of advertising that we did not include in our model because variation in their use, and our ability to discern their specific effects, was minimal.

---

6   We limited the number of agencies so that we could discern the effect a given form might have. We would be less able to discern the effect of a particular form of advertising used by very few or very many departments.

7   Given that advertising is an untransformed dummy variable and "applications" is logged in this model, the percentage effect is calculated as $\exp(0.471) - 1$, which equals 60.

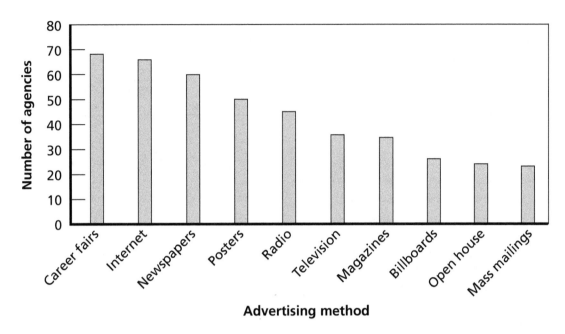

Figure 9.4 Prevalence of Common Advertising Used by Police Departments

RECRUITING INCENTIVES

Departments also use a wide variety of recruiting incentives. Among agencies in our sample, these included

- uniform allowance, used by 97 percent of agencies
- training salary, 84 percent
- college tuition reimbursement, 74 percent
- salary increase for degree, 60 percent
- paid academy expenses, 44 percent
- take-home car, 43 percent
- health club membership, 14 percent
- signing bonus, 14 percent
- tuition for external academy, 13 percent
- other cash bonus, 11 percent
- academy graduation bonus, 9 percent
- mortgage discount, 7 percent
- relocation expenses, 7 percent
- schedule preferences to accommodate coursework, 6 percent.

Table 9.4 Econometric Results for Basic Model of Police Recruits with Select Means of Advertising

	Basic Model: Total	With Common Means of Advertising
Observations	64	64
R-squared	0.546	0.606
Log of the starting yearly compensation at the local police department (standard error)	1.053*** (0.382)	1.196*** (0.397)
Log of the size of the city (standard error)	0.797*** (0.168)	0.743*** (0.185)
Log of the average yearly compensation in all jobs in the area (standard error)	0.152 (0.174)	0.210 (0.152)
Log of the average yearly unemployment rate in the area (standard error)	0.330 (0.254)	0.136 (0.285)
Log of the police department vacancies (standard error)	0.138 (0.131)	0.143 (0.129)
Magazine (standard error)	N/A	−0.028 (0.211)
Radio (standard error)	N/A	−0.360 (0.218)
Television (standard error)	N/A	0.471** (0.224)
Billboard (standard error)	N/A	0.260 (0.203)
Posters (standard error)	N/A	0.040 (0.260)
Mailings (standard error)	N/A	0.054 (0.231)
Open house (standard error)	N/A	−0.180 (0.205)
Constant (standard error)	−17.226*** (4.487)	−18.477*** (4.593)

*, **, and *** indicate a statistically significant difference at the 0.1, 0.05, and 0.01 levels, respectively, indicating that the observed difference is likely not due to chance.

NOTE: Coefficients are unstandardized. Neither multicollinearity nor heteroscedasticity were detected in the models.

We again constructed a statistical model including labor-force variables and those incentives used by a middling range of agencies, or, more specifically, college reimbursement, salary increases for degrees, paid academy expenses, and take-home cars. We found none of the incentives to have a statistically significant effect on the number of applicants (these models also showed no signs of multicollinearity or heteroscedasticity).

Table 9.5 Econometric Results for Basic Model of Police Recruits and Gender-Specific Models

	Basic Model	Base Model for Gender	Male-Only Model	Female-Only Model
Observations	64	46	46	46
R-squared	0.546	0.582	0.491	0.406
Log of the starting yearly compensation at the local police department (standard error)	1.053*** (0.382)	1.354*** (0.475)	2.072* (1.191)	1.633 (1.569)
Log of the size of the city (standard error)	0.797*** (0.168)	0.752*** (0.212)	0.547* (0.312)	0.521 (0.404)
Log of the average yearly compensation in all jobs in the area (standard error)	0.152 (0.174)	0.139 (0.186)	−0.345 (3.397)	−0.326 (4.832)
Log of the average yearly unemployment rate in the area (standard error)	0.330 (0.254)	0.225 (0.320)	−1.100 (0.945)	−1.093 (1.077)
Log of the police department vacancies (standard error)	0.138 (0.131)	0.169 (0.168)	0.228 (0.231)	0.398 (0.326)
Constant (standard error)	−17.226*** (4.487)	−19.709*** (5.153)	−18.124 (27.758)	−15.573 (39.539)

*, **, and *** indicate a statistically significant difference at the 0.1, 0.05, and 0.01 levels, respectively, indicating that the observed difference is likely not due to chance.

NOTE: Coefficients are unstandardized. Multicollinearity was not detected in the models. Heteroscedasticity was detected in the male- and female-specific models so we adjusted the standard errors in these models based on procedures outlined by Davidson and MacKinnon (1993).

RECRUITING BY GENDER AND RACE/ETHNICITY

As noted earlier, most agencies target racial and ethnic minorities, as well as women, for special recruiting efforts. To assess the recruiting environment for male and female recruits, we constructed separate models of labor-force variables for total, male, and female recruits in the 46 departments providing all such information.[8] We found generally similar results, but a greater wage elasticity for male applicants than for the overall sample (Table 9.5). Also, compensation was statistically unrelated to female

8   The sample of agencies represented in the gender models was equivalent to the target population on all agency and community measures except region. Agencies in the Northeast region of the United States were underrepresented (p = 0.09).

Table 9.6 Econometric Results for Basic Model of Police Recruits and Race-Specific Models

	Basic Model	Basic Model for Race	Model for White Recruits	Model for Nonwhite Recruits
Observations	64	47	47	47
R-squared	0.546	0.582	0.307	0.492
Log of the starting yearly compensation at the local police department (standard error)	1.053*** (0.382)	1.349*** (0.475)	1.623 (1.327)	2.624*** (0.800)
Log of the size of the city (standard error)	0.797*** (0.168)	0.750*** (0.212)	0.327 (0.398)	0.810** (0.380)
Log of the average yearly compensation in all jobs in the area (standard error)	0.152 (0.174)	0.136 (0.184)	−0.323 (3.478)	−0.554 (0.354)
Log of the average yearly unemployment rate in the area (standard error)	0.330 (0.254)	0.208 (0.315)	−1.074 (1.286)	−1.345* (0.729)
Log of the police department vacancies (standard error)	0.138 (0.131)	0.173 (0.167)	0.326 (0.268)	0.233 (0.257)
Constant (standard error)	−17.226*** (4.487)	−19.590*** (5.133)	−11.713 (28.473)	−25.632*** (8.689)

*, **, and *** indicate a statistically significant difference at the 0.1, 0.05, and 0.01 levels, respectively, indicating that the observed difference is likely not due to chance.

NOTE: Coefficients are unstandardized. Multicollinearity was not detected in the models. Heteroscedasticity was detected in the model for white recruits, so we adjusted the standard errors in this model based on procedures outlined by Davidson and MacKinnon (1993).

applicants. We did not find any of the advertising strategies or recruiting incentives included in our survey to have a statistically significant effect on numbers of male and female applicants (and hence do not list these in Table 9.5).

Similarly, we assessed the recruiting environment for white and nonwhite recruits, constructing separate models for each among the 47 departments that provided the necessary data (Table 9.6).[9] Again, the results were roughly similar for both groups of recruits. The wage elasticity was greater for the nonwhite applicant group than for the overall group, but wages were statistically unrelated to the number of white applicants. Further investigation is needed to explain why unemployment was inversely related to

9   As in the gender models, the sample of agencies represented in the race/ethnicity models was equivalent to the target population on all agency and community measures except region. Agencies in the Northeast were underrepresented in the sample (p = 0.08).

nonwhite applicants. We found none of the advertising strategies or recruiting incentives to have a statistically significant effect on the number of nonwhite applicants. We also found none of the recruiting incentives to have a statistically significant effect on the number of white applicants. We found a statistically significant negative effect of radio advertising and a statistically significant positive effect of posters on white applicants (results not shown), but the coefficients are unusually high, suggesting extremely large effects—or, more likely, the need for further analysis beyond the scope of this project to discern the true effects of these strategies.

REFERENCES

Alpert, Geoffrey P., "Hiring and Promoting Police Officers in Small Departments: The Role of Psychological Testing," *Criminal Law Bulletin*, Vol. 27, No. 3, May/June 1991, pp. 261–269.

Archbold, C. A., and E. R. Maguire, "Studying Civil Suits Against the Police: A Serendipitous Findings of Sample Selection Bias," *Police Quarterly*, Vol. 5, 2002, pp. 222–249.

Armstrong, Kristen, "Arlington's Police Force Makes It to Full Staffing," *Sun Gazette Newpapers*, November 15, 2006.

Birati, Assa, and Aharon Tziner, "Successful Promotion of Early Retirement: A Quantitative Approach," *Human Resource Management Review*, Vol. 5, No. 1, Spring 1995, pp. 53–62.

Bowyer, Richard F., "Recruiting 21st Century Army Warriors: A Task Requiring National Attention," U.S. Army War College Strategy Research Project, Carlisle, Pa.: U.S. Army War College, 2007.

Braga, Anthony A., "The Effects of Hot Spots Policing on Crime," *The Annals of the American Academy of Political and Social Science*, Vol. 578, 2001, pp. 104–125.

Clarke, R. V., and H. Goldstein, "Reducing Theft at Construction Sites: Lessons from a Problem-Oriented Project," in N. Tilley, ed., *Analysis for Crime Prevention, Crime Prevention Studies*, Vol. 13, Monsey, N.Y.: Criminal Justice Press, 2002.

Clear, T. R., and N. A. Frost, "Informing Public Policy," *Criminology & Public Policy*, Vol. 6, 2007, pp. 633–640.

Cooper, Christine, and Samantha Ingram, "Retaining Officers in the Police Service: A Study of Resignations and Transfers in Ten Forces," London: Home Office Communication Development Unit, NCJ 205347, 2004. As of May 28, 2010: http://www.homeoffce.gov.uk/rds/pdfs04/r212.pdf

COPS Office, *Community Policing Dispatch*, Washington, D.C.: U.S. Department of Justice, Office of Community-Oriented Policing Services, June 2009. As of July 7, 2009: http://www.cops.usdoj.gov/html/dispatch/June_2009/hiring_recovery.htm

Davidson, R., and J. G. MacKinnon, *Estimation and Inference in Econometrics*, New York: Oxford University Press, 1993.

Davis, Lois M., Louis T. Mariano, Jennifer E. Pace, Sarah K. Cotton, and Paul Steinberg, *Combating Terrorism: How Prepared Are State and Local Response Organizations?* Santa Monica, Calif.: RAND Corporation, MG-309-OSD, 2006. As of March 27, 2010: http://www.rand.org/pubs/monographs/MG309/

Davis, Lois M., K. Jack Riley, Greg Ridgeway, Jennifer Pace, Sarah K. Cotton, Paul S. Steinberg, Kelly Damphousse, and Brent L. Smith, *When Terrorism Hits Home: How Prepared Are State and Local Law Enforcement?* Santa Monica, Calif.: RAND Corporation, MG-104, 2004. As of March 27, 2010: http://www.rand.org/pubs/monographs/MG104/

DeRugy, Veronique, "What Does Homeland Security Spending Buy?" Washington, D.C.: American Enterprise Institute for Public Policy Research, Working Paper #18213, December 14, 2006. As of October 11, 2009: http://www.aei.org/docLib/20061214_FactsandFigures.pdf

Draut, Tamara, "Economic State of Young America," New York, N.Y.: Demos, Spring, 2008. As of October 18, 2009: http://www.demos.org/pubs/esya_web.pdf

Draut, Tamara, and Javier Silva, "Generation Broke: Borrowing to Make Ends Meet," New York: Demos, Briefing Paper #2, October 2004. As of October 11, 2009: http://archive.demos.org/pubs/Generation_Broke.pdf

Eck, J. E., and W. Spelman, "Who Ya Gonna Call? The Police as Problem Busters," *Crime and Delinquency*, Vol. 33, 1987, pp. 31–52.

Eckstein, Zvi, and Kenneth I. Wolpin, "The Specification and Estimation of Dynamic Stochastic Discrete Choice Models: A Survey," *The Journal of Human Resources*, Vol. 24, No. 4, Autumn 1989, pp. 562–598.

Egan, Timothy, "Police Forces, Their Ranks Thin, Offer Bonuses, Bounties and More," *New York Times*, December 28, 2005. As of June 24, 2010: http://www.nytimes.com/2005/12/28/national/28police.html

Fechter, Alan E., "Impact of Pay and Draft Policy on Army Enlistment Behavior," in Gates Commission, ed., *Studies Prepared for the President's Commission on an All-Volunteer Armed Force*, Washington, D.C.: U.S. Government Printing Office, 1970, pp. II-3-1 to II-3-59.

Frawley, Kathleen E., *The Effects of 9/11 on the Fire Fighter Labor Market*, Bloomington, Ill.: Illinois Wesleyan University, Economics Department Honors Projects paper 7, 2006. As of June 24, 2010: http://digitalcommons.iwu.edu/econ_honproj/7/

Frost, J. A., "Predictors of Job Satisfaction and Turnover Intention in Police Organizations: A Procedural Approach," Chicago: The University of Chicago, Ph.D. dissertation, 2006.

Fyfe, James J., "Too Many Missing Cases: Holes in Our Knowledge About Police Use of Force," *Justice Research and Policy*, Vol. 4, 2002, pp. 87–102.

Fyfe, James J., Jack R. Greene, William F. Walsh, O. W. Wilson, and Roy McLaren, *Police Administration*, 5th Edition, New York: McGraw Hill, 1997.

"Getting Out of Dodge: Young Cops in Far Rockaway Recite the NYUPD Blues and Try to Flee to Suburban Jobs," *Village Voice*, January 29, 2008. As of March 30, 2010: http://www.villagevoice.com/2008-01-29/news/getting-out-of-dodge/

Gilmore Commission, "Forging America's New Normalcy: Securing Our Homeland, Preserving Our Liberty," *The Fifth Annual Report to the President and the Congress of the Advisory Panel to Assess Domestic Response Capabilities for Terrorism Involving Weapons of Mass Destruction*, 2003. As of March 27, 2010: http://www.rand.org/nsrd/terrpanel/volume_v/volume_v.pdf

Goldstein, Herman, *Policing a Free Society*, Cambridge, Mass.: Ballinger Publishing, 1977.

Gordon, Roger H., and Alan S. Blinder, "Market Wages, Reservation Wages, and Retirement Decisions," *Journal of Public Economics*, Vol. 14, No. 12, October 1980, pp. 277–308.

Gottfredson, Michael R., and Don M. Gottfredson, *Decision Making in Criminal Justice: Toward the Rational Exercise of Discretion*, Second Edition, New York: Plenum Press, 1988.

Greene, William H., *Econometric Analysis*, 4th Edition, Upper Saddle River, N.J.: Prentice Hall, 2000.

Grissmer, David W., and Bernard D. Rostker, "Military Manpower in a Changing World," in Joseph Kruzel, ed., *American Defense Annual: 1991–1992*, New York: Lexington Books, 1992, pp. 127–145.

Gujarati, Damodar N., *Basic Econometrics*, 4th Edition,, New York: McGraw-Hill, 2003.

Hayes, Hennessey, and Kathleen Daly, "Youth Justice Conferencing and Reoffending," *Justice Quarterly*, Vol. 20, No. 4, December 2003, pp. 725–764.

Hickman, Matthew J., and Brian A. Reaves, "Local Police Departments, 2003," Washington, D.C.: U.S. Department of Justice, Office of Justice Programs, Bureau of Justice Statistics, NCJ 210118, 2006. As of July 14, 2009: http://www.ojp.usdoj.gov/bjs/pub/pdf/lpd03.pdf

Hogue, Mark C., Tommie Black, and Robert T. Sigler, "The Differential Use of Screening Techniques in the Recruitment of Police Officers," *American Journal of Police*, Vol. 13, No. 2, 1994, pp. 113–124.

Holtom, Brooks C., Terence R. Mitchell, Thomas W. Lee, and Marion B. Eberly, "Turnover and Retention Research: A Glance At the Past, A Closer View of the Present, and a Venture into the Future," *The Academy of Management Annals*, Vol. 2, No. 1, 2008, pp. 231–274.

Johnston, Lloyd D., Patrick M. O'Malley, Jerald G. Bachman, and John E. Schulenberg, "Various Stimulant Drugs Show Continuing Gradual Declines Among Teens in 2008, Most Illicit Drugs Hold Steady," Ann Arbor, Mich.: University of Michigan News Service, December 11, 2008. As of November 20, 2009: http://monitoringthefuture.org/data/08data.html#2008data-drugs

Jordan, William T., Lorie Fridell, Donald Faggiani, and Bruce Kubu, "Attracting Females and Racial/Ethnic Minorities to Law Enforcement," *Journal of Criminal Justice*, Vol. 37, No. 4, July–August 2009, pp. 333–341.

Kane, Tim, "The Demographics of Military Enlistment After 9/11," Washington, D.C.: The Heritage Foundation, Executive Memorandum #987, November 3, 2005. As of November 11, 2009: http://www.heritage.org/research/nationalsecurity/em987.cfm

Kennedy, D. M., A. A. Braga, A. M. Piehl, and E. J. Waring, *Reducing Gun Violence: The Boston Gun Project's Operation Ceasefire*, Washington, D.C.: U.S. Department of Justice, 2001.

Kondrasuk, Jack N., "The Effects of 9/11 on Human Resource Management: Recovery, Reconsideration, and Renewal," *Employee Responsibilities and Rights Journal*, Vol. 16, No. 1, March 2004, pp. 25–35.

Koper, C. S., E. R. Maguire, and G. E. Moore, *Hiring and Retention Issues in Police Agencies: Readings on the Determinants of Police Strength, Hiring and Retention of Officers, and the Federal COPS Program*, Washington, D.C.: Urban Institute Justice Policy Center, NCJRS No. 193428, 2002.

Langworthy, R. H., "LEMAS: A Comparative Organizational Research Platform," *Justice Research and Policy*, Vol. 4, 2002, pp. 21–38.

Lipsey, M. W., *Design Sensitivity: Statistical Power for Experimental Research*, Thousand Oaks, Calif.: Sage Publications, 1990.

Lynch, Jessica E., and Michelle Tuckey, "Understanding Voluntary Turnover: An Examination of Resignations in Australasian Police Organizations," Payneham, Australia: Australasian Centre for Policing Research, 2004.

Maguire, E. R., *Police Departments as Learning Laboratories*, Police Foundation: Ideas in American Policing, No. 6, 2004.

Maguire, Edward R., and William R. King, "Trends in the Policing Industry," *The Annals of the American Academy of Political and Social Science*, Vol. 593, 2004, pp. 15–41.

Maguire, Edward R., and Stephen D. Mastrofski, "Patterns of Community Policing in the United States," *Police Quarterly*, Vol. 3, No. 1, March 2000, pp. 4–45.

Maguire, E. R., and R. Schulte-Murray, "Issues and Patterns in the Comparative International Study of Police Strength," *International Journal of Comparative Sociology*, Vol. 42, 2001, pp. 75–100.

Maguire, E. R., J. B. Snipes, C. D. Uchida, and M. Townsend, "Counting Cops: Estimating the Number of Police Departments and Police Officers in the USA," *Policing: An International Journal of Police Strategies & Management*, Vol. 21, 1998, pp. 97–120.

Makinen, Gail, *The Economic Effects of 9/11: A Retrospective Assessment*, Washington, D.C.: Congressional Research Service, September 27, 2002. As of November 11, 2009: http://www.fas.org/irp/crs/RL31617.pdf

Manolatos, Tony, "S.D. Cops Flee City's Fiscal Mess, Seek Jobs at Other Departments," *San Diego Union-Tribune*, July 5, 2006. As of November 11, 2009: http://sports.uniontrib.com/uniontrib/20060705/news_1n5gary.html

Martin, S. E., *Breaking and Entering: Policewomen on Patrol*, Berkeley: University of California Press, 1980.

McGarrell, Edmund. F., and Natalie K Hipple,, "Family Group Conferencing and Re-Offending Among First-Time Juvenile Offenders: The Indianapolis Experiment," *Justice Quarterly*, Vol. 24, No. 2, June 2007, pp. 221–246.

McGarrell, E. F., S. Chermak, and A. Weiss, "Reducing Gun Violence: Evaluation of the Indianapolis Police Department's Directed Patrol Project," Washington, D.C.: National Institute of Justice, Special Report, 2002. As of July 22, 2010: http://www.ncjrs.gov/txtfiles1/nij/188740.txt

McGarrell, E. F., S. Chermak, A. Weiss, and J. M. Wilson, "Reducing Firearms Violence Through Directed Patrol," *Criminology & Public Policy,* Vol. 1, 2001, pp. 119–148.

Merck, J. W., and Kathleen Hall, *A Markovian Flow Model: The Analysis of Movement in Large-Scale (Military) Personnel Systems,* Santa Monica, Calif.: RAND Corporation, R-514-PR, February 1971. As of March 30, 2010: http://www.rand.org/pubs/reports/R0514/

Mobley, William H., *Employee Turnover: Causes, Consequences, and Control,* Reading, Mass.: Addison-Wesley, 1982.

National Research Council, Committee on the Youth Population and Military Recruitment, *Attitudes, Aptitudes, and Aspirations of American Youth: Implications for Military Recruiting,* 2003. As of November 20, 2009: http://www.nap.edu/catalog.php?record_id=10478

New South Wales Council on the Cost of Government (NSWCCG), *First Report,* Sydney, Australia, 1996.

Orrick, W. Dwayne, "Maximizing Officer Retention," Presentation at the RAND Summit on Recruitment and Retention, Washington, D.C., June 2008a. As of September 2, 2009: http://www.cops.usdoj.gov/Default.asp?Item=2101

Orrick, W. Dwayne, *Recruitment, Retention, and Turnover of Police Personnel: Reliable, Practical, and Effective Solutions,* Springfield, Ill.: Charles C. Thomas Publishers, 2008b.

Pomfret, John, "Police Finding It Hard to Fill Jobs," *Washington Post,* March 27, 2006. As of June 24, 2010: http://www.washingtonpost.com/wp-dyn/content/article/2006/03/26/ AR2006032600995.html

Proffer, Ben, "More Money, More NYPD Recruits," *New York,* July 6, 2008. As of March 30, 2009: http://nymag.com/news/intelligencer/48332/

Raganella, A. J., and M. D. White, "Race, Gender, and Motivation for Becoming a Police Officer: Implications for Building a Representative Police Department," *Journal of Criminal Justice,* Vol. 32, 2004, pp. 501–513.

Raymond, Barbara, Laura J. Hickman, Laura Miller, and Jennifer S. Wong, *Police Personnel Challenges After September 11: Anticipating Expanded Duties and a Changing Labor Pool,* Santa Monica, Calif.: RAND Corporation, OP-154-RC, 2005. As of May 5, 2009: http://www.rand.org/pubs/occasional_papers/OP154/

Riley, K. Jack, Gregory F. Treverton, Jeremy M. Wilson, and Lois M. Davis, *State and Local Intelligence in the War on Terrorism,* Santa Monica, Calif.: RAND Corporation, MG-394-RC, 2005. As of March 27, 2010: http://www.rand.org/pubs/monographs/MG394/

Rostker, Bernard, *I Want You! The Evolution of the All-Volunteer Force,* Santa Monica, Calif.: RAND Corporation, MG-265-RC, 2006. As of July 21, 2010: http://www.rand.org/pubs/monographs/MG265/

Rostker, Bernard, William M. Hix, and Jeremy M. Wilson, *Recruitment and Retention: Lessons for the New Orleans Police Department,* Santa Monica, CA: RAND Corporation, MG-585-RC, 2007. As of March 27, 2010: http://www.rand.org/pubs/monographs/MG585/

Scrivner, Ellen, *Innovations in Police Recruitment and Hiring: Hiring in the Spirit of Service,* Washington, D.C.: Office of Community Oriented Policing Services, 2006. As of May 5, 2009: http://www.cops.usdoj.gov/RIC/ResourceDetail.aspx?RID=113

Sherman, L. W., and B. D. Glick, "The Quality of Police Arrest Statistics," *Police Foundation Reports,* Washington, D.C.: Police Foundation, 1984.

Sherman, Lawrence, and Heather Strang, "Restorative Justice: What We Know and How We Know It," *Jerry Lee Program on Randomized Controlled Trials in Restorative Justice, Working Paper #1,* Philadelphia: University of Pennsylvania, Jerry Lee Center of Criminology, 2004.

Sherman, Lawrence, Heather Strang, and Daniel Woods, *Recidivism Patterns in the Canberra Reintegrative Shaming Experiments (RISE),* Canberra: Centre for Restorative Justice, Australian National University, 2000.

Slater, Harold R., and Martin Reiser, "A Comparative Study of Factors Influencing Police Recruitment," *Journal of Police Science and Administration,* Vol. 16, No. 3, 1988, pp. 168–176.

Smith, A. R., "Defense Manpower Studies," *Operations Research Quarterly,* Vol. 19, No. 3, September 1968.

Spielman, Fran, "Early Retirement for Cops Helps Budget, Not Force," *Chicago Sun-Times*, July 23, 2009. As of October 12, 2009: http://www.suntimes.com/news/cityhall/1681991,chicago-cops-shortage-retirement-072309.article

Stone, V., and R. Tuffin, "Attitudes of People from Minority Ethnic Communities Towards a Career in the Police Service," *Home Office Police Research Series Paper, 136*, London: Home Office, 2000. As of July 17, 2010: http://rds.homeoffice.gov.uk/rds/prgpdfs/prs136.pdf

Sturm, R., J. S. Ringel, D. Lakdawalla, J. Bhattacharya, D. P. Goldman, M. D. Hurd, G. Joyce, C. W. A. Panis, and T. Andreyeva, *Obesity and Disability: The Shape of Things to Come*, Santa Monica, Calif.: RAND Corporation, RB-9043, 2004. As of November 11, 2009: http://www.rand.org/pubs/research_briefs/RB9043-1/

Switzer, Merlin E., *Recruitment and Retention: Best Practices Update*, Sacramento, Calif.: Commission on Peace Officer Standards and Training, April 2006.

Taylor, Bruce, Bruce Kubu, Lorie Fridell, Carter Rees, Tom Jordan, and Jason Cheney, *Cop Crunch: Identifying Strategies for Dealing with the Recruiting and Hiring Crisis in Law Enforcement*, Washington, D.C.: Police Executive Research Forum, 2006. As of November 11, 2009: http://www.ncjrs.gov/pdffiles1/nij/grants/213800.pdf

Tulgan, Bruce, *Managing Generation X: How to Bring Out the Best in Young Talent*, Oxford: Capstone, 2000.

Twenge, Jean M., and Stacy M. Campbell, "Generational Differences in Psychological Traits and Their Impact on the Workplace," *Journal of Managerial Psychology*, Vol. 23, No. 8, 2008, pp. 862–877.

Uchida, C. D., C. Bridgeforth, and C. F. Wellford, "Law Enforcement Statistics: The State of the Art," *American Journal of Police*, Vol. 5, 1986, pp. 23–43.

Uchida, Craig D., and William R. King, "Police Employee Data: Elements and Validity," *Justice Research and Policy*, Vol. 4, 2002, pp. 11–19.

U.S. Bureau of Labor Statistics, "May 2008 National Occupational Employment and Wage Estimates, United States," Occupational Employment Statistics, last modified May 29, 2009. As of June 24, 2010: http://www.bls.gov/oes/2008/may/oes_nat.htm

U.S. Department of Defense, Office of the Undersecretary of Defense, Personnel, and Readiness, "Population Representation in the Military Services: Trends in Propensity," Washington, D.C.: Department of Defense, March 2003.

U.S. Department of Justice, Bureau of Justice Statistics, Law Enforcement Management and Administrative Statistics (LEMAS): 2003 Sample Survey of Law Enforcement Agencies, ICPSR04411-v1, Washington, D.C.: U.S. Department of Commerce, Bureau of the Census (producer), Ann Arbor, Mich.: Inter-University Consortium for Political and Social Research (distributor), doi:10.3886/ ICPSR04411, 2006. As of August 30, 2010: http://www.icpsr.umich.edu/cocoon/NACJD/STUDY/04411.xml

Van Maanen, J., "Observations on the Making of Policemen," *Human Organization*, Vol. 32, 1973, pp. 407–418.

Walker, Samuel, ed., *Records of the Wickersham Commission on Law Observance and Enforcement*, Bethesda, Md.: University Publications of America, 1997. As of November 11, 2009: http://www.lexis-nexis.com/documents/academic/upa_cis/1965_ WickershamCommPt1.pdf

Walker, Samuel, *Police Accountability: Current Issues and Research Needs*, Washington, D.C.: U.S. Department of Justice, NCJ 218583, November 2006.

Wheeler, Christopher H., "Local Market Scale and the Pattern of Job Changes Among Young Men," *Regional Science & Urban Economics*, Vol. 38, No. 2, March 2008, pp. 101–118.

White, H., "A Heteroscedasticity Consistent Covariance Matrix Estimator and a Direct Test of Heteroscedasticity," *Econometrica*, Vol. 48, 1980, pp. 817–818.

White, Michael D., and Gipsy Escobar, "Making Good Cops in the Twenty-First Century: Emerging Issues for the Effective Recruitment, Selection and Training of Police in the United States and Abroad," *Crime and Criminal Justice*, Vol. 22, No. 1–2, March 2008, pp. 119–134.

Wilson, Jeremy M., *Community Policing in America*, New York: Routledge, 2006.

Wilson, Jeremy M., and Amy G. Cox, *Community Policing and Crime: The Process and Impact of Problem-Solving in Oakland*, Santa Monica, Calif.: RAND Corporation, TR-635-BPA, 2008. As of March 27, 2010: http://www.rand.org/pubs/technical_reports/TR635/

Wilson, Jeremy M., Amy G. Cox, Tommy L. Smith, Hans Bos, and Terry Fain, *Community Policing and Violence Prevention in Oakland: Measure Y in Action*, Santa Monica, Calif.: RAND Corporation, TR-546-BPA, 2007. As of March 27, 2010: http://www.rand.org/pubs/technical_reports/TR546/

Wilson, Jeremy M., Erin Dalton, Charles Scheer, and Clifford A. Grammich, *Police Recruitment and Retention for the New Millennium: The State of Knowledge*, Santa Monica, Calif.: RAND Corporation, MG-959-DOJ, forthcoming.

Wilson, Jeremy M., and Clifford A. Grammich, *Police Recruitment and Retention in the Contemporary Urban Environment: A National Discussion of Personnel Experiences and Promising Practices from the Front Lines*, Santa Monica, Calif: RAND Corporation, CF-261-DOJ, 2009. As of March 27, 2010: http://www.rand.org/pubs/conf_proceedings/CF261/

Wilson, Jeremy M., Bernie Rostker, and Mike Hix, "Police Recruitment and Retention in New Orleans: Crisis as Catalyst," presentation at the RAND Summit on Recruitment and Retention, Washington, D.C., June 2008. As of September 2, 2009: http://www.cops.usdoj.gov/pdf/conference/rand/WilsonPoliceRecruitmentNO.pdf

Wilson, Michael J., "Youth Attitude Tracking Study: 1999 Propensity and Advertising Report," Arlington, Va.: Defense Manpower Data Center, 2000.

Wright, Jerome, "Adding to Police Ranks Rankles," *Memphis Commercial Appeal*, February 1, 2009. As of November 11, 2009: http://www.commercialappeal.com/news/2009/feb/01/adding-to-ranks-rankles/

Zhao, Jihong, Nicholas P. Lovrich, and Quint Thurman, "The Status of Community Policing in American Cities: Facilitators and Impediments Revised," *Policing: An International Journal of Police Strategies & Management*, Vol. 22, No. 1, 1999, pp. 74–92.

The Dynamic Police Staffing Challenge
The Bucket Metaphor

JEREMY M. WILSON, ERIN DALTON, CHARLES SCHEER, AND CLIFFORD A. GRAMMICH

Diminishing sources of recruitment, increasing causes for attrition, and broadening police responsibilities all shape questions of workforce supply and demand. To conceptualize and delineate the distinct forces at work, we use the metaphor of a bucket (Figure 10.1). In this metaphor, the size of the bucket represents the absolute need or demand for police officers, which will vary by agency based on workload determinants and service objectives.

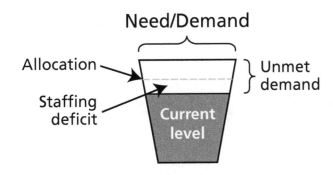

Figure 10.1 The Bucket Metaphor and Demand for Police Officers

THE BUCKET METAPHOR AND DEMAND FOR POLICE OFFICERS

The water inside the bucket represents the current level of police strength. The water level varies over time with accession and attrition and frequently does not fill the bucket because the demand for officers exceeds the ability to meet it (due to resource and other limitations). The difference between the need and the current level represents the true unmet demand for police officers.

Usually somewhere between the current level of officers and the demand for them is the authorized or allocated level of officers. This represents the number of officers for which an agency is budgeted. A somewhat artificial threshold, the allocation level is politically determined by such variables as workload, service orientation, and available resources.

The staffing deficit is the difference between the allocated and actual levels of police strength. Actual staffing levels rarely rise above allocated levels, although this can occur when an agency is building up capacity in anticipation of attrition. The bucket metaphor visually illustrates that an agency can, in fact, be understaffed when it is operating with its full complement of allocated officers.

Three forces can affect the bucket and the amount of water in it. Officers might be "leaked" through a "hole" caused by attrition. New officers might be less likely to "flow" from the "faucet" of new supply. The bucket might expand as police work broadens. These issues might not affect every agency equally or in the same magnitude, but there is evidence of them affecting at least some agencies both in the short and long terms. Every agency has its own unique circumstances that must be considered in workforce planning.

THE HOLE IN THE BUCKET IS WIDENING

Much of the difficulty police agencies face in maintaining their workforce levels is a product of attrition. To be sure, attrition can be positive, as when a department replaces retiring officers with younger, more-skilled ones, or when it loses those who are not committed to being effective, high-performing officers. Nevertheless, attrition can be a problem when it occurs in waves, such as with past hiring booms ultimately resulting in large proportions of staff retiring within a short time of one another. This causes the

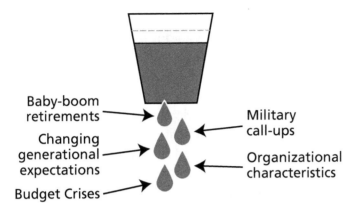

Figure 10.2 Attrition Is Widening the Hole

attrition hole in the bucket to widen, making it increasingly difficult to maintain the actual level of officers, or the water in the bucket.

Figure 10.2 highlights some contributors to the widening of the hole in the bucket: baby-boom generation retirements, changing generational preferences, budget crises, military call-ups, and organizational characteristics.

BABY-BOOM GENERATION RETIREMENTS

Baby-boom generation officers on the cusp of retirement are the greatest pending concern. Officers of this generation are beginning to retire, and the number of retirements is likely to grow considerably in the next few years as the number of officers eligible for retirement increases significantly.

This pending wave of retirements is already affecting departments. In the early 2000s, New York City faced an exodus of officers who had 20 or more years of service, prompting the department to offer retention bonuses and incentives ("NYPD Facing a Flood of 20-and-Out Retirees," 2000). By the end of the decade, facing the additional challenge of paying pensions that the city budget could not afford, New York Mayor Michael Bloomberg proposed abolishing the "20-and-out" rule in his 2009 budget as a way to end the out-migration (Bloomberg, 2009). In Chicago, an early retirement option is expected to increase, from just more than 500 to nearly 900, the deficit of officers below the overall authorized level of 13,500, a problem exacerbated by the department's need to wait for federal funding before scheduling new academy classes (Spielman, 2009). Likewise, the proportion of retirement-eligible officers in Edmonton, Alberta, is expected to increase from less than 10 percent in October 2009 to nearly 20 percent by 2014; this challenge is expected to recur in 2030 as those hired through recent aggressive recruiting become eligible to retire (Edmonton police official, 2009).

The recent downturn in the economy might delay some of these retirements and expand the applicant pool, but retirement requirements and pension reforms will eventually affect all departments and, perhaps, threaten services. In Vallejo, California, for example, recent police retirements coupled with the economic downturn have sparked community concern about the viability of public services (Wolf and Rohrs, 2008). In Boston, changes in pension benefits partially attributable to the economic crisis have led to increased retirement applications across several municipal services (Levenson and Slack, 2009). In Macon, Georgia, early retirement options might debilitate an already thin police force (Womack, 2009). All these trends are widening the hole in the metaphorical bucket, making it difficult to replenish the supply of officers, and even creating a "brain drain" among the most experienced.

Similar trends are evident in other fields, a result both of impending retirements of older workers and of changes in life and career goals of younger ones (Edwards, 2007; Losey, 2005; Graig and Paganelli, 2000). Yet, these trends appear to have affected retention more strongly in policing than in other fields (Taylor et al., 2006; Orrick, 2008a). Increases in law-enforcement turnover have also resulted from police salaries that are lower than private-sector ones, competition with military recruiters, a negative public perception of law enforcement, and lack of interest in policing by younger Americans entering the work force (Jordan et al., 2009; Pomfret, 2006; Egan, 2005; Tulgan, 2000). An increasing number of police are leaving the service prematurely, compounding the macro social trends and their bearing on the police profession (Jordan et al., 2009). Of greater concern are the reportedly low levels of career and organizational commitment of police officers in the United States (Frost, 2006), similar to that in Australia and New Zealand (Lynch and Tuckey, 2004). Low organizational commitment has been seen as an antecedent of a decision to voluntarily leave an organization (Frost, 2006). Yet, other researchers—using evidence that points to fallacies in Bureau of Labor statistics, increasing workforce productivity, baby boomers' willingness to work longer than previous generations, the influx of younger generations into the workforce, and increases in life expectancy—contend that attrition and turnover are not as chronic a problem as social trends would indicate (Edwards, 2007; Graig and Paganelli, 2000; Pikitalis and Morgan, 2003).

Police studies of attrition demonstrate constancy in turnover across multiple locales. Rather than decreasing as a result of turnover, in California, between 1985 and 2005, the number of police officers increased from 63,694 to 84,443 (Switzer, 2006). Transfers to other agencies were fairly stable over the same period, between 3 and 5 percent annually. A survey of 205 North Carolina sheriffs' departments of varying size found steady turnover (12.7 percent) and vacancy (5.5 percent) rates, with 28.6 percent of agencies surveyed noting either a significant or slight increase in turnover rates (Yearwood, 2003).

Retention changes with economic conditions. In times of relative prosperity, other careers and positions might pull officers away from police work with higher salaries and easier work. In times of economic decline, officers might be less likely to leave departments due to concerns about better job security, but departments might be forced to lay off or furlough employees in the wake of budget cuts.

CHANGING GENERATIONAL PREFERENCES AND EXPECTATIONS

Retention also changes with generational preferences. Younger generations of workers might have less organizational commitment than older ones, with many even changing careers (Wheeler, 2008; Twenge and Campbell, 2008).

The changing nature of work has had a pronounced effect on attrition in policing. The movement toward knowledge work, currently transforming career paths, might be reshaping career expectations in law enforcement. The evolution of "boundary-less" careers has required workers to move between employers to gain knowledge and competencies that will enhance expertise and employability (Lynch and Tuckey, 2004). This shift heightens the challenges that police organizations face in retention and succession planning. In Australia and New Zealand, researchers found that police organizations are no longer limited to their traditional crime-detection and law-enforcement functions (Dupont, 2003). They are being reshaped into, among other things, knowledge brokers, social-service referrers, or problem solvers. This transformation might intensify turnover in law enforcement due to unanticipated realities and unfulfilled expectations.

Younger workers might also change jobs more often than older ones, especially in metropolitan areas with diverse economies, in an effort to find the work they like best (Wheeler, 2008; Twenge and Campbell, 2008). This creates difficulties for police departments, which invest considerable time and resources in selecting and training officers, only to have them leave after a short term.

BUDGET CRISES

Decreasing financial support to cover officer salaries has contributed to widening the hole in the bucket through resulting limits both on funding positions and on providing competitive salaries and benefits. Two extreme cases of the effects this can have on retention are evident in New Orleans and San Diego. In New Orleans, many police officers relocating their families to Houston after Hurricane Katrina joined the department there or another elsewhere that offered higher pay and benefits than New Orleans had (see box, facing page). In San Diego, uncompetitive wages and salary freezes led many police officers to seek better opportunities elsewhere, including a lead detective with 21 years on the force who applied for a patrol position in the neighboring community of Chula Vista (Manolatos, 2006).

The recent economic downturn has punctuated this problem. Many communities are struggling to cover the expenses of their police workforces and have responded with tactics ranging from hiring freezes and cancellations of academy classes to furloughs and even layoffs. Officials in Prospect Heights, Illinois, even closed the police station to the public and assigned the police chief and command staff to patrol shifts (J. Byrne, 2009). Those agencies that can hire report a spike in applications and improved ability to hire officers, but some practitioners have raised concerns about the willingness of those who are now pursuing positions to commit to a long-term policing career (DeLord, 2009). The Macon, Georgia, police chief warned that an early retirement option might drain his department of more-experienced and knowledgeable officers (Womack, 2009). Johnstown, Pennsylvania, struggles to replace experienced command staff on an already "depleted roster" (Faher, 2009).

A pattern is emerging: Agencies are increasingly offering early retirements to save costs and trim budgets, but the same budgets do not allow for hiring high-quality candidates—or any candidates at all—to replace those leaving. Limited resources have resulted not just in fewer positions but in attrition of officers from existing positions.

MILITARY CALL-UPS

Military call-ups represent another leak in the bucket. The United States has become increasingly involved in nation-building and peacekeeping missions (Dobbins et al., 2003; Jones et al., 2005; J. Wilson and Grammich, 2009b). The most recent examples of this include Afghanistan and Iraq. This causes the hole in the police staffing bucket to widen because many police officers serve as military reservists and have been called to active duty. During the 12-month period ending June 30, 2003, 21 percent of local police departments and more than 94 percent of agencies serving a population of at least 100,000 had full-time sworn personnel who were called up as full-time military reservists, with call-ups averaging three officers per department and ranging from one to 74 (Hickman and Reaves, 2006a). Such call-ups pose not just manpower but fiscal challenges; federal law requires that health benefits of these officers be maintained and their positions held until they return (Hickman, 2006).

REBUILDING AFTER A CRISIS AND A CATASTROPHE: NEW ORLEANS

As it did on most other elements of the city, Hurricane Katrina had a profound effect on the New Orleans Police Department. In the storm's aftermath, Warren Riley (2008), superintendent of the department, told a RAND summit on recruitment and retention, most officers were homeless, their families had been displaced, and, in some cases, they had to deal with the loss of loved ones. Often, Riley said, "[o]fficers were stranded in flooded police stations, trapped in attics, and in some cases, on rooftops."

The wounds the department suffered proved to be deep and lasting for some time after the storm. "The media coverage following the storm was extensive and often not very positive when it came to the Police Department," Riley said. "It made [the department] appear to be a losing team." The subsequent bleeding to the department would last for some time. From the time of the hurricane until the end of 2005, the department would have 165 separations, with 147 related to officer actions or lack of performance following the storm. Losses would continue past the immediate aftermath of the storm, particularly among lower ranks. Not until 2007 would department hiring exceed separations (Figure 10.3).

By then, separations had claimed one-third of the prestorm force. Complicating matters for the department was the fact that, even before the storm, its staffing level was nearly 8 percent below its allocated level. A year after the storm, its staffing level was nearly 12 percent below its allocated level, even though the budgeted allocation of officers had decreased by nearly one-sixth (Table 10.1).

Although the storm had wounded the department deeply, in some cases, it might have been more a trigger for departures than a cause of them. Over time, New Orleans police salaries and benefits had come to lag those of many other cities (Rostker, Hix, and Wilson, 2007; J. Wilson, Rostker, and Hix, 2008). For nearly all ranks, RAND researchers found that New Orleans' officer pay lagged that of Houston, where many residents relocated at least temporarily after the storm. Officers above the rank of sergeant could earn about $30,000 more per year in Houston than in New Orleans (Table 10.2).

Budget constraints the city faced limited its options for improving recruitment and retention. Fortunately, RAND researchers found, there were several low-cost initiatives the city could take to make its compensation packages more attractive to new officers. While New Orleans police salaries were low, their pensions were generous. Shifting money from pensions to salaries could, in the near term and at no net cost, make the department more attractive to new recruits. Likewise, RAND researchers suggested increasing the frequency of promotional boards, passing only enough officers to fill expected vacancies, to allow talented officers to rise through the ranks more quickly and to create a climate of continual learning.

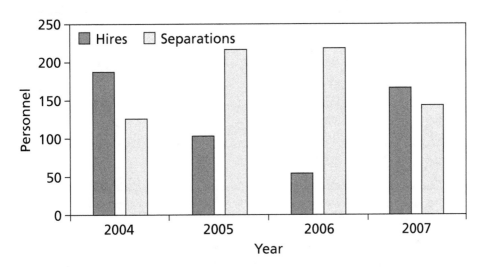

Figure 10.3 New Orleans Police Department Hires and Separations, 2004 to 2007

For the medium term, RAND researchers suggested two low-cost options: converting appropriate jobs from officers to civilians and developing proactive recruiting efforts, such as after-school and summer employment for students interested in police work. Much of the recruiting work done by officers comprised recruiting those who had already volunteered and using the Internet and other tools to conduct background checks, tasks that civilian specialists could perform. For the long term, RAND researchers suggested offering housing to officers as an incentive for a commitment to years of service.

The city government acted quickly to implement many of the recommendations. "The mayor," Riley said, "and the city council . . . immediately bought into it, and it was smooth sailing from there." State law prohibited shifting pension resources to salaries, but the city still substantially increased officer pay and devised several education incentives. These recommendations helped cut department attrition, which averaged 11 officers per month before Katrina, to five officers per month.

Table 10.1 Budgeted and Actual New Orleans Police Officer Levels, Before and After Hurricane Katrina

Level	August 2005	October 2006	Change (%)
Budgeted	1,885	1,600	−15
Actual	1,742	1,421	−18

SOURCE: Stephanie M. Landry, New Orleans Police Department, as cited in Rostker, Hix, and Wilson (2007).
NOTE: Data for 2005 are current as of August 21, 2005. Data for 2006 are current as of October 24, 2006.

Table 10.2 New Orleans and Houston Police Department Salary Comparison, 2006

	Annual Base Salary Without Benefits ($)		
		Houston	
Rank	New Orleans	Minimum	Maximum
Police recruit	30,732	29,164[a]	
Police officer 1[b]	33,111	36,022	50,039
Police officer 2	34,797		
Police officer 3	36,570		55,235
Police officer 4	38,433	51,114	
Police sergeant	42,449	61,784	67,362
Police lieutenant	45,734	69,354	75,606
Police captain	53,750	75,421	86,613
Police major	58,633		

SOURCES: Stephanie M. Landry, New Orleans Police Department, as cited in Rostker, Hix, and Wilson (2007); City of Houston (undated).
[a] Recruits with a bachelor's degree earned up to $33,784 during academy and field training.
[b] A police officer 1 with a bachelor's degree in Houston earns more than $47,000 the first year after the probationary period, including an equipment allowance, shift/weekend pay, and bilingual pay. After one year of service, a New Orleans officer receives $3,600 in annual state supplemental pay. All New Orleans officers also receive an annual uniform allowance of $500.

ORGANIZATIONAL CHARACTERISTICS

Organizational characteristics can also affect attrition. Officers can choose to leave a department for a number of organization-related reasons, including the characteristics of their immediate supervisor, lack of career growth, unmet job expectations, inadequate feedback, insufficient recognition, or lack of training (Orrick, 2008a, 2008b; J. Wilson and Grammich, 2009a).

THE FAUCET (SUPPLY) IS TIGHTENING

Just as trends in attrition are making it difficult to retain police officers, the supply of qualified potential officers might be diminishing. That is, the supply faucet might be tightening (see Figure 10.4). Among contributors to this phenomenon are a general decrease in the qualified applicant pool, changing generational preferences, increased competition, expanded skill requirements, uncompetitive benefits, and organizational characteristics.

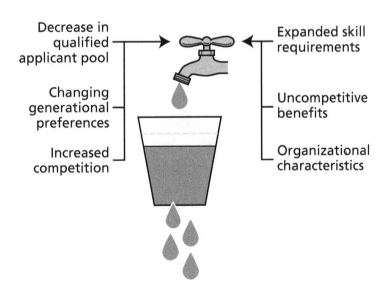

Figure 10.4 The Shrinking Supply Is Reducing the Flow

DECREASE IN QUALIFIED APPLICANT POOL

As noted earlier, the generations replacing the baby-boomers now retiring are smaller. Exacerbating this problem are cohorts of young persons who do not meet the minimum requirements for becoming a sworn officer. Raymond et al. (2005) contend that it is becoming more difficult for the general population to meet minimum qualifications, such as a clean criminal record, little to no drug use, good physical health, and financial stability. Several key statistics support their claim:

- About half of all 12th-graders report having smoked marijuana, and one in four has used some illicit drug *other* than marijuana by the end of the 12th grade, levels of prevalence that are above those of the early 1990s (Johnston et al., 2008).
- Over the past three decades, the obesity rate has more than doubled for adolescents 12 to 19 years of age and has more than tripled for children ages 6–11 (Sturm et al., 2007).
- From 1992 to 2001, credit-card debt among Americans 18 to 24 years of age rose 104 percent to an average of nearly $3,000 per person (in 2001 dollars); the average indebted youth spends almost 30 percent of his or her income on debt maintenance (Draut and Silva, 2004). Younger generations, from which police departments would normally draw recruits, have higher amounts of debt than youths of previous decades (Draut, 2008). In some departments, outstanding debt can disqualify applicants, as it is interpreted as an indicator of bad judgment and a proclivity toward corruption.

Education trends matter too. In the past decade, the percentage of persons 25 to 29 years of age holding college degrees has remained virtually unchanged (Planty et al., 2008). Yet, the length of time to complete a degree has increased as the number of enrollees who complete their degree has decreased (Bound, Lovenheim, and Turner, 2007; Dynarski, 2005). These trends and the increasing costs of college can affect a graduate's career choice. An educated worker might meet law enforcement's increasing education standards but also has more job prospects, in turn making recruiting them into police work more competitive (Bound, Lovenheim, and Turner, 2007).

CHANGING GENERATIONAL PREFERENCES

The militaristic nature of police work, with its emphasis on hierarchy and formality, and the sacrifices that officers must make, from maintaining certain appearances (e.g., no beards or tattoos) to erratic schedules and long shifts, to placing themselves in harm's way, also likely discourage applicants. This same cultural shift has driven military propensity downward since the early 1980s and is compounded in younger generations as realities of military structure conflict with differing youth attitudes about the nature of work (Bowyer, 2007; DoD, 2003; M. Wilson et al., 2000). Moreover, changes in generational values regarding off-duty life have been seen as affecting recruiting (Brand, 1999), whereas the flexibility and emotional control sought by younger generations appears inconsistent with traditional paramilitary police environments (Harrison, 2007; Pew Research Center for the People and the Press, 2007). Less than half of American youths consider a police department or agency a "desirable" or "acceptable" place to work—more than those who view military service that way but fewer than those who view corporations, schools, or other government agencies that way (Sackett and Mavor, 2003). Furthermore, those entering the workforce today expect to have more-rapid advancement opportunities (J. Wilson and Grammich, 2009a) and to have a better balance between work and family (Scrivner, 2008). The youngest generation of workers has shown marked preferences toward extrinsic work values, such as prestige, changing tasks, social and cognitive aspects of work, and flexibility (Lawsson, 2009; Lyons, Duxbury, and Higgins, 2005). Many of these career expectations cannot be met in law enforcement.

INCREASED COMPETITION

As noted earlier, local police agencies look to fill their ranks from a subset of the population that meets minimum qualifications, including a clean criminal record and good physical health. Nevertheless, they are not alone in searching for such candidates. The military, federal and state police agencies, private security firms, and other first-responder agencies recruit similar individuals, and opportunities with them have grown, particularly since the September 2001 terrorist attacks against the United States. The expansion of a security-industrial complex since the attacks has funneled money and personnel into increased private security positions (De Rugy, 2006; Kondrasuk, 2004), spurred demand for fire protection (Frawley, 2006), and stimulated national efforts and capital for security and defense contracting (Makinen, 2002). Military enlistments have increased, particularly among more-educated recruits (Kane, 2005). As a result, the labor market for such public services has become much more competitive. The greater compensation and benefits that other public service agencies can offer exacerbate the problem of competition for local police (Raymond et al., 2005; Rostker, Hix, and Wilson, 2007).

Although recent economic conditions seem to have relieved some competition for applicants, local police agencies still compete for many of the same recruits, particularly as they lure officers and potential recruits away from sister agencies and communities. In recent years, agencies have launched several incentives to attract officers, ranging from signing bonuses and moving expenses to health-club memberships and mortgage discount programs. They have also sought recruits hundreds or even thousands of miles away. In the 12-month period preceding June 2008, the Metropolitan Police Department in Washington, D.C., conducted recruiting trips to Fort Campbell and Fort Knox in Kentucky; Camp Lejeune, North Carolina; Albany, New York; Columbus, Ohio; Tidewater, Virginia; and Oak Creek, Wisconsin (Lanier, 2008). The Arlington County Police Department in Virginia sought recruits as far away as Puerto Rico, albeit with little success (see box, next page).

EXPANDED SKILL REQUIREMENTS

As in other industries (Rich, 2010), the changing nature of police work might also restrict the flow of eligible recruits. Police agencies face growing, more-complex problems in increasingly diverse communities, and policing work has become much more community-oriented. Such changes expand the skills required of police officers. Officers must now be able to work closely with different people, including being able to communicate, collaborate, and interact with a diverse set of stakeholders; have strong analytical, problem-solving, critical and strategic thinking, and technology skills; and be culturally competent (Miller, 2008; Raymond et al., 2005; Scrivner, 2006, 2008; J. Wilson and Grammich, 2009a). Scrivner (2008) also notes the need for officers to focus on service, values, multiple dimensions of performance (not just arrests), and outcomes. These changes call for recruitment efforts to be even more selective, thereby reducing the supply of qualified candidates.

UNCOMPETITIVE BENEFITS

Just as budget crises can widen the hole in the bucket, so too can they tighten the faucet. A key way in which law enforcement limits its supply of qualified applicants is by offering prospective candidates uncompetitive wages and benefit packages (which, as noted earlier, can also contribute to turnover). Officer salaries are not on par with the institutions with which it competes for personnel. In 2003, the average entry-level starting salary was $35,500 for local police officers (Hickman and Reaves, 2006a) and $32,200 for deputies (Hickman and Reaves, 2006b). According to 2008 Bureau of Labor Statistics data, mean

---

RECRUITING AMONG COMPETITORS: ARLINGTON COUNTY (VIRGINIA) POLICE DEPARTMENT

When M. Douglas Scott became chief of the Arlington County Police Department, he found a department below its authorized strength of more than 350 officers (Scott, 2008). It was also facing an attrition rate of 10 percent per year. There were several reasons for this. In addition to the usual lures away, such as other employment or a return to school, the department, because it is located near the heart of the Washington metropolitan area, must compete with federal law-enforcement agencies in addition to neighboring agencies. The department also has an older force, with about one in seven currently serving also eligible for retirement. Complicating its recruiting efforts, Scott said, was a requirement of 60 college credit hours for new hires, with no waiver for military or other police service.

To maintain its numbers and increase its diversity—minority officers comprise 22 percent of the force and female officers 17 percent—the department has tried a variety of strategies. Among the more successful ones have been partnering with local criminal-justice programs, administering monthly exams, offering recruitment bonuses to employees, establishing a recruiting team, and developing recruitment efforts and websites. Some efforts, such as outreach to the Washington-area gay community, were controversial among some residents but not county leaders. Other efforts have been less successful, including a recruiting trip to Puerto Rico, job fairs far removed from the jurisdiction, a cadet program, and venues, such as parades and county fairs, not designed for recruitment. Successful retention initiatives have included increasing salary and retirement benefits. As a result of these efforts, the department was able to reach its authorized strength of 366 officers in 2006, 2007, and 2008.

---

annual wages for all local police and sheriffs' patrol officers, at $52,480 per year, appear competitive with other public service occupations (such as firefighters and correctional officers), but they lag behind other possible professional occupations, such as physical therapists ($74,410 per year), physical- and social-science occupations ($64,280), landscape architects ($64,000), electrical engineers ($85,350), computer-science occupations ($74,500), and construction management ($89,770) (BLS, 2009).

In the past decade, according to Bureau of Labor Statistics figures, benefits and compensation costs were 51.4 percent higher for public than private employees, a figure that had increased steadily throughout the decade (McDonnell, 2002, 2005, 2008). But, looking closer at the discrepancy, wage and work differentials between careers in state and local government (which includes other public service professions) were the main source of the gap: Unionization rates and health-care program participation were seen as driving the discrepancy (McDonnell, 2008). Yet, the perception persists among upper-level police management that the reactive nature of salary and benefit improvements has resulted in a reduced ability to compete with private employment, which is viewed as providing a more attractive lifestyle (Domash, 2002).

ORGANIZATIONAL CHARACTERISTICS

Other organizational characteristics can also limit the supply of prospective qualified officers. The image of law enforcement as a career or of a particular agency, residency policies, length and complexity of the hiring process, and opportunities for advancement and special assignments are just some of the organizational factors that can influence interest in law enforcement (J. Wilson and Grammich, 2009a). Many of these organizational obstacles might affect minority candidates disproportionately (Wright, 2009). All create additional difficulties for police agencies and can change over time.

THE BUCKET (DEMAND) IS EXPANDING

While the staffing-loss hole in the bucket is widening from increased attrition and the flow replenishing it is shrinking from a reduced supply of qualified officers, the demand for officers is increasing the size of the bucket (see Figure 10.5). Without remedy, this serves to exacerbate the true unmet demand for police service (Figure 10.1).

The increasing demand for police officers largely originates from an expansion of their responsibilities. This is perhaps most vividly apparent regarding their roles in community policing, homeland security, and emerging crimes.

COMMUNITY POLICING

The adoption of community policing has broadened the duties of police agencies. In the past two decades, most police agencies have embraced some form of community policing (Maguire and Mastrofski, 2000; J. Wilson, 2006; Zhao, Lovrich, and Thurman,

Figure 10.5 Expanding Duties Increase the Demand for Police Officers

1999). Since 1995, the COPS office (undated [b]), which is the federal agency tasked with advancing community policing, has invested $12.4 billion in community policing, enabling more than 13,000 state, local, and tribal agencies to hire more than 117,000 police officers and deputies. Fifty-eight percent of all local police departments, employing 82 percent of all officers, used full-time community policing officers during 2003, as did 51 percent of all sheriffs' offices, employing 70 percent of all deputies (Hickman and Reaves, 2006a, 2006b).

Community policing increases the number of functions police undertake, particularly for larger departments. Hickman and Reaves (2006a) found that most police agencies in jurisdictions of at least 25,000 residents work with citizen groups to develop community policing strategies, with four-fifths of those in jurisdictions of at least 100,000 having citizen police academies. Such proactive activities require time and resources in addition to those needed for traditional police responsibilities, such as maintaining law and order, preventing crime, and enforcing traffic regulations. In Oakland, California, for example, this required a ten-year, multimillion-dollar voter initiative to address community policing, violence prevention, and fire and paramedic services (see box).

HIRING FOR COMMUNITY NEEDS: OAKLAND, CALIFORNIA

The Oakland Police Department has traditionally faced a hire-and-freeze cycle, under which the department would hire when able but would see its staff dwindle during a hiring freeze (Poulson, 2008). In the early 2000s, for example, the department hired enough officers to boost its number of officers to 740 but, under a hiring freeze, saw this dwindle to 680.

This cycle changed in the wake of an increase in overall violence and in homicide specifically (J. Wilson, Cox, et al., 2007; J. Wilson and Cox, 2008). In 2004, Oakland voters passed the Violence Prevention and Public Safety Act, or Measure Y. This required the city to invest $19 million annually in violence prevention and community policing.

The sudden new demand for officers created difficulties for the department. For example, the community policing component of Measure Y alone required the department to hire at least 63 new officers. Further complicating department hiring was a consent decree requiring personnel for internal affairs, evolving policing requirements, and an ineffective shift schedule resulting in absenteeism rates as high as 40 percent for patrol officers.

Oakland's mayor ultimately sought to boost the department to 803 officers. This required the department to recruit and train 342 officers in just two years (both for new positions and to replace retiring officers). To do so, the department launched several recruitment, training, and retention initiatives. It launched a $1 million saturation advertising campaign, as well as a website, provided regular email updates to applicants, and streamlined its process so that it could hire a candidate passing a background examination within three weeks. It accepted candidates from other, unaffiliated academies. It paid $1,000 to officers who recruited and mentored a new recruit through the first few months on the job. It also boosted pay and adopted a new shift schedule calling for seven 12-hour shifts in a two-week period. As of the end of June 2010, 776 officers work for the department, but 80 of them have received layoff notices as the Oakland City Council attempts to manage a $30.5-million budget deficit (Kuruvila, 2010).

Agencies have sought to meet increased demand in several ways. Some agencies might delay police responses and cut special units, while others rely on cameras and other technologies to do the jobs that absent officers would normally fulfill (C. Fischer, 2009; Wiegler, 2008). The Lower Manhattan Security Initiative, which will blanket the city of New York with video cameras, has coincided with widespread attrition in the New York City Police Department, which has no pending plans to fund or hire additional officers (Winston, 2009).

HOMELAND SECURITY

Increased emphasis on homeland security has also widened the responsibilities of local police officers, increasing the demand for them. Since the September 11, 2001, terrorist attacks against the United States, local police have been asked to perform additional patrol and surveillance, gather and analyze counterterrorism intelligence, conduct risk and threat assessments, participate in various task forces, coordinate and communicate with other agencies, undergo new training and exercises, construct and contribute to fusion centers, formulate new policies, and update mutual-aid agreements and response plans for chemical, biological, and radiological (CBR)–related incidents (Davis et al., 2006; Raymond et al., 2005; K. Riley, Treverton, et al., 2005).

Homeland security duties for local police have also included an expanded role in immigration enforcement. As K. Riley, Treverton, et al. (2005) explain, before the September 11, 2001, attacks, many departments had explicit policies not to arrest and detain someone whose only crime concerned immigration status. Federal policy has since sought more participation of local agencies in immigration enforcement, although some are resisting this. Congressional authorization in 1996 of local agencies to act in immigration-enforcement capacities has also pushed smaller agencies into roles of a more global nature (Khashu and Malina, 2009).

EMERGING CRIMES

As a result of globalization, technological advancement, and greater awareness, the scope of crime the law-enforcement community must now address continues to grow. Over the past decade, police agencies have had to respond to emerging crimes, such as human trafficking, identity theft, cybercrime, and fraud, and take on roles, such as counterterrorism and internal security, usually reserved for the military (Kraska, 2007). Human-trafficking task forces have gained increasing worldwide attention as a local response to the global problem of trafficking in persons; such a strategy relies heavily on international cooperation, information-sharing, and a reconsideration of the local role of police (U.S. Department of State, 2009). Cybercrime and the related problems of intellectual-property theft and fraud are likely to increase, requiring local agencies to train officers to counter this new and evolving threat (FBI, 2008). In sum, local police roles evolved through the community policing era to include benign order-maintenance duties, such as answering noise complaints and solving neighborhood disputes, to new, occasionally militaristic roles, including counterterrorism, information-sharing, and immigration enforcement (Kraska, 2007).

THE WEAKENED ECONOMY

Recent economic changes have had mixed effects on police staffing. In this time of rising unemployment, agencies with the resources to hire officers have been inundated by applications, thereby permitting greater selectivity and, potentially, a more qualified applicant pool. A wave of applicants for six positions in Ventura, California, came from industries as diverse as software and mortgage (Scheibe, 2009). Agencies in states with more-severe and long-term economic shifts are receiving applicants seeking to move from manufacturing to service positions (Goeller, 2009). In Raleigh, North Carolina, applications for police positions more than doubled after the 2008 recession hit, despite the pessimism of command staff that the department's true staffing need might still never be met (S. Chambers, 2009). New York City has seen a flood of applicants to its shrinking department, including those from investment banking, an apparently new source of recruits (Schmidt, 2009).

Police leaders, however, question the long-term commitment of these candidates to their organization, particularly as jobs become more plentiful in other sectors (DeLord, 2009). Concerns about applicants' motivations, which arose in the burst of recruiting following the September 11, 2001, terrorist attacks, have matured into a crisis of confidence among recruiters and command staff about the quality of recruits (Domash, 2002; S. Chambers, 2009). Hiring standards remain the same for inexperienced candidates in areas where the economy has led to increases in applicants (Madrid, 2009). Having more applicants to screen increases the cost and substantive difficulty of assessing and selecting the best candidates for the job. More applications do not necessarily mean more qualified applicants; as one police executive warned, "You can't just hire anybody" (Codispoti, 2009).

At the same time, a weakened economy can also exacerbate staffing problems. Assuming a steady demand for police work, resource shortfalls that lead to furloughs, layoffs, and hiring freezes will expand both the staffing deficit and the true unmet demand for police service (Figure 10.1). Economic problems also highlight the uncertainty of the environments in which police departments must operate. Violent- and property-crime levels decreased during the recessionary year of 2008 (FBI, 2009). Such a decrease can be attributed partly to policing strategies that must continue in order to stave off potential increases but that constricting resources will make difficult to maintain (Camper and Brown, 2008; Moore, 2009).

Police staffing cuts resulting from the recession have occurred in jurisdictions ranging in size, geography, and organization from Santa Rosa, California (McCoy, 2009), to Gwinnett County, Georgia (Fox, 2009), to Toledo, Ohio (Rice, 2009), to Cook County, Illinois, to Sacramento, California (Johnson, 2008). Indeed, a 2008 survey by PERF (C. Fischer, 2009) revealed that 63 percent of responding agencies were preparing plans for funding cuts, with 31 percent of the cuts aimed at funding for sworn personnel, even after many of the agencies already made cuts to staffing via overtime reductions (62 percent), sworn-officer and civilian hiring freezes (27 and 53 percent, respectively), diminished recruit classes (34 percent), reducing employment levels through attrition (24 percent), furloughs (10 percent), and layoffs or forced retirements (7 percent).[1] Budget deficits are also causing cuts among police programs. For example, in addition to 132 sworn-deputy layoffs (after just saving 70 positions), the Sacramento Sheriff's Department grounded its helicopters, cut problem-oriented police units, and returned special weapons and tactics (SWAT) and canine officers to patrol to manage cuts to the department (R. Lewis, 2009). San Francisco police are skeptical that they can afford to fill existing foot-patrol positions, much less add recommended new ones (Sward, 2008). More broadly, the PERF (C. Fischer, 2009) survey indicated that 29 percent of responding agencies anticipated discontinuing special units (e.g., street crimes, narcotics, and community policing units). Such service cuts could intensify the workload of remaining police and increase the true level of unmet demand for police service.

While the economy has made it more difficult for police organizations to meet their workforce needs, the long-term systemic changes highlighted in this chapter suggest that staffing challenges will remain an issue even after the economy improves. Past hiring booms and freezes will create difficulties as they ripple through the organization over time—from field training and promotion to personnel budget consumption and retention. Resulting uneven distributions in the workforce can cause significant administrative challenges even in organizations that are fully staffed.

---

1   The sampling frame for and response rate of this survey is not evident in the report, so the generalizability of these findings is unclear.

CONCLUSION

Police agencies face a threefold challenge in meeting the demand for officers: Attrition is increasing, sources of new recruits might be decreasing, and the demand for their work is expanding.

Attrition might increase as a result of the following:

- baby-boom generation retirements. In some agencies, large proportions of officers are near or eligible for retirement and could lead to a sharp decrease in staffing levels.
- military call-ups. A substantial number of agencies have officers who serve in military reserve forces; their deployment not only drains staff but also poses fiscal challenges through maintenance of benefits for them.
- changing generational expectations. Younger workers might have less organizational commitment than older ones and seek to change jobs more often in "boundary-less" careers.
- budget crises. Decreasing financial support to cover officer salaries limits some agencies' ability to prevent their officers from going to other agencies or even leaving the field.
- organizational characteristics. Immediate supervisors, career growth opportunities, recognition, and feedback can all affect whether an officer will stay or leave.

There are several causes as well to diminishing sources of new officers. Some of these are similar to those contributing to attrition. They include the following:

- a decrease in the qualified applicant pool. Large numbers of youths have used drugs, are out of shape, or have excessive debt.
- changing generational preferences. Similar to those that might get younger workers to leave the profession, changing generational preferences might lead younger workers to seek nonmilitaristic or more-flexible work.
- increased competition. The military, federal and state police agencies, private security firms, and other first-responder agencies recruit similar individuals, and competition for them has grown in the past decade.
- expanded skill requirements. Police work increasingly requires a broad range of skills that not all candidates might have.
- uncompetitive benefits. Police salaries lag those for many professions, although benefits and compensation for public employees have increased faster than those for private ones in the past decade.

- organizational characteristics. The image of a law-enforcement agency and the opportunities it offers, as well as the length and complexity of its hiring process, can all affect how many recruits might be attracted.

The potential for increased attrition and reduced supply makes it increasingly difficulty for police agencies to meet the expanding demand for their services. There are three principal causes of this expanding demand:

- community policing. The adoption of community policing has increased the number of functions local agencies must undertake, functions that require time and resources in addition to those for traditional police responsibilities.
- homeland security. In the past decade, local police have been asked to perform additional patrol and surveillance, gather and analyze counterterrorism intelligence, conduct risk and threat assessments, and participate in many interagency task forces.
- emerging crimes. As a result of globalization, technological advancement, and greater awareness, the scope of crime that local agencies must address has expanded to include emerging crimes, such as human trafficking, identity theft, and cybercrime.

Further complicating these issues, especially recruitment and retention efforts, has been a weakened economy of recent years, reducing or restricting the options available to local agencies. In the next two chapters, we discuss in more depth what local agencies can do to retain and recruit officers. Because retention can reduce the need for recruitment, we focus on it first.

BIBLIOGRAPHY

Ahlrichs, Nancy S., *Competing for Talent: Key Recruitment and Retention Strategies for Becoming an Employer of Choice*, Palo Alto, Calif.: Davies-Black Publishing, 2000.

Alpert, Geoffrey P., "Hiring and Promoting Police Officers in Small Departments: The Role of Psychological Testing," *Criminal Law Bulletin*, Vol. 27, No. 3, May– June 1991, pp. 261–269.

Anderson, Madeleine, and Shalan Gobeil, *Recruitment and Retention in Child Welfare Services: A Survey of Child Welfare League of Canada Member Agencies*, Ottawa: Centre of Excellence for Child Welfare for Child Welfare League of Canada, 2003. As of May 21, 2010: http://www.cwlc.ca/files/file/pubs/Recruitment%20in%20CW.pdf

Anderson, Neil, and Nicole Cunningham-Snell, "Personnel Selection," in Nik Chmiel, ed., *Introduction to Work and Organizational Psychology: A European Perspective*, Malden, Mass.: Blackwell Publishers, 2000, pp. 69–99.

Aronsson, Gunnar, "Influence of Worklife on Public Health," *Scandinavian Journal of Work, Environment and Health*, Vol. 25, No. 6, 1999, pp. 597–604. As of June 23, 2010: http://www.sjweh.fi/show_abstract.php?abstract_id=486

Ash, Philip, Karen B. Slora, and Cynthia F. Britton, "Police Agency Officer Selection Practices," *Journal of Police Science and Administration*, Vol. 17, No. 4, December 1990, pp. 258–269.

Auten, James, "The Paramilitary Model of Police and Police Professionalism," *Policing: An International Journal of Police Strategies and Management*, Vol. 4, No. 67, 1981, pp. 67–72.

Avery, Derek R., and Patrick F. McKay, "Target Practice: An Organizational Impression Management Approach to Attracting Minority and Female Job Applicants," *Personnel Psychology*, Vol. 59, No. 1, Spring 2006, pp. 157–187.

Bacharach, Samuel B., Sharon Conley, and Joseph Shedd, "Beyond Career Ladders: Structuring Teacher Career Development Systems," *Teachers College Record*, Vol. 87, No. 4, Summer 1986, pp. 563–574.

Baker, Nicole, and Max Carrera, "Unlocking the Door to Relationship-Based Corrections Recruitment," *Corrections Today*, Vol. 69, No. 1, February 2007, pp. 36–38.

Bandow, Diane, Barbara D. Minsky, and Richard Steven Voss, "Reinventing the Future: Investigating Career Transitions from Industry to Academia," *Journal of Human Resources Education*, Vol. 1, No. 1, Summer 2007, pp. 23–37. As of June 23, 2010: http://business.troy.edu/JHRE/Issue.aspx?Volume=1&Issue=1

Barber, Alison E., *Recruiting Employees: Individual and Organizational Perspectives*, Thousand Oaks, Calif.: Sage Publications, 1998.

Becker, Wendy S., and W. Mark Dale, "Strategic Human Resource Management in the Forensic Science Laboratory," *Forensic Science Communications*, Vol. 5, No. 4, October 2003, pp. 1–6. As of June 23, 2010: http://www.fbi.gov/hq/lab/fsc/backissu/oct2003/2003_10_research01.htm

Best, Fred, *Work Sharing: The Issues, Policy Options, and Prospects*, Kalamazoo, Mich.: W. E. Upjohn Institute for Employment Research, 1981.

Birati, Assa, and Aharon Tziner, "Successful Promotion of Early Retirement: A Quantitative Approach," *Human Resource Management Review*, Vol. 5, No. 1, Spring 1995, pp. 53–62.

Bloomberg, Michael, "Mayor Mike Bloomberg Lays Out Plan for New York City Budget," *New York Daily News*, February 9, 2009. As of May 28, 2010: http://www.nydailynews.com/opinions/2009/02/09/2009-02-09_mayor_mike_bloomberg_lays_out_plan_for_n.html

BLS—*See* Bureau of Labor Statistics.

Bolhuis, Sanneke, "Alternative Routes to Teaching in Secondary Education in the Netherlands," *European Journal of Teacher Education*, Vol. 25, No. 2–3, October 2002, pp. 223–238.

Bound, John, Michael Lovenheim, and Sarah E. Turner, *Understanding the Decrease in College Completion Rates and the Increased Time to the Baccalaureate Degree*, Ann Arbor, Mich.: University of Michigan Institute for Social Research, Population Studies Center research report 07-626, November 2007. As of June 23, 2010: http://www.psc.isr.umich.edu/pubs/abs/4808

Bowyer, Richard F., *Recruiting 21st Century Army Warriors: A Task Requiring National Attention*, Carlisle Barracks, Pa.: U.S. Army War College, 2007. As of June 23, 2010: http://handle.dtic.mil/100.2/ADA468428

Bradley, Patrick L., "21st Century Issues Related to Police Training and Standards," *Police Chief*, Vol. 72, No. 10, October 2005, pp. 32–39. As of June 23, 2010: http://policechiefmagazine.org/magazine/index.cfm?fuseaction=display_arch&article_id=724&issue_id=102005

Brand, David, "The Future of Law Enforcement Recruiting: The Impact of Generation X," *Police Chief*, Vol. 8, August 1999, pp. 53–63.

Branham, Leigh, *The 7 Hidden Reasons Employees Leave: How to Recognize the Subtle Signs and Act Before It's Too Late*, Saratoga Springs, N.Y.: American Management Association, 2005.

Breaugh, James A., "Employee Recruitment: Current Knowledge and Important Areas for Further Research," *Human Resource Management Review*, Vol. 18, No. 3, September 2008, pp. 103–118.

Breaugh, James A., and Mary Starke, "Research on Employee Recruitment: So Many Studies, So Many Remaining Questions," *Journal of Management*, Vol. 26, No. 3, 2000, pp. 405–434.

Brennan, Adrianne M., Robert D. Davis, Cary D. Rostow, and Matrix Incorporated, "An Investigation of Biographical Information as Predictor of Employment Termination Among Law Enforcement Officers," *Journal of Police and Criminal Psychology*, Vol. 24, No. 2, October 2009, pp. 108–112.

Bureau of Labor Statistics, "Job Openings and Labor Turnover Survey," undated website. As of June 24, 2010: http://www.bls.gov/jlt/

———, "May 2008 National Occupational Employment and Wage Estimates, United States," *Occupational Employment Statistics*, last modified May 29, 2009. As of June 24, 2010: http://www.bls.gov/oes/2008/may/oes_nat.htm

Butler, Martha R., and Joan Felts, "Tool Kit for the Staff Mentor: Strategies for Improving Retention," *Journal of Continuing Education in Nursing*, Vol. 37, No. 5, September–October 2006, pp. 210–213.

Butterfield, Fox, "Urban Police Jobs Are Losing Their Appeal," *New York Times*, July 30, 2001. As of June 23, 2010: http://www.nytimes.com/2001/07/30/national/30POLI.html

Buzawa, Eva Schlesinger, *The Role of Selected Factors upon Patrol Officer Job Satisfaction in Two Urban Police Departments*, East Lansing, Mich.: Michigan State University, Ph.D. dissertation, 1979.

———, "Determining Patrol Officer Job Satisfaction: The Role of Selected Demographic and Job-Specific Attitudes," *Criminology*, Vol. 22, No. 1, February 1984, pp. 61–81.

Buzawa, Eva Schlesinger, Thomas L. Austin, and James Bannon, "The Role of Selected Socio-Demographics and Job-Specific Variables in Predicting Patrol Officer Job Satisfaction: A Reexamination Ten Years Later," *American Journal of Police*, Vol. 13, No. 2, 1994, pp. 51–75.

Byrne, John, "Prospect Heights Police Are on Duty, but Station Shut to Public," *Chicago Tribune*, July 10, 2009. As of June 23, 2010: http://articles.chicagotribune.com/2009-07-10/news/0907090887_1_police-officers-shut-furloughs

Byrne, Roger, "Employees: Capital or Commodity?" *Learning Organization*, Vol. 8, No. 1, 2001, pp. 44–50.

Cable, Daniel M., and Kang Yang Trevor Yu, "Managing Job Seekers' Organizational Image Beliefs: The Role of Media Richness and Media Credibility," *Journal of Applied Psychology*, Vol. 91, No. 4, July 2006, pp. 828–840.

California Commission on Peace Officer Standards and Training, *POST Recruitment Strategic Planning Guide: Finding and Keeping the Right People*, Sacramento, Calif.: California POST Media Distribution, November 2009. As of June 23, 2010: http://lib.post.ca.gov/Publications/RecruitmentStrategicPlanningGuide_11-09.pdf

California Police Chiefs Association, "Demographic Survey, 1994," Sacramento, Calif., 1994.

———, "Demographic Survey, 2001," Sacramento, Calif., 2001.

———, "Demographic Survey, 2004," Sacramento, Calif., November 2004. As of June 23, 2010: http://www.californiapolicechiefs.org/nav_files/research/pdfs/04demosurvey.pdf

Camper, John, and Rick Brown, "'Déjà Vu All Over Again': Meeting the Challenges of Funding Cuts in Patrol Operations," *PERF Subject to Debate*, Vol. 22, No. 12, December 2008, pp. 1–6. As of June 23, 2010: http://www.coronasolutions.com/downloads/perf.pdf

Canadian Association of Chiefs of Police, Canadian Police Association, PricewaterhouseCoopers, and Human Resources Development Canada, *Strategic Human Resources Analysis of Public Policing in Canada*, Ottawa: PricewaterhouseCoopers, 2000.

Cangelosi, Joseph D., F. Scott Markham, and William T. Bounds, "Factors Related to Nurse Retention and Turnover: An Updated Study," *Health Marketing Quarterly*, Vol. 15, No. 3, June 1998, pp. 25–43.

Cantor, Jeffrey A., "Registered Pre-Apprenticeship: Successful Practices Linking School to Work," *Journal of Industrial Teacher Education*, Vol. 34, No. 3, Spring 1997, pp. 35–58.

Carter, David L., and Allen D. Sapp, "College Education and Policing: Coming of Age," *FBI Law Enforcement Bulletin*, Vol. 61, No. 1, January 1992, pp. 8–14.

Cartwright, Susan, and Nicola Holmes, "The Meaning of Work: The Challenge of Regaining Employee Engagement and Reducing Cynicism," *Human Resource Management Review*, Vol. 16, No. 2, June 2006, pp. 199–208.

Castro, Hector, "Bad Economy Good for Police Recruiting," *Seattle Post-Intelligencer*, October 2, 2009. As of June 23, 2010: http://www.seattlepi.com/local/410721_cops02.html

Cavanagh, Michael E., *Policing Within a Professional Framework*, Upper Saddle River, N.J.: Pearson Prentice Hall, 2003.

Chambers, Brad A., "Applicant Reactions and Their Consequences: Review, Advice, and Recommendations for Future Research," *International Journal of Management Reviews*, Vol. 4, No. 4, December 2002, pp. 317–333.

Chambers, Stanley B., "Police Work Looks Good to Many," *Raleigh News and Observer*, May 5, 2009. As of June 23, 2010: http://www.newsobserver.com/2009/05/05/56274/police-work-looks-good-to-many.html

Chapman, Derek S., and Jane Webster, "The Use of Technologies in the Recruitment, Screening, and Selection Processes for Job Candidates," *International Journal of Selection and Assessment*, Vol. 11, No. 2–3, June 2003, pp. 113–120.

Charrier, Kim, "Marketing Strategies for Attracting and Retaining Generation X Police Officers," *Police Chief*, Vol. 67, No. 12, December 2000, pp. 45–51.

Chien, Chen-Fu, and Li-Fei Chen, "Data Mining to Improve Personnel Selection and Enhance Human Capital: A Case Study in High-Technology Industry," *Expert Systems with Applications*, Vol. 34, No. 1, January 2008, pp. 280–290.

City of Houston, Police Department, "HPD Careers," undated Web page. As of July 2, 2010: http://www.houstontx.gov/police/careers.htm

Clem, Connie, Barbara Krauth, and Paula Wenger, *Recruitment, Hiring, and Retention: Current Practices in U.S. Jails*, Longmont, Colo.: National Institute of Corrections Information Center, 2000. As of June 23, 2010: http://nicic.gov/Library/015885

Codispoti, Amanda, "Many Apply for Police Job Slots," *Roanoke Times*, March 11, 2009. As of June 23, 2010: http://www.roanoke.com/news/roanoke/wb/197315

Cohen, Bernard, and Jan M. Chaiken, *Police Background Characteristics and Performance: Summary*, Santa Monica, Calif.: RAND Corporation, R-999/1-DOJ, 1972. As of June 23, 2010: http://www.rand.org/pubs/reports/R999.1/

Cohen-Charash, Yochi, and Paul E. Spector, "The Role of Justice in Organizations: A Meta-Analysis," *Organizational Behavior and Human Decision Processes*, Vol. 86, No. 2, November 2001, pp. 278–321.

Cooper, Cary L., and Derek Torrington, eds., *After Forty: The Time for Achievement?* New York: Wiley, 1981.

Cooper, Christine, and Samantha Ingram, "*Retaining Officers in the Police Service: A Study of Resignations and Transfers in Ten Forces*, London: Home Office Research, Development and Statistics Directorate, NCJ 205347, 2004. As of June 23, 2010: http://www.homeoffice.gov.uk/rds/pdfs04/r212.pdf

"Cop Says Facebook Postings Got Him Fired," *WSBTV.com*, December 8, 2009. As of June 23, 2010: http://www.wsbtv.com/news/21900267/detail.html

Copeland, Thomas N., "Officer Retention: The Next Leadership Challenge," *Criminal Justice Institute Management Quarterly*, Winter 2009. As of June 23, 2010: http://www.cji.edu/Files/MQ2009Winter.pdf

COPS—*See* U.S. Department of Justice, Office of Community Oriented Policing Services.

Crowe, Robert, "Economy Has Folks Feeling the Blue," *San Antonio Express-News*, February 8, 2009. As of June 23, 2010: http://www.mysanantonio.com/news/local_news/Economy_has_folks_feeling_the_blue.html

Cunningham, Sonia, and Melissa Wagstaff, *Reflecting London: Diversity of Police Community Support Officer Recruits Compared to Police Officer Recruits in the Metropolitan Police Service*, London: Metropolitan Police Authority, December 2006. As of June 23, 2010: http://www.mpa.gov.uk/downloads/publications/pcso-diversity-full.pdf

Currier, Joel, "Missouri Police Academies Grow Despite Budget Tightening," *St. Louis Post-Dispatch*, November 2, 2009. As of June 23, 2010: http://www.columbiamissourian.com/stories/2009/11/09/mo-police-academies-seeing-growth/

Dantzker, Mark L., "Designing a Measure of Job Satisfaction for Policing: A Research Note," *Journal of Crime and Justice*, Vol. 16, No. 2, 1993, pp. 171–181.

———, "Measuring Job Satisfaction in Police Departments and Policy Implications: An Examination of a Mid-Size, Southern Police Department," *American Journal of Police*, Vol. 13, No. 2, 1994, pp. 77–101.

Danziger, Nira, Dalia Rachman-Moore, and Rony Valency, "The Construct Validity of Schein's Career Anchors Orientation Inventory," *Career Development International*, Vol. 13, No. 1, 2008, pp. 7–19.

Davenport, Thomas H., Robert J. Thomas, and Susan Cantrell, "The Mysterious Art and Science of Knowledge-Worker Performance," *MIT Sloan Management Review*, Vol. 44, No. 1, Fall 2002, pp. 23–30.

Davis, Lois M., Louis T. Mariano, Jennifer E. Pace, Sarah K. Cotton, and Paul Steinberg, *Combating Terrorism: How Prepared Are State and Local Response Organizations?* Santa Monica, Calif.: RAND Corporation, MG-309-OSD, 2006. As of June 24, 2010: http://www.rand.org/pubs/monographs/MG309/

Dayan, Kobi, Ronen Kasten, and Shaul Fox, "Entry-Level Police Candidate Assessment Center: An Efficient Tool or a Hammer to Kill a Fly?" *Personnel Psychology*, Vol. 55, No. 4, January 2002, pp. 827–849.

DeCicco, David A., "Police Officer Candidate Assessment and Selection," *FBI Law Enforcement Bulletin*, Vol. 69, No. 12, December 2000, pp. 1–6.

Decker, Lisa Kay, and Robert G. Huckabee, "Law Enforcement Hiring Practices and Narrowing the Applicant Pool: A Case Study," *Journal of Offender Rehabilitation*, Vol. 29, No. 3–4, December 1999, pp. 57–70.

———, "Raising the Age and Education Requirements for Police Officers: Will Too Many Women and Minority Candidates Be Excluded?" *Policing: An International Journal of Police Strategies and Management*, Vol. 25, No. 4, 2002, pp. 789–802.

Delaware State Personnel Office, "Research Project: Phase 1," Newark, Del.: University of Delaware, Institute for Public Administration, June 2002.

Del Bueno, Dorothy J., "Reflections on Retention, Recognition, and Rewards," *Journal of Nursing Administration*, Vol. 23, No. 10, October 1993, pp. 6–7, 41.

DeLord, Ron, special counsel to the executive director, Combined Law Enforcement Associations of Texas, interview, "From the Field Experiences," Santa Monica, Calif.: RAND Corporation, June 2009. As of June 24, 2010: http://www.rand.org/ise/centers/quality_policing/cops/resources/field_experiences/ron_delord.html

DeMasi, Michael, "Change in Residency Rule Sought: Police Officials Say Law Hurts Recruitment," *Schenectady Daily Gazette*, August 19, 2003.

Derby, Wade J., "The Impact of Drug Decriminalization on the Future of Police Recruiting Standards," *Police Chief*, Vol. 75, No. 8, August 2008, pp. 92–95.

De Rugy, Veronique, "Facts and Figures About Homeland Security Spending," Washington, D.C.: American Enterprise Institute, December 14, 2006. As of June 24, 2010: http://www.aei.org/docLib/20061214_FactsandFigures.pdf

Dick, Penny, "The Social Construction of the Meaning of Acute Stressors: A Qualitative Study of the Personal Accounts of Police Officers Using a Stress Counselling Service," *Work and Stress*, Vol. 14, No. 3, July 2000, pp. 226–244.

Dobbins, James, John G. McGinn, Keith Crane, Seth G. Jones, Rollie Lal, Andrew Rathmell, Rachel M. Swanger, and Anga R. Timilsina, *America's Role in Nation-Building: From Germany to Iraq*, Santa Monica, Calif.: RAND Corporation, MR-1753-RC, 2003. As of June 24, 2010: http://www.rand.org/pubs/monograph_reports/MR1753/

DoD—*See* U.S. Department of Defense.

Doerner, William G., "Officer Retention Patterns: An Affirmative Action Concern for Police Agencies?" *American Journal of Police*, Vol. 14, No. 3–4, 1995, pp. 197–210.

———, *Introduction to Law Enforcement: An Insider's View*, Boston, Mass.: Butterworth-Heinemann, 1998.

Domash, Shelley F., "Who Wants This Job?" *Police*, Vol. 26, No. 5, May 2002, pp. 34–39.

Donnelly, Daniel, "Policing the Scottish Community," in Daniel Donnelly and Kenneth Scott, eds., *Policing Scotland*, Cullompton, Devon, U.K.: Willan Publishing, 2005, pp. 130–156.

Draut, Tamara, *Economic State of Young America*, New York: Demos, 2008. As of June 24, 2010: http://www.demos.org/pubs/esya_web.pdf

Draut, Tamara, and Javier Silva, *Generation Broke: The Growth of Debt Among Young Americans*, New York: Demos, briefing paper 2, October 2004. As of June 24, 2010: http://archive.demos.org/pubs/Generation_Broke.pdf

Drew, Jacqueline, Sally A. Carless, and Briony M. Thompson, "Predicting Turnover of Police Officers Using the Sixteen Personality Factor Questionnaire," *Journal of Criminal Justice*, Vol. 36, No. 4, August 2008, pp. 326–331.

Dupont, Benoît, *Preserving Institutional Memory in Australian Police Services*, Canberra: Australian Institute of Criminology, Trends and Issues in Crime and Criminal Justice 245, 2003.

Dynarski, Susan M., *Building the Stock of College-Educated Labor*, Cambridge, Mass.: National Bureau of Economic Research, working paper 11604, August 2005. As of June 24, 2010: http://www.nber.org/papers/W11604.pdf

Eaton, Susan C., "If You Can Use Them: Flexibility Policies, Organizational Commitment, and Perceived Performance," *Industrial Relations*, Vol. 42, No. 2, 2003, pp. 145–167.

Edmonton police official, personal communication, October 5, 2009.

Edwards, Gary Scott, *Generational Competence and Retention: A Study of Different Generations in Law Enforcement and How These Differences Impact Retention in the Chesterfield County Police Department*, Richmond, Va.: University of Richmond, thesis, 2007.

Egan, Timothy, "Police Forces, Their Ranks Thin, Offer Bonuses, Bounties and More," *New York Times*, December 28, 2005. As of June 24, 2010: http://www.nytimes.com/2005/12/28/national/28police.html

Ellis, Gene, Greg Marshall, Chris Skinner, and Gary Smith, "Using Visual Technology for Recruitment," *Police Chief*, Vol. 72, No. 1, January 2005, pp. 20–24.

Ensher, Ellen A., and Susan E. Murphy, "Effects of Race, Gender, Perceived Similarity, and Contact on Mentor Relationships," *Journal of Vocational Behavior*, Vol. 50, No. 3, June 1997, pp. 460–481.

Enz, Cathy A., and Judy A. Siguaw, "Best Practices in Human Resources," *Cornell Hotel and Restaurant Administration Quarterly*, Vol. 41, No. 1, February 2000, pp. 48–61.

Eskildsen, Jacob K., and Mikkel L. Nussler, "The Managerial Drivers of Employee Satisfaction and Loyalty," *Total Quality Management and Business Excellence*, Vol. 11, No. 4–6, July 2000, pp. 581–588.

"Even Cops Losing Their Jobs in Recession," Associated Press, June 24, 2009.

Faher, Mike, "City Police Filling Holes in Ranks," *Johnstown Tribune-Democrat*, June 13, 2009. As of June 24, 2010: http://tribune-democrat.com/local/x519194658/City-police-filling-holes-in-ranks

FBI—*See* Federal Bureau of Investigation.

Federal Bureau of Investigation, "The Cyber Threat Today: Major Attacks on the Rise," October 17, 2008. As of June 24, 2010: http://www.fbi.gov/page2/oct08/cyberthreat101708.html

———, "Crime in the United States: Preliminary Annual Uniform Crime Report, January to December 2008," June 1, 2009. As of June 24, 2010: http://www.fbi.gov/ucr/08aprelim/index.html

Fielding, N. G., and J. L. Fielding, "Study of Resignation During British Police Training," *Journal of Police Science and Administration*, Vol. 15, No. 1, March 1987, pp. 24–36.

Fischer, Craig, *Violent Crime and the Economic Crisis: Police Chiefs Face a New Challenge*, Washington, D.C.: Police Executive Research Forum, May 2009.

Fischer, Margaret A., *Best Practices Guide for Generation X Recruits and the Field Training Experience*, Gaithersburg, Md.: International Association of Chiefs of Police, 2006. As of June 24, 2010: http://www.theiacp.org/Portals/0/pdfs/Publications/BP-GenXRecruits.pdf

Fitzgerald, Joan, "The Potential and Limitations of Career Ladders," in Joan Fitzgerald, *Moving Up in the New Economy: Career Ladders for U.S. Workers*, Ithaca, N.Y.: Cornell University Press, 2006, pp. 1–23.

Flood, Patrick C., Thomas Turner, Nagarajan Ramamoorthy, and Jill Pearson, "Causes and Consequences of Psychological Contracts Among Knowledge Workers in the High Technology and Financial Services Industries," *International Journal of Human Resource Management*, Vol. 12, No. 7, November 2001, pp. 1152–1165.

Flynn, Kevin, "As Opportunity Knocks, Police Turn in Badges," *New York Times*, August 12, 2000. As of June 24, 2010: http://www.nytimes.com/2000/08/12/nyregion/as-opportunity-knocks-police-turn-in-badges.html

Folger, Robert, and Mary A. Konovsky, "Effects of Procedural and Distributive Justice on Reactions to Pay Raise Decisions," *Academy of Management Journal*, Vol. 32, No. 1, March 1989, pp. 115–130.

Fox, Patrick, "Proposed Police Cuts Anger Gwinnett Residents," *Atlanta Journal-Constitution*, July 20, 2009. As of June 24, 2010: http://www.ajc.com/news/gwinnett/proposed-police-cuts-anger-96246.html

Frawley, Kathleen E., *The Effects of 9/11 on the Fire Fighter Labor Market*, Bloomington, Ill.: Illinois Wesleyan University, Economics Department Honors Projects paper 7, 2006. As of June 24, 2010: http://digitalcommons.iwu.edu/econ_honproj/7/

Friedman, Raymond A., and Brooks Holtom, "The Effects of Network Groups on Minority Employee Turnover Intentions," *Human Resource Management*, Vol. 41, No. 4, Winter 2002, pp. 405–421.

Fritsch, Eric J., John Liederbach, and Robert W. Taylor, *Police Patrol Allocation and Deployment*, Upper Saddle River, N.J.: Pearson Prentice Hall, 2009.

Frost, Jeffrey A., *Predictors of Job Satisfaction and Turnover Intention in Police Organizations: A Procedural Approach*, Chicago, Ill.: University of Chicago, Ph.D. dissertation, 2006.

Fry, Louise W., and Leslie J. Berkes, "Paramilitary Police Model: An Organizational Misfit," *Human Organization*, Vol. 42, No. 3, Fall 1983, pp. 225–234.

Fulton, Roger, "Recruiting and Hiring New Officers," *Law Enforcement Technology*, Vol. 30, August 2000, p. 130.

Fyfe, James J., Jack R. Greene, William F. Walsh, O. W. Wilson, and Roy Clinton McLaren, eds., *Police Administration*, 5th ed., New York: McGraw-Hill, 1997.

Gaines, Larry K., and Victor E. Kappeler, "Selection and Testing," in Gary W. Cordner and Donna C. Hale, eds., *What Works in Policing? Operations and Administration Examined*, Cincinnati, Ohio: Anderson Publishing, 1992, pp. 107–123.

Geis, Gilbert, and Elvin Cavanagh, "Recruitment and Retention of Correctional Personnel," *Crime and Delinquency*, Vol. 12, No. 3, July 1966, pp. 232–239.

Gettinger, Stephen H., *Assessing Criminal Justice Needs*, Washington, D.C.: U.S. Department of Justice, National Institute of Justice, June 1984.

Glanville, Kathleen, "Portland Police Recruits Hit the Streets Earlier," *Oregonian*, July 11, 2009. As of June 24, 2010: http://www.oregonlive.com/portland/index.ssf/2009/07/portland_police_recruits_hit_t.html

Goeller, Annie, "Economy Leads to Surge in Applications for Government Jobs in Johnson County," *Indiana Economic Digest*, June 29, 2009. As of June 24, 2010: http://www.indianaeconomicdigest.net/main.asp?SectionID=31&ArticleID=48559

Goldstein, Herman, *Policing a Free Society*, Cambridge, Mass.: Ballinger Publishing, 1977.

Golfin, Peggy A., *A Proposed Pilot to Recruit Pretrained Personnel*, Alexandria, Va.: CNA Corporation, January 2006.

Gottfredson, Michael R., and Don M. Gottfredson, *Decision Making in Criminal Justice: Toward the Rational Exercise of Discretion*, 2nd ed., New York: Plenum Press, 1988.

Graig, Laurene, and Valerie Paganelli, "Phased Retirement: Reshaping the End of Work," *Compensation and Benefits Management*, Vol. 16, No. 2, Spring 2000, pp. 1–9.

Greene, Maureen T., and Mary S. Puetzer, "The Value of Mentoring: A Strategic Approach to Retention and Recruitment," *Journal of Nursing Care Quality*, Vol. 17, No. 1, October 2002, pp. 63–70.

Griffin, Gerald R., Roger L. Dunbar, and Michael E. McGill, "Factors Associated with Job Satisfaction Among Police Personnel," *Journal of Police Science and Administration*, Vol. 6, No. 1, March 1978, pp. 77–85.

Gubbins, M. Claire, and Thomas N. Garavan, "The Changing Context and Role of the HRD Professional: Time to Recognize the Importance of Social Networking Competency," paper presented at the Ninth Annual Conference on Human Resource Development, Lille, France, May 2008.

Gunnels-Perry, Sherryl, "Public/Private Partnerships as Recruiting and Retention Strategies," *Employment Relations Today*, Vol. 26, No. 2, January 2007, pp. 1–13.

Haarr, Robin N., "Factors Affecting the Decision of Police Recruits to 'Drop Out' of Police Work," *Police Quarterly*, Vol. 8, No. 4, December 2005, pp. 431–453.

Haggerty, Catherine, lieutenant, recruiting division, Austin Police Department, interview, "From the Field Experiences," Santa Monica, Calif.: RAND Corporation, July 2009. As of June 24, 2010: http://www. rand.org/ise/centers/quality_policing/cops/resources/field_experiences/catherine_haggerty.html

Harrington, Penny E., *Recruiting and Retaining Women: A Self-Assessment Guide for Law Enforcement*, Los Angeles, Calif.: National Center for Women and Policing, a Division of the Feminist Majority Foundation, 2000. As of June 24, 2010: http://www.ncjrs.gov/pdffiles1/bja/185235.pdf

Harris, Louis M., and J. Norman Baldwin, "Voluntary Turnover of Field Operations Officers: A Test of Confluency Theory," *Journal of Criminal Justice*, Vol. 27, No. 6, November–December 1999, pp. 483–493.

Harris, Michael M., Greet Van Hoye, and Filip Lievens, "Privacy and Attitudes Towards Internet-Based Selection Systems: A Cross-Cultural Comparison," *International Journal of Selection and Assessment*, Vol. 11, No. 2–3, June 2003, pp. 230–236.

Harrison, Bob, "Gamers, Millennials, and Generation Next: Implications for Policing," *Police Chief*, Vol. 74, No. 10, October 2007, pp. 150–160.

Hausknecht, John, Julianne M. Rodda, and Michael J. Howard, *Targeted Employee Retention: Performance-Based and Job-Related Differences in Reported Reasons for Staying*, Ithaca, N.Y.: Cornell University School of Industrial and Labor Relations, April 2008. As of June 24, 2010: http:// digitalcommons.ilr.cornell.edu/articles/140/

Hazucha, Joy F., Sarah A. Hezlett, and Robert J. Schneider, "The Impact of 360-Degree Feedback on Management Skills Development," *Human Resource Management*, Vol. 32, No. 2–3, Summer 1993, pp. 325–352.

Hegstad, Christine D., and Rose Mary Wentling, "The Development and Maintenance of Exemplary Formal Mentoring Programs in Fortune 500 Companies," *Human Resource Development Quarterly*, Vol. 15, No. 4, Winter 2004, pp. 421–448.

Herman, Roger E., "HR Managers as Employee-Retention Specialists," *Employee Relations Today*, Vol. 32, No. 2, July 2005, pp. 1–7.

Hickman, Matthew J., "Impact of the Military Reserve Activation on Police Staffing," *Police Chief*, Vol. 73, No. 10, October 2006, pp. 12–14.

Hickman, Matthew J., and Brian A. Reaves, *Local Police Departments, 2003*, Washington, D.C.: Department of Justice, Office of Justice Programs, Bureau of Justice Statistics, NCJ 210118, April 1, 2006a. As of June 24, 2010: http://bjs.ojp.usdoj.gov/index.cfm?ty=pbdetail&iid=1045

———, *Sheriffs' Offices, 2003*, Washington, D.C.: Department of Justice, Office of Justice Programs, Bureau of Justice Statistics, NCJ 211361, April 1, 2006b. As of June 24, 2010: http://bjs.ojp.usdoj.gov/ index.cfm?ty=pbdetail&iid=1217

Hill, E. Jeffrey, Alan J. Hawkins, Maria Ferris, and Michelle Weitzman, "Finding an Extra Day a Week: The Positive Influence of Perceived Job Flexibility on Work and Family," *Family Relations*, Vol. 50, No. 1, January 2001, pp. 49–58.

Ho, Taiping, "Assessment of Police Officer Recruiting and Testing Instruments," *Journal of Offender Rehabilitation*, Vol. 29, No. 3–4, December 1999, pp. 1–23.

Hoffman, J., "Plague of Small Agencies: Turnover," *Law and Order*, Vol. 41, No. 6, June 1993, pp. 25–28.

Hogarty, Kris, and Max Bromley, "Evaluating the Use of the Assessment Center Process for Entry-Level Police Officer Selections in a Medium Sized Police Agency," *Journal of Police and Criminal Psychology*, Vol. 11, No. 1, March 1996, pp. 27–34.

Hogue, Mark C., Tommie Black, and Robert T. Sigler, "Differential Use of Screening Techniques in the Recruitment of Police Officers," *American Journal of Police*, Vol. 13, No. 2, 1994, pp. 113–124.

Holtom, Brooks C., Terence R. Mitchell, and Thomas W. Lee, "Increasing Human and Social Capital by Applying Job Embeddedness Theory," *Organizational Dynamics*, Vol. 35, No. 4, 2006, pp. 316–331.

Holtom, Brooks C., Terence R. Mitchell, Thomas W. Lee, and Marion B. Eberly, "Turnover and Retention Research: A Glance at the Past, a Closer Review of the Present, and a Venture into the Future," *Academy of Management Annals*, Vol. 2, No. 1, August 2008, pp. 231–274.

Hom, Peter W., *Turnover Costs Among Mental Health Professionals*, Tempe, Ariz.: College of Business, Arizona State University, Ph.D. dissertation, 1992.

Hom, Peter W., and Rodger W. Griffeth, *Employee Turnover*, Cincinnati, Ohio: South-Western College Publishing, 1994.

Hurst, Susan, and Stephanie Koplin-Baucum, "Role Acquisition, Socialization, and Retention: Unique Aspects of a Mentoring Program," *Journal for Nurses in Staff Development*, Vol. 19, No. 4, July–August 2003, pp. 176–180.

IACP—*See* International Association of Chiefs of Police.

Idaho State Police, "Realistic Job Preview," undated Web page. As of June 24, 2010: http://www.isp. idaho.gov/hr/trooper_info/realistic_job.html

Ingersoll, Richard M., and Thomas M. Smith, "The Wrong Solution to the Teacher Shortage," *Educational Leadership*, Vol. 60, No. 8, May 2003, pp. 30–33.

International Association of Chiefs of Police, "Discover Policing," undated website. As of June 24, 2010: http://discoverpolicing.org/

International Association of Directors of Law Enforcement Standards and Training, *Reciprocity Handbook*, Meridian, Ida., 2005.

Jackson, Jodie, C. Ken Shannon, Donald E. Pathman, Elaine Mason, and James W. Nemitz, "A Comparative Assessment of West Virginia's Financial Incentive Programs for Rural Physicians," *Journal of Rural Health*, Vol. 19, No. 5, 2003, pp. 329–339.

Jamrog, Jay, "The Perfect Storm: The Future of Retention and Engagement," *Human Resource Planning*, Vol. 27, No. 3, 2004, pp. 26–33.

Jaramillo, Fernando, Robert Nixon, and Doreen Sams, "The Effect of Law Enforcement Stress on Organizational Commitment," *Policing: An International Journal of Police Strategies and Management*, Vol. 28, No. 2, 2005, pp. 321–336.

Johnson, Kevin, "Economy Forces Deep Police Cuts," *Arizona Republic*, October 19, 2008. As of June 24, 2010: http://www.azcentral.com/news/articles/2008/10/19/20081019crime-economy1019.html

Johnston, Lloyd D., Patrick M. O'Malley, Jerald G. Bachman, and John E. Schulenberg, "Various Stimulant Drugs Show Continuing Gradual Declines Among Teens in 2008, Most Illicit Drugs Hold Steady," press release, Ann Arbor, Mich.: University of Michigan News Service, December 11, 2008. As of June 24, 2010: http://monitoringthefuture.org/data/08data.html#2008data-drugs

Jones, Seth G., Jeremy M. Wilson, Andrew Rathmell, and K. Jack Riley, *Establishing Law and Order After Conflict*, Santa Monica, Calif.: RAND Corporation, MG-374-RC, 2005. As of June 24, 2010: http://www. rand.org/pubs/monographs/MG374/

Jordan, William T., Lorie Fridell, Donald Faggiani, and Bruce Kubu, "Attracting Females and Racial/ Ethnic Minorities to Law Enforcement," *Journal of Criminal Justice*, Vol. 37, No. 4, July–August 2009, pp. 333–341.

Kacmar, K. Michele, Martha C. Andrews, David L. Van Rooy, R. Chris Steilberg, and Stephen Cerrone, "Sure Everyone Can Be Replaced ... but at What Cost? Turnover as a Predictor of Unit-Level Performance," *Academy of Management Journal*, Vol. 49, No. 1, February 2006, pp. 133–144.

Kahanov, Leamor, and Lanna Andrews, "A Survey of Athletic Training Employers' Hiring Criteria," *Journal of Athletic Training*, Vol. 36, No. 4, October–December 2001, pp. 408–412.

Kane, Tim, "The Demographics of Military Enlistment After 9/11," Washington, D.C.: Heritage Foundation, executive memorandum 987, November 3, 2005. As of June 24, 2010: http://www.heritage.org/ Research/Reports/2005/11/The-Demographics-of-Military-Enlistment-After-9-11

Kappeler, Victor E., Richard D. Sluder, and Geoffrey P. Alpert, *Forces of Deviance: Understanding the Dark Side of Policing*, Prospect Heights, Ill.: Waveland Press, 1994.

Katz, Jesse, "Past Drug Use, Future Cops," *Los Angeles Times*, June 18, 2000. As of June 24, 2010: http:// articles.latimes.com/2000/jun/18/news/mn-42251

Kearns, Scott Alan, *Recruitment and Retention Challenges for Law Enforcement Agencies: Identifying the Reasons for High Turnover Rates of New Recruits*, Richmond, Va.: University of Richmond, thesis, 2007.

Khashu, Anita, and Mary Malina, *The Role of Local Police: Striking a Balance Between Immigration Enforcement and Civil Liberties*, Washington, D.C.: Police Foundation, April 2009. As of June 24, 2010: http://www.policefoundation.org/pdf/strikingabalance/Narrative.pdf

Kickul, Jill, "Promises Made, Promises Broken: An Exploration of Employee Attraction and Retention Practices in Small Business," *Journal of Small Business Management*, Vol. 39, No. 4, 2002, pp. 320–335.

Kim, Soonhee, "Factors Affecting State Government Information Technology Employee Turnover Intentions," *American Review of Public Administration*, Vol. 35, No. 2, 2005, pp. 137–156.

Kirpal, Simone, "Work Identities of Nurses: Between Caring and Efficiency Demands," *Career Development International*, Vol. 9, No. 3, 2004, pp. 274–304.

Kogi, Kazutaka, "Implications of Flexible Work Systems for Work Studies," *Journal of Human Ergology*, Vol. 26, No. 2, December 1997, pp. 89–97.

Kohn, Paula S., and Marie Truglio-Londrigan, "Second-Career Baccalaureate Nursing Students: A Lived Experience," *Journal of Nursing Education*, Vol. 46, No. 9, September 2007, pp. 391–399.

Kolbitsch, Josef, and Hermann Maurer, "The Transformation of the Web: How Emerging Communities Shape the Information We Consume," *Journal of Universal Computer Science*, Vol. 12, No. 2, 2006, pp. 19–37.

Kolpack, Bryce D., "Assessment Center Approach to Police Officer Selection," *Police Chief*, Vol. 58, No. 9, September 1991, pp. 28–30, 44–46.

Kondrasuk, Jack N., "The Effects of 9/11 and Terrorism on Human Resource Management: Recovery, Reconsideration, and Renewal," *Employee Responsibilities and Rights Journal*, Vol. 16, No. 1, March 2004, pp. 25–35.

Koper, Christopher S., Edward R. Maguire, and Gretchen E. Moore, *Hiring and Retention Issues in Police Agencies: Readings on the Determinants of Police Strength, Hiring and Retention of Officers, and the Federal COPS Program*, Washington, D.C.: Urban Institute, October 2001. As of June 24, 2010: http://www.urban.org/UploadedPDF/410380_Hiring-and-Retention.pdf

Kowal, Julie, Bryan C. Hassel, and Emily Ayscue Hassel, *Financial Incentives for Hard-to-Staff Positions: Cross-Sector Lessons for Public Education*, Chicago, Ill.: Center for American Progress, November 2008. As of June 24, 2010: http://www.americanprogress.org/issues/2008/11/financial_incentives.html

Kraska, Peter B., "Militarization and Policing: Its Relevance to 21st Century Police," *Policing: A Journal of Policy and Practice*, Vol. 1, No. 4, 2007, pp. 501–513.

Kuruvila, Matthai, "80 Oakland Police Officers Get Layoff Notices," *San Francisco Chronicle*, June 29, 2010. As of July 2, 2010: http://articles.sfgate.com/2010-06-29/bay-area/21930012_1_police-union-police-groups-public-safety-program

Lachnit, Carroll, "Employee Referral Saves Time, Saves Money, Delivers Quality," *Workforce*, June 2001.

LaHuis, David M., "Individual Differences in Applicant Reactions: A Job-Search Perspective," *International Journal of Selection and Assessment*, Vol. 13, No. 2, June 2005, pp. 150–159.

Lambert, Eric, "The Impact of Organizational Justice on Correctional Staff," *Journal of Criminal Justice*, Vol. 31, No. 2, March–April 2003, pp. 155–168.

Lambert, Eric, and Nancy Hogan, "The Importance of Job Satisfaction and Organizational Commitment in Shaping Turnover Intent: A Test of a Causal Model," *Criminal Justice Review*, Vol. 34, No. 1, 2009, pp. 96–118.

Landy, Frank J., *Performance Appraisal in Police Departments*, Washington, D.C.: Police Foundation, 1977.

Langworthy, Robert H., Thomas Hughes, and Beth Sanders, *Law Enforcement Recruitment, Selection and Training: A Survey of Major Police Departments in the U.S.*, Highland Heights, Ky.: Academy of Criminal Justice Sciences, Police Section, 1995.

Lanier, Cathy, chief, Metropolitan Police Department, Washington, D.C., "Challenges of Police Recruiting in the District of Columbia," presentation, RAND Center for Quality Policing Recruitment and Retention Summit, Arlington, Va., June 2008. As of June 24, 2010: http://www.cops.usdoj.gov/Default.asp?Item=2101#12

LAPD—*See* Los Angeles Police Department.

Larson, Richard C., *Police Deployment: New Tools for Planners*, Lexington, Mass.: Lexington Books, 1978.

Lavigna, Robert L., "Winning the War for Talent, Part II: Some Solutions," *Government Finance Review*, Vol. 21, No. 2, April 2005.

Lawler, Edward E. III, "Creating High Performance Organizations," *Asia Pacific Journal of Human Resources*, Vol. 4, No. 1, 2005, pp. 10–17.

Lawsson, Robert D., "Identifying and Managing Diversity of Workforce," *Business Intelligence Journal*, Vol. 2, No. 1, January 2009, pp. 215–253.

Lee, Christopher D., *Performance Conversations: An Alternative to Appraisals*, Tucson, Ariz.: Wheatmark, 2006.

Lee, Lori Ann, *Peace Officer Recruitment and Retention: Best Practices*, Sacramento, Calif.: Commission on Peace Officer Standards and Training, July 2001. As of June 23, 2010: http://libcat.post.ca.gov/dbtw-wpd/documents/post/53936324.pdf

Lee, Thomas W., and Terence R. Mitchell, "An Alternative Approach: The Unfolding Model of Voluntary Employee Turnover," *Academy of Management Review*, Vol. 19, No. 1, January 1994, pp. 51–89.

Lee, Wendy, "LAPD May Relax Its Hiring Rules," *Los Angeles Times*, August 29, 2005. As of June 24, 2010: http://articles.latimes.com/2005/aug/29/local/me-lapd29

Levenson, Michael, and Donovan Slack, "Pension Laws Pare Police, Fire Rolls," *Boston Globe*, July 1, 2009. As of June 24, 2010: http://www.boston.com/news/local/massachusetts/articles/2009/07/01/pension_laws_pare_police_fire_rolls/

Levin-Epstein, Jodie, *Getting Punched: The Job and Family Clock*, Washington, D.C.: Center for Law and Social Policy, July 2006. As of June 24, 2010: http://www.clasp.org/admin/site/publications/files/0303.pdf

Lewis, Robert, "70 Deputies' Jobs Saved," *Sacramento Bee*, July 15, 2009. As of June 24, 2010: http://www.sacbee.com/2009/07/15/2026680/70-deputies-jobs-saved.html

Lewis, Suzan, Carolyn Kagan, and Patricia Heaton, "Managing Work-Family Diversity for Parents of Disabled Children: Beyond Policy to Practice and Partnership," *Personnel Review*, Vol. 29, No. 3, 2000, pp. 417–430.

Liebert, Dennis R., and Rod Miller, *Staffing Analysis Workbook for Jails*, Washington, D.C.: Department of Justice, National Institute of Corrections, 2001.

Lim, Nelson, Carl Matthies, Greg Ridgeway, and Brian Gifford, *To Protect and to Serve: Enhancing the Efficiency of LAPD Recruiting*, Santa Monica, Calif.: RAND Corporation, MG-881-RMPF, 2009. As of June 24, 2010: http://www.rand.org/pubs/monographs/MG881/

Litcher, Christopher D., Devon Reister, and Christopher Mason, *Statewide Law Enforcement Officer Retention Study*, Montpelier, Vt.: State of Vermont Law Enforcement Advisory Board, January 4, 2006. As of June 24, 2010: http://www.dps.state.vt.us/LEAB/law_enforcement_retention.pdf

Lloyd Morgan, *Driving Performance and Retention Through Employee Engagement*, undated. As of June 23, 2010: http://www.lloydmorgan.com/PDF/Driving%20Performance%20and%20Retention%20Through%20Employee%20Engagement.pdf

London, Manuel, and Arthur J. Wohlers, "Agreement Between Subordinate and Self-Ratings in Upward Feedback," *Personnel Psychology*, Vol. 44, No. 2, Summer 1991, pp. 375–391.

Los Angeles Police Department, "To Protect and to Serve," undated video, webisode 1. As of June 24, 2010: http://www.joinlapd.com/webisode_01.html

Losey, Michael R., "Anticipating Change: Will There Be a Labor Shortage?" in Michael R. Losey, Susan R. Meisinger, and David Ulrich, eds., *The Future of Human Resource Management: 64 Thought Leaders Explore the Critical HR Issues of Today and Tomorrow*, Alexandria, Va.: Society for Human Resource Management, 2005, pp. 23–37.

Luthans, Kyle W., "Recognition: A Powerful, but Often Overlooked, Leadership Tool to Improve Employee Performance," *Journal of Leadership and Organizational Studies*, Vol. 7, No. 1, 2000, pp. 31–39.

Luthans, Kyle W., and Susan M. Jensen, "The Linkage Between Psychological Capital and Commitment to Organizational Mission: A Study of Nurses," *Journal of Nursing Administration*, Vol. 35, No. 6, June 2005, pp. 304–310.

Lynch, Jessica E., and Michelle Tuckey, *Understanding Voluntary Turnover: An Examination of Resignations in Australasian Police Organizations*, Payneham, Australia: Australasian Centre for Policing Research, report 143.1, 2004.

———, "The Police Turnover Problem: Fact or Fiction?" *Policing: An International Journal of Police Strategies and Management*, Vol. 31, No. 1, 2008, pp. 6–18.

Lyons, Sean, Linda Duxbury, and Chris Higgins, "An Empirical Assessment of Generational Differences in Work-Related Values," *Human Resources Management*, Vol. 26, No. 9, 2005, pp. 62–71.

Madrid, Ofelia, "Officer Applicants Surge at Scottsdale Police Department," *Arizona Republic*, March 26, 2009. As of June 24, 2010: http://www.azcentral.com/news/articles/2009/03/26/20090326sr-pdrecruit0327.html

Maguire, Edward R., and Stephen D. Mastrofski, "Patterns of Community Policing in the United States," *Police Quarterly*, Vol. 3, No. 1, March 2000, pp. 4–45.

Maki, Amos, "Police Residency Tops Agenda," *Memphis Commercial-Appeal*, May 20, 2008. As of June 24, 2010: http://www.commercialappeal.com/news/2008/may/20/police-residency-tops-agenda/

Makinen, Gail E., *The Economic Effects of 9/11: A Retrospective Assessment*, Washington, D.C.: Congressional Research Service, RL31617, September 27, 2002.

Manolatos, Tony, "S.D. Cops Flee City's Fiscal Mess, Seek Jobs at Other Departments," *San Diego Union-Tribune*, July 5, 2006. As of June 24, 2010: http://legacy.signonsandiego.com/news/metro/20060705-9999-1n5gary.html

Martin, Graeme, Martin Reddington, and Mary Beth Kneafsey, *Web 2.0 and Human Resource Management: "Groundswell" or Hype?* London: Chartered Institute of Personnel and Development, 2009.

McCafferty, Francis L., "The Challenge of Selecting Tomorrow's Police Officers from Generations X and Y," *Journal of the American Academy of Psychiatry and the Law*, Vol. 31, No. 1, 2003, pp. 78–88.

McCoy, Mike, "Fire, Police Cuts Loom," *Santa Rosa Press-Democrat*, February 12, 2009. As of June 24, 2010: http://www.pressdemocrat.com/article/20090212/NEWS/902120360

McDevitt, Jack, Amy Farrell, and Russell Wolf, *Promoting Cooperative Strategies to Reduce Racial Profiling*, Washington, D.C.: U.S. Department of Justice, Office of Community Oriented Policing Services, COPS evaluation brief 1, 2008. As of June 24, 2010: http://purl.access.gpo.gov/GPO/LPS115585

McDonnell, Ken, "Benefit Cost Comparisons Between State and Local Governments and Private-Sector Employees," *Employee Benefit and Research Institute Notes*, Vol. 23, No. 10, October 2002, pp. 6–9.

———, "Benefit Cost Comparisons Between State and Local Governments and Private-Sector Employees," *Employee Benefit and Research Institute Notes*, Vol. 26, No. 4, April 2005, pp. 2–5.

———, "Benefit Cost Comparisons Between State and Local Governments and Private-Sector Employees," *Employee Benefit and Research Institute Notes*, Vol. 29, No. 6, June 2008, pp. 2–6.

McEvoy, Glenn M., and Wayne F. Cascio, "Do Good or Poor Performers Leave? A Meta-Analysis of the Relationship Between Performance and Turnover," *Academy of Management Journal*, Vol. 30, No. 4, December 1987, pp. 744–762.

McIntyre, Robert W., *Why Police Officers Resign: A Look at the Turnover of Police Officers in Vermont*, Montpelier, Vt.: Vermont Criminal Justice Center, 1990.

McKay, Patrick F., and Derek R. Avery, "Warning! Diversity Recruitment Could Backfire," *Journal of Management Inquiry*, Vol. 14, No. 4, December 2005, pp. 330–336.

———, "What Has Race Got to Do with It? Unraveling the Role of Racioethnicity in Job Seekers' Reactions to Site Visits," *Personnel Psychology*, Vol. 59, No. 2, Summer 2006, pp. 395–429.

McKeever, Jack, and April Kranda, "Recruitment and Retention of Qualified Police Personnel: A Best Practices Guide," *Big Ideas for Smaller Departments*, Vol. 2, No. 1, Summer 2000, pp. 3–15. As of June 24, 2010: http://www.theiacp.org/LinkClick.aspx?fileticket=Jn02Pt%2BKiWl%3D&tab id=407

Meglino, Bruce M., Elizabeth C. Ravlin, and Angelo S. DeNisi, "A Meta-Analytic Examination of Realistic Job Preview Effectiveness: A Test of Three Counterintuitive Propositions," *Human Resource Management Review*, Vol. 10, No. 4, Winter 2000, pp. 407–434.

Meier, Gretl S., *Job Sharing: A New Pattern for Quality of Work and Life*, Kalamazoo, Mich.: W. E. Upjohn Institute for Employment Research, 1979.

Mestemaker, Michael J., *The Aviation Career Improvement Act and Its Impact on Retention*, Carlisle Barracks, Pa.: U.S. Army War College, 1991. As of June 24, 2010: http://www.dtic.mil/cgi-bin/GetTRDoc?AD=ADA237336&Location=U2&doc=GetTRDoc.pdf

Metropolitan Atlanta Crime Commission, *Manual on Police Patrol Manpower Resource Allocation*, Atlanta, Ga., 1977.

Miller, Laura L., behavioral and social scientist, RAND Corporation, "Police Personnel Challenges After September 11: Anticipating Expanding Duties and a Changing Labor Pool," presentation, RAND Center for Quality Policing Recruitment and Retention Summit, Arlington, Va., June 2008. As of June 24, 2010: http://www.cops.usdoj.gov/pdf/conference/rand/MillerPoliceChallengesafter911.pdf

Mitchell, Terence R., Brooks C. Holtom, Thomas W. Lee, and Ted Graske, "How to Keep Your Best Employees: Developing an Effective Retention Policy," *Academy of Management Executive (1993–2005)*, Vol. 15, No. 4, November 2001, pp. 96–109.

Mitchell, Terence R., Brooks C. Holtom, Thomas W. Lee, Chris J. Sablynski, and Miriam Erez, "Why People Stay: Using Job Embeddedness to Predict Voluntary Turnover," *Academy of Management Journal*, Vol. 44, No. 6, December 2001, pp. 1102–1121.

Mobley, William H., *Employee Turnover: Causes, Consequences, and Control*, Reading, Mass.: Addison-Wesley, 1982.

Moore, Solomon, "Despite Bleak Economy, Crime Numbers Take Positive Turn," *New York Times*, June 1, 2009. As of June 24, 2010: http://www.nytimes.com/2009/06/02/us/02fbi.html

Morgan, Misti M., and William Allan Kritsonis, "A National Focus: The Recruitment, Retention, and Development of Quality Teachers in Hard-to-Staff Schools," *National Journal for Publishing and Mentoring Doctoral Student Research*, Vol. 5, No. 1, 2008, pp. 12–19.

Moriarty, Sean E., "The Leadership in Police Organizations Program in Delaware State Police: Recommendations for Law Enforcement Leadership Development," *Police Chief*, Vol. 76, No. 5, May 2009, pp. 7–13.

Moses, Joseph L., and Virginia R. Boehm, "Relationship of Assessment-Center Performance to Management Progress of Women," *Journal of Applied Psychology*, Vol. 60, No. 4, August 1975, pp. 527–529.

Moyle, Wendy, Jan Skinner, Gillian Rowe, and Chris Gork, "Views of Job Satisfaction and Dissatisfaction in Australian Long-Term Care," *Journal of Clinical Nursing*, Vol. 12, No. 2, March 2003, pp. 168–176.

Mueller, Charles W., and James L. Price, "Some Consequences of Turnover: A Work Unit Analysis," *Human Relations*, Vol. 42, No. 5, 1989, pp. 389–402.

Murphy, David W., and John L. Worrall, "Residency Requirements and Public Perceptions of the Police in Large Municipalities," *Policing: An International Journal of Police Strategies and Management*, Vol. 22, No. 3, 1999, pp. 327–342.

Musser, Linda R., "Effective Retention Strategies for Diverse Employees," *Journal of Library Administration*, Vol. 33, No. 1–2, January 2001, pp. 63–72.

"MySpace, Facebook and Other Social Networking Sites: Hot Today, Gone Tomorrow?" *Universia*, May 31, 2006. As of June 24, 2010: http://www.wharton.universia.net/index.cfm?fa=viewfeature&id=1156&language=english

Nalla, Mahesh K., Michael Lynch, and Michael J. Leiber, "Determinants of Police Growth in Phoenix, 1950–1988," *Justice Quarterly*, Vol. 14, No. 1, March 1997, pp. 115–143.

Nash, James, and Elizabeth Gibson, "Supreme Court: Cities Can't Dictate Where Employees Live," *Columbus Dispatch*, June 10, 2009. As of June 24, 2010: http://www.dispatch.com/live/content/local_news/stories/2009/06/10/asuprme. html

National Institute of Justice, *Assessing Criminal Justice Needs*, Washington, D.C., 1992.

New South Wales Council on the Cost of Government, *First Report*, Sydney, Australia, 1996.

New York City Commission to Combat Police Corruption, *Tenth Annual Report*, February 2008. As of June 24, 2010: http://www.nyc.gov/html/ccpc/downloads/pdf/10th_annual_report_feb_2008.pdf

NIJ—*See* National Institute of Justice

"NYPD Facing a Flood of 20-and-Out Retirees," *Law Enforcement News: A Publication of John Jay College of Criminal Justice*, Vol. 26, No. 527, February 14, 2000. As of June 24, 2010: http://www.lib.jjay.cuny.edu/len/2000/02.14/

O'Brien-Pallas, Linda, Christine Duffield, and Chris Alksnis, "Who Will Be There to Nurse? Retention of Nurses Nearing Retirement," *Journal of Nursing Administration*, Vol. 34, No. 6, June 2004, pp. 298–302.

Oettmeier, Timothy N., and Mary Ann Wycoff, *Personnel Performance Evaluations in the Community Policing Context*, Washington, D.C.: Police Executive Research Forum, July 1997.

OJP—*See* U.S. Department of Justice, Office of Justice Programs.

Olson, Roberta K., Margot Nelson, Carol Stuart, Linda Young, Ardelle Kleinsasser, Rose Schroedermeier, and Phyllis Newstrom, "Nursing Student Residency Program: A Model for Seamless Transition from Nursing Student to RN," *Journal of Nursing Administration*, Vol. 31, No. 1, January 2001, pp. 40–48.

Ontario Office of Fire Marshal, *Resource Book: The Application of Recruitment and Retention Principles*, 2006. As of June 24, 2010: http://www.ofm.gov.on.ca/english/FireProtection/munguide/Volunteer%20Recruitment%20and%20Retention/default.asp

Orrick, W. Dwayne, "Calculating the Cost of Police Turnover," *Police Chief*, Vol. 69, No. 10, October 2002, pp. 100–103.

———, *Recruitment, Retention, and Turnover of Police Personnel: Reliable, Practical, and Effective Solutions*, Springfield, Ill.: Charles C. Thomas, 2008a.

———, "Maximizing Officer Retention," presentation, RAND Center for Quality Policing Recruitment and Retention Summit, Arlington, Va., June 2008b. As of June 24, 2010: http://www.cops.usdoj.gov/Default.asp?Item=2101#11

Palmer, Jonathan, Cheri Speier, Michael Buckley, and Jo Ellen Moore, *Recruiting and Retaining IS Personnel: Factors Influencing Employee Turnover*, Boston, Mass.: Association for Computing Machinery Special Interest Group on Computer Personnel Research, 1998.

Patterson, Bernie L., "Job Experience and Perceived Job Stress Among Police, Correctional, and Probation/Parole Officers," *Criminal Justice and Behavior*, Vol. 19, No. 3, September 1992, pp. 260–285.

PCSO—*See* Pinal County Sheriff's Office.

Pennington, Karen, JoAnn G. Congdon, and Joan K. Magilvy, "Second-Career CNAs in Nursing Homes: Tapping an Underused Resource," *Journal of Gerontological Nursing*, Vol. 33, No. 6, June 2007, pp. 21–28.

Perrons, Diane, "Flexible Working and Equal Opportunities in the United Kingdom: A Case Study from Retail," *Environment and Planning*, Vol. 32, No. 10, 2000, pp. 1719–1734.

Pew Research Center for the People and the Press, *A Portrait of "Generation Next": How Young People View Their Lives, Futures and Politics*, Washington, D.C., January 2007. As of June 24, 2010: http://people-press.org/reports/pdf/300.pdf

Phillips, Jean M., "Effects of Realistic Job Previews on Multiple Organizational Outcomes: A Meta-Analysis," *Academy of Management Journal*, Vol. 41, No. 6, December 1998, pp. 673–690.

Pierce, Jon L., and Randall B. Dunham, "The 12-Hour Work Day: A 48-Hour, Eight-Day Week," *Academy of Management Journal*, Vol. 35, No. 5, December 1992, pp. 1086–1098.

Piktialis, Diane, and Hal Morgan, "The Aging of the U.S. Workforce and Its Implications for Employers," *Compensation and Benefits Review*, Vol. 35, No. 1, 2003, pp. 57–63.

Pinal County Sheriff's Office, *Police Allocation Staffing Analysis*, Florence, Ariz., March 3, 2008. As of June 24, 2010: http://pinalcountyaz.gov/Departments/Sheriff/AboutPCSO/Documents/FinalStaffingReportwithaddendums.pdf

Pitt, Leyland F., and B. Ramaseshan, "Realistic Job Information and Salesforce Turnover: An Investigative Study," *Journal of Managerial Psychology*, Vol. 10, No. 5, 1995, pp. 29–36.

Planty, Michael, Stephen Provasnik, William J. Hussar, Thomas D. Snyder, and Grace Kena, *The Condition of Education 2008*, Washington, D.C.: Claitors Publishing Division, June 2008. As of June 24, 2010: http://nces.ed.gov/pubsearch/pubsinfo.asp?pubid=2008031

Plecki, Margaret L., Ana M. Elfers, and Michael S. Knapp, *Who's Teaching Washington's Children? What We Know—and What We Need to Know—About Teachers and the Quality of Teaching in the State*, Silverdale, Wash.: Center for Strengthening the Teaching Profession, University of Washington College of Education, August 2003. As of June 24, 2010: http://depts.washington.edu/ctpmail/PDFs/WATeacherReport.pdf

Pomfret, John, "Police Finding It Hard to Fill Jobs," *Washington Post*, March 27, 2006. As of June 24, 2010: http://www.washingtonpost.com/wp-dyn/content/article/2006/03/26/ AR2006032600995.html

Poulson, Edward, captain, Oakland (Calif.) Police Department, presentation, RAND Center for Quality Policing Recruitment and Retention Summit, Arlington, Va., June 2008.

Presman, Dylan, Robert Chapman, and Linda Rosen, *Creative Partnerships: Supporting Youth, Building Communities*, Washington, D.C.: U.S. Department of Justice, Office of Community Oriented Policing Services, September 2002. As of June 24, 2010: http://purl.access.gpo.gov/GPO/LPS24105

Prince, Heath J., *Retention and Advancement in the Retail Industry: A Career Ladder Approach*, Boston, Mass.: Jobs for the Future, August 2003. As of June 24, 2010: http://www.jff.org/publications/workforce/retention-and-advancement-retail-industr/310

Pynes, Joan, and H. John Bernardin, "Entry-Level Police Selection: The Assessment Center Is an Alternative," *Journal of Criminal Justice*, Vol. 20, No. 1, 1992, pp. 41–52.

"Q & A Chief Bernard Melekian: Chief Looks Back as Tenure in City Nears Its End," *Pasadena Star-News*, October 18, 2009.

RAND Corporation, "Welcome to the Police Recruitment and Retention Clearinghouse," last updated June 25, 2010. As of June 25, 2010: http://www.rand.org/ise/centers/quality_policing/cops/

Raymond, Barbara, Laura J. Hickman, Laura L. Miller, and Jennifer S. Wong, *Police Personnel Challenges After September 11: Anticipating Expanded Duties and a Changing Labor Pool*, Santa Monica, Calif.: RAND Corporation, OP-154-RC, 2005. As of June 24, 2010: http://www.rand.org/pubs/occasional_papers/OP154/

Reiser, Martin, "Some Organizational Stresses on Policemen," *Journal of Police Science and Administration*, Vol. 2, No. 2, 1974, pp. 156–159.

Reuland, Melissa M., and John Stedman, *Recruitment and Selection for Community Policing: An Analysis of Organizational Change*, Washington, D.C.: Police Executive Research Forum, 1998.

Rice, Laura, "Navarre Speaks Out on Police Cuts," *Toledo on the Move*, April 23, 2009. As of June 24, 2010: http://www.toledoonthemove.com/news/story.aspx?list=194900&id=291244

Rich, Motoko, "Factory Jobs Return, but Employers Find Skills Shortage," *New York Times*, July 1, 2010. As of July 2, 2010: http://www.nytimes.com/2010/07/02/business/economy/02manufacturing.html

Richman, Amy L., Janet T. Civian, Laurie L. Shannon, E. Jeffrey Hill, and Robert T. Brennan, "The Relationship of Perceived Flexibility, Supportive Work-Life Policies, and Use of Formal Flexible Arrangements and Occasional Flexibility to Employee Engagement and Expected Retention," *Community, Work, and Family*, Vol. 11, No. 2, May 2008, pp. 183–197.

Ridgeway, Greg, Nelson Lim, Brian Gifford, Christopher Koper, Carl Matthies, Sara Hajiamiri, and Alexis Huynh, *Strategies for Improving Officer Recruitment in the San Diego Police Department*, Santa Monica, Calif.: RAND Corporation, MG-724-SDPD, 2008. As of June 24, 2010: http://www.rand.org/pubs/monographs/MG724/

Riggio, Ronald E., Bronston T. Mayes, and Deidra J. Schleicher, "Using Assessment Center Methods for Measuring Undergraduate Student Business Outcomes," *Journal of Management Inquiry*, Vol. 12, No. 1, 2003, pp. 68–78.

Riley, K. Jack, Gregory F. Treverton, Jeremy M. Wilson, and Lois M. Davis, *State and Local Intelligence in the War on Terrorism*, Santa Monica, Calif.: RAND Corporation, MG-394-RC, 2005. As of June 24, 2010: http://www.rand.org/pubs/monographs/MG394/

Riley, K. Jack, Susan Turner, John MacDonald, Greg Ridgeway, Terry L. Schell, Jeremy M. Wilson, Travis L. Dixon, Terry Fain, Dionne Barnes-Proby, and Brent D. Fulton, *Police-Community Relations in Cincinnati*,

Santa Monica, Calif.: RAND Corporation, TR-333-CC, 2005. As of June 24, 2010: http://www.rand.org/pubs/technical_reports/TR333/

Riley, Warren, "New Orleans Experience," presentation, RAND Center for Quality Policing Recruitment and Retention Summit, Arlington, Va., June 2008.

Risher, Howard, "Planning a 'Next Generation' Salary System," *Compensation and Benefits Review*, Vol. 19, No. 2, 2002, pp. 13–22.

Roberg, Roy, and Scott Bonn, "Higher Education and Policing: Where Are We Now?" *Policing: An International Journal of Police Strategies and Management*, Vol. 27, No. 4, 2004, pp. 469–486.

Robinson, Sarah, Trevor Murrells, and Michael Clinton, "Highly Qualified and Highly Ambitious: Implications for Workforce Retention of Realising the Career Expectations of Graduate Nurses in England," *Human Resource Management Journal*, Vol. 16, No. 3, July 2006, pp. 287–312.

Rosenholtz, Susan J., "Career Ladders and Merit Pay: Capricious Fads or Fundamental Reforms?" *Elementary School Journal*, Vol. 86, No. 4, January 1986, pp. 513–529.

Ross, Joyce D., "Determination of the Predictive Validity of the Assessment Center Approach to Selecting Police Managers," *Journal of Criminal Justice*, Vol. 8, No. 2, 1980, pp. 89–96.

Rostker, Bernard D., William M. Hix, and Jeremy M. Wilson, *Recruitment and Retention: Lessons for the New Orleans Police Department*, Santa Monica, Calif.: RAND Corporation, MG-585-RC, 2007. As of June 24, 2010: http://www.rand.org/pubs/monographs/MG585/

Russell, Cristel Antonia, *Advertainment: Fusing Advertising and Entertainment*, Ann Arbor, Mich.: University of Michigan Yaffe Center for Persuasive Communication, 2007. As of June 24, 2010: http://www.bus.umich.edu/FacultyResearch/ResearchCenters/centers/Yaffe/downloads/Advertainment_teaching_materials.pdf

Rust, Roland T., Greg L. Stewart, Heather Miller, and Debbie Pielback, "The Satisfaction and Retention of Frontline Employees: A Customer Satisfaction Measurement Approach," *International Journal of Service Industry Management*, Vol. 7, No. 5, 1996, pp. 62–80.

Ryan, Ann Marie, S. David Kriska, Bradley J. West, and Joshua M. Sacco, "Anticipated Work/Family Conflict and Family Member Views: Role in Police Recruiting," *Policing: An International Journal of Police Strategies and Management*, Vol. 24, No. 2, 2001, pp. 228–239.

Rynes, Sara L., Robert D. Bretz Jr., and Barry A. Gerhart, "The Importance of Recruitment in Job Choice: A Different Way of Looking," *Personnel Psychology*, Vol. 44, No. 3, 1991, pp. 487–521.

Saari, Lise M., and Timothy A. Judge, "Employee Attitudes and Job Satisfaction," *Human Resource Management*, Vol. 43, No. 4, Winter 2004, pp. 395–407.

Sackett, Paul R., and Anne S. Mavor, *Attitudes, Aptitudes, and Aspirations of American Youth: Implications for Military Recruiting*, Washington, D.C.: National Academies Press, 2003.

Sánchez, Angel Martínez, Manuela Pérez Pérez, Pilar de Luis Carnicer, and Maria José Vela Jiménez, "Teleworking and Workplace Flexibility: A Study of Impact on Firm Performance," *Personnel Review*, Vol. 36, No. 1, 2007, pp. 42–64.

Sanders, Beth A., "Maybe There's No Such Thing as a 'Good Cop': Organizational Challenges in Selecting Quality Officers," *Policing: An International Journal of Police Strategies and* Management, Vol. 26, No. 2, 2003, pp. 313–328.

Sartain, Libby, and Mark Schumann, *Brand from the Inside: Eight Essentials to Emotionally Connect Your Employees to Your Business*, San Francisco, Calif.: Jossey-Bass Publishers, 2006.

Scheibe, John, "Applicants Seeking Stability of Police Gigs in Shaky Job Market," *Ventura County Star*, February 14, 2009. As of June 24, 2010: http://www.vcstar.com/news/2009/feb/14/well-at-least-somebodys-still-hiring-applicants/

Schein, Edgar, *Career Anchors: Discovering Your Real Values*, San Diego, Calif.: University Associates, 1990.

Schmidt, Michael S., "A Flood of Applicants to a Shrinking Police Dept.," *New York Times*, November 18, 2009. As of June 24, 2010: http://www.nytimes.com/2009/11/18/nyregion/18recruit.html

Scogin, Forest, Joseph Schumacher, Jennifer Gardner, and William Chaplin, "Predictive Validity of Psychological Testing in Law Enforcement Settings," *Professional Psychology: Research and Practice*, Vol. 26, No. 1, February 1995, pp. 68–71.

Scott, M. Douglas, chief, Arlington County (Va.) Police Department, "Competing in a Highly Competitive Job Market," presentation, RAND Center for Quality Policing Recruitment and Retention Summit, Arlington, Va., June 2008. As of June 24, 2010: http://www.cops.usdoj.gov/pdf/conference/rand/ScottCompetinginaHighlyCompetitiveJobMarket.pdf

Scrivner, Ellen M., *Innovations in Police Recruitment and Hiring: Hiring in the Spirit of Service*, Washington, D.C.: U.S. Department of Justice, Office of Community Oriented Policing Services, January 26, 2006. As of June 24, 2010: http://www.cops.usdoj.gov/ric/ResourceDetail.aspx?RID=113

———, "Recruitment and Hiring: Challenge or Opportunity for Change?" presentation, RAND Center for Quality Policing Recruitment and Retention Summit, Arlington, Va., June 2008. As of September 2, 2009: http://www.cops. usdoj.gov/pdf/conference/rand/ScrivnerRecruitmentpresentation.pdf

Searle, Rosalind H., "New Technology: The Potential Impact of Surveillance Techniques in Recruitment Practices," *Personnel Review*, Vol. 35, No. 3, 2006, pp. 336–351.

Seibert, Scott, "The Effectiveness of Facilitated Mentoring: A Longitudinal Quasi-Experiment," *Journal of Vocational Behavior*, Vol. 54, No. 3, June 1999, pp. 483–502.

Shane, Jon M., *What Every Chief Executive Should Know: Using Data to Measure Police Performance*, Flushing, N.Y.: Looseleaf Law Publications, 2007.

Shilling, Dana, *Retention Strategies for Key Employees in B-to-B Companies*, New York: American Business Media, 2004. As of June 24, 2010: http://www.americanbusinessmedia.com/images/abm/pdfs/resources/Retention_Strategies.pdf

Sidener, Carrie J., "Lynchburg Police Department Sees Surge in Applications," *Lynchburg News and Advance*, May 6, 2009. As of June 24, 2010: http://www2.newsadvance.com/lna/news/local/article/lynchburg_police_department_sees_surge_in_applications/15759/

Sigler, Kevin J., "Challenges of Employee Retention," *Management Research News*, Vol. 22, No. 10, 1999, pp. 1–6.

Skolnick, Jerome H., and David H. Bayley, "Theme and Variation in Community Policing," *Crime and Justice*, Vol. 10, 1988, pp. 1–37.

Slater, Harold R., and Martin Reiser, "Comparative Study of Factors Influencing Police Recruitment," *Journal of Police Science and Administration*, Vol. 16, No. 3, September 1988, pp. 168–176.

Smelson, I. Harold, "Psychiatric Screening of Police Candidates," *Journal of the Medical Society of New Jersey*, Vol. 72, No. 3, March 1975, pp. 213–216.

Smith, Thomas M., and Richard M. Ingersoll, "What Are the Effects of Induction and Mentoring on Beginning Teacher Turnover?" *American Educational Research Journal*, Vol. 41, No. 3, September 2004, pp. 681–714.

Sochalski, Julie, "Nursing Shortage Redux: Turning the Corner on an Enduring Problem," *Health Affairs*, Vol. 21, No. 5, 2002, pp. 157–164.

Sparger, Jerry R. and David J. Giacopassi, "Copping Out: Why Police Leave the Force," in Richard R. Bennett, ed., *Police at Work: Policy Issues and Analysis*, Thousand Oaks, Calif.: Sage Publications, 1983, pp. 107–124.

Sparks, Kate, Cary Cooper, Yitzhak Fried, and Arie Shirom, "The Effects of Hours of Work on Health: A Meta-Analytic Review," *Journal of Occupational and Organizational Psychology*, Vol. 70, No. 4, December 1997, pp. 391–408.

Spielman, Fran, "Early Retirement for Cops Helps Budget, Not Force," *Chicago Sun-Times*, July 23, 2009. As of June 24, 2010: http://www.suntimes.com/news/cityhall/1681991,chicago-cops-shortage-retirement-072309.article

Spolar, Matthew, "Camden Acts to Change Police Residency Rule," *Philadelphia Inquirer*, September 9, 2009.

Spuck, Dennis W., "Reward Structures in the Public High School," *Educational Administration Quarterly*, Vol. 10, No. 1, January 1974, pp. 18–34.

Staiger, Douglas O., David I. Auerbach, and Peter I. Buerhaus, "Expanding Career Opportunities for Women and the Declining Interest in Nursing as a Career," *Nursing Economics*, Vol. 18, No. 5, September–October 2000, pp. 230–236.

Stairs, Martin, Martin Galpin, Nicky Page, and Alex Linley, "Retention on a Knife Edge: The Role of Employee Engagement in Talent Management," *Selection and Development Review*, Vol. 22, No. 95, 2006, pp. 19–23.

Stanley, Mary J., "How 'Ya Gonna Keep' Em Down on the Farm: The Problem of Retention," *Indiana Libraries*, Vol. 27, No. 1, 2008, pp. 84–89.

Strawbridge, Peter, and Deirdre Strawbridge, *A Networking Guide to Recruitment, Selection and Probationary Training of Police Officers in Major Departments of the United States of America*, New York: John Jay College of Criminal Justice, 1990.

Sturm, Roland, Jeanne S. Ringel, Darius N. Lakdawalla, Jay Bhattacharya, Dana P. Goldman, Michael Hurd, Geoffrey F. Joyce, Constantijn Panis, and Tatiana Andreyeva, *Obesity and Disability: The Shape of Things to Come*, Santa Monica, Calif.: RAND Corporation, RB-9043-1, 2007. As of June 24, 2010: http://www.rand.org/pubs/research_briefs/RB9043-1/

Sullivan, John, "A Case Study of Google Recruiting," *Dr. John Sullivan's Talent Management Thought Leadership Community*, December 2005. As of June 24, 2010: http://www.drjohnsullivan.com/articles-mainmenu-27/hr-strategy-mainmenu-33/81-a-case-study-of-google-recruiting

Swanberg, Jennifer, "Job-Family Role Strain Among Low-Wage Workers," *Journal of Family and Economic Issues*, Vol 26, No. 1, March 2005, pp. 143–158.

Sward, Susan, "Newsom Likes Police Study, but Cash Is Tight," *San Francisco Chronicle*, November 3, 2008. As of June 24, 2010: http://articles.sfgate.com/2008-11-03/news/17129378_1_newsom-s-comments-new-officers-report-s-proposals

Switzer, Merlin E., *Recruitment and Retention: Best Practices Update*, Sacramento, Calif.: Commission on Peace Officer Standards and Training, April 2006.

Syrett, Michel, and Jean Lammiman, "Advertising and Millennials: Young Consumers," *Insight and Ideas for Responsible Marketers*, Vol. 5, No. 4, 2004, pp. 62–73.

Tadwalkar, Sunil, and Manjira Sen, "Manpower Retention in IT: An Oxymoron?" *Ubiquity*, Vol. 6, No. 14, April 26–May 3, 2005, pp. 2–13.

Taylor, Bruce, Bruce Kubu, Lorie Fridell, Carter Rees, Tom Jordan, and Jason Cheney, *Cop Crunch: Identifying Strategies for Dealing with the Recruiting and Hiring Crisis in Law Enforcement*, Washington, D.C.: Police Executive Research Forum, April 2006. As of June 24, 2010: http://www.ncjrs.gov/pdffiles1/nij/grants/213800.pdf

Tett, Robert P., and John P. Meyer, "Job Satisfaction, Organizational Commitment, Turnover Intention, and Turnover: Path Analyses Based on Meta-Analytic Findings," *Personnel Psychology*, Vol. 46, No. 2, December 2006, pp. 259–293.

Thibaut, John W., and Laurens Walker, *Procedural Justice: A Psychological Analysis*, Hillsdale, N.J.: L. Erlbaum Associates, 1975.

Tigchelaar, Anke, Niels Brouwer, and Jan D. Vermunt, "Tailor-Made: Towards a Pedagogy for Educating Second-Career Teachers," *Educational Research Review*, Vol. 5, No. 2, 2010, pp. 164–183.

Towers Perrin, *Working Today: Understanding What Drives Employee Engagement*, Stamford, Conn.: Towers Perrin, 2003. As of June 24, 2010: http://www.towersperrin.com/tp/getwebcachedoc?webc=hrs/usa/2003/200309/talent_2003.pdf

Truxillo, Donald M., Dirk D. Steiner, and Stephen W. Gilliland, "The Importance of Organizational Justice in Personnel Selection: Defining When Selection Fairness Really Matters," *International Journal of Selection and Assessment*, Vol. 12, No. 1–2, March 2004, pp. 39–53.

Tsang, Eric W. K., and Shaker A. Zahra, "Organizational Unlearning," *Human Relations*, Vol. 61, No. 10, 2008, pp. 1435–1462.

Tulgan, Bruce, *Managing Generation X: How to Bring Out the Best in Young Talent*, Oxford: Capstone, 2000.

Tuomey, Lianne M., and Rachel Jolly, "Step Up to Law Enforcement: A Successful Strategy for Recruiting Women into the Law Enforcement Profession," *Police Chief*, Vol. 76, No. 6, June 2009, pp. 68–73.

Twenge, Jean M., and Stacy M. Campbell, "Generational Differences in Psychological Traits and Their Impact on the Workplace," *Journal of Managerial Psychology*, Vol. 23, No. 8, 2008, pp. 862–877.

U.S. Census Bureau, "U.S. Interim Projections by Age, Sex, Race, and Hispanic Origin: 2000–2050," undated website. As of June 24, 2010: http://www.census.gov/population/www/projections/usinterimproj/

U.S. Department of Defense, Office of the Under Secretary of Defense for Personnel and Readiness, *Population Representation in the Military Services: Trends in Propensity*, Washington, D.C., March 2003.

U.S. Department of Education, Institute of Education Sciences, National Center for Education Statistics, *Digest of Education Statistics, 2005*, Washington, D.C., July 2006. As of June 24, 2010: http://nces.ed.gov/pubsearch/pubsinfo.asp?pubid=2006030

U.S. Department of Justice, Office of Justice Programs, National Institute of Justice, *Policing in Arab-American Communities After September 11*, Washington, D.C., July 2008. As of June 24, 2010: http://purl.access.gpo.gov/GPO/LPS103999

U.S. Department of Justice, Office of Community Oriented Policing Services, "2008 RAND Summit: Summit Proceedings," undated Web page (a). As of June 25, 2010: http://www.cops.usdoj.gov/Default.asp?Item=2101

———, "About," undated Web page (b). As of June 24, 2010: http://www.cops.usdoj.gov/Default.asp?Item=35

———, "COPS Hiring Recovery Program Update," *Community Policing Dispatch*, Vol. 2, No. 6, June 2009a. As of June 24, 2010: http://www.cops.usdoj.gov/html/dispatch/June_2009/hiring_recovery.htm

———, *Law Enforcement Recruitment Toolkit*, Washington, D.C., October 16, 2009b. As of June 24, 2010: http://www.cops.usdoj.gov/ric/ResourceDetail.aspx?RID=542

U.S. Department of Justice, Office of Justice Programs, Office of the Police Corps and Law Enforcement Education, *The Police Corps Annual Report to the President, the Attorney General, and the Congress*, Washington, D.C., 2003.

U.S. Department of State, *Trafficking in Persons Report 2009*, Washington, D.C., June 16, 2009. As of June 24, 2010: http://www.state.gov/g/tip/rls/tiprpt/2009/index.htm

Van Hoye, Greet, and Filip Lievens, "Investigating Web-Based Recruitment Sources: Employee Testimonials vs. Word-of-Mouse," *International Journal of Selection and Assessment*, Vol. 15, No. 4, December 2007, pp. 372–382.

Verhoeven, Helen, Neelofer Mashood, and Bal Chansarkar, "Recruitment and Generation Y: Web 2.0 the Way to Go?" paper presented at the Annual American Business Research Conference, New York, N.Y., April 2009. As of June 24, 2010: http://www.wbiconpro.com/8.Neelofar.pdf

Viney, Claire, Steve Adamson, and Noeleen Doherty, "Paradoxes of Fast-Track Career Management," *Personnel Review*, Vol. 26, No. 3, April 1997, pp. 174–186.

Violanti, John M., and Fred Aron, "Police Stressors: Variations in Perception Among Police Personnel," *Journal of Criminal Justice*, Vol. 23, No. 3, 1995, pp. 287–294.

Walker, Alan G., and James W. Smither, "A Five-Year Study of Upward Feedback: What Managers Do with Their Results Matters," *Personnel Psychology*, Vol. 52, No. 2, Summer 1999, pp. 393–423.

Walker, Samuel, ed., *Records of the Wickersham Commission on Law Observance and Enforcement*, Bethesda, Md.: University Publications of America, 1997.

———, *Police Accountability: Current Issues and Research Needs*, Washington, D.C.: U.S. Department of Justice, NCJ 218583, November 2006.

Webster, Barbara, and Edward F. Connors, *Police Chiefs and Sheriffs Rank Their Criminal Justice Needs*, Washington, D.C.: U.S. Department of Justice, National Institute of Justice, NCJ 113061, August 1988.

Wheeler, Christopher H., "Local Market Scale and the Pattern of Job Changes Among Young Men," *Regional Science and Urban Economics*, Vol. 38, No. 2, March 2008, pp. 101–118.

Whetstone, Thomas S., John C. Reed Jr., and Phillip C. Turner, "Recruiting: A Comparative Study of the Recruiting Practices of State Police Agencies," *International Journal of Police Science and Management*, Vol. 8, No. 1, Spring 2006, pp. 52–66.

White, Michael D., "Identifying Good Cops Early: Predicting Recruit Performance in the Academy," *Police Quarterly*, Vol. 11, No. 1, March 2008, pp. 27–49.

White, Michael D., and Gipsy Escobar, "Making Good Cops in the Twenty-First Century: Emerging Issues for the Effective Recruitment, Selection and Training of Police in the United States and Abroad," *Crime and Criminal Justice*, Vol. 22, No. 1–2, March 2008, pp. 119–134.

Wiegler, Laurie, "Big Brother in the Big Apple," *Engineering and Technology*, Vol. 3, No. 9, 2008, pp. 24–27.

Williams, Charles R., and Linda Parrack Livingstone, "Another Look at the Relationship Between Performance and Voluntary Turnover," *Academy of Management Journal*, Vol. 37, No. 2, April 1994, pp. 269–298.

Wilson, Jeremy M., *Community Policing in America*, New York: Routledge, 2006.

Wilson, Jeremy M., and Amy G. Cox, *Community Policing and Crime: The Process and Impact of Problem-Solving in Oakland*, Santa Monica, Calif.: RAND Corporation, TR-635-BPA, 2008. As of June 24, 2010: http://www.rand.org/pubs/technical_reports/TR635/

Wilson, Jeremy M., Amy G. Cox, Tommy L. Smith, Hans Bos, and Terry Fain, *Community Policing and Violence Prevention in Oakland: Measure Y in Action*, Santa Monica, Calif.: RAND Corporation, TR-546-BPA, 2007. As of June 24, 2010: http://www.rand.org/pubs/technical_reports/TR546/

Wilson, Jeremy M., and Clifford A. Grammich, *Police Recruitment and Retention in the Contemporary Urban Environment: A National Discussion of Personnel Experiences and Promising Practices from the Front Lines*, Santa Monica, Calif.: RAND Corporation, CF-261-DOJ, 2009a. As of June 24, 2010: http://www.rand.org/pubs/conf_proceedings/CF261/

———, "Reconstructing Internal Security in Post-Conflict Societies: The Challenge and Successfulness of Developing Democratic Police and Justice Institutions," *Security Journal*, June 22, 2009b.

Wilson, Jeremy M., Bernard D. Rostker, and Mike Hix, "Police Recruitment and Retention in New Orleans: Crisis as Catalyst," presentation, RAND Center for Quality Policing Recruitment and Retention Summit, Arlington, Va., June 2008. As of June 24, 2010: http://www.cops.usdoj.gov/pdf/conference/rand/WilsonPoliceRecruitmentNO.pdf

Wilson, Michael J., James B. Greenlee, Tracey Hagerty, Cynthia v. Helba, D. Wayne Hintze, and Jerome D. Lehnus, *Youth Attitude Tracking Study: 1999 Propensity and Advertising Report*, Arlington, Va.: Defense Manpower Data Center, June 14, 2000. As of June 24, 2010: http://handle.dtic.mil/100.2/ADA385236

Winston, Ali, "The Eyes Have It: NYPD Plans More Cameras," *City Limits*, June 1, 2009. As of June 24, 2010: http://www.citylimits.org/news/articles/3751/the-eyes-have-it

Wolf, Andrea, and Sarah Rohrs, "Fire and Police Retirement Papers Flooding In," *Vallejo (Calif.) Times Herald*, February 15, 2008.

Womack, Amy Leigh, "Plan Might Cause Police, Fire Exodus," *Macon Sun News*, June 6, 2009. As of June 24, 2010: http://www.macon.com/2009/06/06/739315/plan-might-cause-police-fire-exodus.html

Woska, William J., "Police Officer Recruitment: A Public-Sector Crisis," *Police Chief*, Vol. 73, No. 10, October 2006, pp. 52–59.

Wright, Jerome, "Adding to Police Ranks Rankles," *Memphis Commercial Appeal*, February 1, 2009. As of June 24, 2010: http://www.commercialappeal.com/news/2009/feb/01/adding-to-ranks-rankles/

Yearwood, Douglas L., *Recruitment and Retention Study Series: Sworn Sheriffs' Personnel*, Raleigh, N.C.: North Carolina Sheriffs' Education and Training Standards Commission, April 2003. As of June 24, 2010: http://www.ncgccd.org/PDFs/Pubs/NCCJAC/rrsheriff.pdf

Yearwood, Douglas L., and Stephanie Freeman, "Analyzing Concerns Among Police Admnistrators: Recruitment and Retention of Police Officers in North Carolina," *Police Chief*, Vol. 71, No. 3, March 2004, pp. 43–49.

Zhao, Jihong, Nicholas P. Lovrich, and Quint Thurman, "The Status of Community Policing in American Cities: Facilitators and Impediments Revised," *Policing: An International Journal of Police Strategies and Management*, Vol. 22, No. 1, 1999, pp. 74–92.

ETHICS

Organizational Ethics

ARTHUR D. WEICHMANN

TOPICS

- Values
- Ethics
- Ethical Relativism
- Integrity
- Principle Versus Preference
- Ethical Problems in Law Enforcement

INTRODUCTION

Police organizations and their employees are held to a higher ethical standard than private organizations and their employees. But most police departments have not undertaken active programs to promote an ethical work environment. Management expects their employees to behave in an ethical manner, but they do not take steps to develop this.

By their very nature and structure, many large bureaucracies tend to promote unethical and dishonest behavior ... because many workers find themselves feeling they must compromise their ethical standards to <u>fit in</u>, or to be <u>successful</u>.

> <u>Fitting in:</u> In a police subculture, some officers are verbally abusive to suspects, so a new officer does the same.

> <u>Successful:</u> In a police department, if there is pressure by a supervisor to make drug arrests, an officer may invent probable cause to make vehicle stops which can lead to these arrests.

There are many dynamics involved at work; wanting to fit in, but also wanting to do the right thing. So ... ethics can be very personal, but in this chapter, we will also look at ethics from an organizational level. There can be conflicts between personal and organizational ethics ... they must be congruent.

> For instance ... if an officer has to be unethical to get ahead in the department, the ethics of the officer and the ethics of the department are not congruent.

> **Example:** Everyone is getting along fairly well in an organization. Then comes an announcement that there is going to be a testing process for promotion. Suddenly, a false rumor surfaces about a candidate who is a frontrunner for promotion. Rather than the organization ignoring or quashing the rumor, they perpetuate the process by conducting an investigation on the candidate. The candidate, to save himself, creates rumors about the other candidates, to take the heat off of him and spread it around a little.

TERMS AND CONCEPTS

There are many terms and concepts associated with organizational ethics. Understanding them will provide a good introduction into the subject.

VALUES

<u>Values are the things that are important to the individual ... the things that motivate them.</u> Values are a person's **enduring preferences**, and they are the beliefs that guide

the person's behavior. Values are such things as relationships, money, success, honesty, appearance, and health, just to name a few.

Values vary between social classes. Criminal Justice personnel generally have middle class values, which are conservative. <u>Conflicts can develop when these values are pushed onto others who have different values</u>. Research has even shown that there is a link between hostile, even prejudice activity and conflicts in value systems.

> **Example:** A police officer may be so disgusted by a homeless person's lifestyle, or by someone on welfare that it may lead to an insensitive or hostile confrontation.

So … personnel must make a conscious effort to maintain a neutral stance on imposing their values onto others, which could lead to a negative encounter. The goal of this effort is providing unbiased and fair treatment of all people.

Values are developed during a person's formative years, but they can change as time goes by. People choose their values and prioritize them.

> **Example:** A teenager smokes pot, hangs out with his friends, and takes advantage of his parents. But as he gets older, his values change; he gets a job, cleans up his habits, and helps out his family.

> **Example:** A young man enjoys the company of different women. He always has something going, and gains a reputation as a player. As he gets older, he no longer values the next conquest, but rather, wants to settle down with one woman and have a family.

<u>Many work-related problems are the result of value conflicts. Managers must be aware of their values and the values of others</u>. He must realize that they may not be the same, and take steps to prevent conflict.

> **Example:** A supervisor does not get promoted into that position by accident … it is because he values success and achievement, and has worked hard to get that position. This supervisor has an employee who has no aspirations of supervision or management, he is one of those people who just want to do the job they were hired for and go home at the end of the day. (And there is nothing wrong with that … there are not enough positions at the top of the hierarchy for everyone anyway. Organizations need people like this).

But this supervisor, who values success and achievement highly, views this employee as being lazy and lacking motivation, rather than two people with different values. If this supervisor fails to recognize the distinction, the relationship between him and this employee will suffer, and undoubtedly lead to poor performance by the employee who is now encountering a hostile work environment.

Example: As will be discussed in chapter nine, the emerging workforce culture values recreation time, which makes alternative scheduling so desirable to them. The older workers, many of them supervisors to the younger ones, did not have it as well in their day; they worked five days a week, and were not allowed to use vacation time except once a year.

These new employees are constantly asking for vacation time off, even when they have three or four days off every week. An old school supervisor, who is not aware of changing values from generation to generation, may take a very negative approach to these requests, resulting in hostility between supervision and employees.

So … it is very important for managers and supervisors to recognize that these differences can lead to conflict in the organization. If there is a conflict, it will likely result in a negative outcome for the organization … (In the above example, if the employee is not allowed to take a vacation day because the supervisor does not think he needs it, the employee will just call in sick).

ETHICS

Ethics are the rules which ought to govern human behavior. There are not a lot of them … honesty, truth, the golden rule, hard work, equality, justice. These are the things that we know are right. Ethics involves a process of clarifying what is right and wrong, and acting on what is right.

The real concern about ethics is not in what one does value, but what one should value. Our ethics do not change. We have a choice about following them, which is a choice about who we are.

Remember … <u>it is our values that guide us, not our ethics</u>. Ethics are the "rules" that we are supposed to follow, but that does not mean that we follow them.

> **Example:** A thief knows that it is wrong to steal (ethic), but he has a stronger personal value which creates this choice to be a thief (easy money).

So … knowing the right course of action does not necessarily mean that an individual will follow it. But true leadership instills a desire in others to be ethical. He does this through leading by example.

An ethical person has values that are congruent with ethical standards … they know what the right thing is, and they do it.

Police organizations are very concerned that the employees they hire have high ethical standards. One way that they do this is by conducting a background investigation on candidates. The purpose of this investigation is to determine if the candidate has led an ethical life. This is done by examining their **pattern of behavior**.

> **Example:** If a candidate was arrested for shoplifting when they were 14, and there were no other similar incidents, this would not be a pattern of behavior that the investigator would be concerned about.

> However, if the candidate was also terminated from a job when they were 16 for stealing the petty cash, and a neighbor told the investigator that at age 18 the candidate went joyriding in his car, this would be a pattern of unethical conduct that would be of concern.

Another step that police departments take to determine the ethical standards of potential employees occurs during the oral interview process. Generally, a scenario type question is posed to the candidate, geared toward determining what the candidate values as higher … honesty or loyalty (maintaining membership in the informal group versus telling the truth).

The question will be along the lines of a fellow employee (with seniority and in good standing with the organization), doing something obviously wrong or illegal. The candidate is asked to explain what he will do about it.

Many times, the value of loyalty is so strong that the candidate actually does not know the right answer to the question. He values loyalty so high that he assumes the organization does too. Often, the candidate with this conflict will dance around the issue, and usually stop short of actually reporting it to a supervisor. Unfortunately for this candidate, he has shown the interview panel that to him, there is a gray area when in comes to honesty.

ETHICAL RELATIVISM (ETHICS ARE NOT ALWAYS ABSOLUTE)

This is the belief that some actions are moral in some circumstances and immoral in others ... they are relative to the situation. According to this approach to ethics, there is no absolute right or wrong and no universal rules of conduct.

An example of ethical relativism is **Utilitarianism**. According to this concept, an action is right, compared to other actions, if the result is the greater good for the greatest number of people.

> **Example:** Here is a scenario commonly used to stimulate discussion in ethics workshops ... Five people are on a life raft, and there is only enough food and water for four. If the group kills one person, the rest will live, otherwise, everyone will die. The question is: Would it be ethical to kill someone in this situation?
>
> You can take this even further. What if it is a family of five? Most people would rather face death than live the rest of their lives knowing they had killed a family member so that they could live. But what if none of the people on the boat knew each other? What if one of them was as escaped child molester, who was already injured, and would probably die in a few days anyway?

Many public sector decisions are based on this approach, such as fund allocations. Other decisions that can have a negative effect on some people are also based on utilitarianism, such as a decision to put a freeway through a neighborhood, causing many families to be displaced.

Another area of management, the disciplinary process, is based on the concept of utilitarianism. When a supervisor or manager is considering discipline for an employee, a guideline that is followed is, "The good of the organization must supersede the good of the individual." What this means, is that although the discipline hurts the employee, maintaining discipline benefits the organization.

<u>INTEGRITY</u> (AN ETHICAL PERSON HAS INTEGRITY)

A person with integrity consistently follows an ethical standard which does not compromise values ... because his values are ethical ones. If someone does the right thing only because they are afraid of being caught, that is not integrity.

PRINCIPLE VERSUS PREFERENCE

Organizations lose effectiveness when preference is chosen over principle when making decisions. Preference is the imposition of personal values over doing what is right. Often, this occurs because it is easier, safer, or because of personal benefit or satisfaction.

This conflict between principle (doing the right thing), and preference (doing what you want to do) happens a lot when employees have to follow orders. Line level employees have often been faced with dilemmas involving individual morality versus obedience and loyalty. It is common for employees to succumb to this pressure because it is easier to just follow orders than to be personally accountable for actions.

> **Example:** During the Vietnam War, the My Lai incident involved soldiers killing innocent civilians because they were ordered to. During World War II, Nazi soldiers facing war crime charges said they were just following orders. In both instances, soldiers had to commit crimes disguised as orders, or face a potential firing squad for insubordination during wartime.

So ... we can either excuse the individual from personal moral decisions when they are following orders ... or ... we can <u>condemn</u> the behavior in support of **disobedience** of laws or orders that conflict with ethical principles.

These are difficult positions for employees. There are questions that are difficult to answer, such as ... Where does personal accountability begin? ... and ... Is this accountability absolute, or is someone absolved if they are following orders?

> **Example:** A police sergeant is dealing with a belligerent subject outside of a bar. The sergeant orders an officer to arrest the subject for being intoxicated, when he is not.

If the officer makes the arrest, he is committing an act completely contrary to the standards he has sworn to uphold. If he refuses, the sergeant will make his work life miserable … because if this sergeant is unethical enough to order an unlawful arrest, he is likely unethical enough to retaliate against this officer for his lack of loyalty.

These are the most difficult choices people must make in their careers, choosing personal values that conflict with colleagues or supervisors, which could lead to complete alienation from the work subculture. To add to this difficulty, organizations do not create an atmosphere that helps people to make the right choice.

ETHICAL PROBLEMS IN LAW ENFORCEMENT

No other occupation possesses greater control over personal destiny than law enforcement officers, because of the elements of **authority**, use of **physical force**, and **discretion** inherent in the job. Unethical behavior in the field of law enforcement is usually an abuse of one of those three elements.

Authority: This refers to the authority that police officers have to detain and arrest people. Officers have the ability to control others due to their position. Even when officers obtain consent from people to talk to them (consensual encounters), most people are too intimidated by the uniform to refuse. An abuse of authority amounts to a violation of individual rights.

Physical force: This refers to the use of physical control granted by law to affect arrests, prevent escape, and overcome resistance. Abuse of physical force takes the form of excessive use of force. This occurs when an officer uses more force than is reasonable for the level of resistance that he is encountering.

Discretionary power: This refers to the ability to choose between two or more courses of action, with none of the alternatives potentially being wrong. This is the power that officers have when they decide when and how to enforce laws, how to handle disputes, and how much and what kind of force to use.

Discretion is different than standard decision making, since decision making generally is making a choice between almost right and probably wrong, whereas discretion is choosing between a right course of action and another right course of action. Abuse of discretion occurs when an officer bases his behavior or actions on personal feelings or prejudice rather than doing what is right.

There is a potential for abuse in such a volatile and dynamic occupation which requires critical and immediate decision making. Officers must remain calm in hostile and dangerous situations without succumbing to the temptation to abuse these elements of authority, force and discretion. Because of this, the selection process for police officers is exhaustive since it is so important to hire people that will not abuse their position.

During the testing process, the oral interview will generally contain an "ethical dilemma" question, which will give the interview panel clues as to whether this candidate will uphold the ethics of the organization, or whether he will weaken under pressure or frustration.

CONCLUSION

None of us are perfect. Sometimes we will choose what we know is not right, because of immediate rewards, convenience or lack of courage. That just makes us human.

But ... when we choose that course of action consistently, where it becomes a "pattern of behavior," we choose to be unethical.

How Police Officers Learn Ethics

STEVEN J. ELLWANGER

O ne of the most defining characteristics of the police occupation is the potential use of coercive force to impose the will of the state, especially deadly force (Bittner, 1970). Another defining yet less well understood characteristic is ethics. Just as medicine, law, engineering, or other professions are characterized by ethics that guide individual and group behavior, policing as an occupation contains its own values and value systems that provide a basis by which individual behaviors and attitudes can be measured. In contrast to other professions, however, learning ethics in policing is not entirely the product of education, socialization, and training. In fact, learning often predates formal education and socialization efforts as a result of individual, social, and historical factors. What is more, the process of on-the job police socialization and culturalization may both purposefully and inadvertently threaten the positive ethical ideals and values brought to the police profession by new recruits where a strong and pervasive deviant subculture may passively or actively teach unethical behaviors.

Ethics in policing bears directly on issues of reform, control, and legitimacy of law enforcement institutions in a democratic society that is presenting new challenges as a result of emerging police paradigms and changing social sentiments. The first step in meeting these challenges is to better understand the sources and content of police ethics so that administrators, citizens, legislatures, and the courts can more effectively control police behavior. This chapter attempts to do just this by first identifying and discussing the various frameworks for understanding the sources of police ethics, followed by the identification of several occupational ethics that run the risk of violating legal, organizational, and societal standards. The chapter then concludes with a brief discussion of the various aspects of ethical transformations and implications that police ethics hold for reform, control, and legitimacy in contemporary society.

VALUES, VALUE SYSTEMS, AND POLICE ETHICS

Policing as an occupation is argued to be characterized by a distinct subculture (Crank, 2004; Van Maanen, 1974). The term *culture* is often used to describe differences among beliefs, laws, morals, customs, and other characteristics that set large groups apart. Sometimes there can be cultural differences among people, however, who form a single culture or group. In such an instance, this unique group within the larger social group is referred to as a *subculture*. The primary distinction between cultures and subcultures is that while sharing many of the values and beliefs of the larger culture, the subculture shares values and beliefs that set them apart from the larger culture in which they exist (Kappeler, Sluder & Alpert, 2005).

When considering individual behavior within the subculture of policing, it is often useful to consider the values embraced and transmitted among its members. In fact, Milton Rokeach (1973) argued that individual or group norms and behaviors can often be attributed to particular patterns of adherence to universal value orientations. A *value* as defined by Rokeach is "an enduring belief that a specific mode of conduct or end-state of existence is personally or socially preferable" (Rokeach, 1973:5). Thus, values can be distinguished by the extent to which to they prescribe a specific mode of conduct, or the extent to which they prescribe a socially preferable end-state. A value that identifies a socially preferable end-state is a *terminal value*, while a value that represents the preferred means to achieve that state is an *instrumental value* (Rokeach, 1973; Zhao, He & Lovrich, 1998).

Values, Rokeach continued, could be arranged into a *value system*. Rokeach defined a value system as "an enduring organization of beliefs concerning preferable modes of conduct or end-states of existence along a continuum of relative importance" (Rokeach, 1973:5). What is more, Rokeach contended that the total number of values of primary interest to people was relatively limited. It is these value systems that identify preferable end-states and modes of conduct that provide a basis for human decision-making by providing a socially approved standard by which one can compare his or her actions and decisions.

VALUE-PREDISPOSITION PERSPECTIVE

There are two competing views that seek to explain the source of police ethics: learned and imported. Most students of policing are quick to point to the forging of the "police personality" resulting from the influence of Basic Training Instructors, Field Training Officers, and the impersonal bureaucratic organization that shapes the new recruit during his or her first few years. A competing—yet related—view argues for the existence of an *occupational predisposition*. Persons possessing certain traits and personality characteristics are attracted or "predisposed" to the profession of policing. In other words, policing is just one of many occupations from which individuals choose. Those with a police occupational predisposition are attracted to careers in law enforcement, while those with other personality traits and characteristics will choose alternative occupations (Alpert & Dunham, 1997; Rokeach, Miller & Snyder, 1971).

Chief among these traits and characteristics is a value-predisposition. This *value-predisposition perspective* argues that individuals bring with them an identifiable set of broader societal values into the organization. Personnel selection techniques may actively screen for these values, while the processes of professionalization and culturalization reinforce some and modify and/or replace others during the officer's career. These values ultimately find expression in officer behaviors and attitudes, or ethics. In fact, Pollock (1998) makes a distinction between morals and ethics that is useful in distinguishing between the sources that guide behaviors in both one's personal and professional lives. She notes that in contrast to morals, which are the sum of a person's actions in every sphere of life, ethics are behaviors that are related to an individual's profession. Police ethics are then behaviors and attitudes of police officers that find expression while acting "under the color of law." If one adopts this value-predisposition model and subscribes to this definition of ethics, several value-predispositions and their sources come to mind.

CONSERVATISM AND CONFORMITY

One of the primary goals of police personnel systems is to identify and retain individuals who are conservative—when compared to society as a whole—and conformist. In fact, Wilson (1968) first observed that Chicago police officers tended to be unreceptive to change, while Bayley and Mendelsohn (1969) noted that the Denver police tended to be more conservative and more Republican than the community as a whole, and that age is not related to political orientation. This latter finding suggests that it is the initial selection of officers rather than their socialization that explains this tendency toward conservatism.

The literature seems to suggest that police work tends to attract local and family-oriented individuals who tend to be from the working class (Niederhoffer, 1967). Individuals who are attracted to police work are also inclined to espouse "old-fashioned" values. They tend to see the world in black and white while overlooking the fact that the outcomes of many decisions often involve value tradeoffs. Furthermore, these individuals generally possess military experience and come from families with a history in law enforcement (Caldero & Crank, 2004). Finally, such persons generally perceive police work to be socially significant. They view police work as having a point, weight, interest, and impact on the lives and well-being of other people (Van Maanen, 1974).

This tendency toward political and practical conservatism is reinforced and perpetuated by police personnel selection systems that place a premium on conformity to middle-class values. In fact, police selection practices such as the use of physical agility tests, background investigations, polygraph examinations, psychological tests, and oral interviews are all tools used to screen out applicants who have not demonstrated conformity to middle-class values (Gaines & Kappeler, 2005). Many of these selection techniques may have little to do with actual police work, and more to do with assessing an applicant's "adequacy" to be a moral agent of the state. In fact, Kappeler, Sluder, and Alpert (2005) note that these techniques are designed more to determine an applicant's physical prowess, sexual orientation, gender identification, financial stability, employment history, and abstinence from alcohol or other drug use, rather than to determine their ability to perform the real functions and duties associated with police work (p. 285).

NOBLE CAUSE, EFFICIENCY, AND UTILITARIANISM

In addition to this relative conservatism and conformity among those with an occupational predisposition toward policing, there is also a commitment to the *noble cause*. The noble cause is a moral commitment by police officers to make the world a safer place in which to live (Caldero & Crank, 2004). According to Caldero and Crank (2004), it is this moral predisposition that attracts people to the occupation of policing, while those who join but are not committed to the "noble cause" are quickly liberated from the organization (Conti & Nolan, 2005). The source of this value-predisposition can be traced to enduring societal values.

A long-standing but now debunked myth is that police neutrally and evenhandedly implement the law (Bayley & Bittner, 1984; Bittner, 1970; Lipsky, 1980). The reality is that police exercise an enormous amount of discretion, and values shape behavior in the absence of objective standards by which behavior can measured. An enduring social value that is imported into the occupation is one that has historically evaluated individual and group police performance based on the crime control mandate (Manning, 1997). Society expects police to "control" crime. Unfortunately, the emphasis on the "ends" of catching criminals may often come at a cost to the institution's "duty" to protect the sanctity of the law (Pollock, 2005). In other words, police behaviors were often considered to be ethical if they achieved the desired end of getting the bad guy off the streets—even if this meant compromising individual civil liberties in the process.

The "ends justify the means" value system is reinforced by other imported American values as well. Specifically, police, like American citizens in general, tend to favor the underdog (or the victim, in this instance), emphasize that no one stands above the law (Caldero & Crank, 2004), and often emphasize efficiency (for its perceived neutrality) at the cost of other values, such as effectiveness, equity, and responsiveness (Ford & Morash, 2002; Giacomazzi & McGarrell, 2002; Manning, 1997:31). Efficiency as the criterion by which police performance has traditionally been measured has been rationalized by the concept *utilitarianism*. In other words, ethical police behavior is that behavior that leads to the realization of the "greatest good for the greatest number." The greatest good for the greatest number has often come to mean under the professional paradigm of policing that efficiency (crime control) is *primus inter pares* ("first among equals") among competing values such as equity in due process (individual rights) (Caldero & Crank, 2004; Packer, 1968) and responsiveness in police services (Cordner, 1997).

CRIME FIGHTING

Related to efficiency in crime control is an individual's commitment to the role of "crime fighter." Several theoretical frameworks have been offered by police scholars to distinguish the various roles that police adopt in the performance of their duties (Broderick, 1977; Coates, 1972; Muir, 1977; White, 1972). Although these popular frameworks have yet to yield empirical support (Hochstedler, 1981), they are useful in organizing thoughts and comparing popular notions of various police roles. Consistent among these frameworks is the ideal of police as "crime fighters." Police do more, however, than question suspicious persons, make arrests, collect evidence, and conduct interviews. In fact, police often fulfill a "social worker" (or "human services") role, and some empirical evidence suggests that this is the role that occupies the majority of an officer's time (Wilson, 1968). Police often spend more time acting as brokers who connect citizens with valuable community resources, assist stranded motorists, provide directions, resolve family and neighbor disputes, and help citizens in other important ways. Many new recruits come to policing with a "Dirty Harry" conception of police work, while older, more experienced officers tend to emphasize the human service as well as the crime fighter role because it yields the greatest social rewards (Kraska & Kappeler, 1997; Manning, 1996, 1997).

WHERE DO POLICE VALUES COME FROM?
HISTORICAL, CULTURAL, AND ECONOMIC

According to the predisposition model, ethics in police work are the product of values that are imported (or brought from the larger society) into the organization. They are enduring social values that are actively screened for during the recruitment and selection processes of police personnel systems, with conservatism and conformity being the product of individual and family life experiences. They are also the product of one's socioeconomic status and commitment to "old-fashioned" values that view reality as an objective truth with no shades of gray, while seeing efficiency as a neutral and desirable goal of individual and group actions.

The commitment by individual officers to get the "bad guy" off the street not only comes from previous life and family experience, but also long-standing American values that have favored the underdog, with psychological roots grounded in the idea that anyone can achieve the American Dream if they just work hard enough (Messner & Rosenfeld, 2001). Values-predisposition is also the product of the perceived legitimacy of the law resulting from a democratic process and the perceived neutrality of its application ("all are equal under the law"). The reality is, however, that even the most open and democratic processes run the risk of becoming unduly influenced by either a majority or minority group who may choose to distort the "will of the people" (Green & Shapiro, 1994; Hummel, 1994; Mastrofski, 1988; Stone, 2002). Similarly, the myth of neutral application of the law has long been debunked, as institutional and extralegal factors have been shown to determine how and when the law is applied (Klockars, 1988; Mastrofski, 1988; Spears & Spohn, 1997).

SOCIAL

Popular media depictions along with societal expectations may determine not only who will be attracted to the police occupation, but also who will be deemed qualified for employment. The occupational predisposition perspective argues that individuals with certain traits or characteristics will be attracted to the profession. Much of this attraction is socially constructed—often inaccurately—by images of police in the media. The popular conception of police portrayed in the media is that policing is primarily about "fighting crime."

Despite the various roles played by police and the importance of the social services role in occupying an officer's time, that of crime fighter and "super-cop" are the dominant images portrayed by the media (Manning, 1996). These images misrepresent the actuality of police work, most of which is more mundane and tedious. The media also conveys images of officers with nearly "super human" abilities capable of deducing the motivations of criminals using highly complex and sophisticated forensic approaches. The reality is that in most crimes the criminal is "known" to the complainant or to the police at the time the crime initially comes to the attention of law enforcement (Reiss & Bordua, 1967:43). Such crimes are solved the "old fashioned" way—through interviewing and traditional evidence-gathering procedures. These images not only reinforce the crime-fighter role to attract individuals with such an orientation, but have implications for the organization of police and the provision of their services.

Crime-fighter images portraying individuals possessing nearly super-human abilities attract those persons to the profession whose view of police work is congruent with the dominant media image, while the police institution in turn reacts to the media's depictions (Manning, 1996). For example, partly as a result of popular shows such as *CSI*, police are now feeling increased pressure from juries, the public, and victims to provide "forensic" evidence to secure a conviction. Programs such as *CSI* shape the public's perception of the relationship between police and the criminal justice system. In response, agencies are specializing—creating crime labs and/or specialized investigative units—and relying on reactive forms of policing (science and technology) to control crime (Kraska & Kappeler, 1997).

Equally important is the potential impact that the media has on the police institution with respect to ensuring due process protections for citizens. Of particular relevance are those images depicting officers using "dirty means" to achieve good ends, such as those popularized in *Dirty Harry* movies. Movies such as these were a response to widespread societal sentiments that the police had become "handcuffed" by the Warren Court through such landmark cases as *Mapp v. Ohio* (1961) and *Miranda v. Arizona* (1966). What we can see is that the media and society both influence which types of individuals will find policing to be a desirable occupation while simultaneously shaping the police agency's response to these images. The result is that agencies may feel pressure to actively recruit and screen for both those who adopt a predominantly crime-fighter orientation and those who view efficiency rather than ensuring due process protections as the dominant value to be pursued in police work (Caldero & Crank, 2004; Manning, 1997; Pollock, 1998).

As the occupation of policing has become more professionalized through education requirements demanding two- or four-year degrees, individuals entering law enforcement occupations are increasingly exposed to courses such as criminal justice ethics that have the potential to transmit positive police values. Although the probability of exposure to ethics in policing is greater in some academic programs than others, curricula in most programs do not *require* such training. As a result, exposure to police ethics is most likely to occur informally—if at all—in introductory policing courses. In addition, many policing courses are taught by part-time faculty who usually work, or have worked, in law enforcement (Caldero & Crank, 2004).

Ethics taught by these instructors usually is conveyed through real-world examples that may on occasion tend to reinforce the crime control model and its emphasis on efficiency at the cost of other important values such as protecting individual rights. Because most students interested in law enforcement may already be predisposed to the moral mandate of policing (to make the world a safer place), they may not recognize this value trade-off. Fighting crime and protecting individual rights can be a difficult balance to maintain. Should instructors be critical of certain aspects of the policing institution, students who are morally predisposed toward the noble cause may misinterpret that to mean the professor is anti-police (Caldero & Crank, 2004).

VALUES-LEARNED PERSPECTIVE: SOCIALIZATION AND CULTURALIZATION

A competing perspective of the source of police values argues that police values are not imported from society at large, but are instead learned on the job. This *values-learned perspective* argues that police values are learned through the process of socialization and culturalization within a particular police agency. Although these two frameworks are analytically distinct, in practice they are related (see Figure 12.1). The *socialization* model of police ethics argues that norms and values are learned through the process of *professionalization*. In this regard, police are no different than other professionals, such as physicians and lawyers, who learn their ethics through training and practice (Alpert & Dunham, 1997; Gaines & Kappeler, 2005; Kappeler, Sluder & Alpert, 2005). The process of organizational socialization seeks to "fuse" the officer to the organization by providing him or her with a set of rules, perspectives, prescriptions, techniques, and tools necessary to participate in the organization (Van Maanen, 1974). In a sense, this socialization process seeks to create a "working personality" or "police personality" within the new recruit as he or she experiences distinct occupational phases during his or her career: choice, introduction, encounter, and metamorphosis (see Figure 12.1).

CHOICE

As stated previously, although the values-learned perspective is analytically distinct from the value-predisposition perspective, in practice there is much overlap, and it is at this stage where most of that overlap occurs. This values-learned perspective does not deny that police work attracts individuals with certain traits and characteristics. It further elaborates, however, on the role that police personnel selection systems share with shaping an individual's value system. To a large extent, individuals choose the occupation for what the profession is perceived to offer. Chief among these benefits is the type of work.

The nature of police work that prospective candidates find most appealing is the perceived non-routine, out-of-doors, active, and socially significant aspects afforded by the occupation. In contrast to other occupations in which workers are confined to cubicles performing routine tasks with repetitive motions and relatively close supervision, police work promises much the opposite. It promises individuals the opportunity to go to work not knowing what events or circumstances they will encounter during their shift. Although calls for service may be classified similarly, no two calls are exactly alike. Finally, because most work by police officers is performed in the absence of direct supervision, and because most circumstances encountered by police are too complex to be strictly regulated through Standard Operating Procedures, decisionmaking is highly discretionary (Wilson, 1989). Such discretion and freedom is an attractive lure, especially for those with previous experience in highly bureaucratic work environments.

Perhaps the most important virtue of the occupation for those selecting police work is the perceived "meaningfulness" of the work. In contrast to occupations that exist to generate net profits (like a stockbroker, banker, or salesperson), police work offers the promise of providing a net social benefit. Individuals are often attracted to policing because they believe that the work has a positive impact on the lives and well-being of others. These characteristics of police work are also buttressed by job security and the relatively high salary with respect to the education requirements.

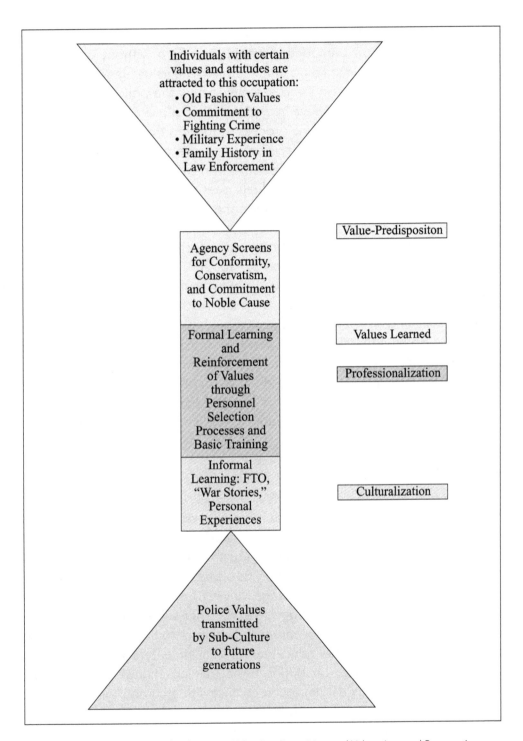

Figure 12.1 Analytic Relationship between Value Predisposition and Values-Learned Perspectives

The value-predisposition perspective would stop here without acknowledging the role of the organization in shaping officer ethics. The values-learned perspective goes further, however, in exploring and examining how the police are socialized by the profession itself to act and behave in a manner that allows them to *continue* their participation in the organization. This process of forging the "working personality" begins when an individual makes a decision to join the organization. It does so by first employing a rigorous and protracted selection process. This process not only ensures a homogeneous group of individuals possessing middle-class values, but also has the effect of creating a sense among the new recruit that the organization is "elite."

Some studies indicate that the recruitment and selection process takes an average of 8.1 months in large departments (Walker & Katz, 2002), while in some agencies it is estimated that only one in 100 applicants will make it to the employment ranks (Gaines & Kappeler, 2005). The fact that the organization would devote so much time and money before selecting an individual to become a member of the organization signals to the prospective recruit that the police agency is an important and challenging place to work (Van Maanen, 1974). It is also during the recruitment and selection phases that the police agency attempts to portray itself in the most favorable light. In addition, potential recruits receive support and encouragement from existing officers, with whom many enjoy relationships via generational or friendship networks.

INTRODUCTION

The optimism and uncritical view held by the recruit of the agency and police work soon begins to fade as the process of professionalization continues during Basic Training. This is where the novice officer begins to learn what police work is "really like." Aside from the technical and mechanical aspects that dominate police recruit training, such as instruction in firearms usage, driving, first aid, self-defense and other use-of-force tactics, the new recruit begins to experience subtle shifts in values and attitudes during this phase of his or her career. In fact, prior to this socialization process, the recruit is said to be at his or her ethical zenith—having entered the profession with high ideals and positive values. It is during Basic Training, though, that the "rookie" begins to adopt negative values that are in conflict with a number of legal standards and core societal values (Conti & Nolan, 2005).

The once-positive view of the agency held by the new recruit is quickly challenged as the recruit learns that the bureaucracy in which he or she now works is highly formal, mechanical, and often arbitrary. In fact, the supportive and positive view of the agency held by the recruit during the *choice* stage now gives way to one that begins to see the agency as a control instrument, concerned primarily with predictability, stability, and efficiency. The new recruit is also taught the value of group cohesion and solidarity as a result of distinguishing training garb, group exercises, training officers' commands to "show unity," and shared experiences with other recruits. The rookie officer also learns that good behavior is likely to go unnoticed, while bad behavior will be punished. Finally, the recruit learns that bad behavior is often punished arbitrarily, based on the context in which it occurs. The new recruits quickly learn that it is in their best interest to remain "under the radar" or become "invisible" to protect themselves from hostile and unsympathetic administrators and other outside groups (Crank, 2004).

Aside from the organizational forces that begin to shape new recruit values and attitudes at this stage, the rookie officer receives lessons in police work through formal and informal instruction. Formally, recruits are introduced to police work through veteran officers and outside experts. The primary goal of this type of instruction is to satisfy criminal and procedural requirements while reducing exposure to civil liability (Buerger, 1998). Informal learning occurs primarily through the use of "war stories," and it is this type of learning that has the greatest potential to generate unethical behavior.

"War stories" are narratives presented to an academy class that describe a particular incident or circumstance (Ford, 2003). These narratives are meant to provide direction for officers by giving them "guidance as to how officers should experience the world if they are to act as police officers within it" (Shearing & Ericson, 1991). War stories also serve to give concrete meaning and highlight the reality of police work. These stories are often used to compliment formal instruction and are given at the discretion of the trainers who are police veterans. War stories often contain two sources of content: manifest and latent.

The "overt or obvious message of the story" is referred to as *manifest content*, while the *latent content* is the covert message of story—or "the message beneath the message" (Ford, 2003). Not all war stories contain latent content, and some instructors inadvertently or unknowing send a message they do not realize is being sent. The latent content of some stories may contradict the primary message of instruction. Such messages are sometimes referred to as *black swans*. For example, Buerger, (1998) cites the following anonymous quotation from police trainers illustrating how war stories often contradict the primary message of instruction:

> ... we're just spouting the official line on everything, all the while strongly suggesting that it was all bullshit and that we would learn the real stuff out on the street – "ya know, we can't tell you to slap

the shit out of those punk gang-bangers back in the alley here, but don't worry about that, you'll learn soon enough."

Although all war stories don't necessarily send messages that contradict social, legal, and societal standards, many still have the potential to transmit negative values and attitudes that threaten to erode positive ones. For example, in his analysis of 269 war stories, Ford (2003) notes that the manifest and latent content of the majority of these stories contained useful messages that taught recruits street skills, while emphasizing the danger and uncertainty surrounding the occupation. There were, however, other stories that contained content ranging from ways to obtain "freebies," to meet women while on duty, and to sleep and shirk duties. In addition, several of these stories contained justifications for using excessive force, such as "just hit the brakes and have the big mouth get waffled on the screen" (p. 92). In the end, Ford's analysis demonstrated that the range of content in police war stories is wide and includes everything from encouraging the violation of rights, racist comments, poor treatment of citizens, failure to perform one's duty, and verbally berating citizens.

ENCOUNTER

The previous stages of the police socialization process set the stage for a fundamental shift in values, rather than the fine tuning of existing ones. In fact, it is here that the popular images constructed of police by the media, the core American values, and the lofty ideals of police practice professed in Basic Training are transformed and replaced by distinct police subculture values. The primary mode of value transmission is through the Field Training Officer, who enjoys the privilege of evaluating the rookie's job performance and ultimately making a recommendation regarding his or her continued employment at the end of their probationary period.

A Field Training Officer (FTO) is a veteran officer who has been patrolling for several years. The FTO is the primary mechanism by which recruits learn how to perform "real" police work. In fact, the new recruit quickly learns that much of what is learned in the academy does not readily translate into practice on the street, and that the police subculture exists to protect itself from hostile and unsympathetic groups. As a result, the first thing that is often told to the new recruit by the FTO is to "forget what you learned in the academy."

This instruction by the FTO is often reinforced when many of the war stories told during Basic Training actually come to life and the new recruit discovers that there often exists a difference between the theory (as taught in Basic Training) and practice (as experienced on the street) of policing. For example, Van Maanen (1974) recounts one officer's experience with attempting to explain the law to a citizen regarding speeding:

> ... Keith was always telling me to be forceful, to not back down and to never try and explain the law or what we are doing to a civilian. I didn't really know what he was talking about until I tried to tell some kid why we have laws about speeding. Well, the more I tried to tell him about traffic safety, the angrier he got. I was lucky to just get his John Hancock on the citation. When I came back to the patrol car, Keith explained to me just where I'd gone wrong. You really can't talk to those people out there, they just won't listen to reason.

Because some of the lessons learned from the recruit's Basic Training experiences fail to readily translate into practice, the FTO becomes the primary mechanism by which the new recruit learns which type of behavior is appropriate for each different situation.

The police uniform and gun are key elements of the occupation that serve to distinguish police from others. They are symbols of power, and such power often provokes challenges from those who are subjected to it. As a result, police often experience open criticisms and taunts, especially from juveniles and minorities (Kappeler & Gaines, 2005). This sometimes hostile reception by the public does not square with the recruit's reasons for becoming an officer—to serve the public. The new recruit also soon discovers that citizens will attempt to manipulate his or her inexperience to achieve some desired end. The result of such exposures is that citizens come to be viewed with suspicion, and in some cases, as enemies and outsiders who can't be trusted (Crank, 2004).

These experiences are subsequently combined with the new recruit's increasing awareness that much of police work is about "patching holes in the social fabric rather than weaving webs to catch criminals" (Sherman, 1982) and that the administration, legal system, and media are as adversarial as the general public (Crank, 2004). The FTO quickly imparts to the new recruit that most police work is mundane and tedious and that only a few calls constitute "real police work." Those calls that do constitute real police work are often referred to as "hot calls," or calls for service that may result in bodily harm for the officer or their partners. How rookie officers respond to these types of calls often serve as the primary basis by which the FTO makes a recommendation for the rookie's retention or severance, as they are a measure of the rookie's willingness to share the risks of police work (Van Maanen, 1974). As a result, responses to these infrequent calls take on new significance and present occasional opportunities to reinforce in the FTO's mind that the rookie is not afraid to use force, protect other officers, and remain loyal.

In addition to testing an individual's commitment to the group by evaluating their response to potentially dangerous calls for service, the new recruit's solidarity is further tested by assessing the extent to which he or she will support or ignore behaviors that run counter to department policy. Examples include conducting personal business while on duty or accepting gratuities. This assessment of an individual's willingness to engage in or ignore behaviors that are prohibited by department policy is a product of the group's recognition that the administration (or the "brass")—like the public—cannot be trusted because they are primarily interested in protecting their own "asses" (Crank, 2004). As a result, officers often attempt to resist administrative control by limiting the flow of information to their supervisors (Manning, 1977, 1997). Recruits who are unwilling to participate in—or, at the very least, ignore—such behaviors quickly find themselves isolated within the police subculture (Caldero & Crank, 2004; Kappeler, Sluder & Alpert, 2005).

Not only has this phase of the recruit's occupational career taught him or her to view the public and administration with cynicism and suspicion, it has significantly altered the rookie officer's view of police work. The new officer has learned at this stage that the legal system tends to be "soft" on crime. Costello (1972) noted that 75 years before the "due process revolution" of the Warren Court, the police were inclined to believe that the courts would not back them up and that punishment, when it did come, was not swift. The new recruit observes that the legal system appears soft on crime when "bad guys get off on a technicality" or prosecutors decide that a case lacks merit or is better adjudicated with a plea-bargain deal.

In contrast to the legal system, which evaluates its decisions and behavior based upon some legal standard (for example, the decision to prosecute based on the worth or merit of a case), police officers tend to evaluate their behavior based upon the "ideal policeman" as described in occupational lore and imagery (Manning, 1978). The "ideal policeman" standard is to get the bad guy off the street, which means using the law or any other tool at the officer's disposal. Furthermore, it is assumed that the ideal police officer is more discerning than the law and knows who is bad (Crank, 2004). In response, the new recruit is often taught to leverage and manipulate the law to achieve the standards of the ideal officer. As a result, the new recruit will often have his or her loyalty tested in such ways as being encouraged to engage in several legal violations: such as to "testily" (to give false testimony), to "dropsy" (remove drugs from a suspect during a pat-down and then discover them in plain sight on the ground), "the shake" (similar to dropsy, only conducted during a vehicle stop), or "stiffing in a call" (calling and reporting a crime as if one is a citizen who had witnessed it) (Caldero & Crank, 2004), all in an attempt to outsmart criminals and leverage the law when they believe someone is guilty.

The legal system also teaches the recruit that because it is soft, slow, and at times arbitrary, deterrence can only be achieved through the immediate concrete exercise of coercion in an attempt to be more aggressive and smarter than criminals. This "street justice" not only includes legal abuses such as those described above, but can also include psychological abuses such as the use of racial epithets and intimidation, or even physical abuses such as administering the "third degree." Each of these examples of misconduct is aimed not only at distributing justice when it is perceived that the legal system cannot be counted on to do so, but to provide a measure of deterrence as well.

METAMORPHOSIS

The final stage of the recruit's occupational career is metamorphosis. This is where the "rookie" morphs both socially and psychologically into a full-fledged officer. This transition in social status and occupational self-identity occurs at the end of the probationary period when the recruit is assigned a position free of institutional dependency

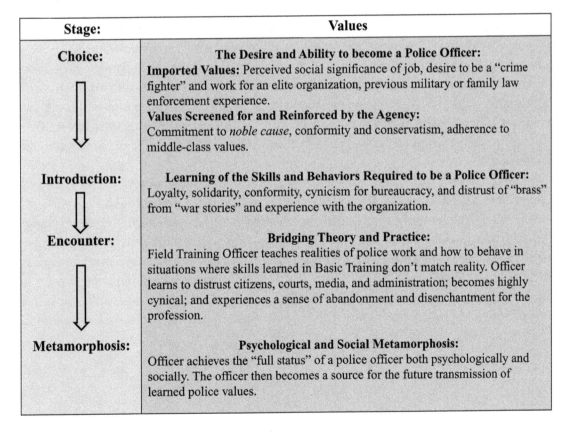

Stage:	Values
Choice: ⬇	**The Desire and Ability to become a Police Officer:** **Imported Values:** Perceived social significance of job, desire to be a "crime fighter" and work for an elite organization, previous military or family law enforcement experience. **Values Screened for and Reinforced by the Agency:** Commitment to *noble cause*, conformity and conservatism, adherence to middle-class values.
Introduction: ⬇	**Learning of the Skills and Behaviors Required to be a Police Officer:** Loyalty, solidarity, conformity, cynicism for bureaucracy, and distrust of "brass" from "war stories" and experience with the organization.
Encounter: ⬇	**Bridging Theory and Practice:** Field Training Officer teaches realities of police work and how to behave in situations where skills learned in Basic Training don't match reality. Officer learns to distrust citizens, courts, media, and administration; becomes highly cynical; and experiences a sense of abandonment and disenchantment for the profession.
Metamorphosis:	**Psychological and Social Metamorphosis:** Officer achieves the "full status" of a police officer both psychologically and socially. The officer then becomes a source for the future transmission of learned police values.

Figure 12.2 Occupational Stages and Values Learned

and where their responsibility and autonomy is more or less equalized with respect to other officers (Van Maanen, 1974). It is during this stage that the officer adopts the self-conception of "cop" that is in part the product of the cynicism, sense of abandonment, and ultimately disenchantment that the recruit now has for the occupation.

After becoming more independent, the officer learns within a short period of time all of the aspects of their work. They learn the geography of their "beat" or district, the social skills of policing, what forms to fill out, and the nuances of the bureaucracy. At this point, there is little left to learn. Police work can become more mundane, tedious, and mechanical. In addition, the police officer begins to realize that police work is more about providing social services and adhering to legal and organizational standards to avoid trouble than it is about solving crimes.

Through war stories, examples witnessed while under the supervision of their FTO, and finally through experience, cynicism and a sense of abandonment may crystallize in the minds of recruits. It is at this point—after achieving institutional independence and assuming equal responsibility—that the forging of the "working personality" may be completed with a psychological morph. Psychologically, the officer may become highly cynical while experiencing a sense of abandonment from what appears to be a hostile, unappreciative, and sometimes unsupportive public. This cynicism and sense of abandonment is further reinforced by the realization and perception that the police bureaucracy is also often arbitrary, mechanical, impersonal, and home to an adversarial administration concerned primarily with self-preservation. These sentiments are further strengthened by the legal system that appears to be more concerned about ensuring due process protections, achieving high conviction rates, and effectively managing correctional populations than about helping police get the bad guys off the street.

What emerges from the socialization process is a relatively consistent set of values that are continually transmitted and reinforced among the police subculture through the process of culturalization. Whether the new recruit accepts these subcultural values is in part determined by the extent to which individual and organizational factors are able to counteract the influences and tendencies of a corrupt and deviant subculture. The content of values transmitted and embraced by this subculture that may contribute to unethical behavior include those governing the use of force, time, group loyalty, fringe benefits, justice, and discretion (see also Sherman, 1982).

THE CONTENT OF POLICE VALUES

Force: *Use of force should not be viewed as a last resort for controlling a situation. In fact, the use of force is necessary to achieve deterrence, convey group loyalty, and achieve some measure of justice.* Instead of being an act of last resort for controlling a situation (Fyfe, 2005; Manning, 1997), force is extolled among the police subculture for its ability to signal to the public that it is not weak, as well conveying to other officers that the officer can be counted on should one become a victim of a violent encounter. As such, force conveys loyalty to the group while providing a measure of deterrence for those who may consider future attacks against the police. Force also acts as a crime deterrent for its immediate and concrete properties where the legal system is viewed by police to operate on the threat of punishment.

Time: *An officer can never respond too quickly to a call for "real" police services, nor can they respond too slowly to a "garbage" call. When not responding to calls for service, an officer's time is his or her own.* Given the complexity of police work and the difficulty in maintaining direct supervision, officers enjoy considerable latitude in defining their work. The consequence of this is that some officers relegate certain calls for service to the status of "garbage"—those that usually relate to the social work or order-maintenance roles—because they do not conform to their conception of what constitutes "real" police work as depicted in the media and reinforced by their FTO and Basic Training instructors. Those calls for service related to the "crime fighter" role (e.g., a robbery in progress) are elevated to a much higher status because they afford the greatest opportunity for social rewards from the public, administrators, and other officers. When not responding to calls for service, an officer's time is his or her own and he or she should not be required to engage in proactive forms of policing. This belief is reinforced by quotas used by administrators that are reinterpreted by officers as production maximums not minimums. Thus, once an officer has met the minimum quota, there exists a strong incentive to shirk duty through sleeping, ignoring opportunities to engage in proactive forms of policing, and/or pretending not to hear a call for service.

Loyalty: *Don't trust anyone except your fellow officer; not the public, the "brass," nor the media. Group loyalty provides protection from the real dangers of police work and from a hostile and unsympathetic administration, and serves to provide emotional support for performing a difficult task.* Officers often feel socially rejected by a public that once inspired them to join the occupation. They learn that even the most seemingly innocuous events and persons may pose a problem for an officer later (e.g., a female motorist smiling and flirting with a male officer while issuing a ticket, only to later file a complaint). The officer also learns that the "brass" is more concerned about reducing exposure to civil liability, managing the department's public image, and satisfying other organizational demands than about helping officers get the bad guys off the street. In a world filled with adversarial and unsympathetic groups, police learn that unbending loyalty is essential for the group's survival. This loyalty comes in the form of physical (use of force when necessary to protect other officers and the institution), legal (fabricating evidence, corroborating false testimony, etc.), and emotional support. Officers who do not provide unconditional loyalty quickly find themselves isolated within the police subculture.

Fringe Benefits: *Police perform a difficult task, one that is dangerous and requires that they deal with society's "social garbage." Given the dangerousness of the occupation and the clientele with which they often interact, police are underpaid. The corollary is that any rewards extended for their service or in appreciation are a form of deserved and appropriate compensation.* Departments generally prohibit the acceptance of gratuities. Although citizens and merchants may wish to extend a gratuity to officers in the form of a discount or free cup of coffee as a gesture of appreciation, organizational policy generally prohibits their acceptance. The rationale for such policies is that acceptance may result in the selective enforcement of the law and/or differential responses to calls for service. Despite these potential problems, gratuities are seen by officers as a form of just compensation for doing a difficult job that is otherwise woefully undercompensated.

Justice: *The legal system is untrustworthy. As a result, justice is sometimes best served on the street based on personal rather than legal considerations.* Due process protections are often at odds with the crime control mandate of police. At the very least, these protections postpone and prescribe punishment in accordance with state statutes. A cop's conception of justice is more personal and immediate. To him or her, it is the concrete exercise of coercion to control situations and individuals. Police generally resist making an arrest for misdemeanor public order offenses if another strategy can resolve the problem. If, however, a suspect is guilty of not being deferential and respectful to an officer (often referred to as "contempt of cop"), an arrest may be desirable for its ability to mete out immediate and concrete justice. This "distributive justice" is different than "legal justice." Distributive justice is about the officer's personal opinion that the individual deserves punishment, rather than legal standards. Many times officers are aware that arrests under such circumstances will not be carried forward by the prosecutors to achieve legal justice, so they may make an arrest based on false charges. At the very least, officers recognize that the arrest—even if charges are not formally filed by the prosecutor—is itself punishment. The social stigma associated with arrest, lost time from work, and legal expenses borne by the citizen are all forms of punishment regardless of the legal system's response.

Discretion: *Enforcement of the law, except in the most serious instances, should be based not only on what the law says but also on individual characteristics.* Whether to enforce the law is as much about the characteristics of the individual suspect as it is about legal considerations. Age, race, socioeconomic status, gender, relationship to the victim, and suspect demeanor are all extralegal factors that determine how and when the law is applied. The young, poor minorities who do not share a close relationship with the victim and who are disrespectful to police are more likely to experience full enforcement of the law than other citizens.

MORAL CAREER

Although the prevalence and strength of these questionable values are not as widespread and strong today as in the past, how officers react to these can be described as an officer's *moral career*. The moral career, as described by Lawrence Sherman (1982), consists of distinct aspects that threaten to move officers from the pinnacle of positive values that drove their desire to protect persons, property, and constitutional rights in an impartial and exemplary manner, to the adoption of behaviors that are contrary to department, legal, and societal standards. The stages of an individual's moral career identified by Sherman are illustrated in Figure 12.3.

The working environments experienced by officers contain a variety of factors that may encourage or discourage the adoption of unethical behaviors. Some of these *contingencies* may include things like levels of supervision and oversight experienced by officers and the type of work. Levels of supervision and type of work (e.g., patrol versus vice crime) may create opportunity and temptations to engage in certain types of unethical behavior. For example, all things being equal, those experiencing low levels of supervision or working vice crimes are more likely than others to have unethical behavior go undetected, while experiencing more opportunity and temptation to engage in such types of misconduct as stealing. Similarly, many types of unethical behavior require the transmission of skills. For example, planting evidence such as a firearm to justify a police shooting may require teaching another officer how to do

Aspect:	Experience:
Contingencies:	Factors experienced by the officer within his or her working environment that encourage or discourage unethical behavior.
Moral Experiences:	Particular experience by officers that challenge their existing morality, or allow for the interpretation of others' morality based on behavior.
Apologia:	Situational justification of unethical behavior.
Stages:	"Slippery slope" progression of unethical behavior.

Figure 12.3 Aspects and Environment of an Officer's Moral Career

so without being detected. This may not only include how to obtain an untraceable firearm and remove fingerprints, but also placing the firearm in the victim's hands and subsequently discharging the firearm to leave gun powder residue to support claims that the officer was fired upon. Contingencies within the individual's work environment, therefore, can produce opportunities, incentives, and skills that encourage or discourage the assimilation of unethical behaviors.

The road to becoming a corrupt or "bent" police officer is also riddled with *moral experiences* that challenge an officer's existing morality. For example, a moral experience will likely arise when an officer witnesses another officer violate department or legal standards. Violation of these standards may run counter to values held by an ethical officer. In these instances, officers will have to make a choice as to whether they should allow or participate in such behavior, or challenge or escape it through employment termination or transfer. A moral experience often leads to the adoption of unethical behavior when it is accompanied by some rationalization.

Apologia encompasses the situationally justified rationalizations that reduce the psychological pain and sense of responsibility experienced by those who engage in behaviors that are not congruent with their ethical values and sense of responsibility. The only way then for the individual to continue the behavior is to provide a rationalization. For example, an officer may steal something from the site of a burglary and justify that behavior by convincing himself or herself that "no one really gets hurt" because the item is covered by the insurance company. Other rationalizations may include convincing oneself that one deserves such rewards because of the dangerousness or nature of the work.

The final aspect of an individual's moral career identified by Sherman (1982) concerns stages. The concept of *stages* recognizes that the process of becoming "bent" is progressive. Unethical behavior begins on a "slippery slope." The transformation of an ethical officer to an unethical one begins with more mild and seemingly innocuous forms of behavior, such as accepting gratuities and small bribes. These actions provide the contingencies, moral experiences, and learning of situational justifications that lead to more aggressive and active forms of unethical behavior, such as stealing, testilying, extortion, and physical and legal violations (or worse, if left unchecked).

POLICE ETHICS AND CONTROL, REFORM, AND LEGITIMACY

Police misconduct is not new. It is as old as the institution itself. What has changed since the emergence of the public police force is the form of misconduct. The learning and teaching of police ethics bears directly on issues of control, reform, and legitimacy of policing in a democratic society. Of particular relevance is the role of emerging police paradigms and changing social sentiments. Police misconduct today is characterized more by the abuse of authority (noble cause corruption) and economic corruption than misconduct associated with using police as political instruments. This is in large part the product of changing social conditions and the "professional era" of policing that witnessed the adoption of a crime control mandate.

Community-Oriented Policing (COP) and Problem-Oriented Policing (POP) present issues with respect to control of the institution where the learning and teaching of police ethics are to some extent the residue of informal on-the-job learning. Specifically, these emerging police paradigms require that officer discretion be increased so that police can effectively engage in proactive forms of policing to *solve* problems. If standard operating procedures (SOPs) are going to give way to discretion, then officer behaviors and attitudes are going to have to be informed by positive police values. The informal on-the-job learning that currently exists and that may facilitate the transmission of negative values presents real challenges for today's police administrators.

If administrators are going to manage the transition to COP and POP effectively, while also controlling police misconduct, learning and teaching police ethics must rely more on formal mechanisms. Specifically, administrators may consider recruiting those who hold a more realistic view of police work, while increasing education requirements. They are also going to have to rely on teaching police ethics through "leading by example." This includes not only emphasizing and acting at the highest ethical standards, but also modifying administrative processes to create incentives favoring such behaviors. For example, individual police performance has historically been evaluated on output measures that may inadvertently introduce incentives to engage in unethical behavior (e.g., "number of arrests or crimes cleared"). Measures of individual police performance that may increase the likelihood of ethical behaviors might include measuring citizen satisfaction with respect to an officer's police work. Administrators will also need to be cognizant of the role that informal messages convey in shaping officer behavior and consider formal training in ethics by Internal Affairs or other investigative divisions.

Not only do these emerging police paradigms present challenges to police behavior that must be met with organizational and administrative reforms, changing social sentiments also introduce challenges with respect to the legitimacy of the institution. The importance of police services has increased in recent years as demonstrated through the increasing variety of police roles. As with other occupations, police are viewed by society to be experts capable of solving many different problems. The extent to which the police are unable to fulfill these expectations is the extent to which the legitimacy of the police institution will likely decline in the eyes of the public.

This is particularly problematic in the era of the "war on drugs," the "war on terror," and the "war on crime." These problems have deliberately been framed as "wars" by politicians because the metaphor implies a sense of urgency, constructs a "we-versus-them" mentality among the police, and fuels the idea of dangerous "foreign enemies." Encouraging such perceptions is useful for generating political capital for (re)election, engaging in deficit spending, and ultimately expanding police power. Police administrators have often been quick to embrace these "wars" as they often increase citizen and fiscal support.

The reality is, however, that politicians may be charging police with impossible tasks. In other words, it may be—and probably very likely is—impossible that these "wars" will ever come to an end. In an era of experts, society expects that "wars" will end with clear winners and losers. The reality is that the sources of these problems span several institutions (economic, politics, education, and religion), many of which are beyond the direct control of the police. These "wars" create incentives among the police subculture and administrators to do whatever it takes to achieve the impossible mandate. Police administrators may do better—in the long run—educating the public regarding their limits so that reasonable expectations may serve as guide for evaluating present and future officer behavior.

REFERENCES

Alpert, G. P. & R.G. Dunham (1997). *Policing Urban America*, 3rd ed. Prospect Heights, IL: Waveland.

Bayley, D.H. & E. Bittner (1984). "Learning the Skills of Policing." *Law and Contemporary Problems*, 47:35–59.

Bayley, D.H. & A. Mendelsohn (1969). *Minorities and the Police*. New York: Free Press.

Bittner, E. (1970). *The Functions of Police in Modern Society*. Washington, DC: National Institute of Mental Health.

Broderick, J.J. (1977). *Police in a Time of Change*. Morristown, NJ: General Learning Press.

Buerger, M. (1998). "Police Training as a Pentecost: Using Tools Singularly Ill-suited to the Purpose of Reform." *Police Quarterly*, 1:27–63.

Caldero, M.A. & J.P. Crank (2004). *Police Ethics: The Corruption of the Noble Cause,* 2nd ed. Newark, NJ: LexisNexis Matthew Bender.

Coates, R. (1972). *The Dimensions of Police-Citizen Interaction: A Social Psychological Analysis*. Unpublished Ph.D. dissertation, University of Maryland.

Conti, N. & J.J.I. Nolan (2005). "Policing the Platonic Cave: Ethics and Efficacy in Police Training." *Policing & Society*, 15:166–186.

Cordner, G.W. (1997). "Community Policing: Elements and Effects." In R.G. Dunham & G.P. Alpert (eds.), *Critical Issues in Policing: Contemporary Readings*, 5th ed. (pp. 451–468). Long Grove, IL: Waveland.

Costello, A.E. (1972). *Our Police Protectors*, 3rd ed. Montclair, NJ: Patterson Smith.

Crank, J.P. (2004). *Understanding Police Culture*, 2nd ed. Cincinnati: Anderson.

Ford, J.K. & M. Morash (2002). "Transforming Police Organizations." In M. Morash & J. K. Ford (eds.), *The Move to Community Policing: Making Change Happen* (pp. 1–11). Thousand Oaks, CA: Sage.

Ford, R.E. (2003). "Saying One Thing, Meaning Another: The Role of Parables in Police Training." *Police Quarterly*, 6:84–110.

Fyfe, J.J. (2005). "The Split-second Syndrome and Other Determinants of Police Violence." In R.G. Dunham & G.P. Alpert (eds.), *Critical Issues in Policing: Contemporary Readings* (pp. 435–450). Long Grove, IL: Waveland.

Gaines, L.K. & V.E. Kappeler (2005). *Policing in America*, 5th ed. Newark, NJ: LexisNexis Matthew Bender.

Giacomazzi, A.L. & E.F. McGarrell (2002). "Using Multiple Methods in Community Crime Prevention and Community-policing Research." In J.K. Ford & M. Morash (eds.), *Transforming Police Organizations* (pp. 61–78). Thousand Oaks, CA: Sage.

Green, D.P. & I. Shapiro (1994). *Pathologies of Rational Choice Theory: A Critique of Applications in Political Science*. New Haven, CT: Yale University Press.

Hochstedler, E. (1981). "Testing Types: A Review and Test of Police Types." *Journal of Criminal Justice*, 9:451–466.

Hummel, R.P. (1994). *The Bureaucratic Experience: A Critique of Life in the Modern Organization*, 4th ed. New York: St. Martin's Press.

Kappeler, V.E. & L.K. Gaines (2005). *Community Policing: A Contemporary Perspective*, 4th ed. Newark, NJ: LexisNexis Matthew Bender.

Kappeler, V.E., R.D. Sluder & G.P. Alpert (2005). "Breeding Deviant Conformity: The Ideology and Culture of Police." In R.G. Dunham & G.P. Alpert (eds.), *Critical Issues in Policing*, 5th ed. (pp. 231–254). Long Grove, IL: Waveland.

Klockars, C.B. (1988). "The Rhetoric of Community Policing." In J.R. Greene & S.D. Mastrofski (eds.), *Community Policing: Rhetoric or Reality* (pp. 239–258). New York: Praeger.

Kraska, P. & V.E. Kappeler (1997). "Militarizing the American Police: The Rise and Normalization of Paramilitary Units." *Social Forces*, 44:1–18.

Lipsky, M. (1980). "Street-level Bureaucracy: The Critical Role of Street-level Bureaucrats." In J.M. Shafritz & A.C. Hyde (eds.), *Classics of Public Administration*. Fort Worth, TX: Harcourt Brace.

Manning, P.K. (1977). "Invitational Edges of Corruption: Some Consequences of Narcotic Law Enforcement." In P. Rock (ed.), *Drugs and Politics* (pp. 279–310). Rutgers, NJ: Society/Transaction Books.

Manning, P.K. (1978). "The Police: Mandate, Strategies, and Appearances." In P.K. Manning & J. Van Maanen (eds.), *Policing: A View from the Street* (pp. 149–193). Santa Monica, CA: Goodyear.

Manning, P.K. (1996). "Policing and Reflection." *Police Forum*, 6: 1–5.

Manning, P.K. (1997). *Police Work*, 2nd ed. Long Grove, IL: Waveland.

Mapp v. Ohio, 367 U.S. 643 (1961).

Mastrofski, S.D. (1988). "Community Policing as Reform: A Cautionary Tale." In J.R. Greene & S.D. Mastrofski (eds.), *Community Policing: Rhetoric or Reality* (pp. 47–68). New York: Praeger.

Messner, S.F. & R. Rosenfeld (2001). *Crime and the American Dream*, 3rd ed. Belmont, CA: Wadsworth / Thomas Learning.

Miranda v. Arizona, 384 U.S. 436 (1966).

Muir, W.K. (1977). *Police: Streetcorner Politicians*. Chicago: Chicago University Press.

Niederhoffer, A. (1967). *Behind the Shield*. Garden City, NY: Doubleday.

Packer, H. (1968). *The Limits of the Criminal Sanction*. Stanford, CA: Stanford University Press.

Pollock, J.M. (1998). *Ethics in Crime and Justice: Dilemmas and Decisions*, 3rd ed. New York: West/ Wadsworth.

Pollock, J.M. (2005). "Ethics in Law Enforcement." In R.G. Dunham & G.P. Alpert (eds.), *Critical Issues in Policing*, 5th ed. (pp. 280–303). Long Grove, IL: Waveland.

Reiss, A. & D.J. Bordua (1967). "Environment and Organization: A Perspective on Police." In D.J. Bordua (ed.), *The Police: Six Sociological Essays*. New York: John Wiley.

Rokeach, M. (1973). *The Nature of Human Values*. New York: The Free Press.

Rokeach, M., M.G. Miller & J.S. Snyder (1971). "The Value Gap Between the Police and the Policed." *Journal of Social Issues*, 27:155–177.

Shearing, C. & R. Ericson (1991). "Culture as Figurative Action." *British Journal of Sociology*, 42:481–506.

Sherman, L. (1982). "Learning Police Ethics." *Criminal Justice Ethics* 1(1): 10–19.

Spears, J.W. & C. Spohn (1997). "The Effect of Evidence Factors and Victim Characteristics on Prosecutors' Charging Decisions in Sexual Assault Cases." *Justice Quarterly*, 14:501–524.

Stone, D. (2002). *Policy Paradox: The Art of Political Decision Making*, 2nd ed. New York: W.W. Norton & Company.

Van Maanen, J. (1974). "Working the Street: A Developmental View of Police Behavior." In H. Jacob (ed.), *The Potential for Reform in Criminal Justice* (Vol. 3, pp. 83–129). Beverly Hills, CA: Sage.

Walker, S. & C.M. Katz (2002). *The Police in America: An Introduction*. Boston: McGraw-Hill.

White, S.O. (1972). "A Perspective on Police Professionalization." *Law & Society Review*, 7:61–85.

Wilson, J.Q. (1968). *Varieties of Police Behavior: The Management of Law and Order in Eight Communities*. Cambridge, MA: Harvard University Press.

Wilson, J.Q. (1989). *Bureaucracy: What Government Agencies Do and Why They Do It*. New York: Basic Books.

Zhao, J., N. He & N.P. Lovrich (1998). "Individual Value Preferences among American Police Officers: The Rokeach Theory of Human Values Revisited." *Policing: An International Journal of Police Strategies and Management*, 21(1): 22–37.

USE OF FORCE

Current Explanations of Police Use of Force

ZACHARY R. HAYS

Before discussing how the social disorganization tradition can be adapted to explain police use of force, it is necessary to understand how policing researchers currently attempt to explain such behavior. As briefly mentioned in Chapter 1, policing researchers have long lamented not only the paucity of theoretical explanations for police behaviors, but also the empirical research that might utilize such explanations as the driving force behind their work (e.g., Bernard and Engel 2001; Garner, Maxwell, and Heraux 2002; Hagan 1989; Klinger 2004). This chapter therefore reviews all of the major *theory-driven* studies of police use of force in the last twenty years[1], in order to help illustrate the continued need for theory (conceptualization and testing) in the policing literature.

One might ask, however, of what consequence is the use of a theoretical framework in policing research? That is, what is the big deal about conducting theory-driven research? Perhaps not surprisingly, many

---

1   The review contained here is restricted to research conducted over the past twenty years in order to limit this chapter to a reasonable length. Additionally, briefly reviewed throughout this chapter, the historical evidence (prior to twenty years ago) has largely produced results similar to the results found in the studies that are reviewed here. Finally, because the research that has been conducted in the last twenty years has the additional benefit of using more sophisticated methodologies and analytic techniques, such research can generally provide more reliable and accurate estimates of how various explanatory variables influence police officers' use of force. This review of the theory-driven empirical tests of existing police use of force theories is therefore limited to the research conducted since the late 1980s.

policing researchers agree with such a sentiment. In fact, many, if not most, empirical studies of police behavior are driven primarily by the availability of data and by examining interesting combinations of explanatory and outcome variables. And, while such research can inform us about *which* factors may be related to police officers' use of force, they cannot explain *why* those factors are related to police officers' use of force. Absent such explanations, studies of this nature cannot help us understand how those factors might be manipulated to help control or reduce police officers' use of force.

For example, if researchers know that neighborhood rates of violence are positively related to police use of force, they might propose that we reduce poverty so that we may also reduce incidents of police use of force. Reducing violence is not so simple a matter, however. If it were, we would have done so a long time ago, for a host of different reasons. Subsequently, simply knowing that violence and police use of force are related can do little to influence "real world" policy without theory to explain why the phenomena are related.

If, on the other hand, some Theory X tells us that increased rates of violence leads to increased levels of strain amongst police officers, and then that increased strain leads to a higher likelihood of police use of force, then researchers can propose new policies for helping officers deal with the stress of their jobs. Thus, if policing researchers wish to truly have an influence on "real world" policy that might reduce unnecessary police use of force, it is necessary that they understand exactly why phenomena are related, not simply that they are. And, since one of the primary goals of this book is to further the theoretical development of the field, it is only those studies that have utilized a theoretical framework to test hypotheses regarding police officers' use of force (i.e., studies that are driven by theory) that are reviewed here.

Another important point to note before jumping into the review of theory-driven literature of the past 20 years is that even though the primary object of this book is to explain police officers' use of *excessive force*, it is useful to expand our focus here to include all types of police use of force behaviors, for two reasons. First, in comparison to the field in general, the number of studies focusing exclusively on police officers' use of *excessive* force is very limited. Second, whether it be the abuse of force (i.e., the use of excessive force), or the legitimate use of either lethal or non-lethal force, research on other forms of police use of force can still provide insight on why police officers' might use excessive force. In other words, if some precipitating factor is sufficient to provoke the legitimate use of (any kind of) force by the police, it may also be sufficient to provoke the use of excessive force by some police officers. Consequently, in an effort to better understand the reasons behind police use of force in general, this review includes studies of any, and all, forms of police use of force.

THEORETICAL FRAMEWORKS EXPLAINING POLICE USE OF FORCE

Nearly all of the theory-driven research on police use of force can be categorized into one of only two broad theoretical frameworks – *social threat theories* and *criminal threat theories.*[2] Studies that are driven by social threat theories generally argue that certain, less powerful, groups within the larger population pose a *social threat* to the existing power hierarchy, and therefore become the primary targets of formal social control efforts, including, but not limited to, police officers' use of force. Studies that are driven by criminal threat theories, on the other hand, generally argue that criminals, as well as other individuals, who pose a *criminal threat* to the physical safety of police officers or other civilians, become the primary targets of police officers' use of force so that their threats might be neutralized.

In addition to these two more popular theoretical frameworks, Klinger (1997) has recently proposed an ecological theory of police *vigor* which might be extended to explain police officers' use of force (although no one has attempted to do so thus far). Unfortunately, no empirical tests of Klinger's theory, as it relates to the explanation of either police vigor or police use of force, have been conducted to date. Nonetheless, as a possible avenue for the further theoretical development of police use of force literature, the basic tenets and arguments of his theory are reviewed in order to assess how they might be used to not only explain police vigor, but police use of force as well.

SOCIAL THREAT THEORIES

Social threat theories were the first theories to be used by researchers to explain police officers' use of force, and can be traced back to Blalock's original theory of minority group relations (1967). Social threat theories generally include any explanations that focus on the formal social control (i.e., police use of force) of less powerful groups within a larger population. Among the more specific aggregate-level theories that fall under the broader heading of social threat theories are the conventional version

---

2   Some might consider police organizational explanations of police officers' use of force to be a third theoretical framework for the study of police use of force. Unfortunately, no unified theoretical framework exists that connects the literatures on the various organizational factors that have been found to influence police use of force. That is, unlike studies testing other theoretical frameworks, there is no common theoretical argument that links organizational measures to police officers' use of force. Instead, researchers have only been able to identify a wide variety of measures (e.g. police subcultures, administrative or departmental use-of-force policies, officer training or experience, etc.) that all explain police use of force in different ways. Thus, generally speaking, any explanations based on various police organizational factors cannot and should not be considered true *theoretical frameworks* of police use of force.

of conflict theory (e.g., Jacobs 1979; Jacobs and Britt 1979; Sorensen, Marquart, and Brock 1993), the political threat hypothesis (e.g., Jacobs and O'Brien 1998), and racial or minority threat hypotheses (e.g., Blalock 1967; Blumer 1958; Bobo and Hutchings 1996; Holmes 2000). At the individual-level, social threat theories include Black's theory of law (Black 1976; Worden 1996), social script theory (Dwyer, Graesser, Hopkinson, and Lupfer 1990), and racial response bias arguments (e.g., Correll, Park, Judd, and Wittenbrink 2002; Correll, Park, Judd, Wittenbrink, Sadler, and Keesee 2007; Correll, Urland, and Ito 2006, Greenwald, Oakes, and Hoffman 2003).

Despite the variety of specific names of different social threat theories, they all generally contend that there is a conflict of interests among the different groups that make up any society, and that it is this conflict that leads to police use of force. More explicitly, social threat theories contend that in many stratified societies, but especially within western, capitalist societies such as our own, the powerful upper classes hold the financial, political, and, to a certain extent, moral authority which they can wield to protect their own interests. Unfortunately, however, the protection of the more power- ful groups' interests usually comes at the expense of the interests of the less powerful groups. In regards to the police use of force, Jacobs (1979) argued that "the more there are inequalities in the distribution of economic power and economic resources, the more one can expect that the social control apparatus of the state will conform to the preferences of monied elites" (914). In another piece he continued, "[because] the state's monopoly of violence is controlled by those who benefit from inequality, it follows that the control agents of the state [i.e., the police] should be more likely to use extreme force when economic inequality is most pronounced" (Jacobs and Britt 1979:403). Thus, according to social threat theories, as tools or agents of the upper-class' interests, the police are expected to formally "control" members of the less powerful racial/ethnic and social class minority groups who pose a threat to the existing status hierarchy through all means available to them, including the use of physical force. Social threat theories therefore predict that members of minority groups will be more likely to experience police use of all kinds of force (legitimate and illegitimate, lethal and non-lethal) than members of majority groups.

EMPIRICAL TESTS OF SOCIAL THREAT THEORIES

The empirical research testing social threat theories has typically utilized what policing researchers refer to as *extra-legal* variables to test their arguments. These variables measure various demographic characteristics of individuals that should have no legal bearing on how or why police officers use force (hence the *extra*-legal term). For ex- ample, researchers testing social threat theories commonly examine the effect of both aggregate- and individual-level measures of race/ethnicity, gender, age, or social class on police officers' use of force. Those researchers then argue that because it is against the interests of those who would benefit from society's inequalities (i.e., the majority groups who tend to hold power) for racial/ethnic minorities and lower-class individuals in particular to rise in power and/or numbers, those same individuals should be the most likely to experience police use of force. As such, the majority of the aggregate-level tests of social threat theories focus primarily on explaining variation in rates of police use of force via the size of racial/ethnic and social class minority populations, while individual-level tests focus on explaining how police officers differentially use force in encounters with racial/ethnic or social class minorities (to a lesser extent[3]) as compared to their encounters with whites and members of the social class majority.

Historically (prior to the set timeframe for this review), the empirical research testing both the aggregate- and individual-level effects of race/ethnicity and social class on police use of force has been supportive of the social threat theoretical framework (e.g., Binder and Fridell 1984; Binder and Scharf 1982; Blumberg 1986; Chamlin 1989; Goldkamp 1976; Hayden 1981; Horvath 1987; Jacobs and Britt 1979; Meyer 1980; Smith 1986). Like their historical counterparts, however, the large majority of the more recent empirical research testing social threat theories have also found that aggregate-level measures of race/ethnicity and social class, to a certain extent, are positively related to the police use of force. At the individual-level, the empirical research generally shows a similar pattern—that racial/ethnic minorities are more likely than whites to experience police officers' use of force (the effects of individual-level social class are less clear).

AGGREGATE-LEVEL EVIDENCE

In one of the most prominent tests of a social threat theory, Jacobs and O'Brien (1998) examined how black population size, income inequality, and racial inequality (white v. black median family income) were related to police use of deadly force across a large number of U.S. cities. The researchers extended Jacobs' earlier research, which also tested social threat theories (Jacobs 1979; Jacobs and Britt 1979), by examining justifiable police killings of civilians (i.e., police use of deadly force). Jacobs and O'Brien's dependent variable came from the FBI's Supplemental Homicide Report (SHR) for 170 cities nationwide with populations 100,000 or greater during the year of 1980. Data for their social threat explanatory measures came from the 1970 and 1980 U.S. census

---

3   At the individual-level, very few studies test how suspects' social class influences police officers' use of force. This is due primarily to the fact that it is extremely difficult to operationalize and measure social class based solely on a suspect's appearance. Thus, most individual-level tests of social threat theories focus primarily on the effect of suspects' racial/ethnic background.

reports. Then, based on what they referred to as "political threat theory," Jacobs and O'Brien hypothesized that rates of police use of deadly force would be the greatest in cities where the black populations were the largest and where both income inequality in general and income inequality (i.e., social class inequality) between whites and blacks were the most pronounced.

In order to test their hypotheses, Jacobs and O'Brien conducted Tobit regression analyses to account for the heavily skewed distribution of their dependent variable. Because incidents of police use of deadly force were, and continue to be, extremely rare, many cities nationwide report zero incidents in any given year. Through the use of Tobit regression, the researchers were able to account for the skewed distribution of their police use of deadly force variable, and were able to obtain more accurate and unbiased estimates as a result. Additionally, the researchers conducted two separate Tobit regression analyses—one to test how city-level black population size, general income inequality, and racial income inequality were related to overall rates of police use of deadly force, and another to test how those same explanatory variables were related specifically to the rates of police killings of blacks.

Jacobs and O'Brien's first set of results revealed that only racial inequality was significantly and positively related to rates of police use of deadly force. Neither city-level black population size nor general income inequality were found to significantly predict changes in the overall rates of police use of deadly force. Interestingly, the results of their second set of analyses revealed that black population size was significantly and positively related to increased rates of police killings of blacks specifically. Thus, Jacobs and O'Brien's study provides only partial support for social threat theories. Unfortunately, however, because they did not examine how their explanatory variables might have been related to other, non-lethal, forms of police force, it is difficult to generalize their findings. That is, because police officers' use of deadly force is restricted specifically to situations in which a dangerous felon is attempting to escape (*Tennessee v. Garner*, 471 U.S. 1, 1985) variation in Jacobs and O'Brien's explanatory variables may have a very different affect other non-lethal, and less restricted, forms of police use of force, including police use of excessive force. Nonetheless, Jacobs and O'Brien's study is among one of the most methodologically sophisticated pieces of research examining police use of force to date, and is consequently one of the most often cited sources documenting (at least partial) support for social threat theories.

In another examination of rates of police use of deadly force, Sorensen and colleagues (1993) found much stronger support for the specific social threat theory that they tested. Like Jacobs and O'Brien, Sorensen and colleagues utilized data from the FBI's SHR on 170 cities with populations over 100,000, but instead examined rates of police use of deadly force over a period of five years (between 1980 and 1984). They also used 1980 U.S. census data to create their measures of social threat, which included city-level measures of overall income inequality (they used the GINI index where 0 indicates no inequality and 1 indicates complete inequality), black population size, and number of individuals living in poverty. Rather than testing political threat hypotheses, though, Sorensen and colleagues used the more traditional version of criminological conflict theory as the basis for three primary hypotheses: that cities with higher levels/ larger populations of 1) income inequality, 2) black residents, and 3) impoverished residents would all experience higher rates of police use of deadly force as well.

Sorensen and colleagues used basic ordinary least squares (OLS) regression analyses to test their hypotheses. Unlike Jacobs and O'Brien (1998), however, Sorensen and colleagues did not adjust for the skewed distribution of their dependent variable. Instead, the researchers conducted a second set of analyses using only cities with populations over 250,000 which effectively circumvented their heteroskedasicity problem by removing a large number of the cities in their analysis that had reported zero incidents of police officers' use of deadly force. Despite their effort to account for such outlying cities, the researchers nonetheless observed similar results in both sets of analyses. They found that regardless of city size, all three of their measures of social threat were significantly and positively related to police killings of civilians. Consequently, unlike Jacobs and O'Brien's later study, Sorensen and colleagues' study provided strong support for social threat theories.

The fact that Sorensen and colleagues did not observe findings similar to those obtained later by Jacobs and O'Brien (1998) is somewhat surprising, especially given that both sets of researchers used largely the same data. One possible explanation for the differences in observed results between the two studies was Jacobs and O'Brien's use of Tobit regression techniques to correct for the skewed distribution of rates of police use of deadly force. However, Sorensen and colleagues conducted separate sets of analyses, in which they had essentially eliminated their heteroskedasicity problems (if only using a different method), and they still obtained significant results. The most likely explanation for the differences between the two studies is therefore the different measures of social threat that were used in each study, as well as the different control variables that were included in each study. That is, it is possible that Sorensen and colleagues found stronger support for social threat theories because they did not include any measures of racial income inequality, as did Jacobs and O'Brien. Regardless of differences between studies, however, both provide at least some support for a social threat theoretical framework of police use of force.

In the final theory-driven examination of rates of police use of deadly force conducted during the past 20 years, Liska and Yu (1992) found support for a social threat explanation as well. Unlike the two above studies, however, they used Vital Statistics data from the National Center for Health Statistics between 1975 and 1979 to construct their dependent variable. In a preemptive effort to avoid heteroskedasicity problems in their dependent variable, Liska and Yu included in their research only cities with populations of 250,000 or more, resulting in a total sample size of 45 cities. In addition to the Vital Statistics data, the researchers also constructed three social threat measures – city-level percent non-white, income inequality (the GINI index), and racial segregation (using a dissimilarity index to measure the percentage of whites who would have to move to another area to produce an even white to non-white population distribution). Based on what the researchers simply called "threat hypotheses," Liska and Yu hypothesized that all three of their social threat measures would be positively related to rates of police use of deadly force.

Liska and Yu tested their hypotheses using two sets of structural measurement models – one using their full sample, and one disaggregated by the race of the victim. The researchers found that percent non-white and racial segregation were two of the strongest predictors in both sets of analyses, net of a variety of controls, thereby providing support for social threat theories once again. Like Jacobs and O'Brien (1998), however, they found no effect of overall income inequality, in either set of analyses. As a result of the three studies reviewed thus far, it therefore appears that aggregate-level measures of race/ethnicity are better predictors of rates of police use of deadly force than are measures of income inequality.

In addition to the findings discussed above, Liska and Yu also found that percent non-white and racial segregation predicted similar rates of police use of deadly force for both whites and non-whites (there was once again no significant effect of income inequality). This finding stands in stark contrast to the findings of Jacobs and O'Brien (1998) that were described earlier. One possible explanation for the differences between these two studies is the different data and measures utilized by each set of researchers. Whereas Jacobs and O'Brien utilized SHR data to analyze rates of police use of deadly force on whites versus blacks in 1980, Liska and Yu utilized Vital Statistics data to analyze rates of police use of deadly force on whites versus non-whites during the 1970s. Consequently, it appears that while blacks were more likely to be victims of police officers' use of deadly force in 1980, racial/ethnic minorities as a whole (i.e. non-whites) were no more likely than whites to be the victim of police officers' use of deadly force during the 1970s. Regardless of these differences, however, Liska and Yu's research provides more (partial) support for social threat theories.

Moving away from the empirical tests of social threat theories that have focused on rates of police use of *deadly* force, Holmes (2000) examined how well social threat theories explained rates of police officers' use of *excessive* force. Data for his dependent variable came from the Department of Justice's (DOJ) Police Brutality Study (PBS), and measured the number of civilian complaints of police officers' use of excessive force that were reported to the DOJ between 1985 and 1990 (Holmes used the terms "police use of excessive force" and "police brutality" interchangeably). All cities with populations of 150,000 or larger that also had municipal police departments with at least two complaints of police use of excessive force annually were included in the study, for a total of 115 cities nationwide. Holmes' dependent variable was therefore the rate of civilian complaints of police use of excessive force per 100,000 individuals in the cities served by each municipal police department. In addition to the data from the PBS study, he also used census measures of city-level percent black, percent Hispanic, and racial income inequality (ratio of white to black and Hispanic median household incomes) to measure social threat.

Using the minority threat theory to guide him, Holmes then hypothesized that cities with larger black and Hispanic populations, and cities with higher levels of racial income inequality would have the highest rates of civilian complaints of police use of excessive force. Holmes tested his hypotheses using basic OLS regression analyses, and corrected for the non-normal distribution of his dependent variable through the use of Poisson estimation techniques. The results of his analyses revealed that that all three of his social threat measures were positively and significantly related to civilian complaints of police use of excessive force. Consequently, Holmes' study is the first to provide full support for social threat theories as explanations for non-lethal police use of force behaviors.

Unfortunately, though, Holmes was not able to distinguish between complaints made by members of minority groups and was therefore unable to determine whether or not the use of force by police was directed primarily at some groups in comparison to others (racial/ethnic and social class minorities vs. whites and social class majority members). Moreover, because his dependent variable relied on civilian reports of police use of force, he may have had measurement error problems in his dependent variable (resulting from civilian reporting bias) which could have affected his results.[4] Since Holmes did not account for the possibility of such problems, his results may subsequently be inaccurate. Nevertheless, because his results were generally consistent with the other tests of social threat theories that have already been reviewed here, it is unlikely that civilian reporting bias significantly affected Holmes' findings.

In another study examining police officers' use of excessive force, Smith and Holmes (2003) attempted to replicate Holmes' (2000) earlier findings using more sophisticated analytic techniques and an additional set of control variables. Like, Holmes' previous study, Smith and Holmes used the PBS and census data to create their dependent variable (rate of civilian complaints of police use of excessive force) and the same three social threat measures (city-level percent black, percent Hispanic, and racial income inequality). They also used the minority threat theory to propose the same

---

4   Civilian reports of police officers' use of excessive force are also utilized as measures of the dependent variable tested in this research, however, any potential measurement error in the dependent variable that might result from civilian reporting bias is held constant. For more details on how civilian reporting bias can be accounted for, see Chapter 5.

hypotheses that Holmes tested earlier. In this study, however, Smith and Holmes included a number of organizational control variables to help determine whether or not the manner in which police departments handled civilian complaints of police use of excessive force might have influenced the rates at which they received those complaints. Additionally, instead of conducting Poisson-based OLS regression analyses, this time the researchers conducted negative binomial regression analyses to correct for the over-dispersion of their dependent variable.

Despite the changes from Holmes' (2000) earlier study, Smith and Holmes more refined analysis yielded generally similar results. That is, like Holmes (2000), the researchers found that both the city-level measures of percent black and percent Hispanic were positively and significantly related to rates of civilian complaints of police use of excessive force, net of a variety of controls, including the organizational measures related to how police departments handled civilian complaints. Unlike Holmes' earlier findings, however, in their more controlled model, the researchers were unable to replicate a significant effect of racial income inequality on civilian complaints. According to the researchers, this difference between study results was most likely due to their more conservative (i.e., more controlled) approach in the later study. Despite this distinction, Smith and Holmes were once again able to provide at least partial support for social threat theories of police use of force. Questions remain, however, regarding the role of racial income inequality. Even so, Smith and Holmes' study improved on Holmes' (2000) earlier study by conducting a more conservative test and provides more aggregate-level evidence that social threat theories can not only explain police officers' use of deadly force, but other forms of police use of force as well.

INDIVIDUAL-LEVEL EVIDENCE

Although many of the more well-known social threat theories (e.g., conflict, racial/minority threat, and political threat theories) are aggregate-level explanations of police use of force, a number of studies have sought to test the framework using individual-level data. These studies typically argue that police officers' (and society in general) tend to take a more punitive view toward, and generally have more negative conscious or unconscious biases against, racial/ethnic minorities, just as social threat theories would expect.[5] Overall, the individual-level tests of the social threat theoretical framework have been just as supportive as the aggregate-level studies, especially when it comes to the effect of race/ethnicity.

---

5 As previously mentioned, because it is difficult to operationalize and measure social class based solely at the individual-level, most of the individual-level empirical tests of social threat theories focus primarily on the effect of suspects' racial/ethnic background.

Much of the individual-level support for social threat theories come from simulation studies in which researchers used computers to assess how civilians (i.e., individuals who had no affiliation with the police or any police training) reacted differently in their decisions to use force against whites in comparison to racial/ethnic minorities. Unfortunately, since most of this research has not directly assessed the use of force responses of actual police officers, the findings of these studies should be considered only suggestive in nature. Nevertheless, the individual-level social threat theories that are at the core of these simulation studies argue that many police officers (just like all individuals within our society) may be prone to what some researchers have called "racial response bias" (Correll et al. 2002). According to these researchers, the concept of "racial response bias" explains how cultural stereotypes related to the negative perception of racial/ethnic minorities can manifest as involuntary or unconscious reactions that, given recognition, time, and training, may be effectively mediated. In the case of having to make split-second decisions in response to potentially dangerous situations, however, researchers expect that racial response bias may cause both police officers and civilians alike to be more likely to use force against minorities than against whites.[6] Thus, even though some of the studies reviewed below do not examine actual police officers' use of force behaviors, they can shed light on how police officers *might* respond.

Much of the simulation research on race/ethnicity and the use of force has been conducted by Correll and colleagues (Correll et al. 2002; Correll et al. 2007; Correll et al. 2006). In their two earlier studies (Correll et al. 2002; Correll et al. 2006), Correll and colleagues drew samples of undergraduate students from the University of Colorado and paid them eight dollars or gave them partial course credit to participate in their study (approximately 40 students for each study). After gathering their respective samples, the researchers then had the students play simple computer video games that presented the students with images of armed or unarmed, white or black, individuals. In the games, the researchers instructed the students to act as if they were police officers and that they should push a "shoot" button if they thought that the individual in the game was armed with a gun. Alternatively, the students were instructed to push a "don't shoot" button if they thought that the individual was holding some other non-weapon item (e.g., a bottle, cell phone, or wallet).

---

6 Some might argue that some of the negative stereotypes about racial/ethnic minorities that persist in our culture may cause individuals to view them as being more dangerous. While such an argument might sound like it belongs in the *criminal* threat theories section discussed later in this chapter, racial response bias arguments are inherently social threat theories. Social threat theorists would argue that the powerful groups in our society have the ability to influence how the racial/ethnic minority groups that pose a threat to the status quo should be viewed by the public (i.e., they can help perpetuate, if not actually create, the negative stereotypes surrounding racial/ethnic minorities). Subsequently, if conscious or unconscious racial response bias does affect individuals' decisions to use force, such evidence would be supportive of social threat theoretical framework, rather than criminal threat one.

Based on the racial response bias argument discussed above, Correll and colleagues then hypothesized that the students in each study would be more likely to incorrectly choose to "shoot" at images of black individuals holding non-weapon items than images of white individuals holding non-weapon items, and that they would be more likely to correctly choose to "shoot" images of black individuals with guns than images of white individuals with guns.[7]

In both studies, Correll and colleagues (Correll et al. 2002; Correll et al. 2006) found support for their racial response bias hypotheses. Using simple analysis of variance (ANOVA) techniques in each study, they observed that, on average, students were more likely to make the correct decision to "shoot" armed blacks, but were also more likely to incorrectly decide to "shoot" unarmed blacks. While the results of these studies are compelling, because the researchers used a non-random sample of compensated civilians, it is difficult to generalize their results to how true, trained, police officers might behave in real world situations. Additionally, the researchers only looked at the mean differences between outcomes (i.e., armed vs. unarmed and black vs. white), instead of conducting multivariate analyses in which they could have accounted for the effects of a variety of control variables (e.g., student participants' demographic characteristics). Subsequently, while the findings of these two earlier studies by Correll and colleagues are supportive of social threat theories in a more general sense, they nonetheless have a number of significant limitations that make their findings less compelling.

Around the same time that Correll and colleagues began their simulation tests, Greenwald and colleagues (2003) began a very similar study in a different part of the country. Greenwald and colleagues recruited 160 University of Washington undergraduate students to take part in a "virtual-reality weapons task" computer game. Unfortunately, the researchers provided no other information on how they obtained their sample (i.e., what sampling strategy they used, whether participants received any compensation, etc.). They do describe their virtual-reality game in detail, however. Similar to how Correll and colleagues implemented their studies (Correll et al. 2002; Correll et al. 2006), students in Greenwald and colleagues' study were also instructed to act as if they were undercover police officers. The researchers then directed the student participants to push a "shoot" button as quickly as possible if the individual displayed in the game was dangerous (i.e., holding a gun). Unlike the Correll and colleagues' studies, however, students also had the option to push a "safety" button

---

7   Correll and colleagues' "racial response bias" hypotheses are consistent with social threat theories, in that the researchers expect that many individuals within our society (obviously including, but not limited to just to police officers and university students) have unconscious biases toward racial/ethnic minorities which make them more prone to perceive them negatively. As a result of this racial response bias, Correll and colleagues expected that racial/ethnic minorities should be more likely to experience all types of formal social control, including police officers' use of deadly force.

if the individual shown in the game was a fellow officer. Finally, the students were also instructed that they could to do nothing if the individual shown in the game was actually just a non-dangerous civilian (i.e., not holding a gun).

Using the same racial response bias argument made by Correll and colleagues (Correll et al. 2002; Correll et al. 2006), Greenwald and his colleagues then hypothesized that their sample of students would similarly be more likely to incorrectly choose to "shoot" unarmed black individuals than they would be to correctly shoot armed white individuals. Unfortunately, Greenwald and colleagues did not explicitly discuss their analytic strategy. Despite this, based on what appeared to be simple comparisons of the proportions of whites incorrectly shot vs. blacks incorrectly shot, the researchers concluded that that both white and black students were more likely to incorrectly choose to shoot unarmed black individuals in their game. If we are to accept Greenwald and colleagues' somewhat questionable methods and findings then, their study was largely successful in replicating the results obtained by the two earlier Correll and colleagues pieces. But, like those studies, Greenwald and colleagues' research suffers from a number of limitations as well, including their use of university students instead of actual police officers and their lack of discussion regarding how they obtained their sample and what analytic strategy they utilized. As a result, it is difficult to draw hard conclusions about what affect race has on actual, trained police officers' decisions to "use force" in real world situations.

Fortunately, the most recent simulation study by Correll and colleagues (Correll et al. 2007) addressed many of the limitations of not only Greenwald and colleagues' study (2003), but of their own earlier studies as well (Correll et al. 2002; Correll et al. 2006). For this piece, the researchers recruited both civilians *and* two separate groups of sworn police officers to participate in their computer simulation experiments. They randomly recruited 135 civilians to voluntarily participate in the study with the help of Colorado Department of Motor Vehicle (each participant was paid $20). Then, in addition to their civilian sample, Correll and colleagues also recruited 124 officers from the Denver Police Department and 113 officers from across the country who were in Denver for a training seminar to voluntarily participate (each officer was paid $50). All 372 civilian and police officer participants were then instructed on how to play the same computer game simulation that Correll and colleagues used in their previous studies (Correll et al. 2002; Correll et al. 2006).

Once again, based on the racial response bias argument, Correll and colleagues (2007) hypothesized that all participants (i.e., both civilians and the two groups of police officers) would be more likely to incorrectly choose to "shoot" images of non-threatening blacks than non-threatening whites. For this study, however, they also hypothesized that the two groups of police officers would be less likely to make mistakes for both images of threatening and non-threatening whites *and* blacks (i.e., incorrectly choose to "shoot" images of unarmed individuals or incorrectly choose "not to shoot" images of armed individuals).

After all their participants had completed the simulation, Correll and colleagues once again conducted simple ANOVA tests. This time, however, they also examined the correlations between their findings and three city-level contextual variables – the total population of the cities in which the participants lived, the rates of violent crime for those cities, and the black population size for each city. Based on their ANOVA analyses, Correll and colleagues found support for both of their hypotheses. That is, they found that both their civilian participants and the two groups of police officers were more likely to incorrectly choose to "shoot" non-threatening blacks than non-threatening whites. They also found that the police officers were less likely to make mistakes than were their civilian participants. Finally, based on their correlational analyses, Correll and colleagues concluded that the mean level of incorrect "shootings" of blacks was related to residence in larger cities, cities with higher violent crime rates, and cities with larger black populations.[8]

Through their examination of both civilians' and police officers' decisions to shoot in their computer simulation game, as well as their correlational analysis of city-level context, Correll and colleagues most recent study provides relatively stronger support for a social threat theoretical framework than their two previous studies. In spite of their improvements, however, their study could still be improved methodologically by drawing random samples of police officer participants to reduce the potential for selection effects (i.e., certain types of police officers being more willing to participate in studies on the use of force). Additionally, by conducting multivariate regression analyses, instead of simple correlational analyses, Correll and colleagues might have more accurately determined how all participants' decision to "shoot" might have been influenced not only by race, but by a host of other control factors as well. Notwithstanding all of the methodological shortcomings of each of the simulation studies reviewed here, such studies provide some compelling, albeit suggestive only, support for racial/ethnic component of social threat theories of police use of force.

Other than the simulation studies reviewed above, there has been only one other individual-level, theory-driven, study of police use of force that has provided support for social threat theories in the past 20 years. Worden (1996) conducted a police officer-civilian encounter-based analysis of police officers' use of excessive force. He utilized systematic observational data of police-civilian encounters from the 1977 Police Services Study (PSS). In the PSS, trained observers accompanied police officers on 900 patrol shifts across 24 police departments in three metropolitan areas (Rochester, New

---

8   Correll and colleagues' research therefore also supports criminal threat theories. For more details on how criminal threat theories applied to this study, see the review in the next section of this chapter.

York, St. Louis, Missouri, and the Tampa-St. Petersburg, Florida, area). During those 900 shifts, observers recorded 5,688 police officer-civilian encounters, of which police officers used excessive force in approximately 74 times (1.3% of all encounters). Then, based on Black's theory of law (Black 1976)[9], Worden hypothesized that racial/ethnic minorities would be more likely to experience excessive use of force by the police.

After conducting both bivariate and multivariate logistic regression analyses, Worden determined that black civilians had greater odds of experiencing the use of excessive force by the police than whites, net of a number of controls, including civilians' mental condition (i.e., signs of inebriation or mental illness), the carrying of a weapon, physically resisting police directions, and having a negative demeanor toward the officers. Based on these results, he concluded that "officers are, on average, more likely to adopt a punitive or coercive approach to black suspects than they are to white suspects" (37), thereby supporting the arguments made by social threat theorists. In addition to a more rigorous methodological approach, Worden was the first researcher to demonstrate that actual police officers were more likely to use force on racial/ethnic minorities in real-life encounters (in comparison to the computer simulation studies reviewed above). Subsequently, Worden's research provides relatively stronger and much more internally and externally valid support for the social threat theoretical framework at the individual-level.

The last empirical test of an individual-level social threat theory reviewed here is the only theory-driven study in the last twenty years to find no relationship between race and police use of force. A few years before the simulation studies reviewed earlier became popular, Dwyer and colleagues (Dwyer et al. 1990) conducted a simple analysis of 60 crime scene vignettes to assess how police officers responded to a variety of individual and situational characteristics, including suspect's race/ethnicity. They enlisted 142 officers from the Shelby County Sheriff's Office (Memphis, Tennessee) to voluntarily participate in their study (officers received no compensation). Each officer was given a booklet with 60 crime scene vignettes and was asked to decide whether they would 1) not draw their weapon, 2) draw, but not aim or fire their weapon, 3) draw and aim their weapon, but not fire it, or 4) draw their weapon, aim it, and shoot the

---

9   Briefly, while Black's theory of law (1976) can most certainly be categorized as a social threat theory, the fit might not be as readily apparent to some. Instead of explaining which groups within a society should receive the most formal social control efforts due to their potential threat to the societal status hierarchy like most social threat theories, Black's theory seeks to explain why those same groups have less capacity to get the law to work in their favor (e.g., obtaining justice against police officers who use excessive force) than majority groups. Then, as a result of their being less able to have the law work toward their advantage, some groups effectively become more suitable targets for police abuses of force. However, because Black argues that it is primarily racial/ethnic minorities and lower social class individuals (he also mentions women) who have the least amount of access to the law, for by and large the same reasons that other social threat theories describe – it is those groups that represent the greatest threat to the status quo – his theory no doubt belongs right alongside each of the other theories/hypotheses discussed in this section.

suspect in the vignette. Across the vignettes a number of factors were manipulated, including the suspect's race (white vs. non-white). Based on what they referred to as "social script theory" (similar to the racial response bias argument made by Correll and colleagues [Correll et al. 2002; Correll et al. 2006; Correll et al. 2007]), Dwyer and colleagues hypothesized that the officers would be more likely to choose to shoot black suspects because of negative social scripts typically associated with racial/ethnic minorities in our society (1990).

In order to test their hypotheses, Dwyer and colleagues conducted multivariate OLS regression analyses. Quite unexpectedly to the researchers, they found that suspects' race *was not* related to officers' decisions to "shoot their weapon," even at a relaxed level of significance ($p > 0.25$). Unlike the simulation studies reviewed earlier, Dwyer and colleagues therefore concluded that police officers were no more likely to use force on non-whites than on whites. Unfortunately, however, due to the nature of their method, it is unlikely that the researchers were truly able to assess any automatic (subconscious) biases that might have affected the officers' decisions to shoot. That is, since the participants were able to take their time to choose their response—rather than being required to respond quickly to a computer simulation—the officers could have simply given the response they thought was more socially desirable or politically correct (i.e., making the decision regardless of race). So, where the simulation studies were specifically designed by psychologists to assess subconscious bias against racial/ethnic minorities, it is highly unlikely that Dwyer and colleagues' method was able to do the same, given the circumstances of their study. Consequently, as theirs was the only theory-driven test of social threat theories to find no significant relationship between race and police officers' decisions to use force, the viability of a social threat theoretical framework should not seriously be called into question.

Overall, based on the aggregate- and individual-level empirical tests reviewed above, the social threat theoretical framework appears to be an adequate, if not strong, explanation for all forms of police use of force. Table 13.1, presented at the end of this chapter, displays condensed summaries of each of the studies reviewed here. Reported in the table are the specific aggregate- and individual-level theories or hypotheses that were tested, the data and methods that were used (when reported), and the major findings of each study. In general, as most of the aggregate-level tests revealed, measures of race/ethnicity appear to be much better predictors of rates of police use of force than are measures of social class (i.e. income inequality). An interesting consequence of these findings is the need for research on *why* threats from lower social class groups are not met with as much police use of force as threats from racial/ethnic minorities. Have changes in the economic structure of the U.S. affected how the level of threat presented by lower social class groups is perceived by the powerful elites? Or, perhaps, the demographic composition of the U.S. has changed enough to make racial/ethnic minority groups even more threatening (the U.S. Census Bureau recently announced that the U.S. will become a "majority minority" nation by 2050 [U.S. Census Bureau 2008])? Future research that examines how the powerful groups in our society perceive threat may help us answer such questions.

In addition to the finding that lower social class groups may not present as much of a social threat as once thought, the general consensus of the studies reviewed above was that blacks are much more likely to be the recipients of police use of force, not only compared to whites, but also compared to other racial/ethnic minorities. Thus, based on both the aggregate- and individual-level research, it appears that blacks are perceived to present the greatest social threat to the powerful groups in our society. However, with the recent increases in the U.S. Hispanic population, it should be interesting to learn whether or not Hispanics begin, or already have begun, experiencing similarly high levels of police use of force. Is there a threshold at which the relative size of a racial/ethnic minority group begins to present enough of a social threat that the group's members also begin to experience more formal social control? In order to determine if such a threshold exists, future research should continue to examine how different racial/ethnic minorities differentially experience police use of force. Regardless of what future research may show, however, social threat theories of police use of force have, to date, received empirical support at both the aggregate- and individual-levels.

CRIMINAL THREAT THEORIES

Criminal threat theories generally contend that police officers use force in response to threatening individuals, situations, and environments (or what they *perceive* to be threatening). So, rather than viewing police use of force as an tool for controlling groups or individuals who pose a social threat to the powerful groups in our society, criminal threat theories posit that police officers will use force on anyone, powerful or powerless, that poses a criminal threat (i.e., a threat of physical harm) to their own safety, the safety of their fellow officers, or the safety of the general public. Among the theories and hypotheses included under the broader heading of the criminal threat theoretical framework are the danger perception theory (Fyfe 1980; MacDonald, Kaminski, Alpert, and Tennenbaum 2001; MacDonald, Alpert, and Tennenbaum 1999; Sherman and Langworthy 1979), community threat or community violence theories (Holmes, Reynolds, Holmes, and Faulkner 1998; Kania and Mackey 1977; Sorenson et al. 1993), and what have been generally referred to as threatening acts hypotheses (Holmes 2000; Liska and Yu 1992; Smith and Holmes 2003; Worden 1996).

MacDonald and colleagues (2001) best described the general criminal threat argument by describing not only how real, physical, and immediate threats were related to police officers' use of force, but also how *perceived* threats might also influence officers' use of force. They asserted that "the level of police use of deadly force is contingent on the danger police officers experience (real or perceived) ... [and that] police officers are more likely to use deadly force during time periods when (or in places where) they encounter greater levels of violence or *view their jobs as being particularly hazardous*" (159, emphasis added). And, even though MacDonald and his colleagues were referring specifically to deadly forms of police force, the danger-perception theory they used, and criminal threat theories in general, all contend that police officers should be more likely to use all types of force (legitimate and illegitimate, lethal and non-lethal) when they receive direct threats to their own safety (e.g., when dealing with an armed criminal suspect), or when they perceive a potential threat to their, or someone else's, safety (e.g., when working in an area with high levels of criminal activity).

EMPIRICAL TESTS OF CRIMINAL THREAT THEORIES

Empirical tests of criminal threat theories have used a variety of measures that assess criminal activity at the aggregate-level, and criminal dangerousness at the individual-level. Among the aggregate-level measures that are most commonly used in the literature are rates of public violence (i.e., riots and violent protests), rates of homicides or other crimes, and even rates of arrest. At the individual-level, criminal threat measures often include individuals' aggressive and violent behaviors toward police officers (i.e., resisting arrest or physically assaulting an officer), the presence and/or displaying of a weapon, and the individual's mental state (i.e., being mental ill or being under the influence of a controlled substance). Using these measures, criminal threat theorists expect that both aggregate-level rates of criminal activity and individual-level measures of dangerousness should be positively related to police use of force behaviors. Not surprisingly, the majority of researchers who have conducted empirical tests of criminal threat theories have found just that.

Historically (again referring to those studies conducted more than 20 years ago), aggregate-level research has consistently shown that areas with high rates of criminal activity also tend to have high rates of police use of force (e.g., Binder and Scharf 1982; Fyfe 1980; Jacobs and Britt 1979; Kania and Mackey 1977; Sherman and Langworthy 1979; Sherman 1986). Similarly, individual-level tests have found that police officers who dealt with more real or perceived criminals, violence, and dangerous crimes in general were significantly more likely to use force (e.g., Binder and Fridell 1984; Binder and Scharf 1982; Copeland 1986; Horvath 1987). Traditionally, then, there has strong support for criminal threat theories of police officers' use of force. More recent empirical tests have been just as consistently supportive.

AGGREGATE-LEVEL EVIDENCE

MacDonald and colleagues (MacDonald et al. 1999) were the first researchers to consider how aggregate-level rates of crime temporally corresponded with rates of police use of force. In particular, they examined how high rates of homicide across the nation covaried with high rates of police use of deadly force over time. They used national homicide data from the FBI's SHR for every month between the years 1976 and 1986 to conduct their study. Based on the danger perception theory, they created a "reactive hypothesis" which argued that increases in rates of certain types of homicides would cause police to perceive higher levels of danger in their jobs, which would subsequently lead to higher rates of police officers' use of deadly force in the same month that the homicide rates spiked. Specifically, they believed that police officers would be most likely to react with deadly force when rates of robbery-related and justifiable civilian homicides (i.e., when a civilian uses deadly force to protect him or herself or loved ones) were high because the circumstances of those types of homicides are also strong indicators of potentially dangerous situations to which police officers might have to respond.

In order to test their hypotheses, MacDonald and colleagues conducted an autoregressive integrated moving average (ARIMA) time series analysis that allowed them to control for the high level of temporal autocorrelation across their 132 months of homicide data. The results of their analyses revealed that during months in which both the rates of robbery-related and justifiable civilian homicides were high, the rates of police officers' use of deadly force were also high. Subsequently, the researchers concluded that "the incidence of police use of deadly force closely follow[ed] the dangerousness of particular time periods" (162). Such evidence strongly supports the criminal threat theoretical framework. Unfortunately, however, while MacDonald and colleagues' research was methodologically sound, they failed to include any potentially confounding measures in their ARIMA models to control for the possibility of an alternative explanation(s) for their results. So, even though MacDonald and colleagues were able to demonstrate a strong temporal relationship between crime rates and police officers' use of deadly force, even they acknowledged that further research was necessary that included not only a variety of covariate control measures, but research that also attempted to predict forms of police behaviors other than the use of deadly force.

In a follow-up to their earlier study, MacDonald and colleagues (2001) reexamined how national homicide rates affected rates of police use of deadly force over time.

This time, however, they expanded the time frame of their analysis to include 21 years (1976 – 1996), and conducted additional stationarity tests to make sure that their findings were as reliable as possible. Monthly homicide data, including their dependent variable (police officers' use of deadly force) once again came from the FBI's SHR. As with their earlier study, they employed the danger-perception theory to propose another "reactive hypothesis," in which they argued that increases in robbery-related and justifiable civilian homicides would be related to increases in police officers' use of excessive force.

In an effort to increase the reliability of their estimates this time around, MacDonald and colleagues not only conducted another set of ARIMA time series analyses, they also conducted several stationarity tests. These stationarity tests allowed them to determine whether the processes driving the temporal relationships between their homicide rate measures and police use of deadly force measure were invariant over time (i.e., stationary), or if those processes changed over time (i.e., non-stationary). Had their tests revealed that the relationships were non-stationary, MacDonald and colleagues would be unable to definitively conclude that some other unmeasured temporal covariate had not influenced both their independent and dependent measures (i.e., the relationships were spurious). Fortunately, the results of their stationarity tests indicated that the relationships they observed were indeed stationary over time, lending added support to their substantive findings. And, as they had observed in their earlier study, MacDonald and colleagues once again found that periods of time which had higher rates of robbery-related and justifiable civilian homicides also tended to have higher rates of police use of deadly force.

As a result of the two separate studies described above, MacDonald and colleagues provided some of the strongest support for the criminal threat theoretical framework. Moreover, in their more recent study (MacDonald et al. 2001), because the researchers were also able to improve their methodology, they were able to obtain more reliable findings as well. Unfortunately, however, while their stationarity tests revealed that the relationship that they had observed was not spurious, they still failed to include any other covariates in their models to control for alternative explanations of changes in police use of deadly force over time. Furthermore, because both of the studies by MacDonald and colleagues focused exclusively on police officers' use of deadly force, the propensity of criminal threat theories for explaining non-lethal police use of force is still unclear.

Fortunately, other research has shown that criminal threat measures are capable of not only explaining other, non-lethal forms of police use of force, but that they are also robust to the inclusion of a variety of control variables. In another recent study in which MacDonald also took part, Alpert and MacDonald (2001) found that violent crime rates positively and significantly predicted police officers' use of all types of force (i.e., both lethal and non-lethal). Data for the researchers' study came from an unidentified national PERF survey of law enforcement agencies that took place in 1998. A total of 265 agencies provided official data on police use of force incidents during the 1996 calendar year, which Alpert and MacDonald then used to calculate rates of police use of force per 100,000 individuals in the areas served by each agency. The violent crime rates for those areas served as the primary measure of aggregate-level criminal threat. Based on a general criminal threat argument (they cited both the "reactive hypothesis" utilized in MacDonald and colleagues' earlier studies [1999; 2001] and the "community violence hypothesis" that other researchers have used [e.g., Sorensen et al. 1993]), Alpert and MacDonald hypothesized that areas with high rates of violent crime would also have high rates of police use of *all types* of force.

To test their hypothesis, Alpert and MacDonald (2001) conducted basic bivariate and multivariate OLS regression analyses. In order to account for the skewed distribution of their police use of force dependent variable (toward zero), they calculated its natural log for use in their analyses (see Jacobs and O'Brien [1998] for precedent). The results of their bivariate analyses revealed that increases in the rates of violent crime were strongly associated with increases in police use of all types of physical force. Alpert and MacDonald then also found that their violent crime rate measure was the strongest predictor of police use of force of all the covariates included in their multivariate analysis. Subsequently, as a result of their focus of all forms of police use of force, and due to their inclusion of a variety of control measures, Alpert and MacDonald's results are not only more generalizable and robust than MacDonald's previous research, they also provide even more evidence in support of a criminal threat theoretical framework of police use of force.

In addition to the research conducted by the above researchers, the inherent logic of criminal threat theories has not escaped those who fall under the banner of "social threat theorists." As such, many of the theory-driven empirical tests of criminal threat theories at both the aggregate- and individual-levels have also included at least one measure of criminal threat. It should therefore be unsurprising that all five of the aggregate-level social threat studies that were reviewed above included measures of criminal threat and accordingly proposed and tested a variety of criminal threat theories as well (Holmes 2000; Jacobs and O'Brien 1998; Liska and Yu; Smith and Holmes 2003; Sorensen et al. 1993). To conserve space, those studies are not reviewed again in specific detail. Instead, only the researchers' measure(s) of criminal threat, the specific criminal threat theories guiding their hypotheses, and their findings as they relate to the broader criminal threat theoretical framework are reviewed below.

Jacobs and O'Brien (1998) used city-level rates of homicides obtained from the FBI's UCR as their measure of criminal threat in order to test the same "reactive hypothesis" that MacDonald and colleagues (1999; 2001) utilized. Specifically, they hypothesized that the rates of homicides in cities across the nation would be positively related to rates of police use of deadly force (FBI's SHR). The results of their Tobit analyses revealed that homicide rates indeed predicted police officers' use of deadly force, net of the social threat measures that they had also found to be related to rates of police use of deadly force. Consequently, because their study was one of the more methodologically sound empirical analyses of police officers' use of force, Jacobs and O'Brien's findings not only provide very strong evidence in support of social threat theories, but very strong in support of criminal threat theories as well.

Sorensen and colleagues' (1993) used city-level violent crime rates (i.e., rates of homicide, rape, robbery, and aggravated assault) obtained from the FBI's UCR to test what they referred to as the "community violence" hypothesis. They expected that increases in violent crime rates would increase the level of dangerousness perceived by police officers, which in turn would result in increased rates of police use of deadly force (FBI's SHR). The results of Sorensen and colleagues' OLS regression analyses revealed that rates of violent crime significantly predicted rates of police officers' use of deadly force, net of their social threat measures, just as Jacobs and O'Brien (1998) had observed. Furthermore, they found that city-level violent crime rates were the strongest predictors of police use of deadly force in each of their models. Thus, even though Sorensen and colleagues' study was not as methodologically sound as Jacobs and O'Brien's study (see review above), it does provide some additional support for the criminal threat theoretical framework of police use of force.

Like their counterparts, Liska and Yu (1992) found support for criminal threat theories as well. They utilized three measures of criminal threat, all of which were obtained from the FBI's UCR: 1) the overall rate of all Index I crimes (homicide/non-negligent manslaughter, rape, robbery, aggravated assault, larceny, burglary, automobile theft, and arson), 2) the rates of violent crimes only (the first four index crimes listed previously), and 3) the rates of homicides on their own. Based on what the researchers referred to as "the threatening acts theory," they hypothesized that all three measures would be positively related to rates of police use of deadly force (FBI's SHR).

The results of Liska and Yu's structural-measurement models revealed that homicide rates on their own were the only significantly predictors of police use of deadly force, but that it had one of the strongest effects. However, because the researchers included three crime rate measures simultaneously, it is not be surprising that the one measure of criminal threat that is the most likely to be perceived as especially dangerous to police officers (i.e., the homicide rate) was also the only measure to significantly predict rates of their use of deadly force. Thus, like the two previous studies of police use of deadly force (Jacobs and O'Brien 1998; Sorensen et al. 1993), Liska and Yu's research provides further support for criminal threat theories.

The final two aggregate studies from the past 20 years that empirically tested both social threat and criminal threat theories were Holmes' (2000) and Smith and Holmes' (2003) examinations of civilian complaints of police use of excessive force. Because the latter study was a replication of the former, and because they utilized the same criminal threat measures to obtain the same results, they are reviewed in concert. For each study, the researchers followed Liska and Yu's (1992) lead and used the same Index I crime rate measure (FBI's UCR) and the same "threatening acts theory" as the basis for their research.

Unexpectedly, however, the researchers found no significant relationship between the Index I crime rates and civilian complaints of police use of excessive force in either study. Given Liska and Yu's (1992) earlier findings, one possible explanation for the researchers' null findings becomes apparent. While Liska and Yu found that overall Index I crime rates were not significantly related to police officers' use of deadly force, they did find that homicide rates alone significantly predicted variation in their outcome variable. Subsequently, it appears that homicide rates on their own (i.e., not when combined with other types of crime rates) are the best predictors of police officers perceptions of criminal threat. Despite their null findings then, the two pieces by Holmes (2000) and Smith and Holmes (2003) help to shed light on just how police officers perceive criminal threats differently for different types of crime. Overall then, the aggregate-level evidence in support of a criminal threat theoretical framework of police use of force is still quite strong.

INDIVIDUAL-LEVEL EVIDENCE

Individual-level criminal threat theories generally contend that police officers will be more likely to use any and all types of force when they perceive a direct threat of physical harm against their own well-being or the well-being of others (i.e., fellow police officers or civilian bystanders). Accordingly, rather than studying how rates of crime influence rates of police use of force, individual-level tests of the criminal threat theoretical framework typically examine how police officers use force during specific encounters with criminals or other potentially dangerous individuals (i.e., mentally unstable individuals or those under the influence of controlled substances).

Holmes, Reynolds, Holmes, and Faulkner (1998) examined a number of factors that might influence how police officers perceive criminal threat. While the researchers did not attempt empirically test any predictors of actual police use of force behaviors, Holmes and colleagues' research helps shed light on the aspects of a police officer-civilian/criminal encounter that may lead police officers to perceive a threat and then use force to either prevent the escalation of the situation or to gain control of the situation once it has already become dangerous. In order to determine what aspects of an encounter might lead police officers to use force, the researchers there-fore conducted a survey of 662 sworn police officers from the London, Ohio, police training academy. In the survey, police cadets were presented with a number of fic-tional vignettes describing a variety of potentially threatening scenarios. Holmes and colleagues then asked the officers to decide whether the circumstances described in each vignette were threatening enough to necessitate the use of force. Based on what they called a "threat presentation" hypothesis, the researchers expected that officers would be more likely to perceive a threat which necessitated the use of force when the characters in the vignette were 1) mentally or emotionally unstable, 2) suspected of committing a serious crime, or 3) physically resisting arrest.

Unfortunately, Holmes and colleagues (1998) do not clearly specify the analytic technique they used to test their hypotheses, but based on the presentation of their results, it appears that they conducted a number of multivariate OLS regression anal-yses. Whatever their actual analytic strategy, the researchers found that the scenarios in which the fictional characters resisted arrest were the most likely to lead officers to perceive a threat serious enough for them to use force. Scenarios in which the characters had committed a more serious crime also caused officers to perceive enough threat to use force. Surprisingly, however, in the scenarios where the officers encountered mentally or emotionally unstable individuals, the officers reported that there was not a strong or immediate enough of a threat that they felt the need to use force. Overall, Holmes and colleagues' research provides some initial support for a criminal threat theoretical framework for explaining police use of force, but because they do not examine police officers' actual use of force behaviors (and, to a lesser extent, because their methods are unclear), no definitive conclusions can, or should, be drawn based upon their findings.

Somewhat surprisingly, Holmes and colleagues' study was the only individual-level research in the last twenty years that exclusively tested a criminal threat theory. Rather, nearly all of the empirical tests of individual-level criminal threat theories are found in the studies testing the social threat theoretical framework reviewed above. To con-serve space once again, the data and methods of those studies are not reviewed in detail. Instead, only the researchers' measure(s) of criminal threat, the specific criminal threat theories guiding their hypotheses, and their findings as they relate to support for criminal threat theories are reviewed below.

In each of the four simulation studies reviewed earlier in this chapter (Correll et al. 2002; Correll et al. 2006; Correll et al. 2007; Greenwald et al. 2003), the researchers presented their participants with images not only of individuals of different racial/ ethnic backgrounds, but also images of individuals with either weapons or some other non-weapon items in their hands (e.g., bottles, cell-phones, wallets, etc.). Based on the threatening acts theory, the researchers all hypothesized that their participants (both civilians and police officers) would be more likely to correctly and more quickly choose to "shoot" images of individuals holding weapons in comparison to individuals holding the other non-weapon items. Not surprisingly, the researchers each independently observed that their civilian participants were more likely to make more correct decisions faster when they were presented with images of individuals holding weapons (Correll et al. 2002; Correll et al. 2006; Greenwald et al. 2003), although police officers responded more quickly and were correct more often in comparison to their civilian counterparts (Correll et al. 2007). Subsequently, the results of all four simulation studies are strongly supportive of not only the social threat theoretical framework, but criminal threat framework as well.

The only other empirical test of both social threat and criminal threat theories over the past 20 years was Worden's (1996) study of police officers' use of excessive force. Unlike the studies reviewed above, Worden utilized systematic observational data from the PSS. He was subsequently able to test how criminal suspects' *actual behaviors* influenced police officers' use of force (as compared to the behaviors of the digitized "suspects" used in the simulation studies above). Once again employing the threatening acts theory used by other researchers, Worden hypothesized that suspects who physically resisted arrest, or who tried to attack officers, would have greater odds of having excessive levels of force used against them. As expected, the results of his logistic regression analyses revealed that those suspects whose actions toward police officers were threatening (i.e., who resisted or tried to attack) had greater odds of experiencing police use of excessive force, net of a variety of other control measures, including all of the social threat measures described earlier in this chapter. As a result, Worden's study helps to substantiate the findings of the simulation studies reviewed above, and provides more evidence that criminal threat at the individual-level is indeed a strong explanation of police officers' use of force.

All together, the aggregate- and individual-level empirical tests reviewed above strongly suggest that the criminal threat theoretical framework is not only a viable explanation for police officers' use of force, but a very powerful one as well. Table 13.1 below presents brief summaries of each of the studies reviewed above that empirically tested a criminal threat theory. Again, for each study, the table displays the specific criminal threat theory that drove the researchers' analyses, the data and methods that were utilized (when reported), and the most important findings that were observed. In general, however, there are three broad conclusions that can be drawn from the criminal threat literature as a whole.

First, in many of the studies that tested both social threat and criminal theories, the measures of criminal threat were usually the strongest predictors of the various measures of police officers' use of force. Although a couple studies found no significant effects of criminal threat measures when controlling for social threat measures

Table 13.1. Theory-Driven Studies of Police Use of Force During the Last 20 Years

Aggregate-Level Studies

Author(s)	Data	Method(s)	Specific Theory Tested	Significant Findings
Alpert & Mac-Donald (2001)	Unidentified Police Executive Research Forum Study	OLS Regression	Reactive/Community Violence (CT)	Violent Crime Rate → (+) **Rates of Police Use of Force**
Holmes (2000)	Police Brutality Study; U.S. Census Report; Uniform Crime Report	Poisson-Based OLS Regression	Minority Threat (ST); Threatening Acts (CT)	Percent Black → (+) Percent Hispanic → (+) Racial Income Inequality → (+) **Rates of Police Use of Excessive Force**
Jacobs & O'Brien (1998)	Supplementary Homicides Report; U.S. Census Report; Uniform Crime Report	Tobit Regression	Political Threat (ST); Reactive (CT)	Racial Income Inequality → (+) Percent Black → (+) Homicide Rates → (+) **Rates of Police Use of Deadly Force**
Liska & Yu (1992)	Vital Statistics; U.S. Census Report; Uniform Crime Report	Structural Measurement Models	Threat (ST); Threatening Acts (CT)	Percent Non-White → (+) Racial Segregation → (+) Homicide Rate → (+) **Rates of Police Use of Deadly Force**
MacDonald, Alpert, & Tennenbaum (1999)	Supplementary Homicides Report	Autoregressive Integrated Moving Average Time Series	Danger Perception (CT)	Robbery-Related Homicide Rate → (+) Justifiable Civilian Homicide Rate → (+) **Rates of Police Use of Deadly Force**
MacDonald, Kaminski, Alpert, & Tennenbaum (2001)	Supplementary Homicides Report	Autoregressive Integrated Moving Average Time Series; Stationarity Tests	Danger Perception (CT)	Robbery-Related Homicide Rate → (+) Justifiable Civilian Homicide Rate → (+) **Rates of Police Use of Deadly Force**
Smith & Holmes (2003)	Police Brutality Study; U.S. Census Report; Uniform Crime Report	Negative Binomial Regression	Minority Threat (ST); Threatening Acts (CT)	Percent Black → (+) Percent Hispanic → (+) **Rates of Police Use of Excessive Force**
Sorensen, Marquart, and Brock (1993)	Supplementary Homicides Report; U.S. Census Report; Uniform Crime Report	OLS Regression	Conflict (ST); Community Violence (CT)	Percent Black → (+) Percent in Poverty → (+) Income Inequality → (+) Violent Crime Rate → (+) **Rates of Police Use of Deadly Force**

Notes: CT = Criminal Threat; ST = Social Threat

Table 13.1. Theory-Driven Studies of Police Use of Force During the Last 20 Years (*Continued*)

Individual-Level Studies

Author(s)	Data	Method(s)	Specific Theory Tested	Significant Findings
Correll, Park, Judd, & Wittenbrink (2002)	University of Colorado	Analysis of Variance	Racial Response Bias (ST); Threatening Acts (CT)	Black Suspect → (+) Presence of a Weapon → (+) **Decision to Use Deadly Force**
Correll, Park, Judd, Wittenbrink, Sadler, and Keesee (2007)	Denver (Colorado) Department of Motor Vehicles; Denver Police Department; Denver Police Training Seminar	Analysis of Variance; Correlational	Racial Response Bias (ST); Threatening Acts (CT)	Black Suspect → (+) Presence of a Weapon → (+) **Decision to Use Deadly Force**
Correll, Urland, & Ito (2006)	University of Colorado	Analysis of Variance	Racial Response Bias (ST); Threatening Acts (CT)	Black Suspect → (+) Presence of a Weapon → (+) **Decision to Use Deadly Force**
Dwyer, Graesser, Hopkinson, & Lupfer (1990)	Shelby County (Tennessee) Sheriff's Office	OLS Regression	Social Script (ST)	No Significant Results
Greenwald, Oakes, & Hoffman (2003)	University of Washington	Unidentified	Racial Response Bias (ST); Threatening Acts (CT)	Black Suspect → (+) **Decision to Use Force**
Holmes, Reynolds, Holmes, & Faulkner (1998)	London (Ohio) Police Department	Unidentified	Threat Presentation (CT)	Physical Resistance → (+) Seriousness of Offense → (+) **Police Decision to Use Force**
Worden (1996)	Police Services Study	Logistic Regression	Black's Theory of Law (ST); Threatening Acts (CT)	Black Suspect → (+) Physical Resistance → (+) Assault Officer → (+) **Police Use of Excessive Force**

Notes: CT = Criminal Threat; ST = Social Threat

(Holmes 2000; Smith and Holmes 2003), the majority of researchers found that their measures of criminal threat predicted police officers' use of force better than their measures of social threat. Upon further consideration, however, this general finding should not be surprising given that criminal threats are more likely to have an immediate and potentially dangerous impact on police officers' well-being than are social threats, which may not directly affect police officers at all. Furthermore, police officers are legally justified to use of force when they (or others) are physically threatened (i.e., presented with a criminal threat), but are not legally justified to use force when they (or others) are threatened socially.

Given these considerations, future research should therefore continue to simultaneously test both theoretical frameworks to further disentangle the direct and indirect relationships between social threat measures, criminal threat measures, and police officers' use of force. For example, does the social threat that racial/ethnic minorities present lead to them be viewed as more of a criminal threat as well? Do any other behavioral (e.g., disrespect, verbal resistance, fleeing, etc.) factors influence police officers' perceptions of criminal threat? What about other factors not related to an individual's behavior (e.g., age, gender, appearance, etc.)? Answers to such questions may help us better understand the processes which lead police officers to use force.

Second, based on some of the aggregate-level studies reviewed above, it appears that homicide rates may be much better indicators of criminal threat than other rates of crime. This suggests that police officers are most likely to use force when they perceive more serious or significant criminal threats. Future research should therefore explore how the threat associated with different types of crimes influence police officers' use of force behaviors. If the overall homicide rate truly is the best predictor of police use of force because it leads officers to be more concerned about their own well-being, what effect might rates of assaults on police officers, or rates of homicides of police officers, have on their use of force behavior? In areas where rates of assaults and homicides of police officers are high, will officers be more likely to use force to preempt more attacks? Will they use more force in retaliation against the attacks on their fellow officers? Future research should consider these questions so that we may better understand how police officers' perceive and respond to different kinds of criminal threats.

Finally, while a number of the aggregate-level tests of the criminal threat theoretical framework have demonstrated that crime rates can influence rates of police use of force, the majority of the theory-driven research at the individual-level has come from simulation studies. It is important to note that there have also been a number of non-theory-driven studies at the individual- or encounter-level that have nonetheless included typical measures of criminal threat (e.g., resisting arrest and assaulting officers) that find that police officers are more likely to use force when threatened (e.g.,

Garner et al. 2002). Unfortunately, in those studies, the researchers simply included as many variables in their analyses as they had available to them, with no theoretical expectations for what they might observe. Consequently, it is difficult to interpret their results in terms of theory. More individual-level, theory-driven, empirical tests of criminal threat theories that utilize other forms of data (i.e., other than simulation and observational studies) are needed to determine exactly how and why police officers respond to criminal threats in the ways that they do.

KLINGER'S ECOLOGICAL THEORY OF POLICE VIGOR

Klinger's (1997) ecological theory of police vigor is the only new theory of police behavior that has been proposed in recent years. While his theory was not specifically intended to explain police use of force, based on the theoretical arguments he makes, it would be relatively easy to empirically determine whether or not his theory constitutes a third viable theoretical explanation of police use of force. In this section, Klinger's theory is reviewed and discussed in regards to how it might be adapted to explain police use of force behaviors.

In 1997, Klinger proposed his "ecological theory of police response to deviance." His primary argument in this theory was that the amount of vigor police officers used to do their jobs should be related to the ecological contexts in which they work. In other words, he believed that the environments that police officers worked in on a day-to-day basis might influence the amount of energy, effort, or desire that officers put into completing their duties. Specifically, he contended that four problems affecting police vigor would arise as a result of police officers working in high crime areas: 1) an increased tolerance for deviant and criminal behavior, 2) decreased perceptions of crime victims' deservingness, 3) increased levels of cynicism toward the value of their crime-fighting efforts, and 4) the increased size of their workloads. Each problem is discussed in more detail below.

First, Klinger argued that officers would put less vigor into the execution of their duties when they believed that the residents within their patrol beats were tolerant, if not accepting, of deviant and criminal behaviors. Essentially, he believed that after working in areas where residents had become desensitized to deviance and/or crime, police officers might also become desensitized such behaviors and consequently use less vigor responding to, or attempting to prevent, said problems since they no longer considered those behaviors to be as serious as an objective outsider might.

For example, if an officer worked in an area where prostitution and drug dealing were tolerated, if not accepted by residents, Klinger argued that police officers might also become tolerant of those behaviors and, as a result, put less effort into enforcing the laws regulating those criminal behaviors. Thus, in high crime areas, police officers might use less vigor because they no longer view certain deviant or criminal behaviors as being unworthy of their time and energy.

Second, Klinger contended that police officers may also use less vigor when they perceive the victims of criminal offenses to be undeserving of their attention or efforts. Specifically, he argued that in areas with high levels of crime, police officers might often deal with crime victims who had helped precipitate their own victimization. For example, if officers responded to a lot of calls where an individual was assaulted or robbed while he or she was under the influence of some illicit substance, Klinger believed that those officers might then start blaming the victim for bringing about their own victimization. That is, if the victim had not been under the influence of an illegal substance in the first place, they would not have been an easier target for being assaulted or robbed in the first place. So, because some victims may help to create the environment that leads to their victimization, Klinger believed that some officers might be less sympathetic to those victims' plights. Subsequently, if police officers were forced to handle a large number of incidents in which the crime victim was not wholly without fault, then Klinger argued that police officers would begin to view those victims as being less worthy of their efforts.

Third, Klinger posited that neighborhoods with high levels of crime may lead the officers working in those neighborhoods to become jaded to the extent that they might even believe that their no matter their vigor, all their efforts to fight crime were futile. In other words, if police officers did their best day-in and day-out to fight crime, but nevertheless continued to see the issues persist despite all of their hard work, Klinger believed that those officers would start becoming cynical about the prospect of their ever really having a chance to be successful. In turn, the officers' cynical attitudes toward the value of their work might then lead to them to put less effort into actually fulfilling their duties. Thus, Klinger expected that in areas where rates of crime had been high for long periods of time, despite police officers' best efforts to control such behaviors, they would become less likely to put forth such effort in the future.

Finally, Klinger suggested that because police officers working in high crime areas often had more crimes with which they had to deal, they also had deal with much heavier workloads. These heavier workloads, he argued, would eventually lead to officers becoming overwhelmed with all the related paperwork, follow-up investigations, and court appearances associated with making many arrests. Subsequently, Klinger believed that those overworked officers might start putting less effort into their jobs, so they might once again find balance in their lives. Then, if those officers' workloads eventually became smaller and more easily manageable due to their lack of vigor, they would then have even less cause (or inclination) to ever go back to fully performing their duties. Thus, Klinger expected that police officers working in high crime areas would use less vigor in the execution of their duties because less work increased the likelihood that they would be able to "get home on time every night."

KLINGER'S THEORY AS AN EXPLANATION FOR POLICE USE OF FORCE

Although Klinger may not have originally intended for this ecological theory to be used as a theoretical framework for explaining police use of force, with some thoughtful interpretation, it has the potential to serve as another valuable tool for helping researchers understand both police vigor and use of force. Unfortunately, however, given the general conclusions of the empirical tests of the criminal threat theoretical framework and the lines of Klinger's original arguments, it is possible that researchers might follow two very different paths for explaining police officers' use of force.

First of all, given that the majority of the research testing criminal threat theories concluded that high crime rates were associated with increased rates of police use of force, it is reasonable to expect that the four problems associated with police vigor in high crime neighborhoods that Klinger originally identified (residents' tolerance of crime, the undeservingness of victims, police cynicism, and heavy workloads) might actually lead to more police use of force. That is, in addition to perceiving greater criminal threats in high-crime neighborhoods, those four problems might also lead police officers to use more force in order to "punish" the people that make their jobs more difficult. Consequently, one might use Klinger's theory to argue that police officers should use *more* force in high-crime areas.

Second, Klinger's ecological theory of police vigor could also be used to argue that police officers should use *less* force in high crime areas too, however. One simple argument for such an effect would simply be that because the use of force can often require a great deal of physical effort, less vigorous police officers should be less inclined to engage in such behaviors. In order to further illustrate how Klinger's theory might be used to explain reduced rates of police use of force in high-crime areas, however, it is useful to independently consider each of the four problems that he originally identified.

Beginning with Klinger's argument that the tolerance of criminal behavior in high-crime areas should decrease police officers' vigor, a compelling argument could be made that if those officers use less vigor in their duties, then they should have fewer encounters with criminals, and fewer encounters means fewer opportunities to use force. It also stands to reason that if police officers believe that crime victims are undeserving of their efforts, then those officers should also be less likely to use force during their investigations of possible suspects or in order to protect the undeserving victims. Next, if officers who worked in high-crime areas did become so cynical that they truly believed that their efforts had little or no effect crime, it would be unlikely that they would feel inclined use force, since doing so would also have very little affect on crime (at least, from those officers' perspective). Finally, as all police officers know, the use of force almost always necessitates a considerable amount of paperwork (i.e., filling out use-of-force reports). Subsequently, this may also cause police officers to use less force, even if they have more opportunities or justifications to do so, if only to avoid filling out more reports. Thus, as laid out above, Klinger's theory can not only be very easily adapted to explaining increased police use of force in high-crime areas, but decreased use of force in those same areas as well.

As a result of the two very different ways in which Klinger's ecological theory of police vigor can be adapted to explain police use of force, it may come down to an empirical test of the theory in order to determine which adaptation, if either, is most appropriate. And, while such a study is a promising direction for future research, the object of this book is not to test Klinger's theory as an explanation for police use of force, but to propose and test an alternative theory for how neighborhood context might affect police behavior. Subsequently, until an empirical test of an adapted version of Klinger's theory aimed at explaining police officers' use of force (such as the one outlined here) can be conducted, it is impossible to determine its true viability.

As a final note, while an adaptation of Klinger's theory is a good start, the general lack of theoretical frameworks for explaining police use of force (i.e., only the two reviewed above – social threat and criminal threat), as well as the lack of empirical tests of those frameworks, clearly indicates that more research is needed. As Table 2.1 above displays, there were only 15 empirical studies over the past 20 years that have utilized theory to drive their analyses. This is regrettable. If researchers do not use theory to help us understand how and why some factor influences police officers' use of force, it is that much more difficult to determine exactly how manipulating that factor might affect police officers' behaviors for better or worse. Consequently, in order to not only further our understanding of police officers' use of force, but also to improve our capacity as researchers to inform real-world policies regarding police actions, more theoretical frameworks must be developed and tested.

REFERENCES

Adams, Kenneth. 1996. "Measuring the Prevalence of Police Abuse of Force." In W.A. Geller & H. Toch (eds.) *Police Violence: Understanding and Controlling Police Abuse of Force*, pp. 52–93. New Haven, CT: Yale University Press.

Alpert, Geoffrey P. and John M. MacDonald. 2001. "Police Use of Force: An Analysis of Organizational Characteristics." *Justice Quarterly* 18:393–409.

Anderson, Elijah. 1999. *Code of the Street: Decency, Violence, and the Moral Life of the Inner City*. New York, NY: W.W. Norton.

Bellair, Paul E. 1997. "Social Interaction and Community Crime: Examining the Importance of Neighborhood Networks." *Criminology* 25:677–703.

Bernard, Thomas J. and Robin Shepard Engel. 2001. "Conceptualizing Criminal Justice Theory." *Justice Quarterly* 18:1–30.

Biderman, Albert D. and James P. Lynch. 1991. *Understanding Crime Incidence Statistics: Why the UCR Diverges from the NCS*. New York: Springer-Verlag.

Binder, Arnold and Lorie A. Fridell. 1984. "Lethal Force as a Police Response." *Criminal Justice Abstracts* 16: 250–280

Binder, Arnold and Peter Scharf. 1982. "Deadly Force in Law Enforcement." *Crime and Delinquency* 28:1–23.

Black, Donald. 1976. *The Behavior of Law*. Orlando, FL: Academic Press.

Blalock, Hubert. 1967. *Toward a Theory of Minority-Group Relations*. New York, NY: Capricorn Books.

Blumberg, Mark. 1986. "Issues and Controversies with Respect to the Use of Deadly Force by the Police." In T. Barker and D.L. Carter (eds.) *Police Deviance*, pp. 222–244. Cincinnati, OH: Pilgrimage Press.

Blumer, Herbert. 1958. "Race Prejudice as a Sense of Group Position." *Pacific Sociological Review* 23:3–7.

Bobo, Lawrence and Vincent Hutchings. 1996. "Perceptions of Racial Group Competition: Extending Blumer's Theory of Group Position to a Multiracial Social Context." *American Sociological Review* 61:951–972.

Bordua, David J. and Larry L. Tifft. 1971. "Citizen Interviews, Organizational Feed-Back, and Police-Community Relations Decisions." *Law and Society Review* 6:155–182.

Brown, Ben and Wm Reed Benedict. 2002. "Perceptions of the Police." *Policing* 25:543–82.

Browning, Christopher R. 2002. "The Span of Collective Efficacy: Extending Social Disorganization Theory to Partner Violence." *Journal of Marriage and Family* 64:833–850.

Browning, Christopher R., Seth L. Feinberg, Robert D. Dietz. 2004. "The Paradox of Social Organization: Networks, Collective Efficacy, and Violent Crime in Urban Neighborhoods." *Social Forces* 83:503–534.

Bursik, Robert J., Jr. 1999. "The Informal Control of Crime through Neighborhood Networks." *Sociological Focus* 32:85–97.

Bursik, Robert J., Jr. and Harold G. Grasmick. 1993. *Neighborhoods and Crime: The Dimensions of Effective Community Control*. New York, NY: Lexington Books.

Cancino, Jeffrey Michael. 2005. "The Utility of Social Capital and Collective Efficacy: Social Control Policy in Nonmetropolitan Settings." *Criminal Justice Policy Review* 16:287–318.

Cao, Liqun, James Frank, and Francis T. Cullen. 1996. "Race, Community Context and Confidence in the Police." *American Journal of Police* 15:3–22.

Carter, David L. 1985. "Hispanic Perception of Police Performance: An Empirical Assessment." *Journal of Criminal Justice* 13:487–500.

Chamlin, Mitchell B. 1989. "Conflict Theory and Police Killings." *Deviant Behavior* 10:353–368.

Chappell, Allison T. and Alex R. Piquero. 2004. "Applying Social Learning Theory to Police Misconduct." *Deviant Behavior* 25:89–108.

Copeland, Arthur R. 1986. "Police Shootings: The Metropolitan Dad County Experience from 1956 to 1982." *American Journal of Forensic Medicine and Pathology* 7:39–45.

Correia, Mark E., Michael D. Reisig, and Nicholas P. Lovrich. 1996. "Public Perceptions of State Police: An Analysis of Individual-Level and Contextual Variables." *Journal of Criminal Justice* 24:17–28.

Correll, Joshua, Bernadette Park, Charles M. Judd, and Bernd Wittenbrink. 2002. "The Police Officer's Dilemma: Using Ethnicity to Disambiguate Potentially Threatening Individuals." *Journal of Personality and Social Psychology* 83:1314–1329.

Correll, Joshua, Bernadette Park, Charles M. Judd, Bernd Wittenbrink, Melody S. Sadler, Tracie Keesee. 2007. "Across the Thin Blue Line: Police Officers and Racial Bias in the Decision to Shoot." *Journal of Personality and Social Psychology* 92:1006–1023.

Correll, Joshua, Geoffrey R. Urland, and Tiffany A. Ito. 2006. "Event-Related Potentials and the Decision to Shoot: The Role of Threat Perception and Cognitive Control." *Journal of Experimental Social Psychology* 42:120–128.

Culliver, Concetta and Robert Sigler. 1995. "Police Use of Deadly Force in Tennessee Following Tennessee v. Garner." *Journal of Contemporary Criminal Justice* 11:187–195.

Darley, John M. and Bibb Latané. 1968. "Bystander Intervention in Emergencies: Diffusion of Responsibility." *Journal of Personality and Social Psychology* 58:377–383.

Davis, John R. 1990. "A Comparison of Attitudes toward the New York City Police." *Journal of Police Science and Administration* 17:233–243.

Dean, Debby. 1980. "Citizen Ratings of the Police: The Difference Contact Makes." *Law and Police Quarterly* 2:445–471.

Decker, Scott H. 1981. "Citizen Attitudes toward the Police: A Review of Past Findings and Suggestions for Future Policy." *Journal of Police Science and Administration* 9:80–87.

Dwyer, William O., Arthur C. Graesser, Patricia L. Hopkinson, and Michael B. Lupfer. 1990. "Application of Script Theory to Police Officers' Use of Deadly Force." *Journal of Police Science and Administration* 17:295–301.

Earls, Felton J., Jeanne Brooks-Gunn, Stephen W. Raudenbush, and Robert J. Sampson. 1997. *Project on Human Development in Chicago Neighborhoods: Community Survey, 1994–1995.* Boston, MA: Harvard Medical School.

Elicker, Matthew K. 2008. "Unlawful Justice: An Opinion Study on the Police Use of Force and How Views Change Based on Race and Occupation." *Sociological Viewpoints* 24:33–50.

Fyfe, James J. 1988. "Police Use of Deadly Force: Research and Reform." *Justice Quarterly* 5:165–205.

------. 1980. "Geographic Correlates of Police Shooting: A Microanalysis." *Journal of Research in Crime and Delinquency* 17:101–113.

------. 1979. "Administrative Interventions on Police Shooting Discretion: An Empirical Examination." *Journal of Criminal Justice* 7:309–323.

Garner, Joel H., Christopher D. Maxwell, and Cedrick G. Heraux. 2002. "Characteristics Associated with the Prevalence and Severity of Force Used by the Police." *Justice Quarterly* 19:705–746.

Garner, Joel H., Thomas Schade, John Hepburn, and John Buchanan. 1995. "Measuring the Continuum of Force Used By and Against the Police." *Criminal Justice Review* 20:146–169.

Geller, William A. and Hans Toch. 1996. *Police Violence: Understanding and Controlling Police Abuse of Force.* New Haven, CT: Yale University Press.

Goldkamp, John S. 1976. "Minorities as Victims of Police Shootings: Interpretations of Racial Disproportionality and Police Use of Deadly Force." *Justice System Journal* 2:169–183.

Gove, Walter, Michael Hughes, and Michael Geerken. 1985. "Are Uniform Crime Reports a Valid Indicator the Index Crimes? An Affirmative Answer with Minor Qualifications." *Criminology* 23:451–502.

Granovetter, Mark S. 1973. "The Strength of Weakness Ties." *American Journal of Sociology* 78:1360–1380.

Greenwald, Anthony G., Mark A. Oakes, and Hunter G. Hoffman. 2003. "Targets of Discrimination: Effects of Race on Responses to Weapons Holders." *Journal of Experimental Social Psychology* 39:399–405.

Hadar, Ilana and John R. Snortum. 1975. "The Eye of the Beholder: Differential Perceptions of Police by the Police and by the Public." *Criminal Justice and Behavior* 2:37–54.

Hagan, John. 1989. "Why is There So Little Criminal Justice Theory? Neglected Macro- and Micro-Level Links between Organization and Power." *Journal of Research in Crime and Delinquency* 25:116–135.

Hagan, John and Celesta Albonetti. 1982. "Race, Class, and the Perception of Criminal Justice in America." *American Journal of Sociology* 88:329–355.

Halim, Shaheen, and Beverly L. Stiles. 2001. "Differential Support for Police Use of Force, the Death Penalty, and Perceived Harshness of the Courts: Effects of Race, Gender, and Region." *Criminal Justice and Behavior* 28:3–23.

Hayden, George A. 1981. "Police Discretion in the Use of Deadly Force: An Empirical Study of Information Usage in Deadly Force Decision Making." *Journal of Police Science and Administration* 9:102–107.

Helsen, Werner F. and Janet L. Starkes. 1999. "A New Training Approach to Complex Decision Making for Police Officers in Potentially Dangerous Interventions: Police Use of Deadly Force." *Journal of Criminal Justice* 24:395–410.

Holmes, Malcolm D. 2000. "Minority Threat and Police Brutality: Determinants of Civil Rights Complaints in U.S. Municipalities." *Criminology* 38:343–368.

Holmes, Stephen T., Michael K. Reynolds, Ronald M. Holmes, and Samuel Faulkner. 1998. "Individual and Situational Determinants of Police Force: An Examination of Threat Presentation." *American Journal of Criminal Justice* 23:83–106.

Homant, Robert J., Daniel B. Kennedy, and Roger M. Fleming. 1984. "The Effect of Victimization and the Police Response on Citizens' Attitudes toward Police." *Journal of Police Science & Administration* 12:323–332.

Horvath, Frank. 1987. "The Police Use of Deadly Force: A Description of Selected Characteristics of Intrastate Incidents." *Journal of Police Science and Administration* 15:226–238.

Hunter, Albert J. 1985. "Private, Parochial and Public School Orders: The Problem of Crime and Incivility in Urban Communities." In G.D. Suttles and M.N. Zald (eds.), *The Challenge of Social Control: Citizenship and Institution Building in Modem Society*, pp. 230–242. Norwood, N.J.: Ablex Publishing.

Jacob, Herbert. 1971. "Black and White Perceptions of Justice in the City." *Law and Society Review* 6:69–89.

Jacobs, David. 1979. "Inequality and Police Strength: Conflict Theory and Coercive Control in Metropolitan Areas." *American Sociological Review* 44:913–925.

Jacobs, David and David Britt. 1979. "Inequality and Police Use of Deadly Force: An Empirical Assessment of a Conflict Hypothesis." *Social Problems* 26:403–412.

Jacobs, David and Robert M. O'Brien. 1998. "The Determinants of Deadly Force: A Structural Analysis of Police Violence." *American Journal of Sociology* 103:837–862.

Jefferis, Eric S., Robert J. Kaminski, Stephen Holmes, and Dena E. Hanley. 1997. "The Effect of a Videotaped Arrest on Public Perceptions of Police Use." *Journal of Criminal Justice* 25:381–395.

Johnson, Devon and Joseph B. Kuhns. 2009. "Striking Out: Race and Support for Police Use of Force." *Justice Quarterly* 26:592–623.

Kaminski, Robert J. and Eric S. Jefferis. 1998. "The Effect of a Violent Televised Arrest on Public Perceptions of the Police: A Partial Test of Easton's Theoretical Framework." *Policing: An International Journal of Police Strategies & Management* 21:683–706.

Kane, Robert J. 2002. "The Social Ecology of Police Misconduct." *Criminology* 40:867–896.

Kania, Richard E. and Wade C. Mackey. 1977. "Police Violence as a Function of Community Characteristics." *Criminology* 15:27–48.

Kasarda, John D. and Morris Janowitz. 1974. "Community Attachment in Mass Society." *American Sociological Review* 39:328–339.

Klinger, David A. 2004. "Environment and Organization: Reviving a Perspective on the Police." *Annals of the American Academy of Political and Social Science* 593:119–136.

------. 1997. "Negotiating Order in Patrol Work: An Ecological Theory of Police Response to Deviance." *Criminology* 35:277–306.

Kornhauser, Ruth Rosner. 1978. *Social Sources of Delinquency: An Appraisal of Analytic Models*. Chicago, IL: University of Chicago Press.

Krivo, Lauren J. and Ruth D. Peterson. 1996. "Extremely Disadvantaged Neighborhoods and Urban Crime." *Social Forces* 75: 619–650.

Lawton, Brian A. 2007. "Levels of Nonlethal Force: An Examination of Individual, Situational, and Contextual Factors." *Journal of Research in Crime and Delinquency* 44:163–184.

Lee, Barrett A. and Karen E. Campbell. 1997. "Common Ground? Urban Neighborhoods as Survey Respondents See Them." *Social Science Quarterly* 78:922–936.

Lersch, Kim M., Thomas Bazley, Thomas Mieczkowski, and Kristina Childs. 2008. "Police Use of Force and Neighbourhood Characteristics: An Examination of Structural Disadvantage, Crime, and Resistance." *Policing & Society* 18:282–300.

Liska, Allen E. and Jiang Yu. 1992. "Specifying and Testing the Threat Hypothesis: Police Use of Deadly Force." In A.E. Liska (ed.), *Social Threat and Social Control,* pp. 53–68. Albany, NY: State University of New York Press.

Lowencamp, Christopher T., Francis T. Cullen, and Travis C. Pratt. 2003. "Replicating Sampson and Groves's Test of Social Disorganization Theory: Revisiting a Criminological Classic." *Journal of Research in Crime and Delinquency* 40:351–373.

MacDonald, John M., Geoffrey P. Alpert, and Abraham N. Tennenbaum. 1999. "Justifiable Homicide by Police and Criminal Homicide: A Research Note." *Journal of Crime and Justice* 22:153–166.

MacDonald, John M., Robert J. Kaminski, Geoffrey P. Alpert, and Abraham N. Tennenbaum. 2001. "The Temporal Relationship between Police Killings of Civilians and Criminal Homicide: A Redefined Version of the Danger-Perception Theory." *Crime & Delinquency* 47:155–172.

MacDonald, John M., Patrick W. Manz, Geoffrey P. Alpert, and Roger G. Dunham. 2003. "Police Use of Force: Examining the Relationship between Calls for Service and the Balance of Police Force and Suspect Resistance." *Journal of Criminal Justice* 31:119–127.

Marenin, Otwin. 1989. "The Utility of Community Needs Surveys in Community Policing." *Police Studies* 12:73–81.

Mastrofski, Stephen and Roger B. Parks. 1990. "Improving Observational Studies of Police." *Criminology* 28:475–496.

McLaughlin, Lindsay M., Shane D. Johnson, Kate J. Bowers, Dan J. Birks, and Ken Pease. 2007. "Police Perceptions of the Long- and Short-Term Spatial Distribution of Residential Burglary." *International Journal of Police Science and Management* 9:99–111.

Meyer, Marshall W. 1980. "Police Shootings at Minorities: The Case of Los Angeles." *Annals of the American Academy of Political and Social Science* 452:98–110.

Micucci, Anthony J. and Ian M. Gomme. 2005. "American Police and Subcultural Support for the Use of Excessive Force." *Journal of Criminal Justice* 33:487–500.

Morenoff, Jeffrey D., Robert J. Sampson, and Stephen W. Raudenbush. 2001. "Neighborhood Inequality, Collective Efficacy, and the Spatial Dynamics of Urban Violence." *Criminology* 39:517–559.

Murty, Komanduri S., Julian B. Roebuck, and Joann E. Smith. 1990. "The Image of the Police in Black Atlanta Communities." *Journal of Police Science and Administration* 17:250–257.

O'Brien, Robert M. 1985. *Crime and Victimization Data.* Beverly Hills, CA: Sage.

Park, Robert E., Ernest W. Burgess, and Roderick D. McKenzie. 1925. *The City.* Chicago, IL: University of Chicago Press.

Parks, Roger B. 1984. "Linking Objective and Subjective Measures of Performance." *Public Administration Review* 44:118–27.

------. 1982. "Citizen Surveys for Police Performance Assessments: Some Issues in Their Use." *The Urban Interest* 4:17–26.

Patillo-McCoy, Mary. 1999. *Black Picket Fences: Privilege and Peril Among the Black Middle Class.* Chicago, IL: University of Chicago Press.

Percy, Stephen L. 1986. "In Defense of Citizen Evaluations as Performance Measures." *Urban Affairs Quarterly* 22:66–83.

------. 1980. "Response Time and Citizen Evaluation of Police." *Journal of Police Science and Administration* 8:75–86.

Peterson, Ruth D., Lauren J. Krivo, and Mark A. Harris. 2000. "Disadvantage and Neighborhood Violent Crime: Do Local Institutions Matter?" *Journal of Research in Crime and Delinquency* 37:31–63.

Raudenbush, Stephen W. and Anthony S. Bryk. 2002. *Hierarchical Linear Models: Applications and Data Analysis Methods, Second Edition.* Thousand Oaks, CA: Sage.

Raudenbush, Stephen W. and Robert J. Sampson. 1999. "Ecometrics: Toward a Science of Assessing Ecological Settings, with Applications to the Systemic Social Observation of Neighborhoods." *Sociological Methodology* 29:1–41.

Reisig, Michael D. and Roger B. Parks. 2000. "Experience, Quality of Life, and Neighborhood Context: A Hierarchical Analysis of Satisfaction with Police." *Justice Quarterly* 17:607–630.

Reisig, Michael D. and Jeffrey Michael Cancino. 2004. "Incivilities in Nonmetropolitan Communities: The Effects of Structural Constraints, Social Conditions, and Crime." *Journal of Criminal Justice* 32:15–29.

Reisig, Michael D. and Andrew L. Giacomazzi. 1998. "Citizen Perceptions of Community Policing: Are Attitudes Toward Police Important." *Policing: An International Journal of Police Strategies & Management* 20:311–325.

Rengart, George F. 1995. "Comparing Cognitive Hotspots to Crime Hotspots." In C. Block, M. Daboub, and S. Fregly (eds.), *Crime Analysis through Computer Mapping*, pp. 33–47. Chicago, IL: Police Executive Research Forum.

Sampson, Robert J. and W. Byron Groves. 1989. "Community Structure and Crime: Testing Social Disorganization Theory. *American Journal of Sociology* 94:774–802.

Sampson, Robert J. and Dawn Jeglum-Bartusch. 1998. "Legal Cynicism and Subcultural? Tolerance of Deviance: The Neighborhood Context of Racial Differences." *Law & Society Review* 32:777–804.

Sampson, Robert J., Jeffrey D. Morenoff, and Felton Earls. 1999. "Beyond Social Capital: Spatial Dynamics of Collective Efficacy for Children." *American Sociological Review* 64:633–660.

Sampson, Robert J., Jeffrey D. Morenoff, and Thomas Gannon-Rowley. 2002. "Assessing 'Neighborhood Effects': Social Processes and New Directions in Research." *Annual Review of Sociology* 28:443–478.

Sampson, Robert J., Stephen W. Raudenbush, and Felton Earls. 1997. "Neighborhoods and Violent Crime: A Multilevel Study of Collective Efficacy." *Science* 277:918–924.

Schafer, Joseph A., Beth M. Huebner, and Timothy S. Bynum. 2003. "Citizen Perceptions of Police Services: Race, Neighborhood Context, and Community Policing." *Police Quarterly* 6:440–468.

Shaw, Clifford R. Henry D. McKay. 1942. *Juvenile Delinquency in Urban Areas.* Chicago, IL: University of Chicago Press.

Sherman, Lawrence W. 1986. "Policing Communities: What Works?" in A.J. Reiss, Jr. and M. Tonry (eds.), *Communities and Crime*, pp. 343–386. Chicago, IL: University of Chicago Press.

Sherman, Lawrence W., Patrick R. Gartin, and Michael E. Buerger. 1989. "Hot Spots of Predatory Crime: Routine Activities and the Criminology of Place." *Criminology* 27:27–56.

Sherman, Lawrence W. and Robert H. Langworthy. 1979. "Measuring Homicide by Police Officers." *Journal of Criminal Law and Criminology* 70:546–560.

Sherman, Lawrence W. and Mark Blumberg. 1981. "Higher Education and Police Use of Deadly Force." *Journal of Criminal Justice* 9:317–331.

Silver, Eric. 2000. "Extending Social Disorganization Theory: A Multi-Level Approach to the Study of Violence Among Discharged Psychiatric Patients." *Criminology* 38:1043–1074.

Silver, Eric and Lisa L. Miller. 2004. "Sources of Informal Social Control in Chicago Neighborhoods." *Criminology* 42:551–583.

Skolnick, Jerome. 1966. *Justice without Trial: Law Enforcement in Democratic Society.* New York, NY: Wiley.

Slovak, Jeffrey. 1986. *Styles of Urban Policing.* New York: New York University Press.

Smith, Douglas A. 1986. "The Neighborhood Context of Police Behavior." In A.J. Reiss, Jr. and M. Tonry (eds.), *Communities and Crime*, pp. 313–41 Chicago: University of Chicago Press.

Smith, Paul E. and Richard O. Hawkins. 1973. "Victimization, Types of Citizen-Police Contacts, and Attitudes Toward the Police." *Law and Society Review* 8:135–152.

Smith, Brad W. and Malcolm D. Holmes. 2003. "Community Accountability, Minority Threat, and Police Brutality: An Examination of Civil Rights Criminal Complaints." *Criminology* 41:1035–1063.

Son, In Soo and Dennis M. Rome. 2004. "The Prevalence and Visibility of Misconduct: A Survey of Citizens and Police Officers." *Police Quarterly* 7:179–204.

Sorensen, Jonathan R., James W. Marquart, and Deon E. Brock. 1993. "Factors Related to Killings of Felons by Police Officers: A Test of the Community Violence and Conflict Hypotheses." *Justice Quarterly* 10:417–440.

South, Scott J. and Kyle D. Crowder. 1997. "Escaping Distressed Neighborhoods: Individual, Community, and Metropolitan Influences." *American Journal of Sociology* 102:1040–1084.

Spano, Richard. 2006. "Observer Behavior as a Potential Source of Reactivity: Describing and Quantifying Observer Effects in a Large-Scale Observational Study of Police." *Sociological Methods & Research* 34:521–553.

------. 2005. "Potential Sources of Observer Bias in Police Observational Data." *Social Science Research* 34:591–617.

Spano, Richard and Michael D. Reisig. 2006. "'Drop the Clipboard and Help Me!': The Determinants of Observer Behavior in Police Encounters with Suspects." *Journal of Criminal Justice* 34:619–629.

Sparger, Jerry R. and David J. Giacopassi. 1992. "Memphis Revisited: A Reexamination of Police Shooting After the Garner Decision." *Justice Quarterly* 9:211–225.

Sun, Ivan Y., Ruth Triplett, and Randy R. Gainey. 2004. "Neighborhood Characteristics and Crime: A Test of Sampson and Groves' Model of Social Disorganization." *Western Criminology Review* 5:1–16.

Tennenbaum, Abraham N. 1994. "The Influence of the Garner Decision on Police Use of Deadly Force." *Journal of Criminal Law and Criminology* 81:241–260.

Terrill, William and Stephen D. Mastrofski. 2002. "Situational and Officer Based Determinants of Police Coercion." *Justice Quarterly* 19:101–34.

Terrill, William, Eugene A. Paoline, III, and Peter K. Manning. 2003. "Police Culture and Coercion." *Criminology* 41:1003–1034.

Terrill, William and Michael D. Reisig. 2003. "Neighborhood Context and Police Use of Force." *Journal of Research in Crime and Delinquency* 40:291–321.

Thompson, Brian L. and James Daniel Lee. 2004. "Who Cares if Police Become Violent? Explaining Approval of Police Use of Force Using a National Sample." *Sociological Inquiry* 74:381–410.

Thurman, Quint C. and Michael D. Reisig. 1996. "Community-Oriented Research in an Era of Community Policing." *American Behavioral Scientist* 39:570–586.

Tienda, Marta. 1991. "Poor People and Poor Places Deciphering Neighborhood Effects on Poverty Outcomes." In J. Huber (ed.), Macro-*Micro Linkages in Sociology.* Newbury Park, CA: Sage.

Triplett, Ruth A., Randy R. Gainey, and Ivan Y. Sun. 2003. "Institutional Strength, Social Control and Neighborhood Crime Rates." *Theoretical Criminology* 7:439–467.

Tuch, Stephen A. and Ronald Weitzer. 1997. "The Polls: Racial Differences in Attitudes Toward the Police." *Public Opinion Quarterly* 61:642–664.

United States Census Bureau. 2008. "An Older and More Diverse Nation by Midcentury." Retrieved September 17, 2009, from http://www.census.gov/newsroom/releases/archives/population/cb08-123.html.

United States Department of Justice. 2005. *Contacts between Police and the Public: Findings from the 2002 National Survey.* Bureau of Justice Statistics.

Velez, Maria B. 2001. "The Role of Public Social Control in Urban Neighborhoods: A Multi-level Analysis of Victimization Risks." *Criminology* 36:441–479.

Veysey, Bonita M. and Steven F. Messner. 1999. "Further Testing of Social Disorganization Theory: An Elaboration of Sampson and Groves's 'Community Structure and Crime'." *Journal of Research in Crime and Delinquency* 36:156–174.

Waegel, William B. 1984a. "The Use of Lethal Force by Police: The Effect of Statutory Change." *Crime and Delinquency* 30:121–140.

------. 1984b. "How Police Justify the Use of Deadly Force." *Social Problems* 32:144–155.

Walker, Samuel and Lorie Fridell. 1992. "Forces of Change in Police Policy: The Impact of Tennessee v. Garner." *American Journal of Police* 11:97–112.

Warner, Barbara D. 2003. "The Role of Attenuated Culture in Social Disorganization Theory." *Criminology* 41:73–98.

Warner, Barbara D. and Glenn L. Pierce. 1993. "Reexamining Social Disorganization Theory Using Calls to the Police as a Measure of Crime." *Criminology* 31:493–517.

Warner, Barbara D. and Pamela Wilcox Rountree. 1997. "Local Social Ties in a Community and Crime Model: Questioning the Systemic Nature of Informal Social Control." *Social Problems* 44:520–536.

Webb, Vincent J. and Chris E. Marshall. 1995. "The Relative Importance of Race and Ethnicity on Citizen Attitudes Toward the Police." *American Journal of Police* 14:45–66.

Weitzer, Ronald. 2002. "Incidents of Police Misconduct and Public Opinion." *Journal of Criminal Justice* 30:397–408.

------. 2000. "White, Black, or Blue Cops? Race and Citizen Assessments of Police Officers." *Journal of Criminal Justice* 28:313–324.

------. 1999. "Citizens' Perceptions of Police Misconduct: Race and Neighborhood Context." *Justice Quarterly* 16:819–46.

Weitzer, Ronald and Steven A. Tuch. 2005. "Determinants of Public Satisfaction with the Police." *Police Quarterly* 8:279–297.

------. 2004. "Race and Perceptions of Police Misconduct." *Social Problems* 51:305–325.

Wilson, James Q. and George L. Kelling. 1982. "Broken Windows: The Police and Neighborhood Safety." *The Atlantic Monthly* 249:29–38.

Wilson, William Julius. 1996. *When Work Disappears: The World of the New Urban Poor.* New York, NY: Vintage Books.

Worden, Robert E. 1996. "The Causes of Police Brutality: Theory and Evidence on Police Use of Force." In W.A. Geller and H. Toch (eds.), *Police Violence: Understanding and Controlling Police Abuse of Force*, pp. 23–51. New Haven, CT: Yale University Press.

Worrall, John L. 1999. "Public Perceptions of Police Efficacy and Image: The 'Fuzziness' of Support for the Police." *American Journal of Criminal Justice* 24:47–66.

Explaining Police Shootings

JAMES P. MCELVAIN

In the previous chapter, it was discussed that seven models were developed for evaluation. Because this study focuses on whether citizen characteristics/behaviors (i.e., alcohol and/or drug intoxication, and prior violent criminal behavior) serve as contributing factors for police shootings, it was decided to also examine officer characteristics (i.e., gender, race/ethnicity, and age) as control variables. This chapter will first, consider the results for each model independently, and then propose alternative models against the other to determine the relationship of citizen behaviors and officer characteristics with officer-involved shootings. Of specific interest, and keeping with the hypotheses outlined in Chapter 6, is whether citizen behavior variables have a stronger impact than officer characteristics.

INDIVIDUAL MODEL RESULTS

Table 14-1 displays Model 1 and Model 2. Model 1 shows the officer characteristics (i.e., the control variables) alone. Each of the variables indicated are significantly related to police use of deadly force. Interpretation of the findings is based on the incident density ratio (IDR) statistics. Essentially, the IDR is interpreted as the ratio of average event rates/counts for every single-unit increase in a model covariate. In Model 1 the rate of male

Table 14-1. Officer-Involved Shootings: Officer Characteristics and Citizen Behaviors (Alcohol)

Covariates	Model 1				Model 2			
			95% CI				95% CI	
	b	IDR	LCU, UCL	χ^2	b	IDR	LCU, UCL	χ^2
Officer Characteristics **Gender**								
Female		1.00	(Reference)			1.00	(Reference)	
Male	1.20*	3.32	1.234, 8.952	5.65	1.15*	3.16	1.173, 8.528	5.18
Race								
White		1.00	(Reference)			1.00	(Reference)	
Non-white	−0.39*	0.67	0.474, 0.961	4.74	−0.39*	0.68	0.474, 0.962	4.73
Age								
Continuous	−0.02*	0.98	0.960, 0.998	4.91	−0.02*	0.98	0.961, 1.000	4.01
Citizen Behavior **Intoxication**								
None	--	--	--	--		1.00	(Reference)	
Alcohol	--	--	--	--	0.80**	2.23	1.347, 3.666	9.77
Drugs	--	--	--	--	--	--	--	--
Alcohol/drugs	--	--	--	--	--	--	--	--
Citizen Behavior **Prior Violence**								
None	--	--	--	--	--	--	--	--
Yes	--	--	--	--	--	--	--	--
Unknown	--	--	--	--	--	--	--	--
Deviance	447.79				439.87			
df	644				643			
Deviance/df	0.695				0.684			
LRS	18.42***				26.34***			
df	3				4			
N	648				648			

*p < .05 **p < .01 ***p < .001

officers being involved in a shooting is 3.3 times greater than female officers (IDR= 3.32, CI = 1.23, 8.95). Non-White officers are 33 percent less likely to shoot than White officers (IDR= 0.67, CI = 0.47, 0.96). It was observed that for every year increase in officer age, the expected number of shootings decrease by 2 percent (IDR= 0.98, CI = 0.96, 0.99).

Model 2 adds the first citizen behavior, alcohol intoxication, to the previous model. Here, the officer characteristics remain significant at the .05 level; however, alcohol intoxication is also significant, but at the higher level of .01. Citizens under the influence of alcohol are expected to be shot or shot at by police officers more than 2.2 times the rate of non-intoxicated persons (IDR= 2.23, CI = 1.35, 3.67).

Models 3 and 4 are shown in **Table 14-2**. Model 3 removes the alcohol intoxication variable for citizen behavior and replaces it with drug intoxication. In this model, the

Table 14-2. Officer-Involved Shootings: Officer Characteristics and Citizen Behaviors (Alcohol and Drugs)

| Covariates | Model 3 | | | | Model 4 | | | |
	b	IDR	95% CI LCU, UCL	χ^2	b	IDR	95% CI LCU, UCL	χ^2
Officer Characteristics								
Gender								
Female		1.00	(Reference)			1.00	(Reference)	
Male	1.00*	2.73	1.009, 7.374	3.91	0.91	2.49	1.089, 6.742	3.21
Race								
White		1.00	(Reference)			1.00	(Reference)	
Non-white	–0.42*	0.65	0.460, 0.932	5.51	–0.43*	0.65	0.459, 0.931	5.56
Age								
Continuous	–0.02*	0.98	0.964, 1.003	2.74	–0.01	0.99	0.966, 1.007	1.78
Citizen Behavior Intoxication								
None		1.00	(Reference)			1.00	(Reference)	
Alcohol	--	--	--	--	1.10***	3.01	1.795, 5.046	17.46
Drugs	0.88***	2.41	1.782, 3.246	32.92	0.98***	2.67	1.962, 3.642	38.83
Alcohol/drugs	--	--	--	--	--	--	--	--
Citizen Behavior Prior Violence								
None	--	--	--	--	--	--	--	--
Yes	--	--	--	--	--	--	--	--
Unknown	--	--	--	--	--	--	--	--
Deviance	418.02				404.52			
df	643				642			
Deviance/df	0.650				0.630			
LRS	48.18***				61.68***			
df	4				5			
N	648				648			

*p < .05 ***p < .001

age of the officer is no longer significant at the .05 range, and citizen drug intoxication is significant at the .01 level. Moreover, the expected number of shootings of citizens under the influence is 2.4 times greater than for citizens who are not drug intoxicated (IDR= 2.41, CI = 1.78, 3.25). Model 4 includes both variables for citizen drug and alcohol intoxication. With the inclusion of these two citizen behavior variables, another officer characteristic variable, gender, lost significance based on conventional criteria; however, both citizen alcohol and drug intoxication were significant at the .01 level. The only remaining significant officer characteristic is race/ethnicity. Non-White officers are still less likely (35 percent) to be in a shooting than White officers.

Table 14-3 depicts Models 5 and 6. In Model 5, those citizens testing positive for being under the influence of a combination of alcohol and illicit drugs were added to the model. As a result of the analysis of this model, no changes were observed in the officer characteristic variables as seen in Model 4. All variables for citizen intoxication were significant at the .001 level. Based on the findings, citizens under the influence of alcohol are targeted by police gunfire 3.4 times more than citizens not inebriated (IDR= 3.42, CI = 2.02, 5.78). Drug intoxicated citizens were shot or shot at by police at a rate that was 3 times higher than that of sober citizens ((IDR= 3.03, CI = 2.20, 4.19). Last, police used deadly force 2.9 times greater against citizens who were under the influence of a combination of alcohol and drugs than citizens who were not under the influence (IDR= 2.93, CI = 1.76, 4.89).

By the time the covariates for prior criminal violence were added to the model (Model 6), none of the officer characteristics remained significant based on conventional criteria. Model 6 shows that citizens with prior or unknown violent criminal participation significantly contribute to police shootings. Although the amount of explanation was reduced, the citizen intoxication variables continue to be significant as well.

Found in **Table 14-4**, Model 7 represents officer characteristics and citizen prior criminal violence variables only; citizen intoxication variables were removed. As in Model 6, officer characteristics remain insignificant in Model 7. This is interesting because before prior criminal violence variables for the citizen were considered in Model 5, the expectation for non-White officers to be involved in a shooting was significantly less than White officers at the .05 level. However, once the variable for prior violent criminal behavior was introduced, officer race was washed out. In Model 7, the expected number of shootings of citizens with prior violent criminal arrest records were 3.7 times greater than citizens with no previous violent criminal contacts with the police (IDR= 3.65 = 2.71, 4.92). In addition, police officers fired their weapons at citizens with unknown prior violent crime contacts 5 times more frequently than citizens who did not have prior violence contacts (IDR= 5.04, CI = 2.51, 10.14).

Table 14-3. Officer-Involved Shootings: Officer Characteristics and Citizen Behaviors (Alcohol, Drugs and Violence)

Covariates	b	IDR	95% CI LCU, UCL	χ^2	b	IDR	95% CI LCU, UCL	χ^2
		Model 5				Model 6		
Officer Characteristics Gender								
Female		1.00	(Reference)			1.00	(Reference)	
Male	0.78	2.22	0.816, 6.029	2.44	0.61	1.83	0.671, 5.003	1.40
Race								
White		1.00	(Reference)			1.00	(Reference)	
Non-white	−0.44*	0.64	0.452, 0.917	5.97	−0.31	0.73	0.512, 1.049	2.88
Age								
Continuous	−0.01	0.99	0.967, 1.008	1.43	−0.01	0.99	0.965, 1.007	1.68
Citizen Behavior Intoxication								
None		1.00	(Reference)			1.00	(Reference)	
Alcohol	1.23***	3.42	2.024, 5.782	21.08	0.92**	2.52	1.473, 4.316	11.37
Drugs	1.11***	3.03	2.198, 4.189	45.54	0.74***	2.10	1.483, 2.968	17.54
Alcohol/drugs	1.08***	2.93	1.762, 4.887	17.11	0.57*	1.77	1.036, 3.008	4.38
Citizen Behavior Prior Violence								
None	--	--	--	--		1.00	(Reference)	
Yes	--	--	--	--	1.00***	2.72	1.960, 3.3773	35.84
Unknown	--	--	--	--	1.61***	4.99	2.475, 10.070	20.17
Deviance	391.04				346.31			
df	641				639			
Deviance/df	0.610				0.542			
LRS	75.17***				119.89***			
df	6				8			
N	648				648			

*p < .05 ***p < .001

Table 14-4. Officer-Involved Shootings: Officer Characteristics and Citizen Behaviors (Violence)

Covariates	Model 7			
			95% CI	
	b	IDR	LCU, UCL	χ^2
Officer Characteristics				
Gender				
Female		1.00	(Reference)	
Male	0.84	2.31	0.852, 6.246	2.71
Race				
White		1.00	(Reference)	
Non-white	−0.24	0.79	0.551, 1.124	1.73
Age				
Continuous	−0.02	0.98	0.964, 1.005	2.29
Citizen Behavior				
Intoxication				
None	--	--	--	--
Alcohol	--	--	--	--
Drugs	--	--	--	--
Alcohol/drugs	--	--	--	--
Prior Violence				
None		1.00	(Reference)	
Yes	1.29***	3.65	2.705, 4.922	71.86
Unknown	1.62***	5.04	2.506, 10.137	20.58
Deviance	368.27			
df	642			
Deviance/df	0.574			
LRS	97.94***			
df	5			
N	648			

*p < .05 ***p < .001

COMPETING MODEL RESULTS

As can be surmised by reviewing the seven equations, it appears that some of the models may be a better fit to the data. In order to measure this assumption, the models were arranged to compete against each other. Because the GENMOD procedure in SAS does not calculate a model chi-square (it gives a deviance), a null model with only the intercept was run in order to compute the likelihood ratio statistic for comparison with each of the subsequent competing models. The null model includes the intercept only, and yields a log-likelihood. To determine whether a subsequent model better fits the data, a model chi-square has to be estimated based on the difference in log-likelihoods. This is accomplished by subtracting the log-likelihood of the null model and multiplying the difference by -2. The formula is stated as follows:

$$LRS = (LL_{null} - LL_{model}) - 2 \qquad \text{(Eq. 2)}$$

The result represents the likelihood ratio statistic (LRS) or model chi-square, which indicates whether the model is significant based on the number of degrees of freedom (i.e., variables) within the model.

Once the LRS is known for each model, a comparison of the models can be made based on the following formula:

$$\rho LRS = LRS_{model\ 1} - LRS_{model\ 2} \qquad \text{(Eq. 3)}$$

where ρLRS = change in the likelihood ratio statistic. If the change in the likelihood ratio statistic from Model 1 to Model 2, based on degrees of freedom, has a significant probability, it may be argued that the second model better fits the data. In other words, the model better explains the dependent variable.

Table 14-5 represents a series of competing or potentially plausible models. Model 1 is the model with the officer characteristics only, and its LRS is 18.42. Looking at the second competing model, which is Model 2, wherein the variable for citizen shot or shot at by police was alcohol intoxication, it is discovered that the model LRS is 26.34. In comparison to Model 1 (with only officer characteristics), Model 2 is a better fit to the data. This is determined by subtracting the LRS for Model 1 from the LRS for Model 2. The difference was 7.92, which is depicted in the ρLRS column. To establish whether the model is a better fit, the difference in degrees of freedom in Model 1 and Model 2 are calculated. Then reference to a chi-square table was made to determine whether the ρLRS is significant. Based on this process, it was established that Model 2 better fit the data than Model 1.

As can be seen in **Table 14-5**, each model (Models 2 through 7) provided a better fit than Model 1. Of particular interest was whether prior violent behavior by the citizen contributed more to police shootings than citizen intoxication. To test this idea, Model 7 (officer characteristics and citizen prior violence) was compared to each varying model with citizen intoxication, (i.e., alcohol alone – Model 2, drugs alone – Model 3, alcohol and drugs – Model 4, and alcohol, drugs and a combination of alcohol and drugs

Table 14-5. Summary of Results for Officer Characteristics and Citizen Behaviors

	Competing Models	LRS	df	prob.	ΔLRS	Δdf	prob.
1.	Officer Characteristics	18.42	3	.001	--	--	--
2.	Model 1 + alcohol	26.34	4	.001	7.92	1	.01
3.	Model 1 + drugs	48.18	4	.001	29.76	1	.001
4.	Model 1 + alcohol and drugs	61.68	5	.001	43.26	2	.001
5.	Model 1 + alcohol, drugs and alc/drugs	75.17	6	.001	56.75	3	.001
6.	Model 1 + violence	97.94	5	.001	79.52	2	.001
7.	Model 5 + violence	119.89	8	.001	101.47	5	.001
8.	Model 7 vs. Model 2	--	--	.001	93.55	4	.001
9.	Model 7 vs. Model 3	--	--	--	71071	4	.001
10.	Model 7 vs. Model 4	--	--	--	58.21	3	.001
11.	Model 7 vs. Model 5	--	--	--	44.72	2	.001
12.	Model 6 vs. Model 5	--	--	--	22.77	2	.001

– Model 5). Despite the fact that the ρLRS from model to model became smaller, in each competing model, the prior violence model (Model 7) remained significantly a better fit at the .01 level. Moreover, when prior violence was added to all the other variables in Model 6 and compared to Model 5 (officer characteristics and citizen intoxication), Model 6 proved to be a better fit to the data.

Of particular interest is the comparison of Models 2 and 3. Although previous studies found a strong correlation between alcohol and violent crime and no significant relationship between drug intoxication and violent crime (Parker 1998; Parker and Auerhahn 1998), here the roles are almost reversed. Even though both substances show a significant correlation with police shootings when examined separately, an assessment of the two models demonstrates that citizen drug intoxication significantly better fits the data at the .001 level.

REFERENCES

Adams, Kenneth. 1999. "What we know about police use of force." Pp. 1–14 in *Use of force by police: Overview of national and local data*. Washington, D.C.: U.S. Department of Justice, BJS and NIJ, October. NCJ 176330.

Agresti, Alan. 1984. *Analysis of Ordinal Categorical Data*. New York: John Wiley & Sons.

Alaniz, Maria L., Randi S. Cartmill and Robert Nash Parker. 1998. "Immigrants and violence: The importance of neighborhood context." *Hispanic Journal of Behavioral Sciences* 20: 155–174.

Alpert, Geoffrey P. and Roger G. Dunham. 1999. "The force factor: Measuring and assessing police use of force and suspect resistance." Pp. 45–60 in *Use of force by police: Overview of national and local data*. Washington, D.C.: U.S. Department of Justice, BJS and NIJ, October. NCJ 176330.

------. 2004. *Understanding Police Use of Force: Officers, Suspects, and Reciprocity*. New York, NY: Cambridge University Press.

Alpert, Geoffrey P. and William C. Smith. 1994. "How reasonable is the reasonable man?: Police and excessive force." *The Journal of Criminal Law and Criminology* 85: 481–501.

Aamodt, Michael G. 2004. *Research in Law Enforcement Selection*. Boca Raton, FL: Brown Walker Press.

Binder, Arnold and Peter Scharf. 1980. "The violent police-citizen encounter." *Annals of the American Academy of Political and Social Science* Vol. 452: 111–121.

Bittner, Egon. 1967. "The police in skid-row: A study of peace keeping." *American Sociological Review* 32: 699–715.

------. 1970. *The Functions of the Police in Modern Society*. Rockville, MD: National Institute of Mental Health.

Blumberg, Mark. 2001. "Controlling police use of deadly force: Assessing two decades of progress." Pp. 559–582 in *Critical Issues in Policing: Contemporary Readings*, edited by Roger G. Dunham and Geoffrey P. Alpert. Prospect Heights, IL: Waveland Press, Inc.

Blumstein, Alfred and Daniel Cork. 1996. "Linking gun availability to youth gun violence." *Law and Contemporary Problems* 59: 5–24.

Blumstein, Alfred, Frederick P. Rivara and Richard Rosenfeld. 2000. "The rise and decline of homicide and why." *Annual Review of Public Health* 21: 505–541.

Boutwell, J. Paul. [1977] 1982. "Use of deadly force to arrest a fleeing felon – A constitutional challenge, parts I and III." Pp. 65–87 in *Readings on Police of Deadly Force*, edited by James J. Fyfe. Washington, D.C.: Police Foundation.

Brown, Michael F. 1984. "Use of deadly force by patrol officers: Training implications." *Journal of Police Science and Administration* 12: 133–140.

Cao, Liqun and Bu Huang. 2000. "Determinants of citizen complaints against police abuse of power." *Journal of Criminal Justice* 28: 203–213.

Centers, Nathan L. and Mark D. Weist. 1998. "Inner city youth and drug dealing: A review of the problem." *Journal of Youth and Adolescence* 27: 395–411.

Chapman, Samuel G. [1967] 1982. "Police policy on the use of firearms." Pp. 224–257 in *Readings on Police of Deadly Force*, edited by James J. Fyfe. Washington, D.C.: Police Foundation.

Cohen, Lawrence E. and Marcus Felson. 1979. "Social change and crime rate trends: A routine activity approach." *American Sociological Review* 44: 588–608.

Cook, Philip, J. and John H. Laub. 2002. "After the epidemic: Recent trends in youth violence in the United States." *Crime and Justice* 29: 1–37.

Correll, Joshua, Bernd Wittenbrink, Bernadette Park, Charles M. Judd, Melody S. Sadler, and Tracie Keesee. 2007. "Across the thin blue line: Police officers and racial bias in the decision to shoot." *Journal of Personality and Social Psychology* 92:1006–1023.

Cullen, Francis. T., Liqun Cao, James Frank, Robert H. Langworthy, Sandra Lee Browning, Renee Kopache and Thomas J. Stevenson. 1996. "'Stop or I'll shoot': Racial differences in support for police use of deadly force." *American Behavioral Scientist* 39: 449–460.

Dine, Kim C. 2005. "Agency culture, training, and the use of force." Pp. 5–7 in *Exploring the Challenges of Police Use of Force*, edited by Joshua A. Ederheimer and Lorie A. Fridell. Washington, D.C.: Police Executive Research Forum.

Donahue, Michael E. and Frank S. Horvath. 1991. "Police shooting outcomes: Suspect criminal history and incident behaviors." *American Journal of Police* 10: 17–34.

Durkheim, Emile. [1895] 2002. *The Rules of Sociological Method*. Pp.63–89 in *Readings from Emile Durkheim*, edited by Kenneth Thompson. New York: Routledge.

Fienberg, Stephen E. 1977. *The Analysis of Cross-Classified Categorical Data*. Cambridge, MA: MIT Press.

Fridell, Lorie A. 1989. "Justifiable use of measures in research on deadly force." *Journal of Criminal Justice* 17: 157–165.

------. 2005. "Improving use-of-force policy, policy enforcement, and training." Pp. 21–55 in *Exploring the Challenges of Police Use of Force*, edited by Joshua A. Ederheimer and Lorie A. Fridell. Washington, D.C.: Police Executive Research Forum.

Fyfe, James J. [1978] 1982. "Administrative interventions on police shooting discretion: An empirical examination." Pp. 258–281 in *Readings on Police of Deadly Force*, edited by James J. Fyfe. Washington, D.C.: Police Foundation.

------. [1981] 1982. "Observations on police deadly force." Pp. 297–314 in *Readings on Police of Deadly Force*, edited by James J. Fyfe. Washington, D.C.: Police Foundation.

------. 1982a. "Introduction." Pp. 3–11 in *Readings on Police of Deadly Force*, edited by James J. Fyfe. Washington, D.C.: Police Foundation.

------. 1982b. "Blind Justice: Police shootings in Memphis." *The Journal of Criminal Law and Criminology* 73: 707–722.

------. [1986] 2001. "The split-second syndrome and other determinants of police violence." Pp.583–598 in *Critical Issues in Policing: Contemporary Readings*, edited by Roger G. Dunham and Geoffrey P. Alpert. Prospect Heights, IL: Waveland Press, Inc.

Garner, Joel H. and Christopher D. Maxwell. 1999. "Measuring the amount of force used by and against the police in six jurisdictions." Pp. 25–44 in *Use of force by police: Overview of national and local data*. Washington, D.C.: U.S. Department of Justice, BJS and NIJ, October. NCJ 176330.

Garner, Joel H., Christopher D. Maxwell and Cedrick Heraux. 2002. "Characteristics associated with the prevalence and severity of force used by the police." *Justice Quarterly* 19: 705–746.

------. 2004. "Patterns of police use of force as a measure of police integrity." Pp. 109–125 in *Police Integrity and Ethics*, edited by Matthew Hickman, Alex Piquero and Jack Green. Belmont, CA: Wadsworth Publishing Company.

Geller, William A. 1982. "Deadly force: What we know." *Journal of Police Science and Administration* 10: 151–177.

------. 1985. "Officer restraint in the use of deadly force: The next frontier in police shooting research." *Journal of Police Science and Administration* 13: 153–171.

Geller, William A. and Kevin J. Karales. 1981. "Shootings of and by Chicago Police: Uncommon crises part I: Shootings by Chicago Police." *The Journal of Criminal Law and Criminology* 72: 1813–1866.

------. 1982. "Shootings of and by Chicago Police: Uncommon crises part II: Shootings by Chicago Police." *The Journal of Criminal Law and Criminology* 73: 331–378.

Geller, William A., and Michael S. Scott. 1992. *Deadly Force: What We Know: A Practitioner's Desk Reference on Police-Involved Shootings*. Washington, D.C.: Police Executive Research Forum.

Goldkamp, John S. [1976] 1982. "Minorities as victims of police shootings: Interpretations of racial disproportionality and police use of deadly force." Pp. 128–151 in *Readings on Police of Deadly Force*, edited by James J. Fyfe. Washington, D.C.: Police Foundation.

Goldstein, Paul J. 1985. "The drugs/violence nexus: A tripartite conceptual framework." *Journal of Drug Issues* 39: 143–174.

Graham v. Connor. 1989. 490 U.S. 386.

Greenfeld, Lawrence A., Patrick A. Langan and Steven K. Smith. 1999. "Revising and fielding the police-public contact survey." Pp. 15–18 in *Use of force by police: Overview of national and local data*. Washington, D.C.: U.S. Department of Justice, BJS and NIJ, October. NCJ 176330.

Harrison, Lana D. 1992. "The drug-crime nexus in the USA." *Contemporary Drug Problems* 19: 203–245.

Henriquez, Mark A. 1999. "IACP national database project on police use of force." Pp. 19–24 in *Use of force by police: Overview of national and local data*. Washington, D.C.: U.S. Department of Justice, BJS and NIJ, October. NCJ 176330.

Herbert, Steve. 1998. "Police subculture reconsidered." *Criminology* 36: 343–369.

Hickman, Matthew J. and Brian A. Reaves. (2003a). *Law Enforcement Management and Administrative Statistics: Sheriff's Offices 2000*. Washington, DC: U.S. Department of Justice, Office of Justice Programs, Bureau of Justice Statistics, January. NCJ 196534.

------. (2003b). *Law Enforcement Management and Administrative Statistics: Local Police Departments 2000*. Washington, DC: U.S. Department of Justice Office of Justice Programs, Bureau of Justice Statistics, January. NCJ 196002.

Holmes, Malcolm D. 2000. "Minority threat and police brutality: Determinants of civil rights criminal complaints in U.S. municipalities." *Criminology* 38: 343–366.

Horvath, Frank. 1987. "The police use of deadly force: A description of selected characteristics of intrastate incidents." *Journal of Police Science and Administration* 15: 226–238.

Hunter, Ronald D. 1999. "Officer opinions on police misconduct." *Journal of Contemporary Criminal Justice* 15: 155–170.

Jacobs, David and David Britt 1979. "Inequality and police use of deadly force: An empirical assessment of a conflict hypothesis." *Social Problems* 26: 403–412.

Jacobs, David and Robert M. O'Brien. 1998. "The determinants of deadly force: A structural analysis of police violence." *American Journal of Sociology* 103: 837–862.

Kappeler, Victor E., Richard D. Sluder and Geoffrey P. Alpert. [1998] 1999. "Breeding deviant conformity: Police ideology and culture." Pp. 238–263 in *The Police and Society* (2nd ed.), edited by Victor E. Kappeler. Prospect Heights, IL: Waveland Press, Inc.

Kelley, Robin D. G. 2000. "Slangin' Rocks ... Palestinian Style." Pp. 21–59 in *Police Brutality: An Anthology*, edited by Jill Nelson. New York, NY: W. W. Norton & Company.

Klockars, Carl B. [1980] 1999. "The Dirty Harry problem." Pp. 368–385 in *The Police and Society* (2nd ed.), edited by Victor E. Kappeler. Prospect Heights, IL: Waveland Press, Inc.

Kposowa, Augustine J. 2006. "Psychiatric care, social disintegration and suicide deaths in U.S. counties, 1990–1992." Unpublished manuscript. Department of Sociology, University of California, Riverside.

Langan, Patrick A., Lawrence A. Greenfeld, Steven K. Smith, Matthew R. Durose and David J. Levin. 2001. *Contacts between police and the public: Findings from the 1999 national survey*. Washington, D.C.: U.S. Department of Justice, BJS and NIJ, February. NCJ 184957.

Lersch, Kim. M. 1998. "Predicting citizen race in allegations of misconduct against the police." *Journal of Criminal Justice* 26: 87–97.

LexisNexis. 2001. Parker's *2002 California Penal and Vehicle Code*. Charlottesville, VA. Matthew Bender & Company, Inc.

Li, Spencer D., Heidi D. Priu and Doris L. MacKenzie. 2000. "Drug involvement, lifestyles, and criminal activities among probationers." *Journal of Drug Issues* 30: 593–620.

Lindgren, James. 1981. "Organizational and other constraints on controlling the use of deadly force." *Annals of the American Academy of Polictical and Social Science* 455: 110–119.

Lipsey, Mark W., David B. Wilson, Mark A. Cohen and James H. Derzon. 1996. "Is there a causal relationship between alcohol use and violence?: A synthesis of evidence." *Recent Developments in Alcoholism, Vol. 13*.

Luna, Andrea M. 2005. "Introduction." Pp. 1–20 in *Exploring the Challenges of Police Use of Force*, edited by Joshua A. Ederheimer and Lorie A. Fridell. Washington, D.C.: Police Executive Research Forum.

MacDonald, John. M., Robert J. Kaminski, Geoffrey P. Alpert and Abraham N. Tennenbaum. 2001. "The temporal relationship between police killings of civilians and criminal homicide: A refined version of the danger-perception theory." *Crime & Delinquency* 47: 155–172.

Manning, Peter K. 1980. "Violence and the police role." *Annals of the American Academy of Polictical and Social Science* 452: 135–144.

Mastrofski, Stephen D., Jeffrey B. Snipes, Roger B. Parks and Christopher D. Maxwell. 2000. "The helping hand of the law: Police control of citizens on request." *Criminology* 3: 307–342.

McCoy, Candace. 1986. "The cop's world: Modern policing and the difficulty of legitimizing the use of force." *Human Rights Quarterly* 8: 270–293.

McElvain, James P., and Augustine J. Kposowa. 2004. "Police officer characteristics and internal affairs investigations for use of force allegations." *Journal of Criminal Justice* 32: 265–279.

-----. 2008. "Police officer characteristics and the likelihood of using deadly force." *Criminal Justice and Behavior* 35:505–521.

Meyer, Marshall W. 1980. "Police shootings at minorities: The case of Los Angeles." *Annals of the American Academy of Political and Social Science* 452: 98–110.

Milton, Catherine, Jeanne Wahl Halleck, James Lardner, and Gary L. Abrecht. [1977] 1982. "Analysis of shooting incidents." Pp. 42–64 in *Readings on Police of Deadly Force*, edited by James J. Fyfe. Washington, D.C.: Police Foundation.

Mirande, Alfredo. 1981. "The Chicano and the law: An analysis of community-police conflict in an urban barrio." *The Pacific Sociological Review* 24: 65–86.

Mundy, Gilbert R. 1996. *A Star Was Born: A Centennial History of the Riverside County Sheriff's Department.* Newport Beach, Ca: Graphic Publishers.

Paoline, Eugene, A. and William Terrill. 2007. "Police education, experience, and the use of force." *Criminal Justice and Behavior* 34:179–196.

Parker, Robert Nash. 1995. "Bringing 'booze' back in: The relationship between alcohol and homicide." *Journal of Research in Crime and Delinquency* 32: 3–38.

------. 1998. "Alcohol, homicide, and cultural context: A cross-national analysis of gender-specific homicide victimization." *Homicide Studies* 2: 6–30.

Parker, Robert Nash. and Kathleen Auerhahn. 1998. "Alcohol, drugs, and violence." *Annual Review of Sociology* 24: 291–311.

Parker, Robert Nash and Randi S. Cartmill. 1998. "Alcohol and homicide in the United States 1934–1995 – or one reason why U.S. rates of violence may be going down." *The Journal of Criminal Law and Criminology* 88: 1369–1398.

Perkins, James E. and Martin J. Bourgeois. 2006. "Perceptions of police use of deadly force." *Journal of Applied Social Psychology* 36: 161–177.

Reaves, Brian A. and Andrew L. Goldberg. 1999. *Law Enforcement Management and Administrative Statistics, 1997: Data for Individual State and Local Agencies with 100 or More Officers.* Washington, DC: U.S. Department of Justice, Office of Justice Programs, Bureau of Justice Statistics, January. NCJ 171681.

Reaves, Brian A., and Pheny Z. Smith. 1995. *Law Enforcement Management and Administrative Statistics, 1993: Data for Individual State and Local Agencies with 100 or More Officers.* Washington, DC: U.S. Department of Justice, Office of Justice Programs, Bureau of Justice Statistics, January. NCJ 148825.

Reiss, Albert J. 1980. "Controlling police use of force." *Annals of the American Academy of Political and Social Science* 452: 122–134.

Robin, Gerald D. 1963. "Justifiable homicide by police officers." *The Journal of Criminal Law, Criminology, and Police Science* 54: 225–231.

------. 1964. "Police slayings of criminals." *Police* 8: 32–35.

Riverside County Sheriff's Department. 2001. *General Orders Manual.*

Roberg, Roy and Scott Bonn. 2004. "Higher education and policing: Where are we now?" *Policing: An International Journal of Police Strategies & Management* 27:469–486.

SAS Institute Inc. 2005. *SAS/stat: The GENMOD Procedure* (Version 9.2) [Computer software]. Cary, NC: Author.

SAS Institute Inc. 1999. *SAS/stat User's Guide* (Version 8) [Manual]. Cary, NC: Author.

Scrivner, Ellen M. 1994. *Controlling police use of excessive force: The role of the police psychologist.* Washington, D.C.: U.S. Department of Justice, BJS and NIJ, October. NCJ 150063.

Sherman, Lawrence W. [1980] 1982. "Execution without trial: Police homicide and the constitution." Pp. 88–127 in *Readings on Police of Deadly Force*, edited by James J. Fyfe. Washington, D.C.: Police Foundation.

------. 1980. "Perspectives on police and violence." *Annals of the American Academy of Political and Social Science* 452: 1–12.

Sherman, Lawrence W. and Mark Blumberg. 1981. "Higher education and police use of deadly force." *Journal of Criminal Justice* 9: 317–331.

Sherman, Lawrence W. and Robert H. Langworthy. [1979] 1982. "Measuring homicide by police officers." Pp. 12–41 in *Readings on Police of Deadly Force*, edited by James J. Fyfe. Washington, D.C.: Police Foundation.

Smith, Brad, W. 2003. "The impact of police officer diversity on police-caused homicides." *The Police Studies Journal* 31:147–162.

Sommers, Ira and Deborah R. Baskin. 1997. "Situational or generalized violence in drug dealing networks." *Journal of Drug Issues* 27: 833–849.

Son, In S., Mark S. Davis and Dennis M. Rome. 1998. "Race and its effect on police officers' perceptions of misconduct." *Journal of Criminal Justice* 26: 21–28.

Swope, Ross. 2001. "Bad apples or bad barrel?" *Law and Order* 49: 80–85.

Takagi, Paul. [1974] 1982. "A Garrison state in a "democratic" society." Pp. 195–214 in *Readings on Police of Deadly Force*, edited by James J. Fyfe. Washington, D.C.: Police Foundation.

Tennenbaum, Abraham N. 1994. "The influence of the "Garner" decision on police use of force." *The Journal of Criminal Law and Criminology* 85: 241–260.

Tennessee v. Garner. 1985. 471 U.S. 1.

Van Maanen, John. 1980. "Beyond account: The personal impact of police shootings." *Annals of the American Academy of Political and Social Science* 452: 145–156.

Walker, Samuel and Lorie Fridell. 1992. "Forces of change in police policy: The impact of Tennessee v. Garner." *American Journal of Police* 11: 97–112.

Weitzer, Ronald. 1999. "Citizens' perceptions of police misconduct: Race and neighborhood context." *Justice Quarterly* 16: 819–846.

------. 2000. "Racialized policing: Residents' perceptions in three neighborhoods." *Law & Society Review* 34: 129–155.

Weitzer, Ronald and Steven A. Tuch. 1999. "Race, class, and perceptions of discrimination by the police." *Crime and Delinquency* 45: 494–507.

Weisburd, David, Rosann Greenspan, Edwin E. Hamilton, Hubert Williams and Kellie A. Bryant. 2000. *Police attitudes toward abuse of authority: Findings from a national study*. Washington, D.C.: U.S. Department of Justice, BJS and NIJ, May. NCJ 181312.

White, Michael D. 2001. "Controlling police decisions to use deadly force: Reexamining the importance of administrative policy." *Crime & Delinquency* 47: 131–151.

CPSIA information can be obtained
at www.ICGtesting.com
Printed in the USA
LVHW051947100119
603478LV00001B/7/P

9 781516 526147